BATTLESHIP
ARIZONA

CONTENTS

PREFACE

Most Americans know something about the battleship *Arizona*. They know that she was sunk with great loss of life at Pearl Harbor on 7 December 1941. They understand that she thus came to symbolize the event that galvanized the nation to action in World War II. And they recall that a memorial was subsequently erected over the hulk of the ship. Aside from those fundamentals, most Americans have only vague ideas about the history of this famous ship. But they want to learn, and more than a million people visit the memorial each year to get to know something more about the *Arizona*.

In fact, the *Arizona* had performed twenty-five years of active service on behalf of the nation by the time the Japanese struck. The events of those twenty-five years were duly recorded in thousands of places—in official records, in news reports, in personal correspondence, and in the minds of the people whose lives the ship touched. Until now, no one has assembled a detailed history of the battleship *Arizona* in one place. This book records the events in the life and death of the ship and does so largely through the activities of her crew members. Theirs was a way of life that was markedly different from the life of U.S. Navy men today, and their stories give the reader an idea of what it was like to serve in a typical U.S. Navy battleship in the time from World War I to the first day of World War II. Indeed, the Navy of the 1920s and 1930s is ripe for further study. Most accounts have dealt with the wartime years, not with the decades of peace that intervened.

Lacking the stimulus provided by combat, the Navy made technological progress only slowly in the interwar years. What technical and tactical progress the Navy did make centered largely on aircraft and aircraft carriers, submarines, and amphibious warfare

rather than battleships. Despite a substantial modernization midway through her career, the *Arizona* still had the same basic mission in 1941 as she did when she was commissioned in 1916. The attack that killed the *Arizona* at Pearl Harbor also did away with a considerable amount of prewar thinking and methods.

A substantial part of the account in this book can be labeled social history. That aspect of the interwar Navy has been even less well documented than its technological changes. There is a shortage of accounts because the men took for granted the way they lived and worked and didn't give a lot of thought to documenting their routines. Life was tougher for Navy men then because the system of discipline was less forgiving than today's and because the Navy was less inclined than it is now to consider the concerns of the individual. In their interviews and letters, the men who served in the *Arizona* describe just what it was like to be battleship sailors when battleships were the predominant representatives of the nation's military power.

One of the drawbacks of writing a book based in large part on oral interviews, nearly all of them dozens of years after the events described, is the matter of determining accuracy. So far, no tape recorder has been invented that has red and green lights on it to indicate whether a given statement is true. I want to include only true or likely stories in this account—so I checked them against documentary sources, other interviews, and what might be called gut feeling. Perhaps a few fables slipped in, and probably some accurate tales got left out because they sounded too good to be true. That's the biggest disappointment: some of the most enjoyable stories are dubious.

One that I encountered several times in the interviews had to do with an ensign who ordered a coxswain to tie up his boat to the starboard yardarm. He really meant the starboard boat boom but misspoke. As the story goes, the coxswain ran several laps around the ship with his boat until challenged by the young officer. The coxswain is reputed to have said something like, "One more lap, sir, and I'll be able to take off." Another tale concerned the time when the *Arizona* was in Turkey right after World War I. Anchored near a British battleship, the *Arizona* dragged anchor in the swift currents of the Bosporus. As the American ship went past, the punctilious British crew rendered the appropriate passing honors. When the *Arizona* got steam up to return to her berth and passed by for a second time, the British man-of-war once again rendered honors.

In 1931, according to another piece of folklore, the crewmen of the battleship got up early one morning, cleaned the ship thoroughly, then put on their best inspection uniforms and stood at attention around the perimeter of the ship to honor visiting President Herbert Hoover. As the tale goes, Mrs. Hoover took a look at the sailors manning the rail and declared that she didn't know why they should be paid because all they did was stand around. In fact, Mrs. Hoover was not on board during her husband's visit. In yet another tale, an enlisted man came to the quarterdeck to go on liberty, and the officer of the deck did not grant permission because the man was not sufficiently respectful in rendering his salute.

Thereupon the enlisted man went to his locker and put on his full collection of decorations, including a Medal of Honor. He then went to the quarterdeck and demanded a salute from the officer of the deck.

Although some stories have failed to check out, I have found many, many cases in which the existing records corroborate the mental pictures. Indeed, that is an eminently satisfying aspect of this work—to see accounts from a variety of sources join to enhance and support one another.

The result of putting together the various stories of what really did happen is that one gets a sense of the personality of the ship and the men who served in her. Many of those men would have a hard time believing that the *Arizona* was an inanimate object. Many—though certainly not all—developed considerable affection for her. Dozens of those men and their families gather each year in the state of Arizona to relive the old memories and to remind themselves of the time when their ship carried the pride of the nation. Each year the gathering gets a bit smaller and the average age of the participants a year older. But they needn't worry about their ship's being forgotten. The *Arizona* is more than just a symbol of America's resolve in World War II. She is more than just a monument to the hundreds of men whose remains were never recovered from inside her hull. She is a visible reminder of an age that helped shape the world of today and tomorrow. New generations will carry that knowledge with them into the future.

ACKNOWLEDGMENTS

When the *Arizona* was nearing her end, in 1940–41, one of the men in the deck force was a seaman, later coxswain, named Ed Marks. His nickname among his shipmates was "Harpo" because he was quiet, like the member of the famous Marx brothers of the movies. He survived the loss of the ship because he was on leave on 7 December, and he died just a few years ago. His widow, Lorraine Marks, became the historian for the *Arizona* Reunion Association so that her work might serve as a tribute to her husband's time in the ship. She has done a spectacular job, traveling widely to collect memories, photographs, and memorabilia to honor the service of the USS *Arizona*. For her, this project is essentially an unpaid full-time job, and she even moved from California to Phoenix, Arizona, so that she could coordinate her efforts with those of the state capitol's museum and spread the word about the ship. She has made immense contributions to this book through her generous sharing of the many things she has collected. It is a far better book than it would have been without her efforts.

Libby and Joe Langdell run the annual reunions for the organization and have also been extremely helpful, putting me in touch with various people and forwarding material for use in the book. Joe, a gregarious man, did some oral-history interviews of his own several years ago concerning the young woman, Madeline Blair, who stowed away in the *Arizona* in 1924. The results of those interviews are incorporated in the text. Jim Vlach, a yeoman in the ship at the time of the Japanese attack, is also an active member of the reunion group and has been most generous in providing material. He has been particularly helpful in checking the list of the ship's crew from 7 December 1941. Jim is the kind of friend everyone would like to have.

Mrs. Nina Hart of Lake Helen, Florida, put together two spiral-bound, paperback books concerning the ship, volumes I and II of *Arizona's Heart Beats*. She generously allowed me to use material from the books, both of which are available for purchase through the reunion association. Mrs. Nellie Main lent me a number of photos from the collection she maintains on behalf of the group. The association does a great deal of good on behalf of the memory of the USS *Arizona*. For information on membership, the address is 1655 West Ajo Way - Space 513, Tucson, Arizona 85713.

Dozens of former *Arizona* men have recorded their recollections of service in the ship for the benefit of this history. I am grateful to them for their contributions. Four of the interviewees were especially memorable because these four were born in the 19th century. For many years Harry Cray, who was in the original crew of the ship in 1916, lived in Tombstone, Arizona, just up the street from the famous O.K. Corral where Wyatt Earp and Doc Holliday had their shoot-out. When I tried to track Cray down, I learned from a friend that he had sold his home and moved to a nursing home in Sierra Vista, Arizona. When I went there, I found he had gone from the nursing home to a local hospital, and that trail in turn led to still another nursing home in Benson, Arizona. Cray sat in a wheelchair as he talked about his experiences in the *Arizona* and other battleships. He died in 1990.

Glenn Frisbie I found living in a cabin with a picture window that afforded a magnificent view of a man-made lake near the Missouri-Arkansas border. Now ninety-four, he lives with his daughter in Independence, Missouri, in the winters and by himself in the cabin in Shell Knob, Missouri, in the summers. On his mantel was a copy of the *Arizona*'s 1917 Thanksgiving dinner menu, and under a bed was a Turkish rug he bought when the ship visited Asia Minor in 1919.

I talked with Joseph Driscoll, his wife, Dorothy, and their son Bernard in the family home in Hartford, Connecticut. Mrs. Driscoll's brother served in the *Pennsylvania* at the same time her future husband was in the *Arizona*. In addition to sharing memories of the time, Driscoll and his son lent more than one hundred postcard-size photos from the ship. Many of those shots illustrate the post–World War I chapter of the book. Bernard has provided excellent follow-up assistance since the death of his father.

The day before Christmas Eve in 1988 I went to the home of retired Admiral Mel Pride in Arlington, Virginia. In his modest, laconic New England fashion, he apologized several times for his poor memory, even though he was recalling an amazing amount of detail about the six months he spent in the *Arizona* as an aviator in 1920. He took me to the basement of his home to show me his scrapbooks and a large framed photo of the ship's entire crew assembled on deck, taken during his time on board. He clearly relished the chance to talk over old times; the tape of the interview is replete with his chuckles and the warmth with which he talked about the old days. Later that evening I got a call from Pride's daughter, who told me that I had left my tape recorder at his house. I had been so captivated by his tales that I had walked away without it. The following day the admiral was visiting his daughter for Christmas Eve, so I went to retrieve the recorder and wish the old gentleman a happy holiday. He reciprocated the greeting, sat down for lunch, watched a football game on television, and died that afternoon while taking a nap.

Sharon Culley and Dale Conley of the National Archives were quite helpful in digging out hundreds of photos of the *Arizona* from that organization's vast collection. Agnes Hoover and Chuck Haberlein were helpful at the Naval Historical Center in Washington, D.C. I am grateful to have been the beneficiary of many kindnesses from Mrs. Hoover prior to her retirement. She was willing to dig for hard-to-find items. Cathy Gilchrist of Blakeslee-Lane in Baltimore did a great deal of excellent camera work, produc-

ing many of the prints of photos that were copied from other collections. There is an art to copying existing photographs, and Ms. Gilchrist has mastered it. James Delgado and Daniel Lenihan of the National Park Service supplied useful material about the submerged cultural resources study conducted on the *Arizona*, including the superb line drawings depicting the present condition of the ship's hull. Ron Brenne of the Bettmann Archive has been patient in dealing with my many requests for specific views. Peter Curtis put me in touch with the *Arizona*'s folder in the old *Baltimore News-American* collection at the University of Maryland.

Larry Wendell and Lou Bushnell of the Universal Ship Cancellation Society's Pearl Harbor Study Group helped me contact Karen Richardson, who was most generous in making available the 1941 letters of her father, Machinist's Mate Ardenne Woodward, that appear in appendix D. John De Virgilio has been consistently helpful in providing both information and diagrams concerning the damage inflicted on the ship and the means by which it was accomplished. Steve McLaughlin provided stories about the ship that appeared in the San Francisco newspapers. Hans Henke and Nerl Reinhart shared material they had bought at sales from the estates of former crew members of the *Arizona*. It's likely, alas, that much other useful material has been discarded as men who have served on the ship have died. Fortunately, Mrs. Janet Joseph preserved the diary of her father, George Leymé, and made it available for this book. It is an amusing and informative document. She also supplied a copy of the very first issue of the ship's newspaper.

Leith Adams of the University of Southern California helped by putting me in touch with material connected with the movie *Here Comes the Navy*. Susan Elter facilitated my use of the collection at the Franklin D. Roosevelt Library. Cora Pedersen and Dwight Miller did so for the Herbert Hoover Presidential Library. The latter has a voluminous collection of material on Hoover's 1931 visit to the *Arizona*. Russell McCurdy, a marine private serving in the *Arizona* in 1941, was most generous in providing recollections, photos, and other material. Admiral Ike Kidd, whose father was the senior officer killed on board the *Arizona*, made available both his recollections and the family scrapbooks. Ted Stone, a friend of long standing, dug into his vast collection of ship photos to provide views of the *Arizona*. Harvey Beigel let me know about the excellent maritime photo collection at the Los Angeles Public Library, and Carol Baldwin facilitated access. Robert Kaplan, a ship enthusiast in New Jersey, has sent numerous communications suggesting sources of photos of the *Arizona*. Mary Marshall Clark of the Columbia University Oral History Research Office made available transcripts, and Alice Creighton of the Naval Academy Library's special collections supplied a useful speech made by Medal of Honor recipient Rear Admiral Samuel G. Fuqua. Billie Clatchey dug into the Naval Academy Alumni Association's files to provide Fuqua's portrait.

Philip Sims supplied some material from the files of the Naval Sea Systems Command, information concerning the *Arizona*'s tussle with rough weather in early 1938. Kempton Baldridge, a chaplain in the Naval Reserve, was very helpful in putting me in touch with Captain Henry Williams, Jr., the individual who put the first bolt into the keel of the *Arizona* in 1914. Baldridge also provided copies of numerous newspaper articles from the scrapbook of Williams, who is a member of his congregation.

The principal source of documentary material for the book has been the National Archives in Washington, D.C. Barry Zerby has been unfailingly helpful in digging out the *Arizona*'s deck logs and other materials. He found a great deal of useful information for me on the ship's material history in the records of the old Bureau of Construction and Repair. Peter Steere of the University of Arizona Library Special Collections spent a good deal of time with me in pulling out a storehouse of material on the ship, both documentary and photographic. The university has the largest collection of which I am aware of the ship's weekly newspaper, *At 'Em Arizona*. The other large repository of material specifically on the ship is the *Arizona* Memorial at Pearl Harbor. During my visit in May 1989 the people there were most kind. Curator Mark Hertig and volunteer museum cataloger Rhoda Rogers Komuro made available dozens of photo prints from the memorial's collection for use in the book. Bruce

Andrae of the Puget Sound Naval Shipyard provided several high-quality photos of the ship taken at Bremerton during various times in her career.

At the Naval Institute, the information services department, including Jim Patterson, Maureen Pease, Linda Miller, and Lee Johnson, has been consistently helpful in facilitating my use of a word processor to assemble the book. The chore was far easier than it would have been without the magic machine. Anthony Chiffolo has used his expertise to do exactly what a good editor should: make the text clearer, smoother, and more concise. He has caught the minor errors that inevitably creep into a text and challenged the things that needed to be. John Cronin, a real pro in the graphic arts area, supervised the production of the book. Karen White demonstrated a great deal of talent and patience in developing the book's elegant design. The volume is composed of many disparate elements, which she has combined beautifully. The dust jacket art is from Tom Freeman, a master at his craft. Alan B. Chesley, who did the ship drawings for my book on the *New Jersey,* has again employed his superb skills in depicting the *Arizona*.

Dr. Thomas Hone, a long-time friend, has been extremely generous with his time and his collection of materials. He has shared his photos, his records of the post-attack investigations of the causes of the ship's traumatic damage, and his specialized knowledge of the pre–World War II U.S. Navy. He read through the entire manuscript and offered many useful suggestions for improvement. Bob Cressman, another old friend, provided copies of the survivor reports and also read portions of the text. Bill Still gave me useful material on the ship's service in European waters after World War I and critiqued the early chapters of the book. Frank Uhlig of the Naval War College also read part of the text and gave me the benefit of his expertise.

My wife, Karen, has also read the entire text and made many useful suggestions. More to the point, she has many times kept our three sons, Joseph, Robert, and James, occupied when I would have enjoyed playing ball or watching TV with them but was glued to the computer screen instead. Love and thanks to all of them for their patience.

BATTLESHIP ARIZONA

1 SUPER DREADNOUGHT
March 1914–November 1918

Hundreds of warmly dressed guests and participants waited expectantly for the arrival of the presiding official at the New York Navy Yard. The date was 16 March 1914, and the official was Assistant Secretary of the Navy Franklin D. Roosevelt. Around 11:30 that morning the tall, thirty-two-year-old FDR arrived, wearing a derby hat. He was greeted by Captain Albert Gleaves, commandant of the navy yard. The receiving ship *Washington* fired seventeen rounds from her saluting guns when the assistant secretary entered the shipyard's gate. A marine guard accompanied Roosevelt and Gleaves, and a band played as they walked to the shipway inside the yard.

The occasion for Roosevelt's presence was the laying of the keel for a new, as-yet-unnamed warship, then known only as battleship number 39. Press reports suggested that the ship would probably be known as the *North Carolina* because Secretary of the Navy Josephus Daniels hailed from that state. The new ship would essentially be a sister to the *Pennsylvania*, which was already under construction at Newport News, Virginia.

Captain Gleaves set the tone for the occasion with a short speech: "We are here today to witness the laying of the keel of the 41st battleship of the United States Navy. We want to make a world's record in length of time between the laying of the keel and the launching of this ship. Judging by the records of the Navy yard in the past, with the *Connecticut*, the *Florida*, and the *New York*, I do not think it is any exaggeration to say that number 39 should be ready to slide down these ways in ten months from today."[1]

Gleaves was counting in his total of forty-one the old *Maine* and *Texas*, officially described as second-class battleships. In fact,

they were essentially coastal-defense vessels. Their construction began in the late 1880s but took so long that they were commissioned only a few months before the first U.S. seagoing battleship in 1895. That ship, the USS *Indiana*, was later designated BB-1; it was with her that the numbering scheme began. The keel being laid in March 1914 was for the United States' thirty-ninth true battleship.

Once the speech was over, shipyard workers put into motion a long-armed crane stretching across the same building ways from which the hull for the *New York* had been launched in October 1912. They lowered into position a fifty-foot-long steel plate, and two more plates followed. Then five small boys came forward, the sons of naval officers.

One by one, the boys put nickel-plated bolts into place to connect the initial keel plates of the ship-to-be. Afterward, they removed the bolts and put them into their pockets as souvenirs, and steel bolts replaced the nickel ones in the keel plates. Then the boys went to the spot in the wooden staging where the ship's bow would emerge in later months and nailed up a horseshoe to bring good luck to the new ship.[2]

The honor of putting in the first of the ceremonial bolts went to three-year-old Henry Williams, Jr., son of a naval constructor. Some seventy-five years after the event, Williams, by then a retired Navy captain, explained that he didn't really know what he remembered about the occasion and what he had heard others tell him. In any event, for some reason he seemed drawn to the handsome young Roosevelt and wrapped his small hand around the assistant secretary's index finger. Alert press photographers captured the moment on their glass-plate negatives, and pictures of young Williams appeared in dozens of newspapers with the future president.

As Williams put it, "I grabbed his finger and hung on for dear life. And they tried to get me away, and, of course, I was a little ham. FDR, being a bit of a ham himself, I guess he saw the possibilities or whatever it might be for all the picture taking . . . . So . . . he shooed them away, and I stayed hanging onto his hand." As the Williams family passed down the story, one of the older boys had been nominated to put in the first bolt, but Henry's impulsive rush toward Roosevelt had stolen the show and won him the job.

In December 1941 Henry Williams, Jr., was a lieutenant on active duty, having graduated from the Naval Academy in 1931, and was serving on the staff of a destroyer flotilla commander at Pearl Harbor. During a spare moment on the night of the seventh, in the wake of the Japanese attack, Williams went out on the deck of his ship and read a newspaper by the light of the inferno consuming a nearby battleship. Henry Williams was

in at the very beginning and at the very end, for battleship number 39 was named not *North Carolina* but *Arizona*.[3]

Ever since the completion in 1906 of the revolutionary HMS *Dreadnought*, the world's first all-big-gun battleship, vessels of the type had been known generically as dreadnoughts. The British *Dreadnought* was armed with a main battery of ten 12-inch guns. Her more modern successors, such as the future *Arizona*, came to be known at the time as super dreadnoughts because of their 14-inch guns.

The keel laying on 16 March was, primarily, a ceremonial milestone in the construction of the U.S. Navy's newest battleship. For several months, workmen had been assembling steel plates and fittings, getting them ready to rivet into place once construction moved from the showy fanfare of Roosevelt's visit to the daily process of building a metal skeleton and then filling in the spaces between the ribs.

Preparing for the construction of the *Arizona* included ordering and assembling

Right: Three-year-old Henry Williams, Jr., grasps the index finger of Assistant Secretary of the Navy Franklin D. Roosevelt at the *Arizona*'s keel laying. The bearded man in the top hat is Senator James O'Gorman, and the naval officer is Captain Albert Gleaves, Commandant of the New York Navy Yard. (Franklin D. Roosevelt Library, 48-22:3626[40])

many pieces that would eventually become part of her structure. Crucial would be her armor plate. Not long after Josephus Daniels became Secretary of the Navy in 1913, the Navy had requested bids for the armor needed to construct the *Arizona*. Daniels was a true activist, and when he looked into the question of armor for the *Arizona*, he was dismayed by the prevailing procurement practices. The previous Secretary of the Navy, George von Lengerke Meyer, who held office from 1909 to 1913, felt it was important to maintain the steel companies as part of the nation's industrial base and thus discouraged competitive bidding. Daniels discovered, for instance, that the Bethlehem Steel Company sold armor plate to foreign navies for prices around $400 per ton but to the U.S. Navy for figures ranging from $440 to $540 per ton.

The three major armor manufacturers—Bethlehem, Carnegie, and Midvale—submitted identical bids of $454 per ton to manufacture the armor plate that would become part of the *Arizona*. They expected that each would receive an order to supply one-third of the total, as had been the custom. Daniels, however, had other ideas and summoned representatives of all three companies to Washington. He told them that competitive bidding would be the rule from then on. To add further impetus to his ideas, he announced that the Navy would build its own plant to produce armor for warships. Construction of the plant did start, but the project never came to fruition. Even so, Daniels's intervention was a boon for the government in its dealings with industry, and the *Arizona*'s armor cost thousands of dollars less than it would have under the previous system.[4]

As the steel plates gradually came together, the creation on the building ways began to look more and more like a ship, with bow and stern, decks and compartments. Naval Constructor Robert Stocker, who was in overall charge of the project, had to ensure that the various components were put together in the right sequence, starting from the bottom and building up. The double bottoms rose above the keel, and then came longitudinal and transverse bulkheads, torpedo-defense bulkheads, oil tanks, shell plating, boiler foundations and boilers, turbine foundations and turbines, armor plating, splinter decks, turret barbettes, roller paths, propeller shafts and struts, bilge keels, and many other compo-

nents. Huge castings were used for her stem, stern, and rudder. After fifteen months of construction, the hull of the *Arizona* was ready to be launched.[5]

Chosen for the honor of naming the ship at the time of launching was Miss Esther Ross,

Above: A crane lowers the *Arizona*'s first keel plate into place at the New York Navy Yard on 16 March 1914. (Franklin D. Roosevelt Library, 62-247)

Left: A derrick made largely of wood lowers a piece of athwartship armor into position after hoisting it over the side on 6 October 1914. (National Archives, 19-LC-19A-8)

the daughter of one of Arizona's pioneer families. Her father, a pharmacist, had moved to the territorial capital of Prescott in 1882. The members of the party from Arizona were treated lavishly during their visit to New York City for the launching and christening. Arizona state flags and other western decorations festooned the lobby of the Waldorf-Astoria Hotel. Theaters provided complimentary tickets and put the spotlight on Arizonans

in the crowd. Among those who made the trip for the festivities was the father of Senator Barry Goldwater. The senior Goldwater was one of Phoenix's earliest merchants.[6]

The launching of a battleship was truly a spectacular event in those years when the century was still young. And the *Arizona* was, after all, the latest and greatest battleship in the world. The date for the ceremony was 19 June 1915. Reporters estimated that between fifty and seventy-five thousand people gathered for the occasion, the largest crowd at that time ever to see an American ship launched. The late spring day was ideal: the sky was blue, and a breeze kept the spectators comfortable. Throughout the New York Navy Yard, other ships were specially decked out with a full dress of signal flags. The collected spectators had tickets of various colors; white tickets, for example, connoted the greatest cachet and preferred places, and marines saw to it that those with tickets of different colors were in the proper spots.[7]

In the hours leading up to the launching, shipyard men were preparing for the day's big event, transferring the massive steel structure from land to water. The sounds of heavy hammers rang through the yard as men under

Above: Newsreel photographers with their hand-cranked cameras prepare to record the keel-laying ceremony. The photographer in the foreground has a precarious perch atop some of the structural members that will be used to frame the ship's double bottoms. In the background, some of the hull plating is already in place before the official keel laying. (Franklin D. Roosevelt Library, 62-272)

Right: A view of the early construction shows the port side, looking aft, on 2 July 1914. The angled pieces are the tops of individual frames, which were four feet apart from bow to stern. The angle was at the intersection of the horizontal armored deck and the vertical side armor belt. (National Archives, 19-LC-19A-15)

Left: By 16 September 1914, the frames were in place for the installation of the armored second deck on top of them. This view is from amidships, looking toward the stern. (National Archives, 19-LC-19A-6)

Below: The hull of the *Arizona*, still surrounded by scaffolding, is only three weeks from launching in this overall view taken 27 May 1915. The cage mast of an older battleship is just to the left of the *Arizona*'s stern. (Brown Brothers)

the ship knocked away the permanent supports that had been holding the hull in place. The weight of the ship was transferred to the sliding ways that she would ride downslope to the river. At 11:00 A.M. the hydraulic launching triggers were successfully tested, and one hundred men poured twenty-five thousand pounds of tallow and lard on the ways—greasing the skids so the ship could slide more easily. At 12:30 a large cantilever crane on tracks near the bow of the dreadnought began moving aft, toward the river, and a large red flag was unfurled to signal to the thousands of people in the yard that the launching was at hand.[8]

The launching was scheduled for 1:00 P.M. to take advantage of the spring tide. The crowd grew quiet as it looked toward the sponsor's stand. An Episcopal bishop from the state of Arizona said a prayer that only those around him could hear. At 1:05 Naval Constructor Robert Stocker, in charge of the launching, gave the order "Saw off," and for a couple of minutes large saws bit into the last holding blocks keeping the hull in place on the ways. The hydraulic levers gave the hull a shove, and at 1:10 it began moving.[9]

Miss Ross then did her part. Bottles of Arizona water and Ohio champagne were

ARIZONA DELEGATION TO CHRISTEN BATTLESHIP ARIZONA AT THE WHITE HOUSE. JUNE. 18, 1915.

Above: President Woodrow Wilson (white suit) poses with the delegation from Arizona on the front porch of the White House on the day before the launching. On one side of Wilson is Arizona's Governor George Hunt, and on the other side is Esther Ross, the ship's sponsor. Secretary of the Navy Josephus Daniels is next to Ross. (Special Collections, University of Arizona Library, 85-6-1)

Right: A framework of scaffolding surrounds the bow of the *Arizona* in this picture made on 26 April 1915, less than two months before launching. (Franklin D. Roosevelt Library)

Far right: The port fore poppet fits the contour of the hull near the bow to help distribute the ship's weight on the launching ways. This photo was taken on 18 June 1915, the day before the launching. (National Archives, 19-LC-19A-13)

suspended on a rope wound with red, white, and blue ribbons. She took a bottle in each hand and hurled them toward the future battleship, which was red that day because it had been painted with an undercoat of primer. As Miss Ross did so, she shouted, "I name thee *Arizona*!" The soon-to-be dreadnought picked up momentum as it went, reaching a speed of more than fifteen knots by the time it hit the river with a splash. It

continued on its way toward the Williamsburg Bridge until reined in by much smaller watercraft. Two hundred sailors rode the hull down the ways so they could handle hawsers sent up from the smaller vessels.[10]

The large crowd whooped and hollered so loudly that it drowned out several bands playing "The Star-Spangled Banner." Ships' whistles and sirens throughout the yard added to the din. Amid the noise, a pack of

tall-stacked steam tugboats set upon the hull and guided the *Arizona* back to the navy yard. There they settled her into a berth so her construction could be completed.

Civic pride played a big part in the christening of the nation's newest battleship, which was named for the nation's newest state (Arizona had been admitted to the union on Valentine's Day 1912). Back in 1906, while Arizona was still a territory, its people had begun building a 248-foot-high dam at the confluence of the Salt River and Tonto Creek, some thirty miles east of Phoenix. The resulting reservoir was to irrigate the Salt River Valley. Rocks for the construction of the dam, which was completed in 1911 and named for President Theodore Roosevelt, came from the nearby Superstition Mountains. However, the area was undergoing such a severe drought that Theodore Roosevelt Lake did not reach capacity until 15 April 1915. The first drops of water that went over the dam that day were bottled and saved for the christening of the new battleship two months later.[11]

Years later, after the *Arizona* had met her unhappy fate at Pearl Harbor, Esther Ross talked about the launching. At one time she recalled, "On the day of the launching, rumor spread in whispered tones that sailors long had considered christening a ship with water a bad omen. Considering that a man had risked his life to obtain the first drops of water that splashed over the spillway of the Roosevelt Dam so that this vast project of Arizona might play a part in the christening ceremony, the superstition was ignored. If ever another vessel should be honored with the name Arizona, may she never be christened with water."[12]

In another interview she told it differently: "Some citizen of my home state caught the first water that had come over the spillway of the new Roosevelt Dam. He sent me the bottle and asked me to use it on the new ship. The sailors later commented that if a ship is christened with water it is a bad omen, but I didn't know it at the time."[13] One of the

Above: A close-up view of the *Arizona*'s stern and rudder, 27 May 1915. (Brown Brothers)

Far left and left: In preparation for the launching of the *Arizona*, a shipyard worker pries open one of the 300 barrels of tallow used to lubricate the ways for the hull's first trip into the water. Another worker uses an ax to cut up the tallow. (Both photos from Franklin D. Roosevelt Library)

The Secretary of the Navy requests the pleasure of your company at the launching of the United States Battleship Arizona on the afternoon of Saturday, the nineteenth of June One thousand, nine hundred and fifteen at one o'clock at the Navy Yard, New York.

pitfalls of oral history is that human memory is sometimes inconsistent.

In any event, the *Arizona* was reported at the time to be the first U.S. warship christened with water. If that was a bad omen, perhaps it was reinforced by the fact that the rocks comprising the Roosevelt Dam came from the Superstition Mountains. Perhaps the ship had bad luck because only the champagne bottle broke when Esther Ross swung the bottles against the bow.[14] Or perhaps Japanese marksmanship at Pearl Harbor, rather than superstition or omens, was the overriding factor.

Right after the ceremony, the dignitaries retired to an official luncheon at the navy yard. The center of attention was a patriotically decorated candy battleship several feet long. As expected, the politicians, including Secretary of the Navy Daniels, took turns making speeches. One long sentence from the address by Arizona's Senator Henry F. Ash-

urst illustrates the flavor of that era's political rhetoric. Speaking of the newly launched *Arizona*, he said, "We send her forth with the proud consciousness that when the storm king gathers his clouds, obscures the fickle moon, opens the mysterious caverns where his hurricanes and tornadoes are imprisoned, and loosens furies to ride on the wings of the wind, fluting the wild and wasteful ocean with tempestuous and angry waves, she will cleave atwain the tumbling billows and send her serene and effulgent rays out upon the deadly waters, lending help, hope, and encouragement to every friendly ship."[15]

Esther Ross's brief speech was much more to the point: "Mr. Secretary, friends. This is the proudest day of my life, because I have christened the largest battleship in the world with the name of the greatest state in the union."[16]

To complete the *Arizona* in the remaining months before she went into commission, the yard workers had to outfit her with a superstructure, turrets, and many other features. Armor was installed around the uptakes leading from the boilers to the smokestack. The stack itself was installed, as was the belt armor that extended much of the length of the ship above and below the waterline. The belt armor would be attached externally, in contrast to the Navy's later practice of installing internal armor in a battleship while the hull was still on the building ways.

The ship's conning tower was built, and aft of it a rudimentary bridge that was little more than a platform with a compass and steering mechanism. Ammunition- and powder-handling equipment was installed inside the turret barbettes. Cage masts were erected fore and aft, the design being one limited almost completely to American battleships. These masts were built of intersecting pieces of metal tubing and had the unhappy characteristic of swaying to and fro when the ship fired her guns. Also installed topside were boat cranes and boat skids, ventilation cowls to scoop up fresh air for the crew below decks, guns, radio masts, searchlight platforms, and teak planking on the weather decks. While all this construction was going on, the ship was being painted gray. No longer the garish red she had been on launching day, the *Arizona* at long last looked like a warship. And after thirty-one months of construction, she was a warship.[17] She had cost the Navy some $16

U.S.S. ARIZONA
Detail - Port Cradle - Aft
Navy Yard, New York, June 19, 1915.
#3018

U.S.S. ARIZONA
...niva... Sponsor...
...New York, June 1...1915.

#3022

Right: The sponsor, Esther Ross, holds a bouquet and two christening bottles shortly before the launching on 19 June. Others, left to right, are Miss Eva Baker, the sponsor's mother Mrs. W. W. Ross, Secretary of the Navy Daniels, and Arizona Governor Hunt. (Special Collections, University of Arizona Library, 85-6-2)

Below: The crowd at the New York Navy Yard cheers as the hull of the *Arizona* goes sliding down the ways into the East River. In the background is the Williamsburg Bridge. (National Archives, 19-N-3340A)

million, nearly $7 million for the work in the shipyard and the rest for the equipment and other components used to build her.

At 4:09 P.M. on 17 October 1916 the newest ship in the fleet officially went into commission at the direction of Rear Admiral Nathaniel R. Usher, Commandant of the New York Navy Yard. The first commanding officer was Captain John D. McDonald. Born during the Civil War, he had graduated from the Naval Academy in 1884 and thus had more than thirty years of commissioned service before becoming the *Arizona*'s captain. On this day he read his orders, and the forty-eight-star flag was raised at the stern as the band played "The Star-Spangled Banner." The crew that gathered on the fantail for the ceremony was still about 150 short of the full allowance of 1,064 officers and men. The rest would arrive in a few weeks.

Many of those who were on hand from the beginning had a good deal of battleship experience already. They were drawn from the *Kansas*, *Vermont*, and *New Hampshire*, which

had been recently transferred to the reserve fleet. All three were less than ten years old, but they were all of the pre-dreadnought type and thus obsolete at an early age. Each of the three had a main battery of four 12-inch guns. The *Arizona*, by herself, had the same number of big guns as the three older ships combined, and the guns in her main battery were larger.

The *Connecticut*, the only remaining pre-dreadnought in active service in the Atlantic Fleet, was herself slated for the reserve fleet. Thus, in only a little more than seven years since the sixteen battleships of the Great White Fleet had completed their around-the-world voyage in 1909, nearly all of them had left active service. Nearby in the navy yard were some of the new battleships whose commissioning had contributed to the modernization of the fleet in the preceding few years: the *Wyoming*, *Delaware*, *New York*, *Texas*, *Arkansas*, *Nevada*, and *Pennsylvania*.[18]

Once the commissioning festivities were over, it was up to the officers and enlisted men to turn this new steel monster into a warship and a home. One of the facets of that process was moving the crew aboard. At the time of commissioning they were still living on board a receiving ship—essentially a floating barracks—until they could get themselves settled in the *Arizona*. In the meantime, only a skeleton crew stayed on board to stand watches, acting essentially as security guards. When it was time to relieve the watch, another shift would come over to the *Arizona* from the receiving ship, and the off-going watchstanders went back.

Among the *Arizona*'s plankowners—members of her commissioning crew—was Seaman First Class Harry Cray. He nearly achieved another type of first, although it was a rather dubious distinction. He remembered being the first man confined to the ship's brig, but he recalled it as a bum rap. One day while the ship was at Brooklyn, he headed down the gangway to the dock so he could buy a snack. A marine in the *Arizona*'s detachment turned him in, claiming that Cray was trying to jump ship. The seaman went up before Captain McDonald, whose message was brief: "What do you have to say for yourself? Three days bread and water." Cray had no chance to respond; punishment was swift and arbitrary. (The ship's log shows that several shipmates preceded Cray to the brig before he was

sentenced on 26 October, nine days after the ship was commissioned.)

There was a certain strange fairness to the sentence, as Cray recounted more than seventy years afterward. Previously, Cray and a shipmate had gone ashore and found comfort in a "gin mill," to use the term of that era. When they emerged, rain was falling, and the shipmate decided he didn't want to walk through the rain to return to the *Arizona*. Instead, they went back to their drinking and were thus late when they eventually returned to the ship. Cray's division officer let him slide, saying he didn't want to besmirch the record of the new ship so soon after commissioning.[19]

Above: A covey of tall-stacked, steam-driven tugboats converges on the *Arizona*'s newly floated hull to tow it to an outfitting pier. (The Mariners' Museum, Newport News, Virginia, PN 2814)

Below: Tugs surround the hull while another pulls on a tow wire (at the lower left). This view shows the barbette for turret two and the beginnings of the superstructure. (UPI/Bettmann Newsphotos, 28770-INP)

On 20 October the engineering department held dock trials to test the ship's propulsion plant. The *Arizona* was originally equipped with twelve Babcock and Wilcox boilers and eight Parsons turbines. Her designed shaft horsepower was 34,000. In comparison, each *Iowa*-class battleship's engineering plant produces a designed horsepower of 212,000. The *Iowa* and her sisters are, of course, bigger and a good deal faster than the *Arizona* was.

Another part of preparing the ship for sea duty included cleaning her up, and the crew conducted field days to eliminate the inevitable industrial grime and trash that are part of shipyard work. In this instance, however, the task was even more distasteful than normal. The sailors discovered that the navy yard's workmen—known as "yard birds" in sailor parlance—had from time to time been too lazy to go ashore to answer calls of nature. Instead of using the restrooms in the shipyard, they merely went into isolated compartments of the *Arizona* to relieve themselves.

Representatives from the Bureau of Medicine and Surgery inspected the new ship and reported, "There were indisputable evidences of this filthy practice and in addition there was

Right: Workmen who took part in the construction of the *Arizona* are shown sitting on turret three, framed by the 14-inch guns, during the commissioning ceremony. (UPI/Bettmann Newsphotos, 45747-INP)

found in many compartments the remains of food carelessly thrown and left by these individuals. This refuse undoubtedly attracted rats that normally inhabit the water front, for quite a number of these rodents were discovered after the ship was placed in commission."[20]

The crew spent much of the last week of October taking aboard the 14-inch projectiles that the new super dreadnought would fire. The *Arizona*'s original big guns could elevate to a maximum of only 15 degrees, producing a range of approximately ten miles. The

Right: Rear Admiral Nathaniel R. Usher and Captain John D. McDonald pose in full-dress uniforms on the deck of the *Arizona* on the day of her commissioning. (Bain Collection, Library of Congress, LC-B2-4026-10)

Below: The flag is raised on the stern as the *Arizona* goes into commission. (Courtesy Ted Stone)

higher the elevation, the longer the range. The principle works up to an angle of 45 degrees. Above that, a higher elevation produces a shorter range. The *Arizona*'s original turrets were in no danger of challenging the maximum.

The big day for sending the *Arizona* to sea was scheduled to be Thursday, 9 November. Thus, on Wednesday, the ship's tall radio masts were removed from the foretop and maintop so the ship could pass safely beneath the Brooklyn Bridge. Liberty expired on board at midnight. Unfortunately, a heavy fog spoiled the ship's planned Thursday debut, so she didn't get under way for the first time until 8:30 on the morning of Friday the tenth. Superstitious sailors have long felt uneasy about beginning voyages on Fridays.

Aided by a covey of tugboats that filled the air with blasts of steam and tooting whistles, the *Arizona* eased out from her berth in the navy yard and began the journey down the East River. News photographers and a press boat were out to record her first journey, which was a festive one, both because of the attention and because of the crew's satisfaction in getting under way after weeks and months in the shipyard.

The first chore was to swing the ship around through the various headings to compensate her magnetic compasses, and then she was off to aid in gunnery practice in the Atlantic off Hampton Roads, Virginia. She was towing targets for her slightly older sister, the USS *Pennsylvania*, which had been commissioned in June, a little more than four months earlier than the *Arizona*. Towing targets and shooting at them would be major themes throughout the *Arizona*'s twenty-five-year service life, and she would be in company with the *Pennsylvania* many times.

While the ship was steaming, she used different combinations of turbines, depending on the situation. On the two outboard propeller shafts were cruising turbines, de-

signed for speeds below seventeen knots. In addition to the cruising turbine, each outboard shaft had a low-pressure turbine for ahead and astern. Each of the outboard shafts had its own engine room. In the center engine room were the two inboard shafts, each of which had two high-pressure turbines, one for ahead and one for astern. This arrangement reduced fuel-oil efficiency, because there was no clutch mechanism to disconnect ahead low-pressure turbines when going astern, and vice versa. At the slower speeds, steam from the boilers had to pass through first the cruising turbines, then the high-pressure turbines, then the low-pressure. Above seventeen knots, the cruising turbines were cut out, and only the high-pressure and low-pressure ones used.[21]

On 12 November Phil Smith, one of the new ship's new crew members, jotted a few lines on a postcard to his wife, Hazel, who lived in Paterson, New Jersey. Crew members had printed the postcard in the ship's print shop, and it provided a rundown of the *Arizona*'s first few weeks in commission. In a sense, the postcard was a predecessor of the current family gram that deployed ships put together to keep relatives back home informed about the doings of the ship and crew. The *Arizona* made it awfully easy. All the crew

member had to do was address the card and put on a one-cent stamp. Smith told his wife that the postcards would be coming out weekly and that he would like her to save them for him. Hazel did, and years later they wound up in the library of the University of Arizona.

After a stop in Newport, Rhode Island, to get a load of torpedoes from the torpedo station there, the *Arizona* was off for Guantanamo Bay, Cuba, and more tests, including standardization runs for the engineering plant and maneuvers to ascertain the ship's tactical data. The ship's first Thanksgiving featured the traditional dinner and an evening of entertainment that included silent movies, boxing, music by the ship's band, songs by a quartet, and dancing. There were no women on board, of course, so the men danced with one another. They also went swimming in Cuban waters, something they would not likely do in late fall in their home port of New York.[22]

Those who look for omens will probably make something of the fact that the *Arizona*'s first major problem occurred on Thursday, 7 December 1916—twenty-five years to the day before the Japanese struck her at Pearl Harbor. The ship had left Guantanamo a couple of days earlier for more engineering

trials. All went well until the seventh when the blades were stripped on the starboard low-pressure turbine. As Phil Smith summarized the problem in the postcard he wrote to his wife a couple of days after the mishap, "In other words one of our engines is on the bum. We are leaving in a couple of days. It will take about 4 months to fix it in N.Y."[23]

Before getting back home, the ship was directed to enter the Chesapeake Bay. She did so for the first time in mid-December and did more testing—this time with the guns. On 19–20 December she tested her 5-inch/51-caliber broadside guns, which were designed to shoot at close-range surface targets. The big day was 23 December, when the *Arizona* fired her 14-inch guns for the first time. Included in that day's activities was a salvo of all twelve big guns. Three-gun turrets were still a novelty in the U.S. Navy, having been introduced in the preceding *Nevada* class. The *Pennsylvania* and *Arizona* were the first U.S. battleships whose main battery consisted

entirely of three-gun turrets. To prevent the projectiles from interfering with one another in the air after being fired, the center gun of each turret was fired a fraction of a second later than the two outer guns.[24]

For the inexperienced men of the *Arizona*, the period before the shooting was a time of apprehension. The reality of the noise, heat, fire, and smoke produced by twelve heavy guns firing virtually simultaneously was impressive. It gave the men of the *Arizona* something to brag about when they went on liberty in New York. And they were going to have a lot of liberty in the next several weeks because the problems with the engineering plant would keep them in New York for some time. Except for a few trial runs, the ship was in the New York Navy Yard from late December 1916 to late March 1917.

Once installed inside a ship, the main engines are intended to stay there. But the starboard low-pressure turbine couldn't be repaired in its engine room. As a result, a

Left: This aerial view from the port quarter is of the *Arizona* approaching the Brooklyn Bridge as she steams down the East River. At the right side of the photo is a ferryboat; another is at the base of the bridge tower. The ship does not yet have 3-inch guns atop turret three, although the platform is in place. (UPI/Bettmann Newsphotos, 46143-INP)

portion of the quarterdeck and sections of the second and third decks had to be removed to provide an opening. Then a giant traveling crane pulled out the casing of the damaged turbine so that it could be taken to a machine shop in the yard. In mid-January the *Arizona* languished in dry dock while the flagship *Pennsylvania* and thirty-one other ships of the Atlantic Fleet headed for sunny Cuba to take part in the annual winter maneuvers and target practice.[25]

In New York, the men of the *Arizona* were putting up with cold drizzle and worse. The seamen who normally had to swab down the decks each morning now had to sweep off the snow as well. Being in dry dock meant that the crew had to go over the side to clean and paint the portion of the ship that was normally underwater. It was unpleasant work at any time and especially so during winter. It was less hazardous if the *Arizona*'s men could stand on floats when the dry dock was partially flooded. Seaman Lawrence Johnson commented in his diary for 9 January: "I went over the side, worked an hour, and knocked off until the drydock filled with water. Captain did not want to spend money on any of us for flowers so had us quit. 100 ft. from

U. S. S. ARIZONA

Navy Yard, New York, N. Y.
Saturday, December 30, 1916.

Dear————

SATURDAY: General Quarters sounded and as soon as all stations reported ready two salvos of one gun from each turret were fired. At 9:38 a. m. a salvo of twelve 14-inch guns was fired. We then proceeded to Lynnhaven Roads and after sending the Board ashore got under way for New York.

SUNDAY: Enroute New York 12½ knots. At 10:15 a. m. held Divine Services. Picked up Ambrose Channel Light vessel at 1:55 p. m. and proceeded up New York Harbor coming to anchor off Tompkinsville at 4:15 p. m.. Furlough party of five hundred men was sent ashore. Received Christmas stores and 27 bags of mail.

MONDAY: Anchored at Tompkinsville, N. Y.

TUESDAY: At 9:36 a. m, got underway for the Navy Yard and at 11:15 a. m. moored, port side, to berth 11. Sent the regular liberty party ashore. The Captain made his round of official calls.

WEDNESDAY: Received stores aboard. Navy Yard workmen began work on ship.

THURSDAY: Navy Yard mechanics employed in dismantling starboard low pressure engine preparatory to its removal to the machine shop on shore.

FRIDAY: Aired bedding. The weather is now very cold.

top deck of ship to bottom of drydock. A nice fall."[26]

The *Arizona*'s time in the New York Navy Yard was a mixed blessing for the crew. On the one hand, shipyard time is dreary, because the ship gets dirty and torn apart and the ship's routine is disrupted. Furthermore, the shipyard's civilian employees, seldom subject to the sort of discipline that Navy men are, work at their own pace. On the other hand, since the ship is in port, the crew has plenty of opportunities for liberty, and the New York area was a great place for it. The liberty parties were largest right after paydays, but sometimes there was a bonus. One night in January, for example, the Broadway Theatre of New York entertained a number of crew members at a free performance of the play *Twenty Thousand Leagues Under the Sea*, the story of a fictitious submarine named the *Nautilus*. Besides the liberty, dozens of *Arizona* crewmen were able to head home for leave. Visitors came aboard for tours of the ship, and the *Arizona*'s men enjoyed the opportunity to make new friends, especially the kind of friends who wore skirts.[27]

On 3 February 1917 the United States broke diplomatic relations with Germany after that nation announced the resumption of unrestricted submarine warfare around the British Isles. Thus, German U-boats were authorized to torpedo ships of all nations without warning. That included merchant ships from neutral countries such as the United States. On the afternoon of 3 February, because of a fear of sabotage against the yard and the ships there, a detail of forty men from the *Arizona* began standing guard duty to provide additional security at the entrance to the navy yard. The new international development gave added impetus to the infantry, artillery, and machine-gun training that the crew of the *Arizona* was receiving while in port. Equipped with belts, rifles, and bayonets, the practice landing parties hiked out to a park in the navy yard and held mock battles. They took along the 3-inch field piece that was stored near the base of the foremast. It was the source of simulated artillery support for the potential naval soldiers.[28]

In early March, after the conclusion of repairs ashore, the troublesome turbine was put back into place. On 14 March a German submarine sank a U.S. commercial ship without warning. Four more American merchantmen went to the bottom by the twenty-first, and the sinkings drew the United States inexorably into the European conflict. On 1 March Congress had approved President Woodrow Wilson's request to arm U.S.-flag merchant ships heading to the war zone. Now the *Arizona* began sending parties of sailors to serve on board those ships as naval gun crews. At the beginning of April the battleship finally managed to shake free from the shipyard after what her crew hoped was the solution of her engine problems. She steamed south to the Chesapeake Bay and dropped her anchor near its southern end. There she encountered many of the Atlantic Fleet warships that had left her behind in January.

On 6 April the U.S. Congress declared war on Germany. War had raged in Europe since the summer of 1914, and the United States had managed to stay neutral during that time. Indeed, in the presidential election of 1916, Wilson successfully ran for another term with the slogan "He kept us out of war." However, the new submarine campaign—combined with the infamous Zimmermann Telegram that suggested a German-Mexican plot against the United States—pushed the nation into a

Opposite page top: This close-up view, taken from a bridge, shows men in the maintop of the *Arizona* as she steams down the East River on her maiden voyage. At the very top, in front of the Lackawanna Railroad pier, is the ship's commissioning pennant. (UPI/Bettmann Newsphotos, 46143-INP)

Opposite page bottom: The ship passes under the Brooklyn Bridge on 10 November 1916. Directly above the *Arizona*'s smokestack is the Woolworth Building in Manhattan; it was then the nation's tallest. (*Baltimore News-American* Collection, McKeldin Library, University of Maryland)

Left: During the nearly six months between the *Arizona*'s commissioning and America's entry into World War I, the ship published weekly postcards that crew members could send home. The postcards were that era's counterpart of today's "family grams." This postcard reported the first time the *Arizona* fired her 14-inch guns. (Christopher Henry William Lloyd Collection, courtesy of Mrs. Virginia Agostini)

conflict then known as The Great War and now as World War I.

The *Arizona*'s new base—and it would remain so for much of the duration of the war—was at the mouth of the York River. Nearby was Yorktown, Virginia, the site of the British surrender at the end of the Revolutionary War. The York River site offered two advantages, having deep enough water to accommodate the *Arizona* and other battleships and being secure from German U-boats. The Navy was able to protect the area with antisubmarine nets and thus provide a safe haven.

Ironically, the Navy's newest battleship would have no opportunity to fight in the war—because she was too modern. In late 1917 the U.S. Navy dispatched a division of battleships to the British Isles to beef up the British Grand Fleet in its conflict with Germany's High Seas Fleet. The ships involved were the *Delaware*, *Florida*, *Wyoming*, *New York*, and *Texas*—all dreadnoughts but all coal-burners. Coal was in much more plentiful

supply than oil in the British Isles, so the older battleships were easier to support than the *Arizona* and her oil-burning contemporaries.

As a result, the *Arizona* spent a great deal of time during the war as a gunnery-training ship in the Chesapeake Bay. Her continuing function was to train the men who would then join the crews of commercial ships and naval escort vessels heading to the war zone. It was a useful role but certainly not a glamorous one. As it happened, the American coal-burners did not get into combat either, because after the Battle of Jutland in May 1916 the High Seas Fleet holed up in German ports and sat out the rest of the war. The presence of U.S. battleships did enable the British to employ some of their other battleships elsewhere while the U.S. ships were part of a force in readiness for a possible clash with the German Navy.

One immediate effect of the onset of war was the rigid censorship imposed on members of the crew. No longer did the *Arizona* supply the chatty postcards every Saturday for

Phil Smith and his shipmates to send their relatives. Now the postcards resembled form letters. All Phil could do was date the card, sign his name, and indicate when he had last heard from his wife. The back of the card contained various preprinted messages, and he could cross out those that didn't apply. Thus, the entire message on his card of 23 April was "I am quite well and am getting along well. I have received your letter dated April 18. Letter follows at first opportunity." If he wanted to tell Hazel he still loved her, he had to communicate that separately. His outgoing letters were also censored to ensure that he didn't violate military security.

Another effect of the beginning of war was that the *Arizona* lost some of her 5-inch broadside guns. They were removed to arm cargo ships. The battleship still had enough to use for training and used them frequently. No German battleships were going to cross the Atlantic to fight it out, but the *Arizona* might encounter U-boats when she ventured outside her secure anchorage into the Atlantic. Thus, torpedo-defense drill became almost a daily staple of her training routine. The 5-inch/51-caliber guns of the secondary battery were intended for just that purpose.

Still another wartime precaution was that of sending out 50-foot motor launches as picket boats to patrol the submarine nets at Yorktown. Seaman Joe Driscoll was among those who went on the patrols in the *Arizona*'s picket boat. Mounted in the bow was a gun that fired 1-pound shells. At best, it was probably intended as an antipersonnel weapon. To take on the submarines themselves, the men of the *Arizona* would need the firepower of the ship's 5-inch guns.[29]

While some of the men were leaving to serve in merchant ships, others were coming aboard to receive training. On 14 April, for instance, a draft of eighty-two men reported aboard after undergoing recruit training at the Great Lakes Naval Training Station in Illinois. The next day the ferryboat from Hampton Roads brought another large draft. The result was that the *Arizona*'s crew regularly consisted of a great many transients. New men would come, be trained, go to new duties, and be replaced by still more new men. By mid-June the crew had swelled to 1,700 because of the influx. Finding places for the new arrivals to sling their hammocks was a problem, although the crowding was relieved

considerably when some five hundred men left to be part of the initial crew of the *New Mexico*, a new battleship.[30]

Even though the *Arizona* was far from the combat zone, the Navy ensured that her men had a great deal to keep them busy. While the ship was at Yorktown or operating out in Chesapeake Bay, the crew's day started with a trip topside to do some calisthenics before breakfast. While today's Navy, much concerned about physical fitness, provides ships with workout facilities such as weights and stationary bicycles, in the *Arizona* about all a man had for the workout were his own body and some instructions from officers or petty officers. One of the activities was called double-timing—essentially jogging—on the ship's quarterdeck. Sometimes the marines did the exercises with their rifles carried in the port-arms position.[31]

After breakfast the men of the deck force swabbed decks topside or perhaps holystoned

Above: A group of sailors with the *Arizona*'s hat bands poses in a model car at a photographer's studio, about 1916. (Courtesy of Gordon Rosen, Naval Historical Center, NH 76593)

them to get them even cleaner. To holystone the *Arizona*'s wooden decks, a man used a piece of brick with a hole bored part of the way into it, inserting a long stick into the hole and then laboriously pushing and pulling the brick across the decks to scrape away the top layer. Normally, the sailors put sand on the decks as well, along with a cleaning agent. The effect was much the same as sandpapering a piece of wood.

During the day each man was occupied in a myriad of ways in the specialties involved in his particular rating, whether it was cooking, working in the machine shop, issuing supplies from storerooms, running the boilers, cleaning clothes, or what have you. No matter what their ratings, however, many of the men were involved in the chipping and painting that are part of the continuous process of preserving a ship against corrosion.

In the evenings, once the day's work and drills were completed, the men of the *Arizona* had the chance to relax. Sometimes they watched silent movies together, or they might read, play cards, or just shoot the breeze. Individual episodes of a movie serial titled *The Shielding Shadow* were shown night after night that April.

On weekends members of the crew went ashore on liberty, visiting places such as Yorktown and Gloucester. They played baseball, took in the sights, and got a chance to eat something other than the customary shipboard fare. Seaman Martin Kos, for instance, particularly enjoyed the fruitcake for sale in the area, so that was a regular Sunday treat for him. Even so, he had to be frugal in his purchases. He received only a few dollars each payday, and the rest of his salary went directly to his parents in the form of an allotment. Even though liberty opportunities were available, life in the York River was far, far different from what the crew had known in New York. On 12 May Seaman Lawrence Johnson lamented in his diary that he had just gone ashore for the first time since the ship left the navy yard nearly a month and a half earlier.[32]

Because of the emphasis on training gun crews for merchant ships, the *Arizona*'s 5-inch broadside guns got a great deal of use during World War I. Each of the 5-inch guns had a

Right: The *Arizona* and *New York* sit across a pier from each other in the New York Navy Yard in this drawing made by Vernon Howe Bailey in early 1917. In the foreground is a small torpedo boat. (Courtesy of Mrs. Wilbur Jenkins, Naval Historical Center, NH 86451)

gunner's mate striker in charge, and each group of two or three guns had a rated gunner's mate over it. Even when the men weren't firing the guns, they rehearsed over and over the techniques of loading projectiles and powder and aiming the guns in terms of elevation and deflection. Much of the Navy's training program involved a seemingly endless repetition of physical drills so that the men could accomplish the movements quickly and smoothly—essentially without thinking. Ammunition allowances dictated how often the guns were actually fired. To save ammunition, the ship used sub-caliber guns attached to the larger ones. The 5-inch guns had .30-caliber guns on top of the barrels, and the 14-inch guns had one-pounders. The sub-caliber pieces enabled the gun crews and trainees to reproduce the trajectories of the larger guns during some of the target practices without using full-size ammunition. At short-range battle practice, the sub-caliber guns were connected to the firing keys of the larger ones. Because the guns were so close to the target, the smaller bullets hit the target where the full-size ones would have.[33]

The guns demanded a lot of routine maintenance and upkeep. On Monday there was general cleaning, wiping off the muzzles and cleaning the muzzle faces, wiping off paint work in the spaces assigned to the crew, and rigging the sub-caliber piece that was mounted atop the barrel and permitted aiming practice without firing the gun itself. On Tuesday the crew added checking and cleaning the ammunition-handling rooms to the routine, along with polishing brightwork, a never-ending chore in the Navy. On Wednesday there was more time in the handling rooms and the checking of spare parts for the guns. On Thursday the men scrubbed guns and cleaned water buckets. On Friday they cleaned the powder charges and battle lamps, worked with the sub-calibers, and shined brightwork.

On Saturday the gun crews prepared for the weekly inspection, and this preparation included removing the tompions, round plugs in the muzzle ends of the barrels. After inspection the men replaced the tompions. Sunday it was time to clean muzzle faces and muzzles again. Cleaning was a continuous battle against the salt, moisture, and dirt that inhibit smooth operation of gun components. During spare time the gunner's mates and their strikers cleaned the ammunition hoists leading from the handling rooms to the guns, and twice a week they worked on maintaining the loading machine.[34]

In this ritual of training and target practice, the repetition produced a great deal of sameness as the days and weeks went on. It was a way of life often considerably removed from the reasons for which the men on the guns had joined the Navy in the first place. In the early months of the war especially, the young sailors were not in the *Arizona* as a result of any great desire to make the world safe for democracy. Years afterward Everett Fore, who had been a seventeen-year-old seaman on board the *Arizona* in 1917, talked about the difference between the United States' war objectives and his own approach: "See, a lot of us were too young . . . to think about that. All we was thinking about was being in the Navy and, you know, doing our duty. . . . A lot of us never even realized when we joined the Navy that we were going to be

in war, you know. We didn't ever realize that at all."[35]

Though Fore had joined the Navy to see the world, the advent of war meant his world would be limited largely to the area near Yorktown, Virginia, and his freedom would be considerably circumscribed by the dictates of the officers and petty officers under whom he served.

In the summer of 1917 the *Arizona* and other ships got some respite from the monotony when they were able go out into the Atlantic and operate as battleships for a change. True, they had had some experience firing their 14-inch guns during target practice in the Chesapeake Bay, but the time at sea afforded the opportunity for mock battles and refreshed the tactical skills of those who stood watches on the bridge and in the conning tower. Caution was a watchword, needed more at sea than behind the submarine nets at Yorktown. At night the *Arizona* and other ships of the fleet operated with their lights turned off. Seaman Joe Driscoll learned just how serious the darken-ship discipline was when he lit a cigarette topside one night while he was standing a gun watch on his 5-inch/51 mount near the bridge. Captain McDonald sent him to the brig for five days on bread and water. It was a costly cigarette.[36]

Besides the sea operations, the summer also brought trips to New York for shipyard work and liberty. Afterward, the Board of Inspection and Survey ran trials to see how well the *Arizona* performed after all the work done on her turbines. Soon after she returned to the York River, a flock of old battleships stood in and anchored: the *Wisconsin, Missouri, Ohio, Kentucky, Kearsarge, Illinois, Alabama, Kansas, Minnesota, Rhode Island, New Jersey,* and *Georgia*. World War I had given many of them a last gasp of active service, but they were near the end of the line. All were of the pre-dreadnought type, and all except the *Alabama* were veterans of the 1907–09 world cruise of the Great White Fleet. Thus, the service life of the new *Arizona* overlapped briefly with that of these aging stalwarts of Teddy Roosevelt's big-stick era.[37]

While at the anchorage, Captain McDonald demonstrated that he was still quick to discipline his men. He confined one of the *Arizona*'s seamen to the brig for five days on a diet of bread and water for spitting tobacco over the side of the ship into the York River.

In addition, a chief gunner's mate found himself disrated to gunner's mate first class because he was insolent to midshipmen.[38]

The *Arizona* spent much of September in Long Island Sound, then returned to the familiar York River. In October the ship's radio equipment—still popularly known as "wireless" in those days—brought in news of baseball's World Series, in Morse code. The crew of the *Arizona*, like the rest of the nation, was eager to learn the outcome of each day's game between the New York Giants and Chicago White Sox. The White Sox won, but two years later the same team would disgrace itself when its members earned the title "Black Sox" by conspiring to throw the World Series to the Cincinnati Reds.[39]

One of the new men who arrived in the ship that fall was a seaman named Glenn Frisbie. After a brief stint in the deck force, he was assigned to work in one of the supply department's storerooms. In the deck force, the boatswain's mates had controlled virtually every move he made. In the main storeroom, however, things were different: he wasn't told to do anything. The man in charge was a senior petty officer with twenty years in the Navy; predictably, he was known as "Pop."

When men from various departments of the *Arizona* came to the storeroom with requisition chits, Pop would go get the desired items and hand them out. Frisbie felt a bit frustrated, because he wasn't getting any direction, so he set out on a do-it-yourself training course. He wandered around the large storeroom and discovered that it resembled a combination of a hardware store and general store. He saw shelves and bins filled with brass, tin, galvanized metal, canvas, nuts and bolts, office supplies, and as Frisbie put it, "everything that you could think of that would be required on a ship." In other storerooms were such things as lumber, canvas, cloth, and paint. Within a month or six weeks Pop perceived that Frisbie knew his way around, and from then on the seaman handled the requisitions, and Pop sat at his desk, quietly being in charge. It was a way of working that Navy chief petty officers have mastered.

As he became more and more knowledgeable, Frisbie came to realize when supplies of various items were getting low, and he would suggest to Pop that it was time for a reorder. Pop filled out a requisition, and it went up the

U. S. S. ARIZONA

THANKSGIVING DINNER
November 29, 1917

Thanksgiving 1917

MENU

OYSTER COCKTAIL

SOUPS

CREAM OF CHICKEN   TOMATO

RELISHES

CELERY   SWEET PICKLES

ENTREES

SPICED VIRGINIA HAM   CANDIED SWEET POTATOES
CAPER SAUCE

ROASTS

PRINCESS ANNE TURKEY   GIBLET GRAVY
OYSTER DRESSING   BAKED NEW POTATOES
ASPARAGUS TIPS   CRANBERRY SAUCE

SALADS

COMBINATION FRUIT   MAYONNAISE

DESSERTS

MINCE PIE   PUMPKIN PIE
ORANGES   APPLES   BANANAS
                 ASSORTED NUTS
COFFEE   COCOA

line to the ship's paymaster. When the items did come, necessarily by boat when the *Arizona* was anchored at Yorktown, Frisbie and other storekeepers had to ask the officer of the deck to summon a working party comprised of sailors from various departments throughout the ship. The working party would haul the things from topside down to the proper storerooms. Of the men who helped shoulder the burden, Frisbie recalled, "You started out with 25, and if you ended up with five, you were lucky." Not only did the men disappear as the work progressed, but so did some of the supplies. If, for instance, candy came aboard for sale in the ship's store, the lights might go out briefly when it was being carried on one of the lower decks. When the lights came back on, less candy belonged to the ship than before.[40]

That fall, Captain McDonald wrote to the Bureau of Construction and Repair in Washington to try to get some improvements in the bridge area. The bridge itself, protected with canvas as a windbreak, was directly aft of the armored conning tower and at about the same level. In the skipper's opinion, this arrangement was unsatisfactory for conning the ship from the conning tower, which was supposed to be his station in battle. Visibility from inside the armored oval was bad enough because only narrow viewing slits pierced the armor, but even worse, the presence of the bridge and its navigation instruments prevented him from seeing more than 20 degrees aft of the beam on either side. Of more personal concern, the rotund McDonald

Above: Even in war-time, the men of the *Arizona* ate well on Thanksgiving. This was the feast of 1917. (Courtesy Glenn H. Frisbie)

Opposite page: Bedding is being aired on the lifelines in this view taken from the foretop and looking toward the stern. The picture was evidently taken in 1917 because the searchlight platform on the mainmast does not yet have the mattresslike padding that came the following year. At the lower edge of the photo, pointing skyward, are two 3-inch antiaircraft guns at the after end of the superstructure. (Courtesy Hans Henke)

requested an enlargement of his emergency cabin; it was cramped and had only a transom, or sofa, on which he could sleep. He had a spacious in-port cabin below the quarterdeck, but it was too far from the bridge and not suitable for use when at sea.[41]

The captain succeeded in half his desires. The visibility problem wasn't solved until a subsequent shipyard period when a mostly enclosed bridge was built aft of the conning tower and high enough to avoid interfering with the view. As for his other request, on 11 October 1917 the bureau authorized the ship's force to enlarge the emergency cabin, and it increased the *Arizona*'s allowance list "to provide for a brass bed with mattresses and pillows."[42]

The *Arizona*'s balky engines continued to plague her during fleet operations that fall. Even though the ship had spent a good deal of time in the New York Navy Yard in 1917 for turbine repairs, the problem wasn't really solved. In January 1918 a new chief engineer, Lieutenant Commander Harold G. Bowen, was assigned, and he was determined to do something about the problem. Once, when the ship anchored in the icy York River after maneuvers, Captain McDonald sent for Bowen and expressed amazement that the engineer hadn't protested backing the turbines at full speed. Years later, in his autobiography, Bowen wrote, "I told him that everyone knew the *Arizona* was no good and the sooner the turbines were completely busted up and some new ones put in the better it would be for everyone."[43]

Bowen began studying engineering blueprints in detail and went over the reports of the various malfunctions the engines had experienced. Then he went inside the casing of the low-pressure turbine when it was open for inspection. It was so large that he could stand up inside the turbine rotor and move with it as it rotated. By doing so, he could participate in what he claimed was "that favorite sport on the *Arizona*—listening for rubbing turbine blades."

He got permission from a reluctant Bureau of Engineering to shave .02 of an inch off all the rotor and casing blades in the most troublesome turbine. Some men from the New York Navy Yard helped, and the results were impressive. Once the rubbing stopped, the danger of damage decreased, and the fuel efficiency improved dramatically. When the ship later visited the navy yard itself, the other turbines got a similar treatment. In assessing the problem in his book, Bowen argued that the *Arizona*'s huge engines represented a real nadir in the development of steam turbines. He suggested that they should have been put in a museum to show young engineers what things were like before the development of better machinery.[44] The problems weren't completely solved until the ship was modernized at the end of the 1920s and received new turbines.

From time to time the ship joined other battleships going out for fleet maneuvers. During drills in mid-January, a storm demonstrated the flimsiness of the cage-type mast, toppling the one just aft of the bridge on board the USS *Michigan*, which was steaming in company with the *Arizona*.[45] During fleet operations in the Atlantic in February, the *Arizona* was involved in battle problems and antisubmarine maneuvers. German U-boats did operate off the U.S. East Coast, so the precautions were justified.

On 18 February Rear Admiral John McDonald was relieved as commanding officer by Captain Josiah McKean. McDonald had

been promoted the year before but remained in command until McKean's arrival.

In late February the crew cut away the ship's starboard whaleboat, rigged in davits for use as a lifeboat, after it had been damaged by rough seas. Alas, the battered boat drifted ashore; its discovery started rumors that the *Arizona* had been sunk. Since her wartime movements were classified, it took some time to quell the untruth that was circulating about her.[46]

Though the war raged on in the trenches of France and the sea-lanes of the Atlantic in 1918, the men of the *Arizona* were still living a lackluster existence far from the front lines. Seaman Larry Flint reported to the ship for duty that year and found the boring routine one that many crew members were eager to get away from. He explained years afterward that it was "no wonder we were pitied by the men we replaced."

Navy life is different in many ways from the civilian version, and learning this difference is part of each recruit's indoctrination. Seaman Flint was on watch shortly after reporting aboard when he was directed to strike the ship's bell to mark the time. The Navy divides the clock into four-hour segments, beginning at midnight. During waking hours one of the watchstanders strikes the correct number of bells every thirty minutes, increasing by one bell each half hour and then starting over after reaching eight bells. The Navy style is to strike them in pairs, so at noon the rhythm would be ding-ding, ding-ding, ding-ding, ding-ding. Flint didn't know that and so just began striking the bell in the same meter, he explained later, used by a cow walking to pasture in his home state of Ohio. He was on the seventh ding when the captain called for the officer of the deck on the speaking tube and demanded, "Who in the [expletive deleted] rang that bell?" The skipper got his answer, and Flint got a lesson in Navy bell ringing.[47]

In 1918 the ship did many of the same things as the previous year. One novelty was the arrival of a group of Naval Academy midshipmen for training; a professor from Annapolis came along to help them with their studies while they were on board. As in 1917, the *Arizona* was often anchored at Yorktown. When she was under way in the Chesapeake Bay, she and other battleships occasionally

Below: This port broadside view, taken in May 1918, captures the essence of the *Arizona*'s World War I service. She is anchored in the York River near Yorktown, Virginia. Some of her casemates for the 5-inch broadside guns have been plated over. The stack has zigzag shapes on it to make the work of the enemy's stereoscopic visual range finders more difficult. (National Archives, 19-N-1979)

fired their 12-inch and 14-inch guns at the old *San Marcos*, the hulk of which was partially sunk in Tangier Sound. Commissioned in 1895 as the second-class battleship *Texas*, she had fought in the Spanish-American War. The nation's only other second-class battleship, the *Maine*, had been sunk at the war's outset. In 1911 the old ship's name was changed to *San Marcos* so that a new battleship could become the *Texas*. After the renaming, she was sunk and served as a target.[48]

For antiaircraft-gunnery practice the *Arizona* shot at large balloons. Members of the ship's marine detachment fired the 3-inch gun mounts—known at the time as "sky guns"—against the nearly stationary balloons with some degree of success, but the guns were of questionable value against the aircraft of the era, even though the planes were slow moving. There were four guns altogether, two atop turret three and two at the after end of the superstructure. They could be fired by percussion or electrically by storage batteries that supplied a current to release the firing pins. The maximum angle of fire was eighty degrees, and the objective was to put up a barrage of thirteen-pound projectiles to keep planes from getting close enough to the ship to bomb her.[49]

The *Arizona*'s gunnery officer, Lieutenant Commander Thomas C. Kinkaid, discovered that the 3-inch guns had sufficient range and power to do some damage if their projectiles hit an airplane, but he was skeptical about the worth of the control system aft on the mainmast. If the barrage were sufficiently heavy, perhaps it would deter planes from getting too close. During an oral-history interview with Columbia University years later, Kinkaid said puckishly that he thought the greatest value of the 3-inch guns would be in scaring the enemy, much like Chinese warriors of old who made noise when they mounted a charge in battle. As a flag officer one war later, Kinkaid played a prominent role in the U.S. victory over Japan.[50]

Even more dubious than the 3-inch guns for use by a battleship were torpedoes. At times the *Arizona* put target boats in the water and practiced firing torpedoes from the ship's submerged tubes. It was definitely a weapon of last resort, to be used only if an enemy somehow got within torpedo range without being stopped by the ship's guns.

Right: The crew gathers on deck to cheer their shipmates in the intradivision race-boat competition at Yorktown, Virginia, on 18 May 1918. As a wartime measure, the tops and searchlight platforms have a mattresslike padding as protection against shell fragments. (National Archives, 19-N-1977)

Left: The crew relaxes on the quarterdeck during wartime. The men on the galley deck are looking down on an impromptu musical concert by the ship's band. The two thin smokestacks to the left of the cage mainmast are for the exhaust from the cooking in the galley. (Arizona Department of Library, Archives and Public Records)

When the *Arizona* was at anchor, her race-boat crews were often in competition with boats from other ships. The oarsmen were surrogates for the rest of their shipmates. The races were spirited, and the men of various ships bet on the outcomes. In addition to the crews that represented the *Arizona* as a whole, several of the divisions had race-boat crews as well.

On 4 July, while the ship was anchored at Yorktown, race-boat crews from the various battleships competed for the Battenberg Cup, donated by the former British First Sea Lord Prince Louis of Battenberg, father of the later Lord Mountbatten. The cup became highly prized as a symbol of athletic supremacy in the U.S. Navy, and on 4 July 1918 the prize went to the crew of the *Arizona*.

Early in the race the boat from the battleship *Virginia* crowded in and broke the oar of one of the *Arizona*'s men. Even so, he kept on with what was left of his oar. The two prime competitors were the crews from the *Arizona* and *Nevada*. They raced head and head for two miles of the course. Near the finish, the men in the *Arizona*'s boat passed their own ship, crowded with men. The enthusiastic cheers of their shipmates gave the rowers the final impetus they needed. They spurted to a three-length lead over the *Nevada*'s boat and maintained it the rest of the way. The winning time for the three-mile race was thirty-two minutes and ten seconds.

So the race-boat crews and other sailors could stay in condition, the *Arizona* had a makeshift rowing machine made of weights and pulleys. The machine was stored in an area known as the "bull ring" at the base of the ship's cage foremast. After the war a more sophisticated rowing machine was set up on one of the ship's lower decks. In addition to the exercise facilities, the bull ring was also a storage site for lengths of mooring line, fire hoses, and other shipboard gear.[51] While such equipment was obviously necessary for running the ship, the Navy's supply system at times went overboard. One day while the ship was at Yorktown, as Storekeeper Glenn Frisbie noted in his diary, a working party loaded eight thousand pounds of Vaseline, an eight-year supply, into the storerooms.[52]

On 12 July the *Arizona* steamed out to shoot short-range battle practice officially and did extremely well; in fact, she achieved a first. Turret two became the U.S. Navy's first triple turret armed with 14-inch guns to earn an E. Two different sets of pointers were used, with each shooting three projectiles per barrel. That amounted to eighteen rounds at a range of 1,800 yards. The turret had seventeen hits on the target in eighteen shots. The first set of pointers made its score in one minute and five seconds, the second set in one minute and twenty-four seconds.

The combination of speed and accuracy had carried the day. The criterion for an E called for each set of pointers to fire its three salvos in one minute and eighteen seconds and make all hits. The second set didn't quite make the

between salvos for the turret crew to clear the barrel, load the new projectile and powder, and then fire. As a reward for their efforts, each man in the turret crew received $20.00 in prize money, and the gun pointers got extra pay per month. It was a tangible incentive for top performance. The 5-inch broadside guns also contributed to the *Arizona*'s fine shooting that day; eight of them achieved E's.[53]

Even while the *Arizona* continued to languish behind the antisubmarine nets, some officers in Washington were anticipating the possibility of sending her overseas. On 13 July the Chief of the Bureau of Ordnance wrote to the Chief of Naval Operations to request the conversion of spaces originally allocated as magazines for the four second-deck 5-inch broadside guns at the ship's stern. The guns had been removed to outfit merchant ships, and the Bureau of Ordnance felt it was appropriate to use the spaces to store 14-inch target-practice projectiles so they could be transported to the war zone.

The requested change was turned down on the grounds that the removal of the 5-inch guns was only temporary and that the ship already had sufficient storage space for main-battery projectiles. Her turret barbettes and handling rooms could accommodate 1,588 projectiles, whereas her wartime allowance was only 1,200 projectiles and her drill allowance, 36.[54] As it happened, the *Arizona* never did get her fantail broadside guns back. The crew was just as happy without those guns since they were so close to the water that they were difficult to operate in anything except a calm sea.

When not south in the York River, the *Arizona* went to the navy yard at New York for upkeep. There her crew members found a variety of ways to pass their time. In early September, for instance, the armored cruiser *Pueblo* stood in and moored alongside the *Arizona*. When commissioned in 1905, the cruiser was the USS *Colorado*, but she was renamed in 1916 so that her original name could be used for one of the new 16-inch–gun battleships due to be built. Thus the *Pueblo* wasn't very old chronologically, but her main battery of four 8-inch guns didn't give her a great deal of pop. Much of the war she spent protecting shipping in the South Atlantic and escorting convoys in the North Atlantic.

George Leymé and other members of the *Arizona*'s signal gang talked to the crewmen

Above: The *Arizona*'s race-boat crew that won the Battenberg Cup in July 1918 poses on deck. Seated to the left of the life ring is the boat coxswain, J. D. Eldridge, chief master-at-arms. (Courtesy Hans Henke)

Right: Captain Josiah S. McKean commanded the *Arizona* for seven months in 1918 before being selected for rear admiral. (Courtesy Hans Henke)

standard, but the average for both sets did. In sum, for the better of the two sets, the three 3-gun salvos had been fired in sixty-five seconds, allowing just over thirty seconds

of the nearby *Pueblo* and the battleship *North Dakota* through visual communications. Leymé, who had just reported aboard, was able to practice what he was learning in the shipboard semaphore course. The ship-to-ship conversations provided a means of finding out what the men of the other ships had been doing, and they enabled the *Arizona*'s signalmen to become more proficient in their duties even when their ship wasn't doing much operating.[55]

On 11 September, which was a chilly day in the New York Navy Yard, the *Arizona* got a new commanding officer. Josiah McKean had been skipper only since February, but he had been selected for rear admiral in late August and thus promoted out of the job because a battleship skipper is a captain's billet. Captain McDonald had been similarly promoted while still on board the *Arizona*, but at that time promotion on the basis of merit rather than seniority was just becoming the rule, and naval procedures had not yet adjusted. Mc-Kean remained on board the ship only about two weeks after being promoted. He was the last of the *Arizona*'s commanding officers to be promoted to flag rank while in the job.

Unlike presidential inaugurations, in which the spotlight is on the new man and what he plans to do, naval change-of-command ceremonies accord the greatest honor to the individual who is being relieved. Admiral McKean spoke to the crew as they mustered aft in dress blues and flat hats. Once he had been relieved by Captain John H. Dayton, McKean left by the starboard gangway, receiving a rousing cheer from the crew. Such cheers were commonplace in the Navy of the era, unlike today's much more sedate way of honoring departing skippers.[56]

Being back in the navy yard gave the crew opportunities for better liberty than they found in Yorktown, and they also didn't have to put up with the inconvenience of riding boats between ship and shore. Seaman George Leymé, for instance, liked to visit Brooklyn's Prospect Park, a couple of miles away from the shipyard. If he had a long weekend of liberty, he could scout the park for girls all day Saturday and Sunday and spend Saturday night in an inexpensive hotel. The hotel room enabled him to get away from the rigors of shipboard routine. Leymé was so enamored of girls at that stage in his life that he made a slight change in his name. Christened George

Russell Leymé, he awarded himself the additional name of Irwin so he could say his initials were G.I.R.L. As he branched out from the borough of Brooklyn, Leymé saw more of the big city. In a late-September diary entry he wrote, "Very beautiful scenery in Bronx; this scenery happens to be chicks."[57]

Another stopping place for Leymé while he was on liberty was the Navy YMCA, because it catered to the low budgets of enlisted men. There he could get a haircut, go for a swim, participate in some of the other recreational activities offered, eat his meals, and stay overnight. This haven enabled him to avoid one of the customary perils of the *Arizona*'s food—weevils in the bread. He had to sleep

Above: Burney gear for the sweeping of mine cables was added to the ship as a wartime precaution. These views, port side and dead ahead, were taken in dry dock at the New York Navy Yard on 24 September 1918. The holes were used for streaming paravanes to push the mine cables out from the side of the ship. Below, a sailor is shown painting the forefoot of the ram bow. (National Archives, 19-N-681 [port side] and 19-N-682 [head-on])

Left: The wartime crew poses on the forecastle in November 1918. Just above the life ring are the executive officer, Commander Walter Stratton Anderson, and the commanding officer, Captain John H. Dayton. Numerals signifying the year are above the ship's bell on the forward searchlight platform. (First Interstate Bank Archives, Phoenix, Arizona)

Inset: While one photographer was shooting the whole crew from the bow in November 1918, another snapped this close-up of the men on the foremast. There is antisplinter padding on the foretop, searchlight platform, and bridge. An enclosed bridge with windows has been added since the views taken in May 1918. (Special Collections, University of Arizona Library, 84-26-104)

on a cot at the YMCA, but it was cheaper than a hotel room.[58]

In October the *Arizona* was back at Yorktown to resume her duties. George Leymé contrasted it with New York by calling it "this mud hole of York river." From the ship's anchorage the men had a good view of the Yorktown monument ashore. In October 1781 British General Cornwallis surrendered to George Washington at Yorktown, and Leymé observed in his diary that "the Kaiser is on the verge of doing the same act." As the weeks passed, rumors continued to float about that the fighting in Europe would soon be over. Until it was, the *Arizona*'s crew continued with its duties: standing watches, cleaning and preserving the ship, standing inspections, and getting under way for torpedo-defense gun-firing drills.

Despite Leymé's preference for New York, he went ashore in Yorktown whenever possible. He returned to the ship somewhat the worse for wear one Saturday. He had rooted himself hoarse in cheering the *Arizona*'s football team to a 23-0 victory over the *Pennsylvania*'s team. What's more, his blues were covered with dust from the playing field, and he had stuffed himself with too much candy and other goodies.

In early November he was confined to sick bay for three days because of a sharp pain in his back. When he returned to his duties on the signal bridge, he joked in his diary, "Feeling fine after getting so much rest and sleep at the sick bay. I believe I will get sick again soon."[59]

The war that wasn't a war for the *Arizona* came to an end on 11 November with the signing of an armistice in Europe. For many years after the Great War, Americans celebrated that date as Armistice Day.

On board the *Arizona* the crew celebrated as well. Seaman Martin Kos observed that the men made so much noise in their excitement that they just about raised the ship out of the water.[60] It was a cold and windy day with the *Arizona* and *Pennsylvania* under way for gunnery practice. When the *Arizona* came in to her anchorage that evening, some of the changes wrought by peace were already apparent. She didn't put out roving picket boats for protection, she had her lights on instead of being at darken-ship condition, and she no longer required her men to stand continuous gun watches. Even though it was cold for the men on watch topside that night, few noticed because they were doing so much skylarking.[61]

2 TOO LATE 'OVER THERE'

November 1918–August 1921

One of the most popular songs of the wartime period was George M. Cohan's spirited "Over There," which included the lyrics, "We won't be back 'til it's over, over there." Generally confined to the York River and Chesapeake Bay during the war, the *Arizona* wouldn't get to Europe until it was over, over there. On the plus side, she could finally be a ship instead of a training platform. A week after the armistice, she was under way for England.

For the experienced sailors the ocean crossing wasn't really a problem, but it was something else for the new men. Winter in the North Atlantic is the worst time for heavy seas, and that season wasn't far away. As the *Arizona* headed eastward, she rolled and pitched—depending on which direction the waves and swells were coming from. The movement was so jarring that men had trouble with normally easy chores such as lashing up their hammocks. The ship pushed her plow-shaped bow down into the seas, and as the bow came up it threw back green water and white spray. One swell forced its way in through a broadside gun port and flooded the deck inside the casemate with two inches of water. Spray coming over the forecastle washed up against the bridge. The ship's seamen didn't have to worry about swabbing the teak decks topside. With choppy seas and rainsqualls, Mother Nature was taking care of the chore several times a day. For those such as Seaman George Leymé who stood their watches topside, the combination of rain and cold wind was not pleasant. It wasn't even safe inside the ship. One night Leymé's hammock lashing broke; he fell to the deck with a thump, biting his tongue and hurting his head and shoulders.[1]

Fog was the enemy as the *Arizona* neared the English coast, but she was finally able to anchor at Portland, where she met up with the battleship *Oklahoma* and a number of other American warships. Before passing through the submarine nets into Portland Harbor, the men of the *Arizona* saw a castle on a high hill; they were a long way from Yorktown. Liberty parties began shoving off for London, Weymouth, and elsewhere. The American sailors bought "Limey" booze, beer, wine, and cigarettes—in part just because those commodities were different from the brands they were used to in the United States. Some men got souvenirs from German prisoners of war who had not yet been repatriated. For Seaman George Leymé, as for many other members of the *Arizona*'s crew, the visit to Portland marked the first time they had been in a foreign country. So fond of the girls back in New York, Leymé found still more in his travels ashore in England. Alas, when one of them visited the ship to see him, he couldn't be with her because he was on watch.[2]

Storekeeper Glenn Frisbie got out for some sight-seeing in the beautiful English countryside, and the British showed him a great deal of gratitude for the American contribution to the recent war effort. When he visited the port city of Weymouth, he found himself even more welcomed because any number of local citizens had essentially the same last name as his, even if the spellings varied.[3]

After nearly two weeks in England, the *Arizona* joined Battleship Division Six and steamed to Brest, France. En route she served as part of the ceremonial escort for the transport *George Washington*, which was carrying President Woodrow Wilson to France for peace-treaty negotiations. The *Pennsylvania* and two divisions of destroyers were already accompanying the transport, which had previously been a passenger ship for the North German Lloyd Line. To honor the president on his arrival in France on 13 December, the other battleships lined up in columns as the *Pennsylvania* and *George Washington* steamed between them.[4]

The men of the *Arizona* manned the rail, rendered honors, played the "The Star-Spangled Banner," and gave three cheers for the president. Wilson acknowledged with a

Above: Followed by another battleship, the *Arizona* enters Brest, France, on 13 December 1918. The close-up shows the maintop, the bottom of the radio mast, and the top of the cage mainmast. (Courtesy Hans Henke)

Right: The crew mans the rail, probably for President Woodrow Wilson at Brest, France, in December 1918. The photo shows the mainmast with padded searchlight platform and the V-front screen on the aft control station for the secondary battery (5-inch/51 broadside guns). (Arizona Department of Library, Archives and Public Records)

wave. Each ship fired a twenty-one–gun salute. Overhead, American seaplanes and balloons joined in the festivities. The *Arizona* and other ships flew large American flags, also known as ensigns, high in each vessel. George Leymé, watching from the signal bridge, observed that it "certainly was a beautiful scene to see the large ensigns floating in the breeze along the columns as far as the eye could see. There was [*sic*] about thirty destroyers, nine battle wagons, and about nine or ten [French] ships." In addition to the *Arizona* and *Pennsylvania*, the U.S. battleship contingent included the *Wyoming*, *New York*, *Texas*, *Oklahoma*, *Florida*, *Utah*, and *Nevada*.[5]

Another milestone event that day was the publication of volume 1, number 1 of the *Arizonian*, the ship's newspaper. Its publication was inspired in part by several British journalists who were riding the ship from England to France. Unlike their homeland, where food was strictly rationed, the *Arizona* served bountiful meals. In fact, the paper joked that the writers wished the ship would get lost so they'd have more time to eat before reaching port. The lead article in the paper reported that Wilson's trip to France marked the first time that a U.S. president had left the country during his term of office. The most intriguing item in the paper was a notice in a column headed "Personals." The entire message read, "G. R. C. Will arrive at Weymouth at 1:40. Meet me. MAUD."

Although the stay in Brest was short—only two days—the crew of the *Arizona* managed

to get ashore to see a culture much different from the one they had seen in England. They observed the quaint costumes and buildings of France, enjoyed the picturesque harbor, ate and drank, bought souvenirs, and saw German and Italian prisoners. True to form, Seaman George Leymé wrote in his diary, "Very pretty place, also some pretty women." Lots of American soldiers were in Brest as

Left: The bow pushes into ice floes, probably on New York's North River, in December 1918. At the lower edge of the picture is the armored optical range finder on the top of turret two. (Arizona Department of Library, Archives and Public Records)

Below: Moored in the North River off New York City, December 1918. (USS *Arizona* Memorial, National Park Service, PR-323)

well, so there was plenty of competition for those pretty women.

On 14 December the *Arizona* and other battleships set course for the United States. On board as passengers were 3 officers and 240 enlisted men, servicemen returning to the United States now that the war was over. Storekeeper Glenn Frisbie and others of the crew enjoyed talking with the veterans,

hearing their tales of the cold, damp existence in the trenches of France. It was a way for the sailors to experience combat vicariously, and it also gave the *Arizona*'s men a chance to feel a bit smug. Even if the months at Yorktown had been boring, the Navy men had certainly lived a more comfortable life on board ship than had the soldiers fighting in France.[6]

The homeward-bound ships, lined up in columns, were an impressive sight. On 15 December, as the ships continued west, the *Oklahoma* apparently suffered a steering casualty. She twice cut through the *Arizona*'s column, barely missing the *Arizona* as she went by. In addition, the *Utah* had engine problems, so the other ships had to slow to accommodate her. The seas were rough initially, and the *Arizona* rolled heavily. Then, as the ship neared the Azores, the Atlantic calmed and the weather warmed, providing an unexpected early Christmas present for the crew. On Christmas Day itself the crew had beans for breakfast and beans for supper, but in between was a bountiful holiday dinner. Beans were a useful item of shipboard food because they could be stored for long periods without refrigeration, and they were frequently served to the ship's crew.[7]

The arrival at New York on 26 December was a triumphal one. Again, the ships were decked out with large American flags. Though

she hadn't served overseas during the war, the *Arizona* was welcomed to her home port as if she had. The crew was at quarters as the *Arizona* led the other battleships in review past the Statue of Liberty, where the yacht *Mayflower* was anchored with Secretary of the Navy Josephus Daniels on board. He had presided at the *Arizona*'s launching three and a half years earlier, and here he was again to join in celebrating victory in The Great War. Despite snowy weather, press boats and movie cameras were on hand to record the event.[8]

As the ships headed up the North River they saw a phalanx of special boats and ferries with welcoming parties on board. After the *Arizona* moored, not far from the tomb of President Ulysses S. Grant, hero of an earlier war, three battalions of her sailors went ashore with a band and bugle corps for a victory parade. Local citizens treated the sailors with cigarettes, candy, and chewing gum. The leader of the *Arizona*'s landing party was her gunnery officer, Lieutenant Commander Thomas Kinkaid.[9]

With the arrival of 1919, the men settled into a postwar routine that included making the ship available for New Yorkers to visit. One of the things the *Arizona*'s men enjoyed doing was taking attractive guests below to show them the Battenberg Cup, which the ship's race-boat crew had won the previous summer.

Soon it was time to head south for the winter, stopping on the way for dry-docking at Norfolk. As usual, the *Arizona* had her sides scraped and wire-brushed. She also had a thorough inspection of her underwater hull. One of the causes of corrosion is the electrolytic action of salt water acting upon metal. To prevent corrosion, the *Arizona*'s hull had, during a previous period in dry dock, been fitted with small, flat pieces of zinc as an experiment. Since zinc is more susceptible to electrolysis than steel, the salt water should attack it and leave the steel alone. The experiment worked exactly as hoped in the *Arizona*. Zincs had been deliberately left off the starboard side at the stern, around the shaft struts and rudder. Sure enough, the starboard side showed evidence of corrosion; none was on the port side, which was protected with zincs.[10]

The next stop was Cuba, where the crew got to go swimming over the side. It was the

sort of opportunity they weren't used to having in February. At night men stretched out on deck topside to sleep because their living compartments were stuffy. That worked all right unless night rain showers sent them scurrying for cover. On such occasions the fleeing crew members formed what was known in shipboard jargon as a "shirt-tail parade."[11]

The *Arizona* and other battleships returned to the kind of maneuvers and target practice that had been the norm for the fleet before the interruption of war. It was a routine that the *Arizona* hadn't really become accustomed to because her turbine problems had taken up a good bit of time between her commissioning and the beginning of World War I.

On 10 March the ship held a big field day, and the crew watched the end of a movie

Above: Although the tops still had antisplinter padding in the immediate postwar period, the padding on the searchlight platforms had been replaced with canvas by the time this photo of the after turrets and superstructure was taken in the winter of 1919. (Courtesy Joseph C. Driscoll)

serial. George Leymé wrote of still another event in his diary, "A kid in our [signal bridge] gang ran into a fellows [*sic*] fist and got his nose broke." Among the stars of the silent movies shown on board the *Arizona* were Charlie Chaplin and Douglas Fairbanks, Sr.[12]

That same month the *Arizona* took a break from training for a liberty visit. She steamed into the Gulf of Paria to Port of Spain, Trinidad, off the coast of South America. Animals were for sale ashore, and many of the sailors and marines came back aboard with

new pets: parrots, monkeys, puppies, and so forth. A tough top sergeant took a look at the menagerie and ordered, "Now listen, you guys, get rid of those animals, and do it now. I don't want one of them here when I come back tonight." The sergeant himself came back to the *Arizona* that night with a snootful and made his way unsteadily up the gangway with a goat in tow.[13]

In early April the *Arizona*'s race-boat crew successfully defended the Battenberg Cup won the year before. A week later she was detached from the rest of the fleet for an

independent assignment. With the Paris Peace Treaty on the verge of being signed, it was time for President Wilson to head home to the United States. Again, the *Arizona* was selected to be an escort. The ship steamed independently across the Atlantic, returning once more to Brest, France. For the watch officers, the business of steaming alone was a distinct pleasure. It was a vivid contrast to normal fleet operations, when the officer of the deck had to keep the *Arizona* in formation, often only five hundred yards from another battleship, constantly monitoring the bearing and range from the other ship.[14]

Another difference was that the crew had more time for liberty than they had had the previous December. Storekeeper Glenn Frisbie and a shipmate from Kansas City caught a train for Paris and gloried in the sights of the beautiful French capital. They found their way around by subway, seeing the Eiffel Tower and the Hall of Mirrors at Versailles where the peace treaty would be signed. They also added to their collections of overseas postcards. When it came time, after two wonderful days and nights, to return to their ship, they were befuddled by the various levels of the Paris railroad station. Their problem was compounded because they neither spoke nor understood French. Fortunately, a war widow and her daughter took them in tow long enough to get them on the right train and headed back to the *Arizona*.[15]

In early May U.S. interest in postwar developments called for the *Arizona*, one of the nation's few battleships with four 3-gun, 14-inch turrets, to go into the Mediterranean Sea rather than returning to the United States as part of the escort for President Wilson. Italy had sent a strong naval force into the vicinity of Smyrna in what was then called Asia Minor—now Izmir, Turkey. Greece had been awarded that area under the terms of the newly concluded Paris Peace Treaty. Italy was one of the major victors in the just-ended war and evidently hoped to influence events so that Italy, rather than Greece, could occupy the area. On 2 May President Wilson directed Chief of Naval Operations William S. Benson, then in Paris as part of the U.S. delegation to the peace conference, to dispatch the *Arizona* immediately to Smyrna. It was a way of ensuring that U.S. naval forces in the area would have enough firepower to influence events if necessary.[16]

Three American destroyers had been waiting at Gibraltar to join up with President Wilson's convoy when it reached the Azores. Instead, the destroyers were directed to join up with the *Arizona* and accompany her eastward across the Mediterranean. The sudden change in plans for both battleship and destroyers provides a 1919 illustration of the flexibility of naval forces in support of national diplomatic objectives.[17]

When the *Arizona* arrived at Smyrna on 11 May, her crew found the situation was tense indeed. Both Greece and Italy thought they should have Asia Minor, so each had a battleship there. The guns of the Italian battleship were pointed at the Greek battleship twenty-four hours a day, and vice versa.

Above: Members of the electrical gang demonstrate the heads that have been shaved as a means of dealing with the tropical heat in March 1919. (Courtesy Hans Henke)

Below: Barefooted sailors holystone the wooden deck under the watchful eye of a marine. At left is the incinerator. (Courtesy Joseph C. Driscoll)

Rear Admiral Mark Bristol was the senior U.S. naval officer in Turkish waters, but his flagship was only a yacht, the *Scorpion*, which he had anchored between the two battleships in the hope of preventing a skirmish. It was a relief to have the *Arizona* and her firepower on the scene.[18]

On the day of arrival the *Arizona*'s officers were busy with diplomatic matters. Not wanting to slight anybody, Captain Dayton paid an official call on Admiral Bristol and entertained calls from the Greek battleship *Giorgios Averoff*, British cruiser *Adventure*, French cruiser *Ernest Renan*, and Italian battleship *Caio Duilio*.[19]

The American battleship had arrived just in time. On 15 May five Greek destroyers and fourteen transports arrived and began sending armed troops ashore to occupy the Turkish territory. Turkey had been one of the few allies of the defeated Germany, so it was bound to lose some of its land as a result. Initially, the Turks offered no resistance, but then fighting broke out in Smyrna because the Turks were understandably reluctant to surrender their land. During the day American citizens came aboard the *Arizona* and stayed overnight until conditions were less precarious ashore.[20]

The *Arizona*'s sailors had been trained to form landing parties, and while at Smyrna they were ordered to don their gear and prepare to go ashore if needed. Seventy years after the fact, Gunner's Mate Joe Driscoll recalled that when the ship's fifth division showed up at quarters in leggings and guard belts, Jerry Couch arrived wearing his leggings all right, but he had forgotten to put on his shoes and socks. It is interesting what will stick in a man's mind.[21] In any event, the Greeks and Turks were left to fight it out among themselves, and the landing party remained on board the *Arizona*. Crew members, however, saw some of the results of battle as the combatants' corpses floated out from the shore.

Driscoll was surprised to see other cage-masted battleships on the scene, but they weren't American—at least not then. They were the Greek *Kilkis* and *Lemnos*. Originally, they had been the USS *Idaho* and *Mississippi*, essentially lemons in the American fleet, because a parsimonious Congress appropriated so little money for the two ships that the

Navy had to use a regressive design instead of a progressive one. In the summer of 1914, with World War I about to break out, Greece was desperate enough to buy the substandard ships from the United States. Five years later, Greece was getting some use from them.[22]

Seaman Howard DeCelles was part of the liberty party at Smyrna. Liberty parties were allowed to go ashore when the situation permitted, but before being allowed to leave the ship, the men of the *Arizona* were cautioned about the possibility of catching venereal disease. The scare tactics included a warning that the Turkish women had the worst kind. Once the men did get their feet on Turkish soil, they discovered a case of mutual curiosity at work. Some sailors undoubtedly did check out the Turkish prostitutes, but for others the mere business of looking around was interesting enough. In the Turks they encountered people who dressed and acted differently from those they had seen in England, France, and America. And the sailors found that they themselves were often being watched with wonder by the Turks.[23] Some of the locals were allowed to visit the *Arizona*. Their first destination when they got aboard was the ship's canteen, to buy chocolate candy bars.[24]

Joe Driscoll went ashore also. There he saw a number of large tanks painted with the insignia of the Standard Oil Company. He concluded that part of the reason for the *Arizona*'s mission to the Mediterranean was to protect John D. Rockefeller's oil.[25] In much more recent times, the United States has dispatched Navy ships to the Persian Gulf to ensure continuing supplies of oil.

After her stop in Smyrna, the *Arizona* steamed to Constantinople (now known as Istanbul), the Turkish capital. She also became the first American battleship to enter the Bosporus, the strait that connects the Sea of Marmara and the Black Sea. Prior to World War I the U.S. Navy had very little presence in the region. The sixteen battleships of the Great White Fleet had gone through the Mediterranean in 1909 but hadn't visited Turkey. The dispatch of battleships to join the British Grand Fleet in 1917 had been a ground-breaking step, and now the *Arizona* was breaking more ground.

When she reached Constantinople, the *Arizona* joined briefly with a large contingent of other foreign warships, notably British.

Left: Sailors from the *Arizona* ride local trucks during sight-seeing in Constantinople on 12 June 1919. (Courtesy Hans Henke)

The British ships were there mainly because Constantinople provided a convenient anchorage at the entrance to the Black Sea, and Great Britain had an active part in the fighting that was going on between the factions in Russia. The British supported the White Russians in their civil war against the red regime, the Bolsheviks who had recently come to power. Constantinople was then full of Russian refugees who had fled their country. Their only resources were what they had been able to bring with them. Britain was also trying to prop up the tottering Turkish dynasty that soon gave way to the forces of Mustafa Kemal, better known as Attaturk.[26]

With her Middle Eastern venture finally concluded, the *Arizona* returned once more to Gibraltar. She had gone to Europe initially as a ceremonial escort but was diverted instead to an assignment that had a good deal more substance than ceremony. President Wilson would have to get home without the *Arizona* this time, because she set course from Gibraltar directly for New York, arriving there more than a week ahead of him.

The men who had enlisted in the Navy for travel and adventure had gotten more than they had bargained for, but there were some drawbacks. For the men of the *Arizona* in the post–World War I era, life on board ship was not so comfortable as life at home, nor was shipboard living as convenient as it would become during the 1930s. In the thirties, for instance, men had metal lockers in which to stow their uniforms and personal items. For the first dozen or so years of the *Arizona*'s service, however, enlisted men lived essentially out of their seabags, which were stowed in their living compartments. From time to time the captain would hold a seabag inspection, in which the members of the crew would spread bag and contents out on the deck as a means of demonstrating that they had the proper uniforms, well cared for.[27]

Members of the crew scrubbed their seabags and hammocks periodically and dropped them over lifelines topside to dry—an exercise known as "air bedding." Fresh water was scarce for any purpose. Saltwater soap was available for baths. The scuttlebutt, or drinking fountain, was open only part of the day. In between, men stayed thirsty. Instead of the electrically powered water cooler that became commonplace later, a scuttlebutt in the early part of the ship's career was a large metal tank with ice water in it. The tank had about half a dozen spigots on it; men pushed a button, and up sprang a stream of water.[28]

Hammocks were taken down each morning and put up each night in individual living compartments. In between they were stowed along the sides of the compartments, along with seabags and ditty boxes. The box represented one of the few manifestations of an individual's personality on board the *Arizona*. The hammocks and seabags were essentially identical, of course. In the ditty box, however, a man kept his shaving gear, toothbrush and tooth powder, soap, stationery, shoe polish, reading material, and other personal items, including the mail he had received. The ditty box, sturdily built of wood, was about 18 inches long and perhaps 10–12 inches high. It could serve as a low stool or, in a sailor's lap, as a writing desk.[29]

The men ate their meals in the same compartments where they slept. One morning, just at 8:00 A.M., Seaman Second Class Ellsworth Ogden was lingering over the last of his breakfast before reporting to his workplace up on deck. Ogden, barely seventeen years old, had joined the ship only a few days before, on 5 July 1919, and had not yet completely assimilated the ways of the Navy. He got a quick lesson during that breakfast. A boatswain's mate, whose left sleeve contained enough hash marks to indicate he had been in the Navy since around the turn of the century, approached Ogden after hearing the shrill notes of a boatswain's pipe.

"Did you hear that whistle, sailor?" the boatswain's mate demanded.

"Yes, sir, I did," replied young Ogden.

"Do you know what it means?"

"I sure do."

"What does it mean?"

"It means turn to," which is the Navy's way of telling people to start work.

"Why aren't you up there?"

"I'm going up there just as soon as I finish this grapefruit."

The boatswain's mate had other ideas and helped the new man on his way to the ladder "with a boot in the ass," as Ogden recalled years afterward. "That's the last thing I should have said," he remembered. "I went up that hatch so damn fast. I never said 'Wait a minute' anymore."[30]

By the time she returned to New York, the ship had reached the highest levels of training readiness. Having served for so many months as a training ship at Yorktown, her gun crews knew their business well. For instance, when Lieutenant John Ballentine took over as division officer for turret two, he found his turret crew to be "well-trained, perfect."[31] What's more, the trips to France, England, and Turkey had also given the ship a chance to exercise her sea legs. The engineers had gotten a lot of experience in answering maneuvering bells, and those with various other underway watches to stand were better prepared as well.

Then the bottom dropped out of the ship's manning. On 11 July 1919 President Wilson signed the annual naval appropriations bill for the new fiscal year. One of the provisions of

the law was that anyone who had enlisted in the Navy, Marine Corps, or Coast Guard for a term of four years between 3 February 1917 and 11 November 1918 was considered to have enlisted for the duration of the war. The first date marked the breaking of diplomatic relations with Germany as a result of the resumption of unrestricted submarine warfare, and the latter, of course, was the date of the armistice in France. The men who met this condition could thus be honorably discharged if they applied by 1 September 1919 and otherwise qualified for that type of discharge. Notices reporting the opportunity for discharge appeared on the *Arizona*'s bulletin boards, and soon her men were departing in droves. Ballentine's turret crew dropped from ninety men to a dozen.[32]

The attempted remedy to the loss of manpower bore at least a passing resemblance to the old press gangs that had rounded up men in the nineteenth century and made them part of ship's crews whether they wanted to be or not. At least the *Arizona* limited her effort to finding more volunteers. Men from the ship went out as recruiting parties on the streets of Brooklyn and the other boroughs of New York. They signed up warm bodies and brought them directly aboard ship, without even sending them through recruit training. It was a desperate measure and fell far short of proving a workable solution. Years later

Ballentine, whose division recruited thirty-three men, explained: "That was an experience I'll never forget, taking these 18-year-old boys into the ship, living with the experienced people, trying to keep their noses clean, trying to keep their clothes clean. It was a great habit of these boys that when their clothes would get dirty, they'd throw them overboard and want to buy new ones, rather than try to keep the ones they had clean." Of those thirty-three men, only fifteen were worth keeping. The rest were so obviously unsatisfactory that they were sent on their way.[33]

Personnel problems such as the *Arizona*'s were common throughout the Navy. The release of the men who had enlisted during the war had a devastating effect on readiness and compelled the Navy to step up its recruiting as a matter of desperation. One of the tools it used was a full-page advertisement that appeared in a number of national magazines. It featured a drawing of the *Arizona* and a resumé of her impressive itinerary during the first six months of the year.

The ship's wretched personnel situation was the cloud; the silver lining was that the absence of operational requirements and the long time in the New York Navy Yard

afforded an opportunity for modernization. New enclosed fire-control tops were constructed atop the two cage masts. The old V-front screens on the cage masts gave way to much more elaborate octagonal torpedo-defense stations on the masts, providing more sophisticated fire-control capability for the 5-inch/51-caliber broadside guns on the main deck and in the superstructure.

During World War I battleships had been able to use their big guns only in the great conflict at Jutland and in a few other isolated engagements. The war had shown the effectiveness of submarines and destroyers. They posed a threat that the *Arizona* had to be able to counter. Probably the best defense was a high volume of fire from the 5-inch guns. Volume could be as effective as accuracy—especially at night—in deterring attacks from destroyers and submarines approaching on the surface. Thus, one factor always emphasized in gunnery practice was the rapidity with which a particular gun could fire off rounds.[34]

The new octagonal fire-control structures were more comfortable than their predecessors because they had roofs and glass windows to protect their occupants. They were only partway up because the cage masts did not have the strength to support that much weight all the way at the top.[35]

While many things had been happening as part of the overhaul, at least one desired change hadn't been made. The *Arizona* requested that the navy yard build a 30-inch by 30-inch soap-mixing tank for the ship's laundry. It was to be made of 1/8-inch-thick brass and would cost $113.00. The request went all the way to Washington, only to be turned down by the Bureau of Construction and Repair. As the bureau pointed out, the Navy supply system was by then providing ships with chip soap instead of the bar soap that had been common up to then. Laundries no longer needed to boil the soap for clothes washing, so the *Arizona* obviously didn't need a soap tank.[36]

For the men of the battleship, one event in the fall of 1919 provided an extraordinary degree of pleasure. To celebrate the third anniversary of the ship's commissioning, the crew threw a big dance for itself on 17 October at the plush Hotel Astor in Manhattan. Seaman Ellsworth Ogden outfitted him-

Below: The Navy ran this full-page recruiting advertisement in national magazines in late 1919 as part of the effort to rebuild its personnel strength after men who had enlisted during the war were discharged. (Courtesy Alfred C. Holden)

self in his best inspection dress uniform and escorted his Long Island girlfriend, who was wearing an evening gown. Many members of the crew were new to the big city. But even for those such as Ogden who grew up in New York, the grand ballroom of the Astor was a rare treat.[37] Gunner's Mate Joe Driscoll and his girlfriend, Dorothy Malone, enjoyed the grand march that was part of the occasion, but he begged off when she asked him to dance, claiming he had two wooden legs. She had known him since she was fourteen years old, so she didn't resent his reluctance. The two got married after he left the Navy in 1921 and were husband and wife for nearly seventy years until his death in 1989.[38]

In 1920 the members of the crew began enjoying similar, though much less formal, entertainment on board the ship. Both in the navy yard and on the North River, when the ship was moored there, the crew periodically held Saturday afternoon dances out on the teak decks. The ship's band played, and girls came by subway and elevated to tour the ship and dance with the crewmen. For the men of the *Arizona* the ship was home, and the dances provided inexpensive entertainment. Ogden spent many of his liberty hours ashore visiting his girl at her home or his on Long Island. As he asked rhetorically, "Where the hell were you going to go on $17.00 a month?"[39]

In December 1919, under the direction of Ensign Sampson Scott, the crew began publishing a newsletter each day. The ship's newspaper, first published a year earlier, had not been continued. Seaman Ogden was involved in the new venture, and he had begun seeking the yeoman rating after he had spent some time in one of the deck divisions. Ensign Scott wrote the contents of the newsletter, and Ogden did the typing and mimeographing. It was distributed free, one copy reaching each mess table and each bulletin board at 7:30 in the morning. The new publication proved so popular that subscriptions were sold at the price of five cents per week to those who wanted to send copies home. Initially, the newsletter was typed on both sides of a legal-sized sheet of paper and was a compendium of news about the ship, doings of members of the crew, jokes, things to do on liberty, ways for getting along successfully on board ship, general information on the Navy, and a strong pitch for reenlisting on active service. Early in the 1920s the physical production of the newsletter became a good deal more sophisticated. Rather than being typed and mimeographed, it was set in type and printed on a printing press, and illustrations were frequently used. Throughout, the publication had a certain small-town charm; the contents were designed to appeal to the inhabitants of the

Below: The *Arizona* at anchor, Guantanamo Bay, Cuba, in January 1920 following modernization. The searchlight platforms have been raised, and enclosed, octagonal, secondary battery–control stations have been built on the cage masts. (Franklin D. Roosevelt Library)

Above: The *Arizona's* baseball team at the base of the mainmast in 1920. (Courtesy Joseph C. Driscoll)

Below: The *Arizona* and another battleship lie at anchor at Guantanamo Bay, Cuba, in January 1920. Boat booms extend out from the sides of the *Arizona*. (National Archives, 19-N-2840)

dancing and . . ." A voice from the congregation rang out, "Where at?"

In August of the following year the newsletter tried to whip up enthusiasm for the first of the Saturday-afternoon dances: "The ship's orchestra will furnish the music and Bandmaster Jones has promised that his jazz hounds will make a cripple sit up and take notice."[41]

One particularly lamentable feature of the newsletter was its publication of demeaning jokes about black people. This was, however, in keeping with the tenor of the times and not considered offensive by the majority of the crew because the stories appeared regularly. Referred to then as "Negroes" or "colored," blacks were depicted in many of the newsletter's jokes as lacking courage and intelligence. In one such story a black man said that there were two people who wouldn't be fighting in the next war, himself and whoever came to get him. In another jibe a black soldier stationed in Vladivostok, Russia, announced at a post office that he was shipping a box of snow to his girlfriend in Georgia because she had never seen any.

In early January 1920, with the major renovations complete, it was time for the *Arizona* to return to the routine of cruising to the Caribbean for the winter. That would give the crew a break from the bad weather and provide training in an attractive climate. On

Arizona, not the wider world. The title was *At' Em Arizona*, and the newsletter survived under that name until the end of the ship's life in 1941.[40] Brittle copies of some of the early issues of the newsletter are still on file at the Library of Congress.

Typical of the brand of humor in the newsletter was an item from the issue of 6 May 1920: "Why do you go to church so often?" "Man, it is a beautiful sight to see one man keep so many women quiet." Another example was from the 7 May 1920 issue. A preacher said, "Young girls, immodestly clothed, spend half their nights shimmy

New Year's Day, shortly before the ship was to sail, she received a draft of 239 recently trained recruits from the naval training station at Great Lakes, Illinois, to augment her crew. The ship's newspaper of 11 December 1919 reported a complement of 927 enlisted men and 74 officers, so the new additions increased the crew to full strength. The recently trained recruits hadn't a great deal of experience, but they were at least better than the people recruited off the streets in earlier months. Nevertheless, the nucleus of trained crew members had a big job ahead to make sailors of the newest *Arizona* men.[42]

The principal base of operations for the fleet in the winter months was Guantanamo Bay, Cuba. Although certainly not a metropolitan environment, it did at least provide the members of the crew a chance to get ashore and reacquire their land legs for a time. A ballpark at Guantanamo was the site of many a baseball game between the *Arizona*'s team and those of other warships. The crew members had practiced some of their baseball skills on the fantail, putting up nets to keep the ball from going overboard when they played catch or practiced their bunting. The crew's loyalty to its team was strong, and the men of the *Arizona* frequently bet on their shipmates. Seaman Ogden once learned the hard way about the follies of gambling. He wagered $10.00 on the outcome of a baseball game. He and a sailor from another ship asked a civilian at the game to hold the stakes for the bet. The *Arizona*'s team won, and when Ogden went to collect his $20.00, the civilian was nowhere to be found.[43]

The real novelty as the southern operations got under way in early 1920 was the beginning of the ship's use of airplanes. During the shipyard period, frameworks for wooden platforms had been built on top of the two high turrets, number two and number three, and runways about 20 feet wide and 50 feet long were rigged atop the guns of those turrets when it was time for flight operations. The *Arizona* was thus adopting the type of flying-off platform that had been tested in March 1919 on board the USS *Texas*. Two naval aviators had reported aboard just before the *Arizona* left Brooklyn: Lieutenant (junior grade) Jacob Wolfer and Ensign Alfred M. "Mel" Pride.

Of necessity, light planes were used. The French Nieuport, located on top of the *Arizona*'s turret three, had a gross weight of 1,625 pounds. The English Sopwith one-and-a-half-strutter, on turret two, had a gross weight of 2,150 pounds. In comparison, the OS2U scout plane that flew from the *Arizona* in 1941 had a gross weight of 6,000 pounds, and some present-day carrier planes weigh more than 60,000 pounds.

Since the battleship hadn't been designed for airplanes and the airplanes hadn't been designed for battleships, putting the planes on the *Arizona* was a makeshift business. The tail skid of the plane normally rested in a trough

Above: A 3-inch antiaircraft gun atop turret three points skyward. The barrel-shaped device to the left of the cage mainmast is a director for the 5-inch broadside guns of the secondary battery. (Courtesy Joseph C. Driscoll)

Left: This view was made looking down on the *Arizona* from a kite balloon in early 1920. A French Nieuport sits atop the wooden platform on turret three. (Courtesy Joseph C. Driscoll)

Above: An officer gunnery observer stands in the basket suspended from the ship's kite balloon. Notice the many lines hanging down from the balloon, probably to help those on deck bring it back onto the fantail. (Courtesy Joseph C. Driscoll)

Below: This close-up of the French Nieuport aircraft on turret three also shows 3-inch antiaircraft guns in the background. The sailor near the propeller has his hand on one of the flotation bags that helped keep the plane on the water after a crash landing. One of the ship's bells is just below the secondary battery–control station. (Courtesy Edward B. Blair, Jr.)

at the top of a wooden stand, somewhat like a sawhorse. The tail was restrained by a pelican hook, a metal fitting of the sort used to hold an anchor in place on deck. When one of the pilots was going to make a flight, he got into the cockpit, warmed up the engine, and then turned it up to full power. On a signal from the pilot, the pelican hook was knocked open, thus removing the restraint and letting the plane go on its way.[44]

With only about fifty feet of runway, the relative wind was crucial in this operation. Today's aircraft carriers use their speed to get thirty knots of wind over the deck because planes generally have to fly directly into the

wind to get sufficient lift for takeoff. Producing a relative wind directly down the axis of each turret's guns called for the proper combination of ship's course and turret position. In these operations the *Arizona* steamed as fast as she could to produce as much wind as possible, and as Pride explained years later, "you wished you had more."[45]

The forward turret was not trained directly over the bow because the planes dropped down when they got to the end of the platform, and it was better to have them drop over the side of the ship instead of toward the forecastle. As Pride put it, "It was always questionable whether you would hit the water or not. I didn't, but some of them [in other ships] did." The after turret was trained as far forward as it could go without pointing the plane toward one of the boat cranes. To produce the correct relative wind for the after turret, the *Arizona* had to steam just about perpendicular to the true wind. A man stood on top of the turret with a hand-held anemometer to determine the speed of the relative wind.[46]

The *Arizona*'s new aircraft had two principal missions, scouting and spotting, although the latter was by far the more significant. At the time of the *Arizona*'s commissioning, spotting the fall of shot depended on the vantage provided by the foretop and maintop on the two cage masts. Later, kite balloons raised the vantage point—and thus extended the distance the spotters could see—even

Above: Bedding airs on the lifelines in this marvelous shot of turret three, the Nieuport, and the mainmast. (National Archives, 19-N-4551)

farther. The new airplanes provided a significant advance. They could fly higher than the kite balloons, and they didn't have to remain tethered to the ship. The pilots sent information about the *Arizona*'s shooting back to the ship in Morse code via radio. Alas, there were drawbacks. Since the planes had wheels rather than pontoon floats, they had to land ashore rather than at sea. The two pilots had gone through land-plane training with the Army Air Service at a base in Florida because the Navy had been flying seaplanes exclusively until then.[47]

After a flight, when the ship was operating out of the base at Guantanamo Bay, Cuba, the planes looked for a spot to land on Hicacal Beach on the island's south coast. Then they had to find a farmer or some other obliging individual with a horse or mule. The farmer would hitch the animal to the tail end of the plane and pull it to a pier or dock at the water's edge. Then a Navy tugboat or some other craft would take the plane aboard and haul it back to the *Arizona*, and finally the ship would lift it aboard and put it back on the platform atop the turret. As a result, the planes could be used only near land; not until pontoon planes and catapults were adopted could ships use their planes far out at sea.[48]

Competition is a way of life in the Navy, and often it is the spur for better performance on the part of those involved. Lieutenant Ballentine, the turret two officer, decided that he would bet $25.00 with the turret three officer, a Naval Academy classmate of his, on which division could rig its airplane platform more quickly. The enlisted men in the two divisions also made bets of their own. When the platform was in place one day, Ballentine and his men marked each piece with chalk to

show its correct position. On the day of the big race Ballentine's men quickly rigged their platform on top of the guns, then smugly went to watch the people from turret three, who fumbled with nuts and bolts for another hour before finishing.[49]

Lieutenant Ballentine's turret crew had to rig and unrig its platform so often that he and his men decided that the aviators were too fussy. Ballentine observed that "the pilot would come up, wet his finger, feel the wind, shake his head—say the signs were not right to fly today." So the crew would unrig the platform for gun drill that day, and then in another day or two they'd go through the

rigging and finger-wetting routine again. Ballentine finally got so disgusted with the process that he applied to become one of the aviators who got to hold up a wet finger and decide whether he would fly.[50]

Actually, he had tried several times before that. During World War I he had requested flight training. The Navy Department's rationale for its refusal was that it needed Naval Academy men like Ballentine to operate ships at sea; plenty of men from civilian colleges were available to be trained as fliers. Now Ballentine tried again. His request for flight training needed an endorsement from Captain Dayton before it went to the Navy Department. The captain called the lieutenant in and spent an hour trying to talk him out of aviation. He told Ballentine that he had a promising future in the surface Navy and shouldn't throw it away on such a sideline as aviation. Dayton sent the request forward, recommending it be disapproved. The commander in chief of the fleet also recommended turning it down. The Navy Department saw it differently, concluding that an officer so promising was just the sort needed to help with the fledgling aviation program.[51]

Some eight years later Ballentine and Dayton crossed paths again. By this time Dayton was the commandant of the Mare Island Navy Yard near San Francisco. Ballentine, who had no hard feelings, decided to stop in for a chat with his old skipper. By that time the Navy's first carrier, the *Langley*, had proved her worth in fleet operations, and two big new carriers, the *Lexington* and *Saratoga*, had just entered the fleet. The visit went well, and when Ballentine got up to leave, Dayton grinned and said, "I want to tell you something. I remember how I tried to talk

you out of this aviation business. If I were younger, I'd like to be in it myself."[52]

The arrival of the airplanes and their associated equipment was sometimes a bitter pill for the traditional battleship officers to swallow. Mel Pride considered Captain Dayton a very fine naval officer and one who liked the tactical advantage that airplane spotting could provide, but the captain was most unhappy with the oil that the planes dripped onto the ship's holystoned wooden decks. Some of the other officers in the ship were a bit envious of the extra pay the aviators received for hazardous duty. And hazardous it was in the early days of aviation.[53]

In early March Lieutenant (junior grade) Wolfer, pilot of the Sopwith on turret two, headed down his wooden runway but never made it off the ship. On this particular day the combination of turret angle and ship's course produced a slight crosswind. Since the plane was so light, it was easily susceptible to such winds. The right wing lifted up a little bit, the left wheel rolled off the platform, and the plane bounced off one of the guns of turret one before coming to rest on the forecastle. The crash killed a man on the forecastle, Seaman G. H. Hall, and injured Apprentice Seaman R. T. Blankenship. Before the day was over, crew members pulled pieces of the plane's fabric outer skin off the wooden skeleton. The plane looked like a fish picked clean by a pack of hungry sharks.[54]

On 17 March Wolfer's cohort Mel Pride, by now a lieutenant (junior grade) himself, also had a mishap. He had gotten his plane into the air, but the Nieuport's engine was sensitive. Every three minutes he had to push a button on the control stick to cut out the ignition momentarily so the engine could cool. Pride was about three or four miles off the beach when the engine quit completely, and he crashed. The planes had been given hydro-vanes to keep them from nosing over when they hit the water and some rudimentary flotation gear, so the Nieuport remained on the surface. A flying boat happened to be operating nearby and landed to rescue Pride.[55]

The crews that accompanied the planes were remarkably compact, especially by today's standards. In addition to the two pilots, there were only about half a dozen enlisted men to do maintenance and otherwise service the planes. Mel Pride was not above doing some of the work himself. He had joined the

Navy in 1917 and served for a time as a machinist's mate before becoming an officer and a pilot. On board the *Arizona* he sometimes spliced wire when it was time to replace a control cable, and he had a hand in repairing the fabric skin of his plane when it got a hole poked in it.[56]

Lieutenant Pride fit into the life of the ship in a number of ways. At nights, when the planes weren't operating, he stood watch as junior officer of the deck on the bridge, viewing the red lights atop the other battleships with a stadimeter to make sure the *Arizona* was the proper distance away. He stood spotting watches high in the maintop for short-range battle practice because the practically point-blank range meant that the airplanes weren't needed. The blast from the 14-inch guns invariably gave him "quite a jolt" atop the none-too-sturdy cage mast.[57]

In port Pride again stood watch as officer of the deck. When the *Arizona* was at Barbados for liberty, Pride would spend part of his time

Above: Sailors bolt metal supports into place on top of the 14-inch guns of turret two. On the supports they then erected a wooden flying-off platform for the Sopwith plane. The forward range clock is just above the plane's right wing. (Courtesy Joseph C. Driscoll)

Below: The minesweeper *Sandpiper* here serves as an aircraft tender in early 1920, returning the *Arizona*'s Sopwith after a mission so it can be hoisted back aboard the battleship. (Courtesy Joseph C. Driscoll)

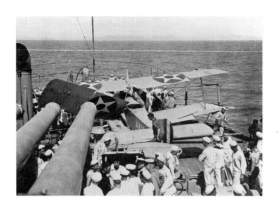

Right: The wrecked Sopwith sits on the forecastle after being blown off the wooden platform by a crosswind. Lieutenant (junior grade) J. F. Wolfer was flying the plane on 4 March 1920 when it wrecked. (Courtesy Edward B. Blair, Jr.)

Far right: Crew members take pieces of wing fabric as souvenirs of the Sopwith plane that crashed on the forecastle. The large structure at left is one of the rotatable ventilation cowls used to provide air to the spaces below decks. (Courtesy Joseph C. Driscoll)

Below: A tugboat lifts the skeleton of the Sopwith over the side of the *Arizona* after the battleship's crew has picked it clean. (Courtesy Joseph C. Driscoll)

looking over the side and marveling at the remarkably clear water that enabled him to see "anchor prints," which showed where other ships had previously anchored. One day, while looking near the bottom of the gangway, Pride saw something curious indeed, a dead guinea pig floating by. He was puzzled since guinea pigs are not normally aquatic mammals, and he became even more intrigued when another passed the foot of the gangway. He dispatched the boatswain's mate of the watch up forward to see what was going on. The boatswain's mate discovered that one of the *Arizona*'s sailors had a brood of guinea pigs in the paint locker as pets. Evidently, the brood had been breeding too quickly to suit the sailor, so he was throwing the extra ones overboard. Pride concluded that the guinea pig experiment was over and had the boatswain's mate get rid of the whole lot of them.[58]

Among his other experiences on board the *Arizona*, Pride enjoyed swapping stories with others in the junior officers' mess in the evenings. The camaraderie was pleasant because even with his aviator's wings he was soon accepted as one of the ship's own. While on board he noticed how proud many in the

crew were about serving in the battleship. Their pride was reflected in the motto "At 'Em *Arizona*" that served as the title for the ship's newsletter and was carried ashore on a banner when sports teams were playing against other ships. It was reflected also in the desire to do things smartly and correctly so as to hold up the ship's standards. The closest rivals of the *Arizona* were the three other ships built about the same time: the *Nevada*, *Oklahoma*, and particularly sister ship *Pennsylvania*.[59]

Even though Pride served in the *Arizona* only about six months, the shipboard experience was beneficial to him later in his career, and it was a distinguished one. He had a hand in devising arresting gear for the carrier *Langley*, flew as a test pilot, commanded the aircraft carrier *Belleau Wood* during World War II, and eventually became Commander Seventh Fleet shortly after the Korean War. He was the first line officer in the U.S. Navy to achieve the rank of vice admiral on active duty without having gone to the Naval Academy.

On 25 April 1920 the race-boat crew from the *Nevada* won the Battenberg Cup, reclaiming the trophy after the *Arizona* had held it for two years. Soon afterward, the winter drill season over, the *Arizona* headed back for her home base at the North River in New York. Then it was back down to the Southern Drill Grounds, with a venture into the Chesapeake Bay. She anchored in the roadstead off Annapolis the first week in June to help celebrate the graduation of the first half of the Naval Academy's class of 1921. During World War I the course at Annapolis had been accelerated to three years. Now that the war was over it was time to get back to the normal four-year curriculum. That meant the top half of the class graduated in June 1920 and the bottom half in June 1921.

When the ship got back into operation, her crew received reports of one of the drawbacks of using kite balloons for observing gunfire. While the ship was anchored near Hampton Roads, balloons from the *Pennsylvania* and *Nevada* were struck by lightning and destroyed. That sent a sobering message to the men whose duty it was to sit in the baskets suspended below the balloons and send their reports down wires to the ships. The cables that connected the balloons to the ships were operated by winches. When it was time to send men aloft, the balloons were winched to the deck so men could climb aboard, then sent aloft again.

Back in New York in the early summer, Captain Dayton wound up his command tour and turned the ship over to Captain William W. Phelps. While in the shipyard, the *Arizona* underwent normal maintenance and upkeep, and she prepared to take on a new role. On 24 August the flag of Rear Admiral Edward Eberle was hoisted, and the *Arizona* became the flagship of Battleship Division Seven, which also included the *Nevada* and *Oklahoma*. Eberle, who sported a distinguished set of white whiskers, later became Chief of Naval Operations.

Later in the year, when she was back in the New York Navy Yard, the ship received modifications so that she would be better suited to have an admiral and his staff on board. The signal searchlights were raised so

that they could be seen from aft as well as from forward and on the beam. When the *Arizona* was leading a column, her admiral needed to be able to send orders by flashing-light signal to battleships steaming astern. In addition, a rudimentary flag plot was constructed in an enclosure at the base of the forward cage mast, thus doing away with the "bull ring" as a storage area. This new enclosure gave the admiral's staff a space for standing watches and communicating while

Above: The ship's Nieuport observation plane, flown by Lieutenant (junior grade) Mel Pride, is airborne soon after flying off the turret three platform on 17 March 1920. (Courtesy Alfred M. Pride)

Below: The crew uses a boom to load torpedoes. The *Arizona* had two submerged torpedo tubes forward and carried an allowance of twelve torpedoes, each twenty-one inches in diameter. (Courtesy Joseph C. Driscoll)

the ship was under way, and it gave them room to plot the positions of ships in company during maneuvers. The ship's force did the remodeling with material supplied by the navy yard. Included was the installation of supports to bear the weight of the plotting room; the structure of the cage mast was not strong enough to carry the additional weight by itself.[60]

One of the criticisms directed at the Imperial Japanese Navy's conduct during World War II was that its officers stuck rigidly to prearranged plans, even when the confusing, changing events of battle indicated the wisdom of flexibility. It is a criticism born

mostly of hindsight, because in the years between the two world wars the U.S. Navy frequently followed a highly rigid format itself when preparing for battle. The doctrine of the era argued that the main purpose of the fleet was to bring the big guns of its battleships to bear on the battleships of an enemy fleet. The Navy spent hundreds of millions of dollars and countless hours of training time to prepare for such an eventuality.

Each year the Office of the Chief of Naval Operations issued orders for gunnery exercise. Following those orders was the fleet's religion, and nearly all else was intended to support that aim. Included in the litany were such events as short-range battle practice, long-range battle practice, day torpedo-defense spotting practice, day individual practice, night battle practice, and so forth. For all of these events, canvas targets, fitted over wooden frameworks, were built on rafts and towed either by large combatant ships for others to shoot at or by smaller vessels such as fleet tugs and minesweepers. The canvas was removed after each practice so that the hits could be counted and scores tabulated. A target-repair party then prepared the wooden framework for still another canvas target and still another round of shooting.

Another part of the ritual called for observers, usually from another ship of the same type, to come aboard the firing ship to see how well the gun crews followed the

Above: Crew members prepare to ram a projectile into one of the ship's 5-inch/51-caliber broadside guns. (USS *Arizona* Memorial, National Park Service, PR-466)

Below: Crew members dance with one another on deck while the ship's band plays during a break between target practices. (Courtesy Joseph C. Driscoll)

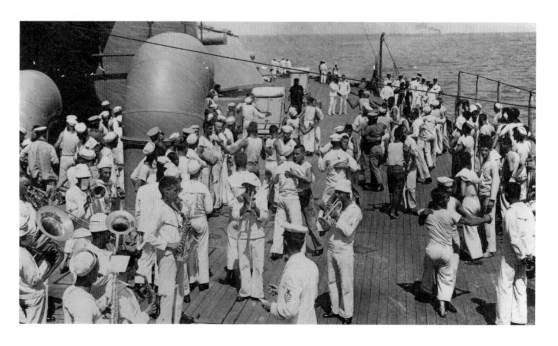

correct procedures for loading, aiming, firing, and maintaining safety. Before each such exercise, the commanding officer of the firing ship prepared what amounted to a detailed script. Indeed, so formal was the process in the early 1920s that these exercise plans were set in type and printed in the ship's print shop, not just typed and mimeographed.

For instance, on 27 September 1920 Captain Phelps of the *Arizona* issued the order for the day torpedo-defense spotting practice to be conducted on Friday, 8 October.[61] The *Oklahoma* was designated as the towing and observing ship. During the initial ten single shots, the target was directed to be on the beam of the *Arizona* at a range of six thousand yards. Later, according to the script, the ranges and bearings for each string of shots would vary as the different guns fired.

On board the *Oklahoma* was a rake party, which used a device known as a rake. It had a series of vertical wooden pegs sticking out of a wooden frame, something akin to the tool used for raking leaves. The pegs were calibrated, so at a given distance from the target, a shell splash in line of sight with a peg so far away from the center indicated a miss of the target by so many yards. It was an exercise in triangulation. The farther the rake was from the target, the larger the triangle, and thus the

larger the number of yards from the target indicated by each peg.

When the *Arizona* fired, the *Oklahoma* used the radiotelephone and auxiliary radio to report the fall of shot in relation to the target. These observations were correlated with the reports from the *Arizona*'s own fire-control spotters to make corrections to be used in subsequent salvos. The highest spotters were those in the foretop and maintop, 122 feet above the waterline, because the *Arizona* had completed her participation in the experiment of flying planes from the turret tops.

There was not much spontaneity in the target-practice routine—whether firing the 14-inch, 5-inch, or 3-inch guns—although it did have the virtue of improving proficiency

Above: The *Arizona*'s marines in a motor launch at the foot of the gangway in 1920. (Courtesy Edward B. Blair, Jr.)

Below: Crew members pose on the quarterdeck in 1920 with flags and a banner that were carried ashore for sports events involving the *Arizona*'s teams. (Courtesy Joseph C. Driscoll)

real thing, a battle practice, in which the scores became a matter of record in determining the performance for a particular gun, battery, turret, or ship for a given competitive year.

Target practice literally had a colorful aspect to it. Before the 5-inch broadside guns were fired to simulate torpedo defense against an approaching destroyer or submarine, the noses of the projectiles were painted different colors. When projectiles missed the target raft, the rake party, on board the tug or another battleship, reported the miss distances. When projectiles hit the target, traces of paint would surround each hole. Since all the projectiles for a single gun were the same color, the observers could determine how many hits each barrel made.

Gunner's Mate Joe Driscoll and others who had been around for a while solemnly explained this whole procedure to new crew members when they reported aboard. Then, with tongue in cheek, they told the gullible recruits how to mark the colors for the 14-inch guns: sit up on the bow with a can of paint and a brush. When a gun fires, they told the greenhorn, hold up the brush and paint the shell as it goes by.[62]

In late October, after still more target practice, the *Arizona* was back in New York. Even so, training continued. The ship's

Above: Part of the morning exercise routine in 1920 included double-timing around the after turrets. (Courtesy Joseph C. Driscoll)

through great repetition. If nothing else, the gun and fire-control crews got very capable at practicing. Each time the ship's log scrupulously recorded the event. It might have been, for instance, an unofficial rehearsal for short-range battle practice. Or an official rehearsal for a practice. Or it might even have been the

newsletter printed an article on ground tackle, for example, making use of something the entire crew would be familiar with, the Woolworth Building in Manhattan, which was the nation's tallest building. The article explained that each of the *Arizona*'s anchors weighed 19,500 pounds, and each had 180 fathoms of chain attached. A fathom is 6 feet, so the total of 1,080 feet per chain was enough to stretch to the top of the 792-foot-tall Woolworth Building with some left over. Each fathom of chain weighed 630 pounds.[63]

As the year 1920 wound down, the officers and enlisted men of the *Arizona* pursued a variety of pleasures in the city that had served as home port for four years but would not do so much longer. Two days after Thanksgiving a number of the *Arizona*'s officers traveled to Harlem at the upper end of Manhattan Island to see the annual Army-Navy football game at the Polo Grounds. The game was then one of the biggest sporting events in the country, and this time the midshipmen of the Naval Academy prevailed 7–0 over the cadets from West Point. A few weeks later Commander Royal Ingersoll, the executive officer, went for a touch of culture when he heard Enrico Caruso, the great Italian tenor, sing *Samson and Delilah* at the Metropolitan Opera House. The phonographs and recordings of the era were still relatively primitive, so hearing Caruso in person was by far the best way to appreciate his talent.[64]

At dawn on 4 January 1921 the Atlantic Fleet got under way from the navy yard in Brooklyn, headed down the East River to Ambrose Channel, and thence entered the Atlantic to steam south for its usual winter maneuvers. Commanded by Admiral Henry B. Wilson, the fleet consisted of seven battleships, eighteen destroyers, and a number of auxiliary vessels for fleet support; the support vessels were known then as the fleet train and included colliers, supply ships, tenders, and repair vessels. The fleet formation called for the battleships—the *Pennsylvania, Arizona, Utah, Delaware, North Dakota, Nevada,* and *Oklahoma*—to steam majestically ahead in column, followed by the train (hence its name), which the old cruiser *Columbia* was shepherding. On both wings of the formation were lines of destroyers, their crew members looking contemptuously at the battleships that could not go nearly so fast and whose

men did not, except rarely, have to endure the rigors of being tossed about by the whims of the ocean.[65]

Gradually, the weather warmed, and whites replaced blues as the uniform of the day. Jumpers and skivvy shirts came off when the fleet was sufficiently far south, and first sunburn, then tan replaced the men's winter pallor. The first stop was Guantanamo, the Atlantic Fleet's home port in winter, and it was set up as a useful training facility. The bay provided a capacious anchorage for dozens of ships and a home base for the big F-5L seaplanes that constituted the fleet's fledgling air force. The U.S. Navy's first aircraft carrier, the *Langley*, was still another year away from being commissioned.

Opposite page, bottom: The *Arizona*'s marine detachment on deck in 1920. (Courtesy Edward B. Blair, Jr.)

Below: The fleet's battleships ride at anchor in New York's North River on 2 May 1920. The picture was taken from the *Arizona*. Next astern is the USS *Pennsylvania*. (UPI/Bettmann Newsphotos, U112907-INP)

Above: A repair party works on a gunnery target. The displaced slats show where projectiles have gone through during previous firings. (N. Moser photo, courtesy Joseph C. Driscoll)

Below: The *Arizona* and the battleship *North Dakota* moored at the New York Navy Yard on Monday, 5 July 1920. They are at full-dress ship in honor of the Independence Day holiday. The *North Dakota*, which was commissioned in 1910, left the fleet in 1923 to comply with the Washington Naval Treaty limitations on battleship tonnage. (Courtesy Joseph C. Driscoll)

Ashore at Guantanamo the Navy rented some thirty-thousand acres from Cuba and has managed to hold onto the possession these seventy years, despite the changes in international relations in that time. The sailors mixed work and play when the fleet was at Guantanamo. The rifle range had space for 264 targets, providing plenty of opportunity for the sailors and marines of the *Arizona*'s landing party to practice their marksmanship. There were also beaches for swimming, a golf course, tennis courts, and ten baseball diamonds. In the small towns of Caimanera and Bucoron, observed one visitor, "rum, roulette, and ruin might be had at a price."[66]

The visitor was journalist Herbert Corey, who accompanied the Atlantic Fleet on that year's winter cruise. The result of his work appeared in a heavily illustrated, fifty-four-page article in the June 1921 issue of *National Geographic*. It's a story well worth looking up

in a library because it was an unofficial status report on the Navy of that period—even if it did have a heavy public-relations flavor. For instance, Corey's article made the following claims: "The American is made into an excellent sailor, as a matter of course; but it is likewise the Navy's effort to make him into a better American. With this end in view, he is offered every opportunity to gain an education; he is taken on jaunts about the world; he is well fed and well clothed and his physical and moral health are guarded. Upon his return to civilian life he has attained to a higher and more intelligent standard of citizenship."[67]

After leaving Guantanamo, the *Arizona* went to Panama and through the Panama Canal for the first time on 19–20 January. Her topside spaces were covered by a sea of white-clad sailors, curious for a look at this engineering marvel completed less than a decade earlier. Partway through the transit the ship anchored overnight in Gatun Lake. Spending time in the freshwater lake was a special treat for the *Arizona*'s crew members, accustomed as they were to bathing in salt water and having only limited access to the scuttlebutt. They broke out fire hoses and went up on deck to wash and spray each other. They also used the fresh water to wash their seabags and hammocks. In 1921 the *Arizona*'s 97-foot beam fit comfortably in the 110-foot-wide canal locks. Later, after blisters were added to her sides for increased protec-

tion against torpedoes, the squeeze was a tight one.

Mail arrived for the crew once the ship got to Panama. Waiting for Seaman Ellsworth Ogden was a package from his girlfriend on Long Island. He opened it eagerly and found two gifts, a can of shoe polish and a can of Planter's peanuts. The shoe polish could wait. He opened the peanuts and popped some into his mouth, only to discover that the heat of the area and the long journey by mail had given the peanuts the taste of shoe polish. In disgust he hurled the can containing the rest of the peanuts over onto the top of the concrete wall forming one side of the canal lock. Panamanian children rushed over to get what they expected to be a treat. Once they tasted the peanuts, they, too, threw them down and took off running.[68]

Panama, like Cuba, offered an attraction not available in the United States—alcohol. Prohibition had become the law of the land in 1919 with the ratification of the Eighteenth Amendment to the Constitution and the passage of the Volstead Act. Men had not been allowed to imbibe on board Navy ships since 1914. Even so, the men of the *Arizona* were able to get a drink once in a while. When the ship visited the Panama Canal Zone,

sailors could go across the boundary into the nation of Panama and drink their fill. If they brought bottles back to the canal zone, shore patrolmen such as Gunner's Mate Joe Driscoll confiscated the bottles at the border after allowing the men to take as many last swigs as they could. Then the shore patrol broke the bottles to comply with the U.S. law, which also applied in the canal zone.[69]

While in Panama the *Arizona* and other ships of the Atlantic Fleet met up with the similarly constituted Pacific Fleet, which was

Left: Gunner's Mate Joe Driscoll, who supplied many of the photos used in this chapter, poses with his 5-inch/51 broadside gun on the starboard side of the superstructure. Immediately above the gun barrel is the armored conning tower with horizontal viewing slits for those inside. (Courtesy Bernard Driscoll)

Below: A broadside view of the *Arizona* steaming through the Panama Canal in 1921. (C. F. Rottmann photo, Naval Photographic Center, USN 1137044, via A. D. Baker III)

Right: Men from the *Arizona* use binoculars to peer into the distance and observe the fall of shot from a battleship astern that is firing target practice. (Courtesy Joseph C. Driscoll)

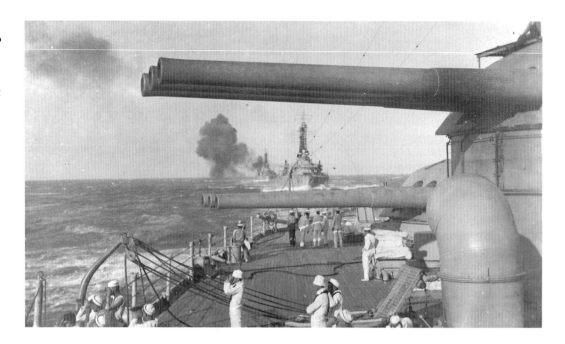

under the command of Admiral Hugh Rodman. The U.S. Navy's combatants had been concentrated in the Atlantic during World War I, but new strategic concerns called for a division of strength soon after war's end. Japan, which had been on the Allied side during World War I, had picked up some of the spoils of war in the Pacific after the defeat of Germany. The oriental nation embraced a strategy that called for wider influence in the Pacific than heretofore, reaching beyond the Asian landmass. To counter Japanese ambitions, the Navy ordered Rodman in 1919 to take some of the Navy's newest dreadnoughts to the West Coast.

Altogether, some sixty warships steamed together once the fleets had been temporarily combined. On 24 January, while the journey continued still farther south, the *Arizona* crossed the equator for the first time in her career. Veteran crew members costumed as Neptunus Rex, Davey Jones, and others gathered to initiate the inexperienced pollywogs into the mysteries of King Neptune's realm. This age-old tradition calls for a good deal of relatively harmless high jinks and merriment. The carpenters built a canvas swimming pool on the teak deck and set up a row of ducking chairs. The hapless pollywogs sat in the chairs, which then tilted over backward and dumped then into the pool. Upon emerging, each man was smacked on the rear end with a paddle. After a few more frivolities, the initiates joined the ranks of the

trusty shellbacks and were given cards attesting to their status.[70]

The equator-crossing initiation is the sort of thing that is much more fun to watch than to be the victim of. One of the watchers was the *Arizona*'s embarked division commander, Rear Admiral Edward Eberle. Gunner's Mate Joe Driscoll observed of the admiral, "He was having a ball. He was sitting up on the wing of the bridge . . . with his feet hanging down, laughing like hell at the guys getting dunked and everything."[71]

Once they were well south of the equator on the Pacific coast of South America, the two fleets divided again. The Atlantic Fleet set its course for the port of Callao, Peru, and the Pacific Fleet continued south to Chile. Because of her draft, the *Arizona* was not able to moor to a pier in Callao. Instead, the Peruvian Navy's two biggest ships, the cruisers *Almirante Grau* and *Coronel Bolognesi*, escorted her to her anchorage in the roadstead. Once the *Arizona* was anchored, her crew rode motor sailers into port for liberty. The boat coxswains had to thread their way gingerly, for the passage was littered with the carcasses of dead cattle, probably thrown overboard from a cattle ship.[72]

The time ashore was a time of learning for the crew, including Ellsworth Ogden, who learned the value of Peruvian currency. He cheerfully handed a street vendor a paper bill for a bunch of grapes. A U.S. citizen who lived in the city witnessed the transaction and told the young sailor that he had just paid the equivalent of $10.00 for his grapes. The civilian was able to persuade the vendor to put things right by returning the bill and accepting the proper coin instead. Other crew members were probably not so lucky.[73] Otherwise, the Peruvians were quite cordial, showing a number of U.S. movies in their theaters so the sailors could feel at home even when far from home.

Eight miles inland from the port city of Callao, the Peruvian capital of Lima beckoned, and many of the *Arizona*'s crew members made their way there. They were armed with small guidebooks that the Navy Department and the National Geographic Society had produced for their benefit. An-

other sight-seeing attraction was the burial place of Francisco Pizarro, the conquistador who had claimed Peru for Spain early in the sixteenth century.[74]

The biggest attraction for the visitors, however, was Lima's bull ring, the world's largest, where the men of the fleet could watch a sport foreign to their own culture. The spectacular show included performances by Belmonte, one of the most celebrated of all Spanish matadors. The size of the ring allowed the bulls plenty of room to roam, so they thus posed more of a challenge than usual for their human predators. Even so, the U.S. sailors saw it as an unfair contest and gave their sympathies and cheers to the bulls. One little brown bull was sufficiently coura-

Top: This crew member is dressed as a "sea lawyer" as part of the equator-crossing festivities. (Courtesy Joseph C. Driscoll)

Above: A sailor is dressed as Davey Jones during the initiation in January 1921. (Courtesy Joseph C. Driscoll)

Left: A stern view of the *Arizona* in one of the locks of the Panama Canal in early 1921. (C. F. Rottmann photo from Library of Congress)

Right: The *Arizona* served as the site for boxing matches between fighters of the Atlantic and Pacific fleets, which gathered at Balboa, Panama, on 16 February 1921. (U.S. Naval Institute)

Below: Dunking stools are used for the initiation of pollywogs on 24 January 1921 during the *Arizona*'s voyage to Callao, Peru. (Courtesy Joseph C. Driscoll)

geous that he cleared out the whole ring with his charges. He left the ring to the applause of the crowd.[75]

The visitors found Peru to be an arid land, one where irrigation was an invaluable remedy to nature's climate. An enterprising foreigner had discovered the remains of an irrigation system built centuries before by the Incas. After clearing away years and years' worth of accumulated sand, he made the system productive once again.[76]

After a week in Peru it was time to get back to work. The two fleets joined again, and the fourteen battleships and thirty-six destroyers staged battle maneuvers.

At that time the Navy was still in its transition from coal to oil as a fuel. The older battleships in the formation thus burned coal, the newer ones, oil. In addition to being much easier to load because it didn't have to be laboriously shoveled into bunkers, fuel oil made less smoke. In fact, if the boilers were operated properly and burners kept clean, the ship could steam largely smoke free. It required skill and vigilance to maintain the proper mix of oil and air to prevent smoke during combustion, but the benefits were worth the extra training and effort. Smoke was a tactical consideration in war games because being able to spot "enemy" ships at a distance was an advantage.[77]

In mid-February the two fleets were back in Panama and had some spirited athletic competition involving the best boxers of the two fleets. The *Arizona* won a boat race, and this time the boats were equipped with sails. It was termed a free-for-all race, in that the boats could carry any amount and kind of sail. The restrictions were that no attachment could be made to the keel, and no leeboard was permitted. Moreover, the boats had to be capable of being restored to service condition after the race. The *Arizona*'s team finished the six-mile course far ahead of the fifteen other boats.[78]

On Washington's birthday the sailing team reported to the *Pennsylvania*, the fleet's flagship, where Admiral Wilson presented a variety of awards for the interfleet athletic events. The *Arizona*'s sailing crew, including Seaman Ellsworth Ogden, got individual medals and a large silver shield for the ship's trophy case. Also in the *Arizona*'s trophy case for two years in a row was the award for overall excellence in athletics. It was a statue of an athlete, perhaps a Greek Olympian of

old, holding his hands aloft in triumph; one hand held the laurel wreath of victory. That trophy was some consolation for the loss of the Battenberg Cup to the *Nevada*.[79]

Soon the fun was over, though, and the *Arizona* and other ships of the fleet got back to their principal business of gunnery. In March new Secretary of the Navy Edwin Denby visited the *Arizona* as part of a swing through the fleet at Guantanamo. Denby was enthusiastic about his Navy job, but he wasn't able to stay in it for a full term. He later got caught up in the Teapot Dome scandal, in which private oil interests paid bribes for leases on land in the western United States

Left: A statue of an Arizona miner with a pick and shovel over his shoulder dominates the decorations for a reception on the quarterdeck. The *Arizona* was the site of the event on 1 August 1921 during her visit to Callao, Peru. The forty-inch-tall bronze statue was presented to the ship by the state in 1916. It normally stood outside the captain's cabin in officers' country. (Courtesy Charles Drake via Joseph K. Langdell)

Below: King Neptune's court parades between the officers and enlisted men of the *Arizona* during the ceremonies of 24 January 1921. (Courtesy Joseph C. Driscoll)

containing rich oil deposits reserved for use by the Navy. Even though not found to be corrupt personally, Denby was considered naive and was removed as part of a general housecleaning.[80]

In early June the *Arizona*'s skipper, Captain Phelps, fell ill and was admitted to the naval hospital in Annapolis. Executive officer Royal Ingersoll became the acting commanding officer. Phelps's illness was not fatal, but it was terminal as far as commanding the *Arizona* was concerned. On 11 June Captain Jehu V. Chase reported aboard and relieved Ingersoll.[81] Soon afterward the *Arizona* headed for the Southern Drill Grounds off the Virginia Capes and there observed bombing tests by army aircraft against captured German submarines. The men of the *Arizona* had been on the lookout for U-boats throughout World War I, and now they got to see the submarines' demise.

In the summer of 1921 the *Arizona* returned to Callao, Peru, this time with only the *Nevada* and *Oklahoma* instead of the entire fleet's battleships. The occasion was the centennial of the beginning of the movement for Peruvian independence. On board was an old friend, John D. McDonald, the *Arizona*'s first commanding officer. By this time he was a vice admiral and Commander Battleship Force Atlantic Fleet. He was concurrently Commander Battleship Division Seven, having relieved Rear Admiral Eberle of that billet at the beginning of July. Eberle was promoted to four stars and took command of the Pacific Fleet.

On 27 July Admiral McDonald and Captain Chase traveled to Lima to attend the official unveiling of a monument to Jose de San Martin, the Argentine liberator who captured the city from Spanish viceroys in 1821. That night and several others the U.S. battleships turned on their large searchlights to join in the festivities. As Admiral McDonald's flagship, the *Arizona* was the site of a large official reception on 1 August. More than one thousand guests, including ambassadors and military men from various nations, attended. When they saw the *Arizona*'s quarterdeck, they had to look twice to see whether they really were on board a ship, because the fantail area was decked out in flags and even had a statue of a miner set up as a symbol of the state for which the ship was named. Less than a month and a half after his arrival, Admiral McDonald departed, replaced as division commander by another former skipper of the *Arizona*, Rear Admiral Josiah McKean.

Although she was already physically in the Pacific as a result of the trip to Callao, the stay in Peru wound up her business with the Atlantic Fleet. Instead of heading for Panama and back to New York as she had at the end of the winter cruise, this time she was going to San Diego, San Francisco, and San Pedro. In the years just ahead, she would see plenty of those cities named for saints.

3 THE TRANQUIL TWENTIES

August 1921–May 1929

Moving from one coast to another, the men of the USS *Arizona* also moved to an entirely different life-style. Gone was New York City, with its boroughs and bridges and subways, its gray concrete canyons, and its cold winters when the North River ice floes scraped away the paint at the ship's waterline. In its place was Southern California, open and sprawling, still uncontaminated by freeways and smog. Sunshine, warmth, palm trees, orange groves, interurban trains, and a more relaxed atmosphere stretched before the newly arriving sailors.

To describe the *Arizona*'s service in the Pacific from 1921 to 1941, this narrative, of necessity, includes much less detail than for the preceding years in the Atlantic. The Pacific years included a great deal of sameness and repetition, and this and subsequent chapters will focus on highlights, on the unusual, and on descriptions of how things were done in the *Arizona* during those twenty years. The account will be told largely through the experiences of the crew, letting those experiences depict the flavor of events and the changing times. Readers who want a detailed account of the ship's movements should refer to the chronology at the back of the book.

As she settled into her new routine on the West Coast, the *Arizona* spent much of her time in her new home port of San Pedro, often traveling north to Puget Sound and less frequently to Hawaii, the Caribbean, and the East Coast.

The change of home port was not, of course, arranged solely or even primarily for the convenience of the ship's crew. The *Arizona* and the other battleships reporting to the Pacific with her were instruments of a changing national policy. In the years since the end of World War I Japan had become increasingly threatening. The term "war scare" was bandied about, and it was not to be taken lightly. Japan sought to dominate East Asia economically and militarily; its navy would be a prominent tool for enforcing such dominance. The U.S. Navy was growing as well, for both the United States and Japan had substantial naval-expansion programs in the works at the beginning of the 1920s. Such a naval arms race had been at least one of the causes of the just-concluded war, and the Navy Department decided that the best counter to Japan was to base the best battleships on the West Coast.

On rather short notice, the Navy reorganized its fleet in the summer of 1921. It was done so quietly that the changes weren't even announced publicly until the following year. Admiral Hilary P. Jones, who had been Commander in Chief Atlantic Fleet, was slated for the new post of Commander in Chief U.S. Fleet, which would consist of almost all of the Navy's warships, but it would be a command really exercised only when they were operating together during exercises. Most of the time only the newly constituted Scouting Fleet—mostly the older, coal-burning battleships and lesser combatants—would operate in the Atlantic. Command of the new Scouting Fleet would go to a former skipper of the *Arizona*, Vice Admiral John D. McDonald. On the West Coast the Pacific Fleet was renamed the Battle Fleet, and it remained under the command of Admiral Edward Eberle, who had had his division flag in the *Arizona* in late 1920 and early 1921.[1]

Under this new setup the *Arizona* remained the flagship of Battleship Division Seven; the other ships in the division were the *Nevada*, *Mississippi*, and *Pennsylvania*. In September Rear Admiral Josiah McKean was relieved as division commander by Rear Admiral Charles F. "Handlebars" Hughes, so known for a

vigorous mustache that gave him a walruslike appearance. He later served as Chief of Naval Operations, 1927–30.[2]

In his excellent book *Prelude to Pearl Harbor: The United States Navy and the Far East, 1921–1931*, which detailed U.S. and Japanese relations in the 1920s and early 1930s, Professor Gerald Wheeler explained the ways in which American thinking toward the Far East was often illogical and at cross purposes with itself. The United States believed in being a big brother to China and the Philippines for both business and religious reasons. Both the commercial market and what Wheeler called the "soul market" were considered useful, but the United States didn't really pursue those markets to advantage. Although businessmen saw China as a potential area for investment, a nation that would buy American goods, the Japanese consistently sold more in China than the Americans did. What's more, the United States did little to support these overseas areas from a military or naval standpoint, depending instead on treaty assurances. Japan had designs on furthering its sphere of control in the Far East and was building the kind of navy necessary for such control.[3]

The senior organization involved in strategic planning and policy making for the U.S. Navy was then the General Board, comprised of senior naval officers. It was seeking to build naval strength at a time when the national mood was moving rapidly toward demanding a naval drawdown. After fighting "the war to end all wars" in 1917–18, Americans in 1920 had elected as president a candidate named Warren G. Harding, who had campaigned on a platform of returning the nation to prewar "normalcy." The losing candidate for vice president on the Democratic Party's ticket, incidentally, was the former Assistant Secretary of the Navy, Franklin D. Roosevelt.

Among the initiatives of the new administration was a dramatic naval-arms-limitation conference held in Washington, D.C., in 1921–22. The idea was to reach an international agreement that would prevent the world's naval powers from getting involved in the sort of shipbuilding competition that preceded World War I. One of the impelling concerns was saving the money that would have to go to build the warships. The conference produced the Washington Treaty of 1922, calling for a ten-year moratorium on the construction of new capital ships. A number of the graduates of the Naval Academy's class of 1922 were encouraged to resign their commissions upon graduating because the naval service didn't seem to offer secure career opportunities.

Under the terms of the Washington Treaty, three U.S. battleships then under construction—the *Maryland*, *Colorado*, and *West Virginia*—would be completed, but a fourth, the *Washington*, would have to be scrapped. Also to be scrapped were a number of the battleships already in commission; included were some, such as the *Delaware* and *North Dakota*, that were only a dozen years old.

As the *Arizona* got involved in the operations of the Pacific Fleet, she encountered another consequence of the money-saving mind-set, the idea that fuel oil had to be used sparingly. Each year's engineering competition among ships of the fleet provided awards for those with the best fuel economy. Indeed, sometimes the competition was so intense that it seemed to become an end in itself. The reward for the ship that did the best was the opportunity for her crew to paint a red E—for excellence—on the smokestack.

Even though he wasn't part of the *Arizona*'s engineering department, Seaman Bob Henderson of the ship's fourth division was involved in this competition. While standing watch as helmsman on the bridge, Henderson had demonstrated that he was among the best on board at steering the ship. He was able to keep her on a straight course with minimum use of the rudder. The less the ship went back and forth, the less fuel she burned, and the better she did in the engineering competition.

Left: Two members of the crew in one of the *Arizona*'s engine rooms. The man at left is watching the shaft revolution counters, and the one at right has his hands on the throttle wheel. (U.S. Navy photo in U.S. Naval Institute Collection)

Below: In this view of an engine room, the man at left is at the throttle wheel for one of the ship's steam turbines. (U.S. Navy photo in U.S. Naval Institute Collection)

Steering a warship well is an art, requiring a knack for anticipating how the movement of wind and waves will affect her and for applying small corrections early rather than large corrections late.

The ship had two principal means of steering, steam and electric, although Henderson recalled that the electric system was most often used during his time on board. The steam system had the traditional large steering wheel, while the electric system had a horizontally operating lever, much like those used by motormen in the trolley cars of those days.[4]

Another measure of fuel economy taken into consideration for the annual competition was the amount of fresh water used. The ship's boilers required a certain quantity of fresh water to make steam for propulsion and to produce electrical power in what were then commonly known as dynamos rather than generators. To keep fuel consumption down, it was important to conserve electricity and to use fresh water sparingly. An early-1923 issue

Above: In this view of the ship's print shop in the early 1920s, printer William Patrick Keeshan is second from left. (Courtesy Nerl Reinhart via Vincent J. Vlach)

of the ship's newspaper chided the crew of the *Arizona* for its freshwater consumption. The figures for November 1922 showed that the *Arizona* used 12.7 gallons of water per man per day, compared with 7.5 gallons by the *Pennsylvania* and 9.3 gallons by the *Mississippi*. The difference in water consumption translated to an extra 15,288 gallons of fuel oil in November. The newspaper added, "Recently one of the Engineer Officers turned off 170 unnecessary lights during a tour of inspection. This represented a waste in power of 9.35 [kilowatt hours] and an extra expenditure of about 5 gallons of fuel per hour or 4 per cent of the total expenditure."[5] It took a while, but the crew finally got its act together to conserve fuel. By the mid-1920s the *Arizona* was wearing the red E on her smokestack, and Bob Henderson, a proficient helmsman, got one on the sleeve of his jumper.

No immediate progress was made in another area, that of shipboard aviation. In the spring of 1922 Captain George Marvell, then the commanding officer of the *Arizona*, sought permission from the Navy Department to get rid of the flying-off platforms that had been installed in late 1919 but not used since the trials in early 1920. The portable parts were stored in a compartment that the ship proposed to use for ammunition. The captain argued that his ship might as well get rid of the airplane equipment "in view of the very remote possibility of the platforms being used for their designed purposes." In its

bureaucratic way, the Navy turned him down, citing directives from the Fleet Commander in Chief and the Chief of Naval Operations that such platforms be retained on board until replaced by catapults. The *Arizona* would not get catapults until 1925, so she would haul the unused platforms around for three more years.[6]

During her time operating in the Pacific in the 1920s and 1930s the *Arizona* regularly went for overhaul and repair work at the Puget Sound Navy Yard at Bremerton, Washington. It was the only navy yard on the West Coast that could handle battleships, which meant it got much of the work for the Battle Fleet. The navy yards on the East Coast, on the other hand, were vastly underused because of the departure of most of the battleships. During her overhaul at Bremerton in May–June 1922 the *Arizona* received four additional 3-inch/50-caliber antiaircraft guns, bringing her total to eight, but they didn't make that much difference since the guns were of little value anyway.[7]

One of the chores for the enlisted crew during the *Arizona*'s time in the shipyard and in port was to work over the side to clean, scrape, and repaint the hull of the ship. Sometimes this was done from a small boat alongside the ship. At other times the side cleaners stood atop the armor belt, a thick layer of armor that protected the ship's vitals in the vicinity of the waterline. The belt projected perhaps a foot or so out from the side of the hull.

One side cleaner who hadn't been in the crew very long fell over the side when the ship was anchored in San Pedro. He swam back to the gangway and climbed aboard. He started to salute the officer of the deck, who asked, "Where the hell did you come from?"

The sailor replied, "Cincinnati, Ohio, sir," and kept right on going.[8]

By tradition, the commanding officer of a Navy ship is known as "Captain," no matter what his actual rank is. In times past, the tradition extended to referring to the executive officer as "the commander," rather than as "XO" or "exec," the terms currently in favor. Prior to World War II the department heads of battleships were generally lieutenant commanders, so the executive officer was frequently the only officer on board with the rank of commander. While the commanding

officer was responsible for maneuvering the ship and conducting her external relations, the executive officer was in charge of the internal administration, subject, of course, to the approval of the captain.

In effect, this made the commander the mayor of a city of some one thousand or more inhabitants and gave him considerable power and influence. One man who held that job in the early 1920s was Commander John J. Hannigan, and he fulfilled his duties in such a way that he was quite popular with the crew. He gave the men of the *Arizona* a great deal of support and enthusiasm in athletic competitions such as boxing, wrestling, and boat racing. The ship did well in those areas while he was there, less well afterward. He also took a generally humane outlook toward enforcing regulations.[9]

For instance, the Navy-issued uniforms of the time were not at all popular with enlisted men. They were baggy-looking, and the white dixie-cup hats just didn't look the way one expected a sailor's hat to look: they were too big and floppy. As a result, nonregulation uniforms were the much-preferred alternative. One can look back through old issues of the biweekly magazine *Our Navy*, which was a staple for sailors of that era, and see a good

many advertisements for tailor-made uniforms and particularly for mail-order white hats. Regulations forbade the wearing of tailor-made uniforms on board ship, but Commander Hannigan permitted nonregulation white hats. What's more, he allowed the enlisted men of the *Arizona* to wear tailor-made uniforms when they left the ship to go on liberty. Men from other ships had to go on liberty in regulation uniforms, then switch into the tailor-mades they had stored ashore in one of the popular locker clubs. Hannigan's policy saved the men of the *Arizona* from having to pay the locker clubs' rental fees, unless they wanted to change into civilian clothes.[10]

Regulation uniforms were required for the weekly inspections. Each Friday the crew held field day throughout the ship to clean up. The next morning the men ate the Navy's traditional Saturday breakfast of beans and corn bread, donned their best uniforms, and mustered topside for the captain's inspection of both personnel and upper-deck spaces. It was a tiring routine, especially since it was so predictable. The practice ensured rigorous adherence to uniform standards but resulted in a lot of unproductive time for those standing around. Seaman Bob Henderson

Above: U.S. battleships steam in column as part of fleet maneuvers near the Panama Canal in early 1923. The small sub-caliber gun on the turret in the foreground was used as part of target practice to save ammunition. While the turret crew went through the usual drills, as did the fire-control party, the small one-pounder gun simulated the firing of the 14-inch turret guns. (Daniel W. Noonan Collection, USS *Arizona* Memorial, National Park Service)

observed, "The only thing that was good about inspections on board every Saturday is that we got the best baked beans in the world for breakfast. I remember that." The other good thing was that men could go on liberty once the inspection was over. Wednesday afternoons were usually free as well, under the label "rope-yarn Sunday," a term that came from an era when sailors used Wednesday afternoons to make and repair uniforms. Thus, the officers and men generally had a five-day work week, although days in the duty section could add to that total.[11]

The Navy's fleet problem of early 1923 got the ship out of the pattern of operations she had followed since arriving in southern California. The scenario was an attack on the Panama Canal. The crew of the *Arizona* drew a map of Central America and parts of North and South America in chalk on the barbette of turret three. Members of the crew thus had an opportunity to keep abreast of the developing strategic situation while playing the annual war game.[12]

On 22 March, while in the Caribbean, the *Arizona*'s men witnessed history of a sort, the deliberate sinking of a U.S. battleship. The old *Iowa*, commissioned in 1897, had been the fourth true U.S. battleship, following the *Indiana*, *Massachusetts*, and *Oregon*. The *Iowa* had fought in the Battle of Santiago in the Spanish-American War in 1898 and had then had a variety of duties over the years before her final decommissioning in 1919. Then, with her guns removed and bull's-eyes painted

on her deck, she had gone into service as a target ship, remotely controlled by radio signals during fleet exercises. By early 1923 she had finished with that job as well and was serving as a real target for gunnery practice near Panama.

On this particular day the *Arizona* was serving as the observing ship near the target, spotting the fall of shot. The USS *Mississippi*, slightly younger than the *Arizona*, steamed in the distance, over the horizon, and shot at the *Iowa*. Watching the proceedings was Seaman Henderson, who remembered, "It took a hell of a lot of ammunition to sink that ship." He could see the 14-inch projectiles flying through the air to work their destruction.[13]

At the end of June a new crop of Naval Academy graduates reported for duty on board the battleships of the fleet. Among those joining the junior officers' mess in the *Arizona* was Ensign Arleigh A. Burke, the same man who later served as a superb destroyer-squadron commander in World War II and as Chief of Naval Operations from 1955 to 1961, the longest tenure in the Navy's history. In the *Arizona* he quickly demonstrated the qualities that would serve him well during his nearly forty years as a commissioned officer. He attacked problems energetically and persisted long after others might have quit.

One example from Ensign Burke's early months in the ship demonstrated the tenacity that was to become his trademark. He was given the unenviable job of inspecting and preserving the *Arizona*'s double bottoms. He took crews of enlisted men down into the spaces between the inner and outer hulls. There, where the air was foul and standing up straight was impossible, they looked for rust and other corrosion and then removed it. Scraping off the rust and repainting the corroded areas were thankless tasks. Consequently, they had often not been performed all that well, and the double bottoms showed the lack of effort. Material inspections soon revealed, however, that the spaces Burke was responsible for were invariably well preserved. The job others shunned, he performed with zest. Thus, not surprisingly, he was given the responsibility for inspecting and fixing all the spaces in the double bottoms. What made it particularly challenging was that the *Arizona*'s malingerers and malcontents were frequently given the undesirable duty because they had not performed well elsewhere. It was on-the-job leadership training, and Burke enjoyed it because he gloried in responding to a challenge that others shirked.[14]

Arleigh Burke had married his fiancée, Roberta Gorsuch, shortly after graduating from Annapolis, and after their arrival in California they had to have a place to live. Initially, they found a small, dingy, furnished apartment in San Pedro. In his biography of Burke, Professor E. B. Potter reported that the newlywed couple's landlady was so suspicious that she photographed her china and told tenants that they would be held responsible for any new cracks that showed up in the pieces while they lived there. There were other difficulties. That one-room apartment—or perhaps it was another they lived in—was so small that it had the kind of bed that swung down out of one wall. On one

occasion Ensign Burke went away to the ship with a trunkful of gear sitting on the floor. His bride discovered that she couldn't go to bed, because the trunk blocked the path of the bed on its way to the floor. So she had to unpack the trunk, which was too heavy for her to move when it was full, and shove it aside to get the bed into a horizontal position.[15]

The Burkes had to be mindful of the meager ensign's pay on which they lived, but they decided to find a better apartment, which they did in Long Beach. A local saying of the time commented on the relative sacrifices to be made by marriage partners: "If you love your husband, you live in San Pedro. If he loves you, you live in Long Beach." Unmarried officers whose entire room and board were available on the ship had no trouble making ends meet financially. For ensigns who had wives to feed, clothe, and house, the

Below: The *Arizona* at Puget Sound Navy Yard on 30 July 1923. Just atop the enclosed bridge in this picture is the forward armored range finder. Forward of that is the armored conning tower. The after armored range finder is on top of turret three. The numbers on the high turrets were added in 1921 to indicate turret deflection to ships operating in company with the *Arizona*. (Courtesy Puget Sound Naval Shipyard)

situation was more of a challenge. For young enlisted men, it was well-nigh impossible, which is why only a relatively small portion of the ship's crew was married.[16]

One enlisted member of the crew had taken a particularly circuitous route to reach the ship. Seaman Second Class Horatio Nelson Warren was born in Canada's province of Prince Edward Island and later migrated to the west to work during wheat harvests. He took a job at age fifteen in the province of Alberta and worked there in a branch of the Royal Bank of Canada for a few years until he developed a problem with nose bleeds. A doctor told him he had high blood pressure and added, "The only reason you're still walking around is to save funeral expenses." The doctor advised a locale near sea level to ease the blood pressure, so young Warren migrated still farther, to southern California. There he fell into the clutches of a U.S. Navy recruiter who quizzed him at some length to ascertain whether he was in trouble with the law. Convinced that he wasn't, the recruiter told him that he would be most welcome in the U.S. Navy because Canadians made particularly good sailors. Warren recalled, "I

knew then that he was blowing smoke at me," but he succumbed to the blandishments anyway.[17]

The eighteen-year-old Warren joined the *Arizona* in September 1923, after boot camp, and was soon put into the radio gang because he had learned Morse code as a boy. At the time, radio was still such a novelty that the radiomen had no division of their own; they were part of the navigation division. The ship's main radio room was on the third deck on the starboard side, behind the armor belt so that communications would be protected against disruption in the event of battle damage. One of Warren's early duties was to take charge of the communications battery room; the ship maintained a large supply of lead-acid storage batteries as further protection against battle damage. If the main power supply were interrupted, the batteries could be used to continue communications.[18]

At nights Warren studied for advancement, mainly electricity: the art hadn't developed sufficiently to earn the more glamorous name of electronics. The first radio equipment he worked with was an old rotating-spark system. During Warren's year on board, the

Arizona installed a new radio setup using vacuum tubes in the transmitter, a system that was a good deal more sophisticated than the first one. The radiomen stood their four-hour watches in main radio with rubber-covered earphones on their heads. They sat at typewriters and typed out the contents of messages addressed to the ship or the embarked flag officer and his staff.[19]

The ship's transmitter was quite powerful, as Nelson Warren learned firsthand when he went back to Alberta on leave the following summer while the ship was in overhaul at Bremerton, Washington. He visited a commercial radio station of the type used for ship-to-shore communication with merchant ships. While chatting with the Morse-code operators there, he learned that they were familiar with the *Arizona*'s call sign NBW— Negative Baker William in the phonetic alphabet of the day—from having heard it

used during various transmissions.[20] Navy ship's call signs now have four letters, still beginning with N, because the Navy is larger now.

In January 1924, as they had a year earlier, the *Arizona* and other ships of the West Coast Battle Fleet steamed to Panama to take part in maneuvers that involved simulated attacks on the Panama Canal. The Navy's first aircraft carrier, the converted collier *Langley*, joined in the games, providing a small glimpse of the growing role that aircraft and carriers would play in the fleet in the years to come.

Once the Caribbean war games were finished, the *Arizona* paid a brief return visit to her previous home port of New York. It was early March, and it was chilly for the ships anchored in the North River. Men went ashore in heavy blue peacoats and blue flat hats for warmth. The flat hat of that time truly

Below: The *Arizona* in dry dock at Bremerton in the mid-1920s. Some 14-inch gun barrels are on a barge at the lower left corner of the photo. The ship still has flying-off platforms on the high turrets, even though the planes have been gone since 1920. (Courtesy Puget Sound Naval Shipyard)

deserved the name, for it looked like a cloth-covered Frisbee held onto the top of a sailor's head by a hat band bearing the name of his ship. The hats were generally worn only for inspections and unusually cold weather. They were not as compact as the later flat hats of the type Donald Duck is seen wearing with his jumper in cartoons. According to Seaman Bob Henderson, sailors quickly discovered the need for a special way of walking on a windy day, bent over and leaning into the wind. Otherwise, a gust could grab hold of the broad-brimmed hat and send it sailing.[21]

Seaman Abe Cohen lamented the departure of Commander Hannigan and his easygoing, tolerant ways. The new regime took a more uptight, by-the-book approach to regulations. An individual who epitomized the tougher approach was the turret three officer, a mustang lieutenant (junior grade) named Joseph E. "Pop" Shaw. Rather than taking it easy on the enlisted men because he had once been one, Shaw was a bit like the reformed sinner who has gotten religion. When he had the quarterdeck, he was extremely demanding of the men's military appearance and smartness. If he saw someone show up in a tailor-made uniform to go ashore, Shaw would literally rip it. When some crew members tried to go ashore with tailor-made flat hats, Shaw made the men throw their hats into the North River. Cohen, a self-styled gigolo, liked to keep his hair longer than regulations allowed, so he had to forgo liberty whenever Shaw was on the quarterdeck.[22]

Although cold, New York offered liberty attractions just not available elsewhere. Members of the crew attended a good many of the stage presentations and burlesque shows popular in an era when radio was still an infant and television only a dream. Seaman Henderson enjoyed the bright lights of the big city because Times Square, Forty-second Street and Broadway, was as well lit up at 3:00 and 4:00 in the morning as most other towns were at 9:00 at night. The men of the *Arizona* were a hardy lot, young and blessed with stamina to keep such hours.[23]

When the men couldn't get ashore to spend their money, the opportunities sometimes sought them out in the North River. An enterprising merchant ran a small boat that came alongside the ships anchored in the river, and he came aboard to sell cakes, ice cream, and what have you. During one of the merchant's visits, a member of the ship's torpedo gang recalled years afterward, he told some officers that the *Arizona* had a woman on board. It was a ridiculous notion, of course, but some rumors are true.[24]

During their stay in the river various Navy ships, including the *Arizona*, were made available for general visiting by the public. The dances the crew had enjoyed in the immediate postwar period were resumed. Some of the gun casemates had pianos in them, and the crew would shine and wax the decks to make them suitable for dancing. Feminine voices could be heard in the ship, and one of them belonged to an attractive nineteen-year-old brunette named Madeline Blair. She has been described in some accounts as a prostitute; another explanation is that she was one of many thousands who had a dream of going to Hollywood to become a movie star. Perhaps both versions are true: she might have been working as a prostitute to bankroll an intended stay in California.

Whatever her reasons, Madeline Blair stowed away in the *Arizona* in early March with the intent of riding the ship to San Pedro, not at all far from Hollywood. In the meantime, accomplices in the crew would

Below: Crew members, wearing flat hats and peacoats, muster on the starboard side of the quarterdeck during the *Arizona*'s visit to New York in 1924. The thin smokestacks near the main stack are for the exhaust from the ship's galley. The two ladders seen at the base of the starboard boat crane lead from the quarterdeck to the upper deck. The point at which the weather deck moves one level higher is known as the break of the deck. There are bearing numbers on turret three. (Irving Underhill photo, Library of Congress)

feed and shelter her, and she in turn would return their kindness and increase her net worth by having sex with them. With her hair cut short, Madeline had either sneaked aboard disguised as a sailor or stayed aboard one of the times when civilians were visiting the ship.[25]

After leaving New York, the *Arizona* visited the Virgin Islands—an ironic port of call, considering the nature of the stowaway. On a regular basis, one of the ship's bakers carried meals to Blair, who lived first in a gun turret and later in the more isolated engineering spaces. The baker hid her food in the bottom of the bucket in which he carried his recently laundered uniforms. This ruse aroused some passing suspicion on the part of one radioman who, seeing the clothes bucket pass by his mess table at mealtimes, commented to his messmates, "That son of a bitch doesn't wash that many clothes."[26]

After a while the young woman became more brazen and ventured topside at night, sitting on top of one of the after turrets to watch silent movies. On one such evening, as described in an early biography of Arleigh Burke, Blair was sitting next to a sailor who needed a match for his cigarette. He didn't have any himself, so he reached into the breast pocket of the person sitting next to him, not taking his eyes off the screen as he did so. He quickly pulled his hand back, explaining later, "What I grabbed hold of didn't belong to no man."[27]

The sailor, however, didn't blow the whistle, probably fearing consequences if he did so. In fact, relatively few men on board the ship knew of Blair's presence until she was caught. The men hiding her apparently thought that the best way to keep a good thing going was to limit the knowledge of her presence to as few as possible.

The end of the caper came rather abruptly on the morning of 12 April when the *Arizona* was anchored at Balboa, Panama, just a few hours away from leaving for San Pedro. During the midwatch a radioman striker (that is, a seaman trying to advance to radioman third class) was taking a drink of water from the third-deck scuttlebutt. He was known in the radio gang for going ashore in the first liberty boat, coming back in the last, and spending his time with women in between. After his drink of water he walked into the radio shack, rubbing his eyes in disbelief.

Speaking of the individual he had just seen at the scuttlebutt, he said to his shipmates, "I'll swear to Christ I just saw a girl I danced with in New York."[28]

Unbeknownst to the striker, Chief Radioman Schuyler Ford was sitting behind a panel in the radio room. The striker couldn't see Ford when he proclaimed his discovery, but Ford could hear him. Concerned about his upcoming retirement, the chief quickly concluded that things might not go well for him if the *Arizona*'s officers later learned that he had known of a woman's presence on board and hadn't acted. So he went up to the quarterdeck and reported what he had heard to the officer of the deck. Not surprisingly, the report was a sensation. A team of masters-at-arms searched the ship. At 3:45 A.M. they found Madeline in a blower room attached to an engine room.[29]

The executive officer and the captain were awakened, and Yeoman Ted Love, who served as the captain's writer (essentially a secretary), was rousted out of the captain's office, where he lived and worked. He slept there on a mattress that he laid across the tops of adjacent desks so that he would be nearby if the captain wanted to do some dictation at night. He showed up in the captain's cabin early on the morning watch, wearing his undershirt and trousers. Then he proceeded to take statements from Blair, from the radioman who had seen her at the scuttlebutt, and from the officer of the deck.

Rounding up the woman's possessions from her hiding place, the master-at-arms found in her purse pictures of a number of the men who had been involved in secreting her away. She had been photographed with them on the deck of the ship when the *Arizona* was still in New York. The commanding officer, Captain Percy Olmsted, questioned Blair at some length, and she posed a question of her own—how was she going to get back to New York? Olmsted, obviously peeved by the whole business, told her she could work her way back to New York the same way she had worked her way to Panama. Yeoman Love was taken aback by the skipper's directness, believing that such a dignified man as the captain wouldn't think in such terms.[30]

At 5:00 A.M. Blair was sent ashore in one of the *Arizona*'s motor whaleboats, accompanied by a police petty officer and Ensign Burt Davis as boat officer. During the forty-five-

Above: Captain Percy N. Olmsted, the *Arizona*'s skipper, poses with the ship's race-boat crewmen and the trophy they won at the Olympic Cup Race in San Francisco on 20 September 1924. (Courtesy Steve Hoza)

minute trip, she treated Davis to nearly forty-five minutes of swearing. He later reported, "It really was something masterful; her profanity shamed eloquence." The ex-stowaway was put aboard a commercial ship for the return trip to New York, but the Madeline Blair affair was far from over.[31]

While she was being questioned, Blair had reported that there were still more women on board the *Arizona*. So at 9:00 o'clock that morning the crew was mustered at quarters on deck so the ship could be searched still more thoroughly and so the woman's accomplices could be identified from the pictures found in her purse. The search went on for a few hours, during which time crew members who had to go to the head were required to unbutton their pants when passing through hatches to demonstrate that they were, in fact, males. The search turned up no other women on board ship; Blair's report had been the act of a defiant captive seeking some small measure of revenge for being discovered before she was able to see her plan through to completion.[32]

One of the victims of the caper was Seaman Melvin Foulds, whose seabag the conspirators had stolen to supply uniforms for Blair to wear while she was on board the *Arizona*. The seabag and those clothes that the young woman hadn't needed were discovered by one of Foulds's shipmates in a pump room in the ship's engineering spaces. Fortunately for Foulds, he had reported the theft to the master-at-arms, so he was cleared of suspicion. He did have to pay for a new seabag and replacement uniforms, but they were cheap

compared with the price paid by those who had abetted Blair's stay on board ship.[33]

After a stop in southern California the *Arizona* proceeded to the navy yard at Bremerton for overhaul, and that was also the site of the courts-martial for those involved in the plot to hide Madeline Blair. She had stayed for a month, a fact that probably contributed to the severity of the justice meted out. When the trials were ended, twenty-three of the *Arizona*'s men were sentenced to naval prison; the longest sentence was ten years. It was an awfully stiff punishment for having sex on a regular basis, but obviously there was a lot more to it than that. The men had willfully flouted Navy regulations and gotten caught.

Naturally, the offenders harbored a good deal of ill will toward Chief Radioman Ford for interfering with their scheme. His life was threatened, and there was talk that he would be thrown overboard. He went ahead with his retirement from the Navy and subsequently settled in southern California. Years later, he ran into former radioman Nelson Warren, by then a civilian again and a banker. Ford showed Warren a pistol that he had gotten a permit to carry to protect himself from those former sailors whose lives he had disrupted so greatly.[34] Another whose life was threatened was Seaman Melvin Foulds, who had testified at the courts-martial about the theft of his seabag, but he also lived for many years afterward.[35]

Admiral Henry Wiley, Commander Battle Fleet, had been in Panama when the discovery of Blair's presence had upset the fleet's departure for California. He concluded that the officers of the *Arizona* should have known a stowaway was on board and directed that critical remarks be entered in their fitness reports, the reports that were all-important for future promotions. The division commander on board the *Arizona*, Rear Admiral William V. Pratt, had been as much fooled as the rest of the officers. He decided that Wiley's retribution was unmerited and later ordered the fitness criticisms removed when he became Chief of Naval Operations in 1930 and had the power to do so.[36]

There was another fallout—publicity. Having a woman stowaway on board for such an extended period was an item made to order for newspapers given to publishing sensational stories. If an account was a bit embellished along the way, that was to be expected in this era of yellow journalism. After the tale of the stowaway made the rounds, relatives and friends of the *Arizona's* men began sending them newspaper clippings about the Madeline Blair case from all over the country. Seaman Bob Henderson had the opportunity to compare a number of the articles and observed, "Hardly any two of them were alike, and hardly any two of them were right." The *Arizona* thus acquired a reputation from the Blair affair as a scandal ship; it was a reputation that persisted for some years afterward.[37]

On 12 June 1924, while operating off San Pedro, the USS *Mississippi* suffered a turret explosion, the sort of casualty that has always been a foremost concern in battleships. As the investigation revealed, a strong wind apparently blew down one of the barrels of her number two turret and prevented the gas-ejection system from blowing out all the burning embers of the silk powder bags from the previous firing. An ember was thus still in the breech of a 14-inch gun when powder for the next round was rammed into the barrel. The result was an explosion that asphyxiated forty-eight men of the turret crew. The accident caught the attention of the entire Battle Fleet, and with good reason. Many lives were at risk. The men of the *Arizona's* turret crews, for instance, went beyond even

their normal safety precautions. As one of them explained, "Believe me, we were careful after that."

One way of making the men of the turret crews safety conscious was to drill them over and over in the motions involved in shooting. Loading practice was held almost daily, even when the guns were not fired. The projectiles were brought up from the handling rooms and rammed into the breech; then up came the powder, and it was rammed into the breech and the breechblock closed. After that, the whole process was reversed and then repeated, and so on.

Ramming a projectile into a barrel was easier than getting it out because there was no reverse rammer. Instead, with the barrels in the horizontal position, as they were when they were loaded, gunner's mates used a backing-out slug. It was a piece of metal that weighed several hundred pounds and had a piece of line attached to an eye at the top. Men out on deck hoisted the slug up to the muzzle and put it in. The barrel was raised, whereupon gravity and momentum took over. The slug fell down against the nose of the dummy projectile and dislodged it from the barrel's rifling so that it could be pulled back out and sent back below in the barbette. The piece of line was then used to pull the slug back out through the muzzle once the barrel was horizontal again. It was a slow process.[38]

Left: Crew members have laid out their hammocks and bedding on the quarterdeck for an admiral's inspection. Captain Olmsted is behind the admiral. (Daniel W. Noonan Collection, USS *Arizona* Memorial, National Park Service)

Right: A stern view of the ship in dry dock at Bremerton on 21 August 1925. (Courtesy Nellie Main, *Arizona* Reunion Association)

Throughout the 1920s gunnery practice continued to be the principal occupation of the *Arizona*. The turrets that did well got tangible rewards. Seaman Bob Henderson was among the members of the turret crew who got distinct pleasure from painting two white Es on turret four in the middle of the decade. The E itself was noteworthy as a mark of achievement. Even better was that all members of the ship's crew were mustered aft for a ceremony. Members of the turret crew stepped forward and were given prize money for their excellent shooting. He recalled receiving about $50.00 in gold altogether, including two $20.00 gold pieces. The prize money resulted from a donation by a woman. As an incentive for excellence in fleet gunnery in World War I, she set up a fund, and each year afterward the interest was used to reward those who did the best shooting.[39]

In December 1924 the *Arizona* began her involvement in a series of Navy experiments that had far-reaching results, culminating in the fleet's ability during World War II to operate for prolonged periods away from shore bases. On 11 January of that year the oiler *Cuyama* had provided fuel under way to the light cruiser *Omaha* and the minesweepers *Tern* and *Kingfisher*. The oiler used a 4-inch hose to refuel the other ships while steaming alongside at bare-steerageway speed.

Encouraged by the results of that first post–World War I effort to refuel at sea, the Navy used the *Arizona* on 4 December to see whether a battleship could be refueled under way. This time the fueling ship was the oiler *Kanawha*, which towed the battleship astern. That initial test was followed in the next two

years by three others involving the *Arizona*. During the first test the oiler was able to steam at speeds of up to ten knots. In three hours the *Arizona* took on 29,186 gallons of fuel, a veritable drop in the tank compared with her rated capacity of nearly 700,000 gallons.

It was a start, but only that. The Commander in Chief of the Battle Fleet considered the rate of delivery by the astern method too small to justify fitting out other oilers for such a role. Future progress depended on increasing the rate of flow and perfecting the method the *Cuyama* had used in January 1924, with both delivering and receiving ships steaming side by side.[40] Nevertheless, the experiments had been a welcome break from the routine of formation cruising.

Maneuvering in formation with other battleships was so routine in fact that members of the *Arizona*'s crew sought diversions to relieve the tedium. Steaming in formation through heavy fog, of course, demanded considerably more attention than usual. One night in the mid-1920s Seaman Bob Henderson was standing lee helm watch in the pilothouse and had the duty of blowing the *Arizona*'s foghorn at regular intervals to warn other ships of her presence. The *Arizona*, with Rear Admiral Pratt embarked as division commander, had the *Pennsylvania* off to the port side. (The *Arizona* by then was the flagship of Battleship Division Four, and after a while she switched to Battleship Division Three. The fleet continued to be reorganized, but the *Arizona* fairly consistently remained a division flagship during the 1920s.)

The admiral was concerned about the nearness of the *Pennsylvania*, so he was listening intently to hear her foghorn. Seaman Henderson, however, was feeling a bit devilish. He was armed with a watch and soon picked out the rhythm of the other battleship's signal. So, just as the *Pennsylvania* was on the verge of sounding off, Henderson blew the *Arizona*'s foghorn and drowned out the other ship's. Henderson recalled of Admiral Pratt, "He knew damn well what I was doing—keeping him from hearing where the 'Pennsy' was. I had to fudge a little bit in order to do it." Once Pratt realized what was happening, he went over to the lee helm and bawled out Henderson directly instead of proceeding down the chain of command. Henderson complained later about this to an unsympathetic officer of the deck, who told him, "After all, that's an admiral. You better keep your goddamn mouth shut."[41]

Until the *Arizona* received her catapult and planes in the mid-1920s, the spotting of projectiles during target practice was done in the old way, from the foretop and maintop. Those stations were equipped with compasses so that men such as Seaman Abe Cohen of the fire-control division could take bearings to the target. He passed the spotting information down to the plotting room by telephone, just as people manning the range finders in the turrets passed on the ranges of the targets. An experienced spotting officer manned each of the tops, one assisting the other. Armed with binoculars, they estimated the corrections a turret needed to make to get on target, sending down orders such as "Left 500, down 200," directing that the subsequent shots should be that many yards different in terms of bearing and range.[42] The men in the plotting room used the inputs to work out the appropriate fire-control solutions and pass them on to the guns.

The F division was one of the ship's elite divisions. When Cohen reported aboard the *Arizona* after duty in the battleship *North Dakota*, he and the other men in the draft lined up on deck, and the officers asked for educated sailors as candidates for operating the fire-control equipment of the F division. Cohen spoke up and volunteered that he had had two years of high school. With that background, more than most of the *Arizona*'s men had, he became a member of the fire-control team. The biggest drawback to topside duty was having to breathe smoke and stack gas when he was in one of the tops for spotting, so he preferred watches in the plotting room.[43]

Some members of the crew left the ship during gunnery exercises to be part of the observer teams. They would be stationed on board boats in the vicinity of the target raft, although not close enough to be hit by stray projectiles if the *Arizona*'s aim was a bit off that day. For Seaman Claude Simpson the most interesting aspect of being in the observing party was watching the three projectiles as they came through the air together, growing larger and larger as they approached the target and either hit it or sent up a geyser of water nearby.[44]

Whenever the ship fired her big guns, her men had to clean up afterward. The 14-inch

guns produced such a powerful concussion and blast that they knocked loose the dust that had accumulated in corners throughout the *Arizona*. Men could see it floating in the air as they returned to their compartments and working spaces after gunnery practice was over.

Although the men of the *Arizona* usually had a great deal of pride in their ship overall, the most cohesive units were the individual divisions. These were the men that worked together and ate and slept in the same compartment. Rivalries existed between the different divisions on board. The *Arizona*'s heads were all the way forward on the main deck, so when a man had to go, he had to walk from his division's compartment. Along the way, which was sometimes fairly long, verbal jibes were passed back and forth with those in other divisions, and occasionally the disagreements got physical. Since the men stored their uniforms in their seabags, theft was common enough, but men took care to steal from those in other divisions, not their own.

Sometimes there were disputes within an individual division. Seaman Abe Cohen was passing through his division's compartment once shortly before mealtime when the mess cook was putting a pork chop on the plate of each sailor. The men would serve themselves for the rest of the meal, but rationing the meat seemed the most effective way of seeing that it was distributed equitably. Even that system had its drawbacks. While on the way to the head, Cohen noticed a big pork chop on his plate and was understandably disappointed when the boatswain's mate piped down chow. When Cohen returned to the compartment, he saw that he now had a puny pork chop; someone else had the one previously on his plate. Angry words led to fisticuffs and a

Above: Two near misses raise splashes near a target raft towed by the *Arizona* for target practice in the mid-1920s. (Arleigh Burke Collection, Naval Historical Center, S-100-A)

comment from still another member of the mess: "Look at that Jew fighting over a pork chop." Although his family was of the orthodox faith, Cohen had made his own pragmatic dietary rules for survival while on shipboard duty. "If you didn't eat pork," he explained, "you'd starve to death."[45]

That wasn't his only problem with the food. Cohen believed that the chief commissary stewards in the fleet in those years lived at the expense of the crews they were supposed to be feeding. They were allotted about forty cents per man per day to pay for the food. If they could feed a man for less than that, Cohen reasoned, they could pocket the difference. And the way to feed for less was to skimp on the quality. More than once Cohen made his way to the ship's gedunk stand—as the snack bar was called—to buy something to eat because he couldn't abide what was being served in the regular mess. Or, when he had the opportunity, he would go to the bake shop because he had friends there who would slip him goodies. Another man who served in the *Arizona* in the 1920s, Seaman Claude Simpson, observed that he could often smell the eggs sent down from the galley from a considerable distance before they reached the

mess tables. They were what might be euphemistically termed "mature."[46]

In 1925 the fleet cruise was far more extensive than normal. It began with war games based on the defense of the Hawaiian Islands, and after that the Battle Fleet spent three months cruising to the South Seas, calling at Samoa, Australia, and New Zealand. It was, in fact, the major deployment of the U.S. Fleet between the world wars. The *Arizona* was among the Battle Fleet ships that gathered at San Francisco before setting out for Hawaii for the maneuvers. The Australian Commissioner was present in San Francisco to offer an advance welcome to some of the Americans who would be coming to his nation. In a memoir written years afterward, Admiral Harris Laning recalled that the commissioner spoke along the following lines:

Officers of the fleet, you should not allow yourselves to gauge Australia's welcome to the fleet by San Francisco's marvelous farewell. I concede the spontaneousnous [*sic*] of that and realize that as a city San Francisco is most generous to the fleet. But last night as I walked

Above: Civilian visitors display the styles of the flapper era as they gather under the guns of turret four. (USS *Arizona* Memorial, National Park Service, PR-35)

Left: A starboard beam view, probably taken in early 1925. The *Arizona* has an aircraft on the stern and an E on her smokestack. She has not yet undergone the overhaul to install her fantail catapult and remove the framework for the flying-off platform from the top of turret two. (Special Collections, University of Arizona Library, 76-6-2)

down Market Street I realized that something was missing when I saw groups of handsome, young sailors and groups of San Francisco's lovely girls parading Market Street with only glances at each other, but your strict American custom demanded formal introductions, so without that they could not meet.

Thank heaven, you will not find introductions necessary in Australia. When your young men encounter Australia's young ladies in Sydney or Melbourne, they will be taken right to their bosoms, and I mean that literally as well as figuratively. Permit me to suggest, gentlemen, that you advise your men accordingly.[47]

The advice was superfluous for the bluejackets of the *Arizona* because their ship was slated for overhaul and modernization at the Puget Sound Navy Yard immediately after the war games.

As she headed west to take part in the fleet problem, the *Arizona* was again operating aircraft. In the years since 1920, when she had flown European land planes off the turret tops, the U.S. Navy had developed floatplanes for scouting and spotting flights. Unlike the big flying boats that the Navy had used during World War I, these floatplanes were small enough to be carried in ships. Some were already operating from catapults in other battleships.

The *Arizona* had a different method for getting them airborne. They were first lifted off the ship with the boom at the stern and set into the water. The pilot then got the engine going and taxied as fast as he could until he had enough speed to break the suction of the water and get some lift from the wind passing the wings. The flights could take place only from relatively calm waters because the planes were not designed to operate from rough seas. Still, the aircraft provided a good deal more flexibility than those that had had to land ashore in 1920.

Lieutenant Charles C. Ferrenz and Lieutenant Samuel H. Arthur were the pilots who flew the *Arizona*'s UO-1 floatplanes. In late April 1925, while flying in the two-seat plane, they ran into trouble when their engine developed problems, reducing its speed. They were able to stay in the air long enough to play their role in that day's battle problem, but afterward they flew to the naval air station on Ford Island in Pearl Harbor. There they could get the plane repaired and refueled before returning to the *Arizona* to be lifted back aboard. But instead of getting the gasoline they wanted, they were "captured" by the defending forces in Hawaii and marched to the brig as simulated prisoners of war. It took a good deal of talking for them to persuade the war game's umpires that they should be released so they could go about their business of getting the airplane fixed, which they did.[48]

Below: The similarity of the sun's reflection off the water indicates that these views of the *Arizona*'s bow and stern were probably taken from the tops within a short time of each other. The crew is at quarters in both shots. Notice the sub-caliber gun on turret two and the soon-to-be removed framework for the flying-off platform. Off center to port is the base for the airplane catapult to be installed during the ship's mid-1925 overhaul at Bremerton. (Bow view, Arleigh Burke Collection, Naval Historical Center, S-100-A; stern view, courtesy Nellie Main, *Arizona* Reunion Association)

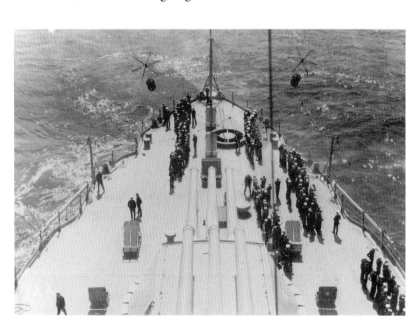

Annual Ball Arizona 1925

Above: Crew members and their dates gather for the ship's ninth annual ball, this one held 27 November 1925 at the Ambassador Hotel in Los Angeles. (Daniel W. Noonan Collection, USS *Arizona* Memorial, National Park Service)

After the war games in the Hawaiian area ended, the fleet steamed west, and the *Arizona* steamed east to the Puget Sound Navy Yard in Bremerton, Washington. One member of the crew who was not particularly unhappy over the ship's missing the cruise to Australia and New Zealand was Seaman Bob Henderson. He said, "As soon as we got off the ship, we grabbed the first ferry and went to Seattle. Believe it or not, that was when the personnel in the Navy did a lot of dancing. We were all pretty good dancers. And Seattle had the best dance halls, the best night clubs." Moreover, with the bulk of the fleet away in the South Pacific, the men of the *Arizona* would have little competition for the girls of Seattle.[49]

Seattle had another valuable attribute as far as sailors were concerned: it was a good deal more open than other liberty ports. Bootleggers offered "rotgut" moonshine for sale, speakeasies accommodated those with more refined tastes, and places for gambling were readily available. Thus, sailors were often inclined to stay in Bremerton only when the ship held periodic dances. Most of the girls who served as dancing partners for the crew members came from—where else?—Seattle. Just as the enlisted men chafed at wearing regulation uniforms on liberty, they also found their shoes to be uncomfortable. Henderson described the regulation shoes as clodhoppers with a big toe area, so he and his shipmates wore special shoes for dancing.[50]

One other activity that took the men of the *Arizona* ashore in the Puget Sound area was landing-force practice. The marine detachment, of course, was well trained and equipped to serve as a landing force if need be, but sailors were also designated to participate. The ship carried a 3-inch fieldpiece on deck for artillery support, and it was dragged ashore in a whaleboat along with sailors outfitted in web belts, leggings, and rifles. After storming ashore, the men staged mock battles with each other. Seaman Henderson had a particular knack for such engagements. "I was very good at dying quick," he said. As soon as he found a convenient shade tree, he simulated being shot and took it easy for the remainder of the battle.[51]

The *Arizona*'s modernization lasted for three months, from mid-June to mid-September, and involved substantial improvements to the ship's combat capabilities. Probably the most visible change was the installation of an aircraft catapult on the stern. The foundation for it had previously been put in place, and now came the catapult itself. The device, though new to the ship, was considered obsolete even when it was put aboard. The USS *Mississippi* already had one that was fired by powder charges. The *Arizona*'s

Right: Sailors on liberty congregate at the fleet landing in San Pedro, the *Arizona*'s home port, in 1925. (Daniel W. Noonan Collection, USS *Arizona* Memorial, National Park Service)

Below: The *Arizona*'s officers pose on the quarterdeck in 1924 with Captain Olmsted in the center of the front row. (Courtesy Mrs. Margaret Gesen)

depended on compressed air and didn't give as much acceleration as the powder type.

New 14-inch and 5-inch broadside guns were installed, equipped with a hydro-pneumatic counterrecoil system. The turrets were further improved with modifications to the sprinkling system and improved flame tightness. To aid in aiming the guns more accurately, an entirely new plotting room was constructed below decks in space previously occupied by storerooms. In the engineering department, the fuel-oil capacity was increased by approximately six hundred tons to give the ship a cruising radius of about nine thousand miles at an economical speed of ten knots. Topside, the navigating bridge was

greatly improved by the construction of necessary bulkheads to enclose it completely and thus improve habitability in cold weather. Although considered a flagship, the *Arizona* still didn't have a suitable flag bridge or battle station for an embarked flag officer.

With the addition of the fantail catapult, the old flying-off platforms were finally taken off the ship. Some other interesting topside weight remained, according to a report that the Board of Inspection and Survey issued after the overhaul. The board discovered that the potato lockers contained more than twenty-five tons of potatoes. For a crew of nearly 1,100 officers and men, that amounted to about fifty pounds per man.[52]

The improvements to the ship had cost a total of approximately $340,000, which exceeded the statutory limit of $300,000 for such work. The austere financial climate of the times demanded a great deal of paperwork to explain and justify the excess cost. The Commandant of the Puget Sound Navy Yard was Rear Admiral Jehu Chase, coincidentally a former skipper of the *Arizona*. He explained that the preoverhaul cost estimates had been made in good faith but that a number of conditions had forced the actual costs higher. Chase had decided that the only way to avoid going over the limit was to stop work in progress, and that step would have left the ship inoperable. The appropriate bureau chiefs in Washington endorsed his decision, and Secretary of the Navy Curtis Wilbur finally approved it. Perhaps a cost overrun of 13 percent on an overhaul would raise eyebrows today, but a difference of $40,000 wouldn't in an era when the most sophisticated destroyers and submarines cost more than $1 billion apiece.[53]

Abe Cohen had transferred from the gunnery department to engineering because he encountered anti-Semitism topside. As a fireman, he did not take kindly to the shipyard time, no matter what it did to help the ship as a whole. His cynical view was that the shipyard workers were paid too much for doing too little. Not only that, he found some of their work counterproductive. After they had worked on pumps, Cohen and other members of the ship's force had to repair the leaks. Or perhaps they had to redo the insulation lagging that was put around steam

lines to protect crew members from burns. The yard workers were inclined to disrupt the lagging during their work but not replace it. Finally, the crewmen seemed to be perpetually cleaning up after the civilian workers. After all, it was the sailors—not the civilians—who would stand the captain's inspection, so it was the sailors who wound up doing the cleaning.[54]

When the *Arizona* got back to Southern California, Cohen was reminded of why the crew liked the Seattle area so much. The girls in California just weren't as accommodating. He liked to go a particular dance hall in the Los Angeles area that had three big orchestras. It cost a quarter to get in and a penny a dance. Cohen bought a sheaf of tickets when he went in, but he couldn't always use them as he would have liked. A type of segregation took place, with Navy men all on one side of the place and civilian men on the other. Many of the girls wouldn't have anything to do with the guys on the Navy side.[55]

Even so, he found women in enough other places in the area that liberty always held its attractions. He found it particularly frustrating to be in the liberty section but not able to get ashore because of the weather. The Los Angeles area was susceptible to sudden brisk winds called Santa Anas that roiled the waters of the harbor and made boating more of an effort than it was worth. All Cohen could do was gaze wistfully over the side at what might have been.

Just as he found it difficult to stay aboard when he wanted to be with a honey on the beach, he also found it difficult to go back to the *Arizona* when he wanted to stay with that honey. Once he returned to the ship a day and a half late. Predictably, he went to captain's mast and was sentenced to five days in the brig on bread and water. Although he had friends in the ship who sympathized with his plight and managed to get some real food to him in his cell, five nights of sleeping on the deck convinced Cohen that the price was too high. He never again got sentenced to brig time.[56]

Although still relatively primitive compared with later versions, submarines continued their development as part of the post–World War I fleet. In 1925 the Navy directed the *Arizona* to supply five ensigns for training at the submarine school in New London, Connecticut. Big-gun ships were still preemi-

Above: UO-1 observation airplanes perch on the newly installed fantail catapult in March 1926. (Courtesy Nellie Main, *Arizona* Reunion Association)

later, described the advantage as being "like looking over somebody's shoulder in a poker hand."[59] Spotting was still done from the tops for short-range battle practice; the planes were put into use for long-range practice. At long range, spotting from aircraft was much more accurate.

As the decade advanced, the handling of aircraft in the ship progressed remarkably over what it had been in 1920. Then the flying-off platforms had to be rigged laboriously on top of the high turrets, and the planes had to be lifted aboard from the boats that returned them to the *Arizona*. With the new catapult and the airplanes equipped with pontoon floats, the men of the *Arizona* slowly learned how to pick up the planes under way. The technique called for the ship to make a sweeping turn as a plane approached for landing, knocking off the tops of the waves and making a slick that lasted long enough for the plane to land on the water. The ship trailed a cargo net from a boat boom as kind of a sled, and the pilot maneuvered to catch hold of the net with a hook on the bottom of his pontoon. Then the boom at the stern was used to pick the plane out of the water and return it to the catapult. Obviously, these new procedures gave a great deal more flexibility than the old way did. But some of the old prejudices remained. In a statement reminiscent of the view of his blackshoe predecessors from 1920, Arleigh Burke said, "No deck officer liked airplanes, because they got oil all over the damn decks, and they were always in the road."[60]

In early 1926 the *Arizona* went into fleet maneuvers with her new catapult. As usual, there were simulated attacks by the opposing fleets, but this time the simulation got a little too realistic. On the morning of 5 March, while operating off the Pacific side of the Panama Canal, the ship was involved in battle torpedo practice when two torpedoes hit her on the port side, one below the conning-tower area and one below the bridge. They dented the hull plates and broke a rivet. Subsequently, the vibration caused by the ship's engines and the firing of the guns loosened the broken rivet and produced a small leak in the hull.

One of the pilots who flew from the *Arizona* as an observer during the maneuvers that spring was Lieutenant Arthur Radford. At the time he was the naval aviator on the

nent, so few evinced a great interest in trying the new craft. To pick the "volunteers," a nickel was flipped, and the losers went to submarines. In one case at least it proved to be a cloud with a silver lining. While Ensign Carl Gesen was at New London he met a student who was going to Connecticut College. She happened to ask for a tour of a submarine. Gesen gave her a tour of the boat and later married her.[57]

When they weren't giving tours to visiting women, the *Arizona*'s wardroom officers often relaxed with nightly games of bridge. The participants depended upon who had the watch on a given night. It was a gentlemanly way to pass the time. For the less gentlemanly, there was gambling in the junior officers' mess. If wardroom officers wanted more action than they could find in the bridge game, they joined the junior officers. On other occasions, the officers watched movies or got involved in sports such as badminton out on deck.[58]

In late 1925 the *Arizona* began realizing the benefits of having airplanes and catapults on board. Because of their immense height advantage, the observers in the planes were much better able to spot the fall of shot than the men in the tops. Jack Arnold, an officer who served in the *Arizona* a number of years

staff of the battleship-division commander; he was later Chairman of the Joint Chiefs of Staff in the 1950s.

In July 1926 Rear Admiral Henry J. Ziegemeier, Commander Battleship Division Three, transferred to the *Arizona* the trophy presented annually on behalf of the President of the United States to the most efficient ship of her type in engineering. The *Arizona* had earned the red E.[61]

During her goings and comings to the Caribbean in the 1920s the *Arizona* stopped for liberty in Panama a number of times. Some of the men who went ashore there got so drunk that they had to be brought back aboard in cargo nets. Abe Cohen recalled standing on the dock while waiting for a boat and getting involved in coconut and banana fights. After the drunken exchange of tropical fruit, the dock would be a slippery mess—littered with mushy bananas.[62]

To enforce the regulation against drinking on board, the men of the quarterdeck watch

would search everybody as he came back aboard ship. That procedure ferreted out the bottles that were hidden in waistbands, socks, and packages. On one occasion, an officers' steward came aboard with a bottle in each hand. The men on the quarterdeck performed the required search, feeling his pants legs and so forth, but they didn't pay any attention to the bottles in his hands. The watchstanders figured that those bottles contained some sort of condiment for the officers' mess. Sometimes, the best hiding place was no hiding place at all.[63]

Enlisted men were far from the only ones who sought to skirt the regulations. One officer was going to get married and have a party when the ship got back home to San Pedro. He ordered a bunch of booze in Panama, and a shore boat was supposed to bring it to the *Arizona* at around 3:00 A.M. while he was standing a watch. Instead, the illicit goods arrived at just about daybreak. Even so, the liquor was unloaded and hidden. Someone reported its presence, and the ship was searched, but the contraband was never

Above: The crew poses for a group portrait on the forecastle, circa 1926. Captain Perrill is in the second row, slightly to port of the life ring. Ensign Burke is in the same row, fourth from right. The azimuth markings are gone from turret two. (Special Collections, University of Arizona Library, 77-7-1)

Right: Captain Harlan P. Perrill commanded the *Arizona* from June 1925 to May 1927. (Daniel W. Noonan Collection, USS *Arizona* Memorial, National Park Service)

Below: Sailors on stages paint the boot topping at the *Arizona*'s waterline with the ship in dry dock. The opening for the port torpedo tube is below the waterline. (USS *Arizona* Memorial, National Park Service, PR-2)

found. The double bottoms were among the popular hiding places on board. In this case, the caper was apparently successful, although, recalled Bob Henderson, "I don't know how the hell he ever got it off ship after he got to San Pedro."[64]

A mustang officer in fourth division ran the ship's service canteen. Once, when the ship was somewhere in the Caribbean, this officer came aboard with cases and cases of bay rum hair tonic. It was not intended to be drunk, but the word went around the ship that straining it through a loaf of bread or a felt hat would take out the poison that was in it. That didn't work, and a number of men got sick. Others sought to slake their thirst by removing some of the alcohol that served as fuel for the ship's torpedoes. One clever chief torpedoman used to spread towels on the deck when he was topping off the torpedoes. He was a bit sloppy in his work, with the result that some of the alcohol inevitably spilled to the towels below. Once the work was completed, he wrung out the towels into a container and had a drink.[65]

From 1925 to 1927 the *Arizona* had a skipper, Captain Harlan Perrill, who had a reputation among some of the junior officers for two qualities—being intimidated by his wife and having no tolerance for subordinates' drinking on board ship. The junior officers had a good lively party going on one occasion while the ship was in port when the captain came aboard unexpectedly. Quickly the word was passed through the *Arizona* that the "Yellow Peril" was on board, and the tipsy officers were secreted away to avoid coming in contact with him.[66]

In addition to his views on alcohol, Captain Perrill was unpopular for other reasons. Arleigh Burke was an ensign when Perrill was skipper and said of him many years afterward, "He didn't realize the necessity to be liked by somebody." As a consequence, he was probably liked by very few. He was a rigid, nervous man who insisted on doing nearly all of the ship handling himself, even though he wasn't particularly good at it. Thus the junior officers didn't get much chance to develop their skills, for ship handling—like riding a bicycle—is something best learned by practice, not by watching and listening to lectures. Perrill was strict and not very understanding. As Burke put it, "He measured everything by the results and that alone. The difficulty of performing, he didn't measure very well." The same pattern held true in disciplinary situations; the skipper was not inclined to take mitigating circumstances into consideration when a sailor did something wrong.[67]

Although his time in the *Arizona* had shunted him from division to division—first fire control, then deck, then engineering—Fireman Abe Cohen developed a great affection for the ship. In fact, when his enlistment came to an end in 1926, he cried genuine tears upon being paid off. The term "paid off" meant literally that. A man was paid five cents per mile for travel back to his home of record, and he was given an additional payment in lieu of salary for any days of unused leave remaining on the books. Cohen traveled from Long Beach to the East Coast and then reenlisted when promised machinist's mate school at Hampton Roads, Virginia. There he got some book-type training in addition to the practical variety that had been customary in the engine rooms of the battleship. When he completed the school, Cohen was rated as a machinist's mate third class and was given his choice of duty. He opted to return to the *Arizona* because by then he considered it home.[68]

One of his duties as a machinist's mate was standing watch in the shaft alleys, the areas near the stern of the ship that the propeller shafts pass through on their way from the engine rooms to the propellers. Watching propellers turn over and over dozens of times per minute was not the most stimulating duty, but there was a purpose to it, as Cohen discovered firsthand when a shaft bearing overheated because of low lube-oil pressure. This was the type of emergency for which he was prepared. Cohen notified the engine room of the problem and then put wet rags on the shaft to cool it down. As he remembered the incident, "They commended me for that, and the next day the chief engineer inspected me, and I had a button off my peacoat, and he bawled the hell out of me. That's the way it goes."[69]

A new man who reported aboard in 1926 was Seaman Second Class Russ Arnett, fresh out of boot camp. As were most of the new men, he was assigned to one of the deck divisions. While in first division he participated in an intraship boxing smoker and did well as a middleweight, winning his bout.

That boxing match led to Arnett's being a part of the ship's last torpedo division. The chief torpedoman was impressed that Arnett had a good deal of strength for his small stature and thus recruited him for service in the *Arizona*'s torpedo room, where the quarters were cramped. Arnett remembered, "There wasn't much room there at all; every inch counted."[70]

The torpedo room was truly an anachronism in a battleship, a holdover from the days early in the century when naval gunfire was generally so inaccurate that ships had to get within a few thousand yards of each other to do some damage. If they had to get that close anyway, the torpedoes could supplement the gunfire. Since then the accuracy of gunfire had

Above: A lighter lies alongside the *Arizona* at San Diego on 17 February 1927 to load a PB-1 flying boat on the quarterdeck for delivery to Guantanamo Bay, Cuba. (Courtesy Nellie Main, *Arizona* Reunion Association)

Below: Crew members use a dolly to move a torpedo on deck during the 1920s. In the lower part of the picture is the face plate for a 14-inch–gun turret. The opening for the barrel is at the lower right. (Bernard Pawlack Collection, USS *Arizona* Memorial, National Park Service)

torpedoes back and forth between the storage racks and the firing tubes. It was no wonder the chief wanted a small, strong man for the duty.[71]

Generally, the *Arizona* fired her torpedoes about once each quarter to keep in practice. Although the tubes could not be trained—they fired perpendicular to the longitudinal axis of the ship—the *Arizona* did not have to be aimed at a right angle to the target. The officers directing the exercise from the bridge used the ship's gyrocompass repeaters to take bearings on the target. Usually, one boat pulled two others as targets. One of the target boats had a mast erected in it to serve as an aiming point. By telephone the officer on the bridge called down to the torpedo room. Arnett and others in the division had been sent to torpedo school to learn the operation and maintenance of the weapons, so they knew how to set the small gyrocompass inside the torpedo to direct it along the desired heading once it entered the water. The firing system worked on compressed air. Once the torpedo was in the tube, the outer door was opened, and the torpedoman first class pulled a lever that expelled a charge of compressed air and fired the torpedo. When the torpedo was clear of the tube, the gyrocompass took over and sent it on its way to the target. Having a torpedo pass under the target boat was considered the equivalent of a hit.[72]

The dummy torpedo used in exercises had a water-filled cavity where the warhead would normally have been. Once the torpedo got to the end of its run, the water was expelled from the cavity, and the torpedo bobbed to the surface. A torpedo-recovery boat then hauled it aboard and returned it to the ship. There the torpedomen brought it aboard on a cable, using a small davit erected for that purpose. Once they had it on deck, they lowered it through a series of hatches to return it to the torpedo room and its space in the storage rack. Men like Arnett, down inside the ship and below the waterline, rarely got to see the results of their work. That was reserved for those topside with binoculars. In 1928 Arnett finally got an opportunity to be in on the topside end of the torpedo operation. Because the *Arizona* was shortly to be modernized and lose her torpedo capability, he was given two choices—duty at the submarine school in New London, Connecticut, or torpedo-recovery duty in Hawaii. For a man who had

Above: Mechanical mules on the wall of one of the Gatun Locks provide the motive power as the *Arizona* makes her transit through the Panama Canal on 6 March 1927. The searchlights have been removed from their platform on the foremast, leaving more room for sight-seeing sailors. (National Archives, 80-G-457050)

Right: This close-up shows a pair of UO-1 observation planes on the *Arizona*'s catapult during the Panama Canal transit on 6 March 1927. Angling upward is the boom used to recover aircraft from the water before the installation of a powered crane in 1934. Notice the air scoops on the portholes forward of the ship's name. (Courtesy O. A. Heinlein, U.S. Naval Institute Collection)

improved considerably, guns could be expected to hit well outside torpedo range. While the weapons were on board, though, the torpedo division operated them. The torpedo room, which was located below the waterline and just forward of turret one, ran from one side of the bow to the other. The ship had one 21-inch-diameter torpedo tube to starboard and another to port. Inside the torpedo room were a dozen torpedoes, stowed in racks along the bulkheads. A chain fall was suspended from a track in the overhead of the torpedo room; it was a heavy block-and-tackle rig that used chain instead of rope in the pulleys. It was with the chain fall that the torpedo gang moved the heavy

PASSING THRU GATUN LOCKS 3-6-27. E

ARIZONA

grown up braving the brisk prairie winds of Kansas, the choice was an easy one—he was soon on his way to Pearl Harbor.[73]

In 1927 some of the sailors in the *Arizona* were formed into a seaman guard to replace part of the marine detachment. The marines had been pulled out of the ship and sent to Nicaragua to take part in one of the many efforts to deal with the wily Augusto Sandino. The man for whom the present-day Sandinistas are named, Sandino was long a thorn in the side of the United States. Seaman First Class Lester Bennett took the role of corporal of the guard in the *Arizona*, although it was a job he didn't particularly relish because it wasn't what he had been trained for.[74]

That year the *Arizona* participated in two presidential reviews. In the first, her crew manned the rail to pay honor to the president of Haiti. A large black man, he came aboard outfitted in stovepipe hat, swallowtail coat, and red cummerbund to receive the honors accorded him. The ship gave him a 21-gun salute.[75] Later, U.S. President Calvin Coolidge reviewed the Fleet at Hampton Roads. In between, the city of New York put on a warm welcome for the *Arizona* and other warships. As usual, the battleships anchored in the North River and decked themselves out with flags and electric lights. In groups of six and seven, local citizens came aboard for guided tours through the ship. Seaman Bennett was delighted with the duty because, as he recalled, "They'd insist on paying you. New York is a great tipping town."[76]

Fireman Ralph Ratcliffe, new to both the Navy and the *Arizona*, managed to get

approval for five days of leave while the ship was in New York. Unfortunately, he miscounted and came back to the ship a day late. Inevitably, he wound up before the skipper, Captain William Tarrant, at captain's mast. Ratcliffe claimed, honestly, that he had not looked at his leave papers when he left the ship, just stuffed them into his pocket and then came back eight hours before he believed his leave was due to expire. He was chagrined when informed that he was not eight hours early but sixteen hours late. Captain Tarrant

Left: As the *Arizona* exits the Gatun Locks, the hull and propeller of the PB-1 flying boat are visible to port of turret three. (National Archives, 80-G-457051)

Below: The crew is at quarters as the *Arizona* takes part in a review of the Fleet by President Calvin Coolidge at Hampton Roads on 4 June 1927. She is wearing an E on her smokestack. (National Archives, 80-G-460111)

believed his story because this sixteen-year-old first offender didn't appear to be trying to beat the system. The chief master-at-arms offered a dissenting opinion. He believed that it was Ratcliffe's responsibility to know when to get back and to do so on time. Obviously, in tempering justice with mercy, the captain's word was law, and Ratcliffe was off the hook. But the chief master-at-arms was, Ratcliffe remembered, "highly pissed" at the captain for giving him a break. It was an opinion the master-at-arms expressed to the seaman, not to the skipper.[77]

In the summer of 1927, after her return to the Pacific from the East Coast, the *Arizona* made her typical summer swing up to the Puget Sound area. While the ship was there, Fireman Ratcliffe fell in love with one of the local girls. "She taught me a few things," Ratcliffe recalled, then added ruefully that she must have been quite an educator because he found out later that "half the fleet knew her."[78]

A new officer who reported to the ship that year was Ensign Clarence Coffin, fresh out of the Naval Academy. Naval aviation was the coming thing then with two large new aircraft carriers, the *Lexington* and *Saratoga*, just joining the fleet. All newly commissioned officers on the West Coast had to report for elimination flight training, a precursor to the real thing. It gave the young officers a taste of flying and measured their aptitude. Those who qualified and desired to do so could then

apply for formal flight training at Pensacola, Florida. Ensign Coffin was eager, but the physical exam discovered astigmatism, which ruled him out for aviation. When Coffin got back to the *Arizona*, the gunnery officer decided that anyone who had studied aviation as the ensign had should have a shipboard role that used that knowledge. He was thus made a spotter for the 3-inch antiaircraft guns.[79]

Part of Coffin's indoctrination as a new naval officer was taking a course that taught him about the *Arizona*. The ensigns had to tour the ship and make notes on what they found. In the engineering plant, for instance, they had to go down to the engine rooms and firerooms and make sketches. They traced steam lines and then drew pictures of the process by which water was heated in the boilers, sent through the various turbines, ranging from high-pressure to low-pressure, and then condensed into water so it could start the cycle all over again. Coffin found it to be excellent practical training, really important background for deck officers to have when they were standing watches on the bridge. To give engine orders intelligently, watch officers had to have an appreciation of what would be happening down below where the orders had to be implemented.[80]

Coffin recalled his department head, Lieutenant Commander Howard A. "Pat" Flanigan, as an effective and energetic gunnery officer, although one who was not always

popular. "A lot of the married guys hated his guts, because he made us stay on board over the weekend. But if we had to work, he was there too, and I thought that was damn good." When a director had to be checked on a Saturday, Flanigan was there, leading the checking. In the jargon that was used in that period to describe a top-notch naval officer or ship, Flanigan was "efficient." The fact was that he got results. Lieutenant (junior grade) Joe Daniel, the turret three officer, said of Flanigan, "He was a crackerjack officer with a wonderful way of leadership." Flanigan was all business on board the ship, but after a successful gunnery practice he would take the gunnery department's officers ashore for a party, let the illicit booze flow, and lead them in a mellow round of the old Navy songs that he knew so well. He drew a definite demarcation between business and pleasure and worked energetically at each.[81]

The officers who served with Flanigan in the *Arizona* were disappointed that he did not continue onward and upward in his naval career. In 1936, because circumstances had prevented his promotion to captain, Flanigan retired prematurely. He had met and married a divorcée who felt that she needed to remarry to provide a father for her growing children. Her former father-in-law, U.S. Senator Hiram Johnson of California, apparently without foundation, concluded that Flanigan had broken up his son's marriage to this woman and exerted pressure to ensure that Flanigan would rise no higher. It was a sad case in which political influence overrode a splendid service record and led to an early retirement. Flanigan was recalled to active duty in 1941 for service in the impending war. He performed so well in Europe as a key officer on the staff of Admiral Harold R. Stark that he was awarded the Distinguished Service Medal and Legion of Merit and was promoted to the rank of rear admiral.[82]

In late October 1927 the *Arizona* steamed to Monterey, California, for the first and only time in her career. The occasion was a Navy Day celebration, giving the citizens of that picturesque seaside city the opportunity to see one of the ships that their tax dollars paid for. For many years Navy Day was celebrated on 27 October, the birthday of President Theodore Roosevelt, because he had done so

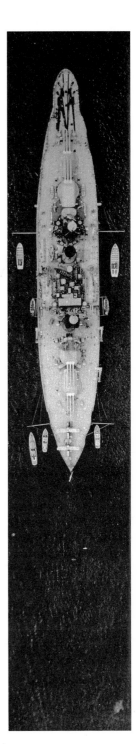

Above: An aerial shot of the *Arizona* anchored off New York City on 2 May 1927. The boxy structure just forward of the mainmast may be an aviation facility installed when the ship got her aircraft catapult. (Naval Historical Center, NH 57655)

much to foster the growth of the U.S. Navy at the beginning of the twentieth century. While the ship was anchored inside the breakwater at Monterey, her junior officers went ashore at the invitation of a group of Army officers stationed at the adjacent Fort Ord. They had an enjoyable party at which the booze flowed. In fact, it was so pleasant that the Navy men decided to reciprocate by inviting the Army officers to bring their wives for a party in the junior officers' mess on board the *Arizona*.

The Army men brought liquor as well as their wives. The officers enjoyed a splendid time of interservice cooperation. When the supply of mix ran low, the ship's junior officers called for a Filipino mess attendant to bring more, putting a towel over his head as he walked through the stateroom area so he wouldn't see the various high jinks going on in individual rooms. The rooms were in a

sufficiently isolated area of the ship that no one was likely to wander in by accident. The party was moving from room to room, and after a while most of the participants were fairly high. Then the ship's navigator, Lieutenant Commander J. H. Wellbrock, Jr., who was the senior officer on board while in port, got wind of the festivities. He showed up on the scene, called for boats to take the Army officers and their wives ashore, and then had the *Arizona*'s participants pledge that there would be no mention of the party in the future. Recalling the occasion more than sixty years after the fact, retired Vice Admiral Joe Daniel said of making the pledge, "If we hadn't, there would have been a lot of officers who never would have been admirals."[83]

Having lied about his age to join the Navy at sixteen and having volunteered for the engineering department to escape the deck scrubbing and holystoning that were part of his lot in the deck force, Fireman Ralph Ratcliffe discovered that there were still obstacles in the way of his getting to do real engineering work. First he had to spend three months as a compartment cleaner, then three months as a mess cook for the boat engineers of A division.

The latter job brought him a highly unexpected benefit on Thanksgiving in 1927. The ship's cooks prepared the usual holiday meal in the galley, and Ratcliffe and the mess cooks from other divisions had to make numerous trips up and down ladders, hauling the food to the compartment.[84] After he had made all those trips and cleaned up the table afterward, there was nothing left for Ratcliffe but grapefruit and some bread and butter—a far cry from turkey and dressing. The next morning he got up to serve breakfast, and he didn't have any customers. Something in the Thanksgiving dinner had been contaminated, producing multiple cases of abdominal distress and diarrhea. As Ratcliffe remembered, "You couldn't buy a seat in the head." The boatswain's mates even had to break out the fire hoses and turn the topside deck-edge waterways into makeshift heads. Ratcliffe's grapefruit looked awfully good in retrospect.[85]

After he finished his tour as a mess cook, Ratcliffe finally got into the real work of the A division. He became the boat engineer in the crew of a 50-foot motor launch. The engine was an old gasoline-burning type, which compelled the crew to be extremely careful during fueling. To diminish the likelihood of an electric spark's starting a fire, the gasoline tank was grounded to the ship, and the hose was grounded as well. Smoking was obviously forbidden during fueling. Changing the oil was a daily chore because it got dirty quickly and lost its lubricating qualities. Since there was no drain plug on the crankcase, Ratcliffe had to take off a little face plate and absorb the dirty oil in a rag to remove it.[86]

Starting the two-cycle engine was also a chore because it wasn't self-starting. Instead, like today's power lawn mowers, it had a flywheel. Ratcliffe had to wrap a piece of line around the flywheel and get two or three members of the crew to join him in vigorously jerking on the cord to get the engine to turn over. Starting it was a special challenge on rainy days when the wet cord was difficult to get hold of and the officer of the deck was shouting, "Get that son of a bitch alongside" because there were sailors waiting on the quarterdeck to become passengers. During the ride the sailors would get as wet as the boat crew, but at least the pleasant experiences of liberty lay ahead.[87]

One of the *Arizona*'s top watchstanders on the bridge in the late 1920s was Lieutenant (junior grade) Harold Page Smith, who came aboard from the USS *Procyon*, trading places with Arleigh Burke. Like Burke, Smith eventually became a four-star admiral, retiring in 1965 as Commander in Chief Atlantic Fleet and Supreme Allied Commander Atlantic. In 1928 he was responsible for conning the *Arizona* during her underway maneuvers. In retrospect, he considered her awfully sluggish in comparison with the far more powerful battleship *Missouri* that he commanded twenty years later. In the *Arizona*, he had to anticipate upcoming movements because the ship took a fair amount of time to respond to changes in the rudder and engines.[88]

Burke had experienced the same situation himself. The trick in getting the *Arizona* to turn smoothly in the wake of the ship ahead—a highly prized attribute in those years—was to give her a goose at the beginning of the maneuver. The wise conning officer started the turn with hard rudder to

overcome the sluggishness, then gradually eased off to standard rudder as she began coming around. In retrospect, Burke explained, a lot of the emphasis on precision ship handling at the time was overrated because of its limited tactical value in combat. "Not that ship handling was so important," he said, "but it was something that could be measured." In that vein, it resembled the competition in such areas as gunnery and fuel economy. The philosophy was that if an officer did well in things that could be measured, he could do well at other things also.[89]

In fog, the watchword was caution. In those days before radar, the ship crept along

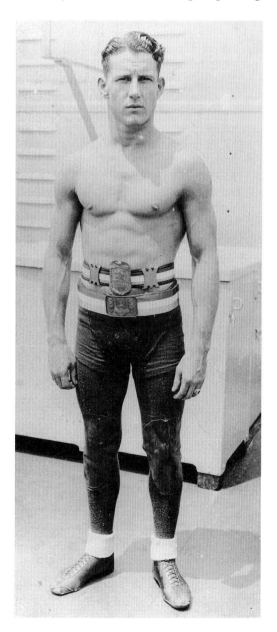

Left: Wrestler Denver Jenkins won the all-Navy belt for 1927–28 while he was in the crew of the *Arizona*. (Special Collections, University of Arizona Library, 63-5-1)

Right: Projectiles splash off the *Arizona*'s starboard quarter during target practice in the late 1920s. Suspended over the side is a patent life buoy, ready for immediate launching in the case of a man going overboard. (Charles E. Legore Collection, USS *Arizona* Memorial, National Park Service)

Below: Crew members use the boat boom during swim call on the way to Hawaii in April 1928. (Courtesy Nellie Main, *Arizona* Reunion Association)

at perhaps five knots. Special fog lookouts were posted at the bow, in what were called the "eyes of the ship," and the bridge windows were rolled down to improve visibility. Lieutenant (junior grade) Smith

discovered he could see better in fog without binoculars than he could with them. When ships were steaming in formation through the fog, those in leading positions trailed floating spars from their sterns. These spars were pieces of timber about six inches square and eight to ten feet long. They had pointed noses and were designed to kick up a rooster tail of spray as they skimmed along the surface of the water. The bow lookouts in trailing ships reported the position of the spars in relation to their own ship. Smith recalled that one advantage of the *Arizona*'s configuration was that the wings of the bridge afforded him a view well aft, a luxury he didn't have years later in the *Missouri*, whose superstructure shielded the stern from view.[90]

Even in good weather, steaming in formation was a challenge. The ships were often only five hundred yards apart in column. That proximity demanded steady vigilance and frequent use of a hand-held device called a stadimeter to take ranges to the ship ahead. When a ship drifted behind in the formation, it was important for her to ease gradually back into position. An officer of the deck didn't want to rush to catch up and then have to take off engine revolutions when practically running into the stern of the ship ahead. Admirals in tactical command enforced the station-keeping by sending out visual signals to those who had strayed beyond the fifty-yard margin for error. The signal went both to the officer of the deck and captain of the offending battleship and was to be avoided if possible. Lieutenant (junior grade) Joe Daniel found there was more slack in station-keeping at night, not only because it was more difficult to judge distances precisely but also because the admirals had gone to sleep, and their subordinates were not so inclined to send out the unpleasant messages.[91]

Each individual in the crew had his own idea of what constituted a desirable liberty location. For some, San Francisco was the best because its policemen were inclined to be more tolerant than those in the ports in Southern California. Claude Simpson remembered that San Francisco's police were not likely to object if sailors smuggled moonshine into dance halls. Bremerton, Washington, site of the principal overhaul yard for the ship, was not hospitable toward sailors. They could gravitate toward the local Navy YMCA, but the command encouraged the men to go across Puget Sound to Seattle for liberty. The police in Bremerton didn't seem to like sailors, a curious attitude in view of the fact that the navy yard was the principal source of livelihood in the town.[92]

Another activity that took crew members off the ship at Bremerton was marksmanship practice. Captain Jesse L. "Cy" Perkins of the marine detachment was in charge, and he was assisted by Ensign Clarence Coffin, who had been on the rifle team at the Naval Academy and would later shoot for the Navy Rifle Team, under the command of an expert marksman, Commander Willis A. Lee, Jr. The program began with the ship's landing party and then expanded to encompass other members of the crew. The *Arizona*'s men used the rifle ranges at Camp Lewis (now Fort Lewis) near Tacoma. Even though the rifle team was expert, it did not excite nearly the attention on board the ship that other sports, notably football, rowing, boxing, and wrestling, did.[93]

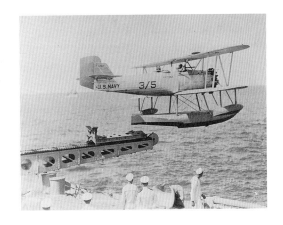

In the late 1920s the state of Arizona gave the ship a brindle-colored pit bull pup as a pet. The pup got along well with the small fox terrier already on board, and the two played together often. When the pit bull got bigger, the sailors took it ashore when they went to practice as a landing force. During one of the mock battles a big Airedale came to investigate and made the mistake of attacking the pit bull—something the little terrier had been far

Left: The fantail catapult launches one of the O2U observation planes in the late 1920s. (Courtesy Sam Femia via Joseph K. Langdell, *Arizona* Reunion Association)

Below: The *Arizona* in overhaul at the Puget Sound Navy Yard on 3 February 1928. Just forward of her is the oiler *Neches*. In the upper right corner of the photo is Crane Ship Number 1, formerly the battleship *Kearsarge*. The *Arizona*'s aircraft catapult has been removed from the ship for maintenance. (Courtesy Puget Sound Naval Shipyard)

Below: Photographer
John W. Proctor made
this handsome shot of
the *Arizona* when she
was anchored at Port
Angeles, Washington,
on 16 August 1928.
(San Francisco Maritime
National Historical
Park)

too smart too try. The pit bull shook off its
initial surprise and retaliated, killing the
Airedale. The men of the *Arizona* came to the
sad realization that they had a born killer on
their hands and had the pit bull put to sleep.[94]

In the spring of 1928 the *Arizona* steamed
to Hawaii as part of the annual fleet problem.

The wives of Lieutenant (junior grade) Page
Smith and another junior officer made the
crossing by passenger ship and rented a
Honolulu apartment in which the two cou-
ples lived comfortably. Still, life had its
challenges, especially when Smith's wife was
ashore nearby and he had to stand a midwatch
on the quarterdeck from midnight to 4:00 in
the morning. It was tough enough being
awake at that time of day anyway, and the
calm, warm atmosphere made it even tougher.
He joked that his feet grew a size or two from
all the pacing he did while standing quarterdeck watches.[95]

From late June to early September of
1928—a period of only nine or ten weeks—
the *Arizona* had Captain Victor A. Kimberly
as commanding officer. This was a remarkably
short command tour, but Kimberly had
apparently pulled some strings in the Navy
Department in Washington because he was
reassigned to command the USS *Maryland*.
The *Maryland* was one of the three newest
battleships in the fleet, the only ones armed
with 16-inch guns. She was considered a
prestigious command. Lieutenant (junior
grade) Joe Daniel, then the turret three
officer, recalled, "We were indignant as hell
that he left to take that job." The feeling in the
Arizona's wardroom was that Kimberly had
let his new shipmates down to fulfill a
personal ambition. In retrospect, the officers
felt that justice had eventually been served, for
Kimberly never was selected for flag rank and
was still a captain when he retired from active
duty in 1934.[96]

Kimberly's relief was Captain Ward K.
Wortman. During his tenure one of the
Arizona's floatplanes was badly damaged on
the fantail. Not all of the planes would fit on
the catapult for stowage, so the others were
put on movable dollies and stored near the
after turrets. On one occasion Joe Daniel in
turret three let one of his observers go to the
head, and while he was gone a gunner's mate
inside the turret trained it around and
depressed the barrels, knocking both wings
off the biplane on the dolly. The accident
upset the operational schedule because the
plane was about to be used to tow a sleeve for
antiaircraft practice. The officers on the type
commander's staff felt that Daniel should
suffer for allowing the accident to happen.
After some fuming, the staff finally turned the
matter over to Captain Wortman to mete out

discipline. Daniel was called to Wortman's cabin at the stern, and there he found the skipper sitting in his underwear. Wortman looked at the turret officer and pronounced sentence: "Daniel, I don't want to go and minimize the enormity of your offense. But after talking it over with the gunnery officer, we have decided to put it on the shelf. I want you to go and sin no more."[97]

Daniel cited that incident as an example of why the *Arizona* was a happy ship during his time on board. The officers were at least reasonable. He contrasted his own experience to a similar case in the *West Virginia*, another of the new 16-inch–gun battleships. The officers of the *West Virginia* seemed intent on winning the E for excellence at all costs and were extremely competitive. Once, Daniel's counterpart in the *West Virginia* didn't make the necessary fire-control compensation when using reduced powder charges rather than full charges for gunnery practice. The result of his mistake was that the projectiles fell so far short of the target that they couldn't be corrected by spotting. The offending turret officer was shortly relieved of duty, detached from the ship, and ordered to the Asiatic Fleet.[98]

In another instance, it was Captain Wortman who was at fault. Some Japanese warships were visiting the United States, and they were at San Francisco at the same time as the *Arizona*. As was the custom of the time, Wortman went to pay an official call of respect on the Japanese admiral. Custom then re-quired the Japanese officer to return the call. As the Japanese admiral ascended the *Arizona*'s gangway and stepped onto the quarterdeck, he saw that Wortman was not there to greet him personally. The visitor immediately turned on his heel, went back down the ladder, boarded his boat, and returned to his flagship. Wortman told Lieutenant (junior grade) Daniel to go to the Japanese flagship and tender the captain's apologies. When Daniel got to the other ship, her junior officers took him to the wardroom and plied him with sake. Thus fortified, he went to see the admiral. He blurted out Wortman's apologies as he was supposed to, but he got only a steely-eyed gaze in return. When it became apparent that the Japanese officer wasn't going to say anything to accept the apology, Daniel turned and left. The United States had affronted the Japanese a number of times in the 1920s, particularly with an immigration act in 1924 that seemed to be aimed toward Japan. Wortman's negligence obviously did nothing to improve the situation.[99]

One of the new members of the crew in the early autumn of 1928 was an eighteen-year-old seaman second class named Sam Femia. It wasn't long before he was involved in the daily routine of scrubbing, cleaning, polishing, chipping, and painting. A lot of this was busywork. Sure, it kept the *Arizona* looking shipshape and thus imparted a good deal of pride to the crew, but the real business of a warship is operating. Today, Femia observed,

Left: The *Arizona*'s race boat is in the center, its flag even with the *Arizona*'s mainmast during this race at San Pedro, California, on 10 December 1928. The *West Virginia*'s boat is at right. The crew from the *Colorado* won that day's race. (Naval Historical Center, NH 69020)

young people are inclined to question, to ask for the explanation that goes with the order. Explanations were neither requested nor offered in the battleship Navy of the late 1920s. When a seaman second class was told to do something, he did it or suffered the consequences.[100]

Life for a seaman on board ship was a continuation of the socialization process that had begun at boot camp. New men learned a lot of new terminology and often a new sense of discipline. Some men rebelled against the

Right: Captain Ward K. Wortman commanded the *Arizona* from September 1928 to April 1930. (Courtesy Nellie Main, *Arizona* Reunion Association)

strict rules. For men such as Femia, the initial reaction was often a shrug. If this was what he had to do, this was what he had to do. He would put his time in and then seek another way of life afterward. As he put it many years later, "You couldn't even dare to talk back to the leading seaman, never mind the coxswain [equivalent to today's boatswain's mate third class]. The leading seaman would start you off, and then you worked up to the coxswain, then there was the boatswain's mate. When you got to the boatswain's mate, that's when you were in trouble."[101]

Since he accepted the system, Femia seldom got in trouble. And then an interesting phenomenon took hold. He got to know people, make friends, and develop a taste for the Navy way of life. In the meantime, he would watch the more senior men come up topside after a meal, walk back and forth on the deck, chat with one another, and sometimes just look at the ocean. At some point, probably without Femia's even realizing it, the Navy way of doing things became his way. He grew accustomed to talking of decks and ladders and bulkheads. After a while he was part of the Navy himself, and that meant until he eventually retired as a chief boatswain's mate.[102]

In addition to being young when he reported to the ship, Femia was often broke, and he was shy as well. When he didn't have enough money for the customary liberty pursuits, he made his way onto the bus tours offered by real-estate promoters trying to sell lots in Hollywood and Beverly Hills. The prices were outrageously low, but still astronomical for a young man making $54.00 a month when he was advanced to seaman first class. Even so, the tours helped pass the time. When he got back to the ship, he had a chance to make additional liberties vicariously because it was the practice for the men of each division to get together afterward and discuss their exploits. In reality, many a man made two liberties on a given day—the real one and the exaggerated version that he bragged about.[103]

But there would not be all that many liberty opportunities for Femia in southern California because the *Arizona* was destined to go to the East Coast for modernization.

A new man who joined the *Arizona* in January 1929 was Electrician's Mate Second Class Oliver Deaton. He came aboard with a short-timer's attitude because he knew he would be in the crew only a few months before the ship went into the navy yard. He was motivated to learn his way around the ship only so that he could find a suitable hiding place in which to avoid work. A buddy pointed out an ideal spot topside. It was a narrow access between the barbette of the number two turret and the housing of a ventilation fan. Deaton weighed only 120 pounds, so he was able to squeeze through the opening. The top two electrician's mates in his division, a chief and a first class, were too well filled out to fit through the opening, so Deaton had a splendid hideout for sleeping and reading when the urge to work was weak.[104]

With the coming of the new year the *Arizona* traveled through the Caribbean on her way to Norfolk. In that period in early 1929 Seaman Femia had what he believed was the best job in the entire first division of the ship. Obviously, these things are in the eye of the beholder because his job was captain of the head. That meant he had to clean up after dozens of his shipmates on a daily basis. But there was a bonus. He got to use as much fresh water as he wanted, while the others had to get by with only part of a bucket of fresh water each day.[105]

When the ship got to Panama City, the crew was surprised to find that the prostitutes advertised their business. As the men walked along the streets the women would yell their going price—twenty-five cents—out their windows. It wasn't a case of competitive bidding, just a statement of fact. Of course, a quarter was worth a good deal more then than it is now. It would buy several beers, so many of the men were able to both get drunk and spend time with the prostitutes before they returned to their anchored gray home.[106]

In Cuba liberty activities were a good deal tamer than in Panama. There were swimming and baseball and maybe a Popsicle at the gedunk stand ashore. Thus, the *Arizona* had a good many willing customers when bumboats pulled up alongside the ship and offered jugs of rum for sale. Lines were dropped down, and the treasure was hauled up, into portholes or to spots on deck away from the eyes of the officers. The men buried a good bit of this treasure in the sand locker, which was all the way forward, near the anchor-chain locker in the forecastle. The sand was there, of

course, to be spread on the wooden decks for holystoning. Somehow the officers got word of the cache and confiscated many jugs of good Havana rum.[107]

In April 1929 the *Arizona* stopped at Gonaives, Haiti, on her swing through the Caribbean. Crew members headed for liberty

Above: A fleet oiler alongside hoists one of the *Arizona*'s O2U observation planes. Oilers provided a depot function for fleet aircraft at the time. (Charles E. Legore Collection, USS *Arizona* Memorial, National Park Service)

Left: The *Arizona*'s forecastle decked out with signal flags in celebration of Navy Day, 27 October 1928. (Charles E. Legore Collection, USS *Arizona* Memorial, National Park Service)

Above: This is a rare photo taken inside one of the *Arizona*'s 14-inch–gun turrets. The gun room was so cramped that the photographer wasn't able to get far enough away to include the breech mechanisms of all three guns. (Special Collections, University of Arizona Library, 71-1-159)

in Port-au-Prince got a warning before leaving the ship that they should carry a canteen of water with them or else promise to drink beer because the water they'd be likely to encounter ashore could make them sick. Fireman Ralph Ratcliffe was like the rest; no self-respecting sailor would carry a canteen on liberty. Barely eighteen and not all that far removed from his growing up in Iowa, Ratcliffe had his first taste of beer and discovered that he didn't particularly like it. He acquired the taste, though, and before long he was joining his shipmates in an activity quite acceptable in Haiti and very much forbidden back in the United States. It would be their last opportunity to drink for a good long while because the ship was soon

headed for Norfolk and the end of her life as a cage-masted ship.[108]

One of the passengers who left once the *Arizona* reached the East Coast was a parrot. It belonged to the captain's wife, but she didn't want to carry it all the way across country on the train when she was rejoining her husband in Norfolk. Thus the captain took the parrot into his cabin at the stern of the ship, and the bird traveled in style. It had plenty of attention, too, because the captain's marine orderlies, who had plenty of time to stand around and do little more than wait to be summoned, were giving it an education in nautical terminology. For instance, they taught the parrot to say, "Forty f. . .ing knots and no smoke." Steaming a ship at forty knots without making smoke would be quite a noteworthy achievement, but Mrs. Wortman quickly decided that the bird's newfound vocabulary was ill-suited to her home and would have nothing more to do with it.[109]

Once the *Arizona* pulled in at the Norfolk Navy Yard, the first phase of her seagoing career was over. Men who had been involved in a variety of occupations while the ship was operating now had a common chore—unloading the ship. She had been filled with fuel and stores when she first went into commission, and they had been replenished on a continuous basis ever since. Out came the food, the hardware, and the many other things that had made a collection of steel into a vital entity. For a while, her vitality would be gone, and with it several thousand tons of steel as well.

4 FIT FOR THE PRESIDENT

May 1929–June 1934

In mid-1929 the *Arizona* entered the Norfolk Navy Yard. Though she had just entered her teen years, she was already obsolescent. Aerial warfare had come of age since the ship was designed, and the accuracy of gunfire was much improved as well. The ship needed a thorough modernization to adapt to these developments. As a result, the entire superstructure was stripped off and replaced during the nearly two years the ship spent in the yard. Even the smokestack was taken down, and a new larger one was put in its place. The bridge area was substantially increased in size, providing a separate flag bridge to accommodate an embarked admiral.

Since her move to the Pacific in 1921 the *Arizona* had gotten her regular overhauls at the Puget Sound Navy Yard in Bremerton. With the movement of the bulk of the Battle Fleet to the West Coast, the workload between shipyards had become unbalanced. Those on the East Coast were underutilized, while those on the West Coast were quite busy. The *Arizona* and her near-contemporaries—the *Pennsylvania*, *Oklahoma*, *Nevada*, *New Mexico*, *Mississippi*, and *Idaho*—all got major face-lifts at the end of the twenties and the beginning of the thirties. When they emerged, they were the most modern battleships in the fleet, because no new ones had been built since the *West Virginia* was commissioned in 1923.

Most of the crew of the *Arizona* left after she got to the Norfolk Navy Yard, which is actually in Portsmouth, Virginia, despite the official name. Offered the choice between the hardships of shipyard life or the opportunity to report for duty in the newly modernized *Nevada*, most opted for the latter. By September 1929 the crew of the *Arizona*—both Navy and Marine Corps—was down to 24 officers and 344 enlisted men.[1]

Those who stayed saw their ship gradually sliced away until the only recognizable structures topside were the turrets, the conning tower, and the fantail airplane catapult. The demolition started at the top as cutting torches ate away the connections between the fire-control tops and the cage masts. A large dockside crane took away the tops, and then the masts grew steadily shorter as more and more sections were sliced off and lifted away. The small bridge went away, and so did the air-scoop funnels, the directors for the 5-inch guns, the smokestack, the boat cranes, and the skids for stowing the boats.[2]

Fireman Ralph Ratcliffe was one of the many who chose to leave the *Arizona* as soon as he could. He was a boat engineer on his duty days when crew members wanted to ride a boat from the *Arizona* to take them between Norfolk and Portsmouth rather than pay the five-cent fare for the ferry. But it was what he had to do in between boat runs that really convinced him to make the move. Unemployed boat engineers wind up being employed at chipping and painting in a shipyard, and it was precisely that sort of duty Ratcliffe had left the gunnery department to avoid. Within a month or two he joined the *Nevada*.[3]

One of the few men who stayed with the *Arizona* all the way through the modernization was Seaman First Class Claude Simpson. Once the topside part of the ship had been removed, it was time for a new superstructure to rise in its place, and that meant virtually constant riveting all day long. Simpson and his shipmates worked to the loud staccato accompaniment of rivet guns pounding the red-hot end of each rivet into a flat shape once it had passed through the matching holes in the two steel plates to be joined together. Years later Simpson remarked, "I believe half the crew couldn't hear after we got out of there."[4]

A few at a time, new men reported to the crew. One such was Seaman Edward Berry, coming aboard from the *Utah*. Under the provisions of the recently concluded London Treaty of 1930, that battleship was to be demilitarized by the removal of her turret guns. She would henceforth serve as a gunnery-training ship and a target for bombs and bullets. When Berry stepped onto the quarterdeck of his new home, he looked down and saw the same view that his predecessors had had in 1917, when the *Arizona* had her low-pressure turbine repaired. He could look right down into an engine room that had no engines in it.[5]

Another new man was Fireman Third Class Walter R. "Sam" Davis, who showed up in early January 1930. He had just finished boot camp and Christmas leave. He reported that the "*Arizona* looked like a wreck, all cut up and torn apart, and I didn't think it could ever be put together again." While it was being put back together, the few members of the crew lived in a nearby marine barracks. The marines were good hosts and fed the visiting

sailors well during the year they stayed there. During that time the engineering department in which Davis served consisted of only about sixty or seventy men—a far cry from normal levels.[6]

Davis was assigned to the boiler division, headed by a watertender first class. He saw to it that a fireman showed Davis through what was left of the *Arizona*, with the new man asking "a million questions." The watertender told Davis that the navy yard's men were there to do the work; it was the job of the skeleton crew to learn and to keep the fireroom clean. Specifically, Davis's assignment was to ensure the fireroom always had a fresh pot of coffee. The watertender also gave Davis a number of tips about how to get along well in the ship: keep a fresh haircut, shave daily, shine his shoes, always carry a flashlight, and never have dirty gloves. His philosophy was that if a man had shined shoes and clean gloves, others would be unlikely to give him dirty jobs. Davis took the advice and wound up with few dirty jobs as a result.[7]

As the year 1930 progressed, more changes took place. Captain Wortman was detached in April, and the executive officer, Commander Thaddeus Thomson, became acting skipper for a while. The turrets' face plates and gun slides had been removed so that new ones could be installed. This modification increased the elevation and thus the range of the guns. Once the new face plates and slides were in place, in went the 14-inch rifles, inserted by a dockside crane. Sturdy new tripod masts were constructed during the course of the year. In September Captain Charles Freeman came aboard and took over the command reins from Thomson. Bit by bit the crew was being put back together at the same time the ship was.[8]

In October 1930 a number of officers reported for duty in the *Arizona*, preparing her to resume active service shortly after the beginning of the new year. When the *Arizona* had gone into the navy yard a year and a half earlier, she had lost many of her men to the *Nevada* because they wanted to be in an operating ship. Now the process was reversed, and the *Arizona* was the beneficiary as other ships temporarily left active service. Ensign John Davidson, like Seaman Ed Berry, reported from the battleship *Utah*.

It wasn't long before Ensign Davidson ran afoul of Commander Thomson. Years later,

Below: The *Arizona* in dry dock at the Norfolk Navy Yard during her modernization. The old superstructure has been taken off and the new tripod masts erected. Construction of the new tops has begun. (Special Collections, University of Arizona Library, 77-3-436)

Davidson said of Captain Freeman, "He was known as somewhat of a sundowner [a strict disciplinarian], but his executive officer was such a so-and-so that it made the captain seem like a pretty nice fellow." For example, the ensign was serving as in-port officer of the deck one day when dozens of enlisted men reported to the *Arizona* to help fill out her crew. When Davidson wrote up the rough deck log for the watch, he attached a copy of the roster of all the new enlisted men. Later, when he had been relieved of duty and was preparing to go ashore, the executive officer's marine orderly intercepted him at the gangway and said, "Commander Thomson would like to see you."

So Davidson went to Thomson's cabin and stuck his head in. The exec looked up and said, "Get the hell out of here!" So Davidson left and began walking away. He hadn't gone far when the marine again stopped him, saying, "Commander would like to see you." Then it finally dawned on Davidson. He had been preparing to go ashore in civilian clothes, as officers customarily did, but Thomson wouldn't talk to him unless he was in uniform. Nor would Thomson stoop to telling him to put on his uniform before coming to the cabin. Davidson had to figure that out for himself. So he went to his room and changed into the uniform of the day. Then the executive officer finally told him that instead of attaching a roster of the enlisted men's orders to the log, Davidson had to print every one of the names in the log himself, including the sailors' serial numbers and rates. Only then could he go ashore. By the time the very disgusted Davidson got done with the task, he was quite late for his planned dinner date.[9]

Some time later Davidson was assigned to the first division. To get oriented, he asked a first class boatswain's mate to show him through the spaces that were the division's responsibility. The ensign and the boatswain's mate were in the enlisted men's head, as far forward in the ship as they could get, when Commander Thomson arrived on the scene as part of an inspection. It was the first time Davidson had been in the space, but Thomson demanded, "Why haven't those tiles been laid?"

"I don't know," replied the ensign. "I just got here." Davidson had neglected to apply his Naval Academy training. There he had

learned to respond in such a situation with "I'll find out, sir." When Thomson heard Davidson's flippant reply, he blew up and said that the ensign certainly ought to know about his own part of the ship. He started chewing out the junior officer in front of the enlisted man, a less-than-desirable way to exert leadership. The exec had known Davidson previously from the Naval Academy and told him that he had been a poor excuse for a midshipman and that it was now obvious he was never going to be worthwhile as an officer either. (Davidson, incidentally, was later promoted to rear admiral and served as superintendent of the Naval Academy in the early 1960s. Thomson retired as a captain.)[10]

While Davidson was learning his way around, more and more people showed up, and the yard workers completed rebuilding the ship from the deck up. The reconstruction of the *Arizona* had cost about $7 million, a bit less than half the cost of her original construction a decade and a half earlier. For that $7 million price she got additional protection against submarine and air attack in the form of 70-pound special-treatment steel added to the armor of the second deck.

Bulges, also known as blisters, were added to her sides to provide additional layers of protection against torpedoes. The bulges also had the effect of increasing her beam; her new outside dimension just barely allowed her to clear the 110-foot-wide locks of the Panama Canal.

The ship got new boilers and new turbines, the latter from the never-completed battleship *Washington*, which had been discarded as a result of the 1922 Washington Treaty on naval disarmament. The more powerful engineering plant enabled the *Arizona* to maintain her speed, despite the increased displacement brought on by the bulges and other additions. The new propulsion equipment was lighter than what was removed, compensating in part for the extra weight in other areas of the ship. The elevation of the *Arizona*'s turret guns was

increased from fifteen degrees to thirty, almost doubling their range. When commissioned, the 14-inch guns could fire a 1,400-pound armor-piercing projectile about 18,000 yards. Now the maximum range was 34,000 yards.[11]

Recognizing that ship-to-ship battles were likely to take place at longer ranges than in the past because of improved accuracy in gunnery, the Navy removed from the *Arizona* and the other battleships the submerged torpedo tubes that were useful mostly for close-in warfare. The change also made the ship less vulnerable to damage by torpedoes fired at her. The underwater openings for the torpedo tubes were necessarily beyond the ends of the waterline armor belt. And the torpedo room extended all the way across the ship. A torpedo exploding in that large, uncompart-

Below: Still partly covered with red-lead primer, the *Arizona* has nearly completed her modernization in this photo from December 1930 at the Norfolk Navy Yard. Notice the structures on deck. Destroyer number 155 is the USS *Cole*. (Norfolk News Service Photo, courtesy Ernest Arroyo, Pearl Harbor History Associates)

mented area could let in a lot of water, and it might also cause the warheads on the ship's own torpedoes to explode. During the reconstruction the torpedo room was compartmented to add to the *Arizona*'s watertight integrity.[12]

In place of the old cage masts, which had tended to sway for a few seconds after the firing of the 14-inch guns, the ship got much more solid tripod masts. The new masts were strong enough to support three-level fire-control tops so that the directors for the main and secondary batteries could be consolidated at a high vantage point; this consolidation would provide greater range for spotting the fall of shot in relation to a target. The secondary battery's 5-inch/51 broadside guns were moved up a level to the main deck so that they wouldn't be so susceptible to getting wet in a seaway. New 5-inch/25-caliber anti-aircraft guns were added, more powerful than the 3-inch/50 guns they replaced. Antiaircraft directors were added atop posts, one on each side of the ship just aft of the bridge.

A new flag bridge and flag quarters were built to supplement the navigating bridge, thus making the *Arizona* a much more capable division flagship than she had been. The compressed-air catapult on the fantail was replaced with a more modern one that used powder charges for firing. Not long after the completion of the modernization, a second catapult was added to the top of turret three. The use of a powder-charge catapult made the second one feasible because it hadn't been possible to run compressed-air lines to the top of a turret.[13]

Still another part of the modernization had to do with interior communications. The age-old method had involved metal voice tubes that ran from one space to another. Sometimes the voices had to travel a considerable distance, and clarity suffered as a result. Another disadvantage was that the tubes pierced bulkheads that were supposed to be watertight. During the 1930s some of the voice tubes were taken out to improve watertight integrity. Another older form of communication had been battery-powered

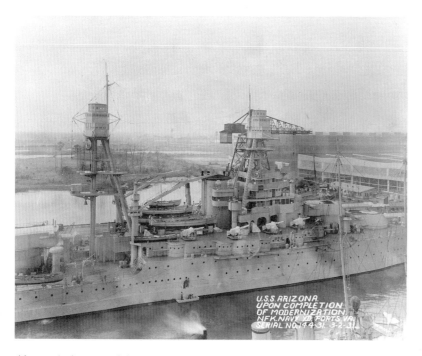

Above: A close-up of the amidships section of the newly modernized *Arizona* at Norfolk, 2 March 1931. The sailors on the punt are painting the blister at the waterline. A searchlight-control platform has been built on each side of the new smokestack. The 5-inch broadside guns have been moved up a deck from before, and 5-inch antiaircraft guns, without shields, have been added on the 02 level. (National Archives, 19-LC-19-B4)

Right: This portrait of Captain Charles S. Freeman, the *Arizona*'s commanding officer, was made during President Hoover's visit to the ship. (National Archives, 80-G-461061)

electrical phone circuits. During the shipyard period sound-powered phones were installed, an improvement over their battery-powered predecessors. Even so, they weren't as reliable or as clear-sounding as today's models.[14]

On 3 March 1931 the *Arizona* left the navy yard at Portsmouth and headed down the Elizabeth River. In some ways, the process of taking the rebuilt ship to sea for the first time resembled the *Arizona*'s sea trials in 1916. The crew had to test-fire guns, check equipment, determine tactical data, compensate the compasses, and so forth. Several technicians from Westinghouse were on board to supervise the use of the newly installed main propulsion turbines. After several days at anchor for inspections and the checking of various systems, she headed into the Atlantic. While she was out getting her sea legs, she got something else—new orders. The *Arizona* was directed to take President Herbert C. Hoover aboard for a vacation cruise in the Caribbean. Presidential trips in naval ships were commonplace in the era, and the *Arizona* needed a shakedown cruise anyway.

Before the president's trip, the *Arizona* returned to the Norfolk Navy Yard for some additional preparations.

The impending arrival of important visitors frequently compels the crews of naval vessels to work long and hard to ensure that their ship's appearance is top-notch. A newspaperman who visited the *Arizona* a few days before President Hoover's scheduled arrival reported Captain Freeman's explanation: "Oh, we aren't doing anything except shining up the old brass knocker on the front door for the company." In fact, wrote the skeptical reporter, the crew was painting, cleaning, and shining the *Arizona* from top to bottom, including applying gray paint up on the tripod masts, more paint in an engine room, and still more paint along the black boot topping at the waterline. The work extended to putting a coat of black paint on a gleaming admiral's barge on the boat deck. The barge would transport Hoover between ship and shore during the coming voyage. Afterward, it would go to the cruiser *Augusta*, which was to be the flagship of the Commander Scouting Fleet.[15]

To look after Mr. Hoover's personal needs, his Filipino cook joined the ship from the presidential retreat on the Rapidan River in Virginia; it was that era's counterpart of Camp David. The *Arizona* didn't have a flag officer embarked, so the admiral's quarters were available for the President. Mrs. Hoover did not make the trip. One presidential perquisite inadvertently provided the *Arizona* with a Navy first. Motion pictures with sound were still a novelty in 1931, and naval vessels were not equipped to show them. The warships had projectors for only the old silent films, so a representative from RCA went aboard shortly before the beginning of the trip and installed new projectors.

Eventually, the rest of the Navy's ships were equipped to show the popular "talkies." For the President's cruise the ship got a supply of the latest movies, some of which had not yet been released to the public. Included in the bill of fare were *Charley's Aunt*, starring Claudette Colbert and Charles Ruggles, and *The Grand Parade*, with Helen Twelvetrees and Fred Scott. To fill out the ship's entertainment schedule, twenty members of the Navy band arrived from Washington. The ship hadn't yet reconstituted its own band after the modernization period. Four radiomen also augmented the crew because of the increased communications load expected while the President was embarked.[16]

Shortly after 7:00 on the morning of 19 March President Hoover and his party boarded the ship. He looked worn out, and with little wonder. By that point he had been in office just over two years and had had only one vacation in that time. For the previous year and a half, Hoover had been bombarded with the bad news of the deepening national Depression. His efforts to spark a recovery had not had much effect. Hoover specified that he wanted the ceremonial aspects of the trip held to a minimum and deliberately boarded at an early hour to avoid some of the pomp and circumstance normally associated with a presidential visit.

The group with Hoover consisted of Secretary of War Patrick J. Hurley, Secretary of the Interior Ray Lyman Wilbur, and twenty-eight others, including Secret Service men and a flock of newspaper reporters and photographers. At 8:00 A.M. the *Arizona* boomed out a twenty-one-gun salute to the chief executive, firing the guns at five-second intervals. Those who fire naval saluting batteries silently recite a little ditty to time the period between shots: "If I weren't a gunner, I wouldn't be here; port, fire. If I weren't a gunner, I wouldn't be here; starboard, fire."

To the newsmen, photographers, politicians, and others on board for the trip, being with Hoover was old stuff. But it was completely new to the intensely curious crew of the *Arizona*. As soon as they could, the men went topside to try to get a look. The lookers included engineers such as Watertender Horace Greer, who later recalled a sense of pride at seeing the presidential flag flying from the truck above the mainmast. It was the first time he had ever seen the President's flag.[17]

When the ship got under way for Puerto Rico, she was heralded by an escort of small craft carrying newsreel cameras and well-wishers. The fanfare was reminiscent of the *Arizona*'s first time under way in New York's East River in late 1916. This time Army and Navy airplanes and blimps flew back and forth overhead to add to the celebration.

Not long into the trip, President Hoover demonstrated an unusual degree of relaxation. Normally intense in both speech and manner, he seemed able to put the concerns of office behind him. He dug out a pipe and went for walks out on deck. Particularly surprising was that he was much more talkative than usual. He was willing to laugh, smile, and engage in small talk on a variety of subjects—also a change for someone who was usually an all-business, workaholic type.[18]

Hoover occupied the flag quarters on the starboard side of the second deck, under the quarterdeck. He had plenty of company at virtually all times. He was with newspaper-

Below: Part of President Hoover's routine for his vacation trip on board the *Arizona* included solitary time for reading, smoking, and relaxing in a lawn chair. Behind him is the stern catapult. A marine orderly stands nearby. (UPI/Bettmann Newsphotos, U148836-Acme)

Dignified to the point of stiffness, Hoover invariably wore a hat and jacket during his forays, but he still managed to acquire on the lower part of his face a sunburn that eventually turned to tan. No such opportunities had been available in wintertime Washington. Surprising those who knew him, he didn't play in any deck sports. Back at the White House the President was known for having a small "medicine ball cabinet" that threw around a heavy, leather-covered exercise ball on the back lawn. One reporter speculated that the bashful Hoover did not want to get involved in that type of exercise on board the *Arizona* because such a large audience was on hand.[19]

At lunch and dinner a few of the *Arizona*'s officers normally joined the President's mess. After lunch each day Hoover was inclined to smoke and chat for a while, then move to a lounge adjoining the dining room in the flag quarters. There he worked on what little official business he had to take care of. He stretched out in a big easy chair in the lounge and sometimes napped in the afternoons on a leather-covered couch. At other times he went

Above: President Hoover and Captain Charles S. Freeman, the commanding officer, inspect the *Arizona*'s crew on Saturday, 21 March 1931. The sailors are in dress whites, a rarely worn uniform with blue cuffs and collar flap. (UPI/Bettmann Newsphotos, U148834-Acme)

Right: The fantail, in front of the catapult and O3U airplanes, is the scene of a formal presidential dinner. Hoover is flanked by Captain Freeman, the *Arizona*'s skipper, and Commander Thaddeus A. Thomson, the executive officer, with whom many had difficulty getting along. (UPI/Bettmann, U149173-Acme)

men at nearly every meal, and the resulting press coverage of the trip was plentiful. During the vacation voyage Hoover was able to sleep later than usual. Before breakfast he customarily went out each day for a brisk half-hour walk around the deck, always accompanied by a newsman or someone else to talk with.

out to sit on a deck chair—smoking, reading, and watching the sunlit ocean pass by. In the evenings he joined the others for the movies and stayed to watch every one of them, even though, in the words of one newsman, "several of them were far below the par of what are rated as first-class pictures."[20]

Hoover did some light reading—mostly of mystery novels—during the voyage. One of his ground rules for the trip was that no newspapers were permitted. As bad as the economic accounts had been in the Depression-plagued months before the trip, the time away from the news was a welcome relief. The only exception came near the end of the voyage, when an Army blimp dropped a day-old copy of a Washington newspaper aboard. Others on board the ship showed much more interest in the paper than Hoover did. The ship's crew did put together a small

newspaper each morning, compiled from reports received by radio.[21]

The weather warmed gradually as the *Arizona* steamed farther and farther south. With a sense of relief the members of the crew shifted from their blue uniforms to white

Left: On Sunday, 22 March, the church pennant flies over the American flag. Hoover's presidential flag flies all the way aloft on the maintop. (National Archives, 80-G-461023)

Below: After the inspection on 21 March, the crew posed on the forecastle and superstructure. President Hoover is front row center. (National Archives, 80-G-461025)

Right: A stiff wind is blowing as President Hoover gets a look at an antiaircraft range finder during a tour of the *Arizona*. The vertical portion was used for measuring the slant range to a plane. At left, with his uniform plastered against his body by the wind, is the President's naval aide, Captain Russell Train. (National Archives, 80-G-461032)

Below: President Hoover looks bored as he stands at the forward part of the bridge. The cranks on the windows allow them to be lowered to keep the concussion of gunfire from breaking them during target practice. At right is the engine-order telegraph. (National Archives, 80-G-461040)

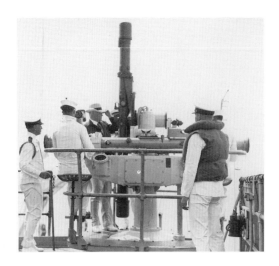

ones. The regular Saturday morning inspection on 21 March was a special occasion because President Hoover, accompanied by Captain Freeman, was the inspecting officer. The crew wore dress white uniforms, which were reserved for special occasions. Unlike the normal jumpers, which were completely white, these were outfitted with blue cuffs and blue back flaps hanging down from the collar.[22]

Once Hoover had made his rounds, the crew gathered on the two forward turrets and up into the superstructure for a photo of themselves and the presidential party. Included were three rousing cheers for the President. They were undoubtedly a welcome sound to a man whose popularity in the nation at large was ebbing rapidly as economic depression sapped the vitality of more and more of the country's citizens.

The failure of one planned event of the journey southward embarrassed the Navy. The destroyer *Taylor*, proceeding ahead, was the *Arizona*'s initial escort. The destroyer *DuPont* was supposed to come out from Guantanamo Bay, Cuba, and join the *Taylor* in steaming by the *Arizona* to render honors as the battleship's crew members manned the rail on 21 March. Alas, the *DuPont*'s navigation was faulty. She wound up some forty miles astern of the *Arizona* and wasn't able to communicate her position because of a malfunctioning radio. Secretary of War Patrick Hurley took delight in teasing the Navy men. He offered to send out an Army Air Corps plane to find the missing ship. After much huffing and puffing, the *DuPont* finally caught up, five hours late. By then, Hoover was dozing in a deck chair and didn't even notice.[23]

The next day Hoover had a brief radiotelephone conversation from the ship with his son, daughter-in-law, and granddaughter in Asheville, North Carolina. They made idle chitchat about the weather, but it marked a step forward in naval communications. Until then the *Arizona* had been able to receive voice radio but not send. Lieutenant Commander Carl Holden, the *Arizona*'s communications officer, had done postgraduate work in the field and was able to devise a small transmitter that made the two-way conversation possible. He was later director of naval communications. Most of the ship's radio communications, of course, were in Morse code.[24]

President Hoover went ashore in Ponce on 23 March. He was the first U.S. President to visit Puerto Rico, just as he would soon be the first to visit the Virgin Islands. The principal reason for his trip in the *Arizona* was to get some relaxation and a respite from the concerns of office. The two Caribbean stops provided some official legitimacy to the voyage. Hoover met with the island's governor, Theodore Roosevelt, Jr., son of the former President. Hoover's message was that he had the same policy as the previous Coolidge administration: he was against proposals that Puerto Rico become either independent or one of the United States. Even so, the Puerto Rican citizens accorded him a sincere, tumultuous welcome during his two-day visit, which included a tour of the island from one end to the other. In an address to the legislature, Hoover thanked the citizens for their courtesies but gently told them that the continued development of the island would depend on their own efforts rather than help from the United States.[25]

The crew of the *Arizona* enjoyed a brief liberty in Ponce. As soon as the liberty launch let the crew off, local citizens jumped aboard, eager to ride out and visit the battleship. Watertender Horace Greer did some sightseeing, had a good meal, and bought enough inexpensive hand-rolled cigars to keep him smoking for a month after the trip. Although few of the sailors spoke Spanish, they had little trouble getting around because the Puerto Ricans were so eager to be hospitable.[26] While in Ponce, the *Arizona* picked up another 250 enlisted men from the battleship *Mississippi*, which was then headed for Norfolk to begin her own radical modernization. That transfer increased the *Arizona*'s reconstituted crew to over 1,200.

After leaving Puerto Rico, the *Arizona* visited St. Thomas in the Virgin Islands. The United States had bought the islands from Denmark for $25 million during World War I to prevent the Germans from establishing a submarine base there. The Navy Department had administered the islands since then. Not

long before Hoover's trip, he had turned the administration of the islands over to the Interior Department and had appointed a civilian governor. In part, Secretary of the Interior Wilbur's need to get a firsthand look at the islands newly placed under his jurisdiction prompted his inclusion in the traveling party.[27] (Another factor was that he was an

Above: The *Arizona* ran into heavy seas on the way north from Puerto Rico and the Virgin Islands while the President was on board. (UPI/Bettmann Newsphotos, U149172-Acme)

Left: Aviators watch from ashore as the *Arizona* arrives at Hampton Roads on 29 March 1931 at the end of President Hoover's Caribbean vacation. (Sargent Memorial Room, Norfolk Public Library)

old friend of the President, their friendship dating back to their days at Stanford University. The presence of familiar company helped Hoover relax.)

While in St. Thomas, Hoover observed a native procession. As one newspaper reporter observed, "Probably one of the oddest parades of all time passed before the President, who saw vendors, school children, and native scratch bands side by side in a colorful picture of insular life."[28] A number of local groups presented requests to Hoover, including one that the prohibition of liquor be repealed as it applied to the Virgin Islands. While Hoover had expressed at least some optimism about Puerto Rico, he couldn't be so sanguine about the Virgin Islands. When talking with reporters during the homeward voyage, he said he had concluded that the islands constituted an economic albatross for the United States.

During the *Arizona*'s homeward trip she staged a mock battle with the accompanying

DuPont for the benefit of Hoover. The President dutifully toured the battleship, and he even climbed to one of the fire-control tops to see the new directors installed during modernization. He went to the bridge and observed other equipment as well, but his expressions in some of the pictures taken during that tour indicate that he was less than enthusiastic. The weather worsened as the ship steamed north along the East Coast, with heavy swells throwing considerable water up onto the decks. The temperatures were cool, and the sunny, fun part of the cruise ended even before the ship got back to Norfolk.[29]

Among the many things the President did during his time on board was to get a couple of haircuts. His barber was Seaman First Class Claude Simpson, who had served in the *Arizona* since 1928. Two marines stood by during each haircut, and Secret Service men were not far away. Simpson was the logical choice because he was the senior barber in the ship. He had been a barber in civilian life before joining the Navy to become an electrician's mate. He never got into electricity because at boot camp the unofficial haircuts he gave his fellow recruits were better than the official ones from the Navy barbers. He thus got pressed into being a barber in the Navy.[30]

In today's setup, barbers are part of the ship's serviceman rating and can go all the way up the advancement ladder. In 1931 those in that specialty were part of the repair division, of all things, and could not advance past seaman first. However, there was an additional incentive that made the job appealing. As the senior barber, Simpson received an additional $125.00 per month taken from the fee paid for each haircut, 15 cents for enlisted men and 25 cents for officers. With this added stipend, he made more than a chief petty officer. The other barbers down the line got monthly bonuses in a descending scale, and the top bonus obviously acted as a powerful incentive for good work. In a normal day each of the *Arizona*'s five barbers did about forty haircuts, which worked out to a rate of about one haircut per week per man. Since the captain held a weekly personnel inspection each Saturday morning, men found their way to the barber shop often. When the ship was in the tropics, many men were inclined to get their hair cut quite short, almost to the point of having their heads shaved. In such circumstances the barber shops were busy from morning to night.[31]

Another who drew extra pay was Fireman Charles Hughlett, who worked as one of the ship's movie projectionists. For his work showing nightly movies he got an additional $10.00 per month. If he didn't want to show the movie some evening, he hired a replacement. He figured that at the rate of thirty 2-hour movies per month, he made about seventeen cents per hour for his extra work. On the other hand, when the regular salary was only $36.00 per month, another $10.00 amounted to a handsome increase.[32]

One of the *Arizona*'s officers was Ensign Richard Hunt, son of a prominent Washington, D.C., socialite. During the cruise he received a radio message from his mother: "In order that you may become more widely known, recommend that you call on Secretary Wilbur." Members of the *Arizona*'s crew

made multiple copies of the message and gave it wide distribution, to the considerable amusement of Ensign Hunt's fellow junior officers. Hunt himself was unfazed by the matter. He was by that time well accustomed to his mother's attempts to steer his career and took the whole thing in stride.[33] Later in his career he did serve for a time as an aide in the White House.

On 29 March the *Arizona* arrived at Hampton Roads and debarked her famous passenger. Those traveling with the President

Left: The Army Air Corps plane also made this close-up of the fantail on 29 March. It shows one of the *Arizona*'s O3U-1s poised on the catapult and another on a dolly near turret three. At this stage, right after her modernization, the ship did not yet have a catapult on turret three. (Naval Historical Center, NH 93552)

Below: The ship's silver service on display on the quarterdeck soon after the *Arizona* was modernized. (Special Collections, University of Arizona Library, 77-3-301)

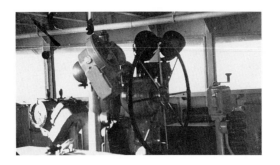

Right: A view of the interior of the *Arizona*'s navigation bridge. The large round wheel is for steam steering. To its right is the small unit for electrical steering, including a lever on top similar to that used by a streetcar motorman. (Courtesy Earl Phares)

concluded that the voyage had been beneficial. Hoover had been able to get away from the usual grind for more than a week. He looked tanned, rested, and refreshed. For the crew members of the newly modernized ship, the trip was also a treat because they had been in the national spotlight and gotten to a warm climate during a cool part of the year. In one sense the cruise had been like the old days in the early 1920s when the ship had routinely gone south for the winter.[34]

In April, once the crew had caught its breath, the *Arizona* was under way again, going north this time to Maine to run trials on the measured mile off the coast at Rockland. As she had more than fourteen years earlier when first commissioned, the ship had turbine trouble. She spent some time in the Boston Navy Yard for repairs before making another trip to Maine.

In May, with the ship back in the Norfolk Navy Yard, Fireman Sam Davis got leave to go home to his native North Carolina. During a visit to his sister in Asheville he met the next-door neighbor's nineteen-year-old daughter. For the first time in his life, Davis was in love. Once he got back to the ship, he was as energetic about romance as he had been about making coffee when the ship was being rebuilt. He wrote to his new sweetheart daily. When the ship was at sea, he still wrote a page per day and then mailed the whole letter when he got to port. His long-distance courtship was successful: in September of that year the girl next-door agreed to accept a ring from Sam Davis and become his wife.[35]

While the shipyard period was coming to an end, another member of the crew had an experience as tragic as Davis's was happy, and it reminded the men of the *Arizona* that service on board naval ships was a hazardous business, even in peacetime. The ship was a giant piece of machinery, with all the attendant hazardous moving parts. During her

twenty-five years in commission the *Arizona*'s officers recorded dozens of deaths and hundreds of injuries in her deck logs. Sometimes the accidents were far from complicated but still deadly. The one that took place in 1931 provides a case in point.

Late on the afternoon of 11 June Seaman Second Class John Howard was part of a crew of men shifting a race boat from one position to another on the boat deck topside. Howard was manning a steadying line attached to the boat to keep it from swinging back and forth while it was being moved. His attention was devoted to the work at hand, with the result that he didn't notice that he was standing on a part of the boat-stowage structure that surrounded an open exhaust trunk for the interior ventilation of the ship. Normally, the trunk had a mushroom-shaped cowl over the top, but the navy yard had removed the cowl as part of its repair work. Waist-high channel bars surrounded the opening, but Howard fell over the top of the bars and four decks straight down through the ventilation trunk. He died about 1:30 the following morning in the naval hospital at the shipyard.[36]

Still the shipyard work continued, and then in July the *Arizona* once more went north to Maine for another try at her postmodernization trials. Even before she could get to the trial waters, however, she had to anchor because of a dense fog. Captain Freeman had his leadsman out, measuring the depth of water. Instinct—undoubtedly combined with years of experience—told him that it would be best to anchor rather than trying to proceed through the fog. The next morning the officers on the bridge heard the sound of cowbells. Sure enough, when the fog cleared they discovered that land was indeed nearby: the bells had marked the sound of cattle on their way to pasture. Freeman had been wise not to try to go farther the night before.[37]

To find out how the *Arizona* would do in battle conditions, those conducting the trials stipulated that she should be at essentially maximum displacement, including fuel, water, stores, and ammunition. When she ran her set of trials on 22 July, she was at 38,113 tons; the displacement was 37,955 tons during trials three days later. She then had a mean draft of about 32 feet. The ship's designed full-load displacement was 32,440 tons when she was new. After modernization the standard, unloaded displacement of the

Arizona at the designer's waterline was 34,207 tons with a mean draft of 28 feet, 10 inches. The comparable figures for the original *Arizona* were 31,400 tons and the same mean draft, 28 feet, 10 inches. The new blisters added enough buoyancy to the ship to offset the added weight and to retain the same unloaded displacement.[38]

After one last tune-up at Norfolk the ship was ready to go. She had been rebuilt, tested, repaired, tested, and repaired yet again. Some in her crew decided to seek transfers and stay on the East Coast. That was wonderful news for Fireman Sam Davis because he got to move into the job and room of a petty officer who was working for the oil king. The job of this monarch was to know at all times how much fuel was on board, what tanks it was in, and the amount in each tank. Since he might be called upon to provide information at any time, Davis literally lived with his records. In a room approximately five feet wide and fourteen feet long were his bed, desk, telephone, and filing cabinets full of fuel and freshwater records. He and the chief master-at-arms were the only two enlisted men in the ship with private rooms.[39]

In August the *Arizona* and the newly modernized *Pennsylvania* steamed together from Norfolk to Panama and thence to California. As the *Arizona* pulled away from the navy yard to begin the long trip, a band on the pier played "California, Here We Come." For young Roy Hubert, a newly arrived seaman from Alabama, it sounded mighty appealing. He had joined the Navy to solve two Depression-related problems for his farm family. By being away, his would be one fewer mouth to feed, and he was also able to send back a portion of his salary, which provided a welcome boost to the family's meager income. What started as a Depression-relief measure turned into a career. Hubert spent twenty-six years on active duty before retiring in 1957.[40]

During their time in company with each other the *Arizona* and *Pennsylvania* engaged in a good many tactical maneuvers to familiar-

Below: The *Arizona* in dry dock number one at the Pearl Harbor Navy Yard in March 1932. The shipyard was then much less developed than it was later in the 1930s when it grew to accommodate the fleet that would fight in World War II. (National Archives, 80-G-409994)

Below: These are two in an often-published series of photos taken of the *Arizona* while she and other battleships were steaming from San Pedro to San Francisco in late April 1932. In the inset the foretop of another battleship can be seen near the *Arizona's* starboard boat crane. (Main photo: National Archives, 80-G-463589. Inset courtesy Ted Stone.)

ize new crews with the ships' handling qualities at sea. Sometimes the maneuvering amounted to a seagoing game of leapfrog. First one ship would be ahead, then the other. Helmsman Edward Berry, who had gotten a good deal of experience steering the USS *Utah* previously, discovered that the *Arizona's* electric steering system left something to be desired.[41]

During one leapfrog game when the bow of the *Arizona* was abreast of the *Pennsylvania's* port quarter, Berry lost steering control. He reported the steering casualty and then tried to match up the rudder-angle indicator

on the steam steering wheel with the position on the electric system. Captain Freeman, no shrinking violet, angrily demanded to know what Berry was doing because the ship continued to swing out of control. Freeman ordered Berry relieved of the watch and put on report. The other people on the bridge quickly found things to appear busy at to avoid the skipper's wrath. As Berry later put it, "the only 2 people who had nothing to do was the Captain and ME!"[42]

Eventually, the steam steering system kicked in and the rudder began responding to the helm. When Captain Freeman calmed down,

he listened to Berry's explanation of why the switch to the steam system took so long, withdrew the order for him to be put on report, and restored Berry to his job as helmsman. Freeman then coached Berry on how to handle the system, which was new to him. Afterward, Berry remarked on the captain's powers as a teacher, saying that he had learned more in five minutes from Freeman about the peculiarities of the electric steering system than he had in hours and hours of instruction before going on watch the first time. Practical experience had focused his concentration far more than a classroom lecture could.[43]

Another time the ship was under way, the officers on the bridge spotted something in the distance before the topside lookout reported it. Since he had the height advantage, the lookout in the foretop should have seen the object first. Freeman called up by phone to find out why the lookout hadn't reported earlier, and he considered the young man's answer unsatisfactory. The captain then summoned the lookout's division officer and sent him climbing up one of the tripod legs to provide on-the-job instruction in how to stand a proper lookout watch.[44]

The men who served under Captain Freeman in the *Arizona* concluded that he was strict but fair. He was also straitlaced, reportedly not allowing his daughters to play cards. Charles Rourk, who was a seaman when Freeman was the skipper, said of him, "He went directly by the book. As long as you did what you were supposed to do . . . the way it said to do it in the book, you were all right." If the book said a white hat was supposed to be worn squarely at all times, that's what he expected—no pushing it to one side or to the back of the head. If people didn't return by the expiration of leave or liberty, they could expect to be punished.[45]

Freeman was fond of conducting inspections. Back when the ship had been in the navy yard in Boston, some members of the crew had to scrape the sides and bottom of the ship. But when it was time for inspection, they had to come out of the dock, put on their best uniforms, and stand by for a look from the skipper.[46] Even more to be feared than Captain Freeman's official inspections were his wife's unofficial ones when the *Arizona* was in port. Rourk joked, "When she went up the starboard side the ship listed to port, and

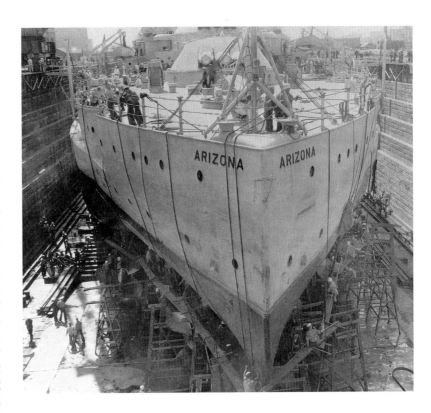

Above: A close-up of the stern in dry dock in the early 1930s. (Courtesy Roy Hubert)

when she came down the port side, the ship listed to starboard." His use of "listing" suggested that all the sailors would rush to the other side to avoid her.[47]

After going through the Panama Canal, the *Arizona* was once again in the Pacific Ocean. Because of the long interruption of service and change of crews, many men were in new jobs. One was Coxswain Carll Gleason, who was appointed coxswain of the captain's gig. The first time he ran the boat for Captain Freeman, the skipper demonstrated anew why his temper (along with his red hair) had earned him the nickname "Red Mike." He got into the gig and ordered Gleason, "Take me ashore." Gleason was new to the port, so he began heading for the landing in San Pedro. About a mile away from the ship, Freeman realized they were going in the wrong direction. He came up out of his cabin and bellowed at Gleason, "No, I want to go to Long Beach." Freeman pointed, and the coxswain went that way. The next day Gleason was relieved of his job as gig coxswain and didn't get it back until a new commanding officer reached the *Arizona* the following year.[48]

In the early 1930s only a small portion of Los Angeles Harbor was protected by a breakwater. Thus the *Arizona* frequently had

Above: A close-up of the bow in dry dock in the early 1930s. There is no longer an opening for the torpedo tube below the waterline because of the removal of the torpedo system during the ship's modernization. (Courtesy Roy Hubert)

to anchor in what amounted to an open roadstead offshore. There she might be subject to long, rolling swells coming in from the Pacific Ocean. The crew members, of course, got used to the phenomenon and learned to compensate for it. When they moved from motor launch to ship, they timed their jumps carefully onto the lower platform of the gangway, and then moved quickly up the steps before another swell rolled the platform down into the water.[49]

Visitors, especially when coming aboard for the first time, learned these techniques the hard way, and most of them got at least their feet wet. For one well-dressed lady the result was far worse. She froze when she got onto the lower platform, unable to summon the presence of mind to climb the ladder. As she stood there the rolling ship and oncoming swell gave her a ducking, billowing her full white dress straight upward. Her broad-brimmed hat with a red ribbon around it stayed precisely in place—about the only dry part of her left.[50]

Now that she was back in California, the ship spent more than half her time anchored, often at San Pedro. As directed, she ventured forth for gunnery practice and tactical maneuvers off the coast of southern California. In

early 1932 the *Arizona* made her first trip to Hawaii since rejoining the fleet. She was involved in a joint Army-Navy exercise that included, prophetically, an air raid on Pearl Harbor by carrier planes. The raid, which came on Sunday morning, 7 February, caught the Army Air Corps defenders completely by surprise.[51]

A few weeks later the *Arizona* herself entered Pearl Harbor for the first time to be dry-docked at the navy yard. On her previous visits to the island of Oahu the ship had anchored in Honolulu Harbor, but by this time the entrance channel to Pearl Harbor had been dredged sufficiently for large ships to enter. Early one morning the ship lay in waiting for a pilot to take her through the channel. The sleepy tranquillity of the area, then hardly built up at all, struck Coxswain Carll Gleason. As he looked out from the ship he saw wisps of smoke rising from houses ashore as some of the residents cooked breakfast on charcoal stoves. Liberty in Hawaii, however, didn't appeal to the big coxswain. A few years later, while Gleason was running the captain's gig, the *Arizona*'s skipper more or less ordered the boat crew to go ashore on Oahu and have a good time. They caught a train ride to a sugar plantation, where they killed enough time to satisfy the captain, and then returned to the ship. Gleason's enjoyment of the occasion was minimal.[52]

In late June, after taking part in Fleet Problem XIII and operations off the West Coast, the *Arizona* got a new commanding officer. Captain Charles S. Kerrick had the same first name and middle initial as Red Mike Freeman but a distinctly different personality. Far less excitable, Kerrick was friendlier and much more easygoing. For the ship's officers and crew, the change was a welcome relief. In appearance, the new skipper looked as if a casting agency had sent him; he fit the part. He was tall, slim, and distinguished looking. As one of the *Arizona*'s ensigns observed of Kerrick, "He *looked* like an officer."[53]

In the summer of 1932 the *Arizona* was at Bremerton for her annual overhaul and repair work. As usual, the shipyard workers were doing the heavy jobs, and the crew members were involved with cleaning, chipping, and painting. Among the less pleasant assignments was that of going down into the double bottoms and the insides of the new antitorpedo blisters. Ensign William Cox, newly reported to the ship from the Naval Academy, joined a group of enlisted men in squeezing through the manholes into the tight spaces inside the blisters. The painting crews had no ventilation except that provided by portable blowers, and after a while the accumulated paint fumes produced what Cox called "cheap drunkenness." As he put it, "Soon the painters wouldn't much care whether they were painting the ship or each other." Singing and loud conversation echoed through the enclosed spaces. When the job was finally done for the day and the men emerged into the welcome fresh air topside, their bodies and clothes were covered with red-lead primer paint. It was an unpleasant but necessary job, and it helped if the painters could find a way to have fun while doing it.[54]

Along with the cheap drunks on board the ship, there were the more expensive ones ashore. Prohibition was still in effect until late 1933, but the junior officers carried on in the fine tradition of their predecessors of the 1920s. Four of them, including Ensign John Davidson, rented a house in an area known as Naples, within commuting distance of the harbor. There they made beer, and they also got brandy, which was manufactured in a government distillery for medicinal use. It wasn't for sale on the open market, but one of the Arizona's junior officers had connections that enabled him to buy it.

The battleship's regular schedule, as it often had been during the 1920s, was to go out for maneuvers and gunnery practice during the weekdays and to anchor overnight in the lee of an island to save fuel. Weekends, the Arizona was back in port, and as Davidson explained afterward, "We always felt that on Friday night and Saturday night you had to drink enough to make up for the fact that you didn't drink Sunday night, Monday night, Tuesday night, Wednesday night, and Thursday night." Actually, he was exaggerating. The officers did have Sunday nights for recreation because the exercise week usually

Below: The Arizona was photographed from a blimp in the spring of 1932 as she took on fuel from the oiler Cuyama at San Pedro. Before World War II, Navy ships typically refueled in port rather than under way. By the time this picture was taken an aircraft catapult had been installed atop turret three. (Security Pacific National Bank Photograph Collection, Los Angeles Public Library, A-000-258)

Right: M. C. "Monty" Matthews models a sweater he earned as a member of the *Arizona*'s race-boat crew in 1933. He is wearing the 13-button trousers of his dress blue uniform and leaning on the barrel of a 5-inch/25 antiaircraft gun. (USS *Arizona* Memorial, National Park Service, PR-70)

Below: Tai Sing Loo, who worked for thirty years as an official photographer at the Pearl Harbor Navy Yard, made this beautiful photograph of Battle Force ships anchored at Lahaina Roads, Maui, in 1933. Left to right: *Saratoga*, *Arizona*, *New York*, and *Lexington*. (Courtesy Evelyn Lee)

didn't start until Monday morning. What's more, there were a good many weeks when the *Arizona* didn't get under way at all.[55]

On at least one occasion Davidson found himself in a considerably different position on the drinking issue. While working as the assistant to the executive officer, he was recorder for a summary court-martial. The president of the court was Commander Charles Best, who had relieved Thaddeus Thomson as exec. Unlike the officers, who had apartments ashore where they could satisfy their thirsts, the accused enlisted man didn't. He had tried to smuggle a bottle aboard and had gotten caught. During the trial Commander Best asked to see the evidence, which was the bottle itself. Davidson passed it to him, whereupon the commander pulled out the cork and took a good-sized swig. He coughed a bit and shook his head. Then he directed Davidson to record his observation: "I declare this bottle to contain a liquid of a very high alcoholic content." He started to pass it back, then said, "But I'd better make sure," and took another good pull from the bottle.[56]

While he was serving on board the *Arizona* Ensign John Kirkpatrick took a wife named Eleanor. In fact, he had gotten one of his fellow ensigns to take a watch for him one night so he could go ashore and propose. The answer that night was maybe, later yes. Marrying Eleanor was a good move for Kirkpatrick, both personally and professionally. One of the ways in which he spent his time while in his new home ashore was doing the assignments for a Naval War College correspondence course in strategy and tactics. As the lessons continued, Eleanor Kirkpatrick decided to help her husband with his assignments. Though he was grateful for her assistance, it caused him some embarrassment when he received his grading officer's feedback. On the first assignment that Eleanor did with her husband, the grader told the ensign that he'd gotten the hang of the thing at long last.[57] Eleanor wound up doing a good deal of the work on the course.

In February 1933 the *Arizona* took part in Fleet Problem XIV, one in the annual series. An interesting aspect of these exercises was that there was essentially a direct relationship between a man's rank and the degree of significance of his involvement in them. Many of the enlisted men did the same kinds of jobs that they would do during normal gunnery practice or other exercises conducted within the *Arizona*'s battleship division. For someone such as a watertender, for instance, looking after a boiler was pretty much the same no matter what the ship was doing tactically or strategically. On the other hand, the higher-ranking officers, especially an embarked admiral, would have a great interest in the outcome of the war games. The performance of the collected ships could have an effect on fleet doctrine; the performance of the *Arizona* herself could affect the fitness reports of her officers and thus their chances for future promotion.[58]

"Fog of war" is a term commonly used to encompass the confusion and limited knowledge that the participants must confront and work with during combat. There were probably also some "fog-of-war games" when a number of the actions had to be simulated and when the "enemy" ships looked exactly like the "friendly" ones because they were all part of the U.S. Navy. Probably the most valuable part of the exercises came afterward when the

officers involved gathered in a large auditorium to look at diagrams of the action and to critique the results. It was during these discussions that the lessons were learned and conclusions drawn.[59]

Those fleet problems of the early 1930s marked a real turning point in naval doctrine. Fleet Problem XII in 1931 was the last gasp of the concepts of the 1920s and earlier. It demonstrated that the battleship was still the backbone of the Navy, the queen of the fleet, or whatever metaphor one might prefer to express the idea of the dreadnought's primacy. The next year, between the surprise carrier attack on Pearl Harbor and Fleet Problem XIII, the aircraft carrier demonstrated that it had substantial potential as an offensive striking force. Before that, the Navy considered it an auxiliary whose primary purposes were spotting and scouting for the big-gun ships. In the fleet problem of 1933 carrier task forces attacked shore targets on the West Coast of the United States. In 1934 the carrier demonstrated its potential in a fleet

Above: Two of the ship's O3Us stored on the fantail between operations, one on the catapult and the other on a dolly. To get the turret three plane back on its catapult, the dolly wheeled it around, and a boat crane lifted it into position. The aircraft carrier *Lexington* can be seen on the horizon. (Courtesy Charles Hughlett)

Below: An O3U observation plane perched atop the catapult on turret three. (Courtesy Charles Hughlett)

Above: A chief petty officer stands by a shattered automobile in this picture of the damage resulting from the Long Beach earthquake of March 1933. (Special Collections, University of Arizona Library, 77-3-370)

problem that allowed offensive carrier task forces to operate independently of the battleships.[60]

Although it would take several more years and the Japanese attack on Pearl Harbor to complete the job, the Navy was in the early 1930s beginning to make its philosophical adjustment from relying on battleships to using aircraft carriers. Part of the reason the change took so long to implement was that the Navy had a huge capital investment in the old way of doing business, and funds were hard to come by. The good news was that some Depression-relief funds in the 1930s were channeled to warship construction and specifically to the building of aircraft carriers. Those built in the 1930s did yeoman work at the outset of World War II. No new U.S. battleships were completed during the 1930s.

On 10 March, after the *Arizona* had completed the fleet problem and returned to her home port, she was rocked by Mother Nature. At 5:54 that afternoon, soon after many in the crew had completed the evening meal, a powerful earthquake hit the Long Beach area and shook the ship for about five seconds. Men on board at the time likened the sensation to what they felt when the *Arizona*'s main battery fired a salvo. Coxswain Carll Gleason, who was below decks during a visit to the War of 1812 frigate *Constitution* then moored in Long Beach, wondered if "Old

Ironsides" had suddenly developed an auxiliary power supply that could produce such a rumble. Despite the shaking, the men on board the *Arizona* were well off because the water acted as a cushion. The ship essentially rolled with the punch and sustained no damage.[61]

The city of Long Beach was not nearly so lucky. Ensign John Davidson and his bride were sitting in their apartment in Long Beach, visiting with a naval aviator friend who had come from Coronado to see them, when the building suddenly began to shake. The couple's new china, a wedding present from the parents of the new Mrs. Davidson, crashed to the kitchen floor and shattered. The startled couple looked out their windows. Across the street another apartment house looked as if it had been sliced open with a knife. The Davidsons and their guest could see into a cross section of the other building; some people were eating, some were in their bathrooms, and so forth. Bricks and other rubble came loose from buildings and tumbled into the street, landing on the tops of parked cars. Mrs. Davidson had the presence of mind to turn off the gas in the apartment so there would be no leaks and resulting explosions.

The Navy quickly responded to provide help. Men from many ships in the harbor performed a variety of useful services. They went on patrol to prevent looting and provide a measure of stability, set up communications ashore, established first-aid stations, fed hungry citizens, built tent towns for those who had become homeless, and helped search damaged buildings for people who were either trapped or dead.[62]

Seaman Charles Rourk was among the crew members detailed for the *Arizona*'s landing party. The men were issued leggings and rifles but no ammunition. Their prevention of looting had to be by deterrence rather than force. Rourk felt the effects of the quake almost as soon as he got off the liberty launch. While he was standing at ease at the fleet landing he noticed that his feet were moving wider and wider apart without any effort on his part. The earthquake-crazed pavement was cracking beneath him, so he quickly scrambled to safety.

Later, as he walked along on patrol, he felt tremors at times and saw the sidewalk rise up. Once he walked past a church, felt a tremor, and then heard a crash behind him. The front of the church had toppled noisily into the street, so Rourk gave buildings a wide berth after that. As time went on, Rourk found that reassurance was also part of his patrolling job. Civilians were fearful of a tidal wave, so Rourk's naval uniform gave him some credibility when he told them there was no threat.

After three days of duty ashore, staying nights in a Long Beach auditorium, Seaman Rourk returned to his floating home in the harbor.[63]

A number of families who lived ashore in the Long Beach/San Pedro area found themselves without adequate accommodations as a result of the earthquake. Many dependents of the *Arizona*'s crew members moved aboard the ship for about a week until they could find new places to live ashore. Among the children who took up residence in the *Arizona* was ten-year-old Edythe Thurber, daughter of Lieutenant Commander Ray Thurber, who was the flag secretary for Rear Admiral Walter Crosley, the embarked Commander, Battleship Division Three. Edythe, her sister, and two brothers lived in the staff quarters; she recalled that they had a separate sitting for meals to avoid interfering with the regular eating schedule for the officers. To make room for the new inhabitants, some of the staff members moved elsewhere in the ship, while others lived in homes still standing ashore.[64]

Ensign Davidson got a considerable surprise when he went into the shower room near the wardroom one day. Lieutenant Horace de Rivera was in the shower already and handed a soap-covered baby out to his shipmate, asking him to hold onto the child while de Rivera washed himself. Years later, Davidson recalled of the incident, "That little

Left: Ships' boats crowd the fleet landing at Long Beach in March 1933 as Navy men come ashore to provide law enforcement and other assistance in the wake of the Long Beach earthquake. (Special Collections, University of Arizona Library, 77-3-389)

monkey was so slippery, I was afraid I was going to drop him right down the drain, but we made out."[65]

Altogether, there were some 150 children on board. Those less fortunate than the Thurber clan slept in cots that were set up in a variety of locations. Their mothers slept in the junior officers' staterooms, and those officers also wound up on cots throughout the ship. The young visitors had their own separate mess on board the *Arizona*. It was a fun time, with no school to attend and a big ship to explore. Ensign John Kirkpatrick observed that after a while he became used to seeing children playing on the quarterdeck while their mothers sat nearby and knitted in the shade of the 14-inch guns. Marines were posted at various places to keep the children out of the superstructure and the bilges. Bridge games kept the wardroom busy all day. The Thurbers' nurse chased and amused Edythe and her siblings because they were pretty well cut off from the rest of the children except at mealtime. The adventure ended for the Thurber clan after about five days when the family was able to move into a cottage at a hotel in Pasadena and subsequently into a house in San Pedro.[66]

In the wake of the earthquake, Fireman Sam Davis got another shock. The deepening Depression had already had something of a roller-coaster effect on his naval career, as it had had on thousands of others. In 1931, a year after joining the ship, he had been advanced to fireman second class, the same

pay grade as a seaman first class in the deck force. He had one payday at the new rate of $54.00 per month, and then his advancement was canceled, along with those of all who had made it when he did. What's more, further advancements were to be frozen for months to come. In the spring of 1932 he finally got back to fireman second. That was a welcome boost because he had recently married the girl next-door who had accepted his mailed proposal. In October 1932, while working for the oil king, he was advanced to fireman first class, the equivalent of a third class petty officer in the deck force. He was optimistic about still another step up and a reenlistment bonus of $200.00. For Davis and his bride, the *Arizona* looked like a home for years to come. Then came the aftershock of 1933. Men were again frozen in grade, and this time there was also a pay cut. The final straw was that there would be no more reenlistment bonuses. Reluctantly, Sam Davis left the Navy, but there would be plenty of others willing to take his place.[67]

One man who was quite happy to stay in the *Arizona* despite having to remain a fireman was Charles Hughlett, the projectionist who worked in the electrical division. At least he had a steady income, and that was more than a good many U.S. citizens could say in the early 1930s. He had a place to stay and three meals a day. Beyond that, he could go ashore and have a good time on liberty those days when he wasn't in the duty section. In his early years on board the *Arizona* he enjoyed going to Los Angeles. He liked to visit the theaters, get something to eat, drink a beer or two, and then head back to the ship.

In early 1933 Hughlett and a shipmate began frequenting a small restaurant in San Pedro. It was that era's version of the fast-food place, although not nearly so plush. The owner was in such straits that Hughlett and his friend each put up $50.00 to help him. Technically, they were part owners, although they didn't really get much for their money except a cup of coffee once in a while. Their real motivation was just to keep the place going because they enjoyed hanging out there. Without the sailors' help, the business might have folded. Even with their help, the restaurant was not exactly prosperous. As Hughlett recalled, "That was some restaurant. If somebody came in and wanted a bacon,

Below: A long-barreled 5-inch/51 broadside gun protrudes from its casemate. Over the top is the canvas curtain used to close off the casemate in normal conditions. To the left, on hinges, is a portion of the metal shutter used to close the casemate in heavy weather. The half-circle cutout goes around the gun barrel. The remaining shutters have to be lifted into position and bolted. The black rubber gasket around the edges of the shutter makes it watertight. Notice the coiled fire hose and the nozzle stored nearby on the bulkhead for firefighting. (Courtesy Earl Phares)

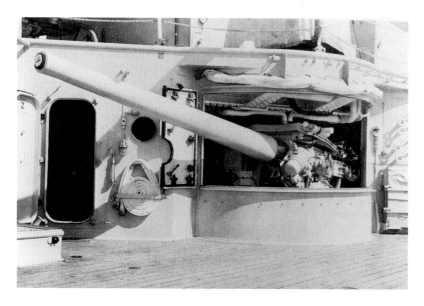

lettuce, and tomato sandwich, you were bound to be short of one of the three. So you had to go out the back door, across the street to the vegetable stand, to get one of them."[68]

Local longshoremen had gone on strike at the time Hughlett was involved in the restaurant, and they were in dire financial need. If they worked for pay anywhere else, they couldn't draw strike benefits from the union. Since he couldn't earn money, one longshoreman used to come in and sweep and swab the restaurant for a sandwich and a cup of coffee. He would eat half the sandwich right away and put the other half in his pocket for a later meal.[69]

The same money-saving measures that sent Sam Davis home affected the Naval Academy as well. Only a portion of the class of 1933 was given officers' commissions upon graduation. Many of the graduates who were in the bottom half of the class standings wound up looking for civilian jobs. One who did get a commission was Ensign Ned Lee. He was delighted by what he found on board the *Arizona* when he reported to the ship, which was at Santa Barbara, California, for that year's Independence Day celebration. Lee remembered it as the most enjoyable time socially during his service on board the *Arizona*. Every day prominent citizens took many of the officers ashore for sumptuous parties and dinners. Lee also enjoyed what the working Navy was about. To a degree, the ship's schedule fell into a repetitive routine after several years, but he still found it so satisfying that he stayed with the ship for five years—considerably longer than the initial tour for most junior officers.[70]

In his time on board the battleship Lee came to have some understanding of how a conglomeration of more than one thousand men could live and work together in a confined space 608 feet long and 106 feet wide. There was a rigidly observed hierarchy of rank and rate, at least somewhat comparable to the feudal system of old. Everyone had a place in the hierarchy, and that place was obvious, indicated by each man's sleeve insignia. Within the hierarchy a vast gulf separated officers and enlisted men—in terms of both status and privilege. The groups could be friendly with each other but not familiar. An officer didn't physically touch an enlisted man, and vice versa. There wasn't a thought

of clapping someone on the back to say hello. Instead, a smartly executed pair of salutes, initiated by the enlisted man and returned by the officer, accompanied the hello.[71]

The officers and enlisted men also had separate territorial rights. As Lee remembered, "If you were proceeding from your room up to the bridge, you didn't go by the crew's quarters just to idly check on what they were doing or see if there was any hanky-panky under way. No more did they peer in your rooms if they were coming back in officers' quarters. You had your place, and you stayed within it. . . . You weren't trying to pry into other things. [If you were curious,] you didn't satisfy your curiosity." Despite these barriers, Lee observed that the men of the *Arizona* got along remarkably well.

As part of its rigidity, the system had a well-defined set of rules. The men who understood and accepted the rules did well. The ship's disciplinary system—both formal and informal—dealt with those who didn't observe the rules. An enlisted man's laziness earned him a kick in the rear end from his petty officer; if he overstayed his time ashore, he went to captain's mast. An officer who was not as professional as he should have been in carrying out his duties was confined to his room for a while.[72]

At the end of 1933 came the ratification of the Twenty-first Amendment to the U.S. Constitution and, with it, the end of Prohibition. Some of the members of the *Arizona*'s crew decided to go into business to take advantage of the new situation. Coxswain Carll Gleason and some other enlisted men got a local woman to rent a house for them in Long Beach. It had several rooms in it, and these were set up as locations for the patrons to do their drinking. Gleason and his group bought a five-gallon tin of 180-proof alcohol and got some lemonade powder and sugar from the ship's galley to flavor the liquid. They obtained a few pitchers, and they were in business. The clientele consisted of their shipmates; Gleason and his partners figured they were on their way to becoming rich. Instead, they found it difficult to charge shipmates, and they wound up giving away most of the pitchers of high-powered lemonade. The whole thing turned into a party rather than a business; each morning found hung-over bodies lying in various places on the floor of the rented house. The whole venture lasted about four days, at which time the too-generous entrepreneurs walked away from their failed enterprise.[73]

After the *Arizona*'s new crew had gotten her off to a new start following her return to the fleet, the inevitable turnover that is part of a ship's life began. The departure of Fireman Sam Davis was one example. Ensign John Davidson concluded that his calling was in the submarine service. Captain Kerrick went on to other duty and was relieved by Captain Macgillivray Milne. Not surprisingly, he signed his official correspondence "M. Milne." Another newcomer to the *Arizona* was far below Captain Milne in the pecking order, but his case illustrates the way in which the Navy provided a lifeline to many a struggling individual during the Depression-ridden 1930s.

Jack Rouse had left home in the 1920s, about the time he reached his teens. Both his father and stepfather had died, so he decided it was time to strike out on his own in San Antonio, Texas. For a while, he worked in a dairy for room and board. During another period he slept in the hayloft of a barn while working as a cleaner and presser. Then he worked in a pants factory. Unfortunately, the reform legislation that was part of the National Recovery Administration of President Franklin D. Roosevelt's New Deal ended his employment. One of the provisions was that participating business establishments could no longer employ underage workers.

In this environment the Navy could afford to be highly selective and take only those men who scored well on its qualification tests. Rouse found that his local congressman's influence also helped. Even with that help, he was on the waiting list for several months before he could enlist in the Navy in December 1933 at Houston and then head to boot camp in San Diego. Once he completed recruit training and a period of leave in Texas, he was transported from San Diego to San Pedro on board a coastal steamer. With him were his hammock, seabag, and orders to the *Arizona*. He and his new shipmates arrived about dusk and were much taken by the sight of the fleet. Lying at anchor in Los Angeles Harbor, the ships had turned on their topside lights for the night ahead. The effect was remarkable. When he got aboard, he took his seabag down to his new living compartment, and there he saw gleaming white enameled bulkheads, red linoleum on the deck, and polished brass fixtures. Far, far from his native Texas, Seaman Second Class Jack Rouse had finally found a home.[74]

5 *HERE COMES THE NAVY*

Spring 1934

In the spring of 1934 the Warner Brothers studio used the *Arizona* as one of the locations for the filming of a movie initially to be titled *Hey, Sailor* but renamed *Here Comes the Navy* before it was released. Now more than fifty years old, it is a valuable historic document about the Navy of the era, primarily because of the Navy Department's unusual degree of cooperation and the Warner cameramen's first-rate photography. Any number of that era's Navy-related commercial movies were filmed largely in studios and included only a modicum of genuine shipboard scenes.

With *Here Comes the Navy* we have a visual record of the men of a warship going about a variety of day-to-day duties, and we get to see shots of different parts of the ship and her equipment. A portion of the movie was also filmed at the giant airship hangar in Sunnyvale, California, home of the USS *Macon*; at that point the giant dirigible was less than a year from her destruction. Warner also did location shooting at the naval training station in San Diego and at the Puget Sound Navy Yard. Stock film footage—probably from newsreel files—was used in some of the sequences involving fleet maneuvers.

Perhaps the records exist somewhere to indicate why the *Arizona*, of all the fleet's battleships, was used. Lacking those, an educated guess is that her operating schedule for the year 1934 best fit in with the scenario for the movie. The bulk of the Battle Force went to New York in the spring of that year for a fleet review by President Roosevelt and an opportunity for East Coast citizens to see the results of their tax dollars. The *Arizona*'s schedule called for her to be in her home port during the early spring and then to travel to Bremerton for a substantial overhaul and modernization.

The Warner Brothers archives for the movie are at the University of Southern California and contain many nuggets of interest for movie fans—daily shooting schedules; the shooting script; dozens of still photos taken while the filming was in progress; contractual arrangements for the female lead, Gloria Stuart, to be rented from Universal Studios for the filming; newspaper advertisements and reviews; and correspondence from lawyers. After the film was released, a number of attorneys came forth to argue that the story was based on previously written scenarios by their clients, rather than Ben Markson, who was credited with the story. None of the claims was substantiated.

Although *Here Comes the Navy* is far from a classic motion picture, it was considered amusing entertainment in the context of 1934 movie-going. The review in the 21 July issue of *The New York Times*, for example, led off, "Some of the heartiest laughs of the current cinema season were recorded last night in the Strand Theatre, where 'Here Comes the Navy' had its metropolitan premiere. A fast-moving comedy enriched by an authentic naval setting, this Warner production has the added advantage, in these parlous times, of being beyond censorial reproach."[1]

Certainly there was nothing to offend the censors. Reproach, if any, would come on other grounds. The movie is truly corny by today's standards. More to the point, the scenario is highly implausible. A number of things just didn't happen in the Navy the way they did in the movie, but such distortions come under the heading of artistic license. Certainly the men of the *Arizona* didn't complain because of the way their ship was used as a vehicle for telling a boy-gets-girl story.

James Cagney, undoubtedly the best known of all those who appeared in the film, por-

Above: In the movie, Frank McHugh portrays a character named Droopy, and here Droopy lives up to the name, sleeping in a drooping hammock because he can't boost himself up into one at normal height. The stencil on the beam indicates this compartment is at frame 41, about the vicinity of turret one. Notice the air inlets from the topside ventilators. Visible just above James Cagney are the ends of two wooden mess tables, suspended from the overhead by metal brackets. (Wisconsin Center for Film and Theater Research)

Right: Pat O'Brien descends a ladder into a shipboard berthing compartment. (Warner Brothers Archives, University of Southern California)

Far right: In the film, O'Connor interrupts the work of polishing a 14-inch–gun tompion to read Droopy Mullins a telegram telling of his girlfriend's request that he come ashore on liberty. (The Museum of Modern Art/Film Stills Archive)

trayed the hero, Chesty O'Connor. Cagney had made his reputation as a screen tough guy by appearing in a series of gangster movies, and he played to that type. He moves from beginning to end of the film with a chip on his shoulder, a major premise of the story line.

To summarize the plot briefly: O'Connor is a civilian riveter at the navy yard in Bremerton. He starts a feud with one of the *Arizona*'s chief boatswain's mates, Biff Martin, played by Pat O'Brien, and then enlists in the Navy to get revenge for being punched out by Martin. O'Connor is assigned to the *Arizona* and gets into several scrapes that label him a "wrong guy" among his shipmates. He is also involved in two heroic actions that essentially redeem him in the eyes of the Navy, extinguishing a turret fire and saving Chief Martin's life in an incident involving the airship *Macon*. Improbably, O'Connor meets and marries Martin's sister, Dorothy, played

by Gloria Stuart. The movie ends with their wedding.

The scenes of boot camp at San Diego provide a brief glimpse of what recruit training was like in the era. Clad in white uniforms, complete with leggings and guard belts, the recruits do calisthenics and then pass in review with bayonetted rifles on their shoulders—an impressive display of precision marching. O'Connor fails to see any applicability of Navy training to shipboard life. Since discipline is not any part of his makeup, the lesson is obviously lost on him. While at boot camp O'Connor makes a pal of Droopy Mullins, a sad-sack sailor portrayed by Frank McHugh, a character actor for many years. Mullins's funny laugh and funny voice give him a distinctive personality throughout the film.

The brand of humor in *Here Comes the Navy* played to a civilian's ignorance of Navy ways. For example, when a chief petty officer at boot camp asks, "Any man here handle a car?" O'Connor, not yet familiar with the Navy's maxim "never volunteer," steps forward, thinking he will get some cushy assignment. The laugh is on him when he winds up driving a pushcart carrying trash cans during a street-sweeping operation. The vignette is revealing, though, because it demonstrates that in the early years of the century, when public transportation was commonplace, the ability to drive an automobile was not a universally held skill on the part of young men.

One of the picture's great men-at-work scenes on board the *Arizona* occurs one morning when O'Connor and Mullins are topside in bare feet, taking part in the washing of the teakwood on the quarterdeck. Fire

hoses supply the water, and the two seamen shove it along with long-handled rubber squeegees. Finally the two sailors realize the applicability of their boot-camp training with push brooms. During the dialogue O'Connor expresses skepticism at one point by saying to Mullins, "Ah, you're full of canal water." Presumably, that phrase adds a nautical flavor to the scene, although it's likely a real sailor would suggest his shipmate is full of something else.

O'Connor makes his first pitch to his female target, blonde, long-legged, good-looking Dorothy Martin, at the telegraph office where she works ashore. Why he, of all the sailors in Long Beach, should appeal to her is not readily apparent, but that appeal is another necessary part of the story line. The street scenes provide a slice of mid-1930s life, with, for example, the boxy-looking automobiles of the era and Dorothy's wearing a hat, as respectable women of the time did. Though intrigued, she demurely declines to invite him up to her apartment that night but gives him her telephone number. He does visit the apartment during a subsequent liberty, and things nearly come apart when he tries to kiss her (horror of horrors) while the potatoes are cooking. It is all quite innocent, and it is no wonder the film had such an easy time satisfying the censors.

When it was made, *Here Comes the Navy* was of interest primarily as entertainment. It is now a rare window into the way the fleet

their appearance wasn't sharp. Enlisted men certainly did not go ashore in civilian clothes as many do now.

In one sequence, Chesty goes ashore without permission during the day to have a date with Dorothy. He is then faced with the problem of how to get back aboard the *Arizona* that night. He catches a ride from the pilot of a commercial water taxi, then jumps off when he gets near the ship, pretending he has fallen overboard from standing his watch on the forecastle. That part of the film lets today's viewers see how the Franklin life buoy worked then. When at sea, sailors stood dull life-buoy watches as a precaution against a man's being swept overboard.

In the movie, the scene occurs in Los Angeles Harbor, and someone on quarter-deck watch pulls the lanyard that trips the equipment, sending the life buoy into the water. The Franklin life buoy was a cylinder bent into the shape of the letter U, and it had flares that ignited when it was used. Thus the preserver held up a man who went overboard, and the light helped the lifeboat crew find him quickly. The ship's 36-inch searchlights, mounted alongside the smokestack, also helped locate him. Most of the ship's boats were stowed in stacks on the boat deck, hoisted in and out of the water by the boat cranes. However, because of the need to get them into the water immediately, the lifeboats

Above: Droopy Mullins, Chesty O'Connor, and Biff Martin handle powder bags in a mock-up of the interior of a 14-inch–gun turret. At left a rammer pushes the base of a projectile into the breech of a gun. These fake powder bags were somewhat less rigid than the real things. (Warner Brothers Archives, University of Southern California)

Right: In this dramatic photo the *Arizona* is launching two lifeboats after Chesty O'Connor has jumped overboard from a water taxi. The boat in the foreground is being lowered from davits; the other, just below the beam of the searchlight, is being lowered by the port boat crane. Pat O'Brien and Frank McHugh are at right center. (Warner Brothers Archives, University of Southern California)

operated in the mid-1930s. The movie illustrates a number of differences in Navy practices between then and now. For example, since nearly all ships today moor at docks or piers, men in liberty status essentially come and go whenever it's convenient. When ships anchored offshore in the 1930s, liberty boats governed the coming and going. That gave officers of the deck the opportunity to scrutinize men carefully as they lined up in ranks and to deny permission to go ashore if

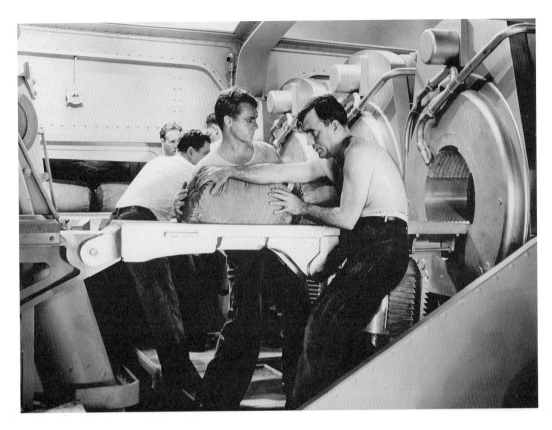

were in davits at the edge of the quarterdeck. The movie shows the lifeboat powered by oarsmen, just as the ship's race boats were.

Soon after that incident, O'Connor is court-martialed and convicted for being absent without leave and for failing to stand his night watch. A subsequent scene demonstrates another phenomenon of the prewar Navy, the publication of court-martial results. As the crew stands at quarters, the offender's sentence is read aloud, presumably as an example for others so they will avoid such behavior. O'Connor is restricted to the limits of the ship for two months and docked $24.00 of his monthly pay for three months. Since a seaman second made only $36.00 per month to begin with, minus the pay reduction resulting from the Depression, the loss of $24.00 would be a pretty stiff jolt.

Following the court-martial, the *Arizona* gets under way with the fleet for battle maneuvers. The scenes show an excellent cross section of the Navy's combat capabilities at that time: biplanes fly from the aircraft carrier *Lexington* and practice dive-bombing; submarines operate in column; destroyers fire torpedoes; and the battleships launch their spotting planes and fire their big guns. Evidently Warner didn't get as much photog-

raphy of the latter as it needed: some of the footage apparently came from 1920s film archives because battleships with cage masts were doing the shooting. Other footage was apparently taken topside on board the *Arizona*; there is a vivid demonstration of the

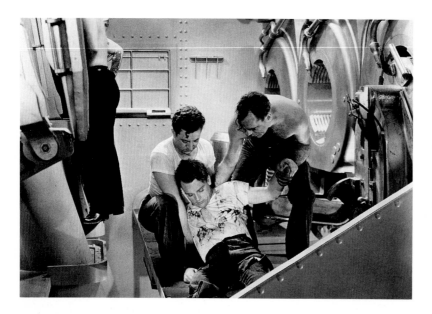

Above: Droopy Mullins and Biff Martin assist O'Connor after the last has extinguished burning powder grains by rolling on them. The breech block of the right gun is in the closed position. The loading tray is folded up and out of the way. The platform holding the three men moves down and up as the guns are elevated for firing and then brought back to the loading position. The loading party has to move out of the way as the men at left have done. (Warner Brothers Archives, University of Southern California)

Opposite page: The *Arizona's* crew musters at quarters for the ceremony at which O'Connor is presented a Navy Cross. The ship's name is painted on the large drum at right center. The officers in the background are saluting during the playing of the admiral's march for the flag officer who has just passed through the rows of side boys at the top of the gangway. (Warner Brothers Archives, University of Southern California)

process of using gas-ejection air to expel waste gases out of the barrels of the guns after shooting.

Several scenes depict the firing of battle practice from inside one of the 14-inch turrets. Part of it was filmed in one of the *Arizona's* turrets, but the remainder was filmed in a studio-built mock-up. Two main reasons prevented Warner Brothers from shooting the gun-chamber sequence on board the *Arizona* herself. For one thing, the area was too small to make room for lights, cameras, microphones, and the other paraphernalia connected with movie-making. In addition, safety concerns prohibited the handling of powder bags the way they are handled in the movie, particularly when in one scene O'Connor rolls on the deck and extinguishes a burning silk ember left over from a previous round. Thus it fell to the movie people to come up with a reasonable facsimile of a turret's interior, and they did an excellent job. In comparison with some of the other mock-ups of military equipment one sees in 1930s-era movies, this was one of the most realistic.

The real value of the mock-up is that it gives today's audiences a fairly close approximation of how the crew of a 14-inch gun went about its business. The film shows the mushroom-shaped breech plug swinging down on its hinge and a loading tray opening up from its jackknife position to swing into place. Then the men ram the projectile and powder bags into place in the breech of the gun. The bags used in the movie are not entirely realistic,

appearing somewhat more flexible and loosely stitched than real ones, but the viewer still gets the idea.

The breech plug is shown with interrupted screw threads that mate up with similar threads in the breech end of the barrel. Once the plug is closed, it is rotated part of a turn so the threads can engage to form a gas-tight and pressure-tight seal that can withstand the force of firing. Probably the most remarkable sequence in the movie occurs when the *Arizona* fires a 14-inch round. The camera appears to rotate—following the grooves of the rifling on the inside of the barrel—as it moves out toward the muzzle end of the gun. The shot gives the viewer the illusion of riding the nose of the projectile out through the barrel. That shot is one of the many that makes *Here Comes the Navy* a delight for those interested in the old battleships.

Ted Turner's organization now owns the rights to the film; to date it has not been colorized or released on videocassette.

One of the perks Coxswain Carll Gleason enjoyed while running the captain's gig during the filming in 1934 was the opportunity to transport the stars of the movie between shore and ship. He usually took them to the *Arizona* in the morning because he and the crew stayed in Long Beach overnight. The coxswain learned that the movie people were not above pulling his leg. The first time the cast members embarked in the boat, Pat O'Brien came aboard smoking a cigar. Because of the potential fire hazard, Gleason asked the actor to put it out. O'Brien was about to throw the cigar over the side into the water, but Gleason told him that wasn't necessary. He could just let it go out by itself and then smoke the rest later. The gig reached the starboard gangway, and the cast members climbed up to begin their location shooting. Once they were off the gig, the seaman tending the stern hook summoned the coxswain back to the covered cabin where the movie people had been riding. There, on each of four seat cushions, was a neat little pile of cigar ashes. The piles weren't big enough to soil the cushions, but they were a small calling card from a man who came from a different culture than did the Navy men.[2]

During their repeated visits to the ship, the actors and production people got to know a number of the officers and crew members.

Above: Photographed on deck during the filming of *Here Comes the Navy* are, left to right, director Lloyd Bacon; Pat O'Brien; Gloria Stuart; Captain Macgillivray Milne, the *Arizona*'s commanding officer; James Cagney; and Frank McHugh. (Courtesy Roy Hubert)

Right: A movie admiral presents the Navy Cross to Chesty O'Connor for his heroism in putting out the burning powder in the turret. Many of the officers in this photo are part of the ship's company. Just beyond the wooden podium is Commander Andrew Denney, the ship's actual executive officer at the time. (The Museum of Modern Art/Film Stills Archive)

The reactions of the sailors were varied, from blasé to star-struck. One yeoman in particular was in the latter category, truly enamored of the film people who were daily coming aboard his ship. His interest made an impression on Gloria Stuart, so she decided to have

some fun. One day the yeoman was part of the in-port watch team on the quarterdeck, a sacrosanct area as far as the ship's crew was concerned but no big deal for the movie folks. Stuart grabbed a photographer from the film crew and asked him to take some still pictures as she began playfully teasing the yeoman, embracing and kissing him while he tried to maintain his on-watch composure.[3]

One officer put off by the casual nature of the movie people was Ensign Ned Lee. To him, Navy uniforms were symbols of a profession in which he took great pride. It was thus understandable that he would be nettled when he saw the actors wearing uniforms in nonregulation fashion or, still in uniform, lying on the deck or lounging against the lifelines. To a Naval Academy graduate such as Lee, these things just weren't done; to the actors, the *Arizona* was just another movie set, and they felt like relaxing when not in front of the cameras. No wonder they were doing what Lee considered "atrociously unmilitary things."[4]

Though the ways of the movie folks bothered Ensign Lee, he was in a minority. Most crew members were simply delighted, especially by the presence of Gloria Stuart. The following observation appeared in the

ALL THE THRILLS AND GLORY OF THE U.S. FLEET...in ACTION!

JAMES CAGNEY   PAT O'BRIEN

HERE COMES THE NAVY

with GLORIA STUART FRANK McHUGH   Directed by LLOYD BACON   A WARNER BROS. FIRST NATIONAL PICTURE

Arizona's newspaper shortly after the filming started: "Everything went lovely until the girls in the cast came aboard Thursday and it went lovingly then. And did our sailors have a treat. From that time on the ship's routine was practically ruined."[5]

An even bigger treat came when Warner Brothers put on an evening smoker for the crew of the ship that was doing so much to cooperate. They gathered on the fantail for a program that obviously had a great deal of professional polish. Cagney demonstrated his versatility with a dance number, while O'Brien and McHugh evoked laughs with a comedy sketch. Several other entertainers, including radio people, sang, danced, and did comedy. Included were a pair of men who painted their faces black in the Negro-minstrel style of comedy that was in vogue then. To top off the evening the studio showed a new film starring O'Brien and Ginger Rogers.[6]

As if all that weren't enough, the studio donated a $1,300 sound system to the ship. Radio reception down inside a large steel ship can be a problem. The new system provided outlets to which individual crew members could hook up to a master antenna. Naturally,

the command invoked a number of regulations to ensure that no one would abuse the new privilege. At the top of the list was the stipulation that the new system was not to be used during working hours.[7]

Fireman Charles Hughlett got more involved than most of the *Arizona*'s men in the filming because he was in the electrical gang. He helped hook up power cables for the large lights that the film crew used, and he helped position large metal reflectors that enhanced the amount of light on the action. Film then wasn't as sensitive as today's, so natural light often wasn't sufficient. After each day's shooting the film was processed and brought back to the ship. Hughlett, one of the projectionists for the evening movies shown regularly on the quarterdeck, ran the projector for these "rushes," as they were called. The director looked at the previous day's scenes to decide whether he was satisfied with what he saw. If not, he reshot those that didn't measure up to expectations before moving on to something else.[8]

A number of the *Arizona*'s crew members had minor parts in the film. For instance, a boatswain's mate was photographed passing the word over the general announcing system. He didn't need any acting training; he just did the same thing he did as part of his shipboard duties. Another crew member was washing a gun barrel. And there were numerous other instances. In addition to the stars, actors in the uniforms of officers and enlisted men played other roles. Members of the film's production crew ate their meals in the ship's chief petty officers' mess during the course of the filming. One of the actors portraying an enlisted man gave his uniforms to a sailor who worked in the chiefs' mess. It was a nice gesture.

Another crew member had a role in facilitating the production, although he didn't appear on camera. He was a chief master-at-arms who shooed the real sailors away from the filming and maintained general watch over the operation. Director Lloyd Bacon was so taken by the work of the chief, who was about to retire from the Navy, that he offered him a security job in Hollywood after he left the Navy. Ship's Cook Ralph Byard saw a later non-Navy film in which the chief had a brief speaking role.

The presence of the film crew affected Byard's own work in the *Arizona*'s galley. When filming was in progress on the quarterdeck, which was near the galley, the cooks were instructed to be quiet so the sound cameras wouldn't pick up their talk. Byard was also ordered to stop chipping paint in the galley once because the sound of his chipping hammer was too noisy for the Warner technicians. It was probably one of the few occasions in the *Arizona*'s history when a crew member was ordered *not* to chip paint. Byard found time to get away from the galley often enough to observe the filming of some of the scenes. He was struck by actor Frank McHugh's peculiar laugh, and years later he observed, "Gloria Stuart, I thought, was the prettiest thing that ever came down the street."[9]

For Coxswain Roy Hubert, the filming of *Here Comes the Navy* provided a glimpse of a culture that was far removed from his experiences as a farm boy in Alabama. He got a behind-the-scenes look at how a movie was made. Things that were routine Hollywood production techniques were fascinating to an outsider. He saw that there was a lot of work involved in filming a scene that might last only a few seconds when it became part of the finished show. The lights and camera had to be set up and makeup adjusted. While the preliminary work was under way, the director employed stand-ins; these were people of about the same size and general appearance as the actors. Meanwhile, the actors themselves relaxed and waited for their turn. Once the director was satisfied with the setup, then Cagney, O'Brien, McHugh, Stuart, and others stepped in and said their lines. At least once, Cagney didn't even play his part at all. Hubert remembered that a stunt man actually played the scene in which Cagney appears to jump overboard from a water taxi and asks to be rescued. The next scene shows Cagney in the water, undoubtedly a tank in a Hollywood studio, not Los Angeles Harbor.[10]

When the ship got to Bremerton for her overhaul in the spring of 1934, some members of the crew thought they might get to travel to Warner's studio in southern California to appear in a turret scene in the movie mock-up. Instead, the movie people evidently decided that they could use the real turret for part of the filming. In the finished movie is a side view of the gun room with the breech ends of the guns included. That is the mock-up. In the portion filmed at Bremerton, the camera was in the turret officer's booth, looking through round viewing ports at the guns as they are elevated.[11]

It didn't take long for Warner to put the finishing touches on the movie once the filming was complete. Location shooting on board the ship hadn't started until late March, and in a little more than four months the movie was finished. Of all the films shown on the *Arizona*'s fantail during the ship's history, probably none had a more eager and appreciative audience than *Here Comes the Navy* at its first screening on board the ship on 30 July. The men whooped and hollered as they recognized themselves and shipmates. But they reserved their loudest cheers of all for blonde Gloria Stuart.[12]

opportunity to swim in a pool at the Puget Sound Navy Yard until a senior officer suddenly put the pool off-limits for enlisted men after his daughter claimed she caught a bad case of gonorrhea from swimming there. Richardson and his shipmates, who were convinced that the young woman contracted the disease through intercourse, were amused.[4]

While in the X division for indoctrination, the new men berthed together. In the evening, while they were in their living compartment, the ship's chaplain said a prayer. They stood with heads bowed until the prayer was over, then put up their hammocks for the night. When he had finished his training in the X division, Seaman Bryan went to the fourth division for duty. The first night he was there, when he heard the chaplain begin his prayer, Bryan took off his hat as he had been trained. The reaction from his new leading petty officer was anything but solemn and religious. He got a firm kick in the rear because the practice in the fourth division was to line up in rows in addition to taking off hats. The kick came from Coxswain John Hostinsky, a man who was both feared and respected in the *Arizona*. Years afterward, Hostinsky has almost the status of a legend among the hundreds of men who served in the ship during the 1930s.[5]

For most of the enlisted men in the *Arizona*, bed was a hammock. The same compartments, which were in some cases the main-deck casemates for the 5-inch broadside guns, served for both eating and sleeping. Throughout the compartment were vertical stanchions extending from deck to overhead. These stanchions had hooks on them for "slinging" hammocks, as it was called. During the daytime the hammocks were rolled up and stowed away in "hammock nettings." The term probably came down from a long-ago period in the Navy when hammocks really were stored in netting. By the 1930s, though, the term was applied to bins along the sides of the compartment.

In the evening the process was reversed, and the hammocks were attached to hooks that suspended them about six feet above the deck. That allowed men to move about the compartment without disturbing those who were sleeping. The hammocks were sufficiently high that sailors had to grab an I-beam in the overhead and swing up into the hammock rather than climbing in. Combined

with a two-inch-thick mattress, the hammock provided a comfortable night's sleep. The more senior enlisted men slept in cots, which had the advantage of being easier to put up and take down, as well as being much easier to get into. In that sense, they were something of a status symbol. The principal disadvantage came in rough weather. The cots followed the motion of the ship, while the hammocks stayed essentially stationary as the ship rolled back and forth.[6]

For sailors newly reported aboard and berthing with the X division, the arrangement was fairly similar to that experienced by men assigned to the *Arizona* in the 1920s. Their seabags served as closets, and in the thirties the men had smaller ditty bags (as opposed to the wooden ditty boxes of a decade earlier) that held toilet articles and other personal items. The situation improved once an enlisted man was assigned to a regular division. There he rated a metal locker that was essentially a cube with three-foot sides. The shelves were more convenient than seabags for storing uniforms, and the fact that they could be locked provided considerably greater security. Even so, theft was still a problem for enlisted men, as it had been for years.[7]

A chore that nearly all junior enlisted men performed was serving as mess cooks. In this case, the word "mess" referred to a group of individuals who habitually ate together. Each separate mess was in a division's living compartment, and a mess cook was responsi-

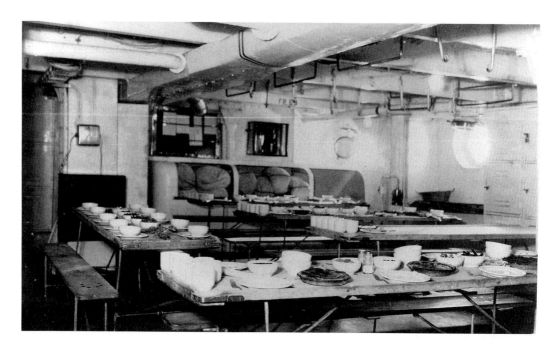

ble for serving two 10-man tables. The wooden tables and benches, equipped with fold-up metal legs, were stored in racks suspended from the overhead of the compartment when not in use. The mess cook got them down for each meal and cleaned them. He went to the bakery for bread, rolls, and pies that were baked on board, to the scullery for dishes and silverware, and to the galley for the rest of the food. Coffee was served in white porcelain mugs without handles, and the mess cook poured it from a pot nearly as large as a water bucket.[8] Along with the nourishment it provided, the meal could be a learning experience in the area of table manners. As Coxswain David McCafferty observed, reaching for extra food before it was time for second helpings could result in a fork in the back of the offender's hand. The lesson was learned quickly.[9]

Along with table manners, sailors also acquired a new vocabulary. As Seaman John Pfeifer learned at mealtime, his mess mates referred to steaks as "snakes," creamed chipped beef on toast as "foreskins on toast," cold cuts as "horse cock" because of the long tube of meat from which they were cut, catsup as "red lead," creamed fried hamburger on toast as "shit on a shingle," and tapioca pudding as "fish eyes." He enjoyed the food, no matter what it was called.[10]

After each meal the mess cook gave the mess gear an initial washing, then took the plates, cups, bowls, and silverware to the scullery to be sterilized in scalding hot water. He folded up the tables and benches and returned them to their storage racks. After having done this three times during the day, the mess cook who had some energy left was free to go ashore on the 6:00 P.M. liberty boat when the *Arizona* was in port.[11]

Each mess cook got an extra $5.00 per month from the Navy, presumably to cover the expense of keeping his white uniforms clean and sanitary. In addition, the mess cook got another bonus on payday. The senior member of the mess passed around a soup bowl for tips that could amount to nearly as much as the mess cook's regular Navy salary.[12] If he was good at his job, he might get fifty cents from each man, an extra $10.00 per payday. The key to getting tips was to hustle to get seconds from the galley, especially seconds of milk, which was strictly rationed.

Married men liked the duty because it meant extra income and the chance to be home every night with their wives. They had to be back aboard in time to serve breakfast, but that was still preferable to staying on board the ship all night. Some of the married men avoided getting advanced to petty officer because that would mean the end of mess-cooking and probably a cut in pay.

Seaman Second Class John Amend found mess-cooking even more lucrative in the chief petty officers' quarters than in a division mess. The space for the *Arizona*'s chiefs had its own range. While part of the meal might come from the galley and cool off during the journey to the table, other parts could be cooked right in the chiefs' quarters. Cooking on the range, young Amend could also cater to individual tastes and increase his tips. In general, the chiefs were better tippers than the lower-rated enlisted men; some kicked in as much as a dollar every payday. One chief signalman did even better than that. He liked to be waited upon, whether it was having fresh coffee poured whenever he wanted, his bunk made for him, or his steaks cooked exactly to order. He was good for a $5.00 tip on each semimonthly payday.

The chief signalman could afford such largess because he was one of the *Arizona*'s loan sharks. The arrangement was simple and not encumbered by the sort of restrictions found in today's truth-in-lending laws. If a sailor was eager for liberty and came up short, he could borrow money in multiples of $5.00. When the next payday came around, he owed $7.00 for every $5.00 he had borrowed. A chief cook in the same mess was also in the money-lending business. Mess cook Amend remembered that this fellow had as much as $500 out on loan at a given time. If so, he stood to collect $700 each payday, a remarkable return on investment. When necessary, the cook turned to boatswain's mates to collect his debts because those individuals exerted great control over the lives of the sailors working under them. If the lender told a boatswain's mate that a certain seaman was behind in his loan repayments, the boatswain's mate could use whatever means were needed to encourage the seaman to honor his obligation. The cook rewarded the boatswain's mate with food during nonmeal hours and perhaps money as well.[13]

Economy was the watchword in the serving of food. The *Arizona*'s commissary stewards were allotted less than fifty cents per day per man to feed the ship's enlisted crew. "They cut all the corners," recalled one crew member. He remembered a time when the commissary steward was behind in his accounts. The steward went into a meat locker, armed with a hypodermic needle. He injected green ink into the joints of a number of

quarters of beef, then told the medical officer that the meat looked as if it had gone bad and thus shouldn't be served to the crew. The doctor certified it for survey, which meant that the meat would no longer be accountable on the galley's books. The commissary steward could then cut out the parts with green ink and serve the rest, which became, in effect, free food.[14]

One of the *Arizona*'s principal butchers during the mid-1930s was Ship's Cook Ralph Byard. When the ship was in her home port of Long Beach/San Pedro, Byard was free to go ashore every night; he wasn't in a duty section. But he paid a stiff price for that freedom. Monday through Saturday he had to get up at 3:30 in the morning and catch the 4:00 A.M. boat to the ship. Once on board, he donned his meat-cutting uniform and went to work, often not knocking off until almost 6:00 in the evening. In that time, he and another man had to cut up the meat for the more than three thousand meals that were served each day on board the ship.[15]

Another crew member who had a hand in food preparation was Seaman Mel Larson. One of the famously dull jobs in military service is peeling potatoes, but Larson enjoyed his duty in the spud locker, partly because it gave him a chance to set up a

Below: Coils of wire for sound-powered telephones are at right and a telephone set is in the center of this shot of the shop used by the *Arizona*'s interior-communications electrician's mates in the 1930s. The limitations of that era's available-light photography have given the sailor in the doorway a ghostly appearance. (Courtesy Charles Hughlett)

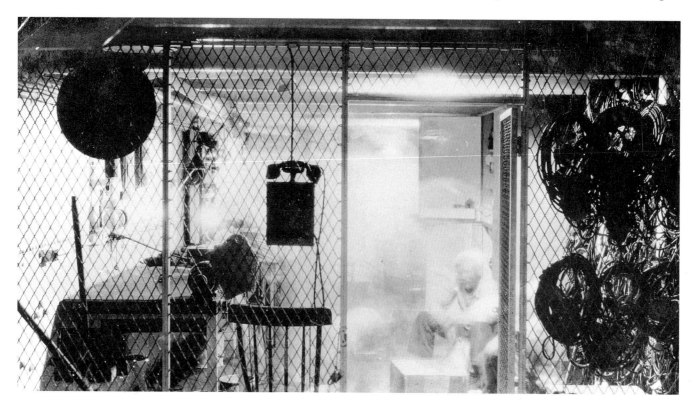

money-making racket. As a potato peeler, he could use all the fresh water he wanted, as opposed to the other crew members whose fresh water was limited, and he could get fresh fruit as well. Larson took advantage of his access to water and started a business of scrubbing sets of blues, fifty cents for a set of undress blues and seventy-five for dress blues. After they were clean, he would put the blues in a bucket with a few apples in the bottom to bribe the men in the press shop to press the uniforms. Being in the spud locker also allowed Larson and others to get extra baked goods from the men in the bakery and steaks from the cooks in the galley. A young man who had come into the Navy underweight after working on a family farm in Iowa, Larson found the spud locker, with its availability of chow, quite an appealing assignment.[16]

The social center for the *Arizona*'s ensigns, and the place where they ate their meals, was the junior officers' mess. They spent much of their nonwork and nonsleep time there. In off-duty hours it was the site of writing, reading, drinking coffee, listening to the radio, and playing two popular Navy pastimes: cribbage and acey-deucey, the latter a board game also known as backgammon. It was more fun being in the JO mess than the wardroom because the former was more boisterous and provided more freedom. One of the *Arizona*'s officers described the atmosphere as similar to that in a college fraternity house. Officers could show up there in casual dress, looking a bit disheveled and perhaps wearing slippers instead of shoes. No one kept a very tight rein on the new officers. As one of them remembered, "You might sneak in and have the mess boy make you up another club sandwich, having only had one an hour before."[17]

There was another aspect to the new-found freedom. After four years at Annapolis, being told when they had to get up and when they had to go to bed, the ensigns could now stay up all night if they wanted to. Ensign Charles Dodds did that several times after he reported to the *Arizona* in 1937. He stayed out hitting the various night spots, then caught the milk boat that came out to the ship first thing in the morning. Once on board, he changed into his uniform, went to morning quarters, and then proceeded with his day's work—to the

extent that he could. After a few times of feeling completely wiped out the day after, Dodds concluded that the freedom to stay out all night was more important than actually using it.[18]

Usually officers from several Naval Academy classes ate in the junior mess, remaining there until they got assigned to a top watch on the bridge, took over a division, or were promoted. These young officers enjoyed a great deal of camaraderie since they spent a great deal of time together, both on board the *Arizona* and when they went ashore. They recognized who was senior among them, but they still had a close relationship with one another.

The junior officers rotated the unpopular chore of supplying their messmates with food. One who was dissatisfied with what he was being served in the mid-1930s was Ensign Jack Arnold. He griped about the food, so he got elected to the job of mess treasurer. He ran on the platform of pleasing one man at every meal. He was elected right away because several others weren't happy with the food either. After about two weeks Ensign Jimmy Vaughan approached Arnold and reminded him of his pledge. Vaughan said he had talked to other members of the mess, and some still didn't like what they were eating. Arnold replied, "Well, I have pleased one guy at every meal."

Vaughan asked, "Who the hell is that?"

Left: Brothers Melvin (left) and Everett Larson pose in front of one of the *Arizona*'s turrets in 1935. At the time, the ship had more than thirty brothers serving in the crew. Both are wearing blue flat hats bearing the ship's name, but the hats are no longer so flat as those of the 1910s and 1920s. On his right shoulder, Melvin has a white stripe (blue on white uniforms) indicating his status as a nonrated man in the deck force. The stripe for nonrated engineers was red. On his left sleeve is a small insignia indicating he is striking for fire controlman. The three white stripes on each cuff indicate that he is a seaman first class; seamen second class had two white stripes, and apprentice seamen had one. As a petty officer, third class gunner's mate, Everett has no shoulder stripe. He has his rating badge on the right sleeve, as did some deck ratings at the time. All are now on the left sleeves. (Courtesy Melvin S. Larson)

Above: Crew members do a stretching exercise on the port side with the ship anchored at San Pedro in early 1934. To the far left is the screen used for evening movies. Just aft of the mushroom-shaped ventilator is the movie-projection booth. (Warner Brothers Archives, University of Southern California)

"Me. I've been happy with every meal we've had."

Eventually, though, Arnold managed to satisfy most of the people in the mess, and they wanted to vote him in again. He concluded that one tour of duty was enough and that others should share the burden.[19] Another who had the duty was Ensign Dodds, who promised he would hold the mess bill to $10.00 per month, about half the normal rate. He thought the kind of austerity demanded by that bill would keep him from being elected, but he was wrong. He kept his promise. He explained, "For a month there, we had beans in every way you can think of." His term was not renewed.[20]

When ensigns reported aboard for duty, they generally were assigned to the junior officers' bunkroom, which was near the wardroom and accommodated perhaps twelve. One of those who joined the ship along with the other members of the Naval Academy's class of 1935 was Fred Borries, Jr. He had starred in football, baseball, and basketball at the academy and attained all-America status in football. Newspapermen of the day delighted in creating alliterative nicknames, so he was widely known as Buzz Borries. To his classmates and messmates, he was "Buster." Something of a lovable imp, Borries enjoyed a good time, sometimes at the expense of someone else, but he was not malicious. One of his favorite weapons when confronted was

a disarming grin. Though he could be blunt at times, his compatriots couldn't get mad at him. As one of them observed, "He was friendly, like a big dog."[21]

A typical example of the Borries touch came one weekend when the *Arizona* was in her home port of San Pedro. He and three other ensigns decided to go out on liberty Saturday night. The night grew long, and one member of the group had reached or surpassed his alcoholic capacity. It happened that he was the owner of the car in which the group was riding. Borries observed that this young officer was in no condition to drive anymore, so Borries drove to the fleet landing, turned the sleeping ensign over to the shore patrol, and asked, "Would you please return this body to the *Arizona?*" With that, Borries and the rest of the group took off. They didn't return until Sunday night, at which time the car's owner demanded, "Buster, where's my car?"

"Well," said Borries, "obviously you couldn't use it. So after we gave you to the shore patrol, we took it up to L.A. for the rest of the night."[22]

Another time, Borries and one of the other ensigns returned to the *Arizona* after taps. Fueled by liquid encouragement, they were in such high spirits that they turned on the lights in the JO bunkroom and drew out their swords. Swords have long been a ceremonial part of the naval officer's uniform, but on this night Borries and friend decided to put theirs to use. They woke up Ensign Dave Mc-Clintock and began prodding him gently with the tips of the swords—all good fun for them, of course. As they got a bit more playful, McClintock concluded it wasn't as much fun for him as for the other two. Clad only in his skivvies, he managed to escape from the bunkroom. As he told the story, "I ran aft in the main corridor. I figured if I ran back towards the skipper's cabin, they would not follow. Well, they did follow. They chased me right by the captain's cabin, right by the Marine orderly—I don't know what he thought—and then back down the other side. I think they were laughing so hard that they let me go back to the sack."[23]

After a year or so on board, McClintock was able to move into a stateroom with one other officer. It was typical for the era: one bunk over the other, a locker for uniforms and civilian clothes, and a small desk. The washroom was down the passageway. Although it afforded more privacy than the bunkroom, the stateroom had hazards of its own. Since it was right over one of the boilers, the stateroom was uncomforatably hot when the ship operated in warm climates. On one trip to Panama, the tropical heat coaxed a phalanx of bedbugs out of hiding. McClintock and his roommate took the mattresses out of the room and worked over the place with a blowtorch for half an hour in an attempt to burn out the bedbugs. They were only partially successful.[24]

The junior officers in the ship led a pleasant, not-too-demanding way of life. The Navy's philosophy was to send the ensigns to big ships where they would be surrounded by a great deal of talent and experience. Then they could make the usual youthful mistakes without causing problems of consequence because the old hands would be around to teach them and back them up. They learned first by observation and then by doing things for themselves. Indeed, the first two years after graduation from the academy were considered a probationary period. The ensigns weren't allowed to marry during that time, supposedly so they could devote all their time to learning. They learned, but had a lot of fun along the way.

Truly a double standard existed for officers and enlisted men in those days, and the difference was readily apparent in their living quarters and in the ways they were treated. In addition to preparing and serving the officers' meals, steward's mates and mess attendants, who were either black or Filipino, functioned as servants: making beds, cleaning staterooms, taking care of the laundry, shining shoes, and fetching things for the officers. Curiously, although the enlisted men were expected to kick in with tips to the mess cooks who served them, the officers didn't tip their steward's mates and mess attendants, even though the salaries of the officers were considerably higher than those of the enlisted men.[25]

There was also a double standard regarding adherence to Navy regulations. If an enlisted man came back late from liberty, he was likely to be punished for it. A late-returning officer was less likely to receive punishment. In general, officers seldom received official punishment for trangressions of regulations, and Borries was particularly well known for being able to get away with things that others wouldn't. It was partly a result of his personality and partly his status as an athlete. On the other hand, an officer was more likely than an enlisted man to be punished for a breach of professional duties. If he made a mistake while maneuvering the ship or failed to show up on time for a watch, for instance, he might well be thrown in hack for a few days. Essentially, that amounted to being suspended from duty and having to spend the time in his stateroom, supposedly contemplating his sins. It was quite similar to the common childhood punishment of being sent to one's room.

One custom that all junior officers were expected to follow was that of making formal calls on the ship's senior officers: the captain, executive officer, and department heads. When the *Arizona* was in her home port, certain hours were designated for calls, and the ensigns showed up at those times without appointment, had one drink, and often left after the obligatory fifteen minutes. If some genuine rapport developed, the call might last longer. As part of the protocol for the occasion, the ensigns left their calling cards in a silver tray. Different ensigns reacted in different ways to the ritual. Some welcomed it as a genuine opportunity to get to know their seniors away from the professional environment. Others thought of it only as a duty to be performed, and a fairly boring one at that.

Personnel inspections were held weekly on board the *Arizona*. Although different inspectors had their own particular concerns, haircuts and shoe shines were the two items the inspecting officers most often looked for. In today's Navy the ship's laundry provides members of the crew with clean uniforms. On board the *Arizona* that responsibility belonged to individual members of the crew. They took their uniforms topside to dry in good weather, a commodity that the ship enjoyed frequently with her fair-weather operating schedule: Southern California in the winter, the Pacific Northwest in the summer, and Hawaii and Panama mixed in between times. The sailors hung their uniforms between boats on the boat deck or perhaps in front of the topside air vents, using clothes pins to make sure they didn't fall down inside the vents. Once the uniforms were dry, men ironed them in their living compartments and then folded them and stowed them away in lockers until it was time for inspection.[26]

For the ship's cooks, the routine was a bit different. Instead of being inspected out on deck, they lined up in the galley on Saturday morning. As soon as breakfast was over, they had to hustle to their compartment and change from the food-stained whites in which they worked to the clean inspection uniforms they stored in their lockers. Then it was back up to the galley to lay out their utensils in rows and stand by for the inspector to look them over. As soon as he had gone, they went down to their lockers again, changed back into their working clothes, and then went back up to the galley to prepare lunch.[27]

During one inspection of the upper decks the crew got permission to keep a pet. A crew member had come across a stray fox terrier at the Pike, an amusement park in Long Beach, and smuggled him aboard under his peacoat. The sailor had set up a box near the ship's incinerator to serve as a home for the dog. The commanding officer, Captain George Baum, came around for an inspection shortly after that and saw the dog—frightened, trembling, and underfed—looking up at him with beseeching eyes. The dog's keeper volunteered to get rid of the terrier if the captain wanted, but Baum said that he could be added to the crew, and he was. The terrier was soon christened "At'em" in honor of the ship's motto and quickly became a favorite among the crew. In time he became quite well fed.

Yeoman Herbert "Zip" Zobel, who worked in the captain's office, observed that the men of the *Arizona* went to some lengths to make At'em part of the ship's routine, including establishing a service record for him, complete with serial number. He had a leather pouch on his harness to hold his identification card and liberty card. The medical crew treated him in sick bay as necessary. Typically, the terrier took care of his calls of nature near the scuppers at the deck edge; these were small troughs that carried water, and his urine, overboard. When At'em got careless about such matters, he was put on report and perhaps denied the opportunity to go ashore on liberty.[28]

At'em's popularity was not universal. He and the A division's compartment cleaner, a fireman named Marion Pulliam, had a mutual antipathy. The terrier watched for his opportunities and did his duty whenever he passed the compartment's fire hydrant and observed that Pulliam wasn't around. (A shipboard fire-main hydrant doesn't look like the kind found in residential neighborhoods, but canine instincts are superb in such matters.)

Opposite page: Hundreds of crew members congregate topside as sight-seers during a trip through the Panama Canal in 1934. Notice the protective metal shields at the front of the walkways around the bridge and conning tower. The circular base for the armored range finder atop the bridge is protected by canvas. (Courtesy Jack Rouse)

Right: A frequent ritual was that of scrubbing seabags and hammocks on deck and drying them topside. Notice the 5-inch/51 broadside gun, one of two in the superstructure rather than in casemates. Lashed to turret two is a paravane used for protection against mines. (Courtesy Earl Phares)

Pulliam directed unpleasant remarks and gestures to the dog whenever he saw it. After one drenching of the fire hydrant, Pulliam hurled a wet swab at the dog, spattering a bulkhead with water just prior to an inspection. At'em, who had evidently studied battleship range finding and fire control, had kept his eye on Pulliam and easily escaped, as one man from the A division described it, "with his usual smug look."[29]

The coxswain of the captain's gig during the mid-1930s was Carll Gleason. He was in overall charge of the boat, including its appearance, and that was a point of great pride, not only in the *Arizona* but for gigs throughout the fleet. He and his crew cleaned and polished the boat with almost loving care. Operationally, Gleason had to master more than seamanship: he had to know protocol as well. Seniority and dates of rank of the various ship's skippers were all-important. Gleason had the list down pat so that he would know when he was expected to render honors to the captain's gig of another ship or when the coxswain of another ship's boat was due to render honors to the *Arizona*'s. When the captains of several ships met on board the flagship for a conference, the gigs went alongside and dropped off skippers according to their sequence on the officer precedence list.[30]

Another member of the gig's crew was Fireman John Clunie, the boat engineer. Above all else, remembered Clunie, Captain Baum was humane. Unlike other skippers, Baum didn't treat his boat crews as lackeys. He respected them for being capable in their specialties. One of Baum's home-port routines was having Gleason drop him off at Long Beach's Pico Street landing in the evening. Baum was likely to say, "I'm going to the Pacific Coast Club to play a little cards tonight. If I win, I'll be back early. If I lose, I'll be back late. Start looking for me at 11:30." So Gleason, Clunie, and the other members of the boat crew used to sit on the rails at the landing and wait for the "old man" to return. They talked with one another, and they watched the passing scene. Said Clunie, "Oh, there was an ebb and flow of all kinds of humanity and lovelies bidding their sailors adieu and sailors bidding their lovelies adieu." There was much to be seen as a liberty evening moved along to its waning hours.[31]

When the night's duty was done, the gig's crewmen left the boat at a slip that the *Arizona* rented in the local yacht basin, and then they went home or wherever they were going to spend the night. The recently married Clunie appreciated the fact that he could join his bride even on duty nights, but it was awfully tough dragging himself out of bed in the morning to head back to the *Arizona*.[32]

Gleason had gotten along well enough with Captain Milne while running his gig, but the coxswain really came into his own with Baum as skipper. The new captain all but adopted him and treated him like a son the rest of his life. When it came time for Gleason to leave for other duty in 1936, he was relieved by Seaman Clyde "Red" Rawson, who had been a loyal deck hand in Gleason's crew much of the time after joining the *Arizona* in 1931.[33] As Gleason had proved himself to Kerrick, Milne, and Baum, Rawson did to subsequent skippers—Captain George Alexander and Captain Alfred Brown.

Rawson was a skilled boat handler, and he could explain his duties well orally; he just wasn't able to pass the written advancement

Above and right: These are water level and aerial views of the *Arizona* when she was moored to a buoy alongside the repair ship *Medusa* at San Pedro in 1934 or 1935. The *Medusa*, a collection of floating shops, was able to provide depot-level repairs and maintenance of equipment in between the battleship's visits to the shipyard at Bremerton, Washington. (Security Pacific National Bank Photograph Collection, Los Angeles Public Library, N-005-138.8; UPI/Bettmann Newsphotos, U738894)

exams. Then, in 1938 came a directive that all boat coxswains had to be rated men—that is, petty officers.[34] Boatswain's Mate First Class Charles Rourk, leading boatswain's mate in the fifth division, asked for and got permission to explain Rawson's situation to Captain Brown. Either Rawson passed the exam, or he could no longer run the gig. Brown said he would speak to the executive officer, and not long after that Rawson was a rated coxswain.

Brown was succeeded by Captain Isaac C. Kidd, the commanding officer in 1938–40. When Kidd came back to the *Arizona* in 1941 as Commander Battleship Division One, Rawson, by then a boatswain's mate first class, served as coxswain of the admiral's barge for him. Rawson and the admiral both died on board the *Arizona* on 7 December 1941.[35]

Both Gleason, who retired from his naval career with the rank of commander, and Rourk, who became a lieutenant, are good examples of the highly professional enlisted men who populated the Navy in the 1930s. They knew their business because they worked at it every day and studied extensively as well. Competition for advancement—and the accompanying pay increase—was fierce because the Navy was not expanding, and jobs in the outside world were scarce. It was common for many more men to pass an advancement exam than there were openings to fill. Those with the highest test scores and best recommendations from their commands got the jobs. Ensign Rod Badger, who served in the *Arizona* from 1935 to 1937, was amazed at Boatswain's Mate Gleason's knowledge of seamanship, and there were many, many others just as capable in their own specialties.

While Rawson had the practical experience but could not pass a written test, some men were able to advance because they learned more from the books than from on-the-job training. Such was the case with a newly reported seaman second class named Jim Vlach. He had studied shorthand and typing in high school, with the result that he was soon reassigned to the executive officer's office and went into training to become a yeoman. Yeomen had traditionally been tapped as telephone talkers on the premise that they can speak more clearly than some of their shipmates. During one exercise Vlach was assigned as a talker in the plotting room, deep inside the ship. Not much was happen-

ing on the phone circuits, so Vlach asked the plotting-room officer for permission to study some training manuals. He essentially memorized the contents and did extremely well on the advancement exam for seaman first class. As he recalled, his practical knowledge of seamanship was almost nil because he spent most of his time with the typewriter. But he could demonstrate a paper knowledge of seamanship, and that got him the higher pay grade.[36]

Throughout the ship's career, her motto was "Up-and-at-'em-*Arizona*," and she engendered a feeling of team spirit, much like that in a high school or college. The comparison is apt because the big ships of the fleet had athletic teams, and the men of the *Arizona* rooted fervently for theirs. The view toward athletes was frequently ambivalent; it really depended on how well the teams did. When the *Arizona* was winning, the sailors felt proud of their shipmates; if her teams didn't do so well, the nonathletes resented the athletes' time off from work for practice and games.

The men of the race-boat crews worked hard to represent the ship. Rowing a race boat was demanding work, requiring that the

Right: Oil derricks dot the skyline as the *Arizona*'s race-boat crew prepares for the *Los Angeles Examiner* race at Long Beach in the mid-1930s. (Courtesy Jack Rouse)

Below left: The 1935 race-boat crew poses on deck with a trophy. (Courtesy Earl Phares)

Below right: Three members of the *Arizona*'s football team take a break. Left to right are John Hostinsky, Carll Gleason, and George Gelius. Hostinsky and Gleason had long terms of service in the ship because the command wanted to keep the football team together. (Special Collections, University of Arizona Library, 84-26-61)

oarsmen be in superb physical condition. The members of the boat crew often got up before the rest of their shipmates and went out to put in a few miles of rowing so they could perfect their timing. After working hours they also did roadwork ashore and sometimes on the deck of the ship, where they used a harnesslike device that enabled them to run in place but still encounter some resistance. They also attached weights to a system of wire ropes and pulleys so that they could build up their arm strength. Seaman Roy Hubert had the feeling at times that the crew member who set the pace during the long runs ashore must have been a marathon runner because he seemed possessed of a great deal of stamina. It was a valuable quality for a race crew that was in arm-to-arm competition against the men of other ships. In part, the races were a test of character as well as conditioning. After a certain amount of maximum sustained exer-

tion, the extra effort required to win came from intestinal fortitude.[37]

Along with the hard work went extra privileges. One benefit was the esteem in which their shipmates held the race-boat crew members. In addition, members of the boat crew had a special mess that included extra steak and other goodies because they were burning so many calories in their exertions. Sometimes they got to go out on excursions of their own. When the ship was in Hawaiian waters on one occasion, the racing crew was ashore on one of the islands for some running. While they were at it, they happened upon a rundown old truck carrying a load of pineapples. Laboring and wheezing under the

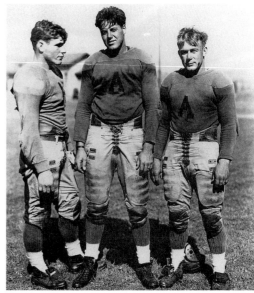

harvest, the truck was having a hard time chugging up a hill. An opportunistic race-boat man jumped on and pitched pineapples off to the rest of his mates.[38]

Football was the *Arizona*'s other major sport. Players on the team were accorded special privileges, including help in advancement in rating, so they would remain happy and stay with the ship. *The* big year for football was 1935. All-American Buzz Borries really put the finishing touch on a team that was talented already. Enlisted men such as Carll Gleason, Charles Rourk, and John Hostinsky had been on the squad since the ship went back into service in 1931. The coach was Lieutenant Hank Hardwick, who was considered talented enough to be the head football coach later at the Naval Academy.

Borries had a tendency to slouch on board ship, and even on the field he seemed to take a casual approach until he got the ball in his hand. As a halfback, he was neither particularly big nor fast, but he was a gifted athlete, one who had a great talent for finding a hole and running through it.[39] Rourk was also in the backfield, and he recalled of Borries, "He was the most relaxed man on the field I've ever seen. When we'd be on defense, he'd lay back there. And you'd look at him, and you'd think he was asleep. That ball would snap, and there he'd be—up there. And when he was on offense, he'd start to run, and you'd think he was in slow motion, but he'd . . . be lifting those legs high and just go."[40]

Rourk had started as a quarterback for the *Arizona*'s team in 1931 when it was just coming out of the doldrums of the modernization layoff and a poor record before that. As additional players came to the ship in later years, Rourk became a running back. He was one of a number of men that the command took care of to keep them motivated enough to stay on as part of the team. One day in 1935, when he was a coxswain and preparing for the exam for boatswain's mate second class, he was standing in one of the 5-inch–gun casemates. Along came Ensign Borries, who handed Rourk a small booklet and said, "Here are all the questions they're going to ask you." Before Rourk could say anything, Borries left, and along came Ensign Fritz Harlfinger. The second ensign put something else into the coxswain's hand and told him, "There are the answers." Rourk was a capable boatswain's mate—and later a ship's commanding officer after he had been commissioned—so he may not have needed the questions and answers at all; they were an insurance policy. He did well as a player that year, but he broke his leg the following season and was done as a football player.[41]

In a game against the team from the carrier *Lexington* during that 1935 season, Captain Baum called Coach Hardwick over and told him that the *Arizona* needed to win by at least forty points. Baum had made a bet with the skipper of the *Lexington*, but because of his own ship's prowess in football, he had to give

Above: A group shot of the 1935 squad, probably *Arizona*'s best-ever football team. Top row, left to right: Coach Hank Hardwick, Fleck, Slade Cutter (borrowed from the USS *Idaho*), Furnarri (77), Buzz Borries, John Hostinsky (14), Banks, Carll Gleason (30), Charles Rourk (90), Bundy, Post (40). Middle row: Pharmacist's Mate Jacobs, Oldham (18), Blevins (66), Benson (70), Keith (13), Paul Nye (11), Leinen (24), W. J. Stromquist, Smith (33), Kruk (44). Bottom row: Boehm (16), Bull Sperandio (12), Frizzell (17), Charlton (22), Parker (20), Buccini (27), and Livingston (55). (Courtesy Earl Phares)

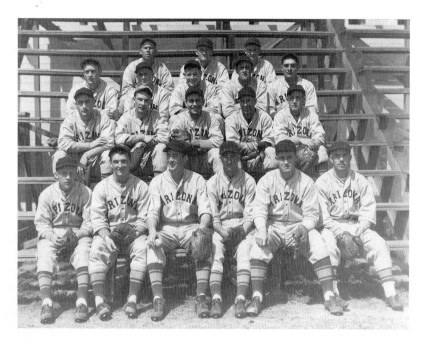

Above: In this photo of the *Arizona*'s 1937 baseball team, pitcher Pat Tobin is second from right in the front row. He later pitched professionally, including one major league game in 1941. Second from left in the second row is Bill Speedie, Tobin's catcher. (U.S. Navy photo in U.S. Naval Institute Collection)

away forty points to make the wager. He needn't have worried. The *Arizona* won 68-0. The team just missed the fleet championship, though, losing a tough game to the *Pennsylvania* at the end of the season.[42]

Late in the year, the *Arizona*'s football team added a "ringer" for a couple of games against civilian teams, including the West Seattle Athletic Club, which had several former collegiate stars on its roster. The *Arizona* and the battleship *Idaho* were both at Bremerton, and the *Arizona*'s team had been hit with injuries, especially at tackle. Coach Hardwick asked Captain Baum to ask the other battleship's skipper if the *Arizona* could borrow Ensign Slade Cutter, an all-America tackle the year before at the Naval Academy and a good friend of Buzz Borries. The prospect was appealing to Cutter because it was a chance to combine football with an unofficial honeymoon: the *Idaho* was due to leave the yard, and the games would give him the opportunity to drive down the coast with his bride to rejoin his ship. As he asked rhetorically, "What could be sweeter?"[43]

Other men from the *Arizona* played baseball. Watertender Joe Giovenazzo enjoyed being on the team, even though he wasn't all that proficient, because he got to eat better than he would have in his normal mess, and he also got out of regular shipboard work whenever he was with the team. The ball team practiced at one of the several diamonds at Trona Field in San Pedro. One day soon after

Giovenazzo had joined, the coach sent him up to the plate to bunt. Giovenazzo didn't have much experience and didn't do well. A man came in from right field to give him some advice on how to do it better. The man was Red Ruffing, a right-handed pitcher for the New York Yankees, then the finest team in major league baseball.[44]

Fireman Bill Speedie was another player on the ship's team. He observed that the *Arizona*'s squad was popular with Ruffing and the other professional players that came out for preseason workouts because it was among the best, winning perhaps 90 percent of its games. The *Arizona*'s caliber of play was closest to their own and thus gave them the best preparation for their own spring training. One of the players who made the *Arizona*'s team so good was pitcher Marion "Pat" Tobin. Speedie, a catcher, caught both Tobin and Ruffing in practice and observed that Tobin had a superb fastball with a good "hop" that made it deceptive to hit. He had a big, roundhouse curveball as well but obviously didn't have the polish of the far more experienced Ruffing. Tobin wasn't nearly as good, for example, at holding runners on first base and didn't have the control that Ruffing did. During the 1937 season Tobin's enlistment in the Navy ended, and he signed a contract with the San Diego Padres, then a minor league team in the Pacific Coast League. Tobin eventually made it to the American League, pitching one inning of one game for the Philadelphia Athletics in 1941. Then came the war, and Tobin never returned to the big leagues.[45]

A chore that was performed over and over during the *Arizona*'s lifetime was the scraping of the hull while she was in dry dock. It was done for more than cosmetic purposes. The marine life that attached itself to the underwater portion of the ship produced a drag effect that could take as much as four or five knots off the speed produced by the engines. Thus it took a greater amount of fuel oil to produce a given speed through the water. As a consequence, the dry-docking was done frequently, sometimes for only a day or two at a time. Crew members went over the side on stages, which were 2 × 12–inch planks suspended by pieces of line. At other times the men stood on wooden platforms that descended gradually as the water flowed out of the dry dock. It was important to scrape off the barnacles before they had a chance to dry and harden. Men used tools that looked like trowels for the scraping. As those lowered in stages descended farther down the side of the ship, they had to be hogged in by lines suspended from the stage because of the hull's inward curve.[46]

Once the scraping was done, the men applied coats of anticorrosive paint and anti-fouling paint. Not every seaman understood the principle completely. An individual taking an advancement exam in another ship was asked to name the two types of paints applied to the ship's hull. His answers were "Annie Carusi" and "Annie Fowler."[47]

On board the *Arizona*, the men of the deck divisions got up at reveille. If a particular sailor didn't get up right after the morning bugle call, the master-at-arms or boatswain's mate could use a forceful persuader, a stick applied to the man's backside through the bottom of the hammock. Once the men were up and dressed, they fell in topside to swab or holystone the decks. Meanwhile, the mess cooks took pots of coffee up to those swabbing decks with bare feet in the chilly water from the ship's fire hoses. After the job was completed to the satisfaction of the boatswain's mates on deck, the men repaired to their division compartments to have breakfast.[48]

The stock-in-trade for the boatswain's mates was a kick in the rear end of a recalcitrant seaman. The boatswain's mates used it as a remedy for slow response to an order or poorly done work, or even as a means of having fun. The junior enlisted men were truly beholden to the petty officers in their division, the men who controlled liberty cards and had the primary say-so in awarding on-the-spot discipline or granting special privileges. Certainly the officers were responsible for the performance of their divisions, but their style of supervision was not so direct as that of the petty officers.[49] As Jack Rouse, who was one of the *Arizona*'s seamen in the 1930s, remembered, "An officer never touched you."

The commanding officer was in many ways aloof from the internal operation of the ship. While the rest of the officers ate in the wardroom or junior officers' mess, the skipper

had his own separate mess. He might go to the various sports events, but often he left that chore to the exec as well. One executive, probably Commander Mervyn Bennion, who served on the *Arizona* in 1936–37, had a way of explaining the situation to seamen second class who were reporting to the *Arizona* from boot camp. He would gather a draft of new men together and tell them, "Don't feel ill at ease. This battleship is just like your own hometown. There's everything on this ship that there is in your hometown. There's the waterworks, boiler works, gedunk counter [soda fountain], policemen [the master-at-arms force]." And he went on to describe any number of other similarities, then explained, "Now, I'm the mayor of this city, and the captain is God." If the recruits laughed, the exec knew he had a pretty good group. If nobody laughed, then he was concerned.

Bennion, who later was killed as commanding officer of the battleship *West Virginia* during the attack on Pearl Harbor, was an exceptional person for the role of commander. The job description generally calls

Above: The *Arizona* is in dry dock at Boston in July 1931, shortly before returning to the Pacific. This shot illustrates an activity typical throughout the ship's career. As the water in the dry dock is lowered, the crew works on stages to scrape marine growth from the bottom before it has a chance to dry and harden. Note the catapult added to turret three since the completion of President Hoover's visit in March 1931. (Courtesy Roy Hubert)

Above: This superstructure view was taken looking forward from the mainmast. The 36-inch searchlights are controlled from inside the houses on the sides of the stack. To port of the stack, covered with canvas, is one of the directors for the 5-inch antiaircraft guns. Just forward of that, a sailor mans a twin-barreled saluting battery. At the top of the photo, on each side of the tripod legs of the foremast, is an optical range finder for the 5-inch antiaircraft guns. (Courtesy Allen T. Peterson)

for the second-in-command to be the head SOB. Bennion, by contrast, was mild-mannered and highly religious. He spoke in a soft, reassuring tone. He didn't drink alcohol but understood that others did. He was not the sort, like his predecessor, Commander Samuel S. Payne, who would make a strong punch and then leave the party to the junior officers. But neither would he prohibit such parties. Though his qualities were unusual for a senior naval officer, he was effective and highly respected by those who served with him. The enlisted men contrasted Bennion's approach with that of Payne, whom they had nicknamed "Summary Sam" because of his penchant for awarding summary courts-martial to those who had committed infractions.[50]

Bennion's successor was Commander Francis S. Craven. Once he was out on deck when Charles Rourk had been supervising some men in a painting project. They hadn't finished, so Rourk picked up a brush to paint the last spot, which was about two feet square. Craven came up behind him and asked, "What is your rate?"

"Good afternoon, Commander," answered Rourk. "I'm a boatswain's mate first class."

"If you're a boatswain's mate, then do the job that a boatswain's mate is supposed to do, not the job that a seaman is supposed to do. The boatswain's mate sees that the seaman does the painting."

Rourk gave the commander a firm "Aye, aye, sir," and felt that he had received a valuable lesson in leadership that day.[51]

Probably the enlisted man who made the biggest impression on the crew of the *Arizona* in the 1930s was John L. Hostinsky, the man who kicked Seaman Bill Bryan during the evening prayer. Hostinsky reported aboard as a coxswain in 1931 when the crew was brought back up to full strength following the rebuilding of the ship. Hostinsky had advanced in rating to first class boatswain's mate by the time he left the crew of the *Arizona* in 1939. During World War II he became an officer, and he eventually retired as a lieutenant commander. He was capable, tough, and colorful. The fourth division was his fiefdom.

One night Hostinsky came back to the ship from liberty and got into an argument with a few members of the marine detachment. Not willing to let the matter lie, Hostinsky posted himself at the top of the ladder that led from the marines' living compartment to the deck above. He challenged the men below to come up the ladder one at a time. Garland Fordyce, one of Hostinsky's teammates on the ship's wrestling team, recalled that Hostinsky took on about six of the marines before he got enough.[52]

When Cletus Schroeder reported aboard as a seaman second class, he was put into the X division, and someone pointed out Boatswain's Mate Hostinsky to him, warning, "There is a tough man." Schroeder's instinct was to stay away from Hostinsky. Soon after that the men of the new draft were divided up, and Schroeder wound up in the fourth division with the tough boatswain's mate. His heart went down to his ankles. One day right after Schroeder joined them, the men in the division were lined up in two ranks, and the division officer said, "Two paces backward."

Schroeder stepped in some wet paint, and right after that someone kicked him in the rear end. Hostinsky saw what had happened. The division officer gave them a pep talk and then told Hostinsky to take over the detail. They saluted each other, and once the officer was gone Hostinsky told his men in rough language to stand at attention. Hostinsky then walked behind Schroeder's row and knocked two heads together, Schroeder's and that of the man who kicked him. Then he wheeled Schroeder around and said, "You little so-and-so, who do you think is boss around here?"

Schroeder said, "You are, sir."

"The next time you call me 'sir,' you'll be spitting teeth all over the place."

Schroeder lay in his hammock that night, thinking about those three years and eight months he still had to do in the Navy. From

Left: George Brunken stands on the fantail catapult at Bremerton in late 1938, preparing to lower the colors. His service ended when he died of a brain tumor in early 1939. (Courtesy Mrs. Mary Brunken, via Lorraine Marks, *Arizona* Reunion Association)

then on, however, the situation improved considerably because Schroeder learned to live life on the boatswain's mate's terms. He did what Hostinsky told him and didn't give him any lip. Later Hostinsky warmed up. He started asking Schroeder questions about math because Hostinsky wanted to go up for warrant officer and needed some help. Schroeder developed considerable respect for the tough boatswain's mate because he knew his job and got things done.[53]

Seaman Nick Richardson was among the many fearful of Hostinsky's intimidating presence and willing to do whatever was necessary to keep the petty officer happy. One day Richardson was scraping paint in a passageway in officers' country when Hostinsky came down a ladder and spotted him. Hostinsky didn't like the way the seaman was doing things, so he slammed him against the bulkhead three or four times. Said Richardson, "That's when my Tennessee temper came out, even though I was scared to death." As he put it, he and the boatswain's mate exchanged "some pretty strong eye contact." Hostinsky realized that Richardson was upset and had a paint scraper in his hand, so he let the seaman go, went back up the ladder, and never said another word about the incident. Richardson thought that Hostinsky was secretly pleased that he had shown some spunk and thus helped him advance more quickly than some of his shipmates. Richardson credited Hostinsky's training for preparing him for what he had to face during World War II.[54]

Because of his aggressiveness as both a football player and a boatswain's mate, Hostinsky acquired a larger-than-life reputation. He settled into his shipmates' memories as a big, tough, mean man. Some were thus surprised to run into him years later at the *Arizona*'s reunions and discover that he was relatively slight in stature. His personality undoubtedly added considerably to his presence.

Another enlisted man had a reputation well beyond his own division, although he wasn't at all frightening. Arky Duckworth was a living example of the country rube who has trouble adapting to the ways of a more sophisticated society. He was a big man of the "gentle giant" stereotype, extremely strong physically but reluctant to use his strength. His nickname was a derivative of his home state of Arkansas, and he was often the butt of

cruel humor. Shipmates joked, for instance, that they might spread some manure on the gangway when Duckworth returned aboard so that he would feel more at home. They also talked about his feet, which were too big to fit into standard Navy-issue shoes.

When the men of the sixth division had some time off, such as a Wednesday afternoon or a weekend, they might wind up relaxing on board the *Arizona* because they weren't in that day's liberty section. With port and starboard duty, chances were one in two that they had to stay aboard. They would have a cheap liberty by buying some ice cream and sitting on the boat deck, talking with each other and eating. When Duckworth came by, the other men in the division often razzed him, and they played little tricks on him, such as hiding his gear or parts of his uniform. Things that might offend other people didn't seem to bother him, although he did confide to Gunner's Mate Dusty Rhodes that at times he was hurt by some of the remarks. But the teasing seemed like a lot of fun to the crew. Jack McCarron, one of the men of the sixth division then, felt a sense of regret years later that he and his shipmates treated Duckworth as they did.[55]

The men who worked on the 5-inch/25-caliber antiaircraft battery needed to be strong to load the guns. The ammunition for the 5-inch broadside guns came in two pieces, a projectile and a powder bag. For the antiaircraft guns, the whole works came in one piece, combining powder and projectile. Because of his size and strength, Duckworth was exceptionally well suited as a loader. Dusty Rhodes recalled him as the fastest loader he ever saw, and speed was important. "He had the strength of an elephant," said Rhodes.[56]

The big man didn't work out so well, however, during an exercise when he was the trainer aiming the gun at an aerial target. In antiaircraft practice, a plane towed a canvas cylinder, known as a "sleeve," that was used as the aiming point for the guns. The customary procedure was for a gunner to aim initially at the plane itself and then shift back to the canvas sleeve before starting to shoot. Duckworth never seemed to figure out how to make the shift when he had his gun in local control. He steadfastly kept tracking the plane itself. Seaman John Amend, who was serving as a safety observer on the mount, kept telling

Duckworth to shift from plane to sleeve, without success. As a result, Amend refused to permit the mount to fire because he was afraid of hitting the plane.[57]

Most of the enlisted men serving in the ship worked hard to advance in rate because of the higher pay and increased privileges that advancement brought. Duckworth struck his shipmates as being entirely content to remain a seaman second class throughout his enlistment, and that he did. Despite his lowly status in the hierarchy of the *Arizona*, he felt that he was still doing far better than he had done in Arkansas.[58]

With his Li'l Abner physique and manners, Duckworth frequently gave the impression on board ship that he had two left feet. Quite the opposite was true when he went dancing ashore. Stacy Barker, a shipmate from the late 1930s, remembered, "Could he dance! I mean, I don't know what kind of a dance came from them hills, but when they was in the Majestic [Ballroom] and Arky would get in there with some girl, first thing you know, there would be no one else dancing. There would just be a ring around about three deep, . . . and Arky would really be kicking up his heels."[59]

During the mid-1930s, because of the Depression, the *Arizona*'s manning level was probably the lowest in her operational career. As a result, men from the engineering department sometimes worked in the ammunition-handling rooms of the 14-inch turrets during gunnery practice, and the deck hands were sometimes assigned to fireroom duty when the ship made full-power runs with all boilers on the line.[60] When the 5-inch antiaircraft guns were to fire a practice, the

Above: Crew members practice with a loading machine for the 5-inch antiaircraft guns in March 1933. The ammunition was the fixed variety, combining both projectile and powder. One shell can be seen in the fuze pot at the left of the mount. At the left of the photo is a leg of a tripod mast and attached ladder. In the upper left corner is a race boat with built-up seats for the oarsmen. At right, ship's boats are nested. (UPI/Bettmann Newsphotos, U217572-Acme)

gun crews would gather on the same side of the ship, fire that half of the battery, then all move to the other side to fire the other half.[61] Boatswain's Mate Joe Vivirito, for instance, was in the sixth division, which manned the 5-inch/25s. During antiaircraft practice he was a gun pointer on a mount on the starboard side; when the port mounts were firing, he was a gun captain. The two roles increased each man's versatility.[62]

Following her modernization at Norfolk from 1929 to 1931, the *Arizona* had six boilers. At least one ran nearly all the time because the ship needed steam for heat and electricity and auxiliaries even when at anchor. The boilers could be shut down completely only when the *Arizona* was alongside a pier or in dry dock and receiving services from shore. When under way, the boilers operated under forced draft so that the air flow could enhance the burning of the heavy, black fuel oil. Ironically, the slower the ship was going and the less steam she was making, the hotter it was for the men in the firerooms.[63] When the *Arizona* was steaming in tropical waters, her watertenders typically wore only their shoes and skivvies while standing fireroom watches.

The boilers put in at Norfolk operated at a maximum steam pressure of 300 pounds per square inch, about twice the pressure of the boilers with which the ship had originally been outfitted. In comparison, the boilers in the *Iowa*-class battleships operate at 600 pounds per square inch, and the more modern steam-turbine ships of the Navy produce 1,200 psi. The higher the pressure, the greater the energy that can be extracted from a given volume of steam.

Each boiler had as many as eight burners, which were perforated cylinders that were inserted into the boiler front and that sprayed fuel onto the fires. When the ship was going slowly, each boiler might need only two burners and a correspondingly slower air flow from the forced draft. At high speed, more burners were used, more fuel was burned, and the draft had to be blowing strongly. The increased air flow made the spaces more comfortable for the watertenders. They had to enter the firerooms through air locks—in effect, double sets of hatches—so that the air pressure couldn't escape when men were coming and going.[64]

Efficient fuel consumption required a proper mixture of oil and air at the time of burning. Too much air, the smoke was white; too much fuel, it came out black. Typically, the B division posted a smoke watch up in the maintop to keep an eye on the stack. The stack was divided into six pie-shaped wedges, one for each boiler. If the topside engineer spotted a problem with the smoke, he would phone a report down to the appropriate fireroom so that the watertenders could correct the mixture. The man on top was usually a boilermaker since he wouldn't have any repair work to do at sea. Being up in the fresh air was preferable to staying in the hot, enclosed spaces down below, so those on smoke watch were loath to complain.[65]

The air that went into the boilers came down along the sides of the smokestack into an area known as the "bull ring." It was an enclosed area on the second deck around amidships. The air itself was drawn in through intakes up on the boat deck and then rushed down through the bull ring to the firerooms. Since the engineers were not permitted to nap in their living compartments in the daytime, they sometimes grabbed some sleep near the bull ring because it was obviously well ventilated. During some periods in the mid-1930s the divisions in the engineering department were so poorly manned that some individuals had to stand essentially port-and-starboard watches—four hours on watch and four hours off. What with the living compartments off-limits in the daytime, Fireman Wes Cole had to look for a place to hole up in the generator room or somewhere on the third deck. The port-and-starboard watch routine invariably fatigued everyone because they had to fit eating, sleeping, shaving, washing, and so forth into their four hours off watch. Cole said that with such a watch rotation, engineers were lucky if they could get five or six hours of sleep out of twenty-four. "You were just a walking zombie," he explained.[66]

At other times it wasn't so bad, especially if the *Arizona* experienced a slow watch during which the ship didn't do much maneuvering. Without a lot of speed changes, the throttlemen didn't have a lot to do, nor did the watertenders need to change the number of burners so often. They might relax by reading magazines or perhaps just shooting the breeze.

One watertender first class had a big interest in hunting. He even had a metal locker in one of the firerooms where he kept his hunting rifles and gunpowder so he could fill his own cartridges. During watches he kept the other watertenders spellbound, telling them of his trips to places such as Canada and Montana, and of his encountering huge grizzly bears and shooting them. Vicariously, the other watertenders had the thrill of the hunt and the treks through the wilds.[67]

Young Joe Giovenazzo was among those enthralled by the tales, so when he came across a fishing and hunting magazine on board the ship, he picked it up and began reading. He found a story about hunting grizzlies in the great north country, and it was remarkably similar to the tale spun by his shipmate. Giovenazzo confronted him, and that was the end of the "first-person" hunting stories. Furthermore, during a subsequent inspection the skipper asked to see the inside of the man's locker, which had remained closed during previous inspections. The captain was appalled by the careless storage of gunpowder and ordered the fireroom hunting locker closed immediately. So ended the hunting career, real or imagined, of one of the *Arizona*'s engineers.[68]

Probably the two most important aspects of life for officers in the *Arizona* in her

Left: Crew members line up in ranks as the *Arizona* passes in review by the fleet flagship *Pennsylvania*, which is out of range of the camera. Other battleships steam in column ahead in the vicinity of San Pedro, California, in March 1933. The *Arizona*'s hull number 39 was painted on top of turret two during much of the 1930s to help pilots and spotters in planes identify the ship from the air. (UPI/Bettmann Newsphotos, U217559-Acme)

twenty-five-year career were gunnery and shiphandling. The latter was necessary to support the former. The ship existed to transport the guns to the places where they might be needed to oppose an enemy. Fleet operations generally involved steaming with other battleships in a battle line. Maintaining proper station in the formation was an exacting responsibility, especially in the days before the use of radio and radar were commonplace. A conning officer had to institute rudder and engine orders in a timely fashion to turn at the proper time and to maintain station when steaming in a straight line.

A quality often known as seaman's eye is valuable for precise station keeping. It is the ability to judge distances accurately and to make necessary corrections when in formation or when steaming to a new station in the formation. A mechanical device known as a stadimeter measured distances, but years of experience enabled officers to make judgments more quickly than the stadimeter and thus enabled them to react faster when

needed. When turning as part of a column of ships, the *Arizona* would ideally turn in the wake of the ship ahead. Conning officers had to know how various combinations of speed and rudder angle would affect the ship, especially since a vessel her size was far less maneuverable than a destroyer, and the interval between ships in column was often only 300–500 yards. Jack Arnold, an ensign on board the *Arizona* in the mid-1930s, likened the process to steering an elephant. As Arleigh Burke had discovered a decade earlier, the rudder had to be over for a while before it began to take effect, especially at slower speeds.[69]

Captain George Baum was representative of the many senior officers who had a well-developed seaman's eye. Ensign Rod Badger recalled a time when he was standing the junior-officer-of-the-deck watch on the *Arizona*'s bridge and operating the stadimeter. A particular maneuver was in progress, and Captain Baum predicted that the *Arizona* would pass another battleship at a distance of 700 yards. At their closest point of approach, Badger looked at the stadimeter, and the reading was 715. From time to time Baum would send groups of officers, armed with stadimeters, out in the ship's boats. Then the ship would go through a series of maneuvers by herself to teach officers the *Arizona*'s tactical data. They would experiment with various combinations of rudder and speed, seeing how long it took for the rudder to have an effect and how big the turning circle was for different speeds and different rudder angles.[70] Coxswain Hugh "Red" Campbell once saw Baum take the *Arizona* alongside a dock in Tacoma, Washington, without the benefit of tugs. He got her in astern of the *West Virginia*—"just eased her in there, just as pretty as you please," said Campbell.[71]

Besides the captain and the officer of the deck, another person of considerable authority during underway periods was the boatswain's mate of the watch, stationed on the bridge to carry out the daily schedule and follow the directions of the officer of the deck. As in so many things in Navy life, the BMOW's ritual had been handed down through the years. One man who served as BMOW was Charles Rourk. His boatswain's call, a silver-plated metal whistle that produced a variety of signals, had two purposes.

Worn attached to a lanyard around the boatswain's mate's neck, it was his badge of authority; it was also an attention-getting device used to precede announcements over the loudspeaker system. Part of the ritual included the litany the BMOW intoned upon taking over a watch: "On deck, the first section. Relieve the watch. Relieve the wheel, lookouts, and life buoy watch. The watch and the lifeboat crew on watch to muster." Then the boatswain's mate had to ensure that everyone was at his assigned station. Each of the horseshoe-shaped Franklin life buoys had a man ready to trip it in case someone fell overboard, and a whaleboat was rigged in davits so that it could be lowered in short order to retrieve someone from the water.[72]

When the *Arizona* was operating, she had men on watch throughout the ship day and night. To maintain their energy for the night watches, men indulged in mid-rats—short for midnight rations. Sometimes the watchstanders ate before going to their posts, sometimes they ate and drank after they got there. Coffee was a staple for nearly all. When Ensign Jack Arnold was learning the ship's propulsion plant by standing watches in the engine room, he observed that the enlisted crew members went to the galley to get freshly baked bread. Back in their spaces, the men would tear out the inside of a loaf and fill the cavity with canned salmon. To make their coffee, they filled a sock—preferably clean—with coffee grounds and put it into a bucket of water. Then they stuck the bucket under a steam line and let a jet of steam heat the water until the drink was sufficiently brewed. Years later, Arnold remarked with a chuckle, "It's a wonder our stomachs survived it, and I'm not sure they did, really."[73]

Sometimes the men of the M division were issued two-pound cans of Vienna sausages for their night rations. To Machinist's Mate First Class Wes Cole the sausages were "hard to eat, even at the very best, so we'd put them up on a big steam valve and heat them up." One night, while a nervous watch officer was on duty in main control, the can of meat stayed on the steam valve too long and exploded. "It sounded like the broadside [guns] had gone off," said Cole, and the watch officer almost jumped straight through the overhead. It took a considerable time to clean up all the sausages.[74]

Although that incident happened by accident, Cole on another occasion laid a trap for a fellow engineer. Chief Watertender Joe Karb stood alongside the throttleman during watches in main control. Whenever the machinist's mate made changes in the ship's speed with his large throttle wheel, Chief Karb communicated the changes to the firerooms so that they could adjust the steam pressure and number of burners in the boilers if needed. Karb followed a certain pattern whenever he arrived in main control to relieve the watch. Before speaking to anyone about the steaming conditions or doing anything else, he went over and poured himself a cup of coffee. Even so, he complained over and over that the coffee in main control was always too weak for his taste.

Cole had the watch before Karb one night and decided he would take care of the chief's complaining. He had his men make a pot of coffee as they normally did. Then they got a fresh set of coffee grounds, but instead of using water for the second batch, they used their newly made coffee. The result, after about thirty or forty minutes, was coffee so thick, according to Cole, that it practically had to be spooned out of the pot rather than poured. Karb took a taste, then quickly jerked the cup away from his mouth. The expressions on the faces of those around him told Karb he had been had, but he was a good sport about it. He drank the rest of the cup and never again complained about the strength of main control's coffee.[75]

Karb, incidentally, had been in the Navy for some fifteen years before reporting to the *Arizona*. She was his first battleship, after he had spent his time mostly in destroyers and minesweepers. Once he had arrived, he wondered why he had taken so long to get there because service in the *Arizona* proved to be a most comfortable existence. The chiefs' quarters were forward in the ship and commodious, including a bunkroom, lounge, and mess area. Even though each chief had his occupational specialty, the men as a group did not share in the rivalries of the various divisions they supervised. They lived together and relaxed together, spending their off-duty hours reading, talking, and playing a lot of acey-deucey and gin rummy. They even had their stashes of booze for occasional use. In a sense, the chiefs had a private club, a perquisite earned through years of service to the Navy.[76]

The *Arizona*'s enlisted men did not explore their ship much because their universe was essentially their living compartment, working place, and battle station. Men of the gunnery department seldom ventured down into the engineering spaces without an invitation, and the engineers did not often issue invitations. And, recalled one sailor, "The snipes [engineering department personnel] were kind of wary about coming up on deck. If they weren't in their dress uniforms, they generally got herded down below, because nobody wanted a spot of grease on the upper decks." Junior enlisted men had little contact with officers, usually encountering them only at quarters and when on watch. If a sailor did have occasion to go into officers' country, he was inclined to walk softly, hat in hand, and conclude his business as quickly as possible.[77]

In addition to their training as landing parties, the members of the ship's marine detachment had other, far more common functions to perform as part of the crew. They served as orderlies for the senior officers on board, often standing long, monotonous watches and acting as "gofers." The marines served as gun crews, provided security for the brig, and handled ceremonial duties, bringing to the ship that military smartness for which the Marine Corps has long been noted. They were loyal, obedient, and mostly unquestioning.[78]

The marines spent a lot of their time making sure that their appearance was impeccable: shining shoes, polishing belt buckles, pressing uniforms. Private Wylie Smith and others found that a Sears-Roebuck catalog had a utility that the Sears people hadn't intended. Rags were scarce, so the marines tore the pages out one at a time and used them to burnish their belt buckles with brass polish. Smith used his handkerchief to give his buckle a last touch-up before inspection. When he was in boot camp, Smith's sergeant had warned him and his fellow recruits that they would need cloth for cleaning their rifles once they got to their duty stations, so he advised them to tear their Marine Corps–issue pajamas into pieces for that purpose. A marine, he told them, didn't wear pajamas.[79]

While many of the men in the *Arizona*'s crew enjoyed their time on board—at least in retrospect—one who didn't was Private Jim McCain, who reported aboard in 1936. He found shipboard duty for marines to be "boring, irritating, frustrating, and generally a waste of good manpower." Many of the things they did, such as cleaning, chipping paint, and operating the 5-inch/51 broadside guns, could just as easily have been done by Navy men, although McCain and most of his marine shipmates enjoyed their work with the guns, both 5-inch and .50-caliber. He also concluded that many of his duties amounted to busywork and didn't serve much of a useful purpose. Standing watch as a brig sentry or senior officers' orderly usually meant several hours of doing essentially nothing except standing around. He described the duty of brig guard as "standing more or less at attention under a ventilation pipe about an inch lower than you were tall, no reading, no talking, maybe one visit in four hours from the corporal of the guard." McCain also spent time in the brig on "piss and punk," the shipboard name for a bread-and-water diet. He gained weight on that regimen, because his marine shipmates smuggled in more regular food than he could reasonably handle.

When he was an orderly, he wore his dress blues and waited outside the officer's door for four hours. Even at night he had to be there, on his feet, ready for the message or errand that probably wouldn't come. He couldn't

Below: Sailors and marines do jumping jacks on the starboard side of the *Arizona*'s quarterdeck in March 1933. Despite the strenuous nature of the exercises, the marines are wearing neckties as part of their uniforms. With the ship at sea, the gangway—that era's name for an accommodation ladder—is stowed on deck. Cylindrical baskets hold coils of line to keep them from interfering with traffic on deck. (UPI/Bettmann Newsphotos, U217565A-Acme)

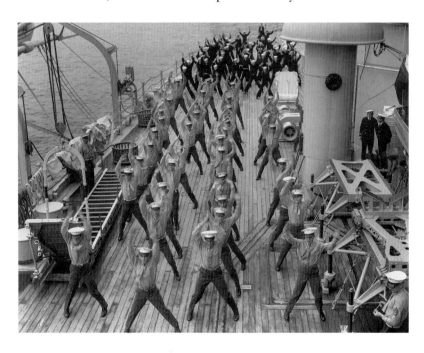

read or talk except in the line of duty; he was just there.[80]

Private McCain was also bothered by the degree to which officers had much greater privileges than enlisted men—even though they were all serving together in the same ship. Enlisted men were quite limited in their use of fresh water. While standing watches in officers' country, he saw "the commissioned officers go by in their bathrobes & slippers, pretty soon the steam rolling out of their showers, while you stood there in your own sweat and felt a bitter resentment." McCain was not alone in his feelings of discontent. He said, "One friend of mine, whom I won't name, shot himself in the foot at the rifle range to get off the ship. I wasn't that desperate of course, but there was very little about seagoing duty that I liked and I was glad to be transferred."[81]

The *Arizona*'s 14-inch turrets were self-contained pieces of machinery that extended through several decks down into the ship. At the very bottom were the magazines and the handling rooms for the bags of powder. Each projectile required a charge of four bags. They were made of silk and were somewhat less rigid than the bags used in modern battleships. The men in the handling rooms took the powder bags out of their storage cans and passed them to the hoist for delivery to the turret above. There they came out of doors at each side of the turret. The bags were put into trays, including being lifted over to the tray for the center gun. The powder bags were rammed mechanically into the breech of the 14-inch gun behind the projectile, which had been rammed in first. (One of the photos in the previous chapter shows a projectile being rammed.)

A red felt pad covered one end of each powder bag; behind the pad was the ignition charge of black powder. To set off the chain reaction that fired the gun, a primerman inserted a primer about the size of a shotgun shell into the firing lock in the breech mechanism. Usually, an electrical circuit fired the primer into the ignition pad. The explosion of the ignition charge, in turn, set off the rapid combustion of the grains of smokeless powder in the bag itself. The rapidly burning fire produced a very high gaseous pressure that expelled the projectile with tremendous force. Since the breech end of the gun was

sealed shut before firing, the projectile was forced to move in the only possible direction—out the muzzle of the gun.

The primerman carried the primers in a sort of cartridge belt around his waist. Waiting down below in the gun pit, he was usually a small man so that he wouldn't be hit by the recoil when the gun fired. When a turret was firing at the maximum elevation of thirty degrees—increased from fifteen degrees during the ship's modernization—each gun recoiled forty inches. The turret was equipped with a pneumatic counter-recoil system. Cylinders containing compressed air absorbed the recoil and then pushed the guns back into position for the next round.[82]

Unlike current battleships, which have subdivided the turret into three individual gun rooms for the sake of safety, the *Arizona*'s guns were all together in one room. A single slide controlled all the guns, elevating or depressing them simultaneously. They had to be in the horizontal position for loading and then followed fire-control orders for elevating.

The men of a turret crew were drilled over and over about how to operate the guns safely. They were told horror stories of what might befall them if they didn't follow procedures correctly. Men in the gun room were warned against carrying anything that might produce a spark, and they were told to

Above: The ship's band holds a jam session on deck in the late 1930s. (Courtesy E. D. Keefe, via Joseph Langdell, *Arizona* Reunion Association)

be sure they were clear of the breech end of the 14-inch gun when they heard the salvo alarm because the rapid recoil could ram the gun into them.[83]

Men were somewhat crowded together in the gun rooms, what with different individuals handling the powder and projectiles and still another man ramming the ammunition into the barrel. The pointer's station down beneath the guns was less crowded. The directions for elevation and bearing came from the main-battery plotting room down inside the ship, although part of the information originated in the turret itself.

Protruding externally from each side of each turret was an "ear" that was one end of a long-base optical range finder. The range-finder operator continuously aimed at the target, and the ranges were transmitted to the plotting room. Bearings to various targets came from the directors in main-battery control stations up in the tops. The plotting room combined this information in the rangekeeper and fed firing instructions back to the turrets. The men in the turret used big brass handwheels to follow signals indicated by mechanical pointers. The turret's hydraulic system translated the movement of the wheels

Right: During a shipyard period 14-inch projectiles lie on a canvas-covered deck. (Special Collections, University of Arizona Library, 77-3-292)

into turret deflection and angle of elevation. Once the gun was loaded and primed, the gun captain closed his ready switch. That meant the gun would fire when the pointer's key was closed or the signal sent from a director. A salvo alarm preceded each salvo by a few seconds. The alarm was a signal for the range-finder operator, such as Seaman Mel Larson, to pull back from the rubber eyepiece on the equipment. If he didn't, the jolt from the firing could poke the eyepiece into his eye.[84]

Behind the gun room was the control booth for the turret. In it stood the turret officer and his sound-powered telephone talker during target practice. They had viewing ports so that they could look through the bulkhead that separated them from the gun room, which was forward of them and somewhat lower. The turret officer was connected by phones with those operating the guns in his turret, with the gunnery officer, and with the plotting room. The turret officer had a selector switch so that the guns could be fired from the turret itself or from a director.

When more than one battleship was firing target practice (or in battle, when it came to that), the ships used dye-loaded projectiles for the 14-inch guns. Thus, if the *Arizona*, *Pennsylvania*, and *Oklahoma* were all firing at the same target, the dye in the nose of the projectile would produce a colored splash when it hit the water. The different colors enabled the spotters from each ship to see how far off target their shots were and to make appropriate adjustments.

The fire-control system was essentially electro-mechanical, up to date for the period but far less sophisticated than the electronic systems of today. The rangekeeper in the plotting room was the heart of the system. The main battery guns were actually aimed from the plotting room, deep within the ship. The pointers and trainers in the turrets just followed the commands from the plotting room. The turret personnel also served as a backup. Once shooting began, the director scopes in the mast-top towers (or an airplane, if it was being used) signaled "overs" and "unders." The plotting room people had to know which salvos the spotters were talking about because more than one could be in the air at the same time.[85]

Fire Controlman Jim O'Donnell had a battle station on one of the directors at the top of the ship. During long-range battle practice, he recalled, there were sometimes as many as nine 14-inch projectiles in the air at the same time from the same turret. The interval between salvos for a good turret crew was just under half a minute. Since the time of flight to a target at long range could be more than a minute, the three projectiles from the third salvo could be fired while those from the first and second were still on their way.[86]

To keep the fire-control equipment effective, the men had to calibrate it from time to time. The primary emphasis was on shooting against ships, although the big guns could also be employed against shore targets. O'Donnell was once in a party of half a dozen men who were put ashore on San Clemente Island, off the southern California coast, to aid in the calibration. The island had benchmarks on it for just that purpose, and O'Donnell and his companions sent the calibration information back to the ship as she steamed some distance offshore. The whole operation took the better part of a day, and when it was over the *Arizona*'s officer of the deck forgot about his shore party. The ship steamed away and left the six men behind. For a time they were especially concerned that some other ship, unaware of their presence, might come along and begin target practice.

Fortunately, they had a radio with them so that they could communicate with the ship during the calibration procedures. They couldn't raise the *Arizona* by the time they realized she was leaving them, but they did contact a shore station, which dispatched the nearby cruiser *Minneapolis* to pick them up. The cruiser's skipper evidently felt like needling the *Arizona* a bit, so he kept the shore party on board for several days, letting them live in style. He even had his crew issue uniform items to the refugees and then sent the bill to the *Arizona*. The *Arizona*'s officer of the deck who left the men behind was given a reprimand and some time to contemplate his oversight.[87]

Also used during the ship's frequent target practices were the 5-inch/51-caliber broadside guns of the secondary battery. This was before the days of the 5-inch/38 dual-purpose guns—surface and antiaircraft—that were commonplace in U.S. warships during World War II. The guns of the secondary battery were for use against surface targets. They had been installed when the ship was new because

the Navy believed that they would be used for defense against torpedo-carrying craft. Theoretically, the broadside guns—like those of the 14-inch main battery—could be used to fire a barrage of projectiles into the water ahead of incoming low-flying torpedo planes. The resulting splashes could intimidate the enemy planes, but it was not a particularly practical solution to the antiaircraft problem.[88]

Thanks to the ship's rebuilding and modernization at the beginning of the 1930s, the

Left: This is a view of the underside of the mainmast. Notice all the shielded electrical cables going up into the bottom of the maintop. Among other things, these cables carried fire-control information to the plotting room far down inside the ship. (UPI/Bettmann Newsphotos, U217738-Acme)

Below: A 5-inch/51 broadside gun erupts in flame as it fires during night battle practice in the 1930s. (Courtesy Lorraine Marks, *Arizona* Reunion Association)

leave, the routine most often called for her to get under way Monday morning and head out to the operating area between San Pedro and San Diego for a variety of exercises, many of them involving some form of gunnery. To save fuel, the ship often anchored at night off Santa Barbara Island or San Clemente Island. Frequently, several of the fleet's ships went out at the same time to observe for one another, tow targets, and serve as reference vessels for spotting drills. By the end of the week, crews were impatient to get back into port for liberty at Long Beach and environs.

When off duty, men frequently spent a lot of time with the other men in their divisions. One event that brought men of different divisions together was the evening movie. They would gather up their folding mess benches and stand poised in passageways, waiting for the master-at-arms's movie call. Then they would go racing out to the quarterdeck to set up the benches in advantageous positions for that evening's film. Chairs were set up in the front for the officers. When all was in readiness, the chief master-at-arms summoned the captain and escorted him to the fantail. At the skipper's signal, the movie began. The films were shown nightly except in bad weather and were usually recent-vintage Hollywood productions. The only flaw in the system was that during a long passage at sea the electrician's mates didn't have an opportunity to swap movies with other ships. Ensign Ned Lee was one of those who made the *Arizona*'s long passage from Bremerton to the East Coast in 1934. One of the pictures that got recycled was *Come and Get It*, starring Edward Arnold. Said Lee, "After about the sixth night of seeing that, it was unendurable."[90]

Another form of entertainment was the boxing and wrestling smokers. A ring was set up on the upper deck, forward of number one and number two turrets. The *Arizona* had some men who were genuinely capable, and it was they who competed against fighters from other ships. But there were also matches in which the various divisions on board the *Arizona* anted up men for the fights. The quality of the bouts varied considerably. As John Clunie, then a fireman, put it, "There was a limited amount of professionals and a lot of windmill-swinging amateurs up there getting knocked on their hind end."[91]

Above: This gun crew from fifth division won an E for its shooting during battle-practice competition in the late 1930s. (V. Weisbrod Company photo courtesy Garland Fordyce)

directors for the 5-inch/51s had been moved into the newly built tops. Second Lieutenant Victor "Brute" Krulak, one of the officers in the ship's marine detachment, had a battle station in secondary aft, which was in the bottom level of the fire-control structure at the top of the mainmast. This height gave a better visual perspective for spotting than had the original control stations on the old cage masts. Through the directors, secondary aft sent commands to the guns in terms of range and bearing. Short-range practice, which essentially amounted to familiarization training for the crews, was like shooting fish in a barrel. Krulak remembered that the *Arizona*'s secondary battery was also accurate enough to score frequent hits at longer ranges, 8,000–10,000 yards.[89]

As the ship's chronology at the back of the book indicates, the *Arizona* spent a great deal of her time in the 1930s at anchor in her home port of San Pedro, California. When she did

Left: New Year's postcard for 1936. (Special Collections, University of Arizona Library, 84-4-13)

Sometimes relaxation came from doing not much at all. After supper Seaman Arthur Williams enjoyed going up onto the boat deck to smoke cigarettes and listen to the music wafting up from a radio in a casemate below. He sang along softly, embarrassed whenever someone approached and overheard him. He watched the ocean pass by and the stars come out with the deepening of twilight. When the ship was anchored off San Clemente Island to save fuel at night, Williams enjoyed looking shoreward at a hill populated with goats and a lighthouse. Often he wished for a camera to photograph sunsets, but by the late 1930s the men could use their cameras only when they went ashore. Crewmen had to turn in their cameras to the master-at-arms to be locked up while on board ship.[92]

Since the ship was very seldom alongside a pier, nearly all the food and drink consumed by the crew had to be brought out from the shore in boats. All divisions contributed members to the working parties that provisioned the ship. These men hoisted the chow out of the boats, up the accommodation ladders, and then to reefers, spud lockers, and other storage areas. At the quarterdeck, the provisions were duly inspected and logged.

More than half a century later, readers can still consult the *Arizona*'s deck logs to see how much and what types of food were brought aboard on a given day. Seaman Second Class Bill Bryan once slipped on the ladder as he was carrying two heavy cans of milk, one under each arm. He lost his balance, nearly hit his head, and wound up dropping both cans of milk into Los Angeles Harbor.[93]

The ship's pharmacist's mates had an advantage over the other men in obtaining their ration of milk, which was a precious commodity in division messes. Regulations called for the ship's medical department to sample the food when it came aboard to ensure that it met quality standards and was safe for the crew. Fred Lager and other pharmacist's mates always took big pitchers with them to get samples from the large metal milk cans hauled up to the quarterdeck from motor launches. They also felt compelled to sample the ice cream. Back down in sick bay, they took care to give some milk to the convalescing patients but always made sure they drank a good-sized portion themselves. Not much was left when it came time for the medical officer to do whatever analysis the regulations required.[94]

Right: A group of officers has already gathered for a bull session on the fantail before the beginning of the evening movie. Many more benches will need to be set up to accommodate the enlisted men in the crew. (Courtesy Allen Peterson)

Lager figured that the doctor could take care of himself. When he was a pharmacist's mate third class, Lager was drawing about $65.00 per month in salary, compared with $54.00 for the hospital apprentices serving with him. So most of the enlisted men were making about $2.00 per day for their work on behalf of ship, Navy, and nation. They looked into the pay tables and discovered that the senior medical officer was making a sum that approached $20.00 per day. Lager recently looked back with bemusement as he recalled the sense of wonderment that he and his fellows had—trying to figure out how in the world a man could spend as much as $20.00 per day.[95]

Since the *Arizona* operated from her home base in Los Angeles Harbor year in and year out, the men followed particular routines when they went on liberty. The *Arizona* almost always anchored in the harbor, and crew members rode either the ship's own motor launches or commercial water taxis to get back and forth between ship and shore. Liberty boats followed a regular schedule, with the result that men went ashore as part of a liberty party, lined up and inspected by the officer of the deck before they climbed down the gangway into the boat.

In fact, the *Arizona* typically had two officers of the deck while she was anchored. The one on the starboard side was the more senior of the two, usually a lieutenant or lieutenant (junior grade). He greeted the distinguished visitors and rendered honors to those who rated them. The junior officer of the deck was on the port side of the quarterdeck, near the break in the deck where ladders led to the upper deck. The junior officer was in charge of keeping the motor launches running to carry enlisted men back and forth to the fleet landing. To keep track of the comings and goings of the ship's boats, the junior officer carried with him a long glass, essentially a small telescope. To this day, in-port officers of the deck in some Navy ships still carry long glasses, and the long glass is now essentially a symbol of authority, a holdover from another era when it had a more practical function.[96]

Ensign Victor Dybdal found the in-port watches to be useful training, especially when he was paired with an officer of the deck who took it upon himself to be a teacher. Dybdal learned that standards had to be enforced to be effective. Thus, if an enlisted man didn't salute properly when he got to the top of the gangway, he should be sent to the bottom of the ladder to repeat the procedure. If there was a bit of slack time in a watch, the officer of the deck pointed to various parts of the ship and asked the ensign for their names and functions. Or he might quiz him on how to handle emergencies such as a fire or man overboard. It was an effective way of training an ensign fresh from the Naval Academy to accept more responsible shipboard positions.[97]

Some of the *Arizona*'s men had families and lived in San Pedro, but the bulk of the liberty boats went to the fleet landing in Long Beach.

Below: The *Arizona* at the Puget Sound Navy Yard on 2 August 1937. A *Maryland*-class battleship is across the pier, her masts visible. (Courtesy Puget Sound Naval Shipyard)

The first thing the men encountered when they reached the landing was the Navy YMCA. Many times it served as bed and breakfast for sailors coming back from liberty. They would sleep on a pool table or a couple of chairs placed side by side. Then they would go to gospel meetings or prayer meetings, which offered free doughnuts and coffee. Bill Huckenpoehler, a seaman second class in the *Arizona*, remembered that reveille or an alarm clock was not really necessary for these men at the YMCA because "it was uncomfortable enough so you generally didn't sleep too late, and there was generally enough noise going on."

Men from various ships staked out specific bars as their turf when in the home port. The men of the *Arizona*, for instance, claimed Jack Roach's place, which was around Ninth and Main in downtown Long Beach. One night some men from the *Colorado* came in and started to push around the *Arizona* sailors who felt they owned the place. This sort of trespassing led to the inevitable fight and the equally inevitable intervention of the shore patrol. On other occasions, the combination of sailors and alcohol was a sufficiently potent one that even a minor disagreement could lead to a fight or even a brawl.[98]

To finance their liberties, the men of the *Arizona* patronized pawn shops between paydays. They might hock a peacoat, camera, or some other item of value and reclaim it the next payday for a higher amount. A peacoat was worth a loan of $3.00, and in the years before World War II that was sufficient for quite an enjoyable liberty.[99] John Amend, a seaman on board the *Arizona* in the late 1930s, expressed the problem succinctly, "You had more liberty than you had money." He was fortunate to have a low-cost alternative when he couldn't afford to hit the bars with his shipmates. He met a Long Beach family whose son had previously served in the

Right: Because the fleet spent so much time at anchor, sailors going on liberty got well acquainted with the motor launches. Here one of the *Arizona*'s boats arrives at the fleet landing in Long Beach in early 1934. Notice the tires used on the pier as fenders to protect the boats from scrapes. (Warner Brothers Archives, University of Southern California)

Arizona before being transferred to duty with the U.S. Asiatic Fleet. The family took Amend in as a sort of surrogate son while theirs was overseas, feeding him home cooking and providing him with a place to stay away from the ship.[100]

Within walking distance from the fleet landing in the *Arizona*'s home port was the Pike, a combination amusement park and honky-tonk area. There were also movies and dance halls nearby. One was the Majestic Ballroom, which sailors knew also as "Gonorrhea Racetrack." The more adventurous might catch the Pacific Electric interurban car for a ride to Los Angeles or Hollywood. A variety of women were available for dating. As Bill Huckenpoehler explained, "Of course, the further you got away from the Pike in Long Beach, the better off you were, because there were a lot of painted women that hung around the Pike: [professional ladies] or semi-professional, or gifted amateurs."[101]

Another sailor referred to some of the Pike women as "ladies of easy virtue." Their price was probably dinner and a few drinks, dinner costing perhaps seventy-five cents, and twenty-five cents being the most a sailor had to pay for a drink in that era. The end result was often pretty much the same as with full-fledged prostitutes, but these women appealed to the sailors who might feel inhibited about the procedures of a brothel. And, of course, there was at least the illusion of conquest with the women near the Pike.[102]

Some of the women were motivated by still another reason—loneliness. One *Arizona* sailor liked to go roller skating at the Pike. Young and innocent as he was, he didn't realize that some women were pickup artists, complete with a "line" to get the conversation going. One redhead began with "Where were you last night?" Her suggestion was that the young sailor had missed their scheduled date when, in fact, he had never seen her before. Her boldness attracted him, so they skated around the rink a few times, and then he accepted an invitation to go home with her. Once he was there, she got him into bed. Since he was inexperienced at sex, he didn't know what to do, but she served as a more than willing instructor. Having thus lost his virginity, the sailor soon discovered that the redhead was a wife and mother. Her two children were sleeping in another room, and her husband was at sea in a merchant ship.

Some women followed the fleet to other ports, such as San Francisco or Seattle, demonstrating considerable loyalty to particular ships. They would look for the same man time after time if he was ashore. If he had the duty on a given day, they might find (or be found by) another man.[103] Seattle had its own willing women, which made it an inviting liberty stop for the *Arizona*'s men. Said David McCafferty, who was a coxswain in the ship in the late 1930s, "The women [of Seattle] were more friendly and easily captured than in any other port that I can remember. They were as wild as the sailors. The result was we had a grand time." He attributed their eagerness to the fact that the sailors were inclined to treat the women better than the civilian men their age in the Seattle area. Much of the attraction had to do with one simple fact: the Navy men had a steady income, and many of the civilians didn't. And the sailors were willing to spend it. Joked McCafferty, "The greatest disgrace a sailor could do was to come back to the ship with money in his pocket."[104]

When liberty came to an end, the sailors at the Navy landing required a fair amount of supervision from the shore patrol. Sailors were tired, often feeling the effects of drink, and sometimes belligerent. They were eager to get back aboard ship to tumble into their hammocks and thus were impatient with waiting for the liberty launch. The potential for trouble multiplied when crew members from a number of ships were waiting at the same time. Rivalries between ships exacerbated their uncomfortable state. Sometimes it didn't take much—a slighting comment or a "my-ship-is-better-than-your-ship" attitude could lead to arguments, shoving matches, or worse. Even the order in which liberty boats came alongside the landing could be a source of dispute. The sooner the boats were loaded and on their way back to the ships, the better.[105]

As the motor launches made their way from the landing to the anchorage, heavy fog often blanketed Los Angeles Harbor. The skilled coxswain thus had to be alert for the periodic ringing of his ship's bell. From time to time a man on board the *Arizona* would strike the ship's hull number—first three gongs and then nine—to serve as a homing beacon for her boats. Expert coxswains such as Red Campbell had other methods of getting home as well. Whenever the ship got into port,

Campbell carefully logged his compass courses for each leg of a boat run for the first trip or two. He marked each heading and the amount of time he stayed on it before turning to the next one. Then, when fog did hit, he just pulled out his book and followed it like a road map.[106]

Junior officers were summoned out of their bunks to supervise the operation of the *Arizona*'s boats when fog descended at night. The coxswains still knew more about the operation of the boats, but standing watch as boat officers taught the junior officers a sense of responsibility at an early age and undoubtedly improved their seamanship skills.[107] It also made them yearn to get married. Ensign

Bill Cox discovered that the single officers were the ones called in the middle of the night to get dressed in the proper uniform and show up topside to man a boat. As he explained, "That's when the bachelors complained about the married men not only getting family allowance pay but also sleeping comfortably ashore with their wives while they were manning boat trips."[108]

When the *Arizona* was under way, either taking part in maneuvers or steaming from one port to another, her boats were stored on the boat deck, lifted there by one of the two boat cranes whose king posts were located at the break of the deck. Stationed up on the post, a crane operator had controls to position the crane and run its hook up and down. When the ship was in port, the boats were seldom lifted aboard between use. They might come aboard from time to time for maintenance and cleaning; otherwise, they stayed in the water, moored below a boat boom.

The boat booms swung out perpendicular to the ship's side when in port. When it was time to put a boat into operation for the day, the coxswain and his crew walked out the catwalk atop the boom, taking care to hold onto the handrail. The footing was a bit tricky at times, especially for the first run in the morning, when the catwalk was likely to be wet from condensed fog. Once out on the boom, the crew descended into the boat by a sea ladder and began the day's activities. At the end of the day the sequence was reversed. Maneuvering along the catwalk and walking up and down the sea ladder might have served as a sobriety test. Thus boat crews were from the day's duty section. Those coming back from liberty after a number of drinks got to go back aboard ship by climbing or being half-carried up the gangway ladder to the quarterdeck. Rather than being vertical like the ladder to the boat boom, the gangway was angled like a normal stairway.[109]

Some of the *Arizona*'s sailors tried to bring a supply of bottled happiness with them when they came back aboard. The officers of the deck dealt with the situation in different ways. The toughest were inclined to put men on report if they tried to smuggle liquor aboard, figuring that punishment was the most effective deterrent. Others took a different approach but still got the same result. As a motor launch arrived at the bottom of the gangway, a lenient officer of the deck would say in a loud voice that the boatswain's mate of the watch was to line the returning liberty party up on deck for a brief inspection. The officer then deliberately stood back from the edge of the deck so he couldn't see what happened next. Forewarned, the crew members tossed their bottles into the harbor. Since the officer hadn't seen their actions, he wasn't in position to put anyone on report; that meant he wouldn't subsequently have to spend time testifying at a captain's mast or court-martial. When the returning sailors got to the quarterdeck, the brief inspection, of course, revealed no liquor, and they were then free to go below to their quarters.[110]

Some officers seemed to enjoy putting enlisted men on report. One such was Lieutenant Cliff Janz. To Coxswain David McCafferty it appeared that Janz even provoked some of the enlisted men into doing things for which he could then put them on report and subject them to the ship's official disciplinary system. McCafferty remembered that another officer, Lieutenant (junior grade) Gordon Chung-Hoon, was upset when Janz used this approach on one of the men in Chung-Hoon's division. He had a dramatic confrontation with Janz, hitting him and knocking him down a ladder.[111]

Chung-Hoon, a man of Chinese-Hawaiian descent, was widely admired in the ship, in part because of his skill as an athlete and partly because he carried himself like a real gentleman. McCafferty felt a bond with the officer because Chung-Hoon took the trouble to learn how to play the boatswain's call. He treated enlisted men as equals rather than being condescending; obviously, the incident with Janz demonstrated Chung-Hoon's downward loyalty to the men working for him.[112]

Chung-Hoon sometimes used an enlisted man's means of discipline—the direct, physical approach—rather than the officers' method of putting someone on report. Seaman Harold McCarty learned this about Chung-Hoon firsthand one day. The seaman was chewing snuff while holystoning the deck. He spit into the waterway so that he wouldn't stain the wood. He concluded that it was all right because the waterway was essentially a deck-edge gutter, and it was hosed down regularly. Chung-Hoon concluded differently and smacked McCarty in the mouth. Even so,

McCarty didn't develop a dislike for the officer because he knew what kind of man Chung-Hoon was.[113]

Another time, Coxswain McCafferty was involved in unofficially disciplining a fellow enlisted man. In the crew were two brothers from Alabama, Daniel and Woodrow Jones. Like Lieutenant Janz, the bigger of the two was something of a bully. He had been in a fight with a baker named James Landry from Massachusetts. Jones was considerably bigger and had knocked out some of Landry's teeth. McCafferty, a New Yorker, figured he had a score to settle on behalf of his friend Landry. The site of the battle was one of the 5-inch-gun casemates. Hatches were closed and lookouts posted to prevent interference.[114]

Though weighing only about 150 pounds, McCafferty, an amateur boxer, had an advantage over the bigger man. He backed Jones up against the bulkhead in the compartment and began whaling away at his midsection with what he described as a "vitriolic hatred." Jones was a street-fighter type, accustomed to intimidating people with his size, and wasn't skillful enough to deflect McCafferty's punishing blows to the midsection. Moreover, his back was cut every time McCafferty backed him up against any sharp edges on the bulkheads. After a time Jones slumped forward onto the deck. In the manner of an ancient Roman gladiator, McCafferty turned the wounded sailor over with his foot and spit on him, making a contemptuous remark about "rebels" because of Jones's southern heritage. McCafferty had avenged Landry's beating, but the spitting convinced a number of men that McCafferty—like Jones—had a streak of meanness in him.[115]

For years, McCafferty carried a sense of shame for the way in which he had dealt with his shipmate. When he encountered his opponent after that on board ship, Jones skulked away, completely shorn of his previous bravado. McCafferty contemplated an apology but never made one.

More than forty years after the fight, McCafferty was in the theater at the *Arizona* visitors' center at Pearl Harbor, watching a film about his old ship. The camera panned down the wall of names of those killed on board the *Arizona* in December 1941. Moving alphabetically, it went first past the names of the Jones brothers and later that of the

small baker, Landry. McCafferty wept openly, perhaps tears of shame. But they had a cleansing, absolving effect, as if he had finally been forgiven after all those years for a long-ago fight on the linoleum-covered steel deck of the USS *Arizona*. McCafferty vividly remembered that moment in the darkened theater; he said, "It was like somebody just reached inside my gut and pulled out something rotten and threw it over the side."[116]

Jimmie Burcham, who was a seaman first class in the *Arizona*, used a euphemistic term for the unofficial discipline process: "making a good sailor of a man." Perhaps the best known of these remedies came for those fellows who didn't take showers or clean their clothes regularly. Burcham recalled taking one particular sailor with a bad case of body odor to the sand locker in the bow of the ship. The sand was normally used for holystoning the wooden decks, but in this case Burcham and some of his shipmates wet down the victim with salt water and then proceeded to give him the sand-and-canvas treatment.[117]

Using pieces of canvas, Burcham and cohorts rubbed sand all over the victim's body until he was red and raw—essentially sandpapered. Then they took the trainee to sick bay, where the *Arizona*'s medical officer exclaimed, "Another one?" He took out a paint brush and covered the wounded body with antiseptic, producing howls of pain. The previously offending seaman remained in sick bay for a couple of days and then returned to his division, where he was a paragon of hygiene thereafter.[118]

Burcham suggested that no one intentionally wanted to be a bad sailor, but some individuals didn't always know what they were supposed to do. Sometimes the more experienced men in a division would take a poorly performing individual into a deserted compartment and conduct some physical "instruction" to get him to see the error of his ways. At times, it happened up on deck as well. Isaac Kidd, who was embarked in the *Arizona* as a rear admiral in 1941, liked to go for daily walks on the quarterdeck. He almost invariably invited someone to go along with him so they could chat. During one of those strolls, Burcham observed a boatswain's mate first class hit a junior man who wasn't doing his job as well as expected. Kidd looked the other way, both literally and figuratively. He gazed out over the ocean rather than remonstrating with the boatswain's mate for the violence. Kidd's approach was like that of the medical officer; he didn't interfere in the domain of the petty officers. The advantage of the system, brutal though it sometimes became, was that the infractions didn't become part of the offender's official record. Burcham explained that it gave a man the opportunity to square himself away and prepare for advancement without having a black mark in his record to slow him down.[119]

One of the chores that fell to the seamen of the *Arizona* from time to time was painting the heavy anchor chains. The procedure called for washing off the links as they came up from the chain locker and then painting them before sending them back down. The seamen used a heavy, black, tarlike paint because an anchor chain that scraped against itself was bound to wear down the paint job. One day, perhaps in 1940, a seaman accidentally spattered another in the face with the paint. The victim retaliated by slapping his assailant with a paint-laden brush, and before long, one man after another was applying black makeup to someone's face. Afterward the men were busy topside with kerosene and rags for an hour or two, getting themselves cleaned up.[120]

Such horseplay was relatively rare, although one seaman named Jim McGowan seemed to revel in finding the comical aspects of routine work. For instance, if he and some other seaman were over the side in a punt to paint the side of the ship, they would contemplate out loud how they could go about scut-

Left: The job of the side cleaners was not a glamorous one. In the upper left corner is the wall of a graving dock. As the water level is lowered, men on floats and punts scrape marine growth off the part of the *Arizona*'s hull normally underwater. In the foreground, tending safety lines, are men standing on top of the antitorpedo blister. (Courtesy James A. McCain, via Lorraine Marks, *Arizona* Reunion Association)

tling the craft. Even when given the dirtiest jobs, McGowan found ways to make fun of the boatswain's mates. Tom Traylor, a fellow seaman, provided a slightly tongue-in-cheek observation of McGowan's supervisors, "Of course, they had to get rid of him, because he was a distraction. . . . Those boatswain's mates wanted to be serious. They wanted everybody to be miserable. They didn't want anybody to be happy. That was against the law."[121]

One of the first chores that fell to Seaman Second Class Jack McCarron after he reported to the *Arizona* was cleaning the paint work and shining the brightwork on the third deck. It was neither interesting nor very challenging work. The supervisor was a senior boatswain's mate who had served in the Asiatic Fleet before returning to the United States and battleship duty. He made sure that subordinates such as McCarron knew that he was in charge. As McCarron remembered, "If he wanted to work you ten hours, you worked ten hours, even if it was cleaning up what you'd already cleaned up." The young seaman was thus ripe for a change when Gunner's Mate First Class Robert Hendon approached him about striking for gunner's mate. To McCarron anything sounded better than what he was doing.[122]

To report to the sixth division, which had the 5-inch antiaircraft guns, McCarron took his gear to the division's living compartment. He approached Boatswain's Mate Sam "Bull" Sperandio, a heavyweight wrestler on the ship's team. Sperandio was turned facing away, so McCarron tapped him on the shoulder to get his attention. Sperandio wheeled around and hit the seaman, knocking him against a row of lockers some ten feet away. There he sat, slightly dazed, with tears in his eyes—shocked by the rude response to his attempt to get the big boatswain's mate's attention. That was when McCarron discovered that one did not touch a petty officer—not even lightly.[123]

Coxswain Red Campbell observed that Sperandio walked around with his shoulders jutting out, as if to advertise his prowess. He and Sperandio went into a beer joint on San Francisco's Market Street one night. A fight started and the police came. They took Sperandio out and handcuffed him to a light pole for safekeeping until things cooled off.

Sperandio told one of the policemen that if he were released, he would go back to the ship and wouldn't cause any trouble. So the policeman opened the cuffs, whereupon the big petty officer knocked him out. He said to Campbell, "That stupid so-and-so. He ain't got no business being a cop, has he?" The two then returned to the *Arizona*, and the matter was never brought up again.[124]

Since she was so badly damaged during the first hour of U.S. participation in World War II, the *Arizona* could not contribute much directly to the war effort. Her indirect contributions to the war are harder to document but real nonetheless. She trained one generation of Navy men and part of another for the war to come. Some of her first officers from 1916 were still on active duty when the war began. The first executive officer, Claude Bloch, for instance, was Commandant of the 14th Naval District at Pearl Harbor in 1941. The first gunnery officer, Walter Stratton Anderson, was Commander Battleships Battle Force. Others of her officers down through the years played prominent roles in the naval war against Germany and Japan: Chester Nimitz, Arleigh Burke, Alan Kirk, Mel Pride, John Ballentine, and Don Moon, to name a few.

Although there were few battleship-versus-battleship gunnery duels during the war, guns were used constantly in combat. Many enlisted men learned their business—in the *Arizona*'s gunnery department and throughout the ship—in the years before the war and used those skills to advantage from 1941 to 1945. Many of the *Arizona*'s Depression-era enlisted men were so capable that they served as commissioned officers during the war. From 1931 to 1941 the *Arizona* and her men went about their business as the operating and overhaul schedules dictated. Their naval service was in many ways different from that experienced in today's electronics, missile, and computer Navy. Some things were the same because seamanship, leadership, and discipline are still important and still require many of the same skills now as then. The bygone Navy is worth documenting as a means of comparison with where we are today. The attack on Pearl Harbor ended more than peace; it also ended the prewar way of life.

7 LAST YEARS OF PEACE

July 1934–December 1941

Evergreen-clad hills provided the backdrop as Warner Brothers completed filming its movie during the *Arizona*'s three-month overhaul at Bremerton in mid-1934. The most visible change during the overhaul itself was the installation of an airplane crane at the stern. It replaced a straight pole with pulleys on it, much like a cargo boom on a merchant ship. Lifting a plane from the sea with the boom had required numerous sailors on deck to heave around on lines. The new dogleg crane was made of metal and powered by electricity, thus requiring considerably less manpower. The crane also had a heavier lifting capacity than the boom—6,000 pounds compared with 4,500 for the boom—permitting the use of heavier floatplanes in the future.[1] The overhaul was the ship's most extensive since the modernization completed in 1931 at Norfolk.[2] The *Arizona* frequently received the services of more than one thousand shipyard workers during the course of a working day. One day in July the number of workers on board the ship was 1,402.[3]

After the overhaul was done and sea trials over, the ship left for southern California to pick up her airplanes and then rejoin the fleet for operations. At 2:20 in the morning of 26 July the *Arizona* was plowing through the black waters near Cape Flattery, where the Strait of Juan de Fuca meets the Pacific Ocean. Her voyage got an abrupt interruption when she collided with the fishing boat *Umatilla*, which was being towed by another vessel. The other boat, the *Emblem*, was lighted, but the *Umatilla* apparently was not, and the *Arizona* hit her on the starboard quarter.

Following the impact, the battleship beamed her 36-inch searchlights down and put a boat in the water to render assistance. One of those who went along was Seaman Don McKinney,

a member of the duty lifeboat crew. When the lifeboat drew near the damaged *Umatilla*, as he recalled, "All you could see was masts above water. And every time we got close enough to the fishing boat, those guys looked like they wanted to jump over and tear us apart or something." That was an understandable reaction. Two members of the *Umatilla*'s crew were lost as a result of the accident.[4]

The *Arizona* resumed her journey south, but she didn't get far, for a radio dispatch directed her to turn around and steam to Seattle for a court of inquiry into the collision. The officer who conducted the inquiry was Captain Frank H. Sadler, commanding officer of the battleship *Pennsylvania*. The court of inquiry recommended that the *Arizona*'s commanding officer, Captain Macgillivray Milne, be court-martialed as a result of the accident. Once the investigation was over, it was time for the *Arizona* to hustle to the East Coast, where the rest of the fleet was operating that summer. Usually the ship steamed in company with other battleships, but this time the *Arizona* proceeded alone. To help break up some of the boredom of the long trip, the crew members turned to sunbathing. Turret tops and wooden decks became popular areas for soaking up the sun.[5]

When the ship had a stopover in Panama, both officers and enlisted men went ashore to find their own versions of pleasure. Ensigns Jack Arnold and Rufus Taylor were among the junior officers who went on liberty there. Taylor, who in later years studied the Japanese language and became the Director of Naval Intelligence, had a keen mind and sometimes carefree spirit. In Panama, as in other places, Taylor was broke, so he asked if they could split Arnold's $20.00. Their path took them to a gambling den, where Arnold's lack of both luck and skill soon deprived him of a

Right: Captain Macgillivray Milne commanded the *Arizona* from September 1933 to December 1934. His tenure ended not long after he was found guilty in a general court-martial. (Frank Meech Collection, USS *Arizona* Memorial, National Park Service)

chunk of his remaining $10.00. When he found Taylor, who had disappeared for a while, Arnold said, "Hey, let's go. I've lost almost half my money in here."

"You just keep right on rolling."

Arnold did so, and the snake eyes kept coming up. Then Taylor returned from another trip around the room and said to him, "Okay, now let's go." At that point, Taylor pulled out a wad of bills totaling $120.00 and peeled off half of it for the crapped-out crapshooter.

"Where the hell did you get that?" asked the incredulous Arnold.

"Look, you are probably the worst crap-shooter in the world. I've been betting against you ever since you've been rolling."[6]

During her Atlantic venture, after passing through the canal, the *Arizona* had evaporator problems, so the crew members were limited to half a bucket of fresh water per day. When a rainsquall appeared on the horizon, the ship steered toward it so the men could go out on deck for showers.

As the ship performed target practice, one of the 5-inch broadside guns got stuck into position and couldn't be trained horizontally. So, after having spent all that time in the Puget Sound Navy Yard, the ship headed up the East River to the New York Navy Yard. In a change from the old days, the ship now had a hinged topmast that could be lowered to pass under the Brooklyn Bridge.

The stay in New York was brief, and then the ship headed south. Shortly after noon on 8 September, while off the coast of New Jersey, the *Arizona* maneuvered into position to stand by in the general vicinity of the passenger ship *Morro Castle*, which was in serious trouble. The liner was burning furiously as the result of an arsonist's work, but the battleship could be of no help as the wind and sea increased in force, rain fell steadily, and the visibility was poor. In fact, the *Arizona* had plenty of troubles of her own. The storm broke the port gangway loose from its lashings on deck, and it stove in the main float of one of the ship's observation planes. While Seaman First Class Y. H. Williams was working on one of the 5-inch broadside guns on the starboard side, a huge wave washed him far aft and deposited him on the quarterdeck, one level lower. He went down to sick bay to get a shot of medicinal alcohol as part of the recovery process. Williams was joined there by six marines who suffered cuts and bruises while rigging the shutters on the same gun.[7]

While she was at the shipyard, the *Arizona* had picked up a gleaming new admiral's barge for Rear Admiral Samuel W. Bryant, the embarked Commander of Battleship Division Two. During the trip south from New York, the heavy seas threw green water and spray as far up as the bridge and boat deck and bashed in the beautiful admiral's barge. The waves also knocked out the centering pins that held the 5-inch antiaircraft guns in position, allowing them to rotate back and forth in response to succeeding cascades of water. Shutters protecting the broadside guns weren't stout enough to hold out the seas in some cases, so water was sloshing back and forth inside the casemates. Water even got down inside the turrets.[8]

The *Arizona* proceeded south to the Caribbean, taking part in battle problems along the way. On 1 October, when the battleship was at Guantanamo, Captain Milne was put under arrest and confined to his quarters. The executive officer, Commander Andrew Denney, took temporary command because the captain was being court-martialed for the July collision with the fishing boat. The trial was conducted with considerable solemnity, including some touches from the old Navy. As the court got under way, the *Arizona* fired a one-gun salute and raised the union jack at the starboard yardarm. Milne stayed in his cabin under the fantail for more than a week, except when court was in session. On 9 October the trial was finally over. Captain Milne was released from arrest and restored to duty when the verdict was in. For the sinking of the *Umatilla*, he was found guilty of culpable inefficiency in the performance of duty and sentenced to lose three seniority numbers in his grade of captain.[9] Milne's penalty was light because of his fine previous record.

In December Captain George Baum relieved Milne as commanding officer. Afterward, the deposed skipper and his Filipino steward were taken ashore. Milne had been dealt with by the Navy's justice system, and the result was a blot on his record. The officer of the deck bid him adieu, but that was about it. To Fireman John Clunie, who observed the scene, his former commanding officer had the demeanor of a fugitive from justice. In fact, Milne had been dealt with by the Navy's justice system, and the blow was a severe one. The commanding officer bears the responsibility for incidents such as collisions and groundings. Now Milne was a former commanding officer.[10] He went on to serve in the Navy billet of governor of Guam but was not selected for promotion to flag rank before his retirement.

Along with learning about gambling, Ensign Jack Arnold was getting his feet wet in the business of being a naval officer. That meant supplementing his Naval Academy

education with practical knowledge. It fell to the experienced petty officers of the fleet to indoctrinate young officers such as Arnold, hazing them but being careful not to go too far because the officers, despite being new, outranked them. Arnold, who was in the academy's class of 1934, eventually became a four-star admiral. That, however, was far in the future when a gunner's mate sought to teach him about the handling of projectiles down in the bowels of turret four. The petty officer said that one of the things the turret crew had to do was move the projectiles from one side of the handling room to the other. Arnold looked around for a crane and, seeing none, observed, "That must be one hell of a job."

The sailor said, "No, it isn't much of a job. Don't they teach you that at the Naval Academy?"

Arnold said, "No, as a matter of fact, they didn't."

"There's nothing to it. Go on. You can move them over there."

"No," Arnold said, "I'd rather see you move them over there."

Right: By the mid-1930s, the *Arizona*'s scout planes were an improved version of the O3U Corsair, with a cowling around the cylinders of the radial engine to reduce drag. Here the observation plane is being lifted back aboard ship following a flight. (Courtesy Edward P. Lee)

Below: The *Arizona* steams past a support tower for the San Francisco–Oakland Bay Bridge during its construction in late 1934. (National Archives, 80-G-1021394)

So the sailor went over and took a 1,400-pound projectile by the nose and pulled it toward him. He got it rocking a little bit and then took it with one hand and walked it across the steel deck. Then the petty officer said, "Okay, you do one of them." As Arnold discovered, it wasn't that difficult, but it did require some care. If a man pulled the shell too far over, it would fall to the deck. Restoring it then to an upright position was a good-sized job. That was Arnold's first indoctrination in the lower handling room. He would learn much more during his time on board the *Arizona*.[11]

One of Arnold's Naval Academy classmates was Second Lieutenant Victor "Brute" Krulak, who had chosen to make his career in the Marine Corps. While serving on board the *Arizona*, the feisty Krulak discovered that he didn't always see eye to eye with Captain Theodore H. Cartwright, the commanding officer of the ship's marine detachment. The gunnery sergeant of the detachment was Walter Holzworth, whom Krulak greatly respected. Holzworth was always willing to give Krulak advice when he asked for it, so the lieutenant said, "Gunny, I want to make a success of this profession. Tell me how to get along with the captain."

He said, "It's real easy, Lieutenant. Just find out what the old son of a bitch wants and give it to him."

Years later, Krulak remembered, "I never forgot that advice. And you'll find Holzworth's name on that white tablet out there at Pearl Harbor. He went down with the *Arizona*."[12]

After the addition of a catapult atop turret three in the early 1930s, the *Arizona* was even better equipped than before to operate floatplanes. Getting them into the air was an exciting experience for those in the aircraft. A powder charge sent the catapult car careening down the track and hurled the plane into the air. The aircraft went from a dead standstill to flying speed in a second or two, which could come as a surprise to the unready.

While the pilot flew each O3U-3 Corsair, an observer rode behind him. One observer was Ensign William Cox, who delighted in the fact that riding in the back seat of the Corsair earned him flight pay, even though he wasn't a naval aviator. In addition to the hazards involved in getting shot off the ship and then brought back aboard, there was also sometimes the problem of finding the ship. Particularly memorable was one day when the *Arizona* was anchored near Santa Barbara Island. When the plane got back from its training mission, the pilot and Cox discovered that the anchorage was covered by a fog bank that extended only about 100 feet off the water, so they could see the tops of the masts of the various battleships.[13]

Cox reported to the *Arizona* by radio that the fog ended about two miles east of the ship and arranged for a rendezvous. Then they flew east and waited. The edge of the fog was so abrupt that the battleship emerged from it just as a person might go from dense jungle into a clearing. Cox described it: "As we were flying overhead, we could clearly see the bow of the ship emerging from the fog bank while the stern was still completely hidden." The water was calm, so the plane landed in normal fashion and was picked up by the crane, only somewhat delayed by the weather.[14]

When an airplane finished its mission, it was recovered at sea through what was known as the cast method, "Cast" being used to represent the letter C in the phonetic alphabet of the time. If there was any chop on the water at all, the helmsman put the rudder over so that the *Arizona* would, as Jack Arnold described it, "knock the tops of the waves off, so that you had about a minute and a half to land the thing in the slick." The pilot approached into the wind, dropped down onto the water, and then caught hold of a cargo net trailed behind the ship. The float at the bottom of the plane had a retractable hook that grabbed the net.

The plane was then hauled near the ship, and the hook from the fantail crane or one of the boat cranes came down above the plane. Then the man in the rear seat had to get out of the cockpit and attach the hook to the plane so it could be hoisted back onto the catapult. With some practice, it became a fairly routine operation. It did require a considerable degree of cooperation on the part of the conning officer, the pilot, the crane operator, and the rear-seat man. Operation of the planes was done almost exclusively in daylight.[15]

While the ship's planes were in the air, they communicated with the *Arizona* via radio, using a Morse code key, not voice. They transmitted spotting and scouting data with the code and, in turn, received their orders

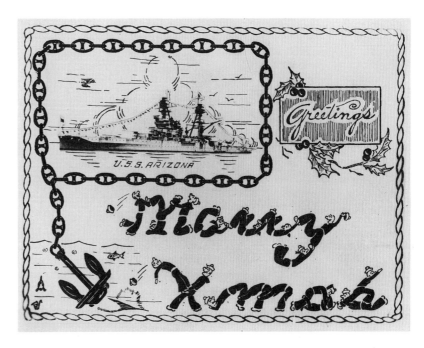

that way. It was a time when naval officers were expected to be a good deal more proficient in Morse code than they are today. As a matter of fact, Ensign Rod Badger thought it was silly to insist that an officer had to handle the communications on board the ship, rather than letting an enlisted radioman do it. Thinking and working in Morse code constituted the essence of the radioman's job, day in and day out, whereas it was only a fraction of an officer's job. The rationale for the rule that officers operate the circuit apparently was that officers were somehow more reliable. Explained Badger, "There was something holy about rank, I guess."[16]

In the summer of 1935 Rear Admiral George T. Pettengill embarked in the *Arizona* as Commander Battleship Division Two. He was an irascible fellow. Knowing his reputation as a nitpicker, Captain Baum and Commander Sam Payne, the executive officer, determined that the admiral's quarters would be perfect. The area where President Hoover had lived several years earlier was cleaned, painted, and polished. Even so, the newly arrived admiral blew his top when he saw his accommodations. The recipient of his wrath was Commander Payne. Payne, normally a most mild-mannered gentleman, was still feeling the sting of the admiral's comments when he stepped out of the cabin and encountered Boatswain's Mate Carll Gleason. "You know," exclaimed the commander, "that son of a bitch doesn't like what we did in his quarters." The reaction amazed Gleason because he didn't realize that senior officers talked that way about other senior officers. The longer Pettengill stayed, the less amazement there was about his unpleasantness, which became commonplace.[17]

One afternoon the admiral was taking a nap when two sailors were standing in a punt to repaint the *Arizona*'s waterline. It was a warm day in Los Angeles Harbor, and there was a slight chop on the water. Since the men weren't up on deck under the direct supervision of a boatswain's mate, they were goofing off. Their game was to try to get the punt's gunwale caught under the ship's scupper as it rolled. They figured this would upset the punt, and they would get a swim. When they ended up in the water, they started laughing and making noise. Soon the telephone rang up on the quarterdeck for Second Lieutenant Krulak, the officer of the deck. The caller was Admiral Pettengill, who ordered, "Come down to my cabin right away." So Krulak went down, and, as he remembered, "He just bawled the hell out of me. I didn't tell them to turn over the punt."[18]

In addition to skylarking seamen, another thorn in the admiral's side that day was At'em, the little terrier that was the *Arizona*'s mascot. After Pettengill had bawled out Krulak, he left his cabin for a while, and when he came back, he found the dog on his bunk. The telephone rang on the quarterdeck, the admiral calling for Krulak again. When the lieutenant showed up, Pettengill growled, "Get that goddamn dog off of my bed, and I don't want to ever see him in the admiral's country again." Krulak took the dog and dragged him up the ladder by his collar to the quarterdeck and had a sailor hide him for the time being. As soon as his watch was over, Krulak went to Lieutenant Commander Donald Mackey, the ship's first lieutenant, and told him, "We've got a problem with the admiral and the dog. The dog likes the admiral, but the admiral doesn't like the dog." Mackey said he would take care of it. Since the crew was crazy about the dog, Mackey and the enlisted men managed to find ways to keep him out of Pettengill's sight as long as the admiral remained on board.[19]

In May 1936 the U.S. Fleet gathered in the vicinity of Panama to stage Fleet Problem

Right: The *Arizona* dry-docked at Hunters Point in San Francisco in the spring of 1935. (USS *Arizona* Memorial, National Park Service, PR-60)

XVII. Seaman Mike Baccala, newly reported to the ship from boot camp, had a much different perspective on the fleet problem than did the ship's officers, who were concerned about the *Arizona*'s tactical performance. In those days before air-conditioning, Baccala and some of his shipmates slept on the upper deck to get some relief from the Caribbean heat. One night he was awakened by a mock war in progress. The battleship *California* was attacked by a submarine and cruiser, and then the *Arizona*—somewhat tardily to Baccala's observation—turned on her searchlights to simulate gunfire. Soon the "enemy" ships disappeared into a smoke screen. He went back to sleep and then was again awakened about 3:00 or so in the morning when the *Arizona* pretended to shoot at a formation of ships in the distance. The seaman couldn't tell whether the *Arizona*'s fleet was winning or losing, but the whole mock war looked exciting to him, like an adventure movie.[20]

The war games continued, and then, after having been a number of years without an equator-crossing initiation, the *Arizona* had one on 19 May 1936. Some of the *Arizona*'s crew members felt that Admiral Joseph M.

"Billy Goat" Reeves, Commander in Chief U.S. Fleet, who was about to retire, just wanted to see one more initiation because he took the fleet some distance out of the way to have the ships cross the line.

As per tradition, the men of the *Arizona*'s crew were charged with various fictitious offenses, sent to kiss the toe of King Neptune, and then directed to various punishment areas. Fireman Charles Hughlett was put onto an "operating table," a ship's mess table covered with a sheet of copper. Before Hughlett was blindfolded, a "surgeon" showed him a large knife to be used for the "operation." Unbeknownst to the fireman, the knife was hooked to a hand-cranking telephone that had magnetos to produce a current of electricity. The "surgeon" and his helpers squirted brine onto Hughlett's bare torso to increase its conductivity, and then drew the dull side of the knife across him while applying the electricity. As Hughlett put it, "I thought I was cut from one end to the other. . . . Oh, that was an awful sensation."[21]

Seaman Baccala was put into a dentist's chair, and when he tried to escape about ten men held him down. One of them squirted into his mouth a mixture of salt, soap, and water. Baccala had by then acquired a rough sailor's vocabulary, so in a sense he was getting the old childhood treatment of having his mouth washed out with soap. He got the knife-across-the-belly treatment and was hit by a rotten egg, hit with clubs a few times, and then dunked into the ocean while suspended from the aircraft crane at the stern. After he was hoisted out, he was put in something like a straitjacket and made to crawl through a canvas tunnel. Finally, he was a shellback. When the whole experience was over, he wrote in his diary, "Today we crossed the line at 8 A.M. & boy was it a lot of fun."[22]

For many of the initiates, the finale involved being dunked not in the ocean but in a tank built of wood and canvas and filled with water. After they had gone through the other parts of the initiation, pollywogs were told that they would be done as soon as they could say, "I'm a shellback." Seaman John Pfeifer discovered that those who were already shellbacks tried to prolong the initiation by pushing a pollywog underwater when he tried to get the words out. He also observed during the initiation that those who were considered wise guys seemed to receive more harassment than the rest of their pollywog shipmates, especially if they were senior to those dishing out the punishment.[23]

One of the reasons for the constant drilling of the *Arizona*'s gun mounts and turrets was to enable men to respond quickly and correctly in the event of an emergency. They practiced things so many times that their reactions were second nature. An example came on 24 July 1936. The *Arizona* was involved in spotting practice for the main battery that morning. After one salvo went on its way, the breeches of the guns in turret two were in the process of being opened for reloading. The first motion of rotating the breech plug blew compressed air into each barrel to clear out the remaining combustion gases from the previous round, along with any remaining embers from the silk powder bags. When the breech of the right gun was pulled open, bore gases came back into the gun chamber, expanded, and burst into flame. In gunnery parlance, it was a flareback.

Seaman First Class Harry Stoll was serving as a tray man in back of the gun. He was burned—painfully but not seriously. The turret officer saw the sheet of flame and dense

Right: This beautiful starboard broadside view of the *Arizona* dates from September 1935. Notice the canvas curtains in place to protect the 5-inch/51 broadside guns. (U.S. Navy photo, USN 423360, U.S. Naval Institute Collection)

smoke from his booth behind the guns, so he activated the turret's sprinkling system. Down below, others turned on sprinklers in the ammunition-handling area and played hoses on the powder in the hoist. Once the fire was out, the sprinklers were turned off, but the water kept coming for another ten or fifteen seconds because sediment in the piping prevented the valves from working properly. Chief Turret Captain Walter C. Ebel finally shut off the valve and got the water stopped. By that time, water from the gun chamber had seeped down into the electric deck below and shorted out the main power panel for the

turret. Soon the turret officer got the word, "Fire on the electric deck." He called the distribution room on the telephone and had all electrical power to the turret shut off. Firefighters were then able to put the blaze out easily.

Turret two was done firing for the day, but the trouble was not over. Rear Admiral Claude C. Bloch, who was embarked as Commander Battleship Division Two, convened a board of investigation. The unanimous testimony of those in the turret was that the gas-ejection system was turned on when the plug was opened and remained open until

the chamber and bore were clear of fire and smoke. The turret officer believed that a strong relative wind, combined with pressure produced about the same time by the firing of nearby turret one, forced the residue gas back down into the turret.

Admiral Bloch refused to accept the conclusions of the board he appointed. He argued that the flareback could not have occurred if the gas-ejection system was working properly, even at a pressure as low as 50 pounds per square inch, compared with the normal pressure of 150. Therefore, he concluded that the ejection air had been turned off "either accidentally or otherwise." The gas-ejection system activated automatically; a crew member had to touch the system's trigger to turn it off. Bloch believed a crew member turned it off before the bore was actually clear. Fortunately, the men had reacted as they were supposed to when the flareback occurred, and for the most part, the system worked. There was no turret explosion. Sprinklers were turned on, and the series of flameproof interlocks between the magazines and the turret kept the fire from spreading to the powder train.[24] Much of the credit for keeping the problem from being worse belonged to Chief Turret Captain Ebel. He served in the ship until he was killed on board in December 1941.

One incident that took place in the mid-1930s spoke volumes about the aging *Arizona*'s inadequacy in antiaircraft gunnery. As usual, the ship had observers on board to serve as umpires for her performance. Ensign Dave McClintock was operating the port director for the battery of 5-inch/25-caliber guns on that side of the ship.

Right: A fleet searchlight display, common for the era, on Navy Day 1935 at San Pedro, California. (Photograph by R. F. McGraw, U.S. Naval Institute Collection)

The fire-control system of the era was adequate for tracking a bomber approaching the ship in a horizontal line. The visual range finder used its split-image system to determine the slant range to the target—that is, the actual distance rather than the distance between the ship and an imaginary line drawn to sea level below the airplane. Two enlisted range-finder operators worked with the vertically oriented equipment, constantly keeping it on target. One operator would call out "Mark," and the other transmitted the range to the director. The job required a degree of concentration, especially during a sustained firing, because the range-finder operators had to do their work for upcoming shots while the noisy 5-inch guns were banging away not far below.[25]

After McClintock had inserted a series of range readings into the director, it was able to

ascertain the speed of the plane and provide a fuze setting for the 5-inch projectiles, based on the plane's anticipated flight path. The projectiles were then inserted into fuze pots on the left side of each gun mount; the fuze setting programmed the projectiles to explode a certain number of seconds after firing. If all went well, the director's prediction would coincide with the fuze setting, and the projectile would explode and spew shrapnel when the airplane reached that slant range from the ship.

The system didn't work very well when a dive-bomber, rather than high-level bomber, was approaching the *Arizona*. The director couldn't respond quickly enough because the speed of approach was too fast. As the antiaircraft portion of one particular exercise progressed, Ensign McClintock watched in futility as carrier dive-bombers zoomed in toward the *Arizona*. The guns were pointed upward but were not really following the approaching planes. The ship's executive officer at the time was Commander Mervyn S. Bennion. Bennion called to McClintock and asked, "Why aren't those guns moving?"

The ensign replied, "We can't handle this kind of an attack with this director."

Bennion told him, "Well, get them moving. We've got the umpires on board. They're looking at us."

McClintock emphasized that Commander Bennion was highly admired on board the *Arizona*, but he was forced to operate within the system then in existence. Because of the competitive grading, form was often as important as substance—or perhaps more so. Even if the equipment wasn't capable, the crew had to appear to be doing something. It was a problem all too common in the prewar fleet.[26]

Just about annually the *Arizona* went to the Puget Sound Navy Yard at Bremerton, Washington, for repairs and overhaul. The ship was in the yard at Bremerton when one of her airplanes came to an untimely end on 9 July 1937. Aviation Cadet Bruce Harwood, one of a new breed of not-yet-commissioned pilots, was flying an O3U-3 biplane when it was caught by a sudden wind that plunged it five hundred feet into Puget Sound. Seaman First Class William H. Meyers, who was riding in the plane as a passenger, was killed. Harwood was injured, suffering a broken nose, cuts, and severe shock. As the wreckage of the aircraft floated on the water near Seattle, the semiconscious Harwood held onto one of the wings. He was rescued by two local civilians. They dove repeatedly beneath the water to pull Meyers out. He apparently died of a skull fracture or broken neck rather than drowning. As one of the rescuers, D. R. Burns, told a reporter, "His body was so limp—it seemed that not one bone was whole." Harwood was delirious during the trip ashore, still struggling as if to free himself from the airplane, but he recovered and later compiled an excellent record in World War II.[27]

Unusually stormy seas marked the *Arizona*'s trip to Hawaii in March 1938. Normal protection for those who lived in the casemates for the 5-inch broadside guns came in the form of canvas coverings to keep out sea spray and relatively small waves. The first of the rough weather hit with little warning. The men reinforced the canvas covers with lumber for greater protection, but one night an especially big wave pushed its way in, shoving aside both lumber and canvas. One man was spun around so tightly in his hammock that he needed help getting out.[28]

The canvas coverings were clearly inadequate, so the crew initiated heavy-weather precautions. When the ship expected heavier seas, the sailors rigged metal shutters to seal off the openings in the casemates. The barrels of the guns still stuck out through the horizontal slots, and the shutters were bolted in place around them. The shutters were sufficiently stout that they required three men to lift and bolt them in place. They had rubber gaskets around the edges to form a watertight seal.[29] Seaman Harold McCarty, protected with a lifeline lashing him to a stanchion, was part of a group trying to dog one of the heavy shutters into place. During the effort a large wave slammed him against a bulkhead and broke one of his ribs. It was like the injuries inflicted on crew members when the *Arizona* steamed off the New Jersey coast in September 1934.[30]

Fireman Harold Gasmann had a chance to look out at times and watch the effects of the heavy seas on other battleships traveling in

Below: This picture was taken on 14 February 1936 to record changes accomplished during the just-completed overhaul at Puget Sound Navy Yard. Most noticeable is the lengthening of the smokestack, presumably to lessen the effect of stack gases on personnel in the superstructure. (Courtesy Puget Sound Naval Shipyard)

company with the *Arizona*. Normally, they were as steady as rocks because of their stout construction and deep draft. Now they were tossing around like chips. Looking aft, Gasmann could see a ship pitching so much that a substantial portion of her keel was exposed when her bow surged out of the water. When he looked at the ships ahead of the *Arizona*, he could often see all four propellers spinning in the air while the stern was out of the water and the bow buried.[31]

Seaman Cletus Schroeder had an underway watch station in the maintop, more than one hundred feet above the water. Getting up and down for watches was no fun when the ship was rolling heavily and the wind was blowing a gale. During one climb, Schroeder lost his footing on the spray-soaked rungs. He held on for dear life with his hands and felt somewhat like a flag fluttering in the breeze. Eventually he was able to reach back and wrap his leg around the tripod leg to secure himself, and then he gradually made his way up. He got into the maintop and began recovering his composure. About five minutes after he got there, another man arrived, his jaw quivering with fright because of what he also had been through. Normally, one man's misfortune might be the subject of some ribbing from his shipmates, but that day nobody in the maintop laughed at anybody.[32]

In the summer of that year, while the *Arizona* was at the navy yard in Bremerton for her annual overhaul, two men from the Bureau of Construction and Repair in Washington visited the ship. Captain A. W. Brown, skipper since the previous December, gave them a set of photos taken during the *Arizona*'s stormy voyage to Hawaii. The photos showed the degree to which heavy seas overflowed the stern of the ship. Walking on deck was difficult, if not impossible, and the seas had thrown the captain's gig out of its storage skids. On a brighter note, the ship's new mushroom-shaped, waterproof ventilator hoods—installed during the 1929–31 modernization—worked effectively, so crew members below had a continuous supply of air, even in rough weather. The new-construction battleships of the 1940s were built with flush decks, not with the stern a deck lower than the forecastle as in the *Arizona*.

One of the visitors afterward wrote a letter that showed that the *Arizona* was still

operating in a time when the visual sighting of targets was essential. He discussed arrangements for combined antiaircraft directors and range finders. Certainly it would be a step forward from manually inserting an aircraft's visual range into the equation for setting the fuzes on projectiles. But it still didn't have the speed and accuracy that were achieved in the

Above: A pool constructed of lumber and canvas is used to initiate pollywogs when crossing the equator on 20 May 1936. (Courtesy Edward P. Lee)

Left: The *Tennessee* and *Arizona* are silhouetted during their cruise to Hawaii in mid-1936. (U.S. Navy photo in U.S. Naval Institute Collection)

Above: The left side of a 5-inch antiaircraft gun has the fuze pots for setting the time between the firing and the detonation of the projectiles. The three black dials near the rear of the mount are for setting the time. Farther forward on the mount is the pair of handwheels used by the mount's pointer for elevating and lowering the barrel. He uses the wheels to match a signal sent from the director. (Special Collections, University of Arizona Library, 71-1-191)

following decade when antiaircraft directors were equipped with fire-control radar. (The *Arizona*'s combined range finder-directors, with no radar, had been in place only about a year when the ship was hit in December 1941. The Japanese planes were too close for the directors to be effective.)

Visibility was still a key to the fire-control problem for the 14-inch guns as well. One of the *Arizona*'s visitors had been on board the *Maryland* during an exercise at sea and noted the difficulty in determining the course of a *New Mexico*–class battleship when she was hull-down at sea—that is, with the hull below the horizon so that only the superstructure could be seen from a distance. When the *New Mexico* and her sisters *Idaho* and *Mississippi* were modernized in the early 1930s, their cage masts were removed and replaced by a single bridge and fire-control structure forward. From a distance, the heading of such a ship was not so readily determined as it was for the bulk of interwar battleships— including the *Arizona*—that had the twin foremast-mainmast arrangement. The advantage of the *Arizona*'s setup was that it provided a second high-level observation point. Once radar came into use, it could be

used to determine the course of an enemy ship, and visual observation was no longer essential.[33]

Near the end of June 1938 the Board of Inspection and Survey issued a report on a thorough material inspection of the ship, conducted 20–23 June at Bremerton. The board's finding indicated the degree to which Depression economy measures limited the operating schedule for the ships of the Battleship Force. In the 1936–37 fiscal year the *Arizona* was at anchor 267 days and under way 98 days and steamed 15,526 miles. For the fiscal year just ending, she would spend 255 days anchored and 110 days under way and would steam 20,234 miles.[34]

Early on the morning of 7 September 1938 the *Arizona* lost her skipper. Captain Brown died of a heart attack in a hotel in Long Beach. His funeral service was held on the fantail of the ship he had commanded. The service drew a large crowd of senior officers, who kept the side boys on the quarterdeck busy saluting as they came aboard in their formal uniforms, including fore-and-aft hats and long coats. Ensign Charles Dodds observed that the quaint-looking hats appeared to ride higher on the heads of the senior officers than on those of juniors. He concluded either that the hats shrank with the passage of time or else that officers' heads got bigger with each promotion.[35]

For many in the crew, it was an emotional moment. However, not all of the ship's men had a chance to pause and mourn the passing of the captain. Ship's Cook Ralph Byard knew that life must go on. While the funeral was in progress, he was in the *Arizona*'s galley, frying scallops for the next meal.[36]

The ship's executive officer took command temporarily, and then the *Arizona* got a new commanding officer, Captain Isaac C. Kidd. He reported to the battleship from Newport, Rhode Island, where he had been at the Naval War College. His son and namesake, Admiral Isaac C. Kidd, Jr., explained that there were three courses of study at the war college, the junior course, the senior course, and the "senile course." The latter was kind of a holding tank for senior officers who had completed the official course and were marking time while waiting for orders. It was also a ready source of qualified officers for just the sort of emergency that had developed in the *Arizona*.[37]

Captain Kidd had previously served as a detailer in the Bureau of Navigation, the agency within the Navy Department that assigned officers. Probably through that connection, Kidd had been slated for command of the fleet's newest battleship, the USS *West Virginia*, armed with 16-inch guns. He got the *Arizona* instead and soon developed great affection for her. He liked the ship's spirit he encountered but was disappointed that her sports teams were on the downswing because he was a great devotee of physical fitness and athletics.

Below: Tai Sing Loo frequently used palm trees as props when photographing warships. This is the *Arizona* at Pearl Harbor in 1936. (Courtesy Evelyn Lee)

Right: Range clocks—this one on the mainmast—were used to communicate shooting ranges in the era before voice radio was common. The two hands indicate thousands and hundreds of yards so that individuals on board other ships can observe with binoculars. The range clocks were known officially as concentration dials. (Courtesy Garland Fordyce)

Below: The *Arizona*, left, leads a column of battleships under the nearly completed Golden Gate Bridge in late 1936. The others are the *Nevada*, *Maryland*, and *Texas*. The sections of roadway have nearly met in the center. (Naval Historical Center, NH 95911)

He soon sought help in beefing up the quality of the *Arizona*'s team. Buzz Borries was gone, so Kidd got in touch with Rip Miller, assistant football coach at the Naval Academy, and asked about prospects. One officer who was assigned to the ship as a result of this contact was Lieutenant (junior grade) Gordon Chung-Hoon, a native of Hawaii and a talented football player at Annapolis. He also wound up as the coach of the team. Others Kidd picked up were a marine officer, Second Lieutenant Martin C. "Moose" Stewart, who had been an all-American center at Louisiana State, and Ensign Ulmont "Monty" Whitehead, captain of the Naval Academy's baseball team. These men became the nucleus of the ship's teams and were about all that Kidd could get away with because there was a limit on how many college men could get into a game at the same time. Whitehead died in the *Arizona* in December 1941; Chung-Hoon survived; Stewart was detached before the attack.[38]

On the same day that Captain Kidd took command, the *Arizona* got a new flag officer as well. Rear Admiral Chester Nimitz took over Battleship Division One. On board the *Arizona* Nimitz demonstrated the same qualities that were noted throughout his career. He preferred to make a point gently rather than taking a heavy-handed approach. One exam-

ple of his method occurred when he was the inspecting officer for one Saturday morning's personnel inspection. When the admiral got to Ensign Victor Dybdal's division, he asked the men to pull up the legs of their bell-bottom trousers. Dybdal was embarrassed to see that an enlisted man in the division was wearing one white sock and one black sock. Nimitz didn't say anything, just smiled. It hadn't even occurred to the ensign beforehand to check his men's socks, but he never failed to do so after that.[39]

Private Dutch Holland served as one of Admiral Nimitz's marine orderlies and enjoyed the duty because the admiral was such a pleasant individual. The role of orderly included being a messenger and errand runner, and there was a body-guard aspect to it as well. Whenever he accompanied Nimitz, Holland wore a holster with a .45-caliber automatic pistol in it. There was a bit of reflected glory in the duty because the orderlies rode along whenever Nimitz went somewhere in his barge or a car. They stood by during meetings or social events. And there was a collateral duty as well. On Sundays Admiral Nimitz brought his wife, Catherine, and their seven-year-old daughter, Mary, to visit the *Arizona*. Admiral Nimitz was in his early fifties by then, and his late-in-life child was spoiled, observed Holland. He and the other orderlies were detailed to play games with young Mary, throwing a ball back and forth or thinking of something else that would keep a girl of seven amused. It brought them some razzing from their shipmates, but they considered it part of the price for working for someone as pleasant as Nimitz.[40]

On one occasion, one of the orderlies couldn't cooperate. Mary Nimitz saw him standing his post outside the admiral's spacious cabin and said, "Come in and play with me."

"I can't," he told her. "I'm on duty."

"You'd better," she replied. "My daddy owns this ship, and he'll fire you."[41]

In early 1939, when the rest of the fleet went to the Caribbean for the annual fleet problem, Nimitz and the *Arizona* stayed behind to do some tactical work that had a valuable payback during World War II. The experiments he conducted as Commander Task Force Seven were far more helpful to the eventual conduct of war against Japan than

were the many and varied target practices that the battleships were wont to engage in. The task force consisted of the battleship, an aircraft carrier, a cruiser, and some destroyers. The antiaircraft problem still remained to be solved, but Nimitz did work on refueling at sea and amphibious landings.

The *Arizona* had been on the receiving end for the initial experiments in the 1920s, and now the process had improved considerably. Instead of having the delivery ship trail a hose to the bow of the receiving ship, the two ships

Above: A close-up of the right side of a 5-inch/25-caliber antiaircraft gun mount. (Courtesy Bruce Edward Thomas, via Lorraine Marks, *Arizona* Reunion Association)

Below: Biplanes fly overhead to welcome the *Arizona* to Hawaii at the conclusion of maneuvers. (National Archives, 80-G-1009378)

steamed alongside. During World War II the only connections were the highlines that supported the hoses, but in the 1930s the battleship still put over spring lines to help keep the ships on parallel headings. The *Arizona*'s boatswain's mates rigged fenders to protect against bumps and scrapes in case the ships got too close together. The refueling was pretty messy the first few times the ship

tried it, spilling oil on those beautifully holystoned teak decks. With time and practice, however, the men got better at it, and underway refueling thus enhanced the fleet's ability to stay at sea for extended periods.[42]

For amphibious exercises, boats filled with armed marines from the various ships approached the shore. These exercises were different from the training situations in which members of the landing force played war games ashore. Then the emphasis had been on maneuvers on land; here the idea was to concentrate on the business of getting the landing force ashore in the face of opposition near the water's edge. Private Dutch Holland, Nimitz's orderly, was among those in the motor whaleboats that were used. He and his shipmates had to hunker down behind the boats' gunwales for protection against presumed gunfire from shore. It was an uncomfortable position, and many of the men got seasick.[43]

When the boats reached the beach at San Clemente Island, the marines had to vault over the bows of the landing boats and then wade ashore. How far they had to walk and

how deep the water was where they landed depended on the boat coxswains. As the name suggests, the whaleboat was designed to provide whalers something to ride while they were being dragged around by a whale at the other end of a harpoon—not something to be run ashore. Again, the requirements for potential wartime operations came up against the realities of the spit-and-polish peacetime fleet. Landing the boat in sand or rocks could damage the beautifully painted bottom, and the crew would then have to repair it before the next inspection. The marines, of course, would be vulnerable to enemy fire at the time they were preoccupied with clambering over the gunwale.[44]

The biggest lesson learned from the exercises was that regular ship's boats were not at all suited for such work. Because they were pointed at both ends, the whaleboats handled all right when waves came in behind them onto the beach, but they couldn't hold many men. The 50-foot motor launches had a larger capacity, but their squared-off sterns made them highly susceptible to broaching—that is, turning parallel to the beach and grounding. Over the next few years the Navy developed specialized landing craft, equipped with a bow ramp that dropped directly onto the landing beach so the embarked troops could run directly ashore. The marines also got different uniforms before the war began. They fought in fatigues during World War II, instead of the shipboard khakis that they wore in the *Arizona*'s landing exercises.[45]

In late June of 1939 several of the ensigns out of the Naval Academy's class of that year reported to the *Arizona* for duty. One of them was Jim Dick Miller, who soon afterward took over as acting division officer for the third division when the regular division officer, a lieutenant, departed for other duty. In the interim, before a new officer showed up, Miller planned to follow his predecessor's advice about how to handle morning quarters. At the beginning of each work day, crew members mustered by divisions all over the ship and got the word passed down from the chain of command. The third division mustered topside, near its turret, and Miller had been advised to have the men march smartly forward, clear of the quarterdeck, before being dismissed.[46]

Left: Captain Alfred W. Brown reads his orders as he takes command of the *Arizona* on 11 December 1937. (Courtesy A. W. Brown, Jr.)

Below: A close-up of the ladder arrangement on the legs of the tripod mainmast. It was a feat to get up and down at night, particularly in rough seas, to stand watches in the maintop. Also visible are empty boat skids, which show the rubber padding used to protect the boat hulls. (Courtesy Bruce Edward Thomas, via Lorraine Marks, *Arizona* Reunion Association)

Above: The *Arizona*'s forecastle, wet with seawater as the ship rolls to port en route to Hawaii. (Courtesy Nick Richardson, via Lorraine Marks, *Arizona* Reunion Association)

Below: The ship's quarterdeck, one level lower than the forecastle, is awash with water as the *Arizona* plows through heavy seas on the way to Hawaii in March 1938. (Courtesy Philip Sims, Naval Sea Systems Command)

On his first morning as acting division officer, Miller gave the order, "Left face, forward march." He stepped out smartly and then looked back and discovered that he was marching all alone. The enlisted men of the division weren't following him because their first class boatswain's mate had said something else to them at the same time as Miller's order. He told them, "All right, all you deck hands, get 'round this boat boom and let's

stow it away." And that's what they were beginning to do as Miller marched away by himself.[47]

Miller learned many things about shipboard life that hadn't been taught at the Naval Academy. One of his discoveries was that Lieutenant Commander Alexander J. Couble—the *Arizona*'s first lieutenant, who was responsible for the overall cleanliness and preservation of the ship—was extremely parsimonious with his paint supplies. Couble's philosophy was, "Scrub it; don't paint." As the division officer, Ensign Miller had to take each paint requisition to the first lieutenant personally and get his signed approval before drawing paint from the paint locker. Even then, the requests weren't always approved, so after the dirt and rust were removed, the bare metal was left to begin rusting again. One day, there was a small touch-up job to do, so one of the third division's boatswain's mates filled out a requisition for one brushful of white paint. Miller took the requisition to Couble, who approved it but warned that the brush was not to be dipped into the paint can more than once.[48]

In their own way, the deck seamen got a measure of revenge. One of the first items of the day's routine was to scrub the ship's wooden decks. Part of the operation called for

the seamen to pound handles into the heads of rubber squeegees, and they did so with particular vigor on the portion of the main deck right over the first lieutenant's stateroom. He never complained, but how could he? They were only doing their jobs.[49]

Some of the *Arizona*'s men liked to carry their own transportation on board ship. One was Ensign Charles Dodds, who took his motorcycle ashore at Bremerton, Washington, and caught the streamlined ferryboat *Kalakala* over to Seattle. As he was about to leave the ferry on one occasion, he saw that one of the foot passengers was Admiral Nimitz. So Dodds graciously offered the admiral a motorcycle ride to downtown Seattle, and Nimitz just as graciously declined.[50]

Seaman Garland Fordyce got the permission of his division officer to have a motorcycle on board ship. In Long Beach, Fordyce and some of the other crew members stored their cycles in a local garage so that they were available to take the men to a variety of places on liberty. When the *Arizona* was ready to go somewhere else, the owners of the motorcycles brought them out to the ship, and the boat cranes lifted them aboard. The men stowed their motorcycles on the ship's boat deck, and they were welcome as long as they didn't get oil on the wooden decks—always an important consideration. Captain Kidd had misgivings but didn't put a stop to the practice. Even so, he talked to Fordyce as a concerned father would to a son. He once gestured toward a hospital ship in the harbor at Long Beach and told Fordyce that many of the men being treated on board were there for motorcycle accidents. Several of Fordyce's shipmates were injured in motorcycle accidents, but he still wasn't deterred.[51]

In fact, the only time Fordyce got in trouble while in the crew of the *Arizona* was when he didn't have his motorcycle with him. The ship was at Bremerton in 1939, and he spent several weekend liberties in Shelton, Washington, because one of his married shipmates lived there. One weekend he rode there with a friend rather than taking his own motorcycle. When it came time to return to the ship, Fordyce's friend overslept and didn't pick him up on time. As a result, they returned late to the ship and were put on report.

Absent over liberty has long been one of the cardinal sins for men in the Navy. Fordyce went to captain's mast to take his medicine. His division's chief petty officer pointed out it was the first time Fordyce had been in trouble in his three years on board. The seaman was sentenced to be restricted to the ship for a period of time, to work extra duty after hours, and to have his conduct grade lowered from 4.0. At the time, Fordyce thought he had gotten a break because he wasn't sentenced to any brig time. However, the sentence was a blot on his record, and that one morning of being late to work held up his advancement to petty officer for months.[52]

Another seaman who ran afoul of the system was Nick Richardson. Like Fordyce, he was late getting back to the ship once because the car in which he and a friend were riding was unreliable. They caught a commercial water taxi and got aboard ship by climbing onto an antitorpedo blister as the *Arizona* headed away from her anchorage at San Pedro. Several other men were in the boat as well, but Richardson was the first to step aboard. When he got to mast, Captain Kidd didn't even listen to his explanation before sentencing him to five days in the brig on bread and water. The rest of the men who returned late got off with a warning. Richardson talked to the ship's chaplain about what seemed unfair treatment. The chaplain suggested that they go see the captain's yeoman,

Below: A close-up of the maintop and storm-tossed seas en route to Hawaii. Another battleship is off the port quarter, two others in the distance to starboard. At the lower edge of the photo is a Curtiss SOC scout-observation plane. The highest level of each of the tops housed the Mark 20 main battery director. The middle level was for main battery spotting, and the bottom level contained two secondary battery directors. (Special Collections, University of Arizona Library, 84-37-3)

Zip Zobel. He pulled out Richardson's record, in which the captain's mast notation was on a loose piece of paper. The chaplain said to Zobel, "Now if that fell into the trash can, nobody would ever know the difference, would they?"

"No," said the yeoman, "I don't guess they would." The service record tilted, the mast record went into the trash, and Richardson has been Zobel's friend ever since.[53]

Many of the men of the *Arizona* looked to Captain Kidd as a kind of father figure. Ensign Miller's third division was responsible for the smartness of the quarterdeck, the

Below: A view from the maintop looking forward. The smokestack is topped by a grating divided into six wedges for the separate firerooms. Notice the pattern of ladders leading up the various levels of the foremast. (Courtesy Garland Fordyce)

passageways outside the captain's and admiral's cabins, and the highly polished gangway that was supposed to be for the exclusive use of the captain and admiral. When something was amiss in those areas, Kidd didn't berate or admonish Miller. Usually, he just put his hand on the ensign's shoulder and said something like, "Now, son, we ought to do such and such." Nor was he strict in enforcing the exclusivity of his gangway and gig. If he saw junior officers waiting on the quarterdeck for a ride in an officers' motorboat, he would ask them to go along in his gig so they could get ashore sooner.[54]

When David McCafferty was advanced to seaman first class, his aunt in New York sent him a long telegram, expressing her great pride in the Navy and in his accomplishment. The commanding officer got copies of incoming dispatches, and the one to young McCafferty intrigued the captain, so he sent for the seaman. Kidd invited McCafferty to his palatial quarters at the stern of the ship and chatted with him for some time, asking about his family, commenting on McCafferty's Scottish birth, and talking about the seaman's aspirations. Before that, McCafferty had sensed that enlisted men were inferior to officers. Here was a senior officer treating him as a human being. Kidd kept an eye on the seaman after that, making a point of speaking with him during their encounters on deck.[55]

Seaman Jack McCarron, a gunner's mate striker, was assigned to one of the 5-inch antiaircraft guns on the boat deck. One of his practices each week was to cut a picture of a pretty girl out of the Sunday paper and tape it to the canvas on the gun mount. More than once Captain Kidd walked by the mount during his strolls about the ship. McCarron snapped immediately to attention and didn't let his eyes stray far enough to see whether the captain was smiling as he looked at the latest feminine decoration on the mount. Kidd never said anything to McCarron about what he had seen. The young gunner's mate took silence to mean consent and continued his practice.[56]

In some cases, the captain's familiarity extended to addressing enlisted men by their first names. In society at large then it was often customary for men to address each other by last names, and especially so in the Navy when officers were talking to enlisted men. On 25 July 1939 Fireman Second Class

Everett Reid was on the quarterdeck of the *Arizona*, talking with Lieutenant J. E. Fitzgibbon, the officer of the deck. Captain Kidd happened up on deck about that time and said to Reid, "Everett, what are you doing in your dress blues."

Fitzgibbon quickly piped up, "He's getting married today, Captain."

They chatted a while longer, and then Kidd said to the officer of the deck, "Call away my gig." The bugler on watch sounded the call for the gig, and soon it came alongside the captain's gangway. Thereupon Kidd said, "Everett, be my guest."

Reid saluted and thanked the captain, saluted the officer of the deck, saluted the flag at the stern, and then headed down the gangway into the waiting boat. Clyde "Red" Rawson, the gig's coxswain, took Reid to a pier in Seattle, whence he would go ashore for his wedding. A lieutenant, serving as shore-patrol officer, came running down the pier because he believed Captain Kidd was coming ashore. When a fireman rather than a captain emerged from the stern sheets of the boat, the breathless lieutenant asked Rawson what his

orders were. "To leave this man at the pier and to return to the ship," replied the coxswain.

Disappointed at not having apprehended a team of hijackers, the lieutenant disgustedly

Left: A detail of enlisted pallbearers puts a flag over the coffin of Captain A. W. Brown prior to taking it ashore from one of the *Arizona*'s motor launches at the fleet landing in Long Beach. The captain's body has just come from a funeral service, held on board the ship on 9 September 1938. (Courtesy A. W. Brown, Jr.)

Below: Pallbearers prepare to carry Captain Brown's body up a brow at the Long Beach landing. In the background is a row of gigs for the assembled battleship skippers on the pier. The boat in the upper right corner is from the USS *Mississippi*; her commanding officer, Captain Raymond Spruance, is in the back row. The ensign with the funeral detail is the late Captain Brown's son and namesake. (Courtesy A. W. Brown, Jr.)

said to Rawson, "Carry out your orders." Reid remembered of the lieutenant, "I think if he'd have had anything on his hip there, he'd have probably shot me. He was so mad he was fuming. We walked the full length of that pier, and he didn't say one word. He was trying to get his breath back." Fireman Second Class Everett Reid had definitely traveled in style on his wedding day.[57]

Many of the crew members of the *Arizona* attended the Golden Gate International Exposition of 1939–40 on man-made Treasure Island in San Francisco Bay. It was the West Coast's counterpart of the New York World's Fair, which was taking place at the same time. America was enjoying a last halcyon fling before the curtain of war ended such fun for a number of years. Among the attractions were scientific exhibits. Many of the nation's top

industrial firms viewed the fairs as showcases for their latest products and those still to come.[58] Seaman Harold McCarty of the *Arizona* was walking by a booth in one of the pavilions when a man called, "Come over here, sailor." He did so, and the man pointed to a television monitor that showed McCarty talking to the man. Then he pointed out the camera of the closed-circuit system. It was the first time McCarty had ever seen television, and he was on it.[59]

Entertainment at the fair included big-band leaders such as Benny Goodman, Tommy Dorsey, and Kay Kyser. The sideshows featured the usual cheap attractions, including partially clad young women for both sailors and civilians to ogle. Private First Class Wylie Smith of the *Arizona*'s marine detachment peeked in on Sally Rand's "Nude Ranch."[60] Rand had made her reputation as a fan dancer

Right: On 17 September 1938 Rear Admiral Chester Nimitz, near the microphone, relieved Rear Admiral Adolphus Watson as Commander, Battleship Division One. Visible between the two is Captain Isaac C. Kidd, who took command of the *Arizona* the same day. His predecessor, Captain Alfred W. Brown, died of a heart attack. (Naval Historical Center, NH 62017)

at the 1933 Century of Progress Exposition in Chicago. Now she was in charge as younger women exposed themselves.

Less than two months after the men of the *Arizona* enjoyed the shows in San Francisco, war broke out in Europe. Chancellor Adolf Hitler of Germany had used one bluff after another to gobble up territory from other countries. England and France finally reacted to his bullying when he invaded Poland, and the fighting began. Security became even tighter than before. Few pictures of the *Arizona* exist from the period between early 1938 and her destruction in late 1941 because of a law enacted by Congress to prohibit, among other things, sketches, photos, or diagrams of military equipment. Because of the likelihood that the United States would eventually become embroiled in the war, Congress wanted to ensure that potential enemies learned as little as possible about the latest changes made to U.S. ships, aircraft, and bases.

An incident that took place on 8 October 1939 demonstrated the seriousness of the situation. The *Arizona* was anchored at San Pedro that afternoon when the sailing yacht *Sans Gene* went past. People topside in the yacht took pictures of the battleship, so the *Arizona*'s officer of the deck dispatched a boarding party commanded by the ship's assistant navigator. He confiscated two rolls of film containing the potentially revealing photos.[61]

The heightened sense of security accompanying the onset of war in Europe was evident also when suspected sabotage in the *Arizona*'s engineering department brought agents of the Federal Bureau of Investigation to the ship. Between 5:00 P.M. on 29 September and 9:00 A.M. on 30 September, while the ship was anchored, someone had opened the reserve lube oil tanks in the port and starboard engine rooms and let the oil drain into the bilges under the center engine room. In addition, nuts, bolts, threading taps, a valve and coil, and pieces of steel wool had been found in the spring bearing housings for three of the four propeller shafts. These bearings supported the shafts as they ran through the long shaft alleys.[62] When the crew members gathered at quarters one Saturday for inspection, they learned that leave and liberty would be canceled for a time so they could be available for questioning. The ship then went out for a week of operations while the FBI men did their work.

One night during the course of the investigation, which took place in early October, the ship was anchored in San Clemente Island's Pyramid Cove. Ensign Jim Miller had the watch as officer of the deck when one of the FBI agents came up on deck, apparently unable to sleep. He struck up a conversation with Miller, asking how deep the water was. Miller told him it was forty fathoms. "That's pretty deep, isn't it?" asked the agent.

"Yes, that's 240 feet."

"Is the anchor all the way down to the bottom?" the FBI man inquired further. Miller didn't say anything, but he thought to

Below: The *Arizona* refuels a four-stack destroyer by means of a hose suspended from the battleship's port boat boom. (Courtesy Richard Van Atta, via Lorraine Marks, *Arizona* Reunion Association)

himself that the FBI man knew more about investigations than about seamanship if he thought the anchor could hold the ship in position just by dangling loose beneath her. Each anchor chain was more than 1,000 feet long, so 240 was no problem.[63]

As a result of all the interviews, inspection of physical evidence, and examination of records, the federal agents produced a report of some two hundred pages. The beginning of the war in Europe raised concern about possible enemy attempts to disable one of the U.S. Navy's battleships. No damage was done, because the tampering was discovered before the engines were started; the spilled oil was able to be recovered. The steel wool had the potential to score the propeller shafts if they had been operated. The agents interviewed all members of the engineering force about their movements when the incident occurred and had detailed discussions with twenty-three men who were on board at the time. Two members of the *Arizona*'s crew

were considered prime suspects, but both denied the charges.

Experienced members of the *Arizona*'s engineering force told the FBI they believed that the sabotage amounted to an attempt to embarrass certain officers of the ship rather than an attempt to do serious damage. Anyone capable of dumping the lube oil and putting in steel wool could just as easily have damaged the turbines, for example, and thus caused far greater disruption. The FBI's wrap-up report on the investigation quoted a letter from an individual in the Eleventh Naval District: "The method used in this case indicates more a desire to delay the ship rather than damage it. This delay would inflict a penalty on the engineering department in annual competition and react on personnel in authority." More than a year after the initial investigation, the FBI again contacted the officers of the *Arizona* and learned of no new information on the sabotage and no similar

Below: Sailors in shorts pull a motor whaleboat onto the beach as part of an amphibious-landing exercise in the late 1930s. The boat appears to have hinged wooden ramps to facilitate movement onto the beach. (Special Collections, University of Arizona Library, 85-4-4)

subsequent occurrences. The case was then closed.[64]

The upshot of this particular incident of sabotage was that the *Arizona* tightened up security procedures within the engineering spaces. When the ship was in port, all spaces that weren't needed for supplying necessary steam and electrical power were locked shut. In all unlocked spaces, in port and at sea, enlisted members of the engineering department had to conduct security inspections. They were outfitted with time clocks of the kind worn by night watchmen. Each engineering space had a key that was attached to a chain; as he made his rounds, the security man had to use the key in the clock to show that he

Left: An overhead view, looking down on a 5-inch/25 antiaircraft gun. Just above the breech of the 5-inch are the twin barrels of a saluting battery on the bridge. (Courtesy Garland Fordyce)

had been in the space to check for unauthorized personnel and for evidence of tampering with the equipment. Those making the rounds had to visit each of the spaces twice during a four-hour watch, with the result that they got a lot of exercise—up and down ladders, in and out of hatches and watertight doors.[65]

In the late 1930s reserve officers began to infiltrate the junior officers' mess. First came the aviation cadets. The Navy had started a program to beef up its growing air arm. To feed men into the system faster than the regular-officer commissioning rate would allow, reservists were sent through flight training as cadets and were later commissioned after a period of satisfactory performance. Then, with the possibility of war looming ever larger, reserve officers were commissioned for deck duty as well. Among the deck officers who reported to the ship in late 1939 was Ensign George Lennig. Whereas the junior officers' mess had for years been populated almost exclusively with Naval Academy graduates, it now included some officers whose training and indoctrination

had been but a fraction of that for the Annapolis men. Perhaps for this reason, Lennig didn't take a condescending approach to the enlisted men who worked for him in the fifth division. Disdaining the practice that forbade fraternization between officers and enlisted men, he went on liberty with some of them while wearing his civilian clothes. Seaman Harold McCarty of the fifth division was among the sailors who went to Lennig's wedding and later visited him and his bride in their apartment.[66]

Santa Claus visited the *Arizona* at Christmas in 1939 while she was anchored at San Pedro. One of the ship's floatplanes picked up Santa, a dressed-up crew member, and flew him to the *Arizona*'s anchorage. The plane taxied to a spot near the stern and was picked up by the fantail airplane crane and deposited on a catapult. Santa evidently got a bargain on roller skates that year and passed out dozens of pairs to the delighted children of the *Arizona*'s crew members. He might have made a wiser choice, at least in the eyes of the boatswain's mates. Those upholders of topside cleanliness were not at all happy by the

Right: Crew members muster on the quarterdeck for the 26 May 1939 change-of-command ceremony when Rear Admiral Willson relieved Rear Admiral Nimitz. (Naval Historical Center, NH 50790)

impressions that roller-skate wheels made on their beautifully holystoned teak decks.[67]

On 3 February 1940 Captain Harold C. Train relieved Captain Isaac C. Kidd as the commanding officer of the ship. (In a remarkable coincidence, his son, Admiral Harry D. Train, relieved Admiral Isaac C. Kidd, Jr., as Commander in Chief, Atlantic Fleet, in 1978.) Captain Train was a low-key individual who remained remarkably calm whatever the circumstances. Seaman First Class John Amend was a member of Train's gig crew. He and other men referred to the skipper as Choo-choo Train, although it was obviously not a label used to the captain's face. He was popular because he wasn't as strict as his predecessor had been. The gig's crew liked Captain Train because he made them feel special. When he saw them on deck during a personnel inspection, he made a point of greeting them.[68] The coxswain during most of Train's command tenure was Russ Ramsey. He and the rest of the crew were real specialists because the boat was virtually their only duty. In port they took the captain wherever he had to go. At sea they spent their days cleaning, polishing, and otherwise caring for the gig, including washing it with fresh water every day, even though it was a highly prized commodity.[69]

The senior naval aviator on board the *Arizona* in 1940 was Lieutenant Clifford H. "Dutch" Duerfeldt. He was a member of the staff of Rear Admiral Russell Willson, who had relieved Nimitz as Commander Battleship Division One. Duerfeldt was also commanding officer of Observation Squadron One, the scoutplanes of the *Arizona*, *Pennsylvania*, and *Nevada*. A three-plane detachment from the squadron served on board each of the ships of the division for scouting, spotting gunfire, and towing targets for antiaircraft practice. The planes were rugged Curtiss SOC biplanes, so well suited to the business of being catapulted from surface ships and recovered under way that a number of ships used them throughout World War II. Lieutenant Duerfeldt had previously been a floatplane pilot in the battleship *Mississippi* when Captain Raymond Spruance was the commanding officer. Spruance used Duerfeldt as an aviation adviser much more than Willson did; Duerfeldt believed it was because Spruance

was more eager to learn about the air capability that was growing in importance in the fleet at the time.[70]

One day the entire squadron of SOCs was in the air when the division was operating together. They were supposed to land into the wind, just as they were catapulted into the wind on takeoff. On this particular day the ships turned so that the planes would have to land while flying downwind, unless Duerfeldt protested. He decided that the wind was light

Right: The *Arizona*'s marines man a Browning .50-caliber water-cooled machine gun on sky aft, a cloverleaf on the mainmast. (Courtesy James A. McCain, via Lorraine Marks, *Arizona* Reunion Association)

started operating from ships. Airplanes were an inconvenience, getting oil on the decks and requiring the ship to conduct various maneuvers to launch and recover them; those disadvantages seemed, at least to some, to outweigh the tactical advantages the planes provided. The fliers did not really convince the rest of the fleet of their legitimacy until after the war had demonstrated their potency. The use of the SOCs in the *Arizona* was limited during Duerfeldt's time on board; he estimated that they flew only about 15–18 hours per month.[72]

In the spring of 1940 the Allied war effort was taking a beating. Germany conquered Scandinavia and the Low Countries and was on the verge of taking France. Japan continued to wage war against China. Following completion of Fleet Problem XXI, the *Arizona* and the other ships of the Battle Force were ordered to remain in Hawaiian waters rather than return to their normal bases on the West Coast. President Franklin D. Roosevelt determined that the fleet's forward location would serve as an effective deterrent against further Japanese incursions on the mainland of Asia. Admiral James O. Richardson, Commander in Chief U.S. Fleet, was disap-

enough that the maneuver could be done safely, and the planes came in for recovery. He was still upset about what he considered a botched maneuver and went to the bridge to protest once he was back aboard the *Arizona*. He started complaining to Lieutenant Commander Victor Long, the flag secretary, because he thought Long had ordered the maneuver.[71]

Duerfeldt started by saying, "Long, it seems to me that with all the equipment you have on battleships nowadays, you ought to be able to find out which way the wind is blowing." Before Long could say anything in reply, Duerfeldt looked over and saw Admiral Willson on the outer part of the flag bridge. Willson beckoned to Duerfeldt with his finger and said, "I made that move." During the course of the discussion that ensued, Duerfeldt thought he finally convinced the admiral that once the planes were in the air, the aviator was in command.

Duerfeldt did take some comfort from the fact that Willson and members of the *Arizona*'s wardroom were not anti-aviation as a number of the "black shoe" surface officers still were at the time. He explained, "It wasn't the aviators they hated as much as the airplanes." The attitude in 1940 was much the same as it had been in 1920 when aircraft first

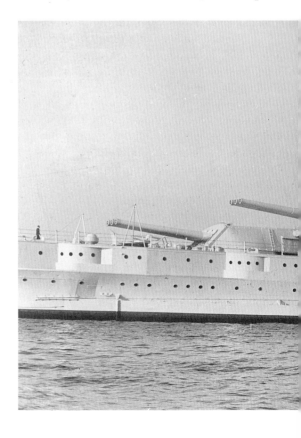

pointed by the move because he believed that the ships could much better prepare for war on the West Coast, which had the appropriate logistics facilities. The navy yard at Pearl Harbor was not equipped to accommodate such a large number of ships.

On board the *Arizona*, the reaction to remaining in Hawaii was mixed. Some men were glad to stay there because the weather was nice, and recreational opportunities were available for those interested in sports. But there were drawbacks as well. One crew member, Bill Huckenpoehler, explained, "Most of the people would much rather have gone back to the States, because of the fact that, really, if you were an enlisted man ashore in Honolulu, you might as well forget about dating anybody. It was either you go to the red-light district, or you go around sightseeing or swimming at the Navy Y, or something like that, drinking pineapple juice, going on tours. Because no self-respecting girl out there would go with a sailor. . . . Whether you participated or not, there were a lot of cathouses out there. It was a pretty common thing [for the most junior enlisted men] just to go there in the afternoon, drink Cokes, and watch the goings-on: watch to see what the big girls and big boys were doing."[73] The "big

boys" evidently didn't feel such timidity because the brothels often had lines of potential customers.

For a while Seaman Milton Hurst didn't get liberty at all. He saw the other men going on liberty, so after a while he worked up his courage to ask his boatswain's mate if he could join them. The boatswain's mate reminded him that he was going ashore already. Hurst and other members of the baseball team went several times a week to practice, so the statement was true. Hurst accepted that answer, in part because he didn't really have much choice. He continued to do his work in satisfactory fashion and to practice with the ball team. Finally, after several more weeks had passed, the boatswain's mate handed him a liberty card, figuring that he had by then earned it. Initially, he became part of the Coke-drinking, sight-seeing crowd. Then one day his shipmates in the second division concluded it was time for his initiation. They took him to a Honolulu bar and introduced him to the boilermaker—a shot of whiskey with a glass of beer for a chaser. It's a combination for an experienced drinker's stomach, something Hurst didn't have. Feeling unsteady and unwell, he went outside the tavern and collapsed. At the end of

Left: A commercial water taxi hurries past the *Arizona*'s port side. For a price, these taxis provided transportation for those who had missed the ship's own motor launch and chose not to wait for the next one. (Security Pacific National Bank Photograph Collection, Los Angeles Public Library)

the evening, his shipmates scooped him up, put him into a ship's boat, and then put him to bed in the *Arizona*.[74]

Shore patrol is often unpopular duty, in part because shore-patrol members see others doing the sorts of things they would like to do but can't while they are on duty. A good deal of the sting was taken out of the duty, however, when various whorehouse madams handed out rain checks—good for use on a later date—to shore-patrol members who did a good job of preserving the peace. The shore patrolmen essentially served as bouncers— preserving order, preventing and breaking up fights, and keeping the places from being damaged. In addition to protecting their property, the madams were making sure they had no trouble that could get them reported to the local authorities. It was a convenient arrangement that served the interests of both shore patrolmen and madams.[75]

However, the relationship wasn't always amicable. Fire Controlman Second Class Jim O'Donnell had the duty in Honolulu and was summoned to a brothel on Beretania Street as the result of a complaint. When he got there, the madam was raising Cain, so he asked, "What's going on?"

"One of your men called my girl a whore," replied the woman.

Right: The principal change evident in this picture taken 30 March 1939 at Bremerton is that the 36-inch searchlights have been moved from the platforms on the smokestack to the cloverleafs on the mainmast. The .50-caliber machine guns are visible on the foremast cloverleafs and at the after end of the bridge. The broadside guns are behind their canvas curtains. (Courtesy Puget Sound Naval Shipyard)

"Lady, when you run a place like this, you can expect that," shot back the petty officer. O'Donnell didn't arrest the kid, who was a young smart aleck, only about seventeen or eighteen; he just sent him on his way. Soon afterward, O'Donnell was directed to report to shore patrol headquarters and was relieved of duty for the day because of his off-the-cuff remark to the woman entrepreneur. Her complaint even got back to the ship but didn't have the desired result. Captain Train gave O'Donnell a "well done" for his actions.[76]

During her operations that summer, which included visits to outlying U.S. bases as part

Left: Midshipman Isaac C. Kidd, Jr., is shown on board the *Arizona*, then commanded by his father, during a visit to the ship in 1939. Young Kidd graduated from the Naval Academy on 19 December 1941, less than two weeks after his father was killed at Pearl Harbor, and eventually became a four-star admiral. (Courtesy Isaac C. Kidd, Jr.)

of the stepped-up readiness effort, the *Arizona* had a Davey Jones party to celebrate crossing the equator on 24 July 1940. The ship had a large number of pollywogs on board because it had been four years since the last initiation. The pollywogs were brought up on the usual ridiculous charges to justify their initiation. One of the more imaginative summonses charged Seaman Second Class Bill Huckenpoehler, "In that you did consolidate all your relatives' names, causing much confusion."[77]

The various tortures imposed on those who hadn't crossed the line before included many of the traditional ones, especially the most traditional of all—getting banged on the bottom with sand-filled clubs made of canvas. Some of the pollywogs made things even worse for themselves. They briefly kidnapped a group of shellbacks and locked them in the boatswain's locker, far forward in the ship. For a while, they blocked access to their imprisoned shipmates. When a rescue party finally freed the shellbacks, they were able to impose vengeance on their erstwhile captors.

Included in the festivities was a royal princess, a crew member who dressed up like a woman. He had on a dress, long wig, woman's hat, and lipstick. He also turned out to be something of a flirt. When pollywogs responded to the flirting, they were appropriately punished—by the customary whack across the backside from a nearby shellback. Seaman Arthur Williams observed that officers probably got the worst of it in the initiation. An equator-crossing was one of those rare occasions when enlisted men could inflict physical pain on officers.[78]

One of the few men who got to be both pollywog and shellback in the *Arizona* was Machinist's Mate Wes Cole. In 1936 he was on the receiving end of the ritual. In 1940 he got to mete out punishment to others who were going through the ceremony for the first time. One of those he initiated in 1940 was Lieutenant Bob Foley, the ship's radio officer. Years later, in 1952, both served together again when Foley was commanding officer of the battleship *Wisconsin* and Cole, by then an officer, was the ship's main propulsion assistant.[79]

On 3 February 1941, a year to the day after he had taken command, Captain Train was relieved by Captain Franklin Van Valkenburgh. The new skipper quickly demon-

strated to his subordinates that he was a top-notch officer, friendly without being familiar, and concerned about the crew. As Chief Watertender Joe Karb observed of the new captain, "It didn't take an act of Congress to make him a gentleman" because he already was one.[80]

The *Arizona* underwent her final overhaul at Bremerton in late 1940 and early 1941. She also underwent a degree of modernization, part of it in anticipation of further updates to be accomplished in a later overhaul, perhaps a year in the future. The main concern during this last updating was to increase the ship's capability in antiaircraft gunnery, an area in which she was woefully deficient. Only a minimal improvement was accomplished in the 1940-41 yard period. She got a pedestal foundation for an air-search radar but not the radar's electronic equipment nor the antenna. She got gun tubs on the main and upper decks to accommodate 1.1-inch antiaircraft guns, but the guns were unavailable.

Below: This fine shot of the *Arizona* was taken at Seattle in 1939 or 1940. It is rare because of the embargo on unofficial photos of military installations and equipment enacted by Congress in 1938. The admiral's barge is at the after starboard boat boom. (Puget Sound Maritime Historical Society)

Left: In this view from the late 1930s, Curtiss SOCs have replaced the Vought O3Us as the *Arizona*'s floatplanes. (Courtesy Mrs. Thomas P. Mullaney, USS *Arizona* Memorial, National Park Service, PR-440)

One real enhancement was the installation of upgraded directors on the port and starboard sides of the bridge to control the 5-inch/25-caliber antiaircraft guns. For the first time, the optical range finder was incorporated in the director itself, so the slant range didn't have to be put in manually after being transmitted by sound-powered phone from another location. In still another change, a type of gun tub known popularly as a "birdbath" because of its shape was installed on the roof of the maintop. It contained four .50-caliber machine guns; the new platform afforded them the highest possible vantage point and no interference from any part of the ship's structure. The *Arizona* was slow in getting such a birdbath. The *Nevada*, for instance, had had one since the mid-1930s. The shipyard built metal shields around the 5-inch antiaircraft guns. The shields provided some protection but far less than that in the enclosed 5-inch–gun mounts being installed in new ships built at the same time. The *Arizona*'s 5-inch mounts themselves were still open.

During this last yard period for the battleship, some of her new men were getting the kind of experience that football coaches refer to as character-building. Seaman Second Class Howard Burk had to go down inside the subdivisions in the blisters to chip and paint the bulkheads. Lights were suspended down into the compartments so that he could see what he was doing. He also served as a fire watch, ready to put out any small blazes caused by the cutting and welding torches of the yard workmen. At other times, he went out on boat patrols in Puget Sound, another manifestation of the wartime concern with security. When the fog came in, the boat's crew had to anchor, and what was supposed to be a four-hour watch might stretch on all night. These were menial chores for Burk but necessary ones for the ship. In the months and years afterward, he looked on that time in the shipyard as valuable training, something that had made a better man of him. At the time, it was work.[81]

Another activity that took place during that last shipyard period was called strip ship. As the situation grew ever more ominous in the Pacific and war seemed a question of when, rather than if, it was time to get rid of the items that were nice to have in peacetime but hazardous in war. Off went the radios for the crew and a good many other things, including the ship's silver service. One of the myths about the *Arizona* is that the silver service was recovered from the hulk at Pearl Harbor. Foresight spared it from that fate. (After World War II, the silver service was put aboard the light cruiser *Tucson* until that ship was decommissioned, and then in the 1950s it was for a time in the amphibious command

ship *Adirondack*. The silver service is now displayed in the state capitol in Phoenix.)[82]

When the overhaul was finished, the *Arizona* picked up new airplanes. Seaman Milton Hurst, who had transferred from the second division to the V division, had a part in making the transition. Monoplane Vought OS2Us replaced the biplane Curtiss SOCs. The aviation division worked ashore at Terminal Island in Long Beach to take the floats off the SOCs and attach wheels so that the planes could operate from land. The procedure was done in reverse for the new aircraft, lining up and attaching the floats so that the OS2Us could operate at sea from the *Arizona*.[83]

On 1 February 1941, while the *Arizona* was en route to Hawaii to rejoin the fleet, Admiral Husband Kimmel relieved Admiral J. O. Richardson to become the Pacific Fleet's Commander in Chief. Richardson had been too blunt in telling President Roosevelt that he didn't believe the fleet should be based in Hawaii. Kimmel was an energetic commander in chief, and he kept the Battle Force ships busy throughout much of the remainder of the year, although the nature of the exercises was changing. The *Arizona* was by then operating on essentially a wartime footing as part of various task forces. Instead of grouping together in battleship divisions, the battleships were integrated into forces that also contained carriers, cruisers, and destroyers.

The tactical importance of the carrier was being recognized, although fleet doctrine still called for the use of the big guns for duels with enemy battleships. In part because U.S. equipment was only slowly catching up to the lessons of combat in Europe, the ships were still not adequately prepared for battles other than the big-gun duels. The old battleships were not fast enough to run with the carriers. Radar was not yet commonplace; it wasn't scheduled to be installed in the *Arizona* until late 1941 or early 1942. Fleet antiaircraft capability was weak, torpedoes were defective, torpedo planes and patrol bombers were fatally vulnerable, and damage control was not battle-tested.

The men of the *Arizona* were forced to operate with what they had. The crew stood watches as if they were facing an actual enemy or might come upon one. Ships steamed darkened at night and took particular care to ensure that watertight integrity was maintained below decks. While the ship was at sea, special watch sections comprised of one officer and a dozen enlisted men patrolled the inside of the ship throughout the night to see that all watertight doors and hatches were closed as they should be.[84]

Although they were trained to follow officers' orders religiously, enlisted men sometimes decided that common sense took precedence over some of the orders. Machinist's Mate First Class Wes Cole discovered he could tell whenever Lieutenant Cliff Janz was the conning officer on the bridge, far above Cole's station as throttleman in main control. Janz had the irritating habit of changing speeds in small increments, presumably to fine-tune the ship's speed while she was operating in formation. Every minute or so he would add one revolution, then shortly take it off again. Cole explained that "all you'd do was log it; you wouldn't touch the throttle. It didn't matter whether we touched the throttle or not, because we knew it would come right back down."

As a senior petty officer, Cole had enough experience and self-confidence to know that his ignoring of orders would prevent a lot of unnecessary action. Then came the day when Lieutenant Janz was transferred to the engineering department as an underway watch officer. Once when Janz was in main control, there was an officer at the conn who gave engine orders almost as often as Janz had. Observing the throttleman, Janz realized that Cole was only logging some of the orders, not carrying them out. He made the big changes

but not the small ones. Lieutenant Janz asked Cole for an explanation and was chagrined when Cole told him he was merely doing what he had been doing when Janz himself was on watch. Cole obeyed all of the orders of most of the officers, but for these exceptional cases he concluded that a bit of discretion made more sense.

In 1941, with the war in Europe having been under way for more than a year and a half, U.S. warships were deliberately overmanned to train as many officers and enlisted men as possible. When Ensign Joe Langdell reported in May of 1941 from midshipman school, some 1,500 souls populated the *Arizona*. The staterooms and junior officers' bunkrooms were already full, so Langdell put up a cot in a passageway and called it home each night. During the daytime he was indoctrinated into the ways of the second division, which operated turret two.

The learning continued at night. When he went to the bridge, he found himself the junior, junior, junior officer of the deck or some such. He concluded that his principal functions were to observe and to stay out of the way until the officer of the deck gave him something to do. After a while, the deck officer might tell him, "Well, Joe, you just go make a tour of the ship and find out what you can." Off he would go, up and down ladders, through hatches, and so forth, trying to discover some system that described the internal labyrinth that constituted a battleship. Before too long he discovered that all the compartments were labeled with letters and numbers. Taken together, the label described how far aft in the ship the compartment was, how far from the centerline, whether it was port or starboard, and what its function was.[85]

When Langdell had to go inside the skin of the ship from a weather deck, the first hatch let him into a light lock. Once he had closed the outer hatch, he could then open the inner one and go into the lighted interior of the ship.[86] During these trips he often walked through poker games in progress—all of them involving men who had been in the Navy longer than he had. He just said, "How do you do?" to the participants and continued on his tour of the ship. He knew that poker games were part of Navy life, so he just left them alone.[87]

Left: This picture, taken 18 January 1941 at the Puget Sound Navy Yard, is the last known close-up view of the *Arizona* prior to the Japanese attack on Pearl Harbor. A birdbath has been built on the maintop for .50-caliber machine guns. Gun tubs are visible for 1.1-inch antiaircraft guns that were never installed prior to the ship's destruction. Shields have been erected outboard of the 5-inch/25 guns. The battleship *Nevada* is across the pier from the *Arizona*. (Courtesy Puget Sound Naval Shipyard)

Above: Posed in front of a flag created for the July 1940 equator-crossing initiation are Captain Harold C. Train, the *Arizona*'s commanding officer; Rear Admiral Russell Willson, Commander Battleship Division One; and Commander Arthur D. Struble, the ship's executive officer. (From the USS *Arizona*'s booklet *Crossing the Line*, courtesy Mrs. Lester Reeves)

Another newly commissioned Naval Reserve officer who reported to the ship that summer was Ensign Guy Flanagan. He had come in through the V-7 program, which required only two years of college. On top of that he got three months of midshipman school at Northwestern University and thus was part of the group known universally as "ninety-day wonders." They had been exposed to the basics about the Navy in what amounted to a boot camp for officers, but they still had a great deal to learn. Flanagan observed a lot of turnover of personnel; in a sense, the *Arizona* was a training ship, just as she had been during World War I at Yorktown, Virginia. The newly reported ensign was assigned to the third division under Ensign Jim Dick Miller and was soon learning about turret operations and a good deal more.[88]

The training was based upon the likelihood of a war against Japan. Silhouettes of Japanese warships were on the bulkheads in junior officers' country, and the officers also studied flash cards with silhouettes of Japanese warships and airplanes. This study did not carry with it a sense of urgency. Rather, the idea was that such a war was probably inevitable, so the officers were acquiring information that would prove useful to them at some time in the future.[89]

Flanagan's practical training included an officer's duties concerning inspections. One Saturday he was detailed to accompany the *Arizona*'s gunnery officer, Lieutenant Commander Bruce Kelley, on an inspection of the mess attendants' living compartment. They had to maintain a clean, sanitary environment for food preparation, but their living quarters did not measure up to the same standards. Kelley reached up with a white glove and ran it along a horizontal beam near the overhead in the compartment. The glove came down filthy, so Kelley chewed out the division officer and told him to get the compartment cleaned up because he would be inspecting again. Then Kelley shooed out everyone except Flanagan and asked him to make a note of the frame number where they had found the offending dirt so that they could follow up. Then Kelley reached up and put a dime on the horizontal surface, figuring that if he found it again later, he would have hard evidence that no cleaning had been done.[90]

A few weeks later, Kelley and Flanagan were again inspecting the mess attendants' compartment. Kelley asked the ensign for the frame number of the beam, and again the commander reached up with a white glove and ran it along the surface. When he opened his hand, he again found a filthy glove, but he now had two nickels in his hand instead of the dime he'd left earlier. After a good laugh at the joke the mess attendants had played at his expense, he proceeded to chew out the division officer again about the dirt.[91]

Ensign Flanagan also got some experience in fleet liberty during the halcyon months of 1941. In the summertime young schoolteachers from the mainland liked to come out for a few weeks of vacation in the island paradise. It was common for young naval officers to go out with a different girl each time they went on liberty. The Waikiki Beach area was popular, especially the Royal Hawaiian Hotel and a steak house known as Lau Ye Chai's. Dancing in the hotel's ballroom with the moonlight reflecting off the Pacific put many a young couple in a romantic mood. There were only two limiting factors for the officers:

they had to stand duty, and their funds were not so plentiful as were the girls.[92]

In the summer of 1941 the *Arizona* made a cruise to the West Coast so her men could spend some time with their families. After the ship returned to Pearl Harbor, Ensign Joe Langdell was sent off on temporary duty to the Fleet Camera Party, based on board the USS *Argonne*. Its function was to support the innumerable target practices conducted by the ships preparing for war. Langdell and a camera party went out on an old four-stack destroyer towing a target for gunnery practice by the big ships. The addition of photography—both still and motion pictures—some years before had added a bit of sophistication to the old rake-party calculations for determining miss distances. The camera party took photos of the splashes and later used trigonometry to ascertain how far from the target the splashes were. Explaining his function, Langdell quipped, "The only reason they needed an ensign on that detail was that an ensign was the lowest grade guy that knew how to work a trigonometry problem." The temporary assignment saved his life. Since he was still attached to the Fleet Camera Party in December, Langdell wasn't in turret two, the one to which he had been assigned on board the *Arizona*.[93]

Other men from the *Arizona* worked with targets throughout the life of the ship, although their detachment was only for a day at a time. At that, it was a long day. Seaman Milton Hurst was one of those assigned to a target-repair party. He and a number of shipmates got up early and loaded supplies into a motor launch, then went a dozen or so miles away from the ship. A vertical spar on each side of the target raft was equipped with lines and pulleys. The men used the lines to raise the canvas targets to a vertical position, much as one would raise a flag. As soon as the target was in place, the target party got back into the boat and temporarily rejoined the tug that was towing the raft; the towline was long enough to provide some security in case the battleship's salvos weren't completely accurate.[94]

The *Arizona* fired a number of salvos, however many were specified for a particular string. Afterward, the repair party motored back over to the raft, took down the target with holes in it, and put up a new one. If one of the dummy projectiles used for target practice managed to hit a spar, the repair party replaced it with one of the spares carried in the boat. The 14-inch projectiles were big enough that the repair-party men could see them as they flew through the air toward the target. They began their flight from over the horizon, then loomed larger and larger as they approached. The repair-party men could see the side of the target and were able to watch as the projectiles passed through on a hit. They also saw the big splashes of water that told them whether the shots were long or short. Once a practice was over, the sailors in the party gathered up the targets that had collected during the day and took them back to the *Arizona* so that the officers of the gunnery department could tell how accurate their fire control had been.[95]

A new enlisted crew member that year was Private Russ McCurdy, who reported to the *Arizona* in June 1941. It didn't take long for him to realize that the commanding officer of the marine detachment, Captain Alan Shapley, was a superb leader. McCurdy spent twenty-four years in the Marine Corps altogether, eventually retiring as a lieutenant colonel. He considered Shapley the finest marine he encountered in that entire time. The detachment's captain took a genuine

Below: For the 1940 equator ceremony, King Neptune's court included one of the *Arizona*'s crewmen dressed as a woman. As the pose suggests, he was quite a flirt. (From the USS *Arizona*'s booklet *Crossing the Line*, courtesy Mrs. Lester Reeves)

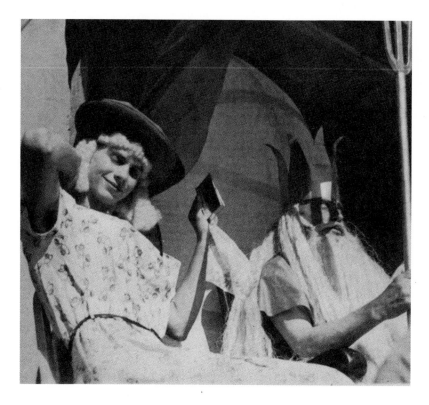

interest in the eighty or so marines in the crew, getting to know their records and their personalities. He treated them with respect, and he cared about them as individuals. They returned that respect in large measure. Unlike the stereotypical marine in command, Shapley was not the gruff type. He was soft-spoken and economical in his use of words, but he got his message across.[96]

Captain Shapley was a Naval Academy man and an athlete, so he strongly supported the marines' race-boat team. When the team beat the ones from the *Arizona's* other divisions, Shapley went to Captain Van Valkenburgh and persuaded him to allow the marine team to represent the ship rather than picking the best of the various divisions, as was the usual practice. Shapley wanted to preserve the teamwork and training that had made them so good. The men of the race-boat team had to get up early in the morning to fit in their daily practice. Shapley got up and watched them, signifying by his presence that what they were doing was important enough for him to lose some sleep.[97]

Russell McCurdy was twenty-four years old when he reported to the *Arizona*, older than the rest of the privates. He was probably assigned as one of the orderlies for Admiral Kidd because of his maturity. As many men on the *Arizona* observed, the admiral had a fetish for physical fitness. McCurdy and the admiral exercised together when the private had orderly watch on the flag bridge. When he had the 4:00 to 8:00 watch in the morning, for instance, McCurdy wouldn't be able to do his normal workout with the race-boat team, so Kidd wanted him to get his exercise on the bridge. Off would come the private's khaki shirt and pistol. The two held each other's feet for sit-ups, for example, and counted the number of repetitions. It was almost a man-to-man relationship at those times, different from when they were in official capacities and the orderly had to keep the prescribed six feet away whenever he accompanied Admiral Kidd somewhere.[98]

In August, when the ship was back in Pearl Harbor after a period of maneuvers, Yeoman First Class Jim Vlach wrote to his wife, Jeanne, in California and hinted that she ought to come out to Hawaii and join him. Both of them had grown tired of the cruise originally scheduled for six weeks but by now stretched to more than a year, so she began making arrangements, even though Vlach's salary was less than $100.00 per month. She borrowed $140.00 from her uncle and bought a first-class ticket on the passenger liner *Matsonia* headed for Honolulu. No less expensive accommodations in the ship were available at that point.[99]

Vlach worked in the executive officer's office and saw a copy of the ship's upcoming schedule that Commander Ellis Geiselman left conveniently lying out. About a day before Jeanne Vlach was due to depart for Hawaii, her husband thus learned that the *Arizona* was scheduled for a trip to the navy yard at Bremerton in December. Vlach asked for permission to go ashore and send a telegram to his wife; he would tell her not to come to Hawaii because in a few months they would be together on the West Coast for the duration of the yard period. The security-conscious executive officer said, "Go ahead, but don't give any reason."[100]

As he walked into the door of the radio company to send the message, Vlach had a change of heart. His telegram was a simple one: "Come on out. Love, Jimmy." That short communication saved his life. He and Jeanne got settled into a newly built apartment near Waikiki. He was there on the morning of 7 December instead of in his battle station in the ship's conning tower.

Right: Yeoman First Class Jim Vlach welcomes his wife, Jeanne, to Honolulu's Aloha Tower on 3 September 1941. Jeanne's arrival in Hawaii saved her husband's life because he was ashore with her on the night of 6 December rather than on board the *Arizona*. (Courtesy Vincent J. Vlach)

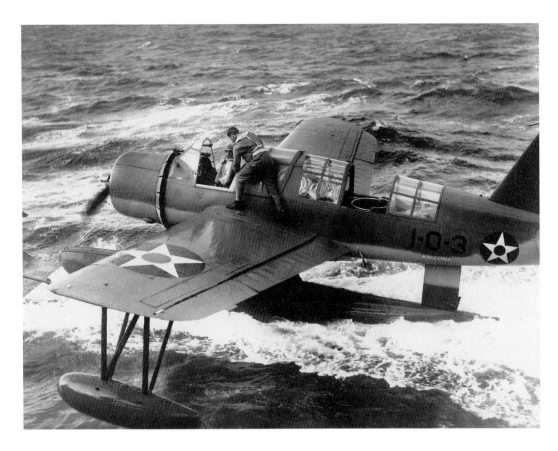

Left and below: One of the *Arizona*'s Vought OS2U Kingfisher planes maneuvers alongside the ship and then hooks on to the airplane crane. The pilot for this maneuver on 6 September 1941 is Ensign Laurence A. Williams, and the rear-seat man is Radioman Third Class Glenn H. Lane. Williams was killed on 7 December; Lane survived. (National Archives, 80-G-66108 and 80-G-66109)

Still single at the time was Gunner's Mate Howard Burk, for whom advancement to third class petty officer came about a year after he enlisted in the Navy. That kind of rapid advancement was unheard-of only a few years before when the openings were scarce and competition fierce. But the Navy was expanding rapidly and needed thousands of petty officers to man its two-ocean fleet. Liberty in Hawaii in the summer and fall of 1941 for Burk usually meant going ashore about twice a week, which was about all his budget could permit, even as a newly advanced petty officer. Included in his itinerary were sight-seeing and the opportunity to sit down and enjoy a steak dinner without having to compete with his messmates for the rations. But the real pleasure of being ashore on Oahu that year came from "drinking some of that rum and Coke, and then we visited the ladies at the houses quite a bit. . . . They had some nice ladies over there." The going price of $3.00 was higher than on the West Coast, but it struck Burk as fair when he compared the supply to the demand.[101]

On board ship, Burk was responsible for operating the aircraft catapult atop turret three. The job fell to a gunner's mate because a charge of smokeless powder fired the catapult. The powder came in a metal cylinder like a 5-inch powder casing and was about two and a half or three feet long. Atop the catapult was a sliding device known as a car, on top of which the OS2U's main float rested. The turret was trained off to the side so that the plane could scoot off along the axis of the turret and fly past the side of the ship. During a launch, the ship was headed on a course that would create a relative wind down the line of the catapult to provide additional lift for the plane. Timing was important in any kind of a rough sea because the plane was best fired off as the ship was rolling upward rather than down.

The months passed, and if anything, the operational tempo picked up even more. The chronology in the back of the book indicates the degree to which the *Arizona* and other ships of the fleet were under way as war approached. It was a far cry from the pace of the 1930s when economy was the watchword. Now the watchwords were readiness for war.

On 22 October, after steaming independently earlier in the day and exercising with submarines, the *Arizona* was joined in column by the *Nevada* and *Oklahoma*. As evening approached, the *Arizona* darkened ship, and the other two battleships sheared out of column to take part in an exercise. From time to time the *Arizona*, which was the formation guide and flagship for the officer in tactical command, bounced a searchlight off low-hanging clouds to serve as a reference for the other two ships. At 6:17 P.M. the *Oklahoma* was approaching from the port side to take station on the *Arizona*. The officers on the bridges of both ships didn't feel comfortable with the proximity of their vessels. The *Arizona* turned on her running lights, and Captain Van Valkenburgh took the conn. He put the rudder hard right and ordered flank speed. Both ships sounded sirens.

Like the *Arizona*, the *Oklahoma* had an old-fashioned ram-type bow. It struck the *Arizona* a glancing blow on the port side, not far behind the break of the deck. Ensign Paul Backus, the signal officer on board the *Oklahoma*, observed that his skipper, Captain Edward Foy, reacted skillfully to minimize the damage when the ships collided. The *Oklahoma* had reciprocating engines, rather than turbines, which meant that she had as much power backing as going forward. Foy used that power to keep the collision from being as hard as it might have been.[102]

When the two ships were separated, the crew assessed the results of the collision. The *Arizona* received far more damage than the *Oklahoma*, winding up with a V-shaped hole, four feet wide and twelve feet long, in her port side blister where the bow of the other battleship had penetrated. A slop chute that had been part of the port side of the *Arizona* was also on the bow of the *Oklahoma*. A slop chute was essentially a vertical cylinder down which garbage was poured when thrown overboard. The chute channeled it downward and kept it from winding up on the side of the ship. As for the *Oklahoma*, her jackstaff was bent out of shape from the force of impact.[103]

The *Arizona* had to go into dry dock for a few weeks at the Pearl Harbor Navy Yard to have new steel plates welded into place to close the hole. Ensign Guy Flanagan stood officer-of-the-deck watch on the quarterdeck during that time and was told to check the identification cards of anyone who came aboard. If the ensign had learned one thing as part of his training as a naval officer, it was that orders were meant to be followed. So he dutifully began checking each yard workman, comparing the face on the card to the face on the man. A considerable backup developed, stretching about one hundred feet from the quarterdeck and preventing the yard workmen from getting on with the job. A more senior officer perceived the problem and quickly modified Flanagan's previous orders since the yard workers had already been checked when they came into the shipyard. Work proceeded smoothly after that.[104]

In November Aviation Machinist's Mate Third Class Milton Hurst returned to the *Arizona* after having attended a Navy school on the East Coast. There he had met a girl who appealed to him a great deal, and they considered the possibility of getting married. All too soon his break from the routine was over, and he returned to his floating home. He was struck by the contrast between the *Arizona* he had left and the one he returned to several weeks later. No longer was she painted light gray all over, the peacetime color scheme. Up to the level of her bridge, the hull and superstructure were painted a dark gray. Only the foretop, maintop, and tops of the tripod masts were still light gray. It was a type of camouflage that would make her more difficult to spot in the distance when seen against the horizon.[105]

Along with the physical change, Hurst encountered a psychological one as well. War with Japan now appeared to be inevitable—at least as far as the fleet was concerned. He had seen the headlines in the East Coast newspapers, which described the U.S.-Japanese negotiations that seemed to go on and on without reaching a solution. Those who argue that President Roosevelt set up Pearl Harbor for attack have some basis. He did not know in advance that the Japanese were going to strike there, nor did he let them come unmolested. His foreign policies, however, pushed the Japanese into a corner from which they felt that war provided the only escape. Earlier in 1941 he had squeezed them economically, cutting off exports of oil and scrap metal as a means of punishing them for continuing a war in China that the United States opposed.

To get these commodities, the Japanese felt they had to move south, into the Dutch East Indies. Such a move was likely to bring U.S. intervention. The way to remove the threat to the Japanese military forces was to attack U.S.

forces in Hawaii and the Philippines. In late November the U.S. Chief of Naval Operations, Admiral Harold R. Stark, sent out a message that came to be known as a "war warning." In addition, the Pacific Fleet's Commander in Chief, Admiral Kimmel, mandated an aggressive training posture. As Hurst saw, the mind-set on board the *Arizona* was that the ship's men had to know how to react when war came. Among other things, they were shown how to inject morphine to counter pain. He and the men in the V division were hanging depth bombs on the OS2Us so they could be used against enemy submarines. As November ended and December began, Hurst knew that war was near. He didn't know how near.[106]

As 1941 progressed, more and more calls went out to the Battle Force to supply experienced men to go back to the United States for assignment to new-construction ships. While the *Arizona* and other older ships continued to train, each new ship needed a nucleus of veteran sailors around which to build a crew.

Late in the year a call went out for volunteers to attend diesel school and then put a new minesweeper into service. Machinist's Mate First Class Wes Cole, on board the *Arizona* since 1935, volunteered but discovered that the ship's personnel people were unwilling to let him go; the *Arizona* preferred to keep as much talent on board as possible. Cole then explained that if he weren't allowed to volunteer for the duty, it was just a matter of time before he would leave the Navy. His enlistment expired in November, but he couldn't be released from the service until the *Arizona* got back to the West Coast; this procedure would save the government transportation costs. Since the ship wouldn't be able to hold onto him anyway, the executive officer reported that the *Arizona* had a volunteer for diesel school. Cole got his orders for transfer and was in charge of the last draft of men to leave the ship prior to the attack. His plucky insistence on going to a new ship saved his life because virtually every member of the engineering department who was on board the ship on 7 December was killed.[107]

During the first week in December, as a Japanese task force steamed silently across the

North Pacific toward Hawaii, the *Arizona* and other ships of her task force were at sea for yet another series of training exercises to enhance their readiness. Near the end of the week the ship's officer of the deck thought he saw the wake of a submarine's periscope in an area where no U.S. submarines were supposed to be operating. Word of the observation spread throughout the *Arizona*. Among the scuttlebutt that made the rounds was that Captain Van Valkenburgh proposed keeping the *Arizona* at sea as a decoy when the rest of the task force returned to Pearl Harbor. An escort of destroyers, which would be ready to pounce if an enemy submarine appeared, would accompany her. Given the worsening diplomatic situation, the idea of a Japanese submarine near Hawaii was plausible to the men in the ship. Chief Watertender Joe Karb was among those who heard that Admiral Kidd sent a dispatch to Admiral Kimmel to propose the idea of the decoy. Instead, the *Arizona* was directed to return to port on schedule.[108]

On Friday, 5 December, the *Arizona* and the other ships of her task force reached Pearl and moored in the pattern that has been depicted many times in various publications since then. She moored starboard side to a pair of concrete quays at Ford Island with her bow pointed toward the channel at the harbor's entrance. During the in-port period just beginning, the *Arizona*, *Oklahoma*, and *Nevada* were to undergo material inspections. Following his usual practice when the ships of his division returned from sea, Admiral Kidd reported to Rear Admiral Walter Stratton Anderson, Commander, Battleships Battle Force, embarked in the *Maryland*. (As a lieutenant commander twenty-five years earlier, Anderson had been the *Arizona*'s first gunnery officer.)[109]

After his talk with Anderson, Admiral Kidd returned to his flagship and, as he customarily did, brought Captain Van Valkenburgh up to date on what was in the offing. The *Arizona* was scheduled to leave the following Saturday, 13 December, for a period of leave and upkeep in her home port of Long Beach/San Pedro, then begin an overhaul. The following morning, 6 December, Lieutenant Commander Samuel G. Fuqua, one of the department heads, was in Van Valkenburgh's cabin prior to the customary Saturday-morning inspection. The skipper remarked, "By this time next week, we will be on our way home for Christmas."

Fuqua, who had been reading in the newspapers about the increasingly tense relations between Japan and the United States, asked, "Captain, don't you think the Japanese situation will cancel the trip to Long Beach?" Van Valkenburgh told him it wouldn't.[110]

Seaman Oree Weller, who had reported to the ship in July from boot camp, had by December been assigned to work for the *Arizona*'s navigator. On Saturday morning he was in the navigator's office on the bridge, giving it a last-minute check prior to the inspection. He heard a strange noise and looked at the overhead to see a drill bit coming through and bits of cork insulation dropping down. Then came a steady dripping of red-lead primer paint onto the navigator's desk. Weller was horrified, what with inspection due shortly, so he hustled up to the signal bridge and discovered there a group of men from the repair ship *Vestal*, which had moored to the *Arizona*'s port side the previous day after the battleship had returned to Pearl Harbor. The *Vestal* was there to supply some technical support for the *Arizona*'s equipment, taking care of some things that then wouldn't need to be fixed during the upcoming yard period in Bremerton.

The repair ship's men were building a shacklike compartment on the after end of the signal bridge, recalled Weller, so it could house the radar equipment that was to be installed in Bremerton. He persuaded them to stop using the red lead for a while so that they wouldn't interfere with the inspection. Then he hustled back down to the navigator's office to clean off the desk and polish it one more time before the captain showed up. Weller succeeded and got his liberty card as a reward.[111]

Another inspection took place that morning on board the *Vestal*. In her crew was Watertender First Class Joe Giovenazzo, who had served in the *Arizona* until a year earlier. His younger brother Mike, a watertender second class, still served in the *Arizona*. Once the inspections in both ships were over, the two men left the ship to head for an apartment where Joe lived with his wife and baby daughter. Mike had arranged a standby so he could spend the weekend with them.[112]

Once they got back to the apartment, Joe was feeling feverish and rundown because he

MICHAEL J. GIOVENAZZO
United States Navy
(Killed in Action)

Most of us knew Mike Giovenazzo . . .

Remember back a few years ago when the American Legion out in Silvis awarded him a medal for outstanding scholarship in school? Remember when Mike was just a kid playing on the baseball lots with the other kids in his Silvis neighborhood? Doesn't seem like so very long ago, does it? It isn't!

Mike wanted to be a Navy man. He wanted to be one so much that he left High School to join Uncle Sam's navy. He was a good one, too . . . on the Battleship Arizona. Mike probably hadn't seen over two Japs in his life. Didn't know much about them. But on that fatal day at Pearl Harbor when he first met a lot of Japs, the world found out what they are. When the Arizona went down under the sneak punch Mike went with it.

Yes, he gave his life! For what? That's up to you and me and all of us. Did he give it for nothing? If we don't eliminate Hitler, Hirohito and all their kind, he did! But when we do that job . . . and do it WE WILL . . . then the tragic loss of Mike Giovenazzo and all the Mikes in Uncle Sam's army and navy will have a new meaning.

Mike's mother didn't only give Mike to her country . . . her other two boys and her son-in-law are in there pitching right now. Their job is to make the Japs and Germans regret to the very bottom of their souls that there ever was a Pearl Harbor or a Sudetenland. And they're doing it!

Now, what's our job? We know it . . . every single one of us! It's to buy these extra war bonds to give these swell kids every chance possible to do their job and come through safely. So when you're asked about bonds in this Fourth War Loan Drive . . . just remember Mike . . . the kid who grew up out in Silvis . . . right next door to you . . . AND BUY TILL IT REALLY HURTS!

Be sure to buy an

EXTRA WAR BOND

as a tribute to our fighting men

had been given a series of shots. He decided to pass up the opportunity to go to the University of Hawaii's football game that afternoon, and his wife went to the ball game with Mike. While they were at the game, Mike ran into a Marine Corps friend from back home in Illinois. He decided to make a liberty with the marine, whom he hadn't seen in some time, and then return to the *Arizona* rather than going back to his brother's apartment. That chance meeting with the marine cost young Mike Giovenazzo his life. He was one of the *Arizona*'s many engineers killed the following morning.[113]

The life of Ensign Leon Grabowsky, an officer in the engineering department, was spared by a botched medical diagnosis a few months earlier. He had been hospitalized in the spring of 1941 because of pneumonia contracted by repeatedly inspecting the steam line, inside the smokestack, leading to the ship's whistle. Because he was slow in recovering his strength after the illness, he underwent a shipboard physical exam in the summer. The verdict at that time was that he

had albuminuria, a symptom of possible kidney disease. As a result, he had to undergo a few weeks of examination at the Pearl Harbor naval hospital. He spent each morning being tested under a variety of conditions and then went out to Waikiki Beach in the afternoon to ride his surfboard.

None of the hospital's test results indicated a kidney problem, so the ensign was sent to a urologist for one more exam. The specialist concluded that Grabowsky's only problem was an enlarged, overactive prostate gland. The doctor wrote in his report that what the *Arizona*'s officer needed to cure the problem was a regular sex life. That report made Ensign Grabowsky instantly famous among the hospital's nurses as the only documented case of a Hawaiian "disease" known as "lackanookie."

Members of the *Arizona*'s medical department were so amused by the new report that they forgot to send it on to Washington. Thus the only one that got to the Bureau of Medicine and Surgery was the one reporting the supposed kidney problem. As a conse-

Below: The *Arizona*'s musicians finished second in a battle-of-bands contest ashore in Pearl Harbor the night of Saturday, 6 December 1941. All were killed on board ship the following morning. (Tai Sing Loo photo courtesy Russell McCurdy)

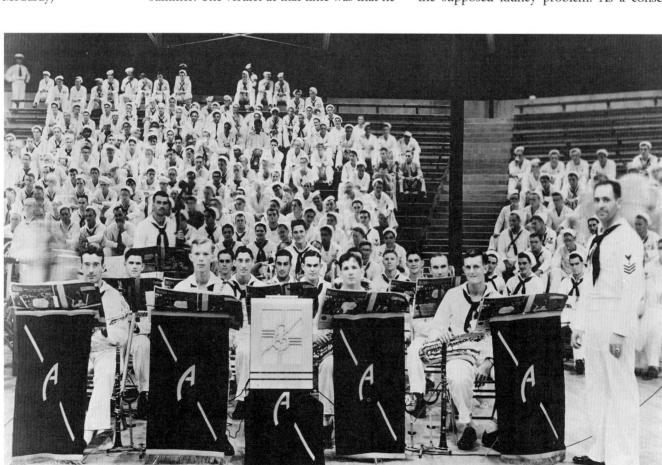

quence, Grabowsky was ordered to the hospital one more time to face a board of medical survey that would determine whether he should be discharged from the Navy. Grabowsky concluded by then that the whole thing was a farce and protested angrily about having to go back to the hospital. But he went anyway on 5 December, and that's where he was when the Japanese struck two days later. The doctor who had made the original incorrect diagnosis was lost with the ship; the patient survived.

The ship's gunnery officer, Lieutenant Commander Bruce Kelley, had head-of-department duty over the weekend, so he brought his family out to the ship for dinner in the wardroom on Saturday evening. During the meal, Lieutenant Commander Fuqua, whose family was back in Long Beach, volunteered to take over the duty so Kelley could spend Sunday ashore with his family. The Kelleys did stay around to see the evening movie in the wardroom, *Dr. Jekyll and Mr. Hyde*, starring Spencer Tracy. By that simple act of kindness, Fuqua unwittingly prepared the ship for the events of the following day. On the morrow, the *Arizona* would need damage control much more than gunnery: he was the ship's first lieutenant and damage-control officer.[114]

The life of Machinist's Mate First Class Everett Reid was saved because of his birth date. He had been born on 6 December 1917 and thus turned twenty-four the day before the Japanese attack. He was slated to stay on board that weekend but got Machinist's Mate Second Class Samuel Gemienhardt to take his duty so he could attend a birthday party with his wife, Barbara, and some shipmates. Like Yeoman Jim Vlach's wife, Barbara Reid had traveled to Hawaii in September to be with her husband. The ship's officers did not encourage the families of crew members to come out because of the possibility that the ship would be going back to the West Coast. Everett Reid had thus asked his wife not to make the trip, but she did anyway.[115]

The Reids went out for dinner and drinks on Saturday night at a Waikiki tavern and then returned to their nearby studio apartment with Elmer Schlund, also a machinist's mate first class who served in the *Arizona*. The Reids offered to set up a place for Schlund to sleep on the floor of the apartment that night so he wouldn't have to make the journey back

to the ship. He declined the offer, saying he would prefer to sleep on board ship. On the following day, Gemienhardt and Schlund died while Reid survived—all because of innocent choices that had dramatic consequences.[116]

Warrant Officer Paxton Carter and Chief Commissary Steward Ralph Byard had dinner together that Saturday evening also. Carter had only recently been promoted to warrant officer after having served as an enlisted man in the ship's supply department for a number of years. He and Byard had become friends in that time and had studied for advancement together. Normally, the Navy transfers newly promoted warrant officers to avoid the awkwardness of having them serve over the men who were formerly their peers. That hadn't happened in Carter's case, but he and Byard still felt compelled to leave the ship separately and meet ashore. Officers and enlisted men weren't supposed to go on liberty together.

After dining in a Honolulu restaurant, they went to Byard's apartment, which was in a building nicknamed "Termite Terrace," near the Bishop Museum. They had a pleasant evening together, and Byard invited Carter to spend the night ashore. Byard had plenty of room, but Carter declined the invitation. He wanted to go back to the *Arizona* so that he could get up early in the morning and grade training courses for some of the crew members who were trying to advance in rate.

Carter's conscientious behavior cost him his life.

The warrant officer's service in the ship is honored through a display of his memorabilia in cases at the *Arizona* Memorial. Photos of Carter's effects were also featured in *Life* magazine on the fortieth anniversary of the Japanese attack. The magazine reported that Carter apparently had a premonition of death during his last visit home in the summer of 1941. He left behind his scrapbooks, which he had never done before, and thus they are now available at the memorial, along with some of his possessions recovered from the wreck of the ship.[117]

On board the *Arizona* and in Honolulu, the other men of the ship found a variety of ways to pass their time as Saturday moved on to its conclusion. They listened to the radio, played cards, read, and talked. When the time came, they went to sleep—many for the last night of their lives.

8 DAY OF INFAMY

7 December 1941

By far, the best known period of the USS *Arizona*'s twenty-five-year career was the hour or two she was under attack by the Japanese on 7 December 1941. To describe the events chronologically, moving in sequence from one part of the ship to another, would be completely chaotic because the scene that morning was chaos itself. Instead, this account focuses on one or a few individuals at a time and then moves on to other experiences. Taken together, the accounts illustrate the reaction of one ship's crew to the near-total destruction of the home where they had lived and worked in peace until the Japanese struck.

At 7:30 that Sunday morning the duty department head, Lieutenant Commander Sam Fuqua, arrived in the wardroom for breakfast and joined the ship's doctor, chaplain, and the just-relieved head of the marine detachment. The latter, Major Alan Shapley, told his table companions that he had been ordered back to the United States, so he would soon be on his way home. At about 7:50 the officer who had just been relieved of the quarterdeck watch came to the wardroom to eat. When the ship's air-raid siren sounded five minutes later, Fuqua asked the recent officer of the deck whether this was a drill and whether the antiaircraft battery was manned. The OOD replied, "I think so" to both questions. Fuqua then tried to call the new officer of the deck, Ensign Henry Davison, to make sure the antiaircraft guns were manned for the customary tracking drill.[1]

Since Fuqua couldn't get Davison on the telephone, he decided to go topside and talk to him directly. He emerged onto the quarterdeck from a hatch on the port side and noticed that the color detail was on deck, preparing to raise the American flag at the stern at 8:00. Just then a plane passed over quite low, guns blazing. Fuqua looked up, saw a red ball on the underside of a wing, and realized it was Japanese. Surmising that it was an isolated aircraft from a Japanese submarine, he felt that the American guns would soon make short work of it. He then double-timed around the after end of turret four to get to the station of the officer of the deck so that he could order the crew to general quarters. As he did so, he looked up and saw a formation of high-level bombers flying down the line of battleships. He also saw, as he described later, "what appeared to be bowling balls and had the terrible realization we were under attack."[2]

Fuqua's next conscious memory was of picking himself up from alongside a crater on the deck near the after gangway and finding fires all around him. A Japanese bomb had penetrated the wood-topped steel deck near him and exploded on the deck below. The bomb's concussion had knocked him unconscious for a time. By then, burning, dying men were pouring onto the quarterdeck from the boat-deck area. With help from the crews of turrets three and four, Fuqua organized teams of fire fighters to try to keep the flames away from the quarterdeck area where wounded men were lying. At that point, Fuqua remembered, "the forward magazine blew up and the whole ship erupted like a volcano."[3] The explosion of the powder magazines for the two forward 14-inch turrets took place right around 8:10 A.M. It was the single most dramatic event that day at Pearl Harbor, turning the battleship *Arizona* into a roaring inferno.

After that, fighting the fires was a futile effort because there was no water pressure in the fire mains. When the valves were opened, the only thing that poured out was smoke. Hand-held fire extinguishers were useful to a degree; they were able to extinguish the flames on men who were burning when they ran from the boat deck to the quarterdeck.[4] Communication was difficult throughout the *Arizona* because the ship's service telephone system was no longer operating. Fuel oil escaped from the stricken *Arizona* and caught fire when it reached the surface of the water.

Because of the overwhelming nature of the damage and the futility of trying to fight fires without water, Lieutenant Commander Fuqua directed the men to abandon their ship. Members of the crew went over the side and swam to the *Arizona*'s boats that were tied up to quays and booms. These boats became rescue vessels, and so did a motor launch that arrived from the hospital ship *Solace* to take away stretcher cases. Men cut down cork life rafts from their stowage places on board ship and threw them into the water, but the rafts were unwieldy and difficult to paddle. Most of the men leaving the ship did so either by swimming or catching a ride in a motor launch.[5]

As Gunner's Mate Second Class Earl Pecotte was leaving the *Arizona*, someone gave him a boost from behind to help him get over the lifelines. He couldn't see but was sure that it was Fuqua. As he reported soon afterward of his view from the water, "The last thing I saw was Mr. Fuqua alone on the quarterdeck and the ship was ablaze from turret three forward."[6]

Ensign Davison, the in-port officer of the deck, was a busy man as the attack planes flew far above the *Arizona* and began pummeling her. He had to sound alarms and notify key people, including the skipper and duty officer, about what was happening. When Fuqua appeared on the quarterdeck, he directed Davison to call the center engine room and order pressure on the fire mains. Davison had just stepped into the officer-of-the-deck booth to make the telephone call when a bomb hit nearby and started a roaring fire. The flames that trapped both him and the boatswain's mate of the watch in the booth had, he

Below: Tom Freeman's fine painting depicts a scene that was not photographed. The *Arizona* and the repair ship *Vestal* are shown moored alongside each other on the morning of 7 December, before the arrival of the Japanese. One detail in particular represents the prewar way of life, the canvas awnings that provided relief from the Hawaiian sun but would be in the way during combat.

recalled, "a sweetish, sickening smell." The two men decided to run through the fire to the quarterdeck but couldn't, so they went over the starboard lifeline into the water. The ensign's first impulse was to return to the ship, but one look at her told him that would be futile because she appeared broken in two. He was pulled from the water into a motor launch and began helping the boat officer, Ensign William Bush from the *Arizona*, rescue as many men as they could.[7]

Even though he had been officially detached, Major Shapley was hanging around so he could play first base that day in a baseball game against the team from the carrier *Enterprise*. He went to his stateroom to change into his baseball uniform when he heard messages passed over the ship's general announcing system. The first order was to get below the armored deck (which was the second deck); then came an order to report to battle stations. Second Lieutenant Carleton Simensen, one of the junior officers in the marine detachment, succeeded in getting a number of sailors turned around, and then he headed up the tripod mainmast to his station in the maintop. On the way, he was badly

wounded in the chest, either by shrapnel, machine-gun bullets, or both. Right behind him was Major Shapley, who was almost blown off the ladder by the same bomb blast. He boosted the mortally wounded lieutenant onto the searchlight platform and continued on up to man the secondary battery director.[8]

When the major arrived, only a few marines were there ahead of him. There wasn't much they could do because their job was to direct the 5-inch broadside guns against surface targets. Japanese surface ships weren't the problem that day. When he looked down from his lofty perch, as Shapley said later, "I thought we were all going to get cooked to death because I couldn't see anything but fire down below after a while." He climbed back down the tripod, talked briefly with Fuqua on the quarterdeck, and then went over to the *Arizona*'s mooring quay to starboard. An explosion blew him off the quay into the water. Whatever hit him was intense because when he arrived on Ford Island, after swimming there, he was wearing nothing but his khaki trousers, and he was dazed.[9]

Another marine whose battle station was in secondary aft was Private Russ McCurdy, Admiral Isaac Kidd's orderly. McCurdy had

Above: This aerial overview was taken by a Japanese pilot shortly after 8:00 A.M. on 7 December. Torpedo wakes can be seen on the water, heading for the *Oklahoma* and *West Virginia*; both have already been hit and are beginning to capsize to port. The ship in the lower left corner is the *Nevada*. Just forward of her is the *Arizona*, with the repair ship *Vestal* moored to port. No torpedo tracks are headed toward the *Arizona*, nor has she yet exploded. (National Archives, 80-G-30550)

been relieved of duty at 7:30 that morning and was waiting to go ashore for a visit with the family of a man who worked in the Pearl Harbor Navy Yard. A number of civilians regularly took sailors and marines home for meals and recreation, in part for the company they provided and in part to keep them away from some of the less wholesome liberty activities available in downtown Honolulu. On this particular morning McCurdy was in the forward part of the *Arizona* when the attack started, so he headed aft and began climbing a leg of the mainmast to get to his battle station in the maintop, the place where he and others had earlier played word games

Right: Marine Private Russ McCurdy wears a broad smile in this picture taken in early 1942 because he is still alive. Only fifteen marines from the *Arizona* survived the events of 7 December. McCurdy, who often stood in this parade-rest position while serving as orderly for Rear Admiral Isaac Kidd, had a panoramic view of the Japanese attack from his battle station in the maintop. (Courtesy Russell McCurdy)

during boring "general quarters" drills. This was no drill, and it certainly wasn't boring. On his way up the mainmast, the private noted the red circles on the wings of the Japanese planes flying close by Battleship Row.[10]

It was a perilous climb because some Japanese planes were strafing while others were bombing. Machine-gun bullets bounced off the legs of the tripod or splintered the deck. McCurdy managed not to be hit. As he looked down from the ladder on the mast, he saw a bomb go through the deck, then explode. The tripod leg shielded him, but Second Lieutenant Simensen didn't have that protection and was badly wounded. McCurdy recalled of the pieces of wood and steel that hurtled past him that morning, "That was my indoctrination. I think at that moment I became a veteran right then. From then on, it seemed the worse it got, the calmer I got."[11]

Once on station, McCurdy tried to set up communications, but there wasn't much else to do because there was no role for the broadside guns. Thus he became a witness to history; high above Pearl Harbor he had a panoramic view of one catastrophe after another. In the distance were Hickam Field, an Army Air Forces base, and closer by was Ford Island, a naval air station; both were under heavy Japanese attack. Torpedo planes bored in with canopies open so McCurdy could see the faces of the Japanese pilots. They launched their deadly missiles toward the port sides of the moored battleships. The *Oklahoma* and *West Virginia* were especially hard hit. McCurdy saw the former capsize slowly to port, exposing the bottom of her hull; she looked like a beached whale.[12]

When the *Arizona*'s forward magazines exploded, McCurdy observed a great upward thrust. He thought that the forward part of the ship came out of the water. The force was so strong that he couldn't keep his knees stiff enough to remain standing. The entire maintop quivered back and forth noticeably, and the vibration threw him and his shipmates off balance. "We ended up in a human ball up there, really," he remembered, but no one was hurt. McCurdy jumped up and looked forward and down, and what he saw looked like a white-hot furnace. Debris had already flown past the maintop. Shapley then said that the communications were out, the ship was burning, and the situation looked bad. There

Left inset: The *Arizona's* forward powder magazines explode at about 8:10 A.M. Part of the force was vented straight up in the vicinity of the smokestack, leading to the erroneous conclusion that a bomb went down the stack and exploded. (National Archives, 80-G-6683)

Left: The forward part of the ship burns furiously in the wake of the initial explosion. (National Archives, 80-G-32920)

was no point in their remaining in the maintop. He told the men to meet at the quarterdeck and stand by for further orders.[13]

The wind was in favor of the maintop crew because it was blowing from the port quarter to the forward part of the ship, giving the marines and sailors up there a path to come down. There were no exits other than the ladders they had used to climb up, which were on the two forward legs of the tripod, the slanting ones. The men burned their hands coming down because the rungs were so hot. They stopped part way down as Shapley waited for more wind. After they got down the ladder, the marines stayed on deck for only five or six minutes before they abandoned ship. They were on the boat deck initially, and they saw charred bodies lying all over. Down on the galley deck McCurdy saw more bodies. Passageways looked like furnaces with blackened men coming out wearing no clothes. The only contrast to the blackness came from the whites of eyes and teeth.[14]

Commander Fuqua was calmly directing things on the quarterdeck, and McCurdy said he did a wonderful job of helping men and trying to get boats lined up for people. On the quarterdeck were people whom McCurdy knew, but he could recognize them only by their voices because they were so badly burned. McCurdy and the rest of the marines swam ashore to Ford Island. By then the ship had sunk somewhat, so the level of the water was not far below the level of the quarterdeck.[15]

The men there essentially stepped off into the water and began swimming through a layer of oil. There were also debris and splinters in the water. Above flew high-level Japanese bombers. "Every bomb, when you looked up, looked like it was pointed right at you," recalled McCurdy. So he and the others swam under the surface of the water as much as they could. Major Shapley was shouting words of encouragement to them as they swam, telling them how good they were on the drill field, the race-boat team, and so forth. McCurdy wasn't a strong swimmer, so he was convinced that Shapley's encouragement helped considerably. When bombs went off in the water, the vibration was so great that it moved the flesh on his legs; he felt as if it was going to pull away from the bones.[16]

At last the private completed the oil-soaked swim to Ford Island, greatly helped by a rest stop on the way at a pipeline. Once he got onto the island, McCurdy went through the gate of some naval officer's quarters. He knocked on the door of a house. No one answered, probably because the occupants had gone to an air-raid shelter. McCurdy went in and walked through the house. He saw oatmeal cooking on the range in the kitchen, so he took the oatmeal off and turned the range off. It is curious what people will do in the face of completely unexpected circumstances.[17]

Private McCurdy was on Ford Island throughout much of 7 December. He spent part of the day with a navy group in an armory, taking weapons out of the Cosmoline grease in which they had been stored and assembling them. From time to time men came around to muster the survivors, and he dutifully gave them his name and service number. Despite his responding to several such requests, the information never got to the right place, and his parents were notified that he had been killed. It was about two weeks later before they learned otherwise from the Marine Corps.[18]

Another marine assigned to the maintop fire-control station was Corporal Earl Nightingale. On his way to his battle station he passed through casemate nine and observed that the crew of the 5-inch broadside gun there had manned the gun and appeared calm and prepared. When he reached the boat deck, Nightingale saw that the 5-inch antiaircraft guns were firing. Some versions of the Pearl Harbor story argue that the *Arizona* did not have a chance to do any firing that morning because the magazine explosion occurred so soon after the beginning of the attack. Nightingale's version deserves strong consideration because it was recorded only a week after the attack, when the events of that Sunday were still fresh in his memory.[19] Commander Fuqua corroborated the marine's statement, saying, "The personnel of the antiaircraft and machine gun batteries on the ARIZONA lived up to the best traditions of the Navy. I could hear guns firing on the ship long after the boat deck was a mass of flames."[20] They did their duty unto death.

When he got up to the searchlight platform on the mainmast, Nightingale came across the wounded Lieutenant Simensen, lying on his back with his shirt front covered with blood. He took him by the shoulders and tried to ask him if there was any help he could provide. Simensen didn't reply because he was already dead or nearly so. After Nightingale had been in the maintop a while, the big explosion rocked the ship. In his statement a week after the attack, Nightingale said, "I reported to the Major that the ship was aflame, which was rather needless, and after looking about, the Major ordered us to leave. I was the last man to leave Secondary Aft because I looked around and there was no one left. I followed the Major down the port side of the tripod mast. The railings, as we descended, were very hot."[21]

Like Shapley, the corporal made his way from the quarterdeck to the quay to which the *Arizona* was moored. He started to take off his shoes, but a bomb blast blew him into the water, probably the same explosion that propelled Major Shapley into the harbor. Nightingale began swimming toward the pipeline fifty yards away and felt his strength give out entirely when he got about halfway there. Shapley was swimming nearby and saw him in distress, so he told the corporal to take hold of his shoulders and he began towing him toward safety. When they were within about twenty-five feet of the pipeline, Shapley's strength failed also, and Nightingale told him to go on and save himself. Shapley

Below: The foremast is engulfed in smoke after toppling forward into the cavity created by the massive explosion forward. (National Archives, 80-G-32420)

refused. He took hold of Nightingale's shirt and pulled him the rest of the way. Nightingale said afterward that he would have drowned if not for the major's help.[22] Shapley's athletic training apparently helped him out: in his late thirties and dazed by the explosion, he saved the man who was a dozen years younger. After leaving the Marine Corps, Nightingale went on to a career in radio as an actor, commentator, and executive. He became widely known for playing a lawman called Sky King in a radio-drama series, and he later had a daily commentary program that was broadcast worldwide.

Boatswain's Mate Second Class Tom White was one of many sailors of the *Arizona* who displayed coolness and presence of mind as the events of Sunday morning unfolded. When general quarters sounded, he went from the quarterdeck to his battle station in the gun pits of turret three. Soon after he heard a big explosion up above, he got orders from the turret booth behind the pits to go out and help fight fires topside. Like so many others, he was frustrated when the fire hoses failed to produce water. He was then ordered to go to an engine room and help the men who were trying to get pressure in the fire mains, but he couldn't get there because a wall of fire in the marines' berthing compartment blocked his way.[23]

When White got back to the quarterdeck, he noticed that the awning there had begun to burn, so he cut it down with a shipmate's knife to prevent it from falling on anyone. Then he went down the admiral's hatch to see if he could find any fire extinguishers below. He couldn't breathe when he got to the second deck and so returned topside. But he discovered that his division officer, Ensign Jim Dick Miller, who had accompanied him down, didn't return with him, so White went below once more. He found Miller searching in the captain's cabin to see whether Captain Van Valkenburgh might be there unconscious. The skipper had already gone to the bridge by then, so White and Miller returned once more to the quarterdeck.[24]

When orders came to abandon ship soon after that, White manned the captain's gig, which had been in the water overnight. The ship had settled so much that the starboard boat boom nearly pinned the gig down.

Left: The mainmast is essentially intact as the forward part of the ship burns. (National Archives, 80-G-32427)

White and some of his shipmates managed to get the boat free and began making rescue runs to Ford Island. During one of the runs the boat's propeller fouled on a piece of canvas in the water. White dived under the water to try to free the screw. Unsuccessful in that, he swam to an empty motor whaleboat from the *Nevada* and began operating it. He picked up a number of men trying to swim through the oily water to Ford Island and carried them to safety.[25]

Once he was on the island, he glanced back at the *Arizona* and realized that because of the chaos, no one had raised the American flag on the battleship's fantail. So he returned once more to his ship and raised a flag on the staff at the stern. He escaped being strafed as he made still more boat runs and finally reported in at the dispensary at the submarine base. To

remove the coat of oil he had picked up while trying to unfoul the screw of the *Arizona*'s gig, he had to take baths in gasoline, glycerin, and hot, soapy water.[26]

Gunner's Mate Second Class Jack McCarron was due to go on shore-patrol duty that Sunday morning. He and the others in the shore-patrol detail dutifully lined up for muster on the quarterdeck shortly before 8:00. They were wearing their service-dress white uniforms, including neckerchiefs and long-sleeved jumpers. While the men were waiting, the Japanese strafed the *Arizona* with machine-gun fire. The neat ranks on the quarterdeck dissolved as the men headed for their battle stations. McCarron was a gun captain for mount seven, one of the 5-inch/25 antiaircraft guns on the starboard side of the

Below: A view of the burning *Arizona* from Ford Island. The pipeline in the foreground was an aid to swimmers because it gave them a place to rest during their journey to the island. At right are a mooring quay and a turret of the *Tennessee*. (National Archives, 80-G-32551)

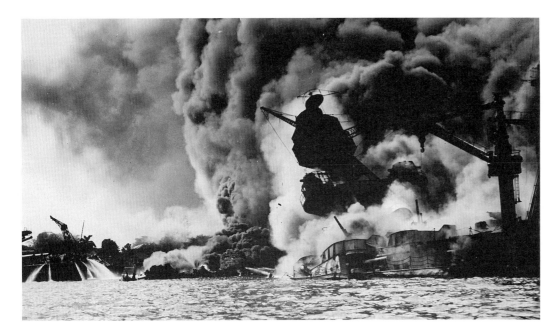

Left: Oil-fed fires from the burning *Arizona* threaten the battleship *Tennessee* just forward. To keep the fires away, the men of the *Tennessee* spray the fire hoses downward and run the ship's propellers to drive away the oil. (National Archives, 80-G-19942)

boat deck. When he arrived, he took off his neckerchief and carefully folded it before setting it down on the ammunition hoist. That's what he habitually did when he put the neckerchief away in his locker, and he was a creature of habit.[27]

Only four men were on the mount when McCarron set about trying to fire at the Japanese aircraft that were swirling about and dropping their deadly calling cards. Other men were nearby but were not reacting, seeming to be frozen in position by a combination of fear and shock. So McCarron and his small group went through the preparations for firing their gun. They didn't worry about headphones or orders from the director; conditions were too chaotic. Instead, they planned to fire with the guns in local control. The gun captain was conscious of noises around him, explosions and the sounds of gunfire, but only on the periphery of his consciousness. He was so intent on preparing his gun to fire that he didn't stop to ascertain what those noises around him actually meant.[28]

The years of repetitive training had had their desired effect. McCarron didn't have to stop and think about each step; he went through the firing preparations essentially by reflex action, just as he had folded his neckerchief before putting it down. McCarron remembered opening the ready-service locker for the ammunition and getting out three 5-inch rounds to put into the fuze pots on the left side of the gun mount. Then he got up onto the platform at the rear of the gun and began putting a round into the breech.[29]

McCarron didn't know whether mount seven fired any rounds that morning because his memory was a blank after the point of putting a round into the breech. The next conscious memory he had was of being in the water, halfway to Ford Island. The massive explosion evidently blew him overboard, and the water revived him. An officer was in the water with him, and when they got to one of the mooring quays, they did an Alphonse-and-Gaston act on who would climb up onto the quay first. A motor launch picked up the pair and took them to Ford Island. McCarron recalled that the boat was strafed, but his memories were really only fragments of that horrible morning. In all likelihood, he was lapsing in and out of consciousness because of the tremendous shock inflicted on him by the traumatic explosion forward.[30]

Like McCarron, Seaman Second Class Oree Weller could not keep from following ingrained habits. His battle station was up in the maintop with the marines whose experiences have been described already. When it came time to descend from the aerial perch, Weller first took off his sound-powered telephone headset, unplugged the cord from the jack, coiled it up, and stowed the cord and headset in their proper place. Then he set out to save his life. As he went down he noticed

Above: In this view from the rear of Battleship Row, the *Arizona* burns, the *Tennessee* sprays her fire hoses downward, and the *West Virginia* lists slightly to port after counterflooding prevented her from capsizing. (National Archives, 80-G-32732)

the remains of the smokestack. Part of the stack had been included in his regular cleaning station, and his first thought when he looked at the stack was, "My God, we're going to have to scrape and paint it."[31]

He scrambled down to the flaming boat deck and saw that the ladder to the quarter-deck was gone, as were the other ladders on the starboard side of the superstructure. So he had to jump down to the quarterdeck. There he took cover under the overhang of turret three for a time to get protection from strafing. He saw many bodies on the deck but was able to recognize only one. Lying there with his eyes burned, able neither to see nor to speak, was seventeen-year-old Charles Brittan. Weller recognized him only by a small tattooed bird on his right shoulder. Weller and Brittan had gone to boot camp together and had ridden from San Pedro to Pearl Harbor in the oiler *Neosho* to report in mid-July for duty on board the *Arizona*. Now his friend was burned so severely that he didn't live long enough to be put aboard a motor launch that had come alongside from the hospital ship *Solace*. Charles Brittan would remain forever seventeen years old.[32]

After helping for a while with the wounded, Weller obeyed when the order came to

abandon ship. As he had done with the phones, the seaman took care to be neat. He took off his shoes and socks and put them together on the deck with his white hat neatly atop them. Then he went over the starboard side of the *Arizona* into the water. As did many others that day, Weller struggled with the heavy coat of oil on the water. The flames advanced closer and closer as he swam toward the officers' landing on Ford Island. Then he looked to his right and saw salvation. Another motor launch from the *Solace* came by, and a member of the crew extended a boat hook. Weller hung on while eager hands hauled him aboard. The coxswain offered a white jumper sleeve so Weller could wipe his mouth, and a pharmacist's mate gave him a wad of gauze to clean his eyes. The young seaman was simultaneously scared, relieved, numb, covered with oil, and breathing heavily from his exertions in the water. But he was safe.[33]

Seaman William Osborne was also in the maintop, although he was assigned to main-battery control, rather than second battery as Weller and the marines had been. Osborne and Seaman Bob Seeley were in the director with the rectangular windows rolled down, as rules specified during general quarters. On this morning the view was gruesome. Before they abandoned the station, Osborne and Seeley looked at the billowing black smoke pouring up from the forward part of the ship. Sometimes the smoke parted enough for them to get a look at the foremast, and they saw men trying to get down. Those men had no choice at all; they could either stay in the foretop and be cooked or could climb down into the fire itself. There were no known survivors from the foretop of the *Arizona*.[34]

Aviation Machinist's Mate Milt Hurst and a buddy began the day on the quarterdeck. They were standing with rackets in hand because they were going to go play tennis. Hurst smoked a cigarette as they waited for 8:00 colors and then the liberty launch to Aiea. "Never did play tennis that day," Hurst offered laconically. The first indication of a problem was the announcement: "Fire and rescue party, muster on the quarterdeck." A hangar on Ford Island had been hit and was emitting a big plume of smoke. The next word he recalled was "All hands get below the armored deck." So that's where he headed. Then general quarters sounded. Not until he got back up from below the armored deck did he really know what was happening. His battle station was up by the aviation shack near the break of the deck, so he headed there.[35]

When he went out on the quarterdeck, he saw people lying on deck badly burned. A bomb hit near a big blower and killed all the people in the aviation shop. It didn't hurt him all that much, just rattled him around a little bit because he was shielded from the full effect. His only injury was the fracture of a small bone in his hand. As with so many other people that day, luck played a truly vital role—his position in relation to the blower meant the difference between a broken hand and a broken body. Once he picked himself up and took stock, Hurst saw smoke coming out of a hatch, so he went down in there to see if he could help anyone who was hurt. He couldn't stay in there because he couldn't breathe in the heavy, acrid smoke. He knew this was officers' quarters.[36]

As he reacted to the chaos around him, Hurst was surprisingly calm. A line from Shakespeare passed through his head—all the world was a stage and the people on it mere players. He remembered also saying a prayer—not for himself but for his girlfriend in New York, the one he had met earlier in the year while going to school there. If the Lord would take care of her, he would go back and marry her. At that point, he knew he would be okay. He felt no panic. Fuqua came around and told them to abandon ship, and that's when Hurst left. He swam over to Ford Island, got into a bomb shelter, and fell asleep. He is still married to the girl from New York.[37]

Back in November, Seaman Carl Christiansen had reported to the *Arizona*, having

Below: Rescue boats ply the waters of Pearl Harbor on 7 December, looking for survivors, as the *Arizona* burns. (Courtesy George Dyson)

requested to serve on the same ship as his older brother Ed. The ship's operating schedule since then had offered them only a couple of opportunities to go ashore together. On the morning of the seventh they were going to Honolulu to find a photo studio where they could have their picture taken together, their first time as Navy men; they would send the portrait home to their parents in Kansas. Carl got to the quarterdeck first and was waiting there for his brother to come down from the galley deck. When Ed arrived, he said he wanted to get something else to take with him. He went away, and Carl never saw him again.[38]

Carl's first awareness of trouble came when water from a bomb or machine-gun strafing splashed Coxswain Ken Edmondson. Edmondson had his head out a port, so he started ordering those around him to close the portholes as a damage-control precaution.[39] At the time, Christiansen thought the coxswain was bossy, but he later realized that it was good that someone was willing to take charge. The ship was hit about that time, and then sounded the call to general quarters.

A member of the fourth division, Christiansen headed down to his battle station in a handling room, near the 14-inch powder magazines for turret four. Before long the electricity failed and the lights went out. The dark was disquieting to those down in the nether regions of the ship, especially when gas began to fill the area. It was not smoke but

had a decided odor, so perhaps it was chlorine gas released by spillage from the lead-acid storage batteries. The batteries were located in the electric deck of each turret as a backup in case the ship's electrical power to operate the turret was cut off.[40]

One member of the group—his name now forgotten—did most of the talking, and his leadership had a calming effect on the men in the handling room. He seemed to know the ship better than most and said that he would lead them to safety. In the darkness the men followed him, each keeping a hand on the shoulder of the man in front. Unable to find their way out, they returned to the handling room. The men were frightened but not panicky, though they seemed to have forgotten some of their normal training. One of them suggested lighting a match to help them see. The others, mindful of the gunpowder all around them and the growing presence of gas, quickly stifled his suggestion.[41]

Then they decided to try another route. They went into a passageway connecting the handling rooms for the two aft turrets and finally managed to get into the handling room for turret three. There the gas was not so unpleasant, although it did increase with time. Then they climbed up the series of ladders from the lower decks to the turret itself—again in darkness. When the sailors got to the top, they felt comforted to a degree by the presence of a small amount of light coming in. At the direction of Ensign Guy

Right: The *Arizona*'s stern has sunk so that the quarterdeck is nearly even with the top of the water. The national ensign still flies; it was taken down later in the day by two of the *Arizona*'s officers. (National Archives, 80-G-32591)

Flanagan, one of the officers in third division, the men in the turret took off their shirts and stuffed them into the telescope slots for the pointer and trainer to keep the smoke out. Finally, they went out the hatch at the rear of the turret and climbed down the ladder on the side of the barbette of turret three and onto the quarterdeck.[42]

At last, Seaman Christiansen was out in the open, able to see again and to breathe air that wasn't quite so stifling as down below. On the other hand, he was now exposed to new hazards, including the machine guns of the Japanese planes. He and others took shelter for a bit under the overhang of turret three. There they took off their shoes and lined them up before jumping into the water to swim ashore. Christiansen didn't get far because of the heavy oil. He made his way back and climbed aboard. After a while a boat came along and began taking men off the *Arizona* at the stern, near where the American flag was still flying. Among that group, Carl Christiansen didn't have far to descend to get into the boat. The main deck, which normally had a freeboard of a little more than 17 feet, was by then only a few feet above the level of the water. The *Arizona* was settling into the harbor.[43]

Ensign Flanagan's experiences largely paralleled those of Seaman Christiansen. Flanagan was dressing in his room when the air-raid siren sounded. He put on his khaki uniform and shoes and headed down and aft to the

turret three powder-handling room, which was his battle station. With him was Ensign Jennings Field, the other junior officer in the division. They had to bang on the door to the handling room because others had gotten there before them and already dogged it down to establish watertight integrity. But nobody inside paid any attention to the banging until Flanagan took off his wristwatch and used it to beat an SOS on the door. As he did so, he was praying out loud.

The lights were already out when the officers finally got into the handling room. Now and then they felt the ship shudder as the bombs hit her. The huge explosion forward was not noticeably louder than the rest because it was some distance away. As time passed, the men in the handling room felt a growing sense of futility because they couldn't raise either the plotting room or the turret booth by sound-powered telephones. The crew grew considerably uncomfortable when fumes started coming in, and confusion reigned briefly. The two ensigns ordered their men to be quiet, and they obeyed quickly. At about that time someone produced a flashlight, and its beam revealed that the room was quite misty with smoke; it was clearly becoming untenable.[44]

The scouts the officers sent out found that the crew from the turret itself was no longer there. Water had already seeped into the handling room to a depth of eight inches above the deck level, so the ensigns decided to take their men out. They were coughing badly before they were able to get through the hatches that led into the gun pits of the turret proper. Flanagan was among those who stuffed shirts into the openings around the guns of turret three, and finally he exited to the quarterdeck. There he saw machine-gun bullets hitting all around, chewing up the teak deck and ricocheting when they hit the steel below the wood. He left the ship on board an admiral's barge after he noted that the life rafts had difficulty floating because they had been painted so many times in peacetime. It was just as well that Flanagan got a boat ride because he didn't know how to swim.[45]

Once on Ford Island, Flanagan and others took shelter under a house until the air raid was over. He reported to the receiving station and was reassigned to the *Maryland*, moored forward of the *Arizona* in Battleship Row. He felt reasonably well until general quarters was

Above and opposite page: Salvage work has already begun on 9 December, even though the *Arizona* is still smoldering. (National Archives, 80-G-32608 and 80-G-32609)

sounded on the night of the seventh; this time American planes were coming in to land. The fumes he had inhaled that morning had a delayed reaction: he collapsed in a passageway of the *Maryland*, and another man walked right over him in his haste to get to his battle station. From there Flanagan got a trip to the hospital.[46]

Seaman First Class Jimmie Burcham was with Flanagan and Field as they sought to get into turret three's lower handling room. He heard Flanagan's prayers and hoped they would be answered. Burcham had begun the morning by eating breakfast and helping to rig the ship for church services that were never held. Then he went down into officers' country, looking for either Ensign Flanagan or Ensign Miller to sign a special-liberty chit for that day. He was standing outside the captain's cabin when he saw a messenger run in to tell Captain Van Valkenburgh that someone was bombing the naval air station on Ford Island. Then the messenger and the skipper ran out of the cabin and up the ladder to the quarterdeck. From there Van Valkenburgh made his way to the bridge.[47]

Burcham decided to go chasing after the other men. He knew that enlisted men didn't use the captain's ladder except in an emergency, and he was sure this qualified. After that he made his way down into the turret three handling room, joining the others as they struggled back up to the quarterdeck. A ride in the admiral's barge from the ship to Ford Island capped the seaman's unusual day. It was the only time in his life he was in an admiral's barge.[48]

Coxswain Edmondson had gotten into the third division, and thereby saved his life, because of a bit of sass to a senior petty officer about six months earlier. On a previous Sunday morning Edmondson had the duty of making sure his men squared away one of first division's messing and berthing spaces after breakfast. Edmondson was playing poker when Boatswain's Mate Second Chester Rose found him and told him to get his mess cooks on the job. Edmondson told Rose that the job had already been done, and he could go see for himself if he wanted to. The senior man didn't take kindly to that, especially since the coxswain, newly advanced to third class, seemed more inclined to hang around with his seaman friends than to join the petty officers' clique. Within half an hour Edmondson was transferred to the third division. Boatswain's Mate Rose, like the rest of first division, died on 7 December.[49]

Poker had also figured in Edmondson's activities on the seventh. That morning he had taken some clothes to the laundry and thought he would go to turret one to collect a poker debt so he would have money for liberty. Instead, he decided to wait until later for his money. As mentioned earlier, Edmondson found out about the attack when a near miss from a Japanese bomb gave him a face full of water. He told whoever was within hearing, "Get your asses to your battle stations," then headed to his own. He went back to the lower-handling-room area for turret three and started climbing a ladder to his station in the upper handling room, just below the turret. As he remembered, "That's when she come up in the air and shook like a dog."[50]

He waited and waited in the dark, but nothing happened. He finally crawled through some hatches and went up into the turret's control booth, but no one else was there. So he dropped out through the hatch in the overhang and went to the quarterdeck. He looked forward and saw nothing but fire and bodies. Coxswain Edmondson quickly concluded that it was a good time to leave the *Arizona*. He looked toward the gangway, which before the attack had slanted down from the quarterdeck to the mooring quay. Now it was essentially level, although turned on its side. He used the bottom handrail as a walkway and held onto the top rail as he crossed over to the quay, where he found some twenty burned men. Two or three called to him by name, but he couldn't tell who they were. He saw a motor launch nearby and loaded the men into that so he could transport them to Ford Island.[51]

He landed at an admirals' pier and put the men into a bomb shelter temporarily. Then he found a station wagon with the keys inside and soon turned it into a makeshift ambulance to haul the burned men to a dispensary for treatment. As he drove along, pieces of hot shrapnel hit the station wagon, but Edmondson wasn't injured. After running the car for some time, he lost it to an ensign who pulled rank and claimed he could do more good with it than the coxswain could. Then Edmondson got himself into the crew of a real ambulance and helped out a while longer, picking up still more of the injured. All he was wearing by then were white shorts, a bloody T-shirt, his boatswain's pipe, and an old pair of galoshes that he had found on Ford Island.

When he was driving the station wagon amid the Japanese strafing, Edmondson non-chalantly steered with one hand while lighting cigarettes and smoking with the other. When he got out and had time to think about what he had been through, the coxswain shook so much that he couldn't light a cigarette even when he tried using both hands.[52]

Seaman Don Stratton of the sixth division was up early on Sunday morning. He ate breakfast in his compartment, then picked up some oranges and stowed them in his white hat so that he could take them down to a shipmate who was in sick bay. He was about to head down to the third deck, near the turret two barbette, when a friend yelled for him to look over at Ford Island, where a bomb had just gone off. Stratton dropped the oranges and headed for his battle station, which was up rather than down. He was a sight-setter on the port-side director for the 5-inch/25 antiaircraft guns.

His station looked like a steel cube. Added to the ship during the last overhaul at Bremerton, the new directors were one level

above the navigation bridge and just out-board of it. They were adjacent to the after legs of the tripod foremast.[53]

A half dozen or so men operated each of the big directors. The director had been doing its job, tracking the Japanese planes, but many of them were too close for the 5-inch guns to have any effect. The projectiles had to go out to a certain range before they would arm and thus be able to explode. The minimum time that could be set on the fuzes was slightly more than three seconds.

Behind each of the 5-inch guns, some ammunition was stored in ready-service boxes. Ensign Frank Lomax knew those projectiles wouldn't last long, so he left the director to see about replenishing the supply. Just then the bomb hit the forward magazines, and Stratton never saw Lomax again.

The director saved Seaman Stratton's life because he was inside it when the forward part of the ship exploded. When the blaze subsided a bit, he opened a hatch on the director and jumped out. He then went hand over hand along a piece of line that stretched from the port side of the director to the repair ship *Vestal* that was moored to port of the *Arizona*. Only six men from the *Arizona* escaped in that fashion, and at least one of those died soon afterward. As he looked

Right: A close-up of the mangled foremast area. The cubelike structure at the top of the pole is the port antiaircraft director for the 5-inch/25 guns. It combined the functions of the previously separate director and optical range finder. Sailors Don Stratton and Russ Lott went hand over hand on a piece of line from this director to reach the repair ship *Vestal* while the battleship was blazing. (Courtesy George Dyson)

across to his ship from his newfound haven, Stratton saw the bodies of men he knew, but there was nothing he could do for them.[54]

Seaman Russell Lott was the man who arranged for the escape route that Stratton and the rest of the director's crew took. To protect himself from the heat of the raging fires, Lott wrapped himself in a blanket and went out to get the attention of the men on board the neighboring *Vestal*. One of them threw over a heaving line, the type used as a light advance messenger for a mooring line when a ship is tying up. Once the heaving line was on the *Arizona*, the *Vestal*'s men then attached a heavier line to it. The director's crew pulled the second line over and tied it to the director platform. That was their lifeline.[55]

Soon afterward Seaman First Class Steve Lukasavitz, who had been part of the crew of one of the *Arizona*'s 5-inch antiaircraft guns, helped free the *Vestal* from alongside the blazing battleship. Lukasavitz had been in a handling room below the gun mount, trying unsuccessfully to feed ammunition upward. When the water in the handling room reached their ankles and continued to rise, he and the men with him escaped by ladder. He went back by the number three turret and vomited, something that helped him feel better. Then he and Aviation Machinist's Mate First Class Donald Graham struggled with the heavy mooring lines on the *Arizona*'s bitts, finally getting them off and letting the repair ship escape. Their first impulse had been to cut the lines with an axe, but an officer on board the *Vestal* asked them to cast off the lines instead so that the ship could use them to moor to a buoy. The *Vestal* grounded instead.[56]

Down in the handling room for turret three, shortly before 8:00 o'clock, one of the first class petty officers of the division directed his men to put away their cots. Unlike most of the divisions, the gunner's mates of the turret divisions didn't eat and sleep in the same compartments. They slept down inside the turret structures themselves so that they would be closer to their battle stations and able to respond more quickly if needed. The gunner's mates had been up to have breakfast in a main-deck compartment near the quarterdeck and were now putting their cots away in a locker for the day. Gunner's Mate Third Class Howard Burk talked about going ashore on liberty, but before he could leave,

the word came over the general announcing system to man battle stations.[57]

The men on duty climbed up from the handling room and took their stations in the gun chamber. Burk was a tray man for one of the 14-inch guns of turret three. Because the Japanese had launched an air attack, and since no Japanese ships were in sight, the *Arizona*'s 14-inch guns had no role to play. The gunner's mates stayed by their stations and then were jolted by the massive explosion in the forward part of the ship. Burk grabbed hold of the tray he operated and used it for support to keep from being pitched off his feet. Ensign Jim Dick Miller, the turret officer, realized there was no point in keeping the men inside the turret and ordered them out. They crawled out of a small hatch at the rear of the turret and went down a few steps to the quarterdeck. There they confronted the horror of their injured, dying, or dead shipmates.[58]

Gunner's Mate Burk joined Fuqua's attempts to fight the fires. Everything forward of the boat deck was ablaze, and men had to jump over holes to get around on the quarterdeck. Buckets materialized from somewhere, and the healthy crew members started a bucket brigade that proved completely futile. Once Fuqua ordered the men to abandon ship, they did so in a variety of ways. Burk described one man who came out of turret four: "He just looked like a wild man. The man was in such a shock that he dove off the ship and went the long distance for the beach, rather than heading for Ford Island, which was near the *Arizona*'s starboard side."[59]

Some men on the fantail threw a life raft into the water. By that time the edge of the

Above: A salvage tug off the port quarter on 10 December. (USS *Arizona* Memorial, National Park Service, PR-52)

Above: The repair ship *Vestal*, which had been moored to the *Arizona*'s port side, is shown beached off Aiea Landing after being freed from alongside the burning battleship. (Naval Historical Center, NH 50273)

junior officers. The man had blood all over his forehead, apparently struck by shrapnel or a strafing bullet, thought Miller. The solicitous Miller asked what had happened, and the officer said that when the bombs began to hit, he had charged up a ladder to get topside. He was in such a rush that he didn't look up and rammed his head right into a closed hatch.[61]

One of the men on the bridge with Captain Van Valkenburgh was Ensign Douglas Hein. Hein had left the junior officers' mess when general quarters sounded. As he made his way to his battle station on the signal bridge, he noticed that some of the *Arizona*'s starboard antiaircraft guns were firing. When he arrived on the signal bridge, he saw he could do nothing there, so he descended a level to the navigation bridge, where the only other people were Captain Van Valkenburgh and a quartermaster. The quartermaster asked the skipper if he wanted to go into the armored conning tower, but Van Valkenburgh said no, remaining instead on the bridge to make telephone calls to various stations within the ship.

A quartermaster reported to Ensign Hein that a bomb had struck turret two. Hein described what happened next: "Suddenly the whole bridge shook like it was in an earthquake, flame came through the bridge windows which had been broken by gunfire. We three were trying to get out the port door at the after end of the bridge during all this shaking, but could not. We staggered to the starboard side and fell on the deck just forward of the wheel. Finally I raised my head and turned it and saw that the port door was open. I got up and ran to it, and ran down the port ladders, passing through flames and smoke. Then I climbed half way down the signal bridge ladder and had to jump to the boat deck as it was bent way under. Then I climbed down a hand railing to the galley deck. The flames and smoke were decreasing in intensity."

From there Hein walked aft and down the ladder to the port quarterdeck. He made his way then to the starboard side and went down the officers' ladder to the admiral's barge, which took him away for medical treatment. Badly burned, Ensign Hein was the only man to escape from the bridge area. He recovered and returned to duty but was killed in an aircraft crash several years later while flying

deck was only about three feet from the water. When Burk and some of his shipmates got into the raft, they discovered there were no paddles, so they set out swimming. Burk came to a dredging line and stopped to rest for a while because he was completely winded from battling the layer of fuel on top of the water. As he stopped, a big wave of oil hit him in the mouth. He swallowed some of it and was sick for a time. Finally, he swam toward Ford Island. Once on land, he got a ride to the Ford Island dispensary for treatment. The Japanese weren't done with him yet, however. While he was in the head, washing oil out of his eyes, the second Japanese air raid came over. One plane dropped a bomb into the courtyard in the center of the dispensary. Fortunately, the bomb didn't detonate, and Howard Burk survived to fight another day.[60]

Ensign Jim Dick Miller of turret three received a Navy Cross for his heroism on board the ship during and after the attack. While trying to deal with the raging fires, he got his turret crew out okay and put the wounded and burned men into boats so that they could be treated. Miller had seen one wounded man after another, many of them in great pain. Then he saw one of his fellow

from the carrier *Antietam* as a lieutenant commander.[62]

On the morning of 7 December Yeoman First Class Jim Vlach and his wife, Jeanne, were in their apartment in the Waikiki area when a chief petty officer's wife, their next-door neighbor, told them to turn on their radio. As soon as he learned of the attack, Vlach donned his whites and made his way to Pearl Harbor. He reported to the receiving station, from which he could see the overturned hull of the *Oklahoma* and the oily black smoke reaching up from the *Arizona*. No one seemed to be in charge at the office, so he went to the Merry's Point boat landing to lend a hand. In came a boatload of wounded men. One of his shipmates from the *Arizona*, badly burned by a ruptured steam line, recognized Vlach and asked him for help in getting out of the boat. The yeoman took hold of the man's arms to pull him out of the boat, and his skin came off in Vlach's hands.[63]

For the rest of the morning Vlach did what he could to help wherever he could. By noon his white uniform was a bloody, oily mess. He went to clothing issue to get some dungarees; the best available pair was still too large, so he had to use a piece of line around his waist to hold them up. Back at the receiving station, he finally had a chance to do some yeoman work. Amid the chaos that was Pearl Harbor

Below: A close-up of the crumpled wreckage of what was once a battleship. Notice the twisted metal shields around the 5-inch antiaircraft guns. (Courtesy George Dyson)

Above: At the top of the foretop is the pedestal for an air-search–radar antenna that was to be installed at Bremerton in early 1942. Two .50-caliber machine-gun positions can be seen just below the foretop. The bridge area has essentially melted and settled onto the top of the conning tower. (Courtesy George Dyson)

that day, Vlach recognized the importance of recording the names of the survivors. He and a yeoman from the *Arizona*'s engineering log room handed out a stack of cards to the gaggle of refugees from various ships and asked them to record their names, rates, service numbers, and duty stations.

Before long an officious officer came in and stopped the two yeomen from distributing the cards. He didn't think the process was orderly enough, so he directed the survivors to line up in two ranks and proceed one by one to the typewriters, where Vlach and his partner could record the pertinent data. Before the yeomen had a chance to get very far, some other officers came in and asked for volunteers to help man the able ships that were going out to fight the Japanese. Many in the receiving station thus charged out the door before the *Arizona*'s two yeomen could get their names on paper. The ships in which the survivors went to sea could not send in their names immediately because of operational commitments and radio silence. Consequently, a number of those men were reported to the Navy Department and to their

relatives back home as missing in action. Vlach and the other yeoman worked on through the rest of the day. Completely bushed, they finally knocked off around midnight on 7 December and went to sleep under a pool table in the receiving station.[64]

Chief Electrician's Mate William Gallagher owed his life to a late game of bridge at the home of Chief Watertender Joe Karb, who lived in the Waikiki area. They played until after the last Saturday night boat had returned to the *Arizona*, so Chief Gallagher stayed the night with his shipmate's family. The next morning Karb was scheduled for a watch, so the pair headed for Pearl Harbor together. When they got to the navy yard, the Japanese planes were still strafing the area; for the first of several times that day, Karb sought protection by diving under something.[65]

During a lull in the action Karb went to Ford Island by boat, thinking perhaps he could render some assistance to his stricken ship. He ran into Major Shapley. Clad in only a pair of khaki pants, Shapley was still in something of a daze from being blown off the mooring quay but managed to relate the highlights to the chief. As the two walked along in single file, a row of Japanese machine-gun bullets stitched a pattern in the ground right alongside them. They raced for a low wall that was part of some structure then under construction. As Karb put it, "Hell, the major—he beat me over, barefooted and all." By then, Shapley was shivering visibly from the shock of the ordeal he had been through.[66]

After they had taken cover once more to avoid being strafed, this time under some piles of steel, the second wave of the attack finally ended. About them were vast amounts of destruction, a temporary hell on earth. When Karb eventually showed up at the receiving station, he sat down and listened to the radio reports that reinforced what he had seen with his own eyes and added still more worries with false reports that the Japanese were staging an amphibious landing on the island of Oahu. "All I could do was cry and throw up," he said later. "I was sick, just looking at all my shipmates there and everything." He had trouble eating for a week.[67]

Still later that Sunday Karb and his friend, Chief Gallagher, were assigned to temporary duty in the *Tennessee*. The ship in which they were billeted was wedged in tightly between the partially sunk *West Virginia* and a mooring quay. She had her main engines turning over to keep away burning oil from the blazing *Arizona* just astern. For Karb and Gallagher, the night of the seventh was a far, far cry from their friendly game of cards just twenty-four hours earlier.[68]

Among the *Arizona's* men saved because they were ashore with their families the night before the attack was Lieutenant Kleber Masterson, the fire-control officer. He reported to Pearl Harbor as soon as he could get there along roads that were being strafed. He soon discovered that his limited knowledge of first aid was not much help in a disaster of this magnitude, so he pitched in and helped Lieutenant Commander Fuqua get things organized ashore once the ship had been abandoned.[69]

Some of the *Arizona's* men have felt a nagging sense of guilt in the years since 1941 because their shipmates died and fate spared them. Not so Masterson, who eventually became a vice admiral. He explained later: "I hated to lose so many shipmates, but I have never wished that I was on board during the bombing, because I couldn't have done a thing about it. I'd have been trapped in the plotting room. We didn't fight the antiaircraft battery on those ships from the plotting room, so I couldn't have helped in the battle. That's the only consolation I have."[70]

At sunset on that traumatic day Lieutenant Masterson and another officer from the *Arizona*, Ensign Leon Grabowsky, got into a motor launch and went over to the still-blazing hulk of their ship. Drooping from the flagstaff at the stern was the American flag raised earlier by Boatswain's Mate White. Part of it was hanging down into the water and stained with oil because the ship had settled steadily throughout the day: the fantail was just about level with the surface of the water. Just at sunset the two officers took down the flag and then reported aboard the *Maryland*, the ship that was to be their temporary home for the next few days. They turned the *Arizona's* oily flag over to the *Maryland's* officer of the deck, expressing their wish that it be preserved as a reminder of their ship. They never saw the flag again, and Masterson never learned what became of it.[71]

Lieutenant Commander Fuqua was in charge of the *Arizona's* detail at the receiving station, and he sent men to various places to spend the night. He told Private Russ McCurdy, Admiral Kidd's orderly, to report to the *Tennessee*. The marine was issued a

Below: The crew of a motor whaleboat pokes at a hatch cover. To the left of turret three, the structure with amplifiers on it is the movie-projection booth. The amplifiers enabled the crew to hear film soundtracks during the nightly shows on the port side of the quarterdeck. (Courtesy George Dyson)

Navy dungaree uniform to wear after he took a shower and had a meal. He decided not to wear the white hat that went with the outfit because it would have made him look even more like a sailor. McCurdy caught a launch to the *Tennessee*, where he was received somewhat skeptically because he had on part of a Navy uniform, was carrying no written orders, only oral ones, and had no identification. One of the marines from the *Tennessee* who had been with McCurdy at sea school had to come down from the maintop and identify him before he was accepted.[72]

After spending some time in the *Tennessee*, Private McCurdy was assigned to a machine gun ashore on Sunday night. The idea was to be ready in case the Japanese launched a follow-up air raid. Instead, the airplanes that came in to land that night were from the U.S. carrier *Enterprise*. Numerous radio warnings told the gunners on duty not to fire because the aircraft were friendly. Initially, fire discipline was observed, but then someone panicked, and the sky was soon full of machine-gun bullets. The American gunners shot down four of their own planes that night, killing three U.S. pilots. McCurdy said that the sky was filled with a "dome of tracers." It was unlike anything the marine witnessed until the very end of the war. He was on Okinawa the night that American machine guns were fired skyward in celebration of Japan's surrender. He had the same vision on the first day of the war and on the last.[73]

Sometime on 7 December, U.S. Navy commands throughout the world received orders to execute WPL-46, the Rainbow Five plan for a multi-theater war. Rear Admiral Robert A. Theobald's Destroyer Flotilla One was one of those commands. While at sea, he and his staff embarked in the light cruiser *Raleigh*; in port, the staff shifted to the destroyer tender *Dobbin*. When Theobald got the order, he didn't have the war plan with him, so he summoned his staff duty officer, Lieutenant Henry Williams, Jr., the same individual who as a three-year-old had put the first bolt into the keel of the *Arizona* in 1914.[74]

Theobald sent Williams to the *Raleigh* to retrieve the plan from the safe in his stateroom. The *Raleigh* had been torpedoed and was listing, so Williams had the coxswain approach the cruiser from astern, and he gingerly clambered aboard over one of the propeller guards. With a flashlight in hand, he made his way to his own room, got the plan, and took it back to Theobald. Ironically, the plan called for the U.S. Fleet to make its way westward to occupy the Marshall and Caroline islands. The plan envisioned a battle-line engagement with the Japanese, but most of the principal ships that were to have executed the war plan lay in shambles there at Pearl Harbor.[75]

That night Pearl Harbor and its environs were blacked out for fear that the Japanese might be planning a follow-up attack or invasion. Williams went out onto the deck of the tender *Dobbin* with a newspaper, just to see if he could read it by the light available from the burning warships. He recalled years afterward, "We were all darkened, of course. It was whatever moon there was and the light of the burning ships, which were pretty bright. And I just stood there and read myself a column or so out of the paper." Williams remembered that the brightest light of all came from the funeral pyre of the *Arizona*.[76]

9 AFTERMATH

1941-Present

In the days following 7 December, the survivors of the attack on Pearl Harbor began to pick themselves up and restore some semblance of order to their lives. There were precious few from the USS *Arizona* left to do that. She lost more men than any U.S. Navy ship before or since. Of the 1,514 men attached, 1,177 were killed—77.7 percent. Of the 337 survivors, a number had been on leave, liberty, or detached duty elsewhere. This means that probably between 80 and 90 percent of those on board the ship at the time of the attack lost their lives. Of eighty-eight marines, only fifteen survived. The *Arizona*—by herself—accounted for more than half the total of 2,117 Navy and Marine Corps fatalities that resulted from the entire attack. Many of the *Arizona*'s crew members, of course, were killed instantly when the magazines exploded; others burned to death in the fires that enveloped the forward two-thirds of the ship. Still others lasted longer—perhaps minutes, perhaps hours. They were in below-decks spaces: engine rooms, firerooms, the plotting room, and other compartments. As the ship settled into the ooze at the bottom of the harbor, they lasted as long as the air pockets did. They could not escape by going up because the inferno blocked their way. In all other directions, decks and bulkheads of steel kept them trapped. Gradually, they asphyxiated or drowned.

Pouring out fire and smoke, the *Arizona* burned from Sunday to Wednesday, 10 December, when the blaze finally went out. It took a while longer for the decks to cool enough to walk on. One morning, a week or so after the attack, Ensign Joe Langdell was eating breakfast at the bachelor officers' quarters on Ford Island. He was still on temporary assignment to the Fleet Camera Party, even though officially attached to the *Arizona*. An officer came into the mess and asked, "Is there an officer here from the *Arizona*?" Langdell raised his hand, and the officer told him what his assignment would be after breakfast. He was to join a crew of some twenty enlisted men and ride a motor whaleboat to the *Arizona*. They were issued sheets and pillowcases so that they could collect the human remains still above the waterline and transfer them ashore for burial. Eventually, a number of the dead men wound up in the Punchbowl Cemetery, which was created in the crater of an extinct volcano.

Ensign Langdell and the other men went aboard and began their grisly task. In one sense their previous assignment to the ship was a help because they knew their way around and might also be able to identify some of the bodies they found. On the other hand, the emotional impact of seeing dead shipmates was even more profound than would have been the case for men who had never known the crew of the USS *Arizona*.[1]

The recovery party wrapped the complete corpses up in sheets and took them to a waiting motor launch for further transfer. The men also retrieved portions of bodies, and sometimes they swept up ashes, storing them in pillowcases for the trip to the cemetery. At the time, Langdell and the others went about the job because they had been ordered to do so. The memory of those days has bothered him many times since then. He thinks of the many who would now be grandfathers but never got the chance.[2]

Gunner's Mate Third Class Howard Burk was among those tapped for the working party. When the boat in which he was riding pulled up to the *Arizona*, he saw a bloated corpse that had floated out of the ship. As he got aboard and walked around, the awful odor of death struck him. The sights of death

had already begun to decompose while in the water. Topside he went onto the boat deck and walked past the charred 5-inch antiaircraft guns. There the fire had cremated some members of the gun crews. He saw piles of ashes that were unmistakably the remains of former shipmates.[4]

Another who went aboard was Lieutenant Commander Sam Fuqua. Fuqua had lived in a stateroom across the passageway from Lieutenant Commander John French, the *Arizona*'s navigator, who hadn't gotten up for breakfast on Sunday morning. So Fuqua borrowed a diver's helmet and went into the ship to look for him. He found French's body floating under his mattress. Fuqua also went into his own room and saw that it had been cut to pieces, including his clothes locker, which was sliced in two. The gold watch his mother had given him for his twenty-first birthday was melted in his desk drawer, but he retrieved it and kept it for many years afterward. He also learned that Captain Van Valkenburgh's Naval Academy class ring and two buttons from his white service uniform had been found under a pile of steel where the bridge had been.[5]

Above: A view looking aft on the starboard side during salvage work on 17 February 1942. A 5-inch broadside gun protrudes from a casemate; on the deck above are the metal shields for the 5-inch antiaircraft guns that have been removed. (USS *Arizona* Memorial, National Park Service, PR-403)

Right: A view looking down and forward from the mainmast during salvage work on 18 May 1942. (USS *Arizona* Memorial, National Park Service, PR-411)

on the boat deck were just as terrible: bones and pieces of charred flesh that had once been his shipmates. And there was an emotional reaction as well: "You're not normal. You're just more or less numb, you know. You're just existing; that's about it."[3]

Chief Watertender Joe Karb assisted in the recovery of one body from below decks, and that was enough to dissuade him from more. Flesh was falling off the corpses because they

Those divers who went inside the *Arizona* found it a spooky place. As they walked along inside the shattered hull, their movements set up currents in the murky waters. In effect, there was a kind of suction, and on more than one occasion divers were hit in the back or in the diving helmet by corpses suspended in the water. One of the divers who had been in the crew of the *Arizona* at the time of the attack never recovered from the experience. He turned first to alcohol for solace but didn't find it. Eventually, he used his Navy pistol to end his life; he was yet another casualty of the Japanese attack on the battleship *Arizona*.[6]

About three days after the attack, Gunner's Mate Second Class Jack McCarron regained consciousness in the hospital at Aiea. His head and hands were swathed in bandages because he had been badly burned. He was convinced that the long-sleeved jumper and long white trousers he was wearing on the morning of the seventh in preparation for shore-patrol duty had saved his life. They had prevented him from being burned over a much larger area of his body. His burns were so bad that he had to be fed through a tube, which entered his mouth through a small opening in his head bandages. In fact, when he became aware of his surroundings, a doctor said to him, "Son, if any miracles come out of this war, you're one of them."[7]

At the time, McCarron wasn't so sure. When doctors peeled off the bandages, the gunner's mate was horrified by what he saw. Later, when a picture was taken for his new identification card, he destroyed it because it didn't resemble the Jack McCarron he remembered—the good-looking six-footer who had been married less than two months before. A friend came by to see him, and McCarron asked him to write to his bride, Roberta, in Long Beach to tell her that she should forget about him. Fortunately, McCarron was persuaded not to follow that line of thinking. He got out of the hospital, went back to sea in a destroyer-minesweeper, and remained in the Navy until his retirement in 1969. He and Roberta celebrated their fiftieth wedding anniversary this year.[8]

On 7 December Seaman Don Stratton had saved himself from being burned to death on board the *Arizona* by going hand over hand along a line to the *Vestal*, which had been moored alongside. That ordeal ended rela-

tively quickly, but another began, and it has lasted for years afterward.

While at his battle station in a 5-inch–gun director near the bridge during the attack, Stratton suffered third-degree burns over some 60 percent of his body. Pieces of skin could be peeled from his arms as if they were gloves. He was hospitalized at Pearl Harbor and heavily bandaged. The hospital personnel didn't think he was strong enough to be moved, but his desire to go back to the West Coast was so strong that he convinced them otherwise. He boarded a ship that got him to the Mare Island Navy Yard near San Francisco at Christmas. He was in a hospital there until September 1942. When he was able to get up and stand on a scale, his weight had dropped to ninety-two pounds.

Stratton has endured years of skin grafts and has worn heavy bandages even in recent years because of the continuing treatment.

Below: A view taken 18 May 1942, looking forward from the mainmast after partial removal of the foremast. The guns of turret two are out of the water. The crumpled bow is at the top of the photo. (USS *Arizona* Memorial, National Park Service, PR-404)

His scars bear painful evidence to his experience at Pearl Harbor. On his legs are lines showing how far down his white shorts extended and how far up his socks came. The flesh in between was cooked. He is grateful that he was wearing shoes when the attack occurred because the decks and bulkheads in the superstructure were so hot during the fire that they singed flesh upon contact.[9]

Seaman Second Class Carl Christiansen was in the hospital for perhaps nine or ten days while recovering from the effects of the noxious gas he had inhaled down in the ammunition-handling rooms. It took even longer than that before he was finally rid of the oil that clung to him after his swim in the harbor. His parents back in Kansas were notified fairly quickly that Carl's brother Ed had perished on board the ship, but the administrative system didn't work so quickly in letting them know that the younger son was still alive.[10]

During Christiansen's time in the hospital, the reality of what he had been through finally hit him. While he had been trying to escape from the ship, mere survival had preoccupied him. In the hospital, with a lot of time to think, he had an attack of nerves. Even now he still has nightmares and flashbacks about that terrible time on board ship.[11]

Once he recovered, Christiansen shipped out on board the heavy cruiser *Chester* and was involved in the first U.S. offensive action of the war, an attack against the Marshall Islands on 1 February 1942. He could help the U.S. forces hit back but never could recover what he had lost on 7 December. He explained, "There's never a day goes by that I

Right: Removing projectiles from turret four, 18 May 1942. (USS *Arizona* Memorial, National Park Service, PR-17)

don't think of my brother—after all these years."[12]

Another who was in the hospital to recover from having breathed noxious fumes was Ensign Guy Flanagan, although his stay was shorter than Christiansen's. The young officer was put on oxygen for a few days until his lungs cleared, and he couldn't talk. Since he hadn't been wearing his khaki shirt, which he had stuffed into an opening in turret three, when he got to the hospital, the chart at the foot of his bed read only, "USS *Arizona*, name unknown." His shipmate, Ensign Joe Langdell, was making the rounds of the hospital to look for other men from the *Arizona* and came upon Flanagan. Langdell sent a telegram to Flanagan's parents in Minnesota, a great Christmas present for them because they had previously received a telegram from the Navy Department reporting that their son was missing in action. As he lay in his hospital bed, Flanagan found himself feeling a kaleidoscope of emotions left over from 7 December: shock, anger, fear, confusion, desire for revenge, and great sadness over the loss of his shipmates.[13]

After he was released from the hospital, Flanagan joined the salvage crew, working with the divers. The original plan was to recover as many bodies as they could. It turned out to be dangerous for the divers to try to pull the bodies out. Striking sharp edges within the ship could sever their air hoses, and the water was murky as well. Flanagan's job was working the pump; it didn't make much difference that he was a commissioned officer. Then the powers that be decided it was a fruitless task and they would leave the rest of the bodies in the ship. Boats took the recovered corpses to Aiea, where medical teams tried to identify the men. Not surprisingly, a number of them could not be identified.[14] One of the divers working on the project was Jack Marcicano. After a day's work, he and others involved in handling the bodies had to wash their hands in kerosene to get rid of the odor of decomposed flesh. He added, "Then we'd go get drunk that night."[15]

Eventually, thirty-nine of the bodies recovered from the *Arizona* were taken to the mainland for burial. Approximately 235 more were buried in various locations on Oahu. As a result, an estimated nine hundred men's remains were left on board the ship, according to Ray Emory, an *Arizona* Memorial volun-

Above: The winch arrangement for hoisting powder from magazines below, 29 June 1942. (USS *Arizona* Memorial, National Park Service, PR-18)

teer who has made a thorough study of the disposition of bodies. Among those buried on the mainland was Seaman First Class Michael Zwarun, Jr. He had been in the crew of the destroyer *Ellet* and had been ordered to stand trial by general court-martial. Since the destroyer didn't have a brig, he was confined on board the *Arizona* while awaiting trial. His offenses were drunkenness, disorderly conduct, and swearing at the shore patrol. Those misdeeds cost him his life because he died in the *Arizona*.[16]

Two of the *Arizona*'s survivors who were qualified divers had a role in the salvage operation. They were Chief Gunner's Mate Robert Hendon and Coxswain Ken Edmondson. They dived on the ship for several months because their service on board had given them a thorough knowledge of the interior layout. The divers were able to get into the officers' quarters at the stern of the ship without difficulty because that area was essentially undamaged. Ken Edmondson remembered that they pulled out a number of

Right: An aerial view of the salvage work done on the *Arizona*, taken 26 January 1943. Temporary boat landings have been built on the ship's port side to facilitate salvage operations. Ford Island is at the top of the picture. (National Archives, 80-G-451256)

Below: Blowers ventilate below-decks spaces during the removal of ammunition from the *Arizona*'s after magazines on 5 October 1942. In the background is a *New Mexico*–class battleship. (USS *Arizona* Memorial, National Park Service, PR-27)

possessions, including uniforms, swords, and personal mementos, and sent them to the families of the officers.[17]

Among other things, the divers came up with the pay records and nearly all of the cash from the disbursing office. Edmondson remembered that it took about three days to get the paymaster's safe opened, even though they had been given the combination. The water had so much oil in it that they had trouble seeing, even with a bright light and their face plates pressed practically against the dial.[18] When the safe was opened, a packet of dollar bills broke loose, and the money escaped.

Machinist's Mate Everett Reid was helping the divers from a motor launch alongside the

Arizona and dropping a weighted gunny sack into the water. Hendon and Edmondson pulled it in through a porthole and put the money inside. When the bag was full, one of the divers gave a couple of tugs on the line attached to the sack, and Reid hauled it up. After a while the whole forward end of the motor launch was filled with wet money. The disbursing officer, Ensign Homan "Bucky" Walsh, was naturally concerned about the money because he was accountable for it. So he soon came by and collected the wet bills from the boat, even before the divers had a chance to come topside and get the satisfaction of seeing what the cache of cash looked like all in one place.[19]

The next day, after Walsh had tallied up the money recovered, he jokingly asked Hendon why he hadn't been able to bring back all of it. Hendon didn't take it as a joke and suggested that the disbursing officer could put on a diving helmet and go look for the rest inside the ship. Walsh declined the offer.[20] Another member of the *Arizona*'s detail, Chief Commissary Steward Ralph Byard, took on the chore of hanging up wet dollar bills to dry on a clothesline rigged in the temporary ship's office at the receiving station.[21]

The pay records weren't brought up until near the end of December. In the meantime, the families of married crew members were having a tough time—both in Hawaii and California. The men couldn't be paid without

pay records, nor could they draw assistance from Navy Relief. The Navy Department in Washington kept changing procedures on how dummy pay records should be set up, and the resulting red tape kept people in limbo. Finally, the money started flowing again. For the single men, the lack of pay was more of an inconvenience than a problem because the Navy was still providing them with meals and places to sleep, whether ashore or on board other ships.[22]

Even though Chief Byard's shipboard experience had been with running the *Arizona*'s galley, he got involved with the pay records because he had been considered for warrant officer and would have wider responsibilities in the supply department than just preparing food. He was part of the detail that remained officially attached to the ship for a few months after her sinking. One of his duties was to work for Ensign Walsh in preserving the crew's pay records to the extent possible.

Byard took the records down to the boiler room of Pearl Harbor's receiving station, where the *Arizona*'s men had set up shop. He spread out the records on the deck, and the heat evaporated the water that had soaked into them. Byard was a perfectionist, so he carefully dried out the records one at a time until he had restored each one to the best condition possible, even putting the pay receipts into numerical order. He was also

Below: A diagram of the type of Japanese 800-kilogram armor-piercing bomb that inflicted devastating damage on the *Arizona* on 7 December 1941. (Courtesy John F. De Virgilio)

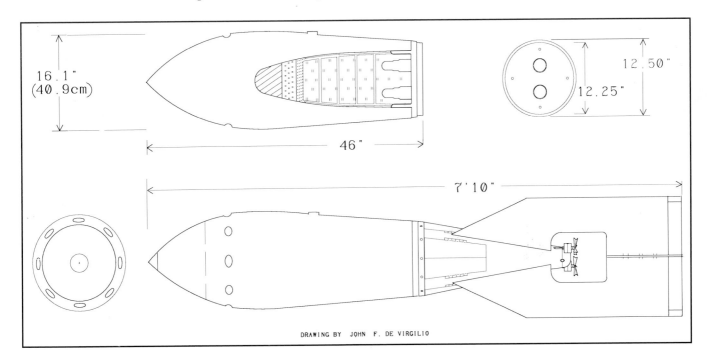

DRAWING BY JOHN F. DE VIRGILIO

Below: Bomb
trajectories and damage
profile of the *Arizona* as
a result of the Japanese
attack. (Courtesy John
F. De Virgilio)

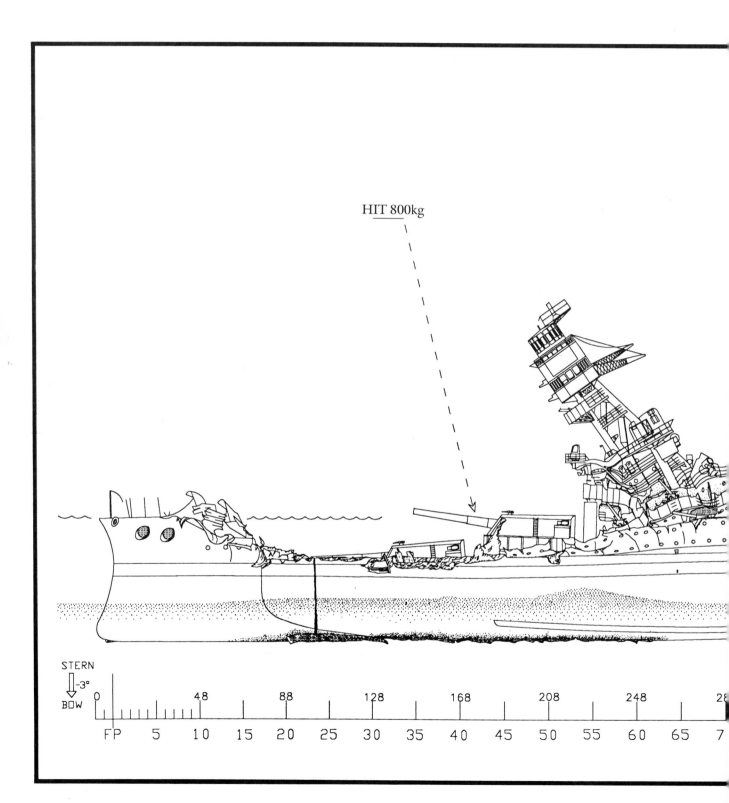

HIT 800kg

STERN
-3°
BOW

0   48   88   128   168   208   248   28

FP   5   10   15   20   25   30   35   40   45   50   55   60   65   7

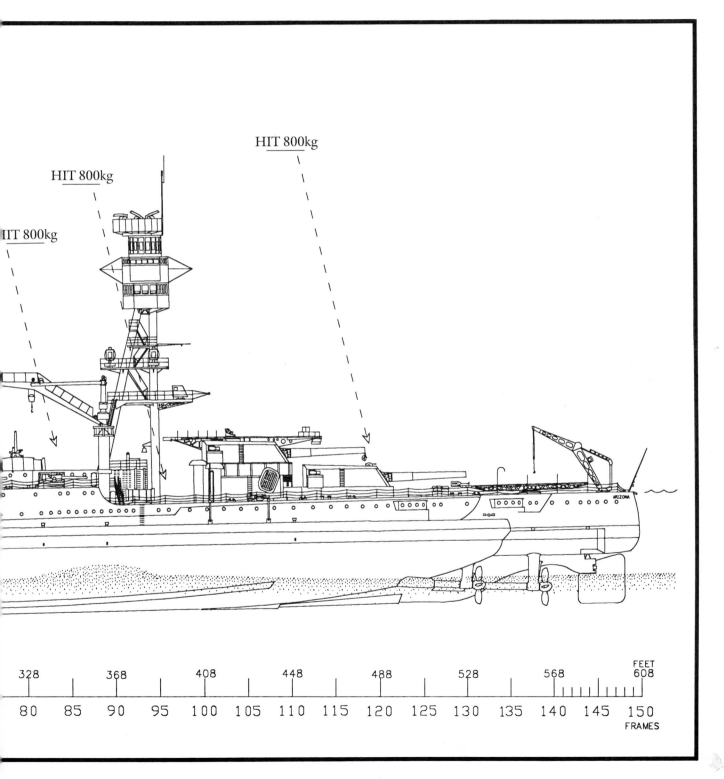

HIT 800kg

HIT 800kg

HIT 800kg

HIT 800kg

328   368   408   448   488   528   568   FEET
608

80   85   90   95   100   105   110   115   120   125   130   135   140   145   150

FRAMES

Below: This overhead view shows the path of the V formations of Japanese Kate high-level bombers approaching Battleship Row during the first wave of the attack. The inset provides a closeup of the hits and near misses of 800-kilogram armor-piercing bombs. The five bombs on and near the *Arizona*'s stern were dropped by planes from the carrier *Kaga*. Then came the five on and near the bow, dropped by planes from the carrier *Hiryu*. (Drawing courtesy of John F. De Virgilio)

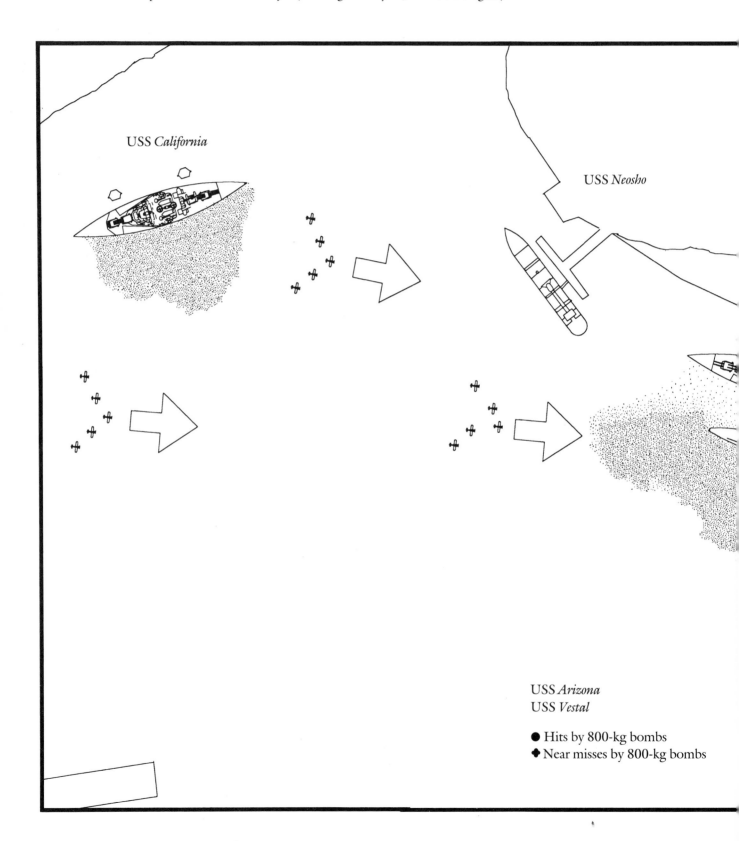

USS *California*

USS *Neosho*

USS *Arizona*
USS *Vestal*

● Hits by 800-kg bombs
◆ Near misses by 800-kg bombs

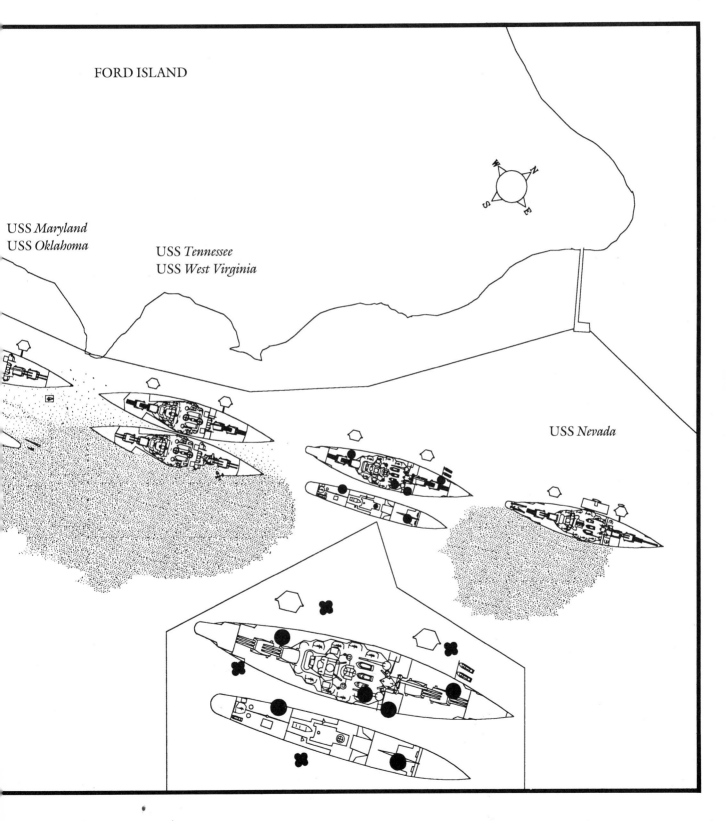

FORD ISLAND

USS *Maryland*
USS *Oklahoma*

USS *Tennessee*
USS *West Virginia*

USS *Nevada*

involved in putting together transfer pay accounts on all the dead and missing crew members. The year before, in an act dated 8 August 1941, Congress had approved a small increase in pay for people on sea duty. In an interview, Byard said of that date—8/8/41—"I wrote that so many times I'll never forget it."[23]

While Byard was working on the pay records, Yeoman Jim Vlach was doing what he could to get together an accurate muster. Initially, he was able to come up with only about 80 names from the total of some 330 who survived. The families of the other 250 were informed that their men were missing in action. It often took days or weeks for accurate information to get through, frequently in the form of a postcard mailed by the man himself to his relatives. But the

postcards weren't going to the *Arizona*'s detail in Pearl Harbor, and so Vlach had only fragmentary information to submit to the Bureau of Navigation in Washington. Divers didn't recover the ship's muster roll from the executive officer's office until around February 1942.[24]

One survivor worked diligently as part of the detail in spite of personal tragedy. Chief Yeoman Tom Murdock had lost two younger brothers, Charles and Melvin, in the attack. Both had been serving in the *Arizona* and were visiting him ashore Saturday night. He urged them to spend the night at his place, but they decided they'd rather go back to the ship. They died there. About three dozen sets of brothers were serving in the *Arizona* at the time of the attack. Only the Warriner combination survived intact. (The Navy

Below: In May 1942 a derrick lifts away the foretop after welding torches have severed the tripod legs of the mast. The boat cranes are at left. (National Archives, 80-G-64595)

continued its practice of assigning brothers together, where feasible, until the loss of five Sullivan brothers when the light cruiser *Juneau* was sunk near Guadalcanal in November 1942.) There was one other family tragedy when two men from Texas were killed on the morning of 7 December. Machinist's Mate First Class Thomas Augusta Free died on board the *Arizona*, and so did his son, Seaman Second Class William Thomas Free.[25]

In addition to his regular work in the aftermath of the loss of the ship, Chief Murdock took upon himself an extra duty—that of traveling around the island of Oahu to talk with people who had been on board the *Arizona* on the morning of 7 December. He collected their descriptions of Lieutenant Commander Fuqua's coolness—even after he had recovered from being knocked unconscious—in directing the others that morning.[26]

One sample can represent many of those statements. Marine Sergeant John Baker of the *Arizona*'s detachment reported, "I also saw Lt. Comdr. Fuqua still on the quarter deck aiding men over the life line and directing others who were shocked too badly to move to abandon ship; there is no doubt in my mind that many men could never have reached safety except for the superb manner in which he (Comdr. Fuqua) kept control of the situation for there was a constant hail of splinters and the ship was being machine gunned continuously. . . . Lt. Comdr. Fuqua

Above: Captain Franklin B. Van Valkenburgh in his cabin on board the *Arizona* in October or November 1941. (Courtesy Franklin B. Van Valkenburgh, Jr.)

Above left: Lieutenant Commander Samuel G. Fuqua was awarded the Medal of Honor for his coolness under fire on board the *Arizona* on 7 December 1941. (Courtesy Billie-Viers Clatchey, Naval Academy Alumni Association)

Left: A posthumous oil portrait of Isaac C. Kidd as a rear admiral. (Naval Historical Center, NH 85226)

was exposed to all this and yet refused to leave the ship as long as he could help the men who were injured."[27]

Murdock's purpose for gathering statements was to put together a Medal of Honor nomination. One consequence of his dili-

an attempt to find heroes in what had been a true catastrophe. Van Valkenburgh was on the bridge of the *Arizona* at the time of the big magazine explosion; Kidd was nearby. Some reports indicate that Kidd stopped to help man a machine gun on the way to his battle station, but that is unlikely. The .50-caliber machine guns were in the birdbath gun platform atop the mainmast, on the side of the smokestack, and on a platform just under the foretop. None of those locations was in a direct line from the admiral's quarters in the stern to the bridge. He probably wouldn't have had time to climb up to any of the three stations and still reach his battle station since there was only about fifteen minutes at the most between the first alarm and the big explosion.

All this is not to say that Kidd and Van Valkenburgh did not act heroically. They may well have, but the witnesses to their actions were all killed—with the exception of Ensign Douglas Hein. His after-action statement mentioned Van Valkenburgh but did not report on any specific act of heroism.[29]

Ensign Jim Dick Miller, the turret three officer, received the Navy Cross, the service's second highest award for bravery. While he was on board the stricken vessel, he displayed much the same calmness as Lieutenant Commander Fuqua while trying to deal with the fires, comfort the wounded, and assist crew members off the ship. He was in the last boatload that left the *Arizona*; he then took charge of a motor launch and used it to rescue

Above: A 150-ton crane lifts the middle section of the rotating portion of turret three on 19 April 1943. (USS *Arizona* Memorial, National Park Service, PR-406)

Right: The upper section of the rotating portion of turret three is lifted clear of the ship on 19 April 1943. (USS *Arizona* Memorial, National Park Service, PR-408)

gence was that he was gone from the office a good deal—so much so that he irritated Fuqua himself, who didn't know the purpose of Murdock's travels. Fuqua put him on report, and Murdock was summoned to captain's mast, which was conducted by the commanding officer of the receiving station. Fortunately, Murdock had cleared his research activities with the skipper. The captain dismissed the charges and told an embarrassed Fuqua what the chief yeoman had been doing. Fuqua did receive the Medal of Honor for his heroism that morning.[28]

He was not the only officer from the *Arizona* to be awarded the Medal of Honor. It also went posthumously to Rear Admiral Isaac Kidd, the commander of the battleship division, and to Captain Franklin Van Valkenburgh, the commanding officer of the ship. Kidd was the first U.S. Navy flag officer killed in action during World War II and one of only about half a dozen during the entire war.

One may speculate that the awards to Kidd and Van Valkenburgh constituted, perhaps,

men both from mooring quays and from the water.

Others earned significant awards. Major Alan Shapley of the marine detachment received the Silver Star medal for risking his life to tow Corporal Earl Nightingale through the oil-covered water to Ford Island. Marine Second Lieutenant Carleton Simensen was initially awarded a posthumous letter of commendation, later upgraded to the Bronze Star medal, for leading his fellow marines up the ladders on the tripod mainmast. The Japanese fire was withering at that point, and Simensen was cut down on the searchlight platform, either by shrapnel or machine-gun bullets. Chief Gunner's Mate Robert Hendon received the Navy and Marine Corps Medal for outstanding performance as chief diver during the salvage operation after the attack.

Without doubt, other men from the *Arizona* performed heroically in the fight against the enemy. Their deeds could not be honored because the witnesses to their actions did not live to report what they had seen.[30]

Some months afterward, when he had gone on to other duty in the wartime Navy, Gunner's Mate Howard Burk received the personal items that had been recovered from his locker in the lower handling room of turret three. The locker had been unlocked at the time of the attack because the men who lived down in the bowels of the turret seldom locked up. The package that came to him included a waterlogged mess that had once been his wallet, watch, and money. Gradually, the Navy assembled a new service record for Burk because his original record was lost with the ship. For a time, his record included pretty much whatever he could recite from memory when he reported for duty in a new

ship. For some particulars, however, the Navy wasn't willing to take chances. Since Burk couldn't produce a written record of his inoculations, he had to endure another whole round of them.[31]

Shortly after the *Arizona* was lost, Ensign Jim Dick Miller was reassigned to the old four-pipe destroyer *Schley* as gunnery officer. After being out for a while on antisubmarine-patrol duty off Pearl Harbor, the ship came in one day to replenish supplies, ammunition, and depth charges. His former shipmate Ensign Walsh came aboard for a visit, so Miller invited him to sit down for a cup of coffee in the wardroom. Walsh put his hands on the wardroom table and tried to get Miller to notice them, but the other officer was wrapped up in his own thoughts. So Walsh took off Miller's Naval Academy class ring, which he had been wearing, and said, "Here, you probably would like to have this back." In his haste to get from his stateroom to his

Right: Two barnacle-covered 5-inch/51 broadside mounts after their removal from the ship. (National Archives, 80-G-41625)

Below: Divers after emerging from their work. The conning tower is at top right. (National Archives, 80-G-41621)

battle station on the morning of the seventh, Miller hadn't taken the time to put on his ring. Some of the gunner's mates from the *Arizona*'s third division were working as divers in the underwater portion of the ship. They knew where Miller's room was and did him the favor of recovering for him something of considerable sentimental value.[32]

In the mid-1970s, while she was living in an apartment a block from the Naval Academy in Annapolis, Mrs. Isaac Kidd fell and broke her hip. She had lived in the same place since 1942, shortly after the destruction of the *Arizona* had made her a widow. Her son, Admiral Isaac Kidd, Jr., and her grandson, then a Naval Academy midshipman, helped to move her possessions to a new home after her fall. The two men went to a storage room in the apartment building, and there Admiral Kidd found his father's sea chest, a big box built for him by some carpenter's mate in some ship during the course of his long naval career. In it were his father's uniforms, sword, and pocket watch, brought up by divers when they went into the admiral's cabin during the salvage operations on the *Arizona*. The watch, with gold chain attached, was a souvenir that the senior Kidd had bought while he was steaming with the Great White Fleet on its around-the-world cruise early in the century.[33]

Also in the storage room was what appeared to Admiral Kidd, Jr., to be a plank of wood. He and his son tried to lift it and discovered it to be extraordinarily heavy. They cleaned it off and discovered it wasn't a plank but the top of a heavy box, addressed in

Naval Academy ring, class of 1906. Captain Cassin Young of the *Vestal*, the repair ship moored alongside the *Arizona* on 7 December, had sent the ring to the admiral's widow. A member of the salvage crew had found it fused to the steel on the top of the *Arizona*'s conning tower. That was all that was left of the man who had commanded the ship as a captain and died in her as an admiral. He may have been on top of the conning tower so he could get a good look at the attacking Japanese planes. An even more likely explanation is that he was on the flag bridge and was blown by the force of the massive explosion onto the nearby conning tower.[34]

While the survivors from the *Arizona* were serving in other ships and stations or putting

Above: Enlisted men at the Pearl Harbor Navy Yard grease the breech end of a 14-inch–gun barrel removed from the *Arizona*. The muzzle is at the extreme right side of the photo. (National Archives photo 80-G-302463 courtesy E. R. Lewis)

Above right: Two sailors prepare turret parts for storage at the Pearl Harbor Navy Yard. This is the three-gun slide for one of the *Arizona*'s turrets. A battleship cage mast can be seen in the upper right corner of the picture. (National Archives photo 80-G-302456 courtesy E. R. Lewis)

Right: Battery Pennsylvania, formerly a 14-inch turret in the *Arizona*, was test-fired in August 1945. (Courtesy E. R. Lewis)

1942 from the Pearl Harbor supply officer to Mrs. Kidd. They pried it open and found a massive brass plaque that had been on the quarterdeck of the *Arizona*. Engraved in the brass were the names of all of the ship's commanding officers, including Captain Kidd, the skipper from 1938 to 1940. Admiral Kidd sent the plaque to the Naval Historical Center. There was one more thing that he found in the apartment. It was his father's

the records in order, other individuals were trying to document the bomb hits and to find an answer to the big question—why did the *Arizona* suffer damage that was so much more devastating than that visited on the other ships hit by bombs? Another question was whether the ship was hit by torpedoes; two ships that were, the *Oklahoma* and *West Virginia*, were opened up with huge holes on their port sides. The *Oklahoma* capsized, and the *West Virginia* was saved from that fate by counterflooding and a superior torpedo-protection system.

Commander Ellis Geiselman, the executive officer of the *Arizona*, had been ashore at the time of the attack. He became the commanding officer of what was left of the ship. In his action report of 17 December 1941, he reported that one bomb, of approximately 500 pounds, had passed through the starboard side of the quarterdeck after bouncing off the faceplate of number four turret. The bomb exploded in the captain's pantry, destroying that and the admiral's pantry and apparently starting a small fire that quickly went out. Another 500-pounder hit at frame 85 on the port gallery deck, making a hole about two feet in diameter. He reported that another bomb, of either 500 or 1,000 pounds, hit at frame 96, on the port side of the quarterdeck in the area where the ship's motorboats were stored; it also produced a hole about two feet wide.

Geiselman estimated that a fifth bomb, of probably 1,000 or 2,000 pounds, went down the *Arizona's* smokestack. This report became the basis for an oft-repeated myth about the attack on the battleship. When the cover of the stack was later recovered, it was still intact, pieces of metal dividing the circle into six pie-shaped wedges, one for each of the ship's firerooms. The undamaged cover thus refuted the notion that a bomb had gone down the smokestack. According to the acting skipper's report, a sixth bomb struck the ship on the port side of the boat deck, at frame 66, near the number four 5-inch/25 antiaircraft gun. A seventh bomb hit at frame 73 on the port side of the boat deck, near the number six 5-inch antiaircraft gun. The eighth bomb, he reported, hit in the vicinity of the forward turrets. It was the culprit that turned the warship into an inferno. Geiselman repeated in his report a claim by the *Vestal's* commanding officer that the *Arizona* apparently was hit

by a torpedo on the port side, around frame 35.[35]

In early 1942, as part of the salvage work, Navy and civilian divers used high-pressure excavating nozzles to blow mud away from the ship. They did not turn up any evidence of torpedo damage. More recently, in the 1980s, a new team of divers surveyed the wreck of the *Arizona*, looking specifically for torpedo effects and finding none. The team members were not able to say with absolute certainty that no torpedoes struck the *Arizona* on 7 December, but it is highly unlikely that the ship was torpedoed.

Dr. Thomas Hone did a splendid study of the destruction of the battle line at Pearl Harbor.[36] His extensive search of documentary evidence revealed that the explosion in

Above: A gun slide and turret for Battery Pennsylvania await assembly at Fort Hase on eastern Oahu on 22 March 1945. (Army Signal Corps photo SC 236035 courtesy E. R. Lewis)

Below: Members of the Hawaiian Seacoast Artillery Command prepare to hoist a gun slide into position for Battery Pennsylvania at Fort Hase, Oahu, on 22 March 1945. (Army Signal Corps photo SC 236036 courtesy E. R. Lewis)

the forward part of the ship had destroyed so much physical evidence that no conclusive cause could really be proven.[37]

David Aiken of Texas and John De Virgilio of Hawaii have reached the same conclusion. These two men have studied the entire attack with the objective of correlating specific Japanese weapon drops with specific damage to U.S. ships. Aiken and De Virgilio have the kind of hobby that becomes compulsive because of the mountain of data to be sifted.

They argue that the *Arizona* was hit by only four of the ten bombs dropped on her from Kate high-level bombers during the first wave of the attack. The damage was so substantial, however, that the aircraft in the second wave wisely sought other targets. In the first wave, the *Arizona* was hit first by a five-plane strike

from the aircraft carrier *Kaga*, soon afterward by five planes from the *Hiryu*. The planes were flying from bow to stern in a V or arrowhead pattern. Aiken and De Virgilio count the following hits on and near the *Arizona*:

—port side, frame 85 on the antiaircraft deck
—port side, frame 96, close to outboard so that it probably detonated in the area of the antitorpedo bulkhead
—a hit outboard on the *Vestal*, outboard of the *Arizona*'s frame 96
—a hit on turret four that ricocheted off turret four and exploded in the captain's pantry
—a near-miss outboard of turret four
—a hit just forward on the starboard side of turret two.

Below: Crew members of the aircraft carrier *Bennington* spell out the name of the *Arizona* as they pass by the hull, with a temporary memorial over the top, on 7 December 1958. Notice the oil around the *Arizona*. (UPI/Bettmann Newsphotos, U1173648)

The last one, of course, was the big one that fatally damaged the ship.[38]

Aiken and De Virgilio suggest that the near-miss in the vicinity of frame 35 threw up a splash of water that mimicked the effect of a torpedo hitting the side of the ship, thus leading nearby observers to believe that the *Arizona* had been torpedoed. The hits by the *Kaga*'s planes, essentially dropping together, were amidships and aft; those from the *Hiryu* hit forward. Lieutenant Commander Fuqua's experiences corroborate this account. The bomb explosions aft knocked him unconscious, but he had regained his senses by the time of the large explosion forward. Aiken and De Virgilio calculate that the bombs struck in two V-shaped patterns that correspond to the formations the planes were in when overflying the ship. As a result of their study, De Virgilio has produced the overhead diagram on pages 264–65 plotting the bomb hits on and near the *Arizona* and *Vestal*.[39]

The Kates dropped bombs that had been 16.1-inch armor-piercing projectiles but that were converted for use by airplanes: they had been ground down to about 12½ inches in diameter at the bases and given fins for stability while falling. Since the projectiles weren't fired from guns, they didn't have the ballistic twist imparted by rifling. The projectile bombs were rated at 796.8 kilograms (1,756.9 pounds). Because of all the metal

needed to punch through armor, the internal cavity held an explosive charge of only fifty pounds.[40]

The projectile bombs were capable of penetrating 5.9 inches of armor plate. The *Arizona*'s second deck was originally almost three inches thick, beefed up with another layer, nearly two inches thick, of special-treatment steel during the 1929–31 reconstruction. The laminated deck would not be as

Above: The current *Arizona* memorial in the early stages of construction. (USS *Arizona* Memorial, National Park Service, PR-309)

Left: The base for the memorial is completed prior to the erection of the superstructure. (USS *Arizona* Memorial, National Park Service, PR-307)

TO THE MEMORY OF THE GALLANT MEN
HERE ENTOMBED AND THEIR SHIPMATES
WHO GAVE THEIR LIVES IN ACTION
ON DECEMBER 7, 1941 ON THE U.S.S. ARIZONA

Above: Retired Rear Admiral Samuel Fuqua poses in front of the wall listing the names of those killed on board the ship in December 1941. This picture was taken at the dedication of the memorial on 30 May 1962. (USS *Arizona* Memorial, National Park Service, PR-122)

Right: One battleship honors another. The USS *New Jersey* steams past the *Arizona* Memorial in September 1968 during a stopover at Pearl Harbor prior to steaming to Vietnam. (Naval Photographic Center, K-58114, courtesy Flora Higgins)

strong as a single five-inch thickness of armor steel. The bombs were equipped with double fuzes in their bases, designed to go off one-fifth of a second after initial penetration.[41]

The intention was for the fuzes to be activated when passing through the outer skin of a ship so that the bombs would explode a fraction of a second later, upon reaching the ship's vitals. Aiken and De Virgilio have found that the Kates were directed to fly over Battleship Row at an altitude of about 3,000 meters (slightly less than 10,000 feet) so that their weapons would have maximum effect. If dropped from a lower altitude, such as 2,000 meters, they wouldn't have generated enough momentum to bore deeply into a ship and thus would probably have exploded before penetrating the armored deck. If dropped from too high an altitude, such as 4,000 meters, the bombs would have been going so fast when they hit that they would have gone entirely through the ship in one-fifth of a second and detonated in the harbor underneath.[42]

The principal matter open to question is just how the projectile bomb near the forward turrets, with a relatively small explosive charge (less than 3 percent of the total weight), wrought such enormous damage. One argument is that it was a spectacularly lucky hit. Of approximately fifty such projectiles dropped by the Japanese bombers, only nine hit targets.

One presumption—in lieu of hard evidence—is that the bomb's armor-piercing nose did indeed enable it to penetrate to a black-powder magazine about thirty feet within the ship. That was the distance from the upper deck to the first platform deck. In that location was a cluster of six magazines

containing smokeless-powder charges for the 14-inch guns, and in the midst of those large magazines was a small one containing black-powder charges for the ship's saluting guns.

Black powder is considerably more volatile than smokeless powder. In fact, each 14-inch powder bag had an ignition pad filled with black powder because the smokeless powder needed an initial kick to cause it to burn. A Japanese pilot wanting to plant his weapon in the most vulnerable part of the ship might well have picked a concentration of black-powder charges.

Discussions with crew members after the event disclosed that each of the forward turrets (including shell decks and handling rooms) contained about three hundred 14-inch projectiles—six hundred in all. The six magazines contained about 1,200 cans of powder. With two bags of powder per can, the magazines could supply four bags per projectile. If a Japanese bomb exploded in the black-powder magazine—the "worst-case scenario"—it would have ignited a charge that, in turn, could have set off the 2,400 bags of smokeless powder.

Another possibility cited by Hone after studying a 1944 Bureau of Ships analysis involved an armored hatch on the third deck, next to the black-powder magazine. If that hatch had been open on the morning of 7 December, and if there were inflammable material in the area, and if a bomb penetrated the second deck, then one of the armor-piercing bombs could have caused a detonation that would have traveled to the main magazines. The Bureau of Ships concluded this was probably a more likely explanation because of the difficulty even an armor-piercing bomb would have penetrating two armored decks and then hitting a small spot of maximum vulnerability. One strength of the 1944 analysis was its careful study of movie film taken of the *Arizona* during the attack. Commander Ernest C. Holtzworth, the study's author, wrote that the film showed evidence of a bomb hit on the forecastle, followed seven seconds later by the massive eruption of the forward magazines. The time it took for fire to travel to the black-powder magazine to set it off could explain this delay.[43]

Aiken and De Virgilio do not accept any theories involving either black powder or aviation gasoline—the latter a source suggested by some. They say the armor-piercing

bomb went directly into a 14-inch powder magazine on the starboard side of the *Arizona*'s forecastle and then exploded. The fifty-pound charge, they argue, had sufficient explosive force to detonate the smokeless powder stored in the ship. The explosion caused an enormously rapid expansion of gases, which then made their way sequentially through the magazines to the port side of the ship, causing greater damage there than to starboard. Aiken and De Virgilio also say that

Left: One of the *Arizona*'s bells is in the memorial; the other is at the University of Arizona in Tucson. This photo was taken during the fortieth anniversary ceremony in 1981. (Courtesy Pearl Harbor Naval Base)

Below: Dressed in white as she was when she christened the original *Arizona* in 1915, the ship's sponsor, now Mrs. Esther Hoggan, reenacts her role with a 27-foot model. She did the reprise at Pearl Harbor on 17 October 1977, the sixtieth anniversary of the ship's commissioning. Mrs. Hoggan died two years later. (Special Collections, University of Arizona Library, 75-5-2)

the angle at which the bomb fell would have prevented it from making its way directly into the black-powder storage.[44]

Whatever the cause, the explosion of the six main magazines around the forward turrets was devastating, making a shambles of the ship forward of frame 88. Because of the wreckage and debris in the area, those who examined the ship afterward could not ascertain a precise path of entry for the Japanese projectile bomb. The massive explosion was vented outward and upward, ripping through the steel in its path. It went through the sides of the *Arizona* in the area extending between about frame 10 and frame 70 and upward through the decks forward of turret one. The decks in the area of the forecastle collapsed and sloped downward from frame 70 forward to about frame 34. The forward turrets and conning tower fell some 25–30 feet. In the diagrams of the *Arizona* in her present condition, the decks in the forecastle are dramatically lower than in the relatively undamaged areas.[45] The internal gutting of the ship produced such a large cavity that the foremast structure tilted down into it.

Even though smokeless powder burns very rapidly in the confines of a gun barrel, the *Arizona*'s main-magazine explosion was so powerful that it hurled grains of the powder off the ship even before they had a chance to burn. The crew of the *Tennessee* found unburned grains of smokeless powder on her quarterdeck, which was four hundred feet in front of the *Arizona*. Some five hundred feet inland of the shoreline of Ford Island, about nine hundred feet away from the *Arizona*'s magazines, were more of her powder grains. Still more grains were found topside on the after part of the *Arizona*, in the mud nearby, and in wreckage in the vicinity of the ship. Exploded powder cans for the 5-inch/51 broadside guns were found hundreds of feet from the *Arizona*, and unexploded 5-inch projectiles were in the mud amidships on the starboard side. Significantly, no intact powder bags at all were found in the forward part of the ship.[46]

In 1942 large pieces of the *Arizona* were cut loose with torches and removed by crane. On 5 May the foremast was taken away; the mainmast went on 23 August. The stern aircraft crane came off on 23 December and the conning tower on 30 December.[47] In a way, it was like 1929 when the old cage masts and original superstructure of the ship had been removed to make way for the modern superstructure. But this time there was no replacement. The after turrets and their guns were subsequently hauled out, and their remaining ammunition was salvaged from inside the waterlogged ship. The guns, slides, deck lugs, and other equipment from turret two were taken away, and turret one was left where it was, lying near the bottom of the ship.[48] As the salvage work went on, workmen also found and removed the bones of former crewmen.

On 1 December 1942, nearly one year after the attack that made her a national symbol, the USS *Arizona* was stricken from the official register of U.S. Navy vessels. One of the enduring myths about the *Arizona* is that she is still in commission today. In fact, she was not officially decommissioned, but ships that sink in action are not decommissioned; they are stricken from the register. Only ships on the register can be in commission, so the *Arizona* is not a commissioned naval vessel.[49]

The *Arizona* was considered so badly damaged that she would not be suitable for further service even if her remains could be salvaged. At that time the priority was to salvage ships that could be used in the war effort. In addition, the harbor bottom around the hull was so porous that Navy salvage experts didn't consider it feasible to build a cofferdam so that the hull could be pumped out and bodies recovered.

Most of the topside material removed from the ship was scrapped. Early in the war the *Arizona* was just an obstacle taking up a berth alongside Ford Island. She was not yet a national shrine, and thus no care was taken to preserve the structures that were removed from her. Among the few pieces of equipment considered to have further combat value were the two after turrets and their six 14-inch guns. In 1942 the idea of a Japanese invasion of Oahu still seemed a very real possibility. The Army had coast-defense batteries to ward off approaching enemy ships, but they were essentially open artillery pieces like other Army guns. Protected by turrets, big guns

Opposite page: A somber view of the memorial taken in the late 1970s. (U.S. Naval Institute Collection)

Below: The aircraft carrier *Coral Sea* passes the memorial in the early 1980s. (Courtesy Pearl Harbor Naval Base)

Right: A fork and remnants of bowls mark the site of the ship's galley during an underwater survey of the *Arizona* in the mid-1980s. (Courtesy Daniel Lenihan, National Park Service)

Below: A survey diver with underwater tablet and tethered marking pen examines the muzzle of a 14-inch gun of turret one, heavily encrusted with marine growth by the mid-1980s. (Courtesy Daniel Lenihan, National Park Service)

had shown their value during the Japanese siege of Manila Bay. Thus the *Arizona*'s turrets, which were immediately available, were potentially useful for coastal defense.[50]

The Army made plans to use the turrets and in December 1942 selected sites for their installation. Construction started in April 1943 at two locations. Battery Arizona was to be on Kahe Point so that the three 14-inch guns could cover a field of fire on the western and southern coasts of the island of Oahu. Battery Pennsylvania was to go in on the tip of Mokapu Peninsula and cover the eastern approaches to Oahu, including the naval air station at Kaneohe Bay.[51]

Work on the two batteries proceeded slowly, in part because the removal of the turrets from the hulk had been crudely done—before their potential for reuse was appreciated. It thus took some effort to realign the turrets' components and to fix the damage sustained during the attack and subsequent immersion in the harbor. Many of the component parts, such as those in motors, had to be repaired or replaced. Even physically moving some of the turrets' components was a challenge, both because of their weight and because of the distance. The barge trip from Pearl Harbor to Battery Pennsylvania was nearly fifty miles. Further difficulties arose when the shipboard turrets were adapted for use on land. For instance, the fire-control equipment needed adequate separation from the guns to minimize problems resulting from

concussion. New ammunition hoists had to be built because magazines encased in dirt, rock, and concrete needed to be deeper than those inside steel barbettes.[52]

The original date for putting the *Arizona*'s after turrets into service as coast-defense batteries was January 1944. However, by then the nature of the war was such that the United States was on the offensive. Oahu no longer faced an immediate threat of invasion, and the batteries would be useful only as part of a postwar defensive system. The pace of work on the two batteries thus slowed down. The construction of the emplacement and the mounting of the guns at Battery Pennsylvania were finally completed in August 1945, just as Japan was surrendering. Its test-firing no longer had any real military significance but was just part of the jubilant celebration of peace after nearly four hard years of fighting in the Pacific. Battery Arizona never was finished. After the war, the turrets and guns were scrapped—again, with no thought to their possible value as memorials. In composing the epitaph for batteries Pennsylvania and Arizona, D. P. Kirchner and E. R. Lewis, authors who have specialized in studying coastal artillery, wrote, "Where the Oahu Turrets once stood to mark the Navy's remarkable contribution to the island's defense, there remain only concrete-lined holes in the ground."[53]

After the end of World War II came a period of neglect for the former battleship—difficult to imagine when one considers the million or so visitors that now come to the *Arizona* Memorial each year. H. Tucker Gratz, a Hawaiian businessman and civic leader, went to the hulk on 7 December one year in the late 1940s to lay a wreath in honor of the dead crew members. There he found the dead wreath he had left a year earlier.[54]

The Navy had by then ceased its efforts to recover the crew members' remains still inside the hull. Two primary factors led to the decision: the cost that would be involved in such recovery and the unlikelihood of being able to identify bodies after the passage of time.[55]

In 1949 the territory of Hawaii—it was still ten years from statehood—established the Pacific War Memorial Commission with Gratz as chairman. The following year Admiral Arthur W. Radford, Commander in Chief

Pacific Fleet, took additional action. He decided to establish a small memorial on the hulk. On 7 March 1950 he directed the erection of a flagpole on the stump of one leg of the tripod mainmast and ordered that an American flag be raised and lowered daily. A wooden platform was built amidships to accommodate boats coming alongside. On 7 December that year Admiral Radford dedicated a plaque to the men of the ship. It carried this benediction: "May God make his face to shine upon them and grant them peace."[56]

In the early 1950s a few organizations called for a permanent *Arizona* memorial. The time was not yet right, nor were the dollars available. In part, the wounds of the day of infamy were still too fresh. The *Arizona* was a reminder of a disastrous defeat for the United States in general and the Navy in particular. At the time, warships were not memorialized as they are today. For instance, Fleet Admiral William F. Halsey mounted a campaign in the 1950s to save his old flagship, the superlative aircraft carrier *Enterprise*, but his efforts were for naught, and the ship was scrapped.

On 7 December 1955 the Navy Club in Hawaii dedicated a plaque on Ford Island to honor the men lost in the *Arizona*. The Commandant of the Fourteenth Naval District, with headquarters at Pearl Harbor, also evinced interest in doing more to memorialize the ship. He indicated his advocacy in a letter to the Secretary of the Navy. The Pacific War Memorial Commission sought to become involved, but the issue of using private funds to build a shrine over a Navy ship complicated the effort. In 1957 Hawaii's nonvoting delegate to Congress, John Burns, introduced

Left: A diver points out the junction of two fire hoses, still joined together. They were of no use on 7 December because there was no water pressure. (Courtesy Daniel Lenihan, National Park Service)

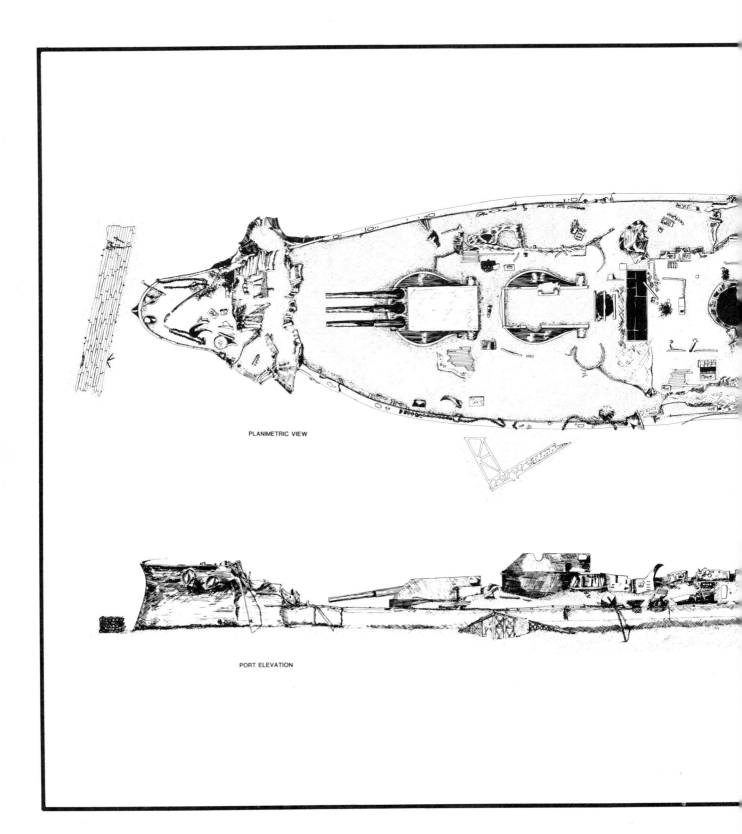

PLANIMETRIC VIEW

PORT ELEVATION

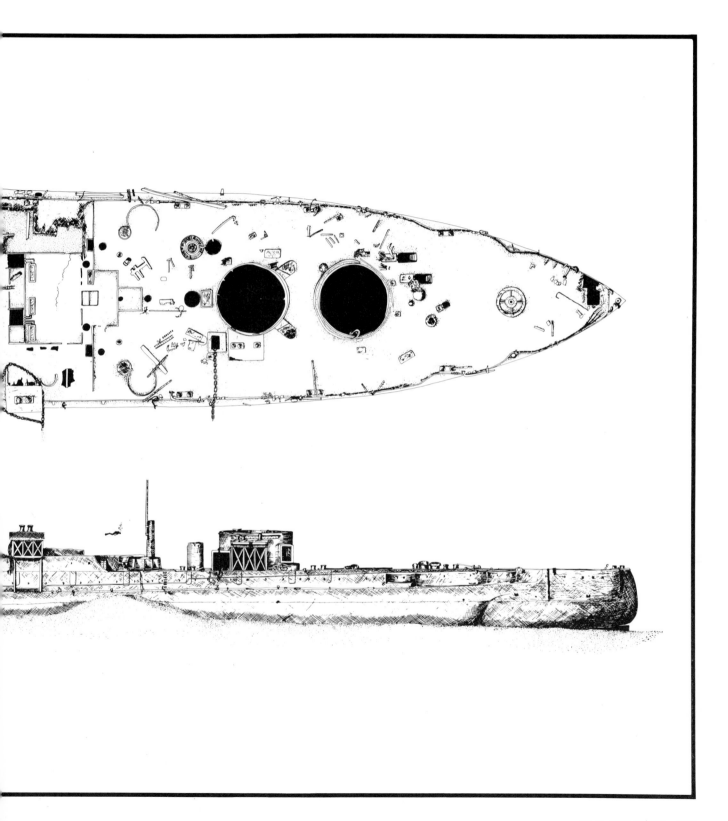

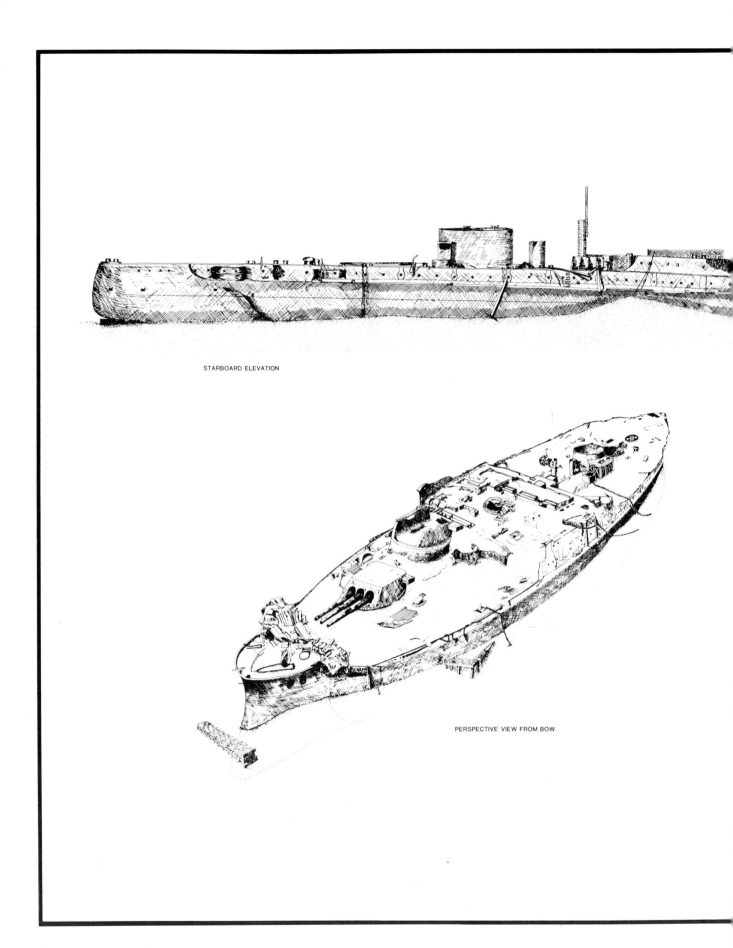

STARBOARD ELEVATION

PERSPECTIVE VIEW FROM BOW

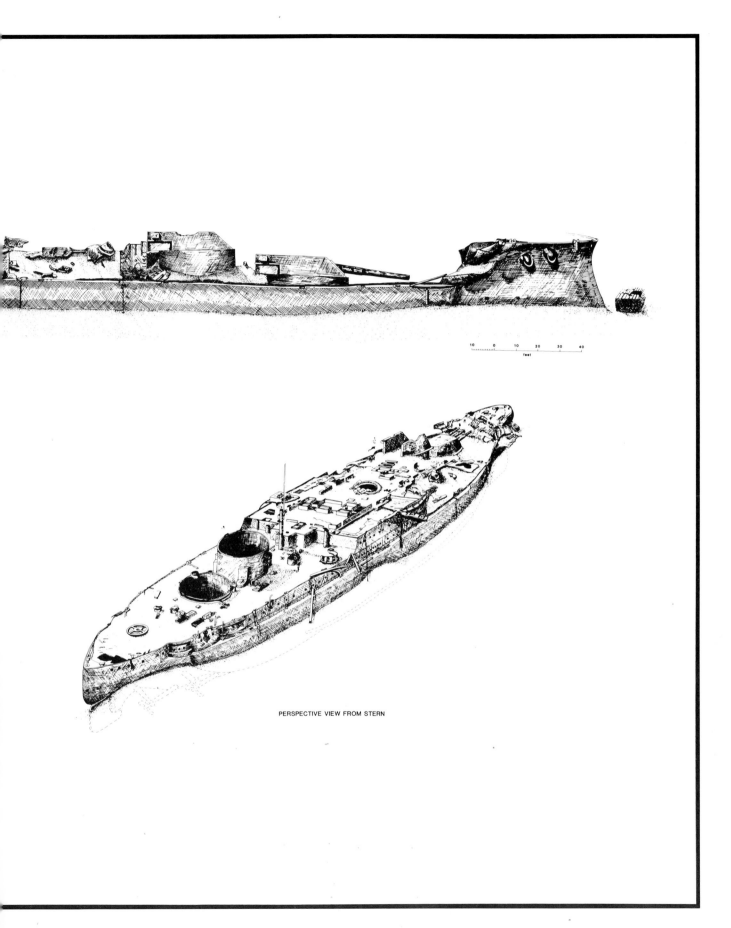

PERSPECTIVE VIEW FROM STERN

a bill to allow construction of the memorial. His proposal gained the support of Samuel Fuqua, the ship's senior surviving officer, who was by then a retired rear admiral. Burns's bill was passed on 15 March 1958, authorizing the Navy to build the memorial and permitting it to accept funds from the Pacific War Memorial Commission.[57]

The fund-raising effort that followed had its ups and downs, as detailed in Michael Slackman's beautifully illustrated book *Remembering Pearl Harbor: The Story Of the USS Arizona Memorial*. Among the more noteworthy contributions were several generous appropriations by Hawaii's legislature. The television program "This Is Your Life" honored the *Arizona*, particularly Rear Admiral Fuqua, in December 1958, generating publicity that helped the campaign to raise $95,000. On 25 March 1961 Elvis Presley sang in a concert at Pearl Harbor's Bloch Arena on behalf of the memorial. The sold-out affair contributed nearly $65,000. National Commander Harold Berc of the AmVets lobbied actively for congressional support. The U.S. Congress finally appropriated $150,000 to finish the effort.[58]

The designer of the memorial was Alfred Preis of a Hawaiian firm. His early efforts included a sort of bridge connecting the hulk of the *Arizona* with Ford Island, but those schemes were rejected, and he came up with the now-famous idea of a structure spanning but not touching the ship's hull. Construction began in late 1960 and lasted until early 1962. Costs eventually mounted to over $500,000. The memorial was dedicated with a flourish on Memorial Day in 1962, indicating that it was in honor of the men of the *Arizona* who had lost their lives, rather than as a commemoration of the Japanese attack.[59]

The memorial was a hit from the outset. As Slackman has written, it became a victim of its own success. It was so popular that visitors became disenchanted with the long waiting lines for the boat ride out from fleet landing. Various organizations sought to enhance the memorial, though each was reluctant to put up the additional money. The Navy was bogged down with the expense of its operations in the Vietnam War. The matter dragged on for years and involved a good deal of legislative and bureaucratic wrangling before Congress finally appropriated money to supplement private donations.

The new visitors' center formally opened on 10 October 1980, and the Navy turned the operation of the memorial over to the National Park Service. The visitors' center includes movie theaters and various displays of photos and artifacts to honor the *Arizona* and her crew. The facility also includes a bookstore and a research area. Attendance at the *Arizona* Memorial has grown steadily since the completion of the center, and its various displays have provided visitors with constructive ways to spend their time.[60]

In 1983–84 Navy and National Park Service divers conducted an underwater archaeological survey of the wreck of the *Arizona*. The project, which was funded by the Arizona Memorial Museum Association, had several objectives:

—establish the wreck's position and chart it in detail
—place reference markers to aid in determining if any shifting or settling occurs in the future

Below: Opened to the public in 1980, the visitors' center contains a movie theater and offers a variety of displays to tell the story of the ship. At left are the Navy launches that take tourists from the visitors' center to the *Arizona* Memorial itself. (Courtesy Daniel Martinez, USS *Arizona* Memorial)

—ascertain the condition of the wreck

—find the location from which fuel oil was still escaping (and does to this day)

—learn whether any unexploded ordnance was still on board

—search for possible torpedo damage to the ship

—clean off an accumulation of coins, combs, cameras, and other things that tourists had thrown or dropped from the memorial over the years.

The results of the study have been published in a book edited by Daniel J. Lenihan, principal investigator for the Submerged Cultural Resources Unit of the National Park Service.[61]

One of the divers on the National Park Service team was Jim Delgado, and he was involved in a follow-up phase of the study in 1988. He has dived on a number of sunken ships, including the collection of naval vessels used for the atomic bomb tests at Bikini Atoll in 1946. Despite his considerable experience in the field, he explains that diving on the *Arizona* was something special. He compares it with being in the Oval Office of the White House or perhaps in Abraham Lincoln's box at Ford's Theater. He says that he and the other divers did not want to enter the ship because they felt they would be trespassing in an area where they weren't supposed to be.

When he was under the water, especially in the area where the *Arizona*'s galley used to be, he could look up and see people watching him from the cutouts in the sides of the white memorial. As he swam around the submerged hull, he was reluctant to touch it or to look too closely into it. He had an eerie feeling that someone might look back from inside, even though reason obviously told him otherwise. He looked into a hatch and saw all sorts of marine growth and twisted metal choking the entrance, and he noted that the deck was covered with silt. Unexpectedly, something emerged from a hatch, startling him. When it floated into the light, Delgado saw that it was a globule of fuel oil, freed from the *Arizona* after nearly fifty years. It rose slowly to the top of the water, then spread out to produce a sheen on the surface.

While he was swimming underwater, Delgado was overcome by a sense of time warp. The world above had changed dramatically since 1941, including the building of the memorial. But the hull of the *Arizona* was largely the same as it had been after the magazine explosion had ripped her asunder. True, she was corroded and covered with marine growth, but the essence was still there—the same hull that had been built seven decades earlier in Brooklyn. Shining his light in through one porthole, he peered into Admiral Kidd's cabin, which was largely

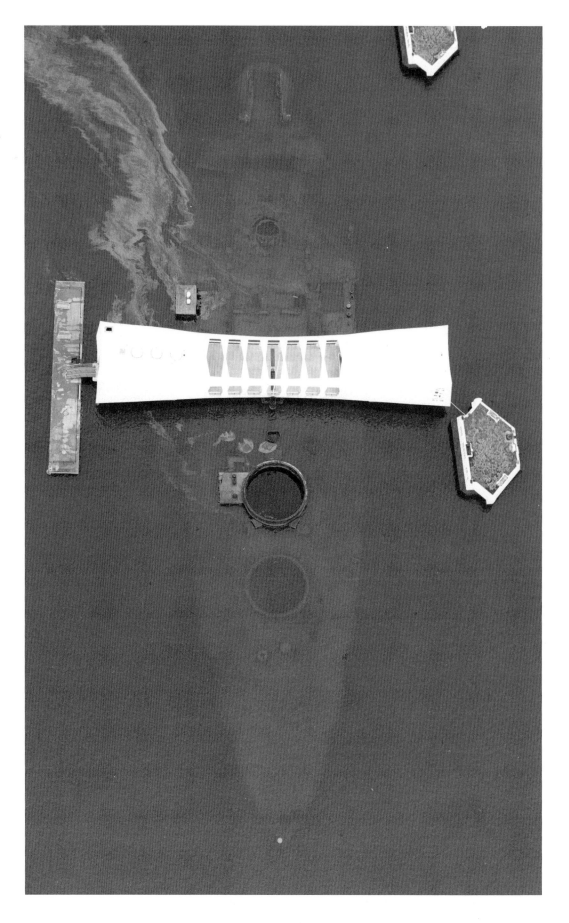

Right: Recent aerial view of the memorial and the remains of the battleship *Arizona*. The stern is in the foreground. Notice the sheen of oil on the water's surface in the upper left corner. (Photo by Gregory Allan Butler, U.S. Naval Institute Collection)

undamaged. He saw heaps on the deck that could have been furniture. On a bulkhead was a telephone; Admiral Kidd had undoubtedly used it many times. Elsewhere he saw the tiles that had been the deck of the galley. On the deck were pieces of silverware and crockery, obvious evidence of human habitation many years earlier. He saw nothing that looked as if it had once been part of a man, and he was relieved not to.

When he swam near the bow, Delgado saw evidence of the cataclysmic explosion that tore the forward part of the *Arizona* apart. The decks were rippled. Pieces of steel appeared to have been crumpled as easily as if they had been made of paper. Beams and decks were twisted into grotesque shapes. The ship showed some evidence of damage aft, but the hull was largely intact—certainly in comparison with the bow. By the time he dived on the wreck, no ordnance was visible, although divers had seen some 5-inch projectiles earlier

in the decade. Delgado and his fellow divers found no sign of the kind of large hole that a torpedo would have made in the side of the ship. When the Park Service diver/historian emerged from the grave of the *Arizona*, he was covered with oil and filled with a profound sense of having been close to something he calls a "temporal touchstone" because it has so much value now as part of American culture.[62]

In the years since the memorial was completed and the remains of the ship became widely accessible, millions of people of many nationalities have come to visit the *Arizona*. Her physical presence is a reminder of the symbolic role she played in rallying Americans to battle in World War II. The battleship *Arizona* lives on, more revered now than she ever was while in active service. Her heritage will endure long after all who ever served in her are gone.

Appendix A

CHRONOLOGY, 1916-1941

This chronology is based on deck logs stored at the National Archives in Washington, D.C. The movements of various flag officers embarked in the *Arizona* are not necessarily complete because of the differing standards used for recording such movements at various times in the ship's career.

1916

17 October–10 November   Moored at the New York Navy Yard. On 17 October Rear Admiral Nathaniel R. Usher, USN, put the *Arizona* into commission. Captain John D. McDonald, USN, read his orders as the first commanding officer.

10–11 November   En route to Hampton Roads.

11–19 November   Under way towing targets for the USS *Pennsylvania*'s battle practice in the Southern Drill Grounds (Virginia Capes) and anchored at Lynnhaven Roads, Virginia.

19–21 November   Moored at Hampton Roads.

21–22 November   En route to Newport.

22–24 November   Anchored at Newport to load torpedoes.

24–29 November   En route to Cuba.

29 November–5 December   Anchored at Guantanamo Bay.

5–7 December   Under way near Cuba for standardization runs and maneuvering for tactical data.

7–12 December   Anchored at Guantanamo Bay.

12–16 December   En route to Lynnhaven Roads.

16–17 December   Anchored at Lynnhaven Roads.

17–18 December   Under way or anchored at Hampton Roads and in the Chesapeake Bay.

18–23 December   Under way or anchored in the Chesapeake Bay. On 19 December the *Arizona* fired her 5-inch guns for the first time. She fired her 14-inch guns for the first time on 23 December; included that day was a salvo of all twelve guns.

23–24 December   En route to New York.

24–26 December   Anchored off Staten Island.

26 December   En route to New York.

26–31 December   Moored at the New York Navy Yard.

1917

1–8 January   Moored at the New York Navy Yard.

8–20 January   Dry-docked at the New York Navy Yard.

20 January–7 March   Moored at the New York Navy Yard.

7–16 March   Dry-docked at the New York Navy Yard.

16 March–3 April   Moored at the New York Navy Yard.

3–4 April   En route to Lynnhaven Roads.

4 April   Anchored at Lynnhaven Roads; under way; anchored in the York River, Virginia.

4–26 April   Anchored in the York River.

26–27 April   Alternately conducted maneuvers in the Chesapeake Bay and anchored in the York River.

27 April–3 May   Anchored in the York River.

3–4 May   Alternately conducted maneuvers in the Chesapeake Bay and anchored in the York River.

4–14 May Anchored in the York River.

14–16 May Alternately conducted maneuvers in the Chesapeake Bay and Southern Drill Grounds and anchored in the Chesapeake Bay and York River.

16–21 May Anchored in the York River.

21–25 May Alternately conducted experimental firing in the Chesapeake Bay and anchored in the Chesapeake Bay.

25–28 May Anchored in the York River.

28–29 May Under way for maneuvers and anchored in the York River.

29 May–5 June Anchored in the York River.

5–9 June Alternately conducted maneuvers in the Chesapeake Bay and anchored in the York River and Chesapeake Bay.

9–18 June Anchored in the York River.

18–22 June Alternately conducted maneuvers in the Chesapeake Bay and anchored in the York River and Chesapeake Bay.

22–25 June Anchored in the York River.

25–28 June Alternately conducted maneuvers in the Chesapeake Bay and anchored in the York River and Chesapeake Bay.

28–30 June Anchored in the York River.

30 June En route to Hampton Roads.

30 June–1 July Anchored in Hampton Roads.

1–2 July En route to New York.

2–3 July Anchored off Staten Island.

3 July En route to New York.

3–18 July Dry-docked at the New York Navy Yard.

18–28 July Moored at the New York Navy Yard.

28–30 July Under way with the USS *Duncan* en route to the Chesapeake Bay.

30 July–2 August Alternately conducted maneuvers in the Chesapeake Bay and anchored in the York River, Chesapeake Bay, and Tangier Sound.

2–10 August Alternately under way in the Chesapeake Bay and anchored in the York River and Hampton Roads.

10–13 August Anchored in the York River, Virginia. On 11 August the deck divisions of the *Arizona* manned the rail in honor of President Woodrow Wilson, who was on board the *Mayflower*, and Secretary of the Navy Josephus Daniels, who was on board the *Sylph*.

13–19 August Steamed in company with other battleships for battle maneuvers, including night torpedo-defense quarters and range-finder and battery drills.

Right: Tugboats provide the escort in New York's East River in 1916. (Enrique Muller, Naval Historical Center, NH 94785)

19–27 August Anchored at Port Jefferson, Long Island Sound.

27–30 August Alternately under way for various drills with the other ships of Battleship Division Eight (USS *Wyoming*, USS *Nevada*, and USS *Pennsylvania*) and anchored at Port Jefferson.

30 August–4 September Anchored at Port Jefferson.

4–7 September Alternately under way for drills with other battleships and anchored at Port Jefferson.

7–10 September Anchored at Port Jefferson.

10–15 September Under way with the fleet for short-range battle-practice rehearsal and other drills.

15–18 September Anchored at Port Jefferson.

18–21 September Alternately anchored at Port Jefferson and under way for drills with other battleships.

21–26 September Anchored at Port Jefferson.

26 September Under way as part of a battle-efficiency inspection.

26 September–1 October Anchored at Port Jefferson.

1–6 October En route to the York River with the fleet.

6–14 October Anchored in the York River.

14–26 October Alternately under way and anchored in Lynnhaven Roads and the York River.

26–27 October En route to New York.

27–28 October Anchored off Staten Island.

28 October En route to New York.

28 October–3 December Moored at the New York Navy Yard.

3–4 December Dry-docked at the New York Navy Yard.

4–7 December Moored at the New York Navy Yard.

7 December En route to Staten Island.

7–9 December Anchored off Staten Island.

9–11 December En route to Lynnhaven Roads with other battleships.

11–12 December Anchored in Lynnhaven Roads.

12 December En route to the York River.

12–16 December Anchored in the York River.

16–17 December Under way for maneuvers with the USS *Paul Jones*.

17–20 December Anchored at Yorktown.

20–21 December Alternately under way and anchored in Hampton Roads.

21–26 December Anchored at Yorktown. On 25 December the *Arizona* hoisted a junior rear admiral's flag, Captain John D. McDonald, USN, having been selected for that rank.

26–27 December Alternately under way and anchored in the Chesapeake Bay.

27–31 December Anchored at Yorktown.

1918

1–14 January Anchored at Yorktown.

14–18 January Under way for maneuvers with other battleships.

18 January–2 February Anchored at Yorktown.

2 February En route to Hampton Roads.

2–4 February Anchored in Hampton Roads.

4 February En route to Yorktown.

4–5 February Anchored at Yorktown.

5–12 February Under way with other battleships for a fleet battle problem and antisubmarine maneuvers.

12–17 February Anchored at Yorktown.

17 February En route to Hampton Roads.

17–18 February Anchored in Hampton Roads. On 18 February Captain Josiah S. McKean, USN, relieved Rear Admiral John D. McDonald, USN, as commanding officer.

18 February En route to the Norfolk Navy Yard.

18–19 February Moored at the Norfolk Navy Yard.

19 February En route to Yorktown.

19–25 February Anchored at Yorktown.

25 February–1 March Under way with other battleships for fleet battle maneuvers.

1–8 March Anchored at Yorktown.

8 March En route to Hampton Roads.

8–11 March Anchored in Hampton Roads.

11 March Under way for short-range director practice.

11–13 March Anchored in Hampton Roads.

13–16 March Alternately under way for torpedo-defense and spotting practice and anchored at Yorktown and in the Chesapeake Bay.

16–18 March Anchored at Yorktown.

18–22 March Under way for maneuvers with the fleet.

22 March–1 April Anchored at Yorktown.

1–5 April Alternately under way for day torpedo-defense practice and anchored in Hampton Roads.

5–8 April Anchored at Yorktown.

8–12 April Under way for battle maneuvers with other battleships.

12–15 April Anchored at Yorktown.

15–19 April Alternately under way for long-range spotting practice and anchored in Hampton Roads.

19–29 April Anchored at Yorktown.

29 April–3 May Under way for battle maneuvers with other battleships.

3–6 May Anchored at Yorktown.

6 May En route to Hampton Roads.

6–8 May Alternately under way for drills and anchored in Hampton Roads.

8–11 May Anchored in Hampton Roads.

11 May En route to Yorktown.

11–21 May Anchored at Yorktown.

21–29 May Under way with the fleet for exercises that included battle maneuvers against a mock enemy fleet.

29 May–4 June Anchored at Yorktown.

4–6 June Alternately under way in the Chesapeake Bay and anchored in Lynnhaven Roads and Tangier Sound.

6 June–8 July Anchored at Yorktown.

8–9 July Alternately under way for short-range battle-practice rehearsal runs and anchored in Tangier Sound.

9–12 July Anchored in Tangier Sound.

12 July Under way to fire short-range battle practice.

Right: A port bow view of the ship when she was anchored in the York River at Yorktown, Virginia, in May 1918. (National Archives, 19-N-1978)

12–15 July Anchored at Yorktown.

15–19 July Alternately under way while firing torpedo-proving practice in the Chesapeake Bay and anchored in the bay.

19–22 July Anchored at Yorktown.

22–26 July Alternately under way while firing torpedo-proving practice in the Chesapeake Bay and anchored in the bay.

26–29 July Anchored at Yorktown.

29 July Alternately under way and anchored in the Chesapeake Bay.

29 July–1 August Anchored in Tangier Sound.

1 August Under way for short-range director practice.

1–9 August Anchored at Yorktown.

9–10 August En route to New York.

10–11 August Anchored off Staten Island.

11 August En route to New York.

11 August–16 September Moored at the New York Navy Yard. A dispatch of 28 August authorized Captain Josiah S. McKean, USN, the commanding officer, to assume the rank of rear admiral and wear the appropriate uniform. On 11 September Captain John H. Dayton, USN, relieved Rear Admiral McKean as commanding officer.

16–25 September Dry-docked at the New York Navy Yard.

25 September–3 October Moored at the New York Navy Yard.

3–4 October En route to Yorktown in company with the USS *Fairfax*.

4–21 October Anchored at Yorktown.

21–25 October Alternately under way in the Chesapeake Bay for torpedo practice and anchored in the bay and Tangier Sound.

25 October–4 November Anchored at Yorktown (under way briefly on 30 October).

4–8 November Alternately under way in the Chesapeake Bay for torpedo-defense practice and anchored in Tangier Sound.

8–11 November Anchored at Yorktown.

11–14 November Alternately under way and anchored in the Chesapeake Bay.

14–18 November Anchored in Hampton Roads.

18–30 November En route to England.

30 November–12 December Moored at Portland, England.

12–13 December En route to France, in company with Battleship Division Six.

13–14 December Anchored at Brest, France.

14–25 December En route to New York with other battleships.

25–26 December Anchored off Ambrose Lightship, New York.

26 December En route to New York.

26–31 December Moored in the North River, New York City.

1919

1–22 January Moored in the North River, New York City.

22–23 January En route independently to Hampton Roads.

23–27 January Anchored in Hampton Roads.

27 January En route to the Norfolk Navy Yard.

27–29 January Moored at the Norfolk Navy Yard.

29 January–1 February Dry-docked at the Norfolk Navy Yard.

1 February En route to Hampton Roads.

2–4 February Anchored in Hampton Roads.

4–8 February En route to Cuba, engaged in fleet maneuvers with other battleships in company.

8–18 February Anchored in Guantanamo Bay.

18 February Under way for standardization trials; highest reported speed was 21¼ knots.

18–19 February Anchored in Guantanamo Bay.

19–28 February Alternately under way for fleet maneuvers and various individual ship exercises and anchored in Guantanamo Bay.

28 February–3 March Anchored in Guantanamo Bay.

3 March Under way for exercises.

3–6 March Anchored in Guantanamo Bay.

6 March Under way for drills, including tactical maneuvers with the USS *Mississippi*.

6–17 March Anchored in Guantanamo Bay.

17–22 March En route to Trinidad with the fleet, engaged in various maneuvers, including battle exercises against a simulated enemy.

22–25 March Anchored at Port of Spain, Trinidad.

26–29 March En route to Cuba with the fleet.

29–31 March Anchored in Guantanamo Bay.

31 March Under way to check range finders and conduct rehearsal for day individual practice.

31 March–4 April Anchored in Guantanamo Bay.

4 April Under way with other ships for day individual practice.

4–9 April Anchored in Guantanamo Bay.

9–12 April En route to Hampton Roads.

12 April Anchored in Hampton Roads.

12–21 April En route to France.

21 April–3 May Anchored at Brest, France.

3–11 May En route to Asia Minor.

11 May–9 June Anchored at Smyrna, Asia Minor (now Izmir, Turkey).

9–10 June En route to Constantinople.

10–15 June Anchored at Constantinople, Turkey (now Istanbul).

15–20 June En route to Gibraltar.

20 June Anchored at Gibraltar.

20–30 June En route to New York.

30 June–3 July Moored in the North River, New York City.

3 July En route to the New York Navy Yard.

3–10 July Moored at the New York Navy Yard.

10–21 July Dry-docked at the New York Navy Yard.

21 July–18 December Moored at the New York Navy Yard.

18–23 December Dry-docked at the New York Navy Yard.

23–31 December Moored at the New York Navy Yard.

1920

1–6 January Moored at the New York Navy Yard.

6–7 January En route to the Southern Drill Grounds.

7–8 January Anchored in the Southern Drill Grounds.

8–13 January En route to Cuba in company with other battleships.

13 January–4 February Anchored in Guantanamo Bay.

4–9 February En route to Barbados with the fleet.

9–14 February Anchored at Bridgetown, Barbados, British West Indies.

14–19 February En route to Panama.

19 February–1 March Anchored at Colon.

Right: Anchored at Constantinople, Turkey, in mid-June 1919. (Imperial War Museum, SP 2108)

1–4 March En route to Cuba with the fleet.

4–15 March Anchored in Guantanamo Bay, Cuba.

15–27 March Alternately under way in the vicinity of Cuba for short-range battle-practice rehearsals and anchored in a variety of locations near Cuba: Cape Cruz, Medano Cay, Carapacho Cay, Cuarto Reales Channel, and Media Luna Cay.

27 March–5 April Anchored in Guantanamo Bay.

5–16 April Alternately under way in the vicinity of Cuba for short-range director-practice rehearsals and anchored in several locations near Cuba: Cuarto Reales Channel, Media Luna Cay, and Guacanayabo Bay.

16–26 April Anchored in Guantanamo Bay.

26 April–1 May En route to New York.

1–17 May Moored in the North River, New York City.

17–18 May En route to the Southern Drill Grounds with Battleship Division Seven.

18–20 May Anchored off Cape Charles, Virginia.

20–21 May Under way for torpedo-defense spotting practice.

21–24 May Anchored in Hampton Roads.

24 May En route to the Southern Drill Grounds.

24–27 May Anchored in the Southern Drill Grounds.

27 May En route to the Chesapeake Bay.

27–28 May Anchored in Tangier Sound, Maryland.

28 May En route to Annapolis.

28 May–7 June Anchored at Annapolis.

7–10 June Alternately under way in the Southern Drill Grounds and anchored in the vicinity: Cape Henry and Virginia Beach, Virginia.

10–16 June Moored at Hampton Roads (under way briefly on 14 June).

16–24 June Alternately under way with the other ships of Battleship Division Seven (USS *Nevada*, USS *Oklahoma*, and USS *Pennsylvania*) for day individual practice rehearsals and division target practice and anchored in the Southern Drill Grounds.

24–25 June En route to New York.

25 June Anchored off Staten Island and en route to the New York Navy Yard.

25 June–9 July Moored at the New York Navy Yard. On 26 June Captain William W. Phelps, USN, relieved Captain John H. Dayton, USN, as commanding officer.

9–15 July Dry-docked at the New York Navy Yard.

16 July–9 August Moored at the New York Navy Yard.

9 August En route to Fort Pond Bay.

10–14 August Anchored in Fort Pond Bay.

14 August En route to Newport.

14–18 August Anchored at Newport.

18–20 August Alternately under way for tactical exercises with other ships and at anchor off Block Island and Montauk Point.

20–30 August Moored in the North River, New York City. On 24 August Rear Admiral Edward W. Eberle, USN, reported aboard the *Arizona* with his staff to take command of Battleship Division Seven.

30 August–3 September Alternately under way with Battleship Division Seven for short-range battle-practice rehearsal and anchored off Fire Island.

3–13 September Moored in the North River, New York City.

13–14 September En route to the Southern Drill Grounds.

Above: Approaching New York in 1920 after operations in the Caribbean. (Levick photo courtesy Ted Stone)

14–24 September Alternately under way for short-range battle-practice rehearsal and anchored in the Southern Drill Grounds.

24–25 September En route to New York.

25–28 September Anchored off Ambrose Light, New York.

28 September En route to New York City.

28 September–4 October Moored in the North River, New York City.

4–5 October En route to the Southern Drill Grounds.

5–14 October Alternately under way for various exercises in the Southern Drill Grounds and anchored in Lynnhaven Roads.

14–15 October En route to New York.

15–25 October Moored in the North River, New York City.

25–26 October En route to the Southern Drill Grounds.

26–28 October Alternately under way for various exercises in the Southern Drill Grounds and anchored in Lynnhaven Roads.

28–29 October En route to New York.

29 October–8 November Moored in the North River, New York City.

8–10 November En route to the Southern Drill Grounds.

10 November Anchored in the Southern Drill Grounds.

10–11 November En route to New York.

11–12 November Anchored off Staten Island.

12 November En route to the New York Navy Yard.

12 November–20 December Moored at the New York Navy Yard.

20–30 December Dry-docked at the New York Navy Yard.

30–31 December Moored at the New York Navy Yard.

1921

1–4 January Moored at the New York Navy Yard.

4–9 January En route to Cuba as part of a fleet formation.

9–17 January Anchored in Guantanamo Bay.

17–19 January En route to Panama as part of a fleet formation.

19 January Anchored at Colon; under way for the first part of the Panama Canal transit.

19–20 January Anchored in Gatun Lake, Panama Canal.

20 January Under way with other battleships for the remainder of the Panama Canal transit.

20–22 January Anchored at Balboa.

22–31 January En route to Peru with the other battleships of the Atlantic Fleet. During this voyage the *Arizona* crossed the equator for the first time on 24 January.

31 January–5 February Anchored at Callao. On 2 February the crew of the *Arizona* manned the rail as the president of Peru circled the fleet.

5–14 February En route to Panama. During this voyage, ships of both the Atlantic and Pacific fleets joined for tactical maneuvers.

14–23 February Anchored at Balboa.

23 February Transited the Panama Canal.

23–26 February En route to Cuba with other battleships.

26–28 February Anchored in Guantanamo Bay.

28 February–4 March Alternately under way off Cuba while rehearsing for day torpedo-defense practice and conducting fleet target practice and anchored in Guantanamo Bay.

4–14 March Anchored in Guantanamo Bay.

14–18 March Alternately under way off Cuba while conducting gunnery and torpedo practice and anchored in Guantanamo Bay.

18–21 March Anchored in Guantanamo Bay.

21–24 March Alternately under way off Cuba while conducting individual and division gunnery practice and anchored in Guantanamo Bay.

24 March–3 April Anchored in Guantanamo Bay.

3–4 April En route to Guacanayabo Bay with other battleships.

4–5 April Anchored in Guacanayabo Bay, Cuba.

5–9 April Alternately under way off Cuba while conducting division maneuvers and torpedo practice and anchored in Guacanayabo Bay.

9–11 April Anchored in Guacanayabo Bay, Cuba.

11 April En route to Cuarto Reales Channel.

11–12 April Anchored in Cuarto Reales Channel, Cuba.

12–15 April Alternately under way off Cuba while conducting division maneuvers and torpedo practice and anchored in Guacanayabo Bay; en route to Guantanamo.

15–24 April Anchored in Guantanamo Bay.

24–27 April En route to Lynnhaven Roads with the Atlantic Fleet.

27–28 April Anchored in Lynnhaven Roads.

28 April En route to Hampton Roads, passing in review for President Warren Harding on board the USS *Mayflower*; anchored in Hampton Roads.

28–29 April En route to New York.

29 April–7 June Moored at the New York Navy Yard. On 30 May Commander Royal E. Ingersoll, USN, became acting commanding officer when Captain William W. Phelps, USN, was hospitalized.

7–10 June Dry-docked at the New York Navy Yard.

10–14 June Moored at the New York Navy Yard. On 11 June Captain Jehu V. Chase, USN, reported aboard and assumed command.

14 June En route to Staten Island.

14–15 June Anchored off Staten Island.

15–16 June En route to Cape Charles.

16–20 June Anchored off Cape Charles, Virginia.

20–22 June Alternately under way in the Southern Drill Grounds while observing gunnery and bombing practice conducted on captured ex-German submarines and anchored in Lynnhaven Roads.

22–25 June Anchored in Lynnhaven Roads.

25–26 June En route to New York.

26 June–9 July Moored in the North River, New York City. On 30 June Rear Admiral Edward W. Eberle, USN, was detached as Commander Battleship Division Seven. On 1 July Vice Admiral John D. McDonald, USN, embarked in the *Arizona* as Commander Battleship Force Atlantic Fleet and Commander Battleship Division Seven.

9–16 July En route to Panama, joined by the USS *Nevada* and *Oklahoma* for short-range battle-practice rehearsal.

16 July Transited the Panama Canal.

16–18 July Moored at Balboa.

18–22 July En route to Peru in company with the USS *Nevada* and *Oklahoma*.

22 July–3 August Anchored at Callao.

3–8 August En route to Balboa in company with the USS *Nevada* and *Oklahoma*.

8–11 August Moored at Balboa. On 10 August Vice Admiral John D. McDonald, USN, hauled down his flag and departed with his staff; that same day Rear Admiral Josiah S. McKean, USN, came aboard with his staff and took command of Battleship Division Seven.

Below: The *Arizona* circa 1921. (Gustave Maurer, Naval Historical Center, NH 2219)

11–21 August En route to San Diego in company with the USS *Nevada* and *Oklahoma*.

21–24 August Anchored at San Diego.

24–26 August En route to San Francisco in company with the USS *Nevada* and *Oklahoma*.

26 August–6 September Anchored at San Francisco.

6–8 September En route to San Pedro with the Pacific Fleet.

8–12 September Anchored at San Pedro.

12–16 September Alternately under way for antiaircraft practice and short-range battle-practice rehearsals and anchored at San Pedro.

16–26 September Anchored at San Pedro.

26–27 September Alternately under way for short-range battle-practice rehearsal and anchored at San Pedro.

27–29 September Anchored at San Pedro, California. On 28 September Rear Admiral Charles F. Hughes, USN, relieved Rear Admiral Josiah S. McKean, USN, as Commander Battleship Division Seven, embarked in the *Arizona*.

29 September–3 October Alternately under way for short-range battle-practice rehearsal and anchored at San Pedro.

3–12 October Anchored at San Pedro.

12 October Under way to fire short-range battle practice.

12–19 October Anchored at San Pedro.

19–21 October Alternately under way for maneuvers with the USS *Pennsylvania* and short-range director-practice rehearsal and anchored at San Pedro.

21–26 October Anchored at San Pedro.

26 October Under way for short-range director-practice rehearsal.

26 October–4 November Anchored at San Pedro.

4 November Under way to conduct short-range director practice.

4–8 November Anchored at San Pedro.

8 November Under way to conduct day torpedo-defense spotting-practice rehearsal.

8–14 November Anchored at San Pedro.

14–16 November Alternately under way for day torpedo-defense practice rehearsals and day torpedo-defense practice and anchored at San Pedro.

16–18 November Anchored at San Pedro.

18–20 November En route to San Francisco in company with the USS *Mississippi*, *Nevada*, and *Oklahoma*, conducting battle torpedo practice.

20 November–1 December Anchored at San Francisco.

1 December En route to Hunters Point.

1–2 December Dry-docked at Hunters Point, the Union Plant of the Bethlehem Steel Shipbuilding Corporation.

2–4 December En route to San Pedro.

4–12 December Anchored at San Pedro.

12–14 December Alternately under way for gunnery practice and anchored at San Pedro.

14–31 December Anchored at San Pedro. On 24 December Captain George R. Marvell, USN, relieved Captain Jehu V. Chase, USN, as commanding officer.

1922

1–3 January Anchored at San Pedro.

3–11 January Alternately under way for night battle-practice rehearsal and anchored at San Pedro.

11–16 January Anchored at San Pedro.

16–17 January Under way for paravane drill and night battle-practice rehearsal.

17–19 January Anchored at San Pedro.

19–21 January En route to San Francisco with Battleship Division Seven.

21 January–15 February Anchored at San Francisco.

15–17 February En route to San Pedro with Battleship Division Seven.

17–23 February Anchored at San Pedro.

23–27 February Alternately under way for battle torpedo-practice rehearsal and anchored at San Pedro.

27 February–14 March Anchored at San Pedro.

14 March Under way briefly for battle approaches to target.

14–27 March Anchored at San Pedro.

27–30 March Alternately under way for division maneuvers and antiaircraft practice and anchored at San Pedro.

30 March–4 April Anchored at San Pedro.

4–7 April Alternately under way for long-range battle-practice approaches and rehearsal and anchored at San Pedro.

7–10 April Anchored at San Pedro.

10 April Under way with other battleships for long-range battle-practice rehearsal.

10–13 April Anchored at San Pedro.

13 April Under way with other battleships to fire long-range battle practice.

13–25 April Anchored at San Pedro.

25–26 April Alternately under way for squadron battle practice and anchored at San Pedro.

26 April–2 May Anchored at San Pedro.

2 May Under way to fire squadron battle practice.

2–5 May Anchored at San Pedro.

5–9 May En route to Bremerton.

9 May–9 June Moored at the Puget Sound Navy Yard.

9–20 June Dry-docked at the Puget Sound Navy Yard.

20–26 June Moored at the Puget Sound Navy Yard.

26 June En route to Blake Island.

26 June–1 July Anchored off Blake Island, Puget Sound.

1 July En route to Seattle.

1–10 July Anchored at Seattle. On 1 July the staff of Commander Battleship Division Seven returned to the *Arizona* after having been embarked in the USS *Pennsylvania* since 4 May, during the *Arizona*'s yard period. Rear Admiral Hughes, who was on temporary duty, rejoined the staff on 17 July.

10 July En route to Port Angeles.

10–11 July Anchored at Port Angeles, Washington.

11–12 July Alternately under way for division maneuvers and anchored at Port Angeles.

12–18 July Anchored at Port Angeles.

18–20 July Alternately under way for division maneuvers and anchored at Port Angeles.

20 July En route to Bremerton.

20–31 July Moored at the Puget Sound Navy Yard. On 27 July Captain John R. Y. Blakely, USN, relieved Captain George R. Marvell, USN, as commanding officer.

31 July En route to Port Angeles.

31 July–4 August Anchored at Port Angeles.

4 August En route to Tacoma.

4–14 August Anchored at Tacoma.

14 August En route to Port Townsend.

14–16 August Anchored at Port Townsend.

16 August Under way for division maneuvers.

Below: Entering dry dock in the early 1920s. (USS *Arizona* Memorial, National Park Service, PR-4)

16–18 August   Anchored at Port Townsend.

18 August   En route to Anacortes.

18–21 August   Anchored at Anacortes, Washington.

21 August   En route to Bellingham.

21–28 August   Moored at Bellingham, Washington.

28 August   En route to Port Angeles.

28 August–2 September   Anchored at Port Angeles.

2–5 September   En route to San Francisco in company with other battleships.

5–12 September   Anchored at San Francisco.

12–13 September   En route to San Pedro. During the voyage the *Arizona* conducted a full-power run at 21+ knots (235 rpms).

13–18 September   Anchored at San Pedro.

18–22 September   Alternately under way for battle torpedo-practice rehearsals in company with the USS *Pennsylvania* and anchored at San Diego.

22–25 September   Anchored at San Pedro.

25–29 September   Alternately under way for various exercises with the USS *Mississippi* and *Pennsylvania* and anchored at San Pedro.

29 September–16 October   Anchored at San Pedro.

16–19 October   Alternately under way for short-range battle-practice rehearsal and anchored at San Pedro.

19–21 October   Anchored at San Pedro.

21–23 October   En route to San Francisco.

23–28 October   Anchored at San Francisco.

28–30 October   En route to San Pedro with the USS *Mississippi* and *Pennsylvania*.

30–31 October   Anchored at San Pedro.

31 October–3 November   Alternately under way for short-range battle-practice rehearsals with the USS *Mississippi* and anchored at San Pedro.

3–13 November   Anchored at San Pedro.

13–16 November   Alternately under way for night spotting practice and night battle practice and anchored at San Pedro.

16–20 November   Anchored at San Pedro.

20–28 November   Alternately under way for night battle-practice rehearsals and serving as a target for torpedo practice by submarines and anchored at San Pedro.

28 November–31 December   Anchored at San Pedro.

1923

1–15 January   Anchored at San Pedro.

15–16 January   En route to San Francisco.

16–17 January   Anchored at San Francisco.

17–19 January   Dry-docked at Hunters Point, San Francisco.

19–22 January   Anchored at San Francisco.

22–23 January   En route to San Pedro.

23 January–8 February   Anchored at San Pedro.

8–21 February   En route to Costa Rica in company with the Battle Fleet, conducting war games.

21–23 February   Anchored at Port Culebra, Costa Rica.

23–26 February   En route to Panama in company with the Battle Fleet.

26 February–12 March   Anchored at Balboa.

12–23 March   Alternately under way for fleet maneuvers, including experimental torpedo practice, and anchored at Balboa. On 22 March the *Arizona* lay to and observed the fall of shot as the USS *Mississippi* sank the ex-battleship *Iowa* with gunfire.

23–31 March   Anchored at Balboa.

31 March–11 April   En route to San Pedro in company with the Battle Fleet.

11–23 April   Anchored at San Pedro.

23–27 April   Alternately under way for gunnery exercises and anchored at San Pedro.

27–30 April   Anchored at San Pedro.

30 April   Under way for gunnery exercises.

30 April–2 May   Anchored at San Pedro.

2 May   Under way to fire long-range battle practice.

2–5 May   Anchored at San Pedro.

5 May   Under way for gunnery exercises.

5–23 May   Anchored at San Pedro.

23 May   Under way for gunnery exercises.

23–25 May   Anchored at San Pedro.

25 May   Under way for gunnery exercises.

25–26 May   Anchored at San Pedro. On 26 May Rear Admiral Charles F. Hughes, USN, Commander Battleship Division Four, and his staff transferred to the USS *Pennsylvania*. Hughes had been Commander Battleship Division Seven until the title was changed in January 1923.

26 May–1 June En route to Bremerton.

1–25 June Moored at the Puget Sound Navy Yard.

25 June–10 July Dry-docked in the Puget Sound Navy Yard.

10–26 July Moored at the Puget Sound Navy Yard.

26 July En route to Seattle.

26–27 July Anchored at Seattle. On 27 July the ship wore full dress for a review by President Warren G. Harding, who was on board the USS *Henderson*.

27 July En route to Bremerton.

27 July–3 August Moored at the Puget Sound Navy Yard.

3 August En route to Seattle.

3–13 August Anchored at Seattle. On 3 August the *Arizona* half-masted her colors and joined other ships in firing a salute to the late President Harding.

13 August En route to Port Townsend.

13–15 August Anchored at Port Townsend.

15 August Under way with Battleship Division Four for maneuvers.

15–17 August Anchored at Port Townsend.

17 August En route to Tacoma.

17–27 August Anchored at Tacoma.

27–31 August En route to San Francisco in company with Battleship Division Four and Destroyer Division 33.

31 August–11 September Anchored at San Francisco.

11–12 September En route to San Pedro with other battleships.

12–18 September Anchored at San Pedro.

18–19 September Alternately under way for torpedo practice and anchored at San Pedro.

19–26 September Anchored at San Pedro.

26–28 September Alternately under way for torpedo and antiaircraft practice and anchored at San Pedro.

28 September–1 October Anchored at San Pedro.

1–3 October Alternately under way for gunnery and torpedo practice and anchored at San Pedro.

3–8 October Anchored at San Pedro.

8–11 October Alternately under way for gunnery practice and anchored at San Pedro.

Above: Firing the 14-inch guns in the early 1920s. (W. E. Greenwood, Naval Historical Center, NH 78118)

11–13 October En route to San Francisco with other battleships.

13–20 October Anchored at San Francisco.

20–21 October En route to San Pedro with other battleships.

21–26 October Alternately under way for gunnery practice and anchored at San Pedro.

26–30 October Anchored at San Pedro.

30 October Under way for gunnery practice.

30 October–2 November Anchored at San Pedro.

2 November Under way for gunnery practice.

2–6 November Anchored at San Pedro.

6 November Under way for gunnery practice.

6–9 November Anchored at San Pedro.

9 November Under way for gunnery practice.

9–20 November Anchored at San Pedro.

20–21 November Alternately under way for gunnery practice and anchored at San Pedro.

21–26 November Anchored at San Pedro.

26 November Under way for gunnery practice.

26 November–7 December Anchored at San Pedro. On 29 November Captain Percy N. Olmsted, USN, relieved Captain John R. Y. Blakely, USN, as commanding officer.

7–10 December En route to San Francisco in company with other battleships.

10–12 December Dry-docked at Hunters Point.

12–13 December Anchored at San Francisco.

13–14 December En route to San Pedro.

14–31 December Anchored at San Pedro. On 17 December Rear Admiral William V. Pratt, USN, embarked in the *Arizona* with his staff and broke his flag as Commander Battleship Division Four.

1924

1–2 January Anchored at San Pedro.

2–16 January En route to Panama in company with the Battle Fleet, conducting various fleet maneuvers.

16 January Anchored at Balboa.

16–17 January Transited the Panama Canal.

17–18 January Anchored at Colon.

18 January Under way for maneuvers with other battleships.

18–25 January Anchored at Colon.

25 January–1 February En route to Culebra with other ships of the U.S. Fleet, conducting war games.

1–11 February Anchored off Culebra Island. On 6 February the *Arizona* joined other ships in firing a gun salute in memory of the late former president, Woodrow Wilson.

11–15 February Under way with other ships for maneuvers under the direction of the Commander in Chief U.S. Fleet.

15–25 February Anchored off Culebra Island.

25 February–3 March En route to New York in company with other battleships.

3–13 March Anchored in the North River, New York City.

13–18 March En route to Culebra in company with other battleships.

18–20 March Anchored off Culebra Island.

20–22 March Alternately under way for torpedo practice and anchored off Culebra Island.

22–31 March Anchored off Culebra Island.

31 March–5 April En route to Panama in cruising formation.

5 April Transited the Panama Canal.

5–12 April Anchored at Balboa.

12–22 April En route to San Pedro with the Battle Fleet, conducting gunnery exercises and tactical maneuvers.

22 April–5 May Anchored at San Pedro.

5–8 May Alternately under way for gunnery practice and anchored at San Pedro.

8–13 May Anchored at San Pedro.

13 May Under way for gunnery practice.

13–16 May Anchored at San Pedro.

16–21 May Alternately under way for gunnery practice and anchored at San Pedro. On 20 May Rear Admiral William V. Pratt, USN, and his Battleship Division Four staff transferred from the *Arizona* to the USS *Tennessee*.

21–26 May En route to Bremerton.

26 May–7 June Moored at the Puget Sound Navy Yard.

7 June–9 July Dry-docked at the Puget Sound Navy Yard.

9–21 July Moored at the Puget Sound Navy Yard.

21 July En route to Port Angeles.

21–24 July Anchored at Port Angeles.

24 July Under way for training maneuvers.

24–28 July Anchored at Port Angeles. On 26 July Rear Admiral Pratt and his Battleship Division Four staff reembarked in the *Arizona*.

28 July En route to Port Townsend.

28 July–4 August Anchored at Port Townsend.

4 August Under way for drills.

4–8 August Anchored at Port Townsend.

8 August Under way for experimental anti-aircraft practice.

8–11 August Anchored at Port Townsend.

11–15 August Under way in company with the Battle Fleet for maneuvers off the Strait of Juan de Fuca.

15–25 August Anchored at Seattle.

25 August En route to Tacoma.

25 August–1 September Anchored at Tacoma.

1–4 September En route to San Francisco with the Battle Fleet.

4–8 September Anchored at San Francisco.

8–12 September Under way with the Battle Fleet for maneuvers and gunnery practice.

12–22 September Anchored at San Francisco.

22–26 September Under way with the Battle Fleet for maneuvers. During this period the *Arizona* was involved in a full-power run and full-power endurance run, registering a top speed of 21.5 knots.

26–29 September Anchored at San Francisco.

29 September–1 October En route to San Pedro with the Battle Fleet.

1–13 October Anchored at San Pedro.

13–22 October Alternately under way off Southern California for fleet maneuvers, gunnery practice, and torpedo practice and anchored at San Pedro.

22–25 October Anchored at San Pedro.

25 October Under way for gunnery practice.

25–28 October Anchored at San Pedro.

28 October Under way for gunnery practice.

28–31 October Anchored at San Pedro.

31 October Under way for gunnery practice.

31 October–10 November Anchored at San Pedro. On 1 November Rear Admiral Pratt and his Battleship Division Four staff transferred to the USS *New Mexico*.

10–13 November Alternately under way for gunnery practice and anchored at San Pedro.

13–18 November Anchored at San Pedro.

18–22 November Alternately under way for gunnery practice and anchored at San Pedro.

22 November–2 December Anchored at San Pedro.

2 December Under way for gunnery practice.

2–4 December Anchored at San Pedro.

4 December Under way to conduct an experimental refueling from the USS *Kanawha*.

4–12 December Anchored at San Pedro.

12–13 December Under way for maneuvers with other battleships.

13–31 December Anchored at San Pedro.

1925

1–5 January Anchored at San Pedro.

5–8 January Alternately under way with other battleships for gunnery practice and anchored at San Pedro.

8–12 January Anchored at San Pedro.

12–16 January Alternately under way with other battleships for gunnery practice and anchored at San Pedro.

16–22 January Anchored at San Pedro. On 19 January Rear Admiral Henry J. Ziegemeier, USN, Commander Battleship Division Three, and his staff embarked in the *Arizona*.

Below: Hanging bedding out to dry, circa 1924. (Courtesy Margaret Gesen)

22–23 January En route to San Diego and fired antiaircraft practice.

23–30 January Moored at San Diego.

30 January En route to San Pedro.

30 January–9 February Anchored at San Pedro.

9 February Under way for night battle-practice rehearsal.

9–12 February Anchored at San Pedro.

12–13 February Under way with other battleships for night battle-practice rehearsal.

13–25 February Anchored at San Pedro.

25–26 February Under way with other battleships for night battle-practice rehearsal.

26 February–2 March Anchored at San Pedro.

2–12 March Under way with the Battle Fleet for Fleet Problem V.

12–16 March Anchored at Coronado.

16 March En route to San Pedro.

16–18 March Anchored at San Pedro.

18–20 March Under way for gunnery practice.

20–23 March Anchored at San Pedro.

23–27 March Alternately under way with other battleships for gunnery practice and anchored at San Pedro.

27 March–3 April Anchored at San Pedro. On 27 March Rear Admiral Ziegemeier and his Battleship Division Three staff transferred to the USS *Oklahoma*. On 28 March Rear Admiral William V. Pratt, USN, and his Battleship Division Four staff embarked in the *Arizona*.

3–5 April En route to San Francisco in company with the Battle Fleet.

5–15 April Anchored at San Francisco.

15–27 April En route to Hawaii with the Battle Fleet.

27–28 April Conducted simulated firing at Haleina, Oahu, and anchored off Haleina.

28 April En route to Honolulu.

28 April–7 May Anchored at Honolulu.

7–9 May Under way for maneuvers as part of the U.S. Fleet.

9–18 May Anchored in Lahaina Roads. On 11 May Rear Admiral Pratt and his Battleship Division Four staff departed.

18–29 May Alternately under way for tactical maneuvers with the U.S. Fleet and anchored in Lahaina Roads. On 23 May the *Arizona* carried out a fueling test with the USS *Kanawha*.

29 May–5 June Anchored at Honolulu.

5–12 June En route to San Francisco.

12 June Anchored at San Francisco.

12–15 June En route to Puget Sound.

15–16 June Anchored off Blake Island.

16 June En route to Bremerton.

16 June–17 August Moored at the Puget Sound Navy Yard, Bremerton. On 27 June Harlan P. Perrill, USN, relieved Captain Percy N. Olmsted, USN, as commanding officer.

17 August–2 September Dry-docked at the Puget Sound Navy Yard.

2–16 September Moored at the Puget Sound Navy Yard.

16–19 September En route to San Francisco independently, conducting school-of-the-ship drills.

19–21 September Anchored at San Francisco.

21–22 September En route to San Pedro.

22 September Anchored at San Pedro.

22–23 September Under way for gunnery practice.

23–25 September Anchored at San Pedro.

25–26 September Under way with the Assistant Secretary of the Navy on board, joining up with the fleet for entry into San Pedro.

26 September–5 October Anchored at San Pedro. On 1 October Rear Admiral Ziegemeier and his Battleship Division Three staff transferred to the *Arizona*.

5–9 October Alternately under way with other battleships for gunnery practice and anchored at Coronado.

9–12 October Anchored at San Pedro.

12 October Under way to fire antiaircraft practice.

12–14 October Anchored at San Pedro.

14–16 October Alternately under way with other battleships for gunnery practice and anchored at San Pedro.

16–19 October Anchored at San Pedro.

19–23 October Alternately under way with other battleships for gunnery practice and anchored at San Pedro.

23–24 October Under way with other battleships for tactical exercises.

24–28 October Anchored at Long Beach.

28 October–5 November Anchored at San Pedro.

5–6 November Under way for full-power endurance run.

6–9 November Anchored at San Pedro.

9–13 November Alternately under way with other battleships for gunnery practice and anchored at San Pedro.

13–17 November Anchored at San Pedro.

17 November Under way to fire gunnery practice.

17–20 November Anchored at San Pedro.

20–21 November Under way for tactical maneuvers with other battleships.

21 November–4 December Anchored at San Pedro.

4 December Under way for exercises during the semiannual inspection of the ship.

4–7 December Anchored at San Pedro.

7–12 December Alternately under way with other battleships for gunnery practice and anchored at San Pedro. On 9 December Rear Admiral Ziegemeier and his staff transferred to the *Pennsylvania*.

12–15 December Anchored at San Pedro.

15–19 December Alternately under way with the battle fleet for various tactical maneuvers and anchored at San Pedro. On 16 December the *Arizona* rehearsed refueling at sea while in tow from the USS *Kanawha* and on 17 December conducted the refueling.

19–31 December Anchored at San Pedro.

1926

1–4 January Anchored at San Pedro.

4–6 January Alternately under way with other battleships for night battle-practice rehearsal and anchored at San Pedro.

6–8 January Anchored at San Pedro.

8–9 January Under way to tow targets for night battle practice.

9–11 January Anchored at San Pedro.

11–13 January Alternately under way for gunnery practice and anchored at San Pedro.

13–15 January En route to San Francisco.

15–16 January Anchored at San Francisco.

16–18 January Dry-docked at Hunters Point, San Francisco.

18–20 January En route to San Pedro.

20–21 January Anchored at San Pedro.

21 January Under way briefly to hoist out target boats for the USS *Idaho*'s torpedo practice.

21–31 January Anchored at San Pedro.

1–15 February En route to Panama in company with the Battle Fleet; during the transit the *Arizona* was involved in a convoy-screening exercise, gunnery exercises, and a battle problem against a simulated enemy.

15–23 February Anchored at Balboa.

23–26 February Under way for maneuvers at sea with the Battle Fleet, including a battle problem against a simulated enemy.

26 February–1 March Anchored at Balboa. On 26 February Rear Admiral

Ziegemeier and his staff embarked in the *Arizona*.

1–5 March Alternately under way for fleet maneuvers and battle problems with the U.S. Fleet and anchored at Balboa.

5–13 March Anchored at Balboa.

13–15 March En route to Costa Rica.

15–20 March Anchored at Port Culebra, Costa Rica.

20 March–1 April En route to San Pedro in company with the Battle Fleet.

1–13 April Anchored at San Pedro.

13–15 April Alternately under way with other battleships for gunnery practice and anchored at San Pedro.

15–19 April Anchored at San Pedro.

19 April Under way to tow a target for the USS *California*.

19–21 April Anchored at San Pedro.

21 April Under way to fire antiaircraft practice.

21–23 April Anchored at San Pedro.

23–24 April Under way for tactical maneuvers with the USS *Nevada* and *Oklahoma*.

24–26 April Anchored at San Pedro.

26–30 April Alternately under way with other battleships for gunnery practice and anchored at San Pedro.

30 April–5 May Anchored at San Pedro.

5 May Under way briefly as part of the ship's annual inspection.

5–10 May Anchored at San Pedro.

10–14 May Alternately under way with other battleships for gunnery practice and anchored at San Pedro.

14–17 May Anchored at San Pedro.

17–22 May Alternately under way for tactical maneuvers and battle problems and anchored at San Pedro. On 19 May Rear Admiral Ziegemeier and his staff shifted to the USS *Pennsylvania*.

22–24 May Anchored at San Pedro.

24–29 May Alternately under way with other battleships for gunnery practice and anchored at San Pedro.

29 May–1 June Anchored at San Pedro.

1–2 June Under way with the Battle Fleet for force battle practice.

2–16 June Anchored at San Pedro.

16–18 June En route to San Francisco with the Battle Fleet.

18–21 June Anchored at San Francisco.

21–27 June En route to Tacoma.

Below: In Miraflores Lock, Panama Canal, in the mid-1920s. (Oscar Levy Collection, Naval Historical Center)

27 June–6 July Anchored at Tacoma.

6 July En route to Port Madison Bay; anchored in Port Madison Bay to transfer torpedoes for overhaul; en route to Port Angeles.

6–19 July Anchored at Port Angeles.

19–23 July Alternately under way for gunnery exercises and anchored at Port Angeles.

23 July En route to Bellingham.

23–26 July Anchored at Bellingham.

26–30 July Alternately under way with other battleships for gunnery practice and anchored at Port Angeles.

30 July–2 August Anchored at Seattle.

2 August En route to Port Angeles.

2–6 August Anchored at Port Angeles.

6 August En route to Tacoma.

6–9 August Anchored at Tacoma.

9 August En route to Seattle.

9–14 August Anchored at Seattle.

14 August En route to Port Angeles.

14–16 August Anchored at Port Angeles.

16–20 August En route to San Francisco, in company with other battleships.

20–30 August Anchored at San Francisco.

30 August–1 September En route to San Pedro.

1–13 September Anchored at San Pedro.

13–17 September Alternately under way with other battleships for gunnery practice and anchored at San Pedro.

17–20 September Anchored at San Pedro.

20–21 September Alternately under way with other battleships for gunnery practice and anchored at San Pedro.

21–23 September Anchored at San Pedro.

23 September–7 October Alternately under way with other battleships for gunnery practice and anchored at San Pedro.

7–22 October Anchored at San Pedro.

22–23 October Under way for tactical exercises.

23–28 October Anchored at Long Beach.

28–29 October Under way for maneuvers and night battle practice.

29 October–2 November En route to Bremerton.

2–19 November Moored at the Puget Sound Navy Yard.

19 November–7 December Dry-docked at the Puget Sound Navy Yard.

7–17 December Moored at the Puget Sound Navy Yard.

17–20 December En route to San Francisco.

20 December Anchored at San Francisco.

20–22 December En route to San Pedro.

22–31 December Anchored at San Pedro.

1927

1–5 January Anchored at San Pedro.

5–7 January Alternately under way for antiaircraft gunnery practice and anchored at San Pedro.

7–10 January Anchored at San Pedro. On 10 January Rear Admiral Henry J. Ziegemeier, USN, Commander Battleship Division Three, and his staff embarked in the *Arizona*.

10–13 January Alternately under way with other battleships for gunnery practice and anchored at San Pedro.

13–14 January Anchored at San Pedro.

14 January Under way to swing ship and check compasses.

14–17 January Anchored at San Pedro.

17–18 January Under way with other battleships for force battle practice.

18–24 January Anchored at San Pedro.

24–27 January Alternately under way with other battleships for gunnery practice and anchored at San Pedro.

27 January–1 February Anchored at San Pedro.

1–4 February Alternately under way with other battleships for advanced battle practice and anchored off Santa Barbara Island.

4–16 February Anchored at San Pedro.

16–17 February En route to San Diego.

17–18 February Anchored at San Diego.

18 February–3 March En route to the Panama Canal Zone in company with the Battle Fleet.

3–6 March Anchored and then moored at Balboa.

6 March Transited the Panama Canal.

6–9 March Anchored at Colon.

9–13 March Steamed with the Battle Fleet as part of a fleet problem, then proceeded independently to Cuba.

13–14 March Anchored in Guantanamo Bay.

14–15 March En route to Haiti.

15–21 March Anchored at Gonaives, Haiti. On 17 March the president of Haiti reviewed the fleet at anchor.

21–25 March Alternately under way with other battleships for gunnery practice and lying to in the vicinity of Haiti.

25–28 March Anchored at Gonaives, Haiti.

28 March–2 April Engaged in tactical maneuvers with the Battle Fleet while in the vicinity of Haiti and en route to Cuba.

2–18 April Anchored in Guantanamo Bay. On 15 April Rear Admiral Jehu V. Chase, USN, Commander Battleship Division Four, and his staff embarked in the *Arizona*.

18–22 April Engaged in gunnery practice and battle problem with other battleships while en route to Haiti.

22 April Anchored at Gonaives, Haiti.

22–29 April En route to New York in company with the U.S. Fleet.

29 April–16 May Moored in the North River, New York City.

16–20 May Engaged in a minor Army-Navy battle problem while en route to Newport, in company with the Battle Fleet.

20–28 May Moored at Newport. On 24 May Captain William T. Tarrant, USN, relieved Captain Harlan P. Perrill, USN, as commanding officer.

28–29 May En route to Hampton Roads with the fleet.

29 May–4 June Moored at Hampton Roads. On 4 June the fleet passed in review for President Calvin Coolidge, who was in the *Mayflower*.

4–11 June En route to the Panama Canal Zone with other battleships.

11–12 June Anchored at Colon.

12 June Transited the Panama Canal.

12–17 June Anchored at Balboa and in Panama Bay.

17–28 June En route to San Pedro with other battleships.

28 June–1 July Anchored at San Pedro.

1–3 July En route to San Francisco.

3–5 July Anchored at San Francisco for Independence Day.

5–6 July Dry-docked at Hunters Point, San Francisco.

6–13 July Anchored at San Francisco.

13–16 July En route to Bellingham with other battleships.

16–25 July Anchored at Bellingham.

25–28 July En route to San Francisco with the USS *Pennsylvania*.

28 July–5 August Anchored at San Francisco.

Right: Anchored in the North River, New York City, 2 May 1927. (Naval Historical Center, NH 57654)

5–8 August En route to Seattle with the USS *Pennsylvania*.

8–15 August Anchored at Seattle.

15 August En route to Port Angeles with the USS *Pennsylvania*.

15–18 August Alternately under way with the USS *Pennsylvania* for tactical maneuvers and anchored at Port Angeles.

18–20 August Anchored at Port Angeles.

20–25 August En route to San Francisco, joining up with other battleships during the voyage.

25 August–2 September Anchored at San Francisco.

2–4 September En route to San Pedro, conducting full-power and endurance runs while under way.

4–19 September Anchored at San Pedro.

19–23 September Alternately under way with other battleships for short-range battle-practice rehearsal and anchored at San Pedro.

23–24 September Under way for tactical exercises with the Battle Fleet.

24–28 September Anchored at San Pedro.

28–29 September Alternately under way with the USS *Pennsylvania* for short-range battle-practice rehearsal and anchored at San Pedro.

29 September–3 October Anchored at San Pedro.

3–6 October Alternately under way with the USS *Pennsylvania* for short-range battle-practice rehearsal and anchored at San Pedro.

6–10 October Anchored at San Pedro.

10–14 October Alternately under way with other battleships for gunnery practice and anchored at San Pedro.

14–17 October Anchored at San Pedro.

17–19 October Alternately under way with other battleships for gunnery practice and anchored at San Pedro.

19–21 October Anchored at San Pedro.

21–22 October Under way with other battleships for fleet tactical exercises.

22–24 October Anchored at San Pedro.

24–25 October En route to Monterey.

25–28 October Anchored at Monterey for Navy Day.

28–29 October En route to San Pedro.

29 October–7 November Anchored at San Pedro.

7–10 November Under way in company with the USS *Pennsylvania* for gunnery and torpedo practice while en route to Santa Monica.

10–12 November Anchored at Santa Monica for Armistice Day.

12 November En route to San Pedro.

12–14 November Anchored at San Pedro.

14–19 November Alternately under way with other battleships for gunnery practice and anchored at San Pedro.

19 November–6 December Anchored at San Pedro.

6–7 December Under way to tow targets for night battle practice.

7–13 December Anchored at San Pedro.

13 December Under way for antiaircraft practice.

13–16 December Anchored at San Pedro.

16–17 December Under way for tactical exercises with the fleet.

17–31 December Anchored at San Pedro.

1928

1–3 January Anchored at San Pedro.

3–5 January Alternately under way for gunnery practice with the USS *Mississippi* and anchored at San Pedro.

5–11 January Anchored at San Pedro.

11 January Under way for antiaircraft practice.

11–17 January Anchored at San Pedro.

17–21 January En route to Bremerton.

21 January–11 February Moored at the Puget Sound Navy Yard.

11–18 February Dry-docked at the Puget Sound Navy Yard.

18–29 February Moored at the Puget Sound Navy Yard.

29 February–3 March En route to San Pedro.

3–5 March Anchored at San Pedro.

5–9 March Alternately under way for long-range battle-practice rehearsal and anchored at Coronado.

9–12 March Anchored at San Pedro.

12–15 March Alternately under way for rehearsals and long-range battle practice and anchored off Santa Rosa Island.

15–22 March Anchored at San Pedro.

22 March En route to San Diego with the USS *New York* and *Pennsylvania*.

22–23 March Anchored at San Diego.

23–24 March Under way with other ships

Right: Anchored, late in the 1920s. (San Diego Maritime Museum, P-6922)

of the Battle Fleet, including the aircraft carrier USS *Langley*, for tactical exercises.

24 March–9 April   Anchored at San Pedro.

9–10 April   En route to San Francisco with other battleships.

10–18 April   Anchored at San Francisco.

18–28 April   En route to Hawaii with other ships of the Battle Fleet as part of Fleet Problem VIII.

28 April–14 May   Anchored at Honolulu.

14–19 May   Alternately under way for tactical maneuvers and anchored in Lahaina Roads.

19–21 May   Anchored in Hilo Bay.

21–27 May   Alternately under way for the fleet problem's mock-battle exercises and anchored in Lahaina Roads.

27–28 May   Anchored at Honolulu.

28–31 May   Alternately under way for tactical maneuvers and anchored at Honolulu.

31 May–1 June   Anchored in Lahaina Roads.

1 June   En route to Honolulu.

1–17 June   Anchored at Honolulu.

17–23 June   En route to San Pedro in company with the Battle Fleet.

23 June–2 July   Anchored at San Pedro. On 27 June Captain Victor A. Kimberly, USN, relieved Captain William T. Tarrant, USN, as commanding officer.

2 July   En route to Santa Monica.

2–5 July   Anchored off Santa Monica for Independence Day.

5–6 July   En route to San Francisco.

6 July   Anchored at San Francisco. Rear Admiral Frank B. Upham, USN, Commander Battleship Division Three, and his staff embarked in the *Arizona*.

6–9 July   En route to Port Angeles.

9–10 July   Anchored at Port Angeles.

10 July   Under way with the USS *Pennsylvania* for tactical exercises.

10–13 July   Anchored at Port Angeles.

13 July   En route to Everett with the USS *Pennsylvania*.

13–20 July   Anchored at Everett.

20 July   En route to Seattle.

20 July–13 August   Anchored at Seattle.

13 August   En route to Port Angeles with other battleships, conducting short-range battle-practice rehearsal runs.

13–17 August   Anchored at Port Angeles.

17 August   Under way with the USS *New York* for short-range battle-practice runs.

17–18 August Anchored at Port Angeles.

18–24 August En route to San Francisco with other battleships.

24–31 August Anchored at San Francisco.

31 August–1 September En route to San Pedro.

1–4 September Anchored at San Pedro. On 4 September Captain Ward K. Wortman, USN, relieved Captain Victor A. Kimberly, USN, as commanding officer.

4 September Under way with the USS *New York* for short-range battle-practice runs.

4–5 September Anchored at San Pedro. On 5 September Rear Admiral Frank B. Upham, USN, Commander Battleship Division Three, and his staff transferred to the USS *Pennsylvania*.

5–7 September Alternately under way for short-range battle-practice rehearsal runs and anchored at San Pedro.

7–10 September Anchored at San Pedro.

10–15 September Alternately under way for gunnery practice and battle problem and anchored off Santa Rosa Island.

15–17 September Anchored at San Pedro.

17–19 September Alternately under way for gunnery practice and anchored off Santa Rosa Island.

19 September–8 October Anchored at San Pedro.

8 October En route to San Diego.

8–9 October Anchored at San Diego.

9–13 October Under way with other battleships for gunnery and torpedo practice.

13–15 October Anchored at San Pedro.

15–16 October En route to Coronado, conducting torpedo practice.

16–19 October Alternately under way for gunnery practice and anchored at Coronado.

19–22 October Anchored at San Pedro.

22–25 October Alternately under way for gunnery practice and anchored at Coronado.

25–29 October Anchored at San Pedro.

29–30 October Alternately under way for torpedo practice and anchored at San Pedro.

30 October–1 November Anchored at San Pedro.

1 November Under way to fire battle torpedo practice.

1–5 November Anchored at San Pedro.

5–7 November Alternately under way for tactical exercises and anchored at San Pedro.

7–10 November En route to San Francisco with the USS *New York* and *Pennsylvania*.

10–15 November Anchored at San Francisco.

15–17 November Dry-docked at Hunters Point, San Francisco.

17–18 November En route to San Pedro.

18 November–3 December Anchored at San Pedro.

3–8 December Alternately under way for gunnery practice and tactical exercises with the USS *Pennsylvania* and anchored at San Pedro.

8–10 December Anchored at San Pedro.

10–14 December Alternately under way for gunnery practice and anchored at San Pedro.

14–17 December Anchored at San Pedro.

17–19 December Alternately under way for long-range battle-practice rehearsals and firing and lying to off Catalina Island.

19–31 December Anchored at San Pedro.

1929

1–15 January Anchored at San Pedro.

15–27 January En route to Panama as part of the black naval force in Fleet Problem IX.

27 January–7 February Anchored at Balboa.

7–8 February Under way for tactical maneuvers.

8–11 February Anchored at Balboa.

11–14 February Under way for tactical problems and torpedo drills.

14–26 February Anchored at Balboa.

26–28 February Under way with the U.S. Fleet for a battle problem.

28 February–5 March Anchored at Balboa.

5 March Transited the Panama Canal.

5–7 March Anchored at Colon.

7–10 March En route to Cuba with other battleships.

10 March–3 April Anchored in Guantanamo Bay.

3 April Under way with the USS *New York* and *Pennsylvania* for division antiaircraft practice.

3–4 April Anchored in Guantanamo Bay.

4 April En route to Haiti with other battleships.

5–9 April Anchored at Gonaives.

9–10 April En route to Cuba with the USS *New York* and *Pennsylvania*.

10–17 April Anchored in Guantanamo Bay.

17 April Under way for the annual inspec-

tion conducted by Commander Battleship Division Three.

17–27 April Anchored in Guantanamo Bay.

27 April–1 May En route to Hampton Roads with other battleships.

1–4 May Anchored in Hampton Roads.

4 May En route to Portsmouth, Virginia.

4–25 May Moored at the Norfolk Navy Yard, Portsmouth.

25 May–12 July Dry-docked at the Norfolk Navy Yard.

12 July–14 August Moored at the Norfolk Navy Yard.

14 August–31 December Dry-docked at the Norfolk Navy Yard.

1930

1 January–25 February Dry-docked at the Norfolk Navy Yard.

25 February–21 June Moored at the Norfolk Navy Yard. On 29 April Commander Thaddeus A. Thomson, Jr., USN, relieved Captain Ward K. Wortman, USN, as commanding officer.

21 June–11 December Dry-docked at the Norfolk Navy Yard. On 20 September Captain Charles S. Freeman, USN, relieved Commander Thaddeus A. Thomson, Jr., USN, as commanding officer.

11–31 December Moored at the Norfolk Navy Yard.

1931

1 January–3 March Moored at the Norfolk Navy Yard.

3 March En route to Lynnhaven Roads.

3–6 March Anchored in Lynnhaven Roads.

6 March En route to Hampton Roads.

6–9 March Anchored in Hampton Roads.

9 March En route to Virginia Beach.

9–10 March Anchored off Virginia Beach.

10 March En route to Lynnhaven Roads.

10–11 March Anchored in Lynnhaven Roads.

11 March Under way for test firing of guns.

11–12 March Anchored in Lynnhaven Roads.

12 March Under way for maneuvering exercises en route to Hampton Roads.

12–16 March Anchored in Hampton Roads.

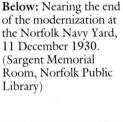
Below: Nearing the end of the modernization at the Norfolk Navy Yard, 11 December 1930. (Sargent Memorial Room, Norfolk Public Library)

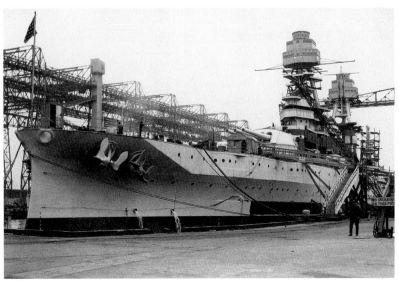

16 March En route to the Norfolk Navy Yard.

16–18 March Moored at the Norfolk Navy Yard.

18 March En route to Hampton Roads.

18–19 March Anchored in Hampton Roads to take aboard President Herbert Hoover.

19–23 March En route to Puerto Rico.

23–24 March Anchored at Ponce.

24–25 March En route to the Virgin Islands.

25 March Anchored at St. Thomas.

25–29 March En route to Hampton Roads.

29 March–6 April Anchored in Hampton Roads; on 29 March President Herbert Hoover and his party disembarked.

6–7 April En route to Annapolis.

7–10 April Anchored at Annapolis.

10–11 April En route to Hampton Roads.

11–13 April Anchored in Hampton Roads.

13 April En route to the Norfolk Navy Yard.

13–18 April Dry-docked at the Norfolk Navy Yard.

18–20 April En route to Rockland, Maine, and ran trial course off Rockland.

20–21 April Anchored at Rockland.

21–22 April En route to Boston.

22–30 April Moored at the Boston Navy Yard.

30 April En route to Maine.

30 April–1 May Anchored off Ragged Island, Maine.

1 May Under way for full-power run.

1–2 May Anchored near Deer Island Light.

2 May En route to Boston.

2–3 May Moored at the Boston Navy Yard.

Left: Flying President Hoover's flag from the main truck, March 1931. (Herbert Hoover Presidential Library, 1931-29C; also National Archives, 19-N-14145)

3–5 May   En route to Portsmouth.

5 May–14 July   Moored at the Norfolk Navy Yard.

14–16 July   En route to Boston.

16–21 July   Dry-docked in South Boston.

21–22 July   En route to Maine.

22–23 July   Anchored at Rockland.

23–24 July   Alternately under way for standardization trial runs and anchored at Rockland.

24–25 July   En route to Hampton Roads.

25–27 July   Anchored in Hampton Roads.

27 July   En route to Portsmouth.

27 July–1 August   Moored at the Norfolk Navy Yard.

1–5 August   En route to Cuba, in company with the USS *Pennsylvania*.

5–8 August   Anchored in Guantanamo Bay.

8–10 August   En route to Panama, in company with the USS *Pennsylvania*.

10–12 August   Anchored at Colon.

12 August   Transited the Panama Canal.

12–15 August   Anchored at Balboa.

15–24 August   En route to San Pedro, in company with the USS *Pennsylvania*.

24 August–21 September   Anchored at San Pedro.

21–24 September   Alternately under way for short-range battle-practice rehearsal and anchored at San Pedro.

24–28 September   Anchored at San Pedro.

28 September–2 October   Alternately under way for short-range battle-practice rehearsal and anchored off Santa Barbara Island.

2–5 October   Anchored at San Pedro.

5 October   Under way with other battleships for short-range battle-practice rehearsal.

5–9 October   Anchored off Santa Barbara Island.

9 October   Under way with other battleships for short-range battle-practice rehearsal.

9–12 October   Anchored at San Pedro.

12–17 October   Alternately under way with other battleships for gunnery practice and anchored off Santa Barbara Island.

17–19 October   Anchored at San Pedro.

19–23 October   Alternately under way with other battleships for gunnery practice and anchored off Santa Barbara Island.

23–28 October   Anchored at San Pedro.

28–30 October   Under way with other battleships for tactical exercises.

30 October–2 November   Anchored at San Pedro.

2 November   Under way to swing ship to compensate the magnetic compass.

2–7 November   Anchored at San Pedro.

7–8 November   En route to San Francisco.

8–12 November   Anchored at San Francisco for Armistice Day.

12–13 November   En route to San Pedro, in company with the USS *Nevada* and destroyers.

13 November–2 December   Anchored at San Pedro. On 1 December Rear Admiral J. R. P. Pringle, USN, Commander Battleship Division Three, embarked in the *Arizona*.

2–4 December   Under way for tactical exercises and a landing in the San Clemente area.

4–31 December   Anchored at San Pedro; under way briefly on 7, 8, 10, 14, and 15 December for various reasons.

1932

1–4 January   Anchored at San Pedro.

4 January   Under way to tow the target for the USS *Oklahoma*'s spotting practice.

4–7 January   Anchored at San Pedro.

7–8 January   Under way with other battleships for tactical exercises and to send a landing force to San Clemente Island.

8–13 January   Anchored at San Pedro.

13–15 January   Alternately under way for antiaircraft rehearsal runs with the USS *California* and *West Virginia* and anchored off Santa Barbara and San Nicholas islands.

15 January–1 February   Anchored at San Pedro.

1–13 February   En route to Hawaii with other battleships while participating in Grand Joint Exercise Number Four.

13–19 February   Anchored in Lahaina Roads.

19 February   Under way for force battle-practice rehearsal.

19 February–1 March   Anchored in Lahaina Roads.

1 March   Under way for force battle-practice rehearsal.

1–2 March   Anchored off the entrance to Pearl Harbor.

2–5 March   Dry-docked at the Pearl Harbor Navy Yard.

5–7 March Moored at Pearl Harbor.

7 March En route to Lahaina Roads.

7–10 March Anchored in Lahaina Roads.

10–22 March En route to San Pedro, in company with Battleship Division Three as part of Fleet Problem XIII.

22 March–3 April Anchored at San Pedro.

3–8 April Under way with other battleships for tactical maneuvers.

8–11 April Anchored at San Pedro.

11–14 April Under way with other battleships for force battle-practice rehearsal.

14–18 April Anchored at San Pedro.

18–23 April En route to San Francisco, conducting tactical maneuvers with the fleet.

23 April–12 May Anchored at San Francisco.

12–13 May En route to San Pedro with other battleships.

13–16 May Anchored at San Pedro.

16–20 May Alternately under way for day spotting practice and antiaircraft practice and anchored off San Nicholas and San Clemente islands.

20–23 May Anchored at San Pedro.

23–27 May Alternately under way with other battleships for gunnery practice and anchored off San Nicholas Island.

27–31 May Anchored at San Pedro. On 28 May Rear Admiral J. R. P. Pringle, USN, Commander Battleship Division Three, and his staff transferred to the USS *Tennessee*.

31 May–1 June Under way; fired long-range battle practice on 31 May.

1–2 June Anchored at San Pedro.

2–3 June Under way for tactical maneuvers.

3–6 June Anchored at San Pedro.

6–9 June Alternately under way for division antiaircraft practice and anchored off San Clemente Island.

9–13 June Anchored at San Pedro.

13–14 June Alternately under way towing targets for the USS *Colorado* and anchored off Santa Barbara Island.

14–28 June Anchored at San Pedro. On 20 June Captain Charles S. Kerrick, USN, relieved Captain Charles S. Freeman, USN, as commanding officer.

28 June–1 July En route to Seattle.

1–5 July Anchored at Seattle for Independence Day.

5 July En route to Bremerton.

5 July–8 August Moored at the Puget Sound Navy Yard.

8–15 August Dry-docked at the Puget Sound Navy Yard.

15 August–3 September Moored at the Puget Sound Navy Yard.

3 September En route to Tacoma.

3–8 September Anchored at Tacoma.

8 September En route to Bellingham.

8–12 September Anchored at Bellingham.

12 September En route to Port Angeles.

12–16 September Anchored at Port Angeles.

16–22 September En route to San Pedro, in company with other battleships.

22–23 September Anchored at San Pedro.

23 September Under way for short-range battle-practice drill.

23–26 September Anchored at San Pedro.

26–29 September Alternately under way for gunnery practice and anchored off Santa Barbara Island.

29 September–3 October Anchored at San Pedro.

3–6 October Alternately under way for gunnery practice and anchored off Santa Barbara Island. On 6 October the *Arizona* fired short-range battle practice.

6–10 October Anchored at San Pedro. On 8 October Rear Admiral Walter S. Crosley, USN, Commander Battleship Division Three, and his staff embarked in the *Arizona*.

10–14 October Alternately under way for night battle practice and night spotting-

Above: Dry-docked at Pearl Harbor, 2 March 1932. (Special Collections, University of Arizona Library, 77-3-241)

practice rehearsal and anchored off Santa Barbara Island.

14–17 October Anchored at San Pedro. On 15 October the Society of the Daughters of the American Revolution presented the *Arizona* with the DAR trophy for excellence in antiaircraft gunnery during the competitive year 1931–32.

17–19 October Alternately under way for night battle practice and night spotting-practice rehearsal and anchored off Santa Barbara Island.

19 October–1 November Anchored at San Pedro.

1–3 November Under way with the USS *Nevada* for antiaircraft spotting-practice rehearsal.

3–4 November Anchored at San Pedro.

4 November Under way to swing the ship and calibrate the radio direction finders.

4–7 November Anchored at San Pedro.

7–10 November En route to San Francisco, conducting antiaircraft practice and fleet tactical maneuvers.

10–14 November Anchored at San Francisco for Armistice Day.

14–15 November En route to San Pedro.

15–28 November Anchored at San Pedro.

28 November Under way for antiaircraft practice.

28–29 November Anchored at San Pedro.

29 November–1 December Under way with the USS *Nevada* for various exercises.

1–2 December Anchored at San Pedro.

2 December Under way for a range finder check.

2–12 December Anchored at San Pedro.

12–14 December Under way with other battleships for tactical exercises.

14–31 December Anchored at San Pedro. On 24 December Rear Admiral Walter S. Crosley, USN, Commander Battleship Division Three, and his staff transferred to the USS *Tennessee.*

1933

1–4 January Anchored at San Pedro.

4–6 January Under way for battle drills with various ships.

6–9 January Anchored at San Pedro.

9–12 January Alternately under way for gunnery practice and anchored off Santa Barbara Island.

12–17 January Anchored at San Pedro.

17–20 January Alternately under way for gunnery practice and anchored at San Pedro.

20 January–9 February Anchored at San Pedro.

9–18 February Under way off the California coast while engaged in Fleet Problem XIV.

18–27 February Anchored at San Francisco.

27–28 February En route to San Pedro with other battleships.

28 February–6 March Anchored at San Pedro.

6–9 March Under way with other battleships for tactical maneuvers.

9–20 March Anchored at San Pedro. On 10 March the Long Beach area suffered an earthquake.

20–24 March Under way with other battleships for tactical exercises.

24–27 March Anchored at San Pedro.

27–30 March Under way with other battleships for exercises.

30 March–3 April Anchored at San Pedro.

3–8 April Under way for maneuvers with other battleships for tactical exercises.

8–10 April Anchored at San Pedro.

10–15 April Under way with other battleships for exercises.

15–19 April Anchored at San Pedro.

19–20 April En route to San Francisco.

20–21 April Anchored at San Francisco.

Below: Anchored at San Pedro, California, on 13 March 1933. (Arleigh Burke Collection, Naval Historical Center, (S-105-X2)

21–23 April   Dry-docked at Hunters Point, San Francisco.

23–25 April   Anchored at San Francisco.

25–26 April   En route to San Pedro.

26 April–3 May   Anchored at San Pedro.

3–5 May   Under way for exercises with other battleships.

5–26 May   Moored at San Pedro alongside the USS *Medusa*.

26 May–5 June   Anchored at San Pedro.

5–6 June   Under way off southern California with the minesweepers *Tern* and *Bobolink*.

6–13 June   Anchored at San Pedro. On 9 June Rear Admiral Ridley McLean, USN, relieved Rear Admiral Walter S. Crosley, USN, as Commander Battleship Division Three, on board the *Arizona*.

13–17 June   Under way, in company with the training ship *Utah* and the minesweepers *Tern* and *Bobolink*.

17–20 June   Anchored at San Pedro.

20–21 June   Under way for main-battery gunnery school, in company with the minesweepers *Pinola* and *Robin*.

21–28 June   Anchored at San Pedro.

28 June   En route to Santa Barbara.

28 June–5 July   Anchored at Santa Barbara.

5–12 July   En route to Seattle, taking part in tactical exercises and battle problems against a simulated enemy.

12–25 July   Anchored at Seattle.

25 July   En route to Bellingham.

25–31 July   Moored at Bellingham.

31 July   En route to Tacoma.

31 July–7 August   Anchored at Tacoma.

7 August   En route to Port Angeles.

7–9 August   Anchored at Port Angeles.

9–11 August   En route to San Francisco with other battleships.

11–23 August   Anchored at San Francisco.

23–24 August   En route to San Pedro with other battleships.

24 August–13 September   Anchored at San Pedro.

13–15 September   Alternately under way for gunnery practice and anchored off San Nicholas Island.

15–18 September   Anchored at San Pedro.

18–23 September   Alternately under way for gunnery practice and anchored off San Nicholas Island.

23–25 September   Anchored at San Pedro.

25–28 September   Alternately under way for gunnery practice and anchored off Santa Barbara Island.

28 September–3 October   Anchored at San Pedro. On 30 September Captain Macgillivray Milne, USN, relieved Captain Charles S. Kerrick, USN, as commanding officer.

3–6 October   Under way for fleet exercises.

6–9 October   Anchored at San Pedro.

9–12 October   Under way for exercises with other battleships.

12–23 October   Anchored at San Pedro.

23–24 October   Under way for exercises with other battleships.

24–25 October   Anchored at San Pedro.

25–27 October   Under way for exercises with other battleships.

27–30 October   Anchored at San Pedro.

30 October–2 November   Under way for exercises with other battleships.

2–6 November   Anchored at San Pedro.

6–7 November   Under way for tactical exercises.

7–9 November   Anchored at San Pedro.

9 November   En route to Santa Barbara.

9–13 November   Anchored at Santa Barbara for Armistice Day. On 12 November the *Arizona*'s embarked division commander, Rear Admiral Ridley McLean, USN, died while visiting the USS *Nevada*.

13 November   En route to San Pedro.

13 November–1 December   Moored at San Pedro alongside the USS *Medusa*.

1–4 December   Anchored at San Pedro.

4–8 December   Alternately under way for night spotting and night battle practice and anchored off Santa Barbara Island.

8–31 December   Anchored at San Pedro. On 12 December Rear Admiral Henry V. Butler, USN, assumed command of Battleship Division Three on board the *Arizona*.

1934

1–3 January   Anchored at San Pedro.

3–6 January   Under way with other battleships for tactical exercises.

6–8 January   Anchored at San Pedro.

8–12 January   Alternately under way for tactical exercises and anchored off Santa Barbara Island.

12–15 January   Anchored at San Pedro.

15–17 January   Alternately under way for

battle-line maneuvers and anchored off San Clemente Island.

17–22 January Anchored at San Pedro.

22–26 January Alternately under way for long-range battle-practice rehearsal and anchored off San Clemente Island.

26 January–12 February Anchored at San Pedro.

12–14 February Alternately under way for antiaircraft spotting practice and anchored off San Clemente Island.

14–19 February Anchored at San Pedro.

19–22 February Under way for fleet tactical exercises.

22–26 February Anchored at San Pedro.

26 February–3 March Alternately under way for airplane recovery tests and target towing and anchored off Santa Catalina and San Clemente islands.

3 March–18 April Anchored at San Pedro. On 26 March Rear Admiral Henry V. Butler, USN, Commander Battleship Division Three, transferred his flag to the USS *Maryland*. At various dates during this period a Warner Brothers location crew was on board to shoot scenes for a movie tentatively titled "Hey, Sailor."

18–22 April En route to Bremerton.

22 April–24 May Moored at the Puget Sound Navy Yard.

24 May–29 June Dry-docked at the Puget Sound Navy Yard.

29 June–14 July Moored at the Puget Sound Navy Yard.

14 July Under way in Puget Sound for trials.

14–25 July Moored at the Puget Sound Navy Yard.

25–27 July En route to San Pedro. On 26 July the *Arizona* collided with the small vessel *Umatilla*, striking her on the starboard quarter while she was being towed by the fishing boat *Emblem* of Tacoma. As a result of the collision, the *Arizona* was ordered on 27 July to reverse course and return to Puget Sound.

27–29 July En route to Puget Sound.

29 July–4 August Anchored at Seattle. From 30 July to 3 August a court of inquiry was held as a result of the collision with the *Umatilla*.

4–7 August En route to San Pedro.

7–9 August Anchored at San Pedro.

9–17 August En route to Panama.

17 August Transited the Panama Canal.

17–22 August En route to the Southern Drill Grounds.

22–23 August Anchored in the Southern Drill Grounds off the coast of Virginia.

23 August Under way with other battle-

Right: Steaming in Puget Sound, circa 1934. (Courtesy Warren Kaiser, via Joseph Langdell, *Arizona* Reunion Association)

ships for short-range battle-practice rehearsal.

23–27 August Anchored in Hampton Roads, Virginia.

27 August–1 September Alternately under way off the coast of Virginia for short-range battle practice, anchored in the Southern Drill Grounds, and anchored in Hampton Roads.

1–2 September En route to New York.

2–8 September Moored at the New York Navy Yard. On 4 September Rear Admiral Samuel W. Bryant, USN, assumed command of Battleship Division Two on board the *Arizona*.

8–9 September En route to Hampton Roads, Virginia. On 8 September the *Arizona* spent some time steaming at various courses and speeds while standing by in the vicinity of the passenger ship SS *Morro Castle*, which had caught fire off the coast of New Jersey.

9–10 September Under way for short-range battle practice in the Southern Drill Grounds.

10–15 September Anchored in Hampton Roads.

15–21 September En route to Cuba, taking part in war games.

21 September–10 October Anchored in Guantanamo Bay. From 1 to 8 October

Captain Macgillivray Milne, USN, commanding officer of the *Arizona*, was placed under arrest by order of Commander Battleships Battle Force, because of his trial by court-martial; during this period the ship's executive officer, Commander Andrew D. Denney, USN, served as acting commanding officer.

10–12 October Under way in the drill grounds off Cuba for tactical exercises.

12–20 October Anchored in Guantanamo Bay.

20–21 October En route to Haiti.

21–22 October Anchored at Gonaives.

22–24 October En route to Panama.

24 October Anchored at Colon.

24–25 October Transited the Panama Canal. Many ships of the U.S. Fleet made the canal transit at the same time, one right after the other.

25–29 October Anchored at Panama City.

29 October–9 November En route to San Pedro, taking part in war games.

9 November–5 December Anchored at San Pedro.

5–7 December En route to San Francisco, taking part in war games.

7–17 December Anchored at San Francisco. On 10 December Captain George M. Baum, USN, relieved Captain Macgillivray Milne, USN, as commanding officer.

17–18 December En route to San Pedro.

18–31 December Anchored at San Pedro.

1935

1–14 January Anchored at San Pedro.

14–16 January Under way with other ships for tactical exercises and battle problem.

16–21 January Anchored at San Pedro.

21–26 January Alternately under way for battle practice, night spotting practice, night battle practice, and anchored off Santa Barbara Island.

26–28 January Anchored at San Pedro.

28–30 January Alternately under way for machine-gun practice, to serve as a reference ship for night battle practice, and anchored off Santa Barbara Island.

30 January–7 February Anchored at San Pedro.

7–8 February Under way with other battleships for antiaircraft-defense drills.

8–11 February Anchored at San Pedro.

11–13 February En route to San Francisco with other battleships for battle practice. Joined in forming a scouting line on 12 February to search for the downed airship USS *Macon* and her survivors.

13–23 February Anchored at San Francisco.

23–24 February En route to San Pedro.

24 February–4 March Anchored at San Pedro.

4–8 March Alternately under way for various gunnery exercises and anchored off San Clemente Island.

8–25 March Anchored at San Pedro; under way for machine-gun practice on 11 March.

25–28 March Under way for the U.S. Fleet's tactical exercises.

28 March–4 April Anchored at San Pedro. On 30 March Rear Admiral George T. Pettengill, USN, relieved Rear Admiral Samuel W. Bryant, USN, as Commander Battleship Division Two, on board the *Arizona*.

4 April Under way for annual military inspection.

4–22 April Anchored at San Pedro. From 20 April to 1 May Rear Admiral Pettengill shifted his flag to the USS *Nevada*, then returned to the *Arizona*.

22–23 April En route to San Francisco.

23–30 April Anchored at San Francisco.

30 April–1 May Dry-docked at Hunters Point.

1–3 May Anchored at San Francisco.

3–12 May En route to Pearl Harbor while engaging in Fleet Problem XVI.

12–16 May Moored at Pearl Harbor.

16–26 May Under way for the resumption of Fleet Problem XVI, which included maneuvers in the vicinity of Midway Island.

26–31 May Moored at Pearl Harbor.

31 May–10 June En route to Coronado while engaging in Fleet Problem XVI.

10 June Anchored at Coronado.

10–11 June En route to San Pedro.

11 June–3 July Moored at San Pedro alongside the USS *Medusa*.

3–6 July Anchored at San Pedro.

6–12 July En route to Tacoma, conducting ship-handling drills and tactical maneuvers.

12–25 July Anchored at Tacoma.

25 July En route to Bremerton.

25–31 July Moored at the Puget Sound Navy Yard.

31 July En route to Seattle.

31 July–5 August Moored at Seattle.

5–9 August En route to San Francisco with other battleships.

9–19 August Anchored at San Francisco.

19–23 August En route to Coronado with other battleships.

23–30 August Anchored at Coronado.

30 August En route to San Pedro.

30 August–16 September Anchored at San Pedro.

16–20 September Alternately under way for short-range battle-practice rehearsal and anchored off San Clemente and Santa Catalina islands.

20–23 September Anchored at San Pedro.

23–26 September Alternately under way for short-range battle-practice rehearsal and anchored off Santa Catalina Island.

26–30 September Anchored at San Pedro.

30 September–3 October Under way with the U.S. Fleet, engaging in battle-line tactics.

3–24 October Anchored at San Pedro.

24–25 October Under way with other battleships for radio-direction-finder calibration and night-spotting drill.

25–29 October Anchored at San Pedro.

29 October–2 November Alternately under way for various gunnery exercises and anchored off San Clemente Island.

2–4 November Anchored at San Pedro.

4–5 November Alternately under way for short-range battle-practice rehearsal and lying to off San Clemente Island.

5–6 November Anchored at San Pedro.

6–8 November En route to San Francisco with other battleships.

8–12 November Anchored at San Francisco for Armistice Day.

12–15 November En route to Bremerton.

15 November–31 December Moored at the Puget Sound Navy Yard.

1936

1–14 January Moored at the Puget Sound Navy Yard.

14–30 January Dry-docked at the Puget Sound Navy Yard.

30 January–8 February Moored at the Puget Sound Navy Yard.

8 February Under way for post-repair trial run.

8–15 February Moored at the Puget Sound Navy Yard.

15–18 February En route to San Francisco.

18–19 February Anchored at San Francisco.

19–20 February En route to San Pedro.

20 February–2 March Anchored at San Pedro.

2–6 March Alternately under way with other battleships of the U.S. Fleet for various exercises and anchored outside the breakwater of Los Angeles Harbor.

6–9 March Anchored at San Pedro.

9–13 March Alternately under way for antiaircraft and fire-control drills and anchored off San Clemente Island.

13–16 March Anchored at San Pedro.

16–18 March Alternately under way for antiaircraft and main-battery gunnery practice and anchored off Santa Barbara Island.

18–20 March Anchored at San Pedro.

20–21 March Under way with other battleships for tactical maneuvers.

21–30 March Anchored at San Pedro.

30 March–2 April Alternately under way with other battleships for gunnery practice and anchored off San Clemente Island.

2–6 April Anchored at San Pedro.

6 April Under way to exercise at drills and maneuvers as part of the annual military inspection conducted by Commander Battleship Division Two.

6–27 April Anchored at San Pedro.

27 April–9 May En route to Panama, engaged in a variety of maneuvers and simulated battle exercises as part of Fleet Problem XVII.

9–16 May Anchored at Balboa.

16–22 May Under way as part of the resumption of Fleet Problem XVII. On 19 May the *Arizona* held initiation ceremonies in conjunction with crossing the equator.

22–26 May Anchored at Balboa.

26 May–6 June En route to San Pedro with other ships of the U.S. Fleet as part of Fleet Problem XVII.

6–30 June Anchored at San Pedro. On 8 June Captain George A. Alexander, USN, relieved Captain George M. Baum, USN, as commanding officer. On 23 June, on board the *Arizona*, Rear

Admiral Claude C. Bloch, USN, relieved Rear Admiral George T. Pettengill, USN, as Commander Battleship Division Two.

30 June–1 July En route to San Francisco with the USS *Pennsylvania*, *West Virginia*, *Idaho*, and *Texas*, conducting tactical exercises.

1–7 July Anchored at San Francisco for Independence Day.

7–15 July En route to Pearl Harbor with other battleships.

15–18 July Dry-docked at the Pearl Harbor Navy Yard.

18 July–3 August Moored at Pearl Harbor; under way for various fire-control drills on 23–24 July and for gunnery practice on 28 July.

3–9 August Alternately under way with other battleships for various drills and anchored in Lahaina Roads and at Honolulu.

9–12 August Moored at Pearl Harbor.

12 August Under way for damage-control practice problem.

12–13 August Anchored in Mamala Bay.

13–22 August En route to San Pedro with other battleships, conducting battle-line tactical maneuvers.

22 August–14 September Anchored at San Pedro.

14–18 September Alternately under way with other battleships for short-range battle-practice rehearsal and anchored off San Clemente Island.

18–21 September Anchored at San Pedro.

21–25 September Alternately under way with other battleships for short-range battle-practice rehearsal and anchored off San Clemente Island.

25–29 September Anchored at San Pedro.

29–30 September Alternately under way to observe tactical data and calibrate radio direction finders and anchored at San Pedro.

30 September–5 October Anchored at San Pedro.

5–7 October Under way with the battle line for tactical exercises.

7–8 October Anchored at San Pedro.

8–24 October Moored at San Pedro alongside the USS *Medusa*.

24–26 October Anchored at San Pedro.

26–31 October Alternately under way with the USS *Nevada* for night battle-practice rehearsal and anchored off San Clemente and Santa Barbara islands.

31 October–3 November Anchored at San Pedro.

3–4 November Alternately under way to fire night-battle practice and anchored off Santa Barbara Island.

4–9 November Anchored at San Pedro.

9–10 November En route to San Francisco with other battleships, conducting main-battery-director drill.

10–16 November Anchored at San Francisco for Armistice Day.

16–18 November En route to San Pedro with other battleships.

18 November–7 December Anchored at San Pedro.

7–11 December Alternately under way with other battleships for long-range battle-practice rehearsal and anchored off San Clemente Island.

11–14 December Anchored at San Pedro.

14–17 December Alternately under way with other battleships for long-range battle-practice rehearsal and anchored off San Clemente Island.

17–31 December Anchored at San Pedro.

1937

1–18 January Anchored at San Pedro. On 2 January, on board the *Arizona*, Rear Admiral John W. Greenslade, USN, relieved Rear Admiral Claude C. Bloch, USN, as Commander Battleship Division Two.

18–19 January Under way for antiaircraft drill with other battleships.

19–20 January Anchored at San Pedro.

20–22 January Under way for a battle problem with the U.S. Fleet.

22–25 January Anchored at San Pedro.

25–29 January Alternately under way with the USS *Pennsylvania* and *Oklahoma* for gunnery practice and anchored off Santa Barbara Island.

29 January–16 February Anchored at San Pedro.

16–18 February Under way for exercises with other battleships.

18 February–8 March Anchored at San Pedro.

8–12 March Alternately under way to calibrate radio direction finders and

anchored or lying to off Santa Barbara Island.

12–29 March Anchored at San Pedro.

29 March Under way for formation battle practice with other battleships.

29 March–5 April Anchored at San Pedro.

5–6 April Under way for a battle problem with other battleships.

6–24 April Anchored at San Pedro. On 13 April Rear Admiral John W. Greenslade, USN, Commander Battleship Division Two, and his staff transferred to the USS *Maryland*.

24–29 April En route to Bremerton.

29 April–28 June Moored at the Puget Sound Navy Yard.

28 June–15 July Dry-docked at the Puget Sound Navy Yard.

15–22 July Moored at the Puget Sound Navy Yard.

22 July Under way for post-repair trials and ship-handling training.

22 July–3 August Moored at the Puget Sound Navy Yard.

3–6 August En route to San Francisco.

6–10 August Anchored at San Francisco. On 7 August Rear Admiral Manley H. Simons, USN, Commander Battleship Division One, and his staff embarked in the *Arizona*.

10–14 August Conducted battle problem and mock attacks against other ships while en route to San Pedro.

14–30 August Anchored at San Pedro.

30 August–3 September Alternately under way with other battleships for gunnery practice and anchored off San Clemente Island.

3–7 September Anchored at San Pedro.

7–10 September Alternately under way with other battleships for gunnery practice and anchored off San Clemente Island.

10–13 September Anchored at San Pedro.

13–17 September Alternately under way with other battleships for gunnery practice and anchored off San Clemente Island.

17–28 September Anchored at San Pedro.

28 September Under way for radio-direction-finder calibration.

28–30 September Anchored at San Pedro.

30 September Under way for a battle problem.

30 September–4 October Anchored at San Pedro.

4–8 October Alternately under way with other battleships for a mock battle problem and anchored off San Clemente Island.

8–11 October Anchored at San Pedro.

11–14 October Alternately under way with other battleships for gunnery practice and anchored off San Clemente Island.

14–18 October Anchored at San Pedro.

18–21 October Alternately under way with other battleships for gunnery practice and anchored off San Clemente Island.

21 October–8 November Anchored at San Pedro. On 26 October Rear Admiral Adolphus Watson, USN, assumed command of Battleship Division One.

8–9 November En route to San Francisco with other battleships.

9–15 November Anchored at San Francisco for Armistice Day.

15–19 November Conducted tactical exercises with other battleships en route to San Pedro.

19–22 November Anchored at San Pedro.

22–24 November Under way with the USS *Pennsylvania* for gunnery practice.

24–29 November Anchored at San Pedro.

29 November–2 December Alternately under way for gunnery practice and anchored off Santa Barbara Island.

2–31 December Anchored at San Pedro. On 11 December Captain Alfred W. Brown, USN, relieved Captain George A. Alexander, USN, as commanding officer.

Below: In Hawaii, mid-1930s. (Tai Sing Loo photo, courtesy Evelyn Lee)

1938

1–3 January   Anchored at San Pedro.

3–7 January   Alternately under way with other battleships for a variety of gunnery exercises and anchored off San Clemente Island.

7–10 January   Anchored at San Pedro.

10–12 January   Alternately under way with other battleships for gunnery exercises and anchored off San Clemente Island.

12 January–1 February   Anchored at San Pedro.

1–4 February   Under way with other battleships for tactical exercises.

4–7 February   Anchored at San Pedro.

7 February   Under way for machine-gun practice.

7–15 February   Anchored at San Pedro.

15–16 February   En route to San Francisco independently.

16–17 February   Anchored at San Francisco.

17–19 February   Dry-docked at Hunters Point, San Francisco.

19–23 February   Anchored at San Francisco.

23–24 February   En route to San Pedro.

24 February–15 March   Anchored at San Pedro.

15 March–1 April   En route to Hawaii with other ships as part of Fleet Problem XIX.

1–4 April   Anchored in Lahaina Roads, Hawaii.

4–8 April   Under way with other battleships as part of Fleet Problem XIX.

8–21 April   Moored at Pearl Harbor, Hawaii.

21–28 April   En route to San Pedro with other battleships as part of Fleet Problem XIX.

28 April–4 May   Anchored at San Pedro.

4–8 May   En route to Bremerton.

8 May–20 July   Moored at the Puget Sound Navy Yard.

20–22 July   En route to San Francisco.

22–25 July   Anchored at San Francisco.

25–29 July   Alternately under way with other battleships for training exercises and anchored in Drake's Bay.

29 July–9 August   Anchored at San Francisco.

9–12 August   En route to San Pedro with other battleships, conducting tactical maneuvers.

12–15 August   Anchored at San Pedro.

15–19 August   Alternately under way with other battleships for training exercises and anchored off Santa Barbara Island.

19–22 August   Anchored at San Pedro.

22–26 August   Alternately under way for tactical and gunnery exercises and anchored off Santa Barbara and San Nicholas islands.

26–29 August   Anchored at San Pedro.

29 August   Under way with other battleships for gunnery exercises.

29 August–1 September   Anchored off San Clemente Island.

1 September   Under way for short-range battle-practice rehearsal.

1–19 September   Anchored at San Pedro. On 7 September Captain Alfred W. Brown, USN, commanding officer of the *Arizona*, died of a heart attack ashore in Long Beach. The executive officer, Commander Wallace B. Phillips, USN, took over temporary command. On 17 September Captain Isaac C. Kidd, USN, assumed command of the ship. Also on 17 September, on board the *Arizona*, Rear Admiral Chester W. Nimitz, USN, relieved Rear Admiral Adolphus E. Watson, USN, as Commander Battleship Division One.

Above: Arthur Beaumont's painting of the *Arizona* and *New Mexico* completing an exercise at sea in 1938. (Naval Historical Center, NH 89577)

19–23 September Alternately under way for a variety of drills and anchored off San Clemente Island.

23–26 September Anchored at San Pedro.

26–30 September Alternately under way with other battleships for day battle practice and day spotting-practice rehearsals and anchored off San Clemente Island.

30 September–3 October Anchored at San Pedro.

3 October Under way for turret spotting practice.

3–5 October Anchored at San Pedro.

5–6 October Alternately under way for long-range battle-practice rehearsal and anchored off Santa Barbara Island.

6–17 October Anchored at San Pedro.

17–20 October Alternately under way with other battleships for tactical and gunnery exercises and anchored off Santa Barbara Island.

20–24 October Anchored at San Pedro.

24–25 October En route to San Francisco with the USS *Nevada* and *Oklahoma*.

25–31 October Anchored at San Francisco for Navy Day.

31 October–4 November Alternately under way with the USS *Nevada* and *Oklahoma* for gunnery practice and anchored off Santa Barbara and San Clemente islands.

4–7 November Anchored at San Pedro.

7–10 November Under way with other battleships for fleet tactical exercises.

10–28 November Anchored at San Pedro.

28 November–1 December Alternately under way for gunnery exercises and anchored off San Clemente Island.

1–5 December Anchored at San Pedro.

5–6 December Alternately under way for antiaircraft machine-gun training and anchored off Santa Barbara Island.

7–28 December Anchored at San Pedro.

28–29 December En route to San Francisco independently.

29 December Anchored at San Francisco.

29–31 December En route to Seattle.

1939

1 January En route to Seattle; anchored at Seattle; en route to Bremerton.

1 January–27 February Moored at the Puget Sound Navy Yard.

27 February–15 March Dry-docked at the Puget Sound Navy Yard.

15–28 March Moored at the Puget Sound Navy Yard.

28 March Under way for post-repair trials.

28–31 March Moored at the Puget Sound Navy Yard.

31 March–3 April En route to San Francisco.

3 April Anchored at San Francisco.

3–4 April En route to San Pedro.

4–14 April Anchored at San Pedro.

14–15 April En route to San Diego.

15–17 April Moored at San Diego.

17–21 April Alternately under way with the USS *Oklahoma* for landing-force exercises and radio-direction-finder calibration and anchored off San Clemente Island.

21–24 April Anchored at San Pedro.

24–28 April Alternately under way for gunnery practice and radio-direction-finder calibration and anchored off San Clemente Island.

28 April–1 May Anchored at San Pedro.

1–5 May Alternately under way with battleships and heavy cruisers for landing-force exercises and anchored off San Clemente Island.

5–8 May Moored at San Diego.

8–9 May Alternately under way with the USS *Oklahoma* for antiaircraft practice and anchored off Santa Barbara Island.

9–10 May Anchored at San Pedro.

10–12 May Alternately under way with the USS *Oklahoma* and *Nevada* for antiaircraft practice and anchored off San Clemente Island.

12–15 May Anchored at San Pedro.

15–17 May Alternately under way with other battleships for firing advance day battle practice and anchored off San Clemente Island.

17–20 May Anchored at San Pedro.

20 May Under way for annual military inspection and annual damage-control practice.

20–31 May Anchored at San Pedro. On 27 May, on board the *Arizona*, Rear Admiral Russell Willson, USN, relieved Rear Admiral Chester W. Nimitz, USN, as Commander Battleship Division One.

31 May Under way for antiaircraft practice.

31 May–5 June Anchored at San Pedro.

5–9 June Alternately under way with the

USS *Nevada* and *Tennessee* for ship-handling drill and radio-direction-finder calibration and anchored off San Clemente Island.

9–15 June   Anchored at San Pedro.

15 June   Under way for magnetic-compass compensation.

15–30 June   Anchored at San Pedro.

30 June–1 July   En route to San Francisco in company with battleships and cruisers of the Battle Force.

1–17 July   Anchored at San Francisco.

17–20 July   En route to Tacoma in company with other battleships, conducting tactical maneuvers.

20–24 July   Anchored at Tacoma.

24 July   En route to Seattle with other battleships.

24–31 July   Anchored at Seattle.

31 July–4 August   En route to San Pedro with other battleships, conducting tactical maneuvers.

4–21 August   Anchored at San Pedro.

21–25 August   Alternately under way with other battleships for antiaircraft practice and short-range battle-practice rehearsal and anchored off Santa Barbara Island.

25–28 August   Anchored at San Pedro.

28 August   Under way with other battleships for short-range battle-practice rehearsal.

28–31 August   Anchored off Santa Barbara Island.

31 August   Under way for firing of short-range battle practice and anchored off Santa Barbara Island.

31 August–5 September   Anchored at San Pedro.

5–8 September   Alternately under way with other battleships for ship-handling drills, radio-direction-finder and range-finder calibration, and division tactics and anchored off San Clemente Island.

8–26 September   Anchored at San Pedro.

26–29 September   Under way with battleships, cruisers, and the aircraft carrier *Enterprise* for fleet tactical maneuvers, including simulated attacks by destroyers.

29 September–2 October   Anchored at San Pedro.

2–6 October   Alternately under way with battleships and cruisers for day battle-practice rehearsal and division maneuvers and anchored off Santa Barbara Island.

6–9 October   Anchored at San Pedro.

9–13 October   Alternately under way with other battleships for day and night battle practice and anchored off Santa Barbara Island.

13–16 October   Anchored at San Pedro.

16–18 October   Alternately under way with other battleships for antiaircraft spotting practice and anchored off San Clemente Island.

18 October–2 November   Moored alongside the USS *Medusa* at San Pedro.

2–6 November   Anchored at San Pedro.

6–10 November   Alternately under way with the USS *Pennsylvania* and *Nevada* for ship-handling training and night battle-practice rehearsal and anchored off San Clemente Island.

10–13 November   Anchored at San Pedro.

13–17 November   Under way with other battleships for fleet tactical maneuvers, including repelling destroyer and aircraft attacks.

17–20 November   Anchored at San Pedro.

20–22 November   Alternately under way for gunnery exercises and other drills and anchored off San Clemente Island.

22–27 November   Anchored at San Pedro.

27–28 November   Alternately under way for gunnery practice and anchored at San Pedro.

28–29 November   Anchored off San Clemente Island.

29 November–3 December   Under way for collision drill and antiaircraft battle practice, then en route to Seattle.

3–4 December   Anchored at Seattle.

4 December   En route to Bremerton.

4–5 December   Moored at the Puget Sound Navy Yard.

5–16 December   Dry-docked at the Puget Sound Navy Yard.

16–19 December   En route to San Pedro independently.

19–31 December   Anchored at San Pedro.

1940

1–4 January   Anchored at San Pedro.

4–5 January   Alternately under way with other battleships for machine-gun practice and anchored at San Pedro.

5–8 January   Anchored at San Pedro.

8–12 January   Alternately under way for

various drills and anchored off San Clemente.

12–15 January Anchored at San Pedro.

15–19 January Alternately at sea with other battleships for a battle problem and anchored off San Clemente.

19 January–5 February Anchored at San Pedro. On 3 February Captain Harold C. Train, USN, relieved Captain Isaac C. Kidd, USN, as commanding officer.

5–6 February Alternately under way and anchored off San Clemente.

6–9 February Anchored off San Clemente.

9 February En route to San Pedro.

9–12 February Anchored at San Pedro.

12–16 February Alternately under way with other battleships and anchored off San Clemente.

16–26 February Anchored at San Pedro.

26 February–1 March Under way in company with other battleships for various drills.

1–4 March Anchored at San Pedro.

4–7 March Alternately under way with other battleships for drills and anchored off San Clemente.

7–11 March Anchored at San Pedro.

11–13 March Alternately under way with other battleships for various drills and anchored off San Clemente.

13 March–2 April Anchored at San Pedro.

2–10 April En route to Hawaii with other elements of the U.S. Fleet as part of Fleet Problem XXI.

10–14 April Anchored in Lahaina Roads.

14–24 April Under way for continuation of Fleet Problem XXI.

24–25 April Anchored in Lahaina Roads.

25–26 April En route to Pearl Harbor.

26 April–14 May Moored at Pearl Harbor.

14–15 May En route to Lahaina Roads with other battleships.

15–20 May Anchored in Lahaina Roads.

20–23 May Alternately under way for various exercises and anchored in Lahaina Roads.

23–24 May En route to Pearl Harbor.

24 May–10 June Moored at Pearl Harbor.

10–13 June Alternately under way for various exercises and anchored in Lahaina Roads.

13–17 June Anchored in Lahaina Roads.

17–21 June Alternately under way for various exercises and anchored in Lahaina Roads.

21 June En route to Pearl Harbor.

21–24 June Moored at Pearl Harbor.

24–25 June Dry-docked at Pearl Harbor.

25 June–15 July Moored at Pearl Harbor.

15 July En route to Lahaina Roads.

15–19 July Alternately under way for various exercises and anchored in Lahaina Roads.

19–29 July Under way with other battleships to outlying bases; on 21 July the *Arizona* was in the vicinity of Palmyra Island; on 24 July the *Arizona* crossed the equator and initiated pollywogs; on 26 July the *Arizona* was in the vicinity of Christmas Island; on 27 July the *Arizona* was in the vicinity of Jarvis Island.

29–30 July Anchored in Lahaina Roads.

30 July–1 August Alternately under way for various exercises and anchored in Lahaina Roads.

1–2 August En route to Pearl Harbor.

2–19 August Moored at Pearl Harbor.

19–30 August Alternately under way for various exercises and anchored in Lahaina Roads.

30 August–3 September Anchored at Honolulu.

3–5 September Under way for maneuvers with other battleships.

5–9 September Anchored in Lahaina Roads.

9–13 September Under way with other ships of the U.S. Fleet for a simulated fleet engagement.

13–23 September Moored at Pearl Harbor.

23–30 September En route to Long Beach as part of Task Force One.

30 September–17 October Anchored at Long Beach.

17–20 October En route to Puget Sound in company with the USS *New Mexico* and *Mississippi*.

20–21 October Anchored off Port Orchard, Washington.

21 October En route to Bremerton.

21 October–27 December Moored at the Puget Sound Navy Yard.

27–31 December Dry-docked at the Puget Sound Navy Yard.

1941

1–9 January Dry-docked at the Puget Sound Navy Yard.

9–13 January Moored at the Puget Sound Navy Yard.

13 January Under way for post-repair trial.

13–19 January Moored at the Puget Sound Navy Yard.

19–22 January En route to San Pedro.

22–25 January Anchored at San Pedro. On 23 January, on board the *Arizona*, Rear Admiral Isaac C. Kidd, USN, relieved Rear Admiral Russell Willson, USN, as Commander Battleship Division One.

25 January Under way for calibration exercises.

25–27 January Anchored at San Pedro.

27 January–3 February En route to Pearl Harbor, joining up with a fleet exercise in the Hawaiian operating area.

3–12 February Moored at Pearl Harbor. On 3 February Captain Harold C. Train, USN, was detached from the *Arizona* and Commander Ellis H. Geiselman, USN, took temporary command. On 5 February Captain Franklin B. Van Valkenburgh, USN, reported for duty in command.

12–19 February Alternately under way with other battleships for battle practice and anchored in Maalaea Bay, Hawaii.

19–26 February Moored at Pearl Harbor.

26 February–5 March Under way with other battleships for tactical exercises and day and night battle practice.

5–12 March Moored at Pearl Harbor.

12–20 March Under way at various times with Task Force One and Task Force Two for night battle practice, night spotting practice, a battle-line engagement, and other exercises.

20–26 March Moored at Pearl Harbor.

26 March–4 April Under way at various times independently, with other battleships, and as part of Task Force One and Task Group Five for advanced battle practice, division antiaircraft practice, and advanced light force practice.

4–18 April Moored at Pearl Harbor.

18–26 April Under way at various times with Task Force One, Task Force Five, and Battleship Division One for antiaircraft practice and torpedo-battle prac-

Below: Remains of the *Arizona*, December 1941. (National Archives, 80-G-413510)

tice. On 21 April the *Arizona* and the destroyer USS *Davis* collided while the *Davis* was refueling.

26 April–14 May   Moored at Pearl Harbor.

14–23 May   Under way at various times with other battleships and as part of Task Force One to repel bomb, torpedo, and destroyer attacks, antiaircraft practice, and other exercises.

23 May–10 June   Moored at Pearl Harbor.

10–17 June   En route to San Pedro as part of Task Group 11, which included the cruiser USS *Trenton*, tender USS *Dobbin*, and three destroyers, conducting short-range practice.

17 June–1 July   Anchored at San Pedro.

1–8 July   En route to Pearl Harbor in company with other warships, conducting short-range practice.

8–24 July   Moored at Pearl Harbor.

24 July–1 August   Under way at various times with the USS *Oklahoma* for standardization, tactical data, and range-finder calibration, independently for antiaircraft practice, and as part of Task Force Two and Task Force Four for various exercises.

1–14 August   Moored at Pearl Harbor.

14–22 August   Under way at various times independently and with the USS *Nevada* and *Oklahoma* for short-range practice, towing exercises, and other drills. On 20 August the *Arizona* refueled from the oiler USS *Sabine*, which was connected to the battleship by two tow lines. The *Arizona* later joined Task Force Two.

22 August–4 September   Moored at Pearl Harbor.

4–10 September   Under way with Task Force Two for antisubmarine and anti-aircraft exercises and independently for range-finder calibration.

10–15 September   Moored at Pearl Harbor.

15–19 September   Dry-docked at the Pearl Harbor Navy Yard.

19–24 September   Moored at Pearl Harbor.

24 September–2 October   Under way with Task Force Two for short-range practice and antiaircraft drills.

2–7 October   Moored at Pearl Harbor.

7–8 October   Under way with the USS *Nevada* for night spotting practice.

8–18 October   Moored at Pearl Harbor.

18–26 October   Under way at various times independently and with other ships for short-range practice and night-battle practice. On the evening of 22 October the *Arizona* and *Oklahoma* collided.

26–27 October   Moored at Pearl Harbor.

27–31 October   Dry-docked at the Pearl Harbor Navy Yard.

The *Arizona*'s deck logs for November and December 1941 were not sent to Washington, D.C., prior to the ship's destruction and thus are not available for research.

Appendix B
COMMANDING OFFICERS

Captain/Rear Admiral John D. McDonald, U.S. Navy
17 October 1916–18 February 1918

Captain/Rear Admiral Josiah S. McKean, U.S. Navy
18 February 1918–11 September 1918

Captain John H. Dayton, U.S. Navy
11 September 1918–26 June 1920

Captain William W. Phelps, U.S. Navy
26 June 1920–30 May 1921

Commander Royal E. Ingersoll, U.S. Navy
30 May 1921–11 June 1921

Captain Jehu V. Chase, U.S. Navy
11 June 1921–24 December 1921

Captain George R. Marvell, U.S. Navy
24 December 1921–27 July 1922

Captain John R. Y. Blakely, U.S. Navy
27 July 1922–29 November 1923

Captain Percy N. Olmsted, U.S. Navy
29 November 1923–27 June 1925

Captain Harlan P. Perrill, U.S. Navy
27 June 1925–24 May 1927

Captain William T. Tarrant, U.S. Navy
24 May 1927–27 June 1928

Captain Victor A. Kimberly, U.S. Navy
27 June 1928–4 September 1928

Captain Ward K. Wortman, U.S. Navy
4 September 1928–29 April 1930

Commander Thaddeus A. Thomson, Jr., U.S. Navy
29 April 1930–20 September 1930

Captain Charles S. Freeman, U.S. Navy
20 September 1930–20 June 1932

Captain Charles S. Kerrick, U.S. Navy
20 June 1932–30 September 1933

Captain Macgillivray Milne, U.S. Navy
30 September 1933–10 December 1934

Captain George M. Baum, U.S. Navy
10 December 1934–8 June 1936

Captain George A. Alexander, U.S. Navy
8 June 1936–11 December 1937

Captain Alfred W. Brown, U.S. Navy
11 December 1937–7 September 1938

Commander Wallace B. Phillips, U.S. Navy
7 September 1938–17 September 1938

Captain Isaac C. Kidd, U.S. Navy
17 September 1938–3 February 1940

Captain Harold C. Train, U.S. Navy
3 February 1940–3 February 1941

Commander Ellis H. Geiselman, U.S. Navy
3 February 1941–5 February 1941

Captain Franklin B. Van Valkenburgh U.S. Navy
5 February 1941–7 December 1941

Below: Captain George A. Alexander, left, and Captain Alfred W. Brown, right, confer in the captain's cabin about their upcoming change of command in December 1937. In the center is the ship's executive officer, Commander Francis S. Craven. (Wide World Photos)

CREW LIST – 7 DECEMBER 1941

This list includes the officers and enlisted men of the ship's company, Navy and Marine Corps, the staff of Commander Battleship Division One, and members of Observation Squadron One (VO-1) attached to the ship. The list of fatalities includes individuals who died on board other ships, particularly the hospital ship *Solace*, after being transported there from the *Arizona*.

KEY

NAVY

Commissioned Officers
RADM—Rear Admiral
CAPT—Captain
CDR—Commander
LCDR—Lieutenant Commander
LT—Lieutenant
LTJG—Lieutenant (junior grade)
ENS—Ensign
CHC—Chaplain Corps
DC—Dental Corps
MC—Medical Corps
SC—Supply Corps

Warrant Officers
CARP—Carpenter
CHGUN—Chief Gunner
CHMACH—Chief Machinist
ELECT—Electrician
MACH—Machinist
PAYCLK—Pay Clerk

Chief Petty Officers
ACCM—Acting Chief Machinist's
    Mate
CBM—Chief Boatswain's Mate
CCM—Chief Carpenter's Mate
CCStd—Chief Commissary Steward
CEM—Chief Electrician's Mate
CGM—Chief Gunner's Mate
CMM—Chief Machinist's Mate
CMsmith—Chief Metalsmith
CPhm—Chief Pharmacist's Mate
CPrtr—Chief Printer
CQM—Chief Quartermaster

CRM—Chief Radioman
CSF—Chief Shipfitter
CSK—Chief Storekeeper
CSM—Chief Signalman
CTC—Chief Turret Captain
CWT—Chief Watertender
CY—Chief Yeoman

Other Petty Officers
AMM—Aviation Machinist's Mate
AMsmith—Aviation Metalsmith
AOM—Aviation Ordnanceman
Bkr—Baker
BM—Boatswain's Mate
Bmkr—Boilermaker
Bug—Bugler
CM—Carpenter's Mate
Cox—Coxswain
EM—Electrician's Mate
FC—Fire Controlman
GM—Gunner's Mate
MAtt—Mess Attendant
Mldr—Molder
MM—Machinist's Mate
Msmith—Metalsmith
Mu—Musician
OC—Officers' Cook
OS—Officers' Steward
PhM—Pharmacist's Mate
Pmkr—Patternmaker
Ptr—Painter
QM—Quartermaster
RM—Radioman
SC—Ship's Cook
SF—Shipfitter
SK—Storekeeper

SM—Signalman
TC—Turret Captain
WT—Watertender
Y—Yeoman
1/c—First Class
2/c—Second Class
3/c—Third Class

Nonrated Enlisted Men
F1/c—Fireman First Class
F2/c—Fireman Second Class
HA—Hospital Apprentice
S1/c—Seaman First Class
S2/c—Seaman Second Class

MARINE CORPS

Commissioned Officers
LCOL—Lieutenant Colonel
MAJ—Major
CAPT—Captain
2LT—Second Lieutenant
1LT—First Lieutenant

Enlisted Men
AsstCook—Assistant Cook
Cpl—Corporal
FldCk—Field Cook
FldMus—Field Music
FldMusCpl—Field Music Corporal
1stSgt—First Sergeant
MGySgt—Master Gunnery Sergeant
PFC—Private First Class
PltSgt—Platoon Sergeant
Pvt—Private
Sgt—Sergeant

Navy Fatalities

Name	Rank/Rate	Name	Rank/Rate
Aaron, Hubert	F2/c	Bandy, Wayne Lynn	Mus2/c
Abercrombie, Samuel Adolphus	S1/c	Bangert, John Henry, Jr.	FC1/c
Adams, Robert Franklin	S1/c	Bardon, Charles Thomas	S2/c
Adkison, James Dillion	S1/c	Barker, Loren Joe	Cox
Aguirre, Reyner Aceves	S2/c	Barner, Walter Ray	S2/c
Aguon, Gregorio San	MAtt3/c	Barnes, Charles Edward	Y3/c
Ahern, Richard James	F1/c	Barnes, Delmar Hayes	LTJG
Alberovsky, Francis Severin	BMkr1/c	Barnett, William Thomas	S2/c
Albright, Galen Winston	S1/c	Bartlett, Paul Clement	MM1/c
Alexander, Elvis Author	S2/c	Bates, Edward Munroe, Jr.	ENS
Allen, Robert Lee	SF3/c	Bates, Robert Alven	PhM3/c
Allen, William Clayborn	EM1/c	Bator, Edward	F1/c
Allen, William Lewis	SK2/c	Bauer, Harold Walter	RM3/c
Alley, Jay Edgar	GM1/c	Beaumont, James Ammon	S2/c
Allison, Andrew "K"	F1/c	Beck, George Richard	S1/c
Allison, J. T.	F1/c	Becker, Marvin Otto	GM3/c
Alten, Ernest Mathew	S2/c	Becker, Wesley Paulson	S1/c
Amon, Frederick Purdy	S1/c	Bedford, Purdy Renaker	F1/c
Anderberg, William Robert	F2/c	Beerman, Henry Carl	CM3/c
Anderson, Charles Titus	CM2/c	Beggs, Harold Eugene	F1/c
Anderson, Delbert Jake	BM2/c	Bell, Hershel Homer	F1/c
Anderson, Donald William	SM3/c	Bell, Richard LeRoy	S2/c
Anderson, Harry	S1/c	Bellamy, James Curtis	OS3/c
Anderson, Howard Taisey	F2/c	Benford, Sam Austin	Bkr2/c
Anderson, Irwin Corinthias	MAtt1/c	Bennett, William Edmond, Jr.	Y3/c
Anderson, James Pickens, Jr.	S1/c	Benson, James Thomas	S1/c
Anderson, Lawrence D.	ENS	Bergin, Roger Joseph	F2/c
Anderson, Robert Adair	GM3/c	Berkanski, Albert Charles	Cox
Andrews, Brainerd Wells	CCM	Bernard, Frank Peter	SF2/c
Angie, Earnest Hersea	F2/c	Berry, Gordon Eugene	F2/c
Anthony, Glenn Samuel	S1/c	Berry, James Winford	F2/c
Aplin, James Raymond	CWT	Bersch, Arthur Anthony	S1/c
Apple, Robert William	F1/c	Bertie, George Allan, Jr.	S2/c
Aprea, Frank Anthony	Cox	Bibby, Charles Henry	F2/c
Arledge, Eaton	SM2/c	Bickel, Kenneth Robert	F1/c
Arnaud, Achilles	F3/c	Bicknell, Dale Deen	S1/c
Arnold, Claude Duran, Jr.	F3/c	Bircher, Frederick Robert	RM3c
Arnold, Thell	SC1/c	Birdsell, Rayon Delois	F2/c
Arrant, John Anderson	MM1/c	Birge, George Albert	S1/c
Arvidson, Carl Harry	CMM	Bishop, Grover Barron	S1/c
Ashmore, Wilburn James	S2/c	Bishop, Millard Charles	F3/c
Atkins, Gerald Arthur	HA1/c	Bishop, Wesley Homer, Jr.	RM3/c
Austin, Laverne Alfred	S1/c	Blais, Albert E.	RM3/c
Autry, Eligah T., Jr.	Cox	Blake, James Monroe	F2/c
Aves, Willard Charles	F2/c	Blanchard, Albert Richard	Cox
Aydell, Miller Xavier	WT2/c	Blankenship, Theron Andrew	S1/c
Ayers, Dee Cumpie	S2/c	Blanton, Atticus Lee	SF3/c
Badilla, Manuel D.	F1/c	Blieffert, Richmond F.	S1/c
Baird, Billy Byron	S1/c	Block, Ivan Lee	PhM2/c
Bajorims, Joseph	S1/c	Blount, Wayman Boney	S1/c
Baker, Robert Dewey	CMM	Boggess, Roy Eugene	SF2/c
Ball, William V.	S1/c	Bohlender, Sam	GM3/c

Name	Rank/Rate	Name	Rank/Rate
Bolling, Gerald Revese	S1/c	Caldwell, Charles, Jr.	F3/c
Bolling, Walter Karr	F3/c	Callaghan, James Thomas	BM2/c
Bonebrake, Buford Earl	F2/c	Camden, Raymond Edward	S2/c
Bonfiglio, William John	EM1/c	Camm, William Fielden	Y2/c
Booth, Robert Sinclaire, Jr.	ENS	Campa, Ralph	S1/c
Booze, Asbury Legare	BM1/c	Campbell, Burdette Charles	S1/c
Borger, Richard	CMM	Caplinger, Donald William	SC3/c
Borovich, Joseph John	S1/c	Carey, Francis Lloyd	SK3/c
Bosley, Kenneth LeRoy	EM3/c	Carlisle, Robert Wayne	S1/c
Boviall, Robert Walter	AMM2/c	Carlson, Harry Ludwig	SK3/c
Bowman, Howard Alton	S2/c	Carmack, Harold Milton	F2/c
Boyd, Charles Andrew	CM3/c	Carpenter, Robert Nelson	MAtt1/c
Boydstun, Don Jasper	S2/c	Carroll, Robert Lewis	S1/c
Boydstun, "R" "L"	S2/c	Carter, Burton Lowell	S2/c
Brabbzson, Oran Merrill	Mus2/c	Carter, Paxton Turner	PAYCLK
Bradley, Bruce Dean	S2/c	Casey, James Warren	S1/c
Brakke, Kenneth Gay	F3/c	Casilan, Epifanio Miranda	OS3/c
Bridges, James Leon	S1/c	Caskey, Clarence Merton	S1/c
Bridges, Paul Hyatt	S1/c	Castleberry, Claude William, Jr.	S1/c
Bridie, Robert Maurice	F1/c	Catsos, George	F1/c
Brignole, Erminio Joseph	S2/c	Chace, Raymond Vincent	CSK
Brittan, Charles Edward	S2/c	Chadwick, Charles Bruce	MM2/c
Broadhead, Johnnie Cecil	F2/c	Chadwick, Harold	MAtt1/c
Brock, Walter Pershing	S1/c	Chapman, Naaman "N"	S1/c
Bromley, George Edward	SM3/c	Charlton, Charles Nicholas	WT1/c
Bromley, Jimmie	S1/c	Chernuca, Harry Gregory	Mus2/c
Brooks, Robert Neal	ENS	Chester, Edward	S1/c
Broome, Loy Raymond	SM3/c	Christensen, Elmer Emil	MM2/c
Brooner, Allen Ottis	S1/c	Christensen, Lloyd Raymond	F1/c
Brophy, Myron Alonzo	F2/c	Christiansen, Edward Lee	Bkr3/c
Brown, Charles Martin	S2/c	Cihlar, Lawrence John	PhM3/c
Brown, Elwin LeRoy	EM3/c	Clark, George Francis	GM3/c
Brown, Frank George	QM3/c	Clark, John Crawford Todd	F3/c
Brown, Richard Corbett	S1/c	Clark, Malcolm	Bkr3/c
Brown, William Howard	S2/c	Clark, Robert William, Jr.	FC3/c
Browne, Harry Lamont	CMM	Clarke, Robert Eugene	S1/c
Browning, Tilmon David	S1/c	Clash, Donald	F2/c
Brune, James William	RM3/c	Clayton, Robert Roland	Cox
Bryan, Leland Howard	S1/c	Clemmens, Claude Albert	S1/c
Bryant, Lloyd Glenn	BM2/c	Clift, Ray Emerson	Cox
Buckley, Jack "C"	FC3/c	Cloues, Edward Blanchard	ENS
Budd, Robert Emile	F2/c	Clough, Edward Jay	GM1/c
Buhr, Clarence Edward	S1/c	Cobb, Ballard Burgher	S1/c
Burden, Ralph Leon	RM3/c	Coburn, Walter Overton	S1/c
Burdette, Ralph Warren	Mus2/c	Cockrum, Kenneth Earl	MM1/c
Burke, Frank Edmond, Jr.	SK2/c	Coffin, Robert	SF3/c
Burnett, Charlie Leroy	S2/c	Coffman, Marshall Herman	GM3/c
Burns, John Edward	F1/c	Cole, David Lester	ENS
Busick, Dewey Olney	F3/c	Colegrove, Willett Stillman, Jr.	S2/c
Butcher, David Adrian	F2/c	Collier, John	F2/c
Butler, John Dabney	F1/c	Collier, Linalda Long, Jr.	Bkr3/c
Byrd, Charles Dewitt	S1/c	Collins, Austin	SF3/c
Cabay, Louis Clarence	S1/c	Collins, Billy Murl	S1/c
Cade, Richard Esh	S2/c	Conlin, Bernard Eugene	S2/c

Name	Rank/Rate	Name	Rank/Rate
Conlin, James Lee	F2/c	Donohue, Ned Burton	F1/c
Connelly, Richard Earl	CQM	Dority, John Monroe	S1/c
Conrad, Homer Milton, Jr.	S1/c	Dougherty, Ralph McClearn	FC1/c
Conrad, Robert Frank	S2/c	Doyle, Wand B.	Cox
Conrad, Walter Ralph	QM2/c	Driver, Bill Lester	RM3/c
Cooper, Clarence Eugene	F2/c	Ducrest, Louis Felix	S1/c
Cooper, Kenneth Erven	F2/c	Duke, Robert Edward	CCStd
Corcoran, Gerald John	S1/c	Dullum, Jerald Fraser	EM3/c
Corey, Ernest Eugene	PhM3/c	Dunaway, Kenneth Leroy	EM3/c
Cornelius, P. W.	SC3/c	Dunham, Elmer Marvin	S1/c
Corning, Russell Dale	RM3/c	Dupree, Arthur Joseph	F2/c
Coulter, Arthur Lee	S1/c	Durham, William Teasdale	S1/c
Cowan, William	Cox	Dvorak, Alvin Albert	BM2/c
Cowden, Joel Beman	S2/c	Eaton, Emory Lowell	F3/c
Cox, Gerald Clinton	Mus2/c	Ebel, Walter Charles	CTC
Cox, William Milford	S1/c	Eberhart, Vincent Henry	Cox
Craft, Harley Wade	CM3/c	Echols, Charles Louie, Jr.	EM3/c
Crawley, Wallace Dwight	Cox	Echternkamp, Henry Clarence	S1/c
Cremeens, Louis Edward	S1/c	Edmunds, Bruce Roosevelt	Y2/c
Criscuolo, Michael	Y2/c	Eernisse, William Frederick	Ptr1/c
Criswell, Wilfred John	S1/c	Egnew, Robert Ross	S1/c
Crowe, Cecil Thomas	GM2/c	Ehlert, Casper	SM3/c
Crowley, Thomas Ewing	LCDR (DC)	Ehrmantraut, Frank, Jr.	S1/c
Curry, William Joseph	WT2/c	Ellis, Francis Arnold, Jr.	EM3/c
Curtis, Lloyd "B"	S1/c	Ellis, Richard Everett	S1/c
Curtis, Lyle Carl	RM2/c	Ellis, Wilbur Danner	RM2/c
Cybulski, Harold Bernard	S1/c	Elwell, Royal	S1/c
Cychosz, Francis Anton	S1/c	Embrey, Bill Eugene	F3/c
Czarnecki, Stanley	F1/c	Emery, Jack Mendeville	ENS
Czekajski, Theophil	SM3/c	Emery, John Marvin	GM3/c
Dahlheimer, Richard Norbert	S1/c	Emery, Wesley Vernon	SK2/c
Daniel, Lloyd Maxton	Y1/c	Enger, Stanley Gordon	GM3/c
Danik, Andrew Joseph	S2/c	Erickson, Robert	S1/c
Darch, Phillip Zane	S1/c	Erwin, Stanley Joe	MM1/c
Daugherty, Paul Eugene	EM3/c	Erwin, Walton Aluard	S1/c
Davis, John Quitman	S1/c	Estep, Carl James	S1/c
Davis, Milton Henry	S1/c	Estes, Carl Edwen	S1/c
Davis, Murle Melvin	RM2/c	Estes, Forrest Jesse	F1/c
Davis, Myrle Clarence	F3/c	Etchason, Leslie Edgar	S1/c
Davis, Thomas Ray	SF1/c	Eulberg, Richard Henry	FC2/c
Davis, Walter Mindred	F2/c	Evans, Evan Frederick	ENS
Day, William John	S2/c	Evans, Mickey Edward	S1/c
Dean, Lyle Bernard	Cox	Evans, Paul Anthony	S1/c
De Armoun, Donald Edwin	GM3/c	Evans, William Orville	S2/c
DeCastro, Vicente	OS3/c	Ewell, Alfred Adam	WT1/c
Deritis, Russell Edwin	S1/c	Eyed, George	SK3/c
Dewitt, John James	Cox	Fallis, Alvin E.	PhM2/c
Dial, John Buchanan	S1/c	Fansler, Edgar Arthur	S1/c
Dick, Ralph "R"	GM1/c	Farmer, John Wilson	Cox
Dine, John George	F2/c	Fegurgur, Nicholas Sam	MAtt2/c
Dineen, Robert Joseph	S1/c	Fess, John, Jr.	F1/c
Dobey, Milton Paul, Jr.	S1/c	Fields, Bernard	RM3/c
Doherty, George Walter	S2/c	Fields, Reliford	MAtt2/c
Doherty, John Albert	MM2/c	Fife, Ralph Elmer	S1/c

Name	Rank/Rate	Name	Rank/Rate
Filkins, George Arthur	Cox	Gove, Rupert Clair	S1/c
Firth, Henry Amis	F3/c	Granger, Raymond Edward	F3/c
Fischer, Leslie Henry	S1/c	Grant, Lawrence Everett	Y3/c
Fisher, Delbert Ray	S1/c	Gray, Albert James	S1/c
Fisher, James Anderson	MAtt1/c	Gray, Lawrence Moore	F1/c
Fisher, Robert Ray	S2/c	Gray, William James, Jr.	S1/c
Fisk, Charles Porter III	Y1/c	Green, Glen Hubert	S1/c
Fitch, Simon	MAtt1/c	Greenfield, Carroll Gale	S1/c
Fitzsimmons, Eugene James	F3/c	Griffin, Reese Olin	EM3/c
Flannery, James Lowell	SK3/c	Griffiths, Robert Alfred	EM3/c
Floege, Frank Norman	Mus2/c	Grissinger, Robert Beryle	S2/c
Flory, Max Edward	S2/c	Grosnickle, Warren Wilbert	EM2/c
Fones, George Everett	FC3/c	Gross, Milton Henry	CSK
Ford, Jack C.	S1/c	Grundstorm, Richard G.	S2/c
Ford, William Walker	EM3/c	Gurley, Jesse Herbert	SK3/c
Foreman, Elmer Lee	F2/c	Haas, Curtis Junior	Mus2/c
Fortenberry, Alvie Charles	Cox	Haden, Samuel William	Cox
Fowler, George Parten	S2/c	Haffner, Floyd Bates	F1/c
Frank, LeRoy George	S1/c	Haines, Robert Wesley	S2/c
Frederick, Charles D.	EM2/c	Hall, John Rudolph	CBM
Free, Thomas Augusta	MM1/c	Halloran, William Ignatius	ENS
Free, William Thomas	S2/c	Hamilton, Clarence James	MM1/c
French, John Edmund	LCDR	Hamilton, Edwin Carrell	S1/c
Frizzell, Robert Niven	S2/c	Hamilton, William Holman	GM3/c
Fulton, Robert Wilson	AMsmith1/c	Hammerud, George Winston	S1/c
Funk, Frank Francis	BM2/c	Hampton, "J" "D"	F1/c
Funk, Lawrence Henry	S1/c	Hampton, Ted W., Jr.	S1/c
Gager, Roy Arthur	S2/c	Hampton, Walter Lewis	BM2/c
Gargaro, Ernest Russell	S2/c	Hanna, David Darling	EM3/c
Garlington, Raymond Wesley	S1/c	Hansen, Carlyle "B"	MM2/c
Garrett, Orville Wilmer	SF2/c	Hansen, Harvey Ralph	S1/c
Gartin, Gerald Ernest	S1/c	Hanzel, Edward Joseph	WT1/c
Gaudette, William Frank	S1/c	Hardin, Charles Eugene	S1/c
Gaultney, Ralph Martin	EM3/c	Hargraves, Kenneth William	S2/c
Gazecki, Philip Robert	ENS	Harrington, Keith Homer	S1/c
Gebhardt, Kenneth Edward	S1/c	Harris, George Ellsworth	MM1/c
Geer, Kenneth Floyd	S2/c	Harris, Hiram Dennis	S1/c
Geise, Marvin Frederick	S1/c	Harris, James William	F1/c
Gemienhardt, Samuel Henry	MM2/c	Harris, Noble Burnice	Cox
Gholston, Roscoe J.	Y2/c	Harris, Peter John	Cox
Gibson, Billy Edwin	S1/c	Hartley, Alvin	GM3/c
Giesen, Karl Anthony	Y2/c	Hartsoe, Max June	GM3/c
Gill, Richard Eugene	S1/c	Hartson, Lonnie Moss	SM3/c
Giovenazzo, Michael James	WT2/c	Hasl, James Thomas	F1/c
Givens, Harold Reuben	Y3/c	Haverfield, James Wallace	ENS
Gobbin, Angelo	SC1/c	Havins, Harvey Linfille	S1/c
Goff, Wiley Coy	S2/c	Hawkins, Russell Dean	SM3/c
Gomez, Edward, Jr.	S1/c	Hayes, John Doran	BM1/c
Good, Leland	S1/c	Hayes, Kenneth Merle	F1/c
Goodwin, William Arthur	S2/c	Haynes, Curtis James	QM2/c
Gordon, Peter Charles, Jr.	F1/c	Hays, William Henry	SK3/c
Gosselin, Edward W.	ENS	Hazdovac, Jack Claudius	S1/c
Gosselin, Joseph Adjutor	RM1/c	Head, Frank Bernard	CY
Gould, Harry Lee	S1/c	Heater, Verrel Roy	S1/c

Name	Rank/Rate	Name	Rank/Rate
Heath, Alfred Grant	S1/c	Iak, Joseph Claude	Y3/c
Hebel, Robert Lee	SM3/c	Ibbotson, Howard Burt	F1/c
Heckendorn, Warren Guy	S1/c	Ingalls, Richard Fitch	SC3/c
Hedger, Jess Laxton	S1/c	Ingalls, Theodore A.	SC3/c
Hedrick, Paul Henry	BM1/c	Ingraham, David Archie	FC3/c
Heely, Leo Shinn	S2/c	Isham, Orville Adalbert	CGM
Heidt, Edward Joseph	F1/c	Isom, Luther James	S1/c
Heidt, Wesley John	MM2/c	Iversen, Earl Henry	S2/c
Helm, Merritt Cameron	S1/c	Iversen, Norman Kenneth	S2/c
Henderson, William Walter	S2/c	Ivey, Charles Andrew, Jr.	S2/c
Hendriksen, Frank	F2/c	Jackson, David Paul, Jr.	S1/c
Herring, James Junior	SM3/c	Jackson, Robert Woods	Y3/c
Herriott, Robert Asher, Jr.	S1/c	James, John Burditt	S1/c
Hess, Darrell Miller	FC1/c	Jante, Edwin Earl	Y3/c
Hessdorfer, Anthony Joseph	MM2/c	Janz, Clifford Thurston	LT
Hibbard, Robert Arnold	Bkr2/c	Jastrzemski, Edwin Charles	S1/c
Hickman, Arthur Lee	SM3/c	Jeans, Victor Lawrence	WT2/c
Hicks, Elmer Orville	GM3/c	Jeffries, Keith	Cox
Hicks, Ralph Ducard	Ptr2/c	Jenkins, Robert Henry Dawson	S2/c
Hill, Bartley T.	AOM3/c	Jensen, Keith Marlow	EM3/c
Hilton, Wilson Woodrow	GM1/c	Johann, Paul Frederick	GM3/c
Hindman, Frank Weaver	S1/c	Johnson, David Andrew, Jr.	OC2/c
Hodges, Garris Vada	F2/c	Johnson, Edmund Russell	MM1/c
Hoelscher, Lester John	HA1/c	Johnson, John Russell	RM3/c
Holland, Claude Herbert, Jr.	S2/c	Johnson, Samuel Earle	CDR (MC)
Hollenbach, Paul Zepp	S1/c	Johnson, Sterling Conrad	Cox
Hollis, Ralph	LTJG	Jolley, Berry Stanley	S2/c
Hollowell, George Sanford	Cox	Jones, Daniel Pugh	S2/c
Holmes, Lowell D.	F3/c	Jones, Edmon Ethmer	S1/c
Homer, Henry Vernon	S1/c	Jones, Floyd Baxter	MAtt2/c
Hopkins, Homer David	S1/c	Jones, Harry Cecil	GM3/c
Horn, Melvin Freeland	F3/c	Jones, Henry, Jr.	MAtt1/c
Horrell, Harvey Howard	SM1/c	Jones, Homer Loyd	S1/c
Horrocks, James William	CGM	Jones, Hugh, Jr.	S2/c
Hosler, John Emmet	S1/c	Jones, Leland	S1/c
House, Clem Raymond	CWT	Jones, Thomas Raymond	ENS
Housel, John James	SK1/c	Jones, Warren Allen	Y3/c
Howard, Elmo	S1/c	Jones, Willard Worth	S1/c
Howard, Rolan George	GM3/c	Jones, Woodrow Wilson	S2/c
Howe, Darrell Robert	S2/c	Joyce, Calvin Wilbur	F2/c
Howell, Leroy	Cox	Judd, Albert John	Cox
Hubbard, Haywood, Jr.	MAtt2/c	Kagarice, Harold Lee	CSK
Huffman, Clyde Franklin	F1/c	Kaiser, Robert Oscar	F1/c
Hughes, Bernard Thomas	Mus2/c	Katt, Eugene Louis	S2/c
Hughes, Lewis Burton, Jr.	S1/c	Keller, Paul Daniel	Mldr2/c
Hughey, James Clynton	S1/c	Kelley, James Dennis	SF3/c
Huie, Doyne Conley	HA1/c	Kellogg, Wilbur Leroy	F1/c
Hunter, Robert Frederick	S1/c	Kelly, Robert Lee	CEM
Huntington, Henry Louis	S2/c	Keniston, Donald Lee	S2/c
Hurd, Willard Hardy	MAtt2/c	Keniston, Kenneth Howard	F3/c
Hurley, Wendell Ray	Mus2/c	Kennard, Kenneth Frank	GM3/c
Huval, Ivan Joseph	S1/c	Kennington, Charles Cecil	S1/c
Huys, Arthur Albert	S1/c	Kennington, Milton Homer	S1/c
Hyde, William Hughes	Cox	Kent, Texas Thomas, Jr.	S2/c

Name	Rank/Rate	Name	Rank/Rate
Kidd, Isaac Campbell	RADM	Legros, Joseph McNeil	S1/c
Kiehn, Ronald William	MM2/c	Leigh, Malcolm Hedrick	GM3/c
Kieselbach, Charles Ermin	CM1/c	Leight, James Webster	S2/c
King, Gordon Blane	S1/c	Leopold, Robert Lawrence	ENS
King, Leander Cleveland	S1/c	Lesmeister, Steve Louie	EM3/c
King, Lewis Meyer	F1/c	Levar, Frank	CWT
King, Robert Nicholas, Jr.	ENS	Lewis, Wayne Alman	CM3/c
Kinney, Frederick William	Mus1/c	Lewison, Neil Stanley	FC3/c
Kinney, Gilbert Livingston	QM2/c	Lightfoot, Worth Ross	GM3/c
Kirchhoff, Wilbur Albert	S1/c	Linbo, Gordon Ellsworth	GM1/c
Kirkpatrick, Thomas L.	CAPT (CHC)	Lincoln, John William	F1/c
Klann, Edward	SC1/c	Lindsay, James Mitchell	SF2/c
Kline, Robert Edwin	GM2/c	Linton, George Edward	F2/c
Klopp, Francis Lawrence	GM3/c	Lipke, Clarence William	F2/c
Knight, Robert Wagner	EM3/c	Lipple, John Anthony	SF1/c
Knubel, William, Jr.	S1/c	Lisenby, Daniel Edward	S1/c
Koalajajck, Brosig	S1/c	Livers, Raymond Edward	S1/c
Koch, Walter Ernest	S1/c	Livers, Wayne Nicholas	F1/c
Koenekamp, Clarence Dietrich	F1/c	Lock, Douglas A.	S1/c
Koeppe, Herman Oliver	SC3/c	Lohman, Earl Wynn	S1/c
Konnick, Albert Joseph	CM2/c	Lomax, Frank Stuart	ENS
Kosec, John Anthony	BM2/c	Lomibao, Marciano	OS1/c
Kovar, Robert	S1/c	Long, Benjamin Franklin	CY
Kramb, James Henry	S1/c	Louastanau, Charles Bernard	S1/c
Kramb, John David	MSmth1/c	Lounsbury, Thomas William	S2/c
Kramer, Robert Rudolph	GM2/c	Loveland, Frank Crook	S2/c
Krause, Fred Joseph	S1/c	Lucey, Neil Jeremiah	S1/c
Krissman, Max Sam	S2/c	Luna, James Edward	S2/c
Kruger, Richard Warren	QM2/c	Luzier, Ernest Burton	MM2/c
Kruppa, Adolph Louis	S1/c	Lynch, Emmett Isaac	S2/c
Kukuk, Howard Helgi	S1/c	Lynch, James Robert, Jr.	GM3/c
Kula, Stanley	SC3/c	Lynch, William Joseph, Jr.	S1/c
Kusie, Donald Joseph	RM3/c	Maddox, Raymond Dudley	CEM
Laderach, Robert Paul	FC2/c	Madrid, Arthur John	S2/c
La France, William Richard	S1/c	Mafnas, Francisco Reyes	MAtt2/c
Lake, John Ervin, Jr.	PAYCLK	Magee, Gerald James	SK3/c
Lakin, Donald Lapier	S1/c	Malecki, Frank Edward	CY
Lakin, Joseph Jordan	S1/c	Malinowski, John Stanley	SM3/c
La Mar, Ralph B.	FC3/c	Malson, Harry Lynn	SK3/c
Lamb, George Samuel	CSF	Manion, Edward Paul	S2/c
Landman, Henry	AMM2/c	Manlove, Arthur Cleon	ELECT
Landry, James Joseph, Jr.	Bkr2/c	Mann, William Edward	GM3/c
Lane, Edward Wallace	Cox	Manning, Leroy	S2/c
Lane, Mancel Curtis	S1/c	Manske, Robert Francis	Y2/c
Lange, Richard Charles	S1/c	Marinich, Steve Matt	Cox
Langenwalter, Orville John	SK2/c	Maris, Elwood Henry	S1/c
Lanouette, Henry John	Cox	Marling, Joseph Henry	S2/c
Larson, Leonard Carl	F3/c	Marlow, Urban Herschel	Cox
La Salle, Willard Dale	S1/c	Marsh, Benjamin Raymond, Jr.	ENS
Lattin, Bleecker	RM3/c	Marsh, William Arthur	S1/c
Lee, Carroll Volney, Jr.	S1/c	Marshall, Thomas Donald	S2/c
Lee, Henry Lloyd	S1/c	Martin, Hugh Lee	Y3/c
Leedy, David Alonzo	FC2/c	Martin, James Albert	BM1/c
Leggett, John Goldie	BM2/c	Martin, James Orrwell	S2/c

Name	Rank/Rate	Name	Rank/Rate
Martin, Luster Lee	F3/c	Morris, Owen Newton	S1/c
Mason, Byron Dalley	S2/c	Morrison, Earl LeRoy	S1/c
Mastel, Clyde Harold	S2/c	Morse, Edward Charles	S2/c
Masters, Dayton Monroe	GM3/c	Morse, Francis Jerome	BM1/c
Masterson, Cleburne Earl Carl	PhM1/c	Morse, George Robert	S2/c
Mathein, Harold Richard	Bmkr2/c	Morse, Norman Roy	WT2/c
Mathison, Charles Harris	S1/c	Moss, Tommy Lee	MAtt2/c
Matney, Vernon Merferd	F1/c	Moulton, Gordon Eddy	F1/c
Mattox, James Durant	AM3/c	Muncy, Claude	MM2/c
May, Louis Eugene	SC2/c	Murdock, Charles Luther	WT1/c
Maybee, George Frederick	RM2/c	Murdock, Melvin Elijah	WT2/c
Mayfield, Lester Ellsworth	F1/c	Murphy, James Joseph	S1/c
Mayo, Rex Haywood	EM2/c	Murphy, James Palmer	F3/c
McCary, William Moore	Mus2/c	Murphy, Jessie Huell	S1/c
McClafferty, John Charles	BM2/c	Murphy, Thomas J., Jr.	SK1/c
McClung, Harvey Manford	ENS	Myers, James Gernie	SK1/c
McFaddin, Lawrence James, Jr.	Y2/c	Naasz, Erwin H.	SF2/c
McGlasson, Joe Otis	GM3/c	Nadel, Alexander Joseph	Mus2/c
McGrady, Samme Willie Genes	MAtt1/c	Nations, James Garland	FC2/c
McGuire, Francis Raymond	SK2/c	Naylor, "J" "D"	SM2/c
McHughes, John Breckenridge	CWT	Neal, Tom Dick	S1/c
McIntosh, Harry George	S1/c	Necessary, Charles Raymond	S1/c
McKinnie, Russell	MAtt2/c	Neipp, Paul	S2/c
McKosky, Michael Martin	S1/c	Nelsen, George	SC2/c
McPherson, John Blair	S1/c	Nelson, Harl Coplin	S1/c
Means, Louis	MAtt1/c	Nelson, Henry Clarence	BM1/c
Meares, John Morgan	S2/c	Nelson, Lawrence Adolphus	CTC
Menefee, James Austin	S1/c	Nelson, Richard Eugene	F3/c
Meno, Vicente Gogue	MAtt2/c	Nichols, Alfred Rose	S1/c
Menzenski, Stanley Paul	Cox	Nichols, Bethel Allan	S1/c
Merrill, Howard Deal	ENS	Nichols, Clifford Leroy	TC1/c
Miles, Oscar Wright	S1/c	Nichols, Louis Duffie	S2/c
Miller, Chester John	F2/c	Nicholson, Glen Eldon	EM3/c
Miller, Doyle Allen	Cox	Nicholson, Hancel Grant	S1/c
Miller, Forrest Newton	CEM	Nides, Thomas James	EM1/c
Miller, George Stanley	S1/c	Nielsen, Floyd Theodore	CM3/c
Miller, Jessie Zimmer	S1/c	Noonan, Robert Harold	S1/c
Miller, John David	S1/c	Nowosacki, Theodore Lucian	ENS
Miller, William Oscar	SM3/c	Nusser, Raymond Alfred	GM3/c
Milligan, Weldon Harvey	S1/c	Nye, Frank Erskine	S1/c
Mims, Robert Lang	S1/c	O'Bryan, George David	FC3/c
Mlinar, Joseph	Cox	O'Bryan, Joseph Benjamin	FC3/c
Molpus, Richard Preston	CMsmth	Ochoski, Henry Francis	GM2/c
Monroe, Donald	MAtt2/c	Off, Virgil Simon	S1/c
Montgomery, Robert Eugene	S2/c	Ogle, Victor Willard	S2/c
Moody, Robert Edward	S1/c	Oglesby, Lonnie Harris	S2/c
Moore, Douglas Carlton	S1/c	Oliver, Raymond Brown	S1/c
Moore, Fred Kenneth	S1/c	Olsen, Edward Kern	ENS
Moore, James Carlton	SF3/c	Olson, Glen Martin	S2/c
Moorhouse, William Starks	Mus2/c	O'Neall, Rex Eugene	S1/c
Moorman, Russell Lee	S2/c	O'Neill, William T., Jr.	ENS
Morgan, Wayne	S1/c	Orr, Dwight Jerome	S1/c
Morgareidge, James Orries	F2/c	Orzech, Stanislaus Joseph	S2/c
Morley, Eugene Elvis	F2/c	Osborne, Mervin Eugene	F1/c

Name	Rank/Rate	Name	Rank/Rate
Ostrander, Leland Grimstead	PhM3/c	Rawson, Clyde Jackson	BM1/c
Ott, Peter Dean	S1/c	Ray, Harry Joseph	BM2/c
Owen, Fredrick Halden	S2/c	Reaves, Casbie	S1/c
Owens, Richard Allen	SK2/c	Rector, Clay Cooper	SK3/c
Owsley, Thomas Lee	SC2/c	Reece, John Jeffris	S2/c
Pace, Amos Paul	BM1/c	Reed, James Buchanan, Jr.	SK1/c
Parkes, Harry Edward	BM1/c	Reed, Ray Ellison	S2/c
Paroli, Peter John	Bkr3/c	Register, Paul James	LCDR
Patterson, Harold Lemuel	S1/c	Restivo, Jack Martin	Y2/c
Patterson, Richard, Jr.	SF3/c	Reynolds, Earl Arthur	S2/c
Paulmand, Hilery	OS2/c	Reynolds, Jack Franklin	S1/c
Pavini, Bruno	S1/c	Rhodes, Birb Richard	F2/c
Pawlowski, Raymond Paul	S1/c	Rhodes, Mark Alexander	S1/c
Pearce, Alonzo, Jr.	S1/c	Rice, William Albert	S2/c
Pearson, Norman Cecil	S2/c	Rich, Claude Edward	S1/c
Pearson, Robert Stanley	F2/c	Richar, Raymond Lyle	S1/c
Peavey, William Howard	QM2/c	Richardson, Warren John	Cox
Peckham, Howard William	F2/c	Richison, Fred Louis	GM3/c
Peery, Max Valdyne	S2/c	Richter, Albert Wallace	Cox
Peleschak, Michael	S1/c	Rico, Guadalupe Augustine	S1/c
Peltier, John Arthur	EM3/c	Riddell, Eugene Edward	S1/c
Penton, Howard Lee	S1/c	Riganti, Fred	SF3/c
Perkins, George Ernest	F1/c	Riggins, Gerald Herald	S1/c
Peterson, Albert H., Jr.	FC3/c	Rivera, Francisco Upingoo	MAtt2/c
Peterson, Elroy Vernon	FC2/c	Roberts, Dwight Fisk	F1/c
Peterson, Hardy Wilbur	FC3/c	Roberts, Kenneth Franklin	BM2/c
Peterson, Roscoe Earl	S2/c	Roberts, McClellan Taylor	CPhM
Pettit, Charles Ross	CRM	Roberts, Walter Scott, Jr.	RM1/c
Petyak, John Joseph	S1/c	Roberts, Wilburn Carle	Bkr3/c
Phelps, George Edward	S1/c	Roberts, William Francis	S2/c
Philbin, James Richard	S1/c	Robertson, Edgar, Jr.	MAtt3/c
Pike, Harvey Lee	EM3/c	Robertson, James Milton	MM1/c
Pike, Lewis Jackson	S1/c	Robinson, Harold Thomas	S2/c
Pinkham, Albert Wesley	S2/c	Robinson, James William	S2/c
Pitcher, Walter Giles	GM1/c	Robinson, John James	EM1/c
Pool, Elmer Leo	S1/c	Robinson, Robert Warren	PhM3/c
Poole, Ralph Ernest	S1/c	Roby, Raymond Arthur	S1/c
Post, Darrell Albert	CMM	Rodgers, John Dayton	S1/c
Povesko, George	S1/c	Roehm, Harry Turner	MM2/c
Powell, Thomas George	S1/c	Rogers, Thomas Spurgeon	CWT
Presson, Wayne Harold	S1/c	Romano, Simon	OC1/c
Price, Arland Earl	RM2/c	Rombalski, Donald Roger	S2/c
Pritchett, Robert Leo, Jr.	S1/c	Romero, Vladimir Mendoza	S1/c
Puckett, Edwin Lester	SK3/c	Root, Melvin L.	S1/c
Pugh, John, Jr.	SF3/c	Rose, Chester Clay	BM1/c
Putnam, Avis Boyd	SC3/c	Rosenberry, Orval Alert	SF2/c
Puzio, Edward	S1/c	Ross, Deane Lundy	S2/c
Quarto, Mike Joseph	S1/c	Ross, William Frazer	GM3/c
Quinata, Jose Sanches	MAtt2/c	Rowe, Eugene Joseph	S1/c
Radford, Neal Jason	Mus2/c	Rowell, Frank Malcolm	S2/c
Rasmussen, Arthur Severin	CM1/c	Royals, William Nicholas	F1/c
Rasmusson, George Vernon	F3/c	Royer, Howard Dale	GM3/c
Ratkovich, William	WT1/c	Rozar, John Frank	WT2/c
Rawhouser, Glen Donald	F3/c	Rozmus, Joseph Stanley	S1/c

Name	Rank/Rate	Name	Rank/Rate
Ruddock, Cecil Roy	S1/c	Simpson, Albert Eugene	S1/c
Ruggerio, William	FC3/c	Skeen, Harvey Leroy	S2/c
Runckel, Robert Gleason	Bug1/c	Skiles, Charley Jackson, Jr.	S2/c
Runiak, Nicholas	S1/c	Skiles, Eugene	S2/c
Rush, Robert Perry	S1/c	Sletto, Earl Clifton	MM1/c
Rusher, Orville Lester	MM1/c	Smalley, Jack "G"	S1/c
Ruskey, Joseph John	CBM	Smart, George David	Cox
Rutkowski, John Peter	S1/c	Smestad, Halge Hojem	RM2/c
Ruttan, Dale Andrew	EM3/c	Smith, Albert Joseph	LTJG
Sampson, Sherley Rolland	RM3/c	Smith, Earl, Jr.	S1/c
Sandall, Merrill Keith	SF3/c	Smith, Earl Walter	FC3/c
Sanders, Eugene Thomas	ENS	Smith, Edward	GM3/c
Sanderson, James Harvey	Mus2/c	Smith, Harry	S2/c
Sanford, Thomas Steger	F3/c	Smith, John "A"	SF3/c
Santos, Filomeno	OC2/c	Smith, John Edward	S1/c
Sather, William Ford	PMkr1/c	Smith, Luther Kent	S1/c
Savage, Walter Samuel, Jr.	ENS	Smith, Mack Lawrence	S1/c
Savin, Tom	RM2/c	Smith, Marvin Ray	S1/c
Savinski, Michael	S1/c	Smith, Orville Stanley	ENS
Schdowski, Joseph	S1/c	Smith, Walter Tharnel	MAtt1/c
Scheuerlein, George Albert	GM3/c	Soens, Harold Mathias	SC1/c
Schiller, Ernest	S2/c	Sooter, James F.	RM3/c
Schlund, Elmer Pershing	MM1/c	Sorensen, Holger Earl	S1/c
Schmidt, Vernon Joseph	S1/c	South, Charles Braxter	S1/c
Schrank, Harold Arthur	Bkr1/c	Spence, Merle Joe	S1/c
Schroeder, Henry	BM1/c	Spotz, Maurice Edwin	F1/c
Schuman, Herman Lincoln	SK1/c	Spreeman, Robert Lawrence	GM3/c
Schurr, John	EM2/c	Springer, Charles Harold	S2/c
Scilley, Harold Hugh	SF2/c	Stallings, Kermit Braxton	F1/c
Scott, "A" "J"	S2/c	Starkovich, Charles	EM3/c
Scruggs, Jack Leo	Mus2/c	Starkovich, Joseph, Jr.	F2/c
Seaman, Russell Otto	F1/c	Staudt, Alfred Parker	F3/c
Seeley, William Eugene	S1/c	Steffan, Joseph Philip	BM2/c
Sevier, Charles Clifton	S1/c	Steigleder, Lester L.	Cox
Shannon, William Alfred	S1/c	Steinhoff, Lloyd Delroy	S1/c
Sharbaugh, Harry Robert	GM3/c	Stephens, Woodrow Wilson	EM1/c
Sharon, Lewis Purdie	F1/c	Stephenson, Hugh Donald	S1/c
Shaw, Clyde Donald	S1/c	Stevens, Jack Hazelip	S1/c
Shaw, Robert K.	Mus2/c	Stevens, Theodore "R"	AMM2/c
Sheffer, George Robert	S1/c	Stewart, Thomas Lester	SC3/c
Sherrill, Warren Joseph	Y2/c	Stillings, Gerald Fay	F2/c
Sherven, Richard Stanton	EM3/c	Stockman, Harold William	FC3/c
Shiffman, Harold Ely	RM3/c	Stockton, Louis Alton	S2/c
Shiley, Paul Eugene	S1/c	Stoodard, William Edison	S1/c
Shimer, Melvin Irvin	S1/c	Stopyra, Julian John	RM3/c
Shive, Malcolm Holman	RM3/c	Storm, Laun Lee	Y1/c
Shiveley, Benjamin Franklin	F1/c	Strange, Charles Orval	F2/c
Shores, Irland, Jr.	S1/c	Stratton, John Raymond	S1/c
Shugart, Marvin John	S1/c	Suggs, William Alfred	S1/c
Sibley, Delmar Dale	S1/c	Sulser, Frederick Franklin	GM3/c
Sidders, Russell Lewis	S1/c	Summers, Glen Allen	Y1/c
Sidell, John Henry	GM3/c	Summers, Harold Edgar	SM2/c
Silvey, Jesse	MM2/c	Sumner, Oren	S2/c
Simon, Walter Hamilton	S1/c	Sutton, Clyde Westly	CCStd

Name	Rank/Rate	Name	Rank/Rate
Sutton, George Woodrow	SK1/c	Wallenstien, Richard Henry	S1/c
Swisher, Charles Elijah	S1/c	Walters, Clarence Arthur	S2/c
Symonette, Henry	OC1/c	Walters, William Spurgeon, Jr.	FC3/c
Tambolleo, Victor Charles	SF3/c	Walther, Edward Alfred	FC3/c
Tanner, Russell Allen	GM3/c	Walton, Alva Dowding	Y3/c
Tapie, Edward Casamiro	MM2/c	Ward, Albert Lewis	S1/c
Tapp, Lambert Ray	GM3/c	Ward, William E.	Cox
Targ, John	CWT	Watkins, Lenvil Leo	F2/c
Taylor, Aaron Gust	MAtt1/c	Watson, William Lafayette	F3/c
Taylor, Charles Benton	EM3/c	Watts, Sherman M.	HA1/c
Taylor, Harry Theodore	GM2/c	Watts, Victor E.	GM3/c
Taylor, Robert Denzil	Cox	Weaver, Richard Walter	S1/c
Teeling, Charles Madison	CPrtr	Webster, Harold Dwayne	S2/c
Teer, Allen Ray	EM1/c	Weeden, Carl Alfred	ENS
Tennell, Raymond Clifford	S1/c	Weidell, William Peter	S2/c
Terrell, John Raymond	F2/c	Weller, Ludwig Fredrick	CSK
Theiller, Rudolph	S1/c	Wells, Floyd Arthur	RM2/c
Thomas, Houston O'Neal	Cox	Wells, Harvey Anthony	SF2/c
Thomas, Randall James	S1/c	Wells, Raymond Virgil, Jr.	S1/c
Thomas, Stanley Horace	F3/c	Wells, William Bennett	S1/c
Thomas, Vincent Duron	Cox	West, Broadus Franklin	S1/c
Thompson, Charles Leroy	S1/c	West, Webster Paul	S1/c
Thompson, Irven	S1/c	Westcott, William Percy, Jr.	S1/c
Thompson, Robert Gary	SC1/c	Westerfield, Ivan Ayres	S1/c
Thorman, John Christopher	EM2/c	Westin, Donald Vern	F3/c
Thornton, George Haywood	GM3/c	Westlund, Fred Edwin	BM2/c
Tiner, Robert Reaves	F2/c	Whitaker, John William, Jr.	S1/c
Tisdale, William Esley	CWT	Whitcomb, Cecil Eugene	EM3/c
Triplett, Thomas Edgar	S1/c	White, Charles William	Mus2/c
Trovato, Tom	S1/c	White, James Clifton	F1/c
Tucker, Raymond Edward	Cox	White, Vernon Russell	S1/c
Tuntland, Earl Eugene	S1/c	White, Volmer Dowin	S1/c
Turnipseed, John Morgan	F3/c	Whitehead, Ulmont Irving, Jr.	ENS
Tussey, Lloyd Harold	EM3/c	Whitlock, Paul Morgan	S2/c
Tyson, Robert	FC3/c	Whitson, Ernest Hubert, Jr.	Mus2/c
Uhrenholdt, Andrew Curtis	ENS	Whitt, William Byron	GM3/c
Valente, Richard Dominic	GM3/c	Whittemore, Andrew Tiny	MAtt2/c
Van Atta, Garland Wade	MM1/c	Wick, Everett Morris	FC3/c
Van Horn, James Randolf	S2/c	Wiclund, John Joseph	S1/c
Van Valkenburgh, Franklin	CAPT	Wilcox, Arnold Alfred	QM2/c
Varchol, Brinley	GM2/c	Will, Joseph William	S2/c
Vaughan, William Frank	PhM2/c	Willette, Laddie James	S2/c
Veeder, Gordon Elliott	S2/c	Williams, Adrian Delton	S1/c
Velia, Galen Steve	SM3/c	Williams, Clyde Richard	Mus2/c
Vieira, Alvaro Everett	S2/c	Williams, George Washington	S1/c
Vojta, Walter Arnold	S1/c	Williams, Jack Herman	RM3/c
Vosti, Anthony August	GM3/c	Williams, Laurence "A"	ENS
Wagner, Mearl James	SC2/c	Williamson, Randolph R., Jr.	MAtt1/c
Wainwright, Silas Alonzo	PhM1/c	Williamson, William Dean	RM2/c
Wait, Wayland Le Moyne	S1/c	Willis, Robert Kenneth, Jr.	S1/c
Walker, Bill	S1/c	Wilson, Bernard Martin	RM3/c
Wallace, Houston Oliver	WT1/c	Wilson, Comer A.	CBM
Wallace, James Frank	S1/c	Wilson, Haurschel Woodrow	F2/c
Wallace, Ralph Leroy	F3/c	Wilson, John James	S1/c

Name	Rank/Rate	Name	Rank/Rate
Wilson, Neil Mataweny	CHMACH	Fincher, Dexter Wilson	Sgt
Wilson, Ray Milo	RM3/c	Finley, Woodrow Wilson	PFC
Wimberley, Paul Edwin	GM3/c	Fitzgerald, Kent Blake	Pvt
Winter, Edward	MACH	Fleetwood, Donald Eugene	PFC
Wojtkiewicz, Frank Peter	CMM	Fox, Daniel Russell	LCOL
Wolf, George Alexanderson, Jr.	ENS	Griffin, Lawrence John	PFC
Wood, Harold Baker	BM2/c	Hamel, Don Edgar	FldMus
Wood, Horace Van	S1/c	Harmon, William Daniel	PFC
Wood, Roy Eugene	F1/c	Herrick, Paul Edward	Pvt
Woods, Vernon Wesley	S1/c	Holzworth, Walter	MGySgt
Woods, William Anthony	S2/c	Hope, Harold Wyatt	Pvt
Woodward, Ardenne Allen	MM2/c	Hudnall, Robert Chilton	PFC
Woody, Harlan Fred	S2/c	Huff, Robert Glenn	Pvt
Woolf, Norman Bragg	CWT	Hughes, Marvin Austin	Pvt
Wright, Edward Henry	S2/c	Hultman, Donald Standly	PFC
Wyckoff, Robert LeRoy	F1/c	Hux, Leslie Creade	PFC
Yates, Elmer Elias	SC3/c	Jerrison, Donald Dearborn	Cpl
Yeats, Charles, Jr.	Cox	Jones, Quincy Eugene	PFC
Yomine, Frank Peter	F2/c	Kalinowski, Henry	Pvt
Young, Eric Read	ENS	Keen, Billy Mack	Pvt
Young, Glendale Rex	S1/c	Krahn, James Albert	PFC
Young, Jay Wesley	S1/c	Lindsay, James Ernest	PFC
Young, Vivian Louis	WT1/c	Lovshin, William Joseph	PFC
Zeiler, John Virgel	S1/c	McCarrens, James Francis	Cpl
Ziembicki, Steve Anthony	S1/c	Minear, Richard John, Jr.	PFC
Zimmerman, Fred	Cox	Mostek, Francis Clayton	PFC
Zimmerman, Loyd McDonald	S2/c	Nolatubby, Henry Ellis	PFC
Zwarun, Michael, Jr.	S1/c	O'Brien, Joseph Bernard	PFC
		Patterson, Clarence Rankin, Jr.	PFC

Marine Corps Fatalities

Name	Rank/Rate		
Amundson, Leo Devere	Pvt	Pedrotti, Francis James	Pvt
Atchison, John Calvin	Pvt	Piasecki, Alexander Louis	Cpl
Bailey, George Richmond	PFC	Powell, Jack Speed	PFC
Baraga, Joseph	Sgt	Power, Abner Franklin	Pvt
Bartlett, David William	Cpl	Reinhold, Rudolph Herbert	Pvt
Beaton, Freddie	Pvt	Schneider, William Jacob	PFC
Belt, Everett Ray, Jr.	PFC	Scott, Crawford Edward	PFC
Black, James Theron	Pvt	Scott, George Harrison	PFC
Bond, Burnis Leroy	Cpl	Shive, Gordon Eshom	PFC
Borusky, Edwin Charles	Cpl	Simensen, Carleton Elliott	2LT
Brickley, Eugene	Pvt	Sniff, Jack Bertrand	FldMusCpl
Chandler, Donald Ross	Pvt	Stevenson, Frank Jake	PFC
Cole, Charles Warren	Sgt	Stovall, Richard P.	PFC
Davis, Virgil Denton	Pvt	Swiontek, Stanley Stephen	FldCk
Dawson, James B.	Pvt	Szabo, Theodore Stephen	Pvt
De Long, Frederick Eugene	Cpl	Webb, Carl Edward	PFC
Dreesbach, Herbert Allen	Pvt	Weier, Bernard Arthur	Pvt
Dunnam, Robert Wesley	Pvt	Whisler, Gilbert Henry	PFC
Durio, Russell J.	PFC	Windish, Robert James	Pvt
Duveene, John	1stSgt	Windle, Robert England	PFC
Erskine, Robert Charles	PFC	Wittenberg, Russell Duane	Pvt
Evans, Donald Delton	Pvt		
Fincher, Allen Bradley	AsstCook		

Navy Survivors

Name	Rank/Rate
Amacher, Charles Andrew	S1/c

Name	Rank/Rate	Name	Rank/Rate
Anderson, John Delmar	BM2/c	Czarnecki, Anthony Francis	MM1/c
Bagby, Walter Franklin	SF3/c	Daniel, Alfred Eugene	GM1/c
Ball, Masten "A"	F1/c	Dare, James Ashton	ENS
Ballard, Galen Owen	F1/c	Davis, Carl Everette	GM3/c
Barth, DeWayne	BM1/c	Davis, Elvin Clay	S1/c
Bass, Edward Forester	F2/c	Davison, Henry Donald	ENS
Baumeister, William Nicolas	ACMM	Dean, William Ernest	BM1/c
Becker, Harvey Herman	GM2/c	Dearing, John Davis	WT2/c
Bemis, Edwin Wallace	S1/c	Decker, Deward	Cox
Bennett, Earl Dean	GM3/c	Deserano, Joseph Charles	Mldr1/c
Berdollt, George Anthony	FC3/c	Dickerson, William Charles A.	RM2/c
Bird, Leroy Alexander	CTC	Dickinson, Merle Edward	GM3/c
Birdsell, Estelle	MM1/c	Dobson, Clarence Junior	GM3/c
Birtwell, Daniel Thomas, Jr.	LCDR	Doherty, John Andrew	CGM
Bodey, Edward Raymond	BM2/c	Donegan, Timothy Albert	Prtr1/c
Bowen, Andrew Jackson, Jr.	CMM	Doucett, John Walter	GM3/c
Bradshaw, Harry Frederick	S1/c	Duncan, Henry Barnett	FC3/c
Braydis, John	S1/c	Duncan, Tommie Wilson	BM2/c
Brown, Gene Rachar	S1/c	Edmondson, Kenneth Eugene	Cox
Browning, Robert James	S2/c	Egan, Paul Howard	FC3/c
Bruce, John Franklin	GM3/c	Elkins, Merle	S1/c
Bruner, Lauren Fay	F3/c	Elliott, Lawrence Emmitt	MM1/c
Bruns, Martin Benjamin	Y2/c	Ellis, George William	SC1/c
Buehl, Herbert Vincent	F3/c	Enos, James R.	S/2c
Burcham, Jimmie Charles	S1/c	Eskew, Weldon Virgil	MM1/c
Burk, Leland Howard	GM3/c	Evans, John Willard	S1/c
Bush, William Jack	ENS	Eversole, Elmer Everett	S1/c
Byard, Ralph Duncan	CCStd	Eyman, Lawrence Oliver	S1/c
Campbell, Frank Monroe	ENS	Falge, Francis Marion	LT
Campbell, George Kilgore	CTC	Farquhar, Lawrence Albert	FC2/c
Carlson, Roy Christian	S2/c	Faulkner, Paul Harding	S1/c
Carson, Carl Malvin	S1/c	Fay, Lawrence Edward	GM3/c
Chandler, Edwin Ray	S1/c	Felton, Nathaniel	MAtt1/c
Chapman, Noel "B"	S2/c	Field, Jennings Pemble	ENS
Chappell, William Robert	S1/c	Finger, William Ralph	SM1/c
Christiansen, Harlan Carl	S2/c	Fitch, Harry Lionel	ENS
Chung-Hoon, Gordon Patea	LT	Flanagan, Guy Spalding, Jr.	ENS
Clouser, Marion Howard	GM1/c	Flannery, Wendell Lee	Cox
Coburn, George W.	S1/c	Flory, Dale Frederick	WT2/c
Coker, Charles Walter	LT	Forbis, James Leamon	Cox
Combs, Clyde Jefferson	S1/c	Foster, James Park, Jr.	S1/c
Condon, Daniel Jerome	LTJG	Fowler, Ralph Edward	BM1/c
Conter, Louis A.	QM3/c	Fowler, Robert Dale	S2/c
Cook, Lonnie David	S1/c	Frazier, Glen	CGM
Coole, Lloyd Edward	S1/c	Frye, Everett Ellsworth	S1/c
Coplin, Norman Walter	S1/c	Fuqua, Samuel Glenn	LCDR
Corbin, Ralph Victor Leon	S1/c	Gallagher, William Fred	CEM
Cornelius, Lyle Richard	S2/c	Garfield, Jerome Harold	ENS
Cosby, Ray Charles	S1/c	Gaskins, Walter James	S1/c
Cox, John Madison, Jr.	LCDR	Gaut, Harold Woodson	S1/c
Cozad, Francis Burnard	S2/c	Geiselman, Ellis Hugh	CDR
Crothers, Lee Raymond	BM1/c	Genest, Dayton Merrill	S1/c
Cruz, Henry Mesa	MAtt1/c	Gibbin, A.	SC1/c
Culp, Donald Arthur	S2/c	Gibson, Claude Clenton	S1/c

Name	Rank/Rate	Name	Rank/Rate
Gilbert, Arthur Barnes	S1/c	Johnston, Brooxey J., Jr	GM3/c
Gillem, Charles "M"	S1/c	Jones, Hubert Hayes	CWT
Gillenwater, Charles Ervin	S1/c	Karb, Joe Frank	CWT
Gillespie, David William	S1/c	Keener, "C" "H"	GM3/c
Glenn, Richard Clyde	ENS	Keffer, Carl Emerson	S1/c
Goldsberry, William Joseph	S1/c	Kelley, Bruce Draper	LCDR
Gordon, Donald Eugene	GM2/c	Kirk, Guy Duane	S1/c
Goshen, William Eugene	S1/c	Kissinger, Walter Marlond	MM1/c
Grabowsky, Leon	ENS	Kuhn, Harold Joseph	S1/c
Graham, Donald Alexander	AMM1/c	Kurtz, Stanley Robert	S1/c
Gray, James Victor	S1/c	Lancaster, James Daniel	S1/c
Green, Clay Douglas, Jr.	S1/c	Landreth, Ralph William	GM2/c
Green, James William	GM3/c	Lane, Glenn Harvey	RM3/c
Grim, George Edwin	GM1/c	Langdell, Joseph Kopcho	ENS
Guerin, Charles William, Jr.	S1/c	Lawrence, Thomas Hurshel	S1/c
Guna, Andrew	BM1/c	Lawson, James Lenox	GM3/c
Haerling, Howard Gustave	BM1/c	Lawson, Leonard George	S1/c
Haerry, Raymond John	Cox	Leighton, Lindsay Ray	WT1/c
Hamilton, Elsworth Fonzo	ACMM	Lencses, Louie	GM3/c
Hamilton, James Edward	S1/c	Lennig, George Birmingham	ENS
Hand, Vernon	S1/c	Leopard, Curtis James	BM1/c
Hargis, Paul Eugene	Y3/c	Lewis, William Edward	LTJG (MC)
Harr, Oliver Virgil	MM1/c	Lindsey, Jack Lawton	S1/c
Harrell, Allen Boyd	S1/c	Lott, Russell Ardell	S1/c
Harris, Henry Sherman	S1/c	Lukasavitz, Steven J.	S1/c
Harris, John David	S1/c	MacQueen, Donald Elmer	ENS
Hart, James Willard	F1/c	Mainwaring, Billy Braun	F3/c
Hartland, Alfred Jack	S1/c	Malaski, John	S1/c
Hauff, Richard	GM3/c	Malcolm, Everett Allen	ENS
Hein, Douglas	ENS	Mancuso, Joseph	S1/c
Heinz, Robert Henry	S1/c	Mann, Charles Clark	LT
Hendon, Robert Marvin	CGM	Marcum, Harry Bedford	CEM
Henry, John William	ENS	Marks, Edward Joseph	Cox
Hetrick, Clarendon Robert	S1/c	Masterson, Kleber Sandlin	LT
Hill, Robert Howe	Y2/c	Mattlage, Herbert	ENS
Hinton, John Harold	CSM	McCarron, John Harry	GM2/c
Hjelle, Clarence Otto	S2/c	McDonald, Don Erwin	S1/c
Holland, Fred McKenzie	S1/c	McFall, Charles William	GM1/c
Holmes, Roy Willard	S1/c	McKenna, Kenneth Kermit	SM1/c
Homann, Alfred James	LT	Melvin, Earle Thomas	CFC
Hooks, Woodrow Robert	S2/c	Metcalf, John Howard	S2/c
Hooper, Clifford Charles	RM2/c	Migliaccio, Thomas William	S2/c
Howatt, John Paul	ENS	Milhorn, Harvey Hollis	GM3/c
Hughes, James Curtis	S1/c	Miller, Jim Dick	ENS
Hull, Lester DeLance	S1/c	Millikin, Donald Hugh	S2/c
Hurst, Milton Thomas	AMM3/c	Mini, James Haile	LTJG
Hutchins, Edward Francis	LT	Mode, Stanley Robert	EM1/c
Huzar, Peter	WT1/c	Mommer, Rolland Earl	BM2/c
Hyslope, Charles Edward	F1/c	Murdock, Thomas Daniel	CY
Inselman, Donald	S1/c	Musick, Clay Henry	S1/c
Janikowski, Edward Joseph	Cox	Mylan, Jack Clement	SM2/c
Jeffers, Warren Edwin	S1/c	Nelson, Grady Lee, Jr.	S2/c
Johnson, Donald R.	S/1c		
Johnson, Neil Francis	Cox		

Name	Rank/Rate	Name	Rank/Rate
Newell, Bobby Earl	S2/c	Shew, Martin Luther	MM2/c
Nichols, John Edward	RM1/c	Simmons, Claude William, Jr.	S1/c
Niemara, Stanley Joseph	S1/c	Smith, Clyde Crockett	CEM
O'Brion, Edward Francis Joseph	S1/c	Smith, Harold Francis	BM2/c
Oliphant, Harold Eugene	GM3/c	Smith, Roscoe Bryant	GM3/c
Olsen, Vernon James	S1/c	Smith, William Hansford, Jr.	Cox
Osborne, William Daniel, Jr.	S1/c	Snow, Rutherford Hayes	WT1/c
Osmond, Robert Hugh	FC3/c	Stanborough, Thomas William, Jr.	S1/c
Osterberg, Vernon Magnus	ENS	Starks, Don Harrison	MM1/c
Otterman, Clarence Wayne	GM2/c	Stoffer, Bernald Henry	AMM1/c
Owen, Paul Ralph	S1/c	Stratton, Donald Gay	S1/c
Pablo, Patrocinio	OS1/c	Strong, Herbert Ronald	Cox
Pacitti, Louis John	GM3/c	Stuart, Jean Marcelle	S1/c
Parker, William Whiteford	S1/c	Sullivan, Aubry Randolph	Cox
Parson, C. M.	S1/c	Tagtmeyer, Laurence Ernest	CHGUN
Pecotte, Earl Henry	GM2/c	Tapp, Murray L.	S2/c
Peil, William John	BM2/c	Teslow, Stanley Merlin	GM2/c
Perry, Seth Harold	S2/c	Thomas, Steven Joseph	EM3/c
Phipps, Berwyn Robert	SF2/c	Thompson, Norman	MACH
Phraner, George Dewey	S2/c	Trantham, Glenwood Orris	BM1/c
Pittard, George Franklin	LT	Traviola, Vernon Alva	S2/c
Pitz, Robert Leo	S1/c	Tucker, Edward Daniel	BM2/c
Pollack, Francis Lee	SC3/c	Turner, Richard Newton, Jr.	S1/c
Port, Stanley Harrison, Jr.	Cox	Urbaniak, Edmund Leo	CARP
Posey, Ernest Mendum	MM1/c	Van Winkle, Edward Laverne	F2/c
Potts, Howard Kenton	Cox	Velia, Keith Lloyd	S2/c
Pousson, Alfred Andrew	S2/c	Vessels, James Allard	GM3/c
Probst, Richard William	S1/c	Vidal, Daniel	MAtt1/c
Puckett, Louis Alford	CDR (SC)	Vlach, Vincent James, Jr.	Y1/c
Purvis, William Robinson	F3/c	Von Spreckelsen, Charles A.	Ptr2/c
Quillin, Wallace Franklin	S1/c	Wagner, Robert Eugene	S1/c
Rahn, Carl Frederick, Jr.	S1/c	Wagner, Rudolph Louis	CBM
Rampley, John Watson	GM3/c	Walker, James Edward	QM2/c
Ramsdell, Millard Arthur	ENS	Walsh, Homan Leavell	ENS (SC)
Reid, Everett Owen	MM1/c	Ward, James Robert	S1/c
Reifert, Eldon Ray	Cox	Warriner, Kenneth T.	S/2c
Rider, Maurice David	BM1/c	Warriner, Russell Walter	S1/c
Ridley, William Hull	RM3/c	Washington, Joseph Henry	MAtt1/c
Riner, Earl William	GM3/c	Watson, Howard Lincoln	BM2/c
Robinson, Lewis Perrin	S1/c	Weaver, Richard Duncan	BM1/c
Rourke, John Paul	S1/c	Welch, Frank, Jr.	ENS
Rowley, Welton Dana	LCDR	Weller, Oree Cunningham	S2/c
Ruhlman, Fred Lee	LT	Wells, Harold Leroy	S1/c
Sadler, Jack Ivan	S2/c	Welter, Eddie Charles	S2/c
Sadowski, Joseph Steven	S1/c	Wentzlaff, Edward Louis	AOM2/c
Sanders, Elmer Larimore	GM1/c	West, Mark Austin	CMM
Sargent, Robert Isaac, Jr.	S2/c	Westbrook, Clinton Howard	S1/c
Schafer, Herman Leroy, Jr.	ENS	White, Thomas Arthur	BM2/c
Schubert, Anthony Robert	ENS	Williams, John Francis	GM3/c
Schumacher, William James	WT1/c	Wilson, Charles Leo	S1/c
Seeley, Robert Fox	S2/c	Wilson, Harold Green, Jr.	F2/c
Shaffer, John Jackson III	LT	Wise, James Louis	S1/c
Shawn, Ernest Maurice	GM3/c	Zadik, Edward Albert	S2/c
Shebak, Joseph	S1/c		

Marine Corps Survivors

Name	Rank/Rate
Baker, John McR.	Sgt
Brahm, Edward J.	PFC
Cabiness, Frank R.	PFC
Carter, Edward J.	PltSgt
Cory, James E.	PFC
Coursey, John P.	1LT
Crawford, Lamar S.	PFC
Earle, John H., Jr.	CAPT
Goodman, Kenneth D.	PFC
Hardy, Charles L.	Pvt
McCurdy, Russell J.	Pvt
Nightingale, Earl C.	Cpl
Shapley, Alan	MAJ
Soley, Michael	Cpl
Young, Donald G.	PFC

Fatalities

	Recovered	Entombed in Ship	Total
Officers	3	45	48
Enlisted	229	900	1,129
Totals	232	945	1,177

NOTE: Of the 229 enlisted men's bodies recovered from the *Arizona*, 124 could not be identified. Thus, there is no way to compile an accurate list of the names of the men entombed in the ship.

Survivors

	Wounded	Not Wounded	Total
Officers	7	44	51
Enlisted	33	253	286
Totals	40	297	337

The total muster roll for all components was 1,511. Of this total, a number of the unwounded survivors were either on leave or liberty at the time of the attack. Still others were on temporary assignment to other commands, such as the Fleet Camera Party, but still carried on the *Arizona*'s muster roll.

This list is largely the work of Lieutenant Commander Vincent James Vlach, U.S. Navy (Retired). In December 1941 he was a yeoman first class in the crew of the *Arizona*. He reported casualty lists as part of the *Arizona* detail, that is, those crew members still officially attached to the ship after 7 December. About forty years after the attack, Vlach obtained microfilm copies of the muster roll and the report of changes submitted by the ship's detail. In addition, he obtained records from several other sources to compile a record of the fatalities and survivors. He obtained information on the recovery of remains from Chief Boatswain's Mate Raymond D. Emory, who was serving in the light cruiser *Honolulu* at the time of the Japanese attack. Emory has done extensive research on the disposition of bodies to various grave sites, information not included in this book for reasons of space. In a few cases, the various source materials do not agree concerning the names of the *Arizona*'s crew at the time of the attack, so in those cases the spellings presented amount to likely guesses. This list, which comprises Lieutenant Commander Vlach's compilation from a variety of sources, represents his most accurate reconstruction of names.

Appendix D
A SAILOR'S LETTERS

Ardenne Allen "Bill" Woodward was born on 9 June 1921. He enlisted in the Navy at Richmond, Virginia, on 11 July 1938 for the remainder of his time as a minor; the expiration date of his enlistment was 8 June 1942, the day before his twenty-first birthday. Woodward was 5 feet 6 inches tall and weighed 129 pounds. He had brown eyes, auburn hair, and a ruddy complexion. On 10 November 1938, following recruit training at Norfolk, he reported to the USS *Arizona* for duty. In August 1939 he switched his rate from seaman second class to fireman third class. That December he was advanced in rate to fireman second class and the following August to fireman first class. In 1940 he married Miss Virginia Greenwood of Daly City, California; he had met her at the Long Beach Pike while on liberty from the *Arizona*. He spent considerable time with his new in-laws, who found him to be shy and polite—the result of his upbringing in the state of Virginia. Virginia Woodward was pregnant with the couple's first child when the ship left San Pedro on 1 July 1941 to steam to Pearl Harbor. That same day Bill Woodward became a machinist's mate second class. Following are condensed versions of ten letters he wrote to Virginia in Huntington Beach, California, in the ensuing months. The spelling and punctuation are from the originals. The paragraph indentations have been added to facilitate reading.

Far left: Machinist's Mate Bill Woodward. (Courtesy Karen Richardson)

Left: Virginia Woodward in 1941. (Courtesy Karen Richardson)

My Very Own Precious Darling Wife:

Darling I sure do wish I could hurry up and find out what the dope is, wheather I am a pappa or not. I am pretty sure I will be though by the time you receive this letter. Darling I do love you so terribly much and miss you more than you will ever know. Darling if I am a pappa now, then kiss the little fellow for me will you please darling.

Honey I have been doing quite a bit of scrubbing this morning. I have just finished scrubbing my cot, bedding bag, sea bag and three suits of dirty blues. No darling dont go getting excited. I didnt scrub the blues because I thought we were going back to the states. I have just had my rating badges sewed on the jumpers, and they are old badges that I have collected in the last three years and were pretty dirty. So instead of buying new ones I had them sewed on and scrubbed them blues and all. Then I will put them away somewhere until that happy day that we head for the States.

I should go to church this morning but I dont feel like listening to the guy preach, that kept me from getting 30 days emergency leave. Yes darling I could have gotten 30 days emergency leave if it had not been for the Chaplain; he said child birth is no emergency. Then he started telling me how much this navy means to us. I then told him that I didnt know how much the Navy meant to him but to me the Navy or anything connected with it doesnt mean even a little bit to me compared to my wife, who I love with all my heart and soul.

Precious I will be the happiest fellow in the whole wide world when I receive that message saying that you and the baby are doing fine. Darling I am the luckiest man in the whole world to have you, the sweetest girl in the whole wide world for the mother of _our_ child. Darling be sure to let me know what you decide to name (him or her). Darling all the fellows in the pump house have all ready told me what kind of cigars they want so I guess I will have to buy them.

Your Bill

My Very Own Precious Darling Wife:

Oh God darling I do so much wish that I would hurry up and receive a telegram saying that you and the baby are doing fine, then I would not worry so much.

We are going in Friday I hope because then we will get the mail that's there waiting for us and I think that I will probably have to walk half of the night on shore patrol playing nurse maid to a bunch of drunk sailors.

Dont look for me back before about the 20th of Dec because we dont have any idea that we will get back before, but we do _think_ we will get to spend Xmas in the

States with our love ones. That will probably be the only time that we will be back to the States until next June when the ship goes back for its yard overhaul and I get paid off. Thank god.

Well precious we will be drawing Second class pay this time I get paid. It will sure make me feel a lot better to be able to send you more money. I may get a little back money, I dont know.

Honey it is really hot out in this ungodly hole now. 122° at all times down in the Pump House. The Dr. makes us take salt tablets once every hour to keep us from getting sick from perspiring. The only thing any of us wear down there is a pair of shoes and a pair of under pants. And they're soaking wet by the time you have been there five minutes.

I forever remain your worshiping true loving husband,

Bill

Karen Joan Woodward was born on 30 July 1941.

Sept. 24, 1941
At Sea thinking only of you my sweet.

My Very Own Precious Darling Wife & Baby:

Oh my darling I will be so terribly glad when I can see you both. This is just hell having a daughter and not even having seen her or her mother since she was born. But I will be with you when the next one arrives my sweet, if I have to go through hell and high water to do it.

We are in a pretty bad storm right now. This old battle wagon is tossing like a chip on the ocean. There are an awful lot of these new recruits that are really seasick right now but it will take just you my sweet to cure what's wrong with me.

There was a plane off of the Nevada that cracked up this afternoon trying to land on the rough water. And the Enterprise an aircraft carrier has two planes that are lost somewhere; they didn't come in from this afternoons flight. All ships have their searchlights trained up in the sky now trying to guide them in if they are anywhere in seeing distance.

They have put me in charge of a watch underway now, so all I have to do at sea now is just sit around and see that the fellows keep the pumps running. Its a pretty soft job but not soft enough to even make me think about staying in this outfit. I would rather dig ditches all day and be with you at night than to do nothing all the time and be away from you my sweet.

Honey I am just wondering what Mother will say if we stay out on this coast when I get paid off instead of going back east. But really I had rather stay out here on this coast. And being as we have our own lives to live together the way we want to there it doesnt make much difference what anyone says or thinks. We will decide definitely what we want to do though my sweet when we get together again which wont be so terribly much longer I hope.

Your Bill

My Very Own Precious Darling Wife & Baby:

We are still at sea cruising around in circles and it is really rough weather. It's been storming something terrible ever since we have been out. I am awful sleepy. I had a 12–4 watch last night and then at 4:30 this morning we manned all battle stations just another of these make believe wars. I think we won because we are still floating anyhow.

Two destroyers ran together out here last night; there were a couple or three men killed on each I think. Honey I sure will be glad when Sunday comes so that we will get some mail on this big hunk of pig iron. I do so much want to hear from you as to how you and Karen are feeling and how you like our new house. Honey the happiest day of my life will be when I step off of that bus in H.B. [Huntington Beach] and head for 317-9th St.

The next best thing to seeing you is to get letters from you and pictures of you. Dont worry my sweet I am saving every one of them and I will bring them all home when I come. Ed [an *Arizona* crewman who lived in Hawaii with his wife] is still after me to go out to his house with him for dinner some day. I guess maybe I will go sometime or other I dont know when. I dont even like to leave the ship over in this godforsaken place. It might take a notion to head for the States and leave me out here and then they really would have to keep me in a padded cell.

Your Bill

Nov. 14, 1941
Somewhere at Sea

My Very Own Precious Darling Wife & Baby:

Darling I am not sure but I am afraid that this Japan situation is going to hold up our going back to the states for awhile. Oh my darling I do love you so terribly much and I would give any thing in the world to see you and to take you in my arms and tell you how terribly much I miss you.

We have been firing anti air craft battery and machine guns all day yesterday and today and we are going to fire night battle on the main battery (big guns) tomorrow night. And then we go in Monday we think and I should have some letters from you waiting for me I hope. Darling I have all ready picked out your Xmas present. No I wont tell you what it is. It has to be ordered from the States so I am going to wait untill around the 5th of Dec and order it then and have it sent directly to you from the store instead of from out here. [The Christmas gift was a camphor wood chest.]

Honey if Shirley [Virginia Woodward's younger sister] sleeps with you then tell her not to get to used to it because I am sure going to take her place when we get back and I have an idea that it would be very embarrassing for her to be around in sight or hearing distance dont you???

Boy is it hot down here now. I am sitting around with my shirt and pants off and the sweat is still streaming down my whole body. Maybe its just because I am writing to you that I am so hot. You know you effect me that way quite a bit.

Honey I sure wish we would make a peace treaty with the Japs then we could leave this place and be in the states for good. Honey have you gotten our daughter to drink orange juice yet? Maybe I should send her some pineapple juice goodness knows there enough of it out here. Honey I was going to get you a little breakfast cloth up at the Ships Store but it had "Honolulu the paradise of the Pacific" on it and I couldnt stand to have that big a lie in our house. So I will wait awhile and maybe I will run across one without that on it. Well sweetheart I must close and check upon my men on the pumps.

Your own
Bill

Nov. 18, 1941
Pearl Harbor

My Very Own Precious Darling Wife & Baby:

Darling I am terribly glad that you have had Karens pictures taken and I can hardly wait to get one of them. As you have no idea my precious how hard I want to see her and how I feel about not having seen her or <u>you</u> since she was born.

Honey I sure hope that they let me out of here as soon as my time is up instead of holding me in a couple of months or so. That would really be the last straw. I sure wish I could be with you thanksgiving day my sweet.

Honey they gave us two shots in the left arm today and mine's so sore I can hardly move it. One for typhoid and one for lock jaw. I think I had all most as leave have lock jaw. I sure am getting tired of this Dr. sticking a needle in me any time he wants to. In fact I am tired of all this bunch of bull——.

We are getting paid Wednesday. I will send you all I can in my next letter. Oh my sweet I will be so terribly happy when we are together again. It seems like years since I last held you in my arms.

We are still hoping and praying that we will get to go back before so very much longer. I sure hope that the president and that slant eye come to some sort of an agreement up in Washington. Maybe we will get to come back for good if they compromise or at least we will get back more often. But I hope I wont have to worry about it but six months more. Honey the time seems to pass so slow that I nearly go crazy waiting for the 8th of the month so I can check off another month as being one more less that we will be apart.

Your own—
Bill

Nov 22 1941
Pearl Harbor

My Very Own Precious Darling Wife & Baby:

We are still hoping and praying that we will leave for the states one of these days before long. I dont know wheather our hoping will do any good or not. But I am going to keep on hoping any way. Darling a couple of the fellows and I have just been sitting around telling each other about our loved ones. Neither of them are married but they have hopes. Oh my darling it does make me so happy to tell someone about you, how sweet you are and that you are the most precious and perfect wife in the whole wide world and how I love you and your family.

You know a fellow doesnt usually get the sweetest wife in the world and an awful sweet mother in law together as I did. And I am terribly proud of you both. Darling I do love you so terribly much and I can hardly wait untill I can sit around the house with you in my arms and getting in your way when you are trying to cook or something as I kiss you. It will be so heavenly when we do get together again.

Darling if I had more time to do and had the money I sure would bring you out here. But since I only have six months then I dont think it wise. Do you? Do you think you can stand another six months of this?

Well darling I must close for today. This letter will probably seem a little mixed up to you but its all because I love you so much that I don't even know how to tell you.

Your own—
Bill.

Nov 24, 1941
Pearl Harbor

My Very Own Precious Darling Wife & Baby:

I trust and pray that this will find you fine and I do hope that Karen's ear is well by this time.

Darling from now on be sure to address all my letters to "<u>M</u>" Div. instead of "B" as I have been transferred along with another machinists mate and eight firemen. They transferred us because they want some experienced men in the engine rooms. Darling I sure do envy Ellis [a man from Huntington Beach who was one of Woodward's new in-laws] his thirty days leave in the states but I sure dont envy him the two years he has to do now. When you ship over now you sign up for the duration of the national emergency, and god only knows how long that will be.

Darling I want you to myself every minute that I can possibly have you when I do get home. Of course I will share you with our little one but thats only natural. Do you think I am being hoggish? I hope not. I sure will be glad when the steamer comes in Wednesday. I should have at least three letters from you. And I will read each and every one of them six times.

Just your Own
Bill

My Very Own Precious Darling Wife & Baby:

Oh my precious angel I do want to see you and hold you in my arms so terribly much. I dont see how I can stand this being away from you much longer. I think only of you all day every day and I dream of you every night. Not <u>that</u> kind of dream all ways but any dream of you is the sweetest thing in the world to me next to seeing you and hearing from you.

Darling I am so anxious to receive the picture of Karen. I do so terribly much want to see her or at least a large picture of her. I have a place all fixed for her picture right by her mother's picture. They will be the sweetest pair in all the whole wide world. And your both twice as sweet as any picture could ever picture you. Well darling we go to sea again Friday for another week. Will be back in the 4th of Dec. I think. I only hope that the next time we go out we will be going to the states.

Honey I sure hope they pay us that back money and that $10.00 raise this pay day. They probably wont though as this Navy never does any thing you want them to do. Well darling I must close for tonight and go to bed and have one of <u>our</u> dreams. I only wish it could be real, but it will be forever one of these days.

Your own—

Bill

P.S. I love you truly with all my heart and all the rest of me and shall forever.
PSS Kiss Karen for her loving Dad.

My Very Own Precious Darling Wife & Baby:

Oh darling I do so much hope that we go back to the states before long. There is a lot of talk that we will and a lot that we wont. Myself I am afraid to say. I have built myself and you too up so many times for an awful let down that its just about to drive me out of my mind. So I am just praying and hoping and letting the rest of the men do the talking. It shouldnt be so very long before we know one way or the other and oh god how I hope its the right away.

Well darling our little one was four months old the 30th wasn't she? Darling I do hope that you at least have some idea of how badly I want to see you both. I know you aren't having a very good time yourself sitting around the house by yourself taking care of the little one.

It was so rough last night when I came up off of a 8–12 watch that I could hardly stay in my bunk. How is our little one my sweet? Fine I hope. Oh darling I can hardly wait to see her as I have dreamed and thought about her so terribly much. I would like to see her at least once before she gets old enough to walk.

After six more months my sweet you will never have to be alone for a whole day again. I will be terribly glad when we get back in because it will be that much closer to the 13th and I want to get my mail that I <u>should</u> have waiting for me there from you. I only received one letter this week. So I should make up for it next week. I have an 8–12 watch this time out and its really a killer. It seems as though you are on watch all the time. But it has its good points too such as making the time pass faster. Well darling I must close for today and go on watch.

Your own—
<u>Bill</u>

Bill Woodward, age twenty, was among the 1,177 men killed on board the *Arizona* on 7 December 1941. His widow later remarried, had a son with her second husband, and now lives in Oregon. These photos and letters are printed through the kindness of Karen Richardson, the daughter that Woodward never saw.

Appendix E

SHIP'S DATA

As of Commissioning, October 1916

General

Displacement
—at designer's waterline—31,400 tons
—full load—35,852 tons

Dimensions
—length overall—608 feet, 0 inches
—length at waterline—600 feet, 0 inches
—maximum beam—97 feet, 0½ inches
—mean draft—28 feet, 10 inches
—maximum draft at full load—29 feet, 8¼ inches

Anchors
Three 20,000-pound anchors (two to port, one to starboard); 180 fathoms of chain for the port anchors, 120 fathoms of chain for the starboard.

Personnel Complement
1,087 total (including 72 marines)—56 officers, 1,031 enlisted

Armament
—twelve 14-inch/45-caliber in four triple turrets
—twenty-two 5-inch/51-caliber in single mounts (ten removed prior to modernization)
—two 21-inch submerged torpedo tubes
—four 3-inch/50-caliber antiaircraft guns (soon after comissioning; four more were added in 1922, for a total of eight)
—four 3-pounder saluting cannons
—one 3-inch field piece for landing party
—four 1-pounder subcaliber guns, one on each turret
—two 1-pounder boat guns
—two .30-caliber machine guns

Armor

Total weight
8,422 tons

Belt
Frames 20 to 127: 13.5 inches from the top of the second deck to 2 feet, 4 inches below the normal waterline, then tapered uniformly to 8 inches at the bottom, which was 8 feet, 9¾ inches below the waterline. The total width of the armor belt was 17 feet, 4⅝ inches.
Frame 127 to the stern post: 13 inches from the top of the third deck to 2 feet, 4 inches below the normal waterline, then tapered as indicated for the forward part of the belt.

Ends
Forward at frame 20: 13 inches between the second deck and the second platform, tapering to 8 inches below the first platform for a total width of 17 feet, 4⅝ inches.
Aft at frame 127: 13 inches between the second and third decks.
Aftermost: athwartship from just abaft the rudder stock to the third deck, 13 inches down to 2 feet, 4 inches below the normal waterline, tapering uniformly to 8 inches at the bottom, 8 feet, 9¾ inches below the waterline.

Decks
A 120-pound (2.94-inch) protective deck covered the armor belt. The splinter deck was 40 pound (0.98 inches) on the flat and 60 pound (1.47 inches) on the slope behind the belt.

Uptakes
An octagonal tapering shield surrounded the stack uptakes between the second and upper decks. The dimensions were 15-inch sides, 12-inch quarter plates, and 9-inch ends.

Turrets
—face plates—18 inches
—sides—9 inches, increased to 10 inches near the front

—rear—9 inches
—top—5 inches
—exposed undersides—2 inches

Barbettes

13 inches above the second deck; 4½ inches between the second and third decks.

Conning Tower

16 inches on the sides; two 4-inch layers on top.

Conning Tower Tube

5-foot inside diameter from the third deck to the base of the conning tower; 16 inches above the second deck, 6 inches below.

Longitudinal Torpedo Bulkheads

Two continuous bulkheads on each side ran from frames 20 to 127: two layers of 60-pound (1.47-inch) special-treatment steel plating formed the outer bulkhead, normal structural steel for the inner bulkhead. The total width of protection on each side was 11 feet, 9 inches.

Transverse Torpedo Bulkheads

Four 40-pound (0.97-inch) special-treatment steel bulkheads ran outboard the outer longitudinal bulkhead at frames 23, 30, 90, and 120.

Machinery

Total Weight

2,399 tons

Boilers

twelve Babcock and Wilcox

Turbines

Eight Parsons type on four shafts: two high-pressure ahead and two high-pressure astern on the inboard shafts; two low-pressure ahead and astern and two cruising turbines on the outboard shafts. All shafts turned outboard.

Shaft Horsepower

34,000 maximum ahead

Maximum Speed

21 knots at 226 shaft rpm

Endurance

—3,240 nautical miles at 19 knots
—4,750 nautical miles at 15 knots
—6,950 nautical miles at 10 knots
(These figures assume that 95 percent of the fuel was usable.)

Generators

four 300-kilowatt, 240-volt direct-current turbo-generator sets

Propellers

four 4-bladed: 12 feet, 1½ inches in diameter

Rudder

one balanced, tapered type: 443 square feet in area

Fuel Oil Capacity

2,332 tons (694,830 gallons)

Reserve Boiler Feed Water

313.5 tons

Potable Water

187.5 tons

Following Modernization, March 1931

General

Displacement

—at designer's waterline—34,207 tons
—full load—37,654 tons

Dimensions

—length overall—608 feet, 0 inches
—length at waterline—600 feet, 0 inches
—maximum beam—106 feet, 2¾ inches
—mean draft at designer's waterline—28 feet, 10 inches
—maximum draft at full load—30 feet, 1¾ inches
—freeboard at bow—25 feet, 1¼ inches
—freeboard at stern—17 feet, 4¼ inches

The increase in beam resulted from the addition to the antitorpedo bulges on each side. These bulges were each 4 feet, 7⅛ inches wide.

Anchors

Same as before.

Stern Crane

—6,000 pounds lifting capacity

Boat Cranes

—25,687 pounds lifting capacity each

Personnel Complement

1,731 total—92 officers, 1,639 enlisted

Armament

—twelve 14-inch/45-caliber in four triple turrets
—twelve 5-inch/51-caliber in single mounts (two removed in 1940)
—eight 5-inch/25-caliber antiaircraft guns
—four 3-pounder saluting cannons

—four 1-pounder sub-caliber guns, one for each turret
—eight .50-caliber antiaircraft machine guns

Armor

The armor was the same as before modernization, except for two additions. A layer of 70-pound special-treatment steel plating (about 1.7 inches thick) was added to the armored second deck, and an armored grating was added inside the funnel at the level of the upper deck.

Machinery

Boilers
six Bureau Express type: 300 pounds of pressure per square inch

Turbines
—two Westinghouse geared impulse-reaction, 3,600-rpm high-pressure main turbines
—two Westinghouse geared impulse-reaction 3,600-rpm cruising turbines
—two Parsons 226-rpm low-pressure ahead and astern turbines
—two Parsons 226-rpm high-pressure astern turbines

Shaft Horsepower
35,081 maximum ahead

Maximum Speed
21.23 knots at 231 shaft rpm (July 1931)

Endurance
—8,500 nautical miles at 20 knots
—13,600 nautical miles at 15 knots

Generators
four 300-kilowatt, 120/240-volt direct-current turbo-generator sets

Propellers
four 3-bladed: 12 feet, 7 inches in diameter

Rudder
Same as before.

Fuel Oil Capacity
—4,630 tons normal
—6,180 tons in emergency

Diesel Oil
75 tons for boats

Reserve Boiler Feed Water
—323 tons normal
—392 tons emergency

Potable Water
400 tons

The above information is drawn from three main sources:

General Information: Battleship No. 39: U.S.S. Arizona. New York Navy Yard, 1916 (Washington, D.C.: U.S. Government Printing Office, 1918).

General Information Book: U.S.S. Arizona (BB39). Puget Sound Navy Yard, 1941 (Washington, D.C.: Bureau of Ships, Navy Department, 1941).

Norman Friedman, Arthur D. Baker III, Arnold S. Lott, and Robert F. Sumrall. *USS Arizona (BB-39).* Annapolis: Leeward Publications, 1978.

Copies of the general information books are on file in Record Group 19, National Archives. The data are not always as clear cut as they appear in this appendix, being subject to some interpretation. For instance, in the 1916 book the standard displacement is calculated with the ship at the designer's waterline; in 1941 the standard displacement and the D.W.L. displacement differ. The lifting capacity for the aircraft crane at the stern is rated variously at 6,000 and 6,500 pounds, but a note also indicates that the crane was successfully tested with an overload that made its true capacity greater than rated capacity. The general information books contain a treasure trove of specific technical information about the *Arizona* and her equipment.

The Leeward Press booklet contains several inaccuracies. For instance, it reports that the *Arizona* was equipped with four submerged 21-inch torpedo tubes at the time of commissioning. The general information books and ship's deck logs indicate only two torpedo tubes. The booklet reports that the ship had sixteen 1.1-inch antiaircraft guns in 1941. The gun tubs for the four quadruple mounts were installed during the last overhaul, but the guns themselves were never put aboard because they were not available in time. The Leeward booklet contains a useful table of ballistic data not included here.

The *Arizona* as Outfitted in May 1917

Scale = 1:600

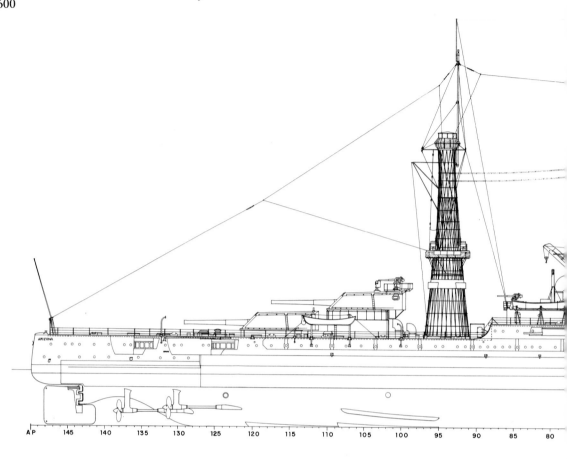

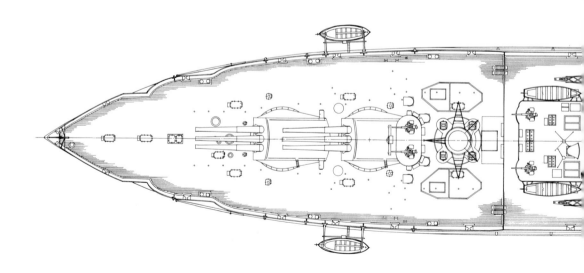

Drawings by Alan B. Chesley

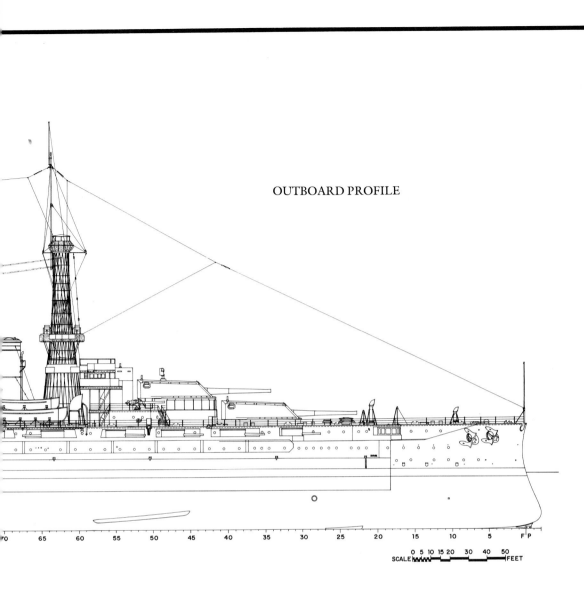

OUTBOARD PROFILE

70   65   60   55   50   45   40   35   30   25   20   15   10   5   F P

SCALE 0 5 10 15 20 30 40 50 FEET

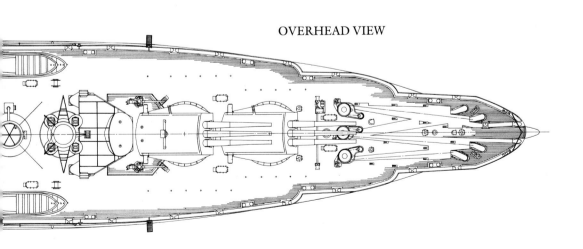

OVERHEAD VIEW

# The *Arizona* as Outfitted in June 1922
Scale = 1:600

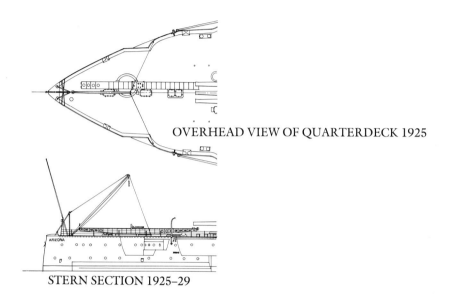

OVERHEAD VIEW OF QUARTERDECK 1925

STERN SECTION 1925–29

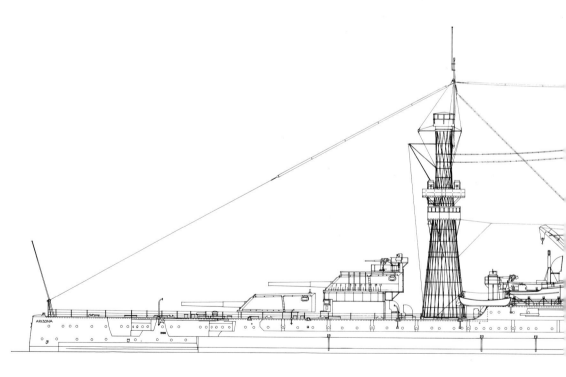

Drawings by Alan B. Chesley

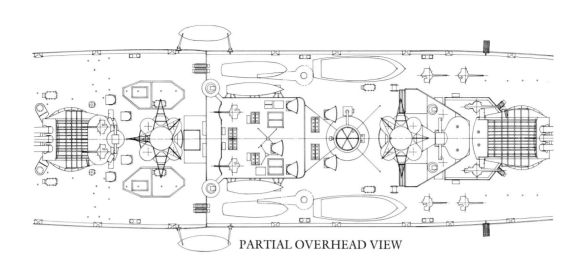

PARTIAL OVERHEAD VIEW

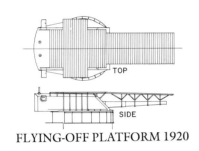

TOP

SIDE

FLYING-OFF PLATFORM 1920

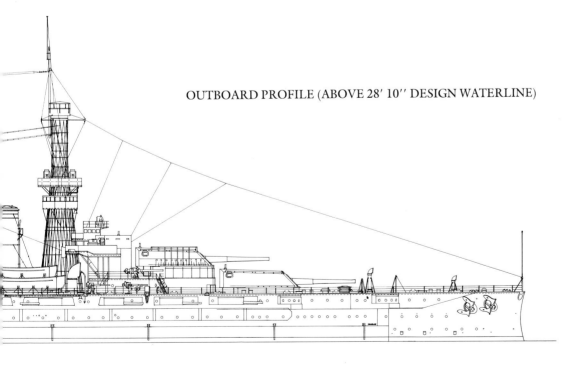

OUTBOARD PROFILE (ABOVE 28′ 10″ DESIGN WATERLINE)

The *Arizona* as Outfitted in March 1936

Scale = 1:600

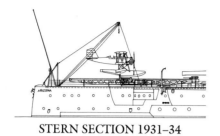

STERN SECTION 1931–34

14″ TURRET GLACIS PLATE

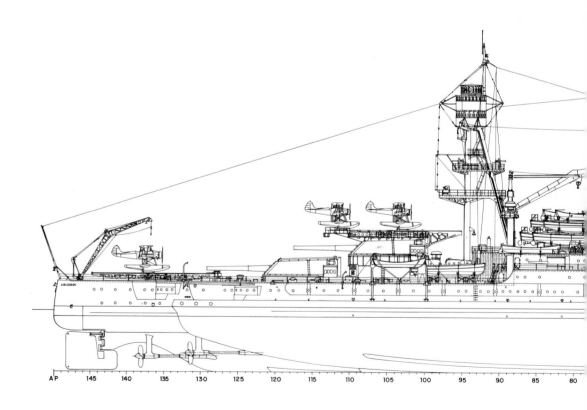

Drawings by Alan B. Chesley

FUNNEL AND SEARCHLIGHT PLATFORM—PRE-1936
(FUNNEL WAS HEIGHTENED IN 1936)

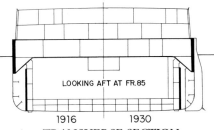

LOOKING AFT AT FR.85

1916   1930

TRANSVERSE SECTION

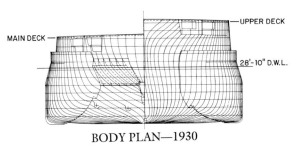

MAIN DECK

UPPER DECK

28'-10" D.W.L.

BODY PLAN—1930

OUTBOARD PROFILE

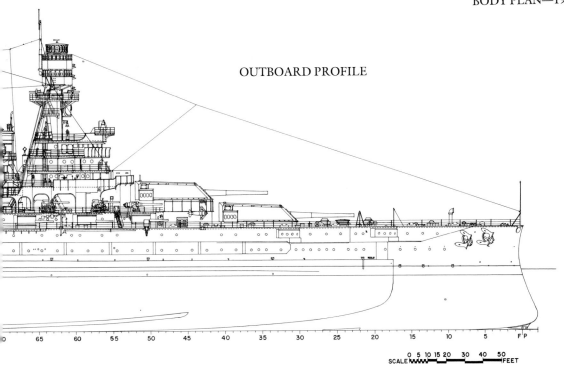

65   60   55   50   45   40   35   30   25   20   15   10   5   F.P.

0 5 10 15 20   30   40   50
SCALE   FEET

# The *Arizona* as Outfitted in June 1941
Scale = 1:600

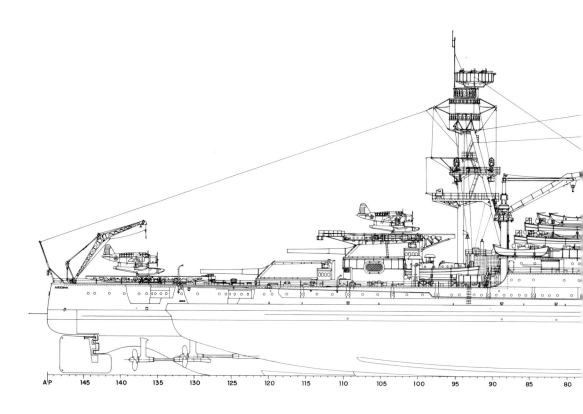

A|P   145   140   135   130   125   120   115   110   105   100   95   90   85   80

Drawing by Alan B. Chesley

OUTBOARD PROFILE

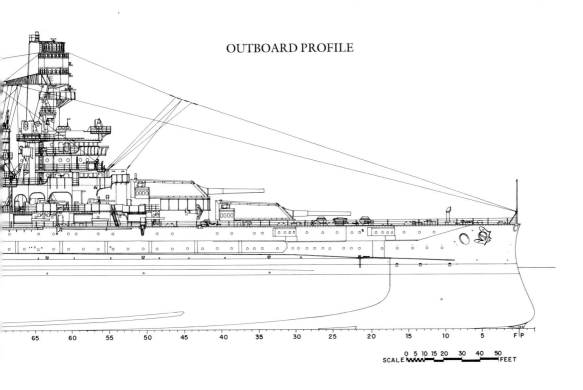

65   60   55   50   45   40   35   30   25   20   15   10   5   F P

0 5 10 15 20   30   40   50
SCALE   FEET

# The *Arizona* as Outfitted in June 1941
Scale = 1:600

1 CPO Wash Room and Head
2 Crew's Wash Room
3 Chain Pipe
4 Wildcat
5 Windlass Shaft
6 Windlass Machinery
7 CPO Quarters
8 Supply Department Stores
9 Paravane Gear and Supply Department Stores
10 CPO Mess
11 Sick Bay
12 Cobbler's Shop
13 Electrical Stores
14 Chain Locker
15 Sprocket
16 CPO Suitcases
17 Switch Room
18 Passage
19 CPO Stores
20 Access Trunk
21 Supply Department Paint Stores
22 Aviation Stores
23 Gasoline Stowage Tanks
24 Oil Room
25 Boatswain's Stores
26 Kerosene Stowage
27 Running Gear
28 Peak Tank
29 Cofferdam
30 Sand Locker
31 Crew's Quarters
32 Carpenter's Shop
33 Repair Shop
34 14″-Gun Turret, Barbette, and Handling Room
35 Shell-Handling Room
36 Plotting Room
37 Dynamo Room (Forward and Aft)
38 Dynamo Condenser Room (Forward and Aft)
39 Distribution Room (Forward and Aft)
40 Central Room
41 Wiring Passage
42 Port and Starboard Firerooms
43 Starboard Engine Room

44 Port Engine Room
45 Fuel Oil Tanks
46 Diesel Oil Tanks
47 Steam Steering Room
48 14″ Powder Room
49 5″ Antiaircraft Magazine
50 Ship's Service and Admiral's Stores
51 Radio School Room
52 Junior Officers' Stateroom
53 Wardroom Officers' Stateroom
54 Wardroom Officers' Country
55 Electric Capstan
56 After Gyrocompass Room
57 Chemical Defense Equipment
58 Port Inboard Propeller
59 Rudder
60 Steering Gear
61 Steering Motor Room
62 Wardroom
63 Wardroom Pantry
64 Flag Radio Room
65 Aircraft Crane Training Gear
66 Aircraft Crane Hoisting Gear
67 General Workshop
68 Vent Trunk
69 Blower Room
70 Blower Space
71 Construction & Repair Canvas Stores
72 Air Intake Space
73 Firemen's Head

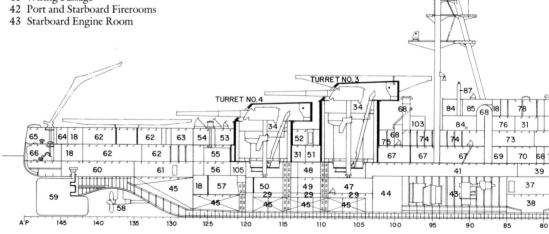

Drawings by Alan B. Chesley

74 Wardroom Officers' Mess
75 Junior Officers' Quarters
76 Crew's Reading and Recreation Room
77 Dumbwaiter
78 Crew's Galley
79 Officers' Galley
80 Scullery
81 Bakery
82 Coppersmith and Pipefitter's Shop
83 Blacksmith, Metal, and Aviation Workshop
84 Vegetable Locker
85 Potato (Spud) Locker
86 General Mess and Community Issuing Room
87 Antenna Trunk
88 Navigator's Office
89 Clipping Room
90 Conning Tower Tube
91 Conning Tower
92 Flag Plotting Room
93 Flag Commander's Office
94 Chart House
95 Admiral's Emergency Cabin
96 Radio Direction Finder Hut
97 Uptake
98 Pilothouse
99 Head
100 Secondary Battery Control Station (Forward and Aft)
101 Air Defense Station (Forward and Aft)
102 Main Battery Gun Director (Forward and Aft)
103 Chair Locker
104 Fireman's Passage
105 Small Arms

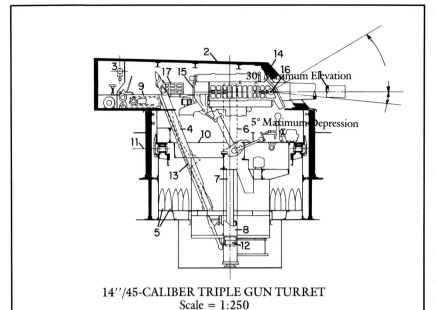

14″/45-CALIBER TRIPLE GUN TURRET
Scale = 1:250

1 14″/45-Caliber Rifle
2 Turret Roof
3 Left Range Finder
4 14″ Projectile Hoist
5 14″ Projectiles
6 Left Powder Hoist
7 Central Column
8 Right Powder Hoist
9 Rammer
10 Pan Floor
11 Roller Path
12 Powder Bag
13 Auxiliary Powder Hoist
14 Glacis Plate
15 Breech
16 Trunnions
17 Door to Powder-Transfer Tray

INBOARD PROFILE

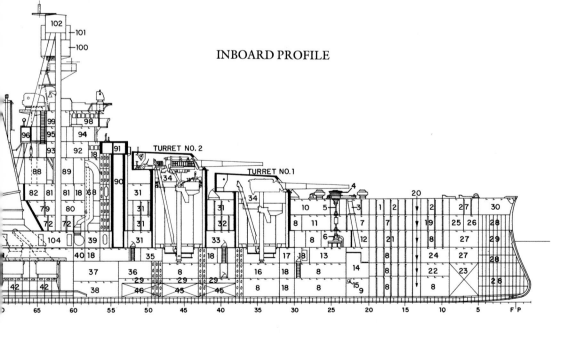

The *Arizona* as Outfitted in June 1941

Scale = 1:600

OVERHEAD VIEWS

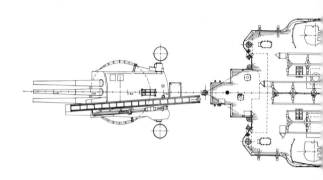

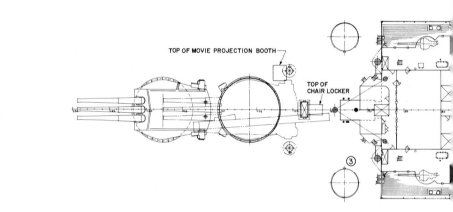

TOP OF MOVIE PROJECTION BOOTH

TOP OF
CHAIR LOCKER

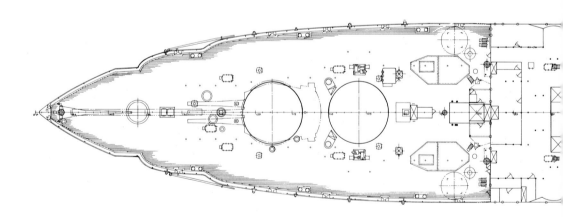

Drawings by Alan B. Chesley

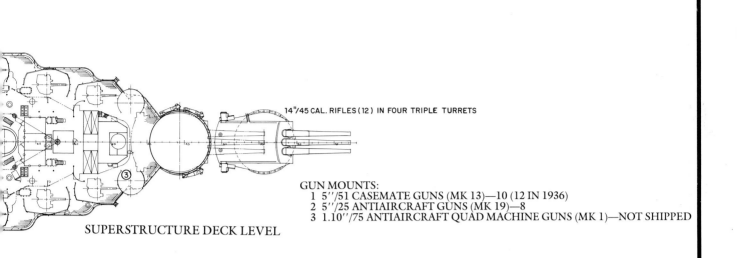

14"/45 CAL. RIFLES (12) IN FOUR TRIPLE TURRETS

GUN MOUNTS:
1 5''/51 CASEMATE GUNS (MK 13)—10 (12 IN 1936)
2 5''/25 ANTIAIRCRAFT GUNS (MK 19)—8
3 1.10''/75 ANTIAIRCRAFT QUAD MACHINE GUNS (MK 1)—NOT SHIPPED

SUPERSTRUCTURE DECK LEVEL

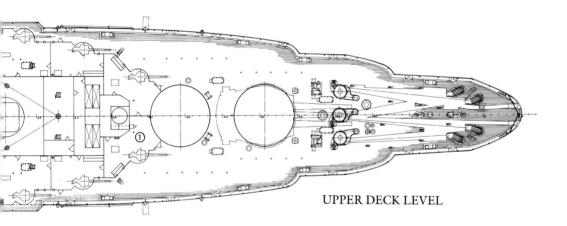

UPPER DECK LEVEL

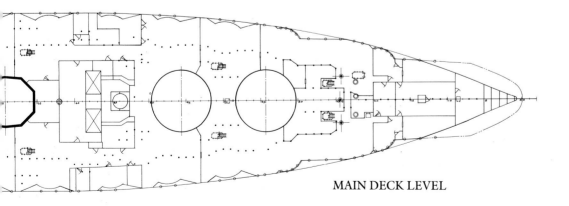

MAIN DECK LEVEL

# The *Arizona* as Outfitted in June 1941
Scale = 1:600

OVERHEAD VIEWS

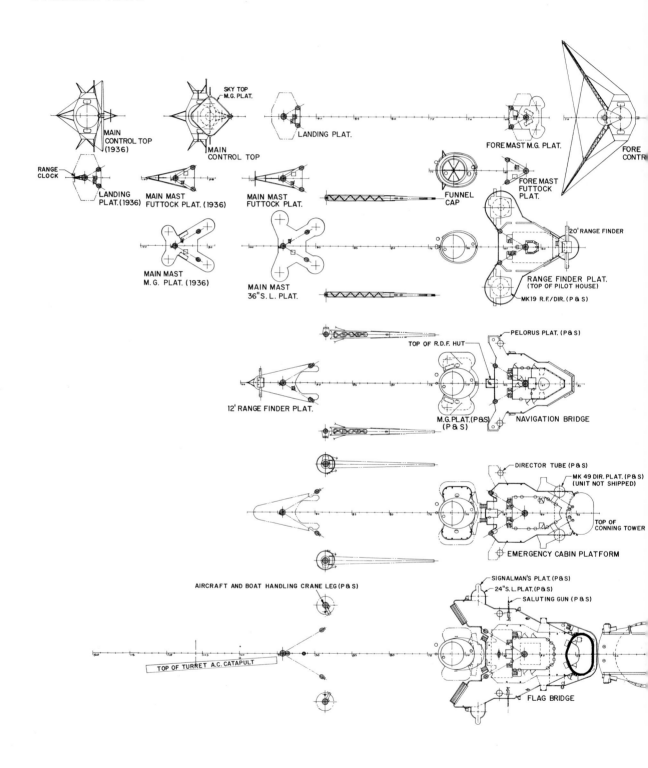

Drawings by Alan B. Chesley

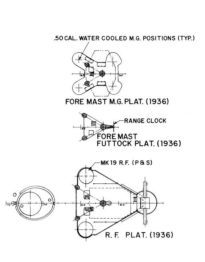

.50 CAL. WATER COOLED M.G. POSITIONS (TYP.)

FORE MAST M.G. PLAT. (1936)

RANGE CLOCK

FORE MAST FUTTOCK PLAT. (1936)

FORE CONTROL TOP (1936)

MK19 R.F. (P & S)

R.F. PLAT. (1936)

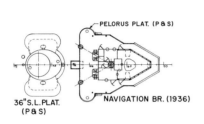

PELORUS PLAT. (P & S)

36"S.L.PLAT. (P & S)

NAVIGATION BR. (1936)

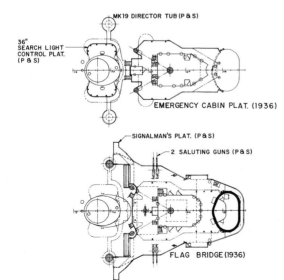

MK19 DIRECTOR TUB (P & S)

36" SEARCH LIGHT CONTROL PLAT. (P & S)

EMERGENCY CABIN PLAT. (1936)

SIGNALMAN'S PLAT. (P & S)

2 SALUTING GUNS (P & S)

FLAG BRIDGE (1936)

NOTES

Chapter 1 — Super Dreadnought

1. *New York Tribune*, 17 Mar. 1914.
2. *New York Evening Sun*, 16 Mar. 1914, and *The New York Press* and *New York Herald*, 17 Mar. 1914, give details of the ceremony.
3. Henry Williams, interview with author, 17 May 1989.
4. Daniels, *The Wilson Era*, 351-63.
5. Folder 110-B39-1, Box 2036, Record Group 19, National Archives, contains month-by-month progress reports on the *Arizona*'s construction.
6. "Launching of Ship Arizona is Recalled," *Yavapai Associated*, 1945. The copy was in the files of the Arizona Historical Society, Tucson, Arizona.
7. "Arizona Afloat as 75,000 Cheer," *The New York Times*, 20 June 1915.
8. Ibid.
9. Ibid.
10. Ibid.
11. Jennings, *The Treasure of the Superstition Mountains*, 108-9.
12. "Launching of Ship Arizona is Recalled," *Yavapai Associated*.
13. "Esther Ross Hoggan, 82, Christened Arizona in 1915," *Los Angeles Times*, 27 Aug. 1979.
14. *Courtland Arizonan*, 26 June 1915.
15. Copy of the speech from the files of the Arizona Historical Society, Tucson, Arizona.
16. "Launching of Ship Arizona is Recalled," *Yavapai Associated*.
17. Folder 110-B39-1, Box 2036, Record Group 19, National Archives.
18. "The Mighty Arizona Now a Part of Navy," *The New York Times*, 18 Oct. 1916, gives details of the commissioning.
19. Cray, interview with author, 30 Nov. 1989.
20. Bureau of Medicine and Surgery letter of 4 Apr. 1917 to Bureau of Construction and Repair, File 125135, Folder AP-AR, Box 378, Record Group 52, National Archives.

21. "Turbine Topics," *At 'Em Arizona*, 10 Nov. 1920.
22. USS *Arizona* postcard, 2 Dec. 1916.
23. USS *Arizona* postcard, 9 Dec. 1916.
24. "Our Latest Dreadnought, the 'Arizona', " *Scientific American*, 25 Nov. 1916, 471, 485.
25. USS *Arizona* postcards, Jan. 1917.
26. Johnson, 1917 diary.
27. USS *Arizona* postcards, Jan. 1917.
28. Johnson, 1917 diary.
29. Driscoll, interview with author, 17 July 1989.
30. Johnson, 1917 diary.
31. Kos, interview with Lomonaco, 19 Dec. 1984.
32. Johnson, 1917 diary.
33. Reilly, interview with author, 28 Nov. 1990.
34. Driscoll, 1917–21 journal, gives the gun crew routine.
35. Fore, interview with Johnson, 31 May 1983.
36. Driscoll, interview with author, 17 July 1989.
37. USS *Arizona*, 1917 deck log.
38. Ibid.
39. Johnson, 1917 diary.
40. Frisbie, interview with author, 25 July 1988.
41. Folders 3-B39-42 and 3-B39-43, Box 582, Record Group 19, National Archives.
42. Ibid.
43. Bowen, *Ships Machinery and Mossbacks*, 32.
44. Ibid, 33.
45. Hough, *Dreadnought: A History of the Modern Battleship*, 39, has a dramatic photo of the *Michigan*'s badly misshapen foremast.
46. USS *Arizona*, 1918 deck log; Driscoll, interview with author, 17 July 1989.
47. Larry Flint, *Youngstown, Ohio, Vindicator*, Dec. 1941.
48. USS *Arizona*, 1918 deck log.
49. "The Antiaircraft Battery," *At 'Em Arizona*, 15 Oct. 1920.
50. Kinkaid, interview with Mason, 6 Mar. 1961.

51. Driscoll, letter to author, 3 Mar. 1990.

52. Frisbie, 1918 diary.

53. *At 'Em Arizona*, 11 Dec. 1919.

54. Folder 3-B39-57, Box 582, Record Group 19, National Archives.

55. Leymé, 1918 diary.

56. Ibid.

57. Ibid.

58. Ibid.

59. Ibid.

60. Kos, interview with Lomonaco, 19 Dec. 1984.

61. Leymé, 1918 diary.

Chapter 2 – Too Late 'Over There'

1. Leymé, 1918 diary.

2. Ibid.

3. Frisbie, interview with author, 25 July 1988.

4. USS *Arizona*, 1918 deck log.

5. Leymé, 1918 diary.

6. Frisbie, interview with author, 25 July 1988.

7. Leymé, 1918 diary.

8. USS *Arizona*, 1918 deck log.

9. USS *Arizona*, 26 Dec. 1918 deck log.

10. USS *Arizona*, 1919 deck log.

11. Driscoll, interview with author, 17 July 1989.

12. Leymé, 1919 diary.

13. Flint, *Youngstown, Ohio, Vindicator*, Dec. 1941.

14. Ballentine, interview with Mason, 11 Apr. 1961.

15. Frisbie, interview with author, 25 July 1988.

16. Chief of Naval Operations letter of 6 May 1919 to Secretary of the Navy, reel 42, Josephus Daniels papers, Library of Congress.

17. Ibid.

18. Ballentine, interview with Mason, 11 Apr. 1961.

19. USS *Arizona*, 1919 deck log.

20. Ibid.

21. Driscoll, interview with author, 17 July 1989.

22. Ibid.

23. DeCelles, undated questionnaire for U.S. Army Military History Research Collection.

24. Driscoll interview with author, 17 July 1989.

25. Ibid.

26. Snook, "British Naval Operations in the Black Sea, 1918–1920," 36–50. Ballentine, interview with Mason, 11 Apr. 1961. Still, letter to author, 8 Jan. 1991.

27. Ogden, interview with author, 28 Sept. 1990.

28. Ibid.

29. Ibid.

30. Ibid.

31. Ballentine, interview with Mason, 11 Apr. 1961.

32. Ibid. "In Congress: Naval Appropriation Act of July 11," *Army and Navy Register*, 19 July 1919, 65.

33. Ballentine, interview with Mason, 11 Apr. 1961.

34. Hone, letter to author, 30 Sept. 1990.

35. Friedman, *U.S. Battleships*, 175.

36. Folder 3-B39-91, Box 583, Record Group 19, National Archives.

37. Ogden, interview with author, 28 Sept. 1990. *Army and Navy Journal*, 18 Oct. 1919, 212.

38. Driscoll, interview with author, 17 July 1989.

39. Ogden, interview with author, 28 Sept. 1990.

40. Ibid.

41. "Crew's Dances to [Start] Saturday," *At 'Em Arizona*, 2 Aug. 1920.

42. Ballentine, interview with Mason, 11 Apr. 1961. USS *Arizona*, 1920 deck log.

43. Ogden, interview with author, 28 Sept. 1990.

44. Pride, interview with author, 23 Dec. 1988.

45. Ibid.

46. Ibid.

47. Ibid.

48. Ibid.

49. Ballentine, interview with Mason, 11 Apr. 1961.

50. Ibid.

51. Ibid.

52. Ibid.

53. Pride, interview with author, 23 Dec. 1988.

54. Ballentine, interview with Mason, 11 Apr. 1961. Driscoll, interview with author, 17 July 1989. USS *Arizona*, 1920 deck log.

55. Pride, interview with author, 23 Dec. 1988.

56. Ibid.

57. Ibid.

58. Ibid.

59. Ibid.

60. Folder 3-B39-97, Box 583, Record Group 19, National Archives.

61. A copy of the order may be found at the National Archives in Record Group 52, Box 378, file 125135, folder AP-AR.

62. Driscoll, interview with author, 17 July 1989.

63. "Anchor Gear," *At 'Em Arizona*, 11 Oct. 1920.

64. Ingersoll, 1920 diary.

65. Corey, "Across the Equator with the American Navy," 571–624.

66. Ibid.

67. Ibid.

68. Ogden, interview with author, 28 Sept. 1990.

69. Driscoll, letter to author, 12 July 1990.

70. Ogden, interview with author, 28 Sept. 1990.

71. Driscoll, interview with author, 17 July 1989.

72. Ogden, interview with author, 28 Sept. 1990.

73. Ibid.

74. Corey, "Across the Equator with the American Navy," 571–624.

75. Ibid.

76. Ibid.

77. Ibid.

78. "Sailing Race," *At 'Em Arizona*, 20 Feb. 1921. "Yesterday's Race," *At 'Em Arizona*, 21 Feb. 1921.

79. "Awards this Morning," *At 'Em Arizona*, 23 Feb. 1921.

80. Gerald E. Wheeler, "Edwin Denby," in Coletta, *American Secretaries of the Navy*, 583-603.

81. Ingersoll, 1921 diary.

Chapter 3 — The Tranquil Twenties

1. Wheeler, *Prelude to Pearl Harbor*, 75.

2. *At 'Em Arizona*, Christmas 1922 issue.

3. Wheeler, *Prelude to Pearl Harbor*, 75.

4. Henderson, interview with author, 1 Dec. 1988.

5. *At 'Em Arizona*, 13 Jan. 1923.

6. File 3-BB39-111, Box 584, Record Group 19, National Archives.

7. USS *Arizona*, 1922 deck log.

8. Henderson, interview with author, 1 Dec. 1988.

9. Ibid. Cohen, interview with author, 2 Dec. 1988.

10. Henderson, interview with author, 1 Dec. 1988.

11. Ibid.

12. *At 'Em Arizona*, 3 Mar. 1923.

13. Henderson, interview with author, 1 Dec. 1988.

14. Potter, *Admiral Arleigh Burke*, 27–29.

15. Mrs. Roberta Burke, interview with author, 17 Feb. 1991.

16. Potter, *Admiral Arleigh Burke*, 24–25.

17. Warren, interview with author, 16 Nov. 1990.

18. Ibid.

19. Ibid.

20. Ibid.

21. Henderson, interview with author, 1 Dec. 1988.

22. Cohen, interview with author, 2 Dec. 1988.

23. Henderson, interview with author, 1 Dec. 1988.

24. Boyle, interview with Langdell, 4 Dec. 1982.

25. Warren, interview with author, 15 Nov. 1990.

26. Ibid.

27. Jones and Kelley, *Admiral Arleigh (31-Knot) Burke*, 64–65.

28. Warren, interview with author, 15 Nov. 1990.

29. Ibid.

30. Love, interview with Langdell, 4 Dec. 1983.

31. Jones and Kelley, *Admiral Arleigh (31-Knot) Burke*, 65–66.

32. Warren, interview with author, 15 Nov. 1990.

33. Foulds, interview with Langdell, 3 Dec. 1982.

34. Warren, interview with author, 15 Nov. 1990.

35. Foulds, interview with Langdell, 3 Dec. 1982.

36. Potter, *Admiral Arleigh Burke*, 32–33.

37. Henderson, interview with author, 1 Dec. 1988.

38. H. P. Smith, interview with author, 26 Oct. 1990.

39. Henderson, interview with author, 1 Dec. 1988.

40. Dyer, *On the Treadmill to Pearl Harbor*, 206–7. USS *Arizona*, 1924 deck log.

41. Henderson, interview with author, 1 Dec. 1988.

42. Cohen, interview with author, 2 Dec. 1988. H. P. Smith, interview with author, 26 Oct. 1990.

43. Cohen, interview with author, 2 Dec. 1988.

44. Simpson, interview with author, 30 Nov. 1988.

45. Cohen, interview with author, 2 Dec. 1988.

46. Ibid. Simpson, interview with author, 30 Nov. 1988.

47. Laning, book-length memoir.

48. *At 'Em Arizona*, 2 May 1925.

49. Henderson, interview with author, 1 Dec. 1988.

50. Cohen, interview with author, 2 Dec. 1988.

51. Henderson, interview with author, 1 Dec. 1988.

52. Board of Inspection and Survey, Pacific Coast Section, report dated 6 Oct. 1925, folder BB39/S3-(5), Box 753, Record Group 19, National Archives.

53. Rear Admiral Jehu V. Chase letter of 31 Oct. 1925 to Chief, Bureau of Construction and Repair, folder BB39/L9, Volume 1, Box 749, Record Group 19, National Archives.

54. Cohen, interview with author, 2 Dec. 1988.

55. Ibid.

56. Ibid.

57. Gesen, letter to author, 5 Apr. 1990.

58. H. P. Smith, interview with author, 26 Oct. 1990. Daniel, interview with author, 17 Nov. 1990.

59. Arnold, interview with author, 11 Apr. 1989.

60. Arleigh Burke, interview with author, 17 Feb. 1991.

61. USS *Arizona*, 1926 deck log.

62. Cohen, interview with author, 2 Dec. 1988.

63. Henderson, interview with author, 1 Dec. 1988.

64. Ibid.

65. Ibid.

66. Daniel, interview with author, 17 Nov. 1990.

67. Arleigh Burke, interview with author, 17 Feb. 1991.

68. Cohen, interview with author, 2 Dec. 1988.

69. Ibid.

70. Arnett, interview with author, 15 Nov. 1990.

71. Ibid.

72. Ibid.

73. Ibid.

74. Bennett, interview with Marks, 18 July 1990.

75. Ibid.

76. Ibid.

77. Ratcliffe, interview with author, 24 Oct. 1990.

78. Ibid.

79. Coffin, interview with author, 3 Dec. 1989.

80. Ibid.

81. Ibid. Daniel, interview with author, 17 Nov. 1990.

82. Daniel, interview with author, 17 Nov. 1990.

83. Ibid.

84. Ratcliffe, interview with author, 24 Oct. 1990.

85. Ibid.

86. Ibid.

87. Ibid.

88. H. P. Smith, interview with author, 26 Oct. 1990.

89. Arleigh Burke, interview with author, 17 Feb. 1991.

90. H. P. Smith, interview with author, 26 Oct. 1990.

91. Daniel, interview with author, 17 Nov. 1990.

92. Simpson, interview with author, 30 Nov. 1988.

93. Coffin, interview with author, 3 Dec. 1989.

94. H. P. Smith, interview with author, 26 Oct. 1990.

95. Ibid.

96. Daniel, interview with author, 17 Nov. 1990.

97. Ibid.

98. Ibid.

99. Ibid.

100. Femia, interview with author, 2 Dec. 1989.

101. Ibid.

102. Ibid.

103. Ibid.

104. Oliver Deaton, undated letter to Nina Hart, ed., *Arizona's Heart Beats*, volume 1, 72.

105. Femia, interview with author, 2 Dec. 1989.

106. Ibid.

107. Ibid.

108. Ratcliffe, interview with author, 24 Oct. 1990.

109. Ibid.

Chapter 4 — Fit for the President

1. USS *Arizona*, 1929 deck log.

2. Ratcliffe, interview with author, 24 Oct. 1990.

3. Ibid.

4. Simpson, interview with author, 30 Nov. 1988.

5. Edward Berry, undated letter to Nina Hart, ed., *Arizona's Heart Beats*, volume 1, 27.

6. Walter R. Davis, undated letter to Nina Hart, ed., *Arizona's Heart Beats*, volume 2, 48–50.

7. Ibid.

8. USS *Arizona*, 1929 deck log.

9. Davidson, interview with author, 23 Aug. 1985.

10. Ibid.

11. Friedman and others, *USS Arizona (BB-39)*, 10, 25.

12. Reilly, interview with author, 28 Nov. 1990.

13. Folder BB-39/L9, Volume 1, Box 749, Record Group 19, National Archives, gives information on the ship's modernization.

14. Hughlett, interview with author, 16 Jan. 1989.

15. "Arizona Shines as Crew Makes Ready for Trip With President," *Norfolk Virginian-Pilot*, 18 Mar. 1931.

16. Ibid. Greer, "Fifteen Minute Talk."

17. Greer, "Fifteen Minute Talk."

18. Young, "When the President Takes a Vacation," 1.

19. Ibid, 2.

20. Ibid, 1–2.

21. Ibid, 2.

22. Greer, "Fifteen Minute Talk."

23. Theodore C. Wallen, "Warship Astray, Sea Review by President Fails," *New York Herald Tribune*, 22 Mar. 1931, 1.

24. William P. Flythe, "Hoover Happy As He Chats With Family," *Washington Herald*, 23 Mar. 1931.

25. Richard V. Oulahan, "Hoover Promises to Help Porto Rico; He Resumes His Trip," *The New York Times*, 25 Mar. 1931, 1.

26. Greer, "Fifteen Minute Talk."

27. Edward T. Folliard, *The Washington Post*, 15 Mar. 1931, 1.

28. "President Steams Toward Norfolk," *New York Evening Post*, 26 Mar. 1931.

29. Richard V. Oulahan, "President's Ship Plows Heavy Seas," *The New York Times*, 28 Mar. 1931.

30. Simpson, interview with author, 30 Nov. 1988.

31. Ibid.

32. Hughlett, interview with author, 16 Jan. 1989.

33. Davidson, interview with author, 29 Feb. 1988.

34. Richard V. Oulahan, "Benefit to Hoover by Cruise Evident," *The New York Times*, 29 Mar. 1931.

35. Walter R. Davis, undated letter to Hart, ed., *Arizona's Heart Beats*, volume 2, 48–50.

36. W. B. Woodson letter of 27 July 1931, folder BB-39/L11-1, Box 752, Record Group 19, National Archives.

37. Davidson, interview with author, 29 Feb. 1988.

38. Folder BB-39/S8, Box 754, Record Group 19, National Archives.

39. Walter R. Davis, undated letter to Hart, ed., *Arizona's Heart Beats*, volume 2, 48–50.

40. Hubert, interview with author, 3 Dec. 1988.

41. Edward Berry, undated letter to Hart, ed., *Arizona's Heart Beats*, volume 1, 28.

42. Ibid, 29.

43. Ibid, 29–30.

44. Rourk, interview with author, 3 Dec. 1988.

45. Ibid.

46. Hubert, interview with author, 3 Dec. 1988.

47. Rourk, interview with author, 3 Dec. 1988.

48. Gleason, interview with author, 29 Nov. 1989.

49. Rear Admiral John E. Kirkpatrick's speech to the *Arizona* Reunion Association in Dec. 1983, printed in Hart, ed., *Arizona's Heart Beats*, volume 1, 39–40.

50. Ibid.

51. Admiral Arthur Radford, "Aircraft Battle Force," in Stillwell, *Air Raid: Pearl Harbor!*, 18–19.

52. Gleason, interview with author, 29 Nov. 1989.

53. Lee, interview with author, 15 Apr. 1989.

54. Rear Admiral William R. Cox, letter of 10 Apr. 1986 to Hart, ed., *Arizona's Heart Beats*, volume 2, 13–14.

55. Davidson, interview with author, 23 Aug. 1985.

56. Ibid, 29 Feb. 1988.

57. Rear Admiral John E. Kirkpatrick's speech to the *Arizona* Reunion Association in Dec. 1983, printed in Hart, ed., *Arizona's Heart Beats*, volume 1, 41.

58. Lee, interview with author, 15 Apr. 1989.

59. Ibid.

60. Keith, *United States Navy Task Force Evolution*.

61. USS *Arizona*, 1933 deck log. Gleason, interview with author, 29 Nov. 1989.

62. Greer, "Fifteen Minute Talk."

63. Rourk, interview with author, 3 Dec. 1988.

64. Donovan, letter to author, 22 Mar. 1988.

65. Davidson, interview with author, 23 Aug. 1985.

66. Donovan, letter to author, 27 Oct. 1990. Rear Admiral John E. Kirkpatrick's speech to the *Arizona* Reunion Association in Dec. 1983, printed in Hart, ed., *Arizona's Heart Beats*, volume 1, 39.

67. Walter R. Davis, undated letter to Hart, ed., *Arizona's Heart Beats*, volume 2, 48–50.

68. Hughlett, interview with author, 16 Jan. 1989.

69. Ibid.

70. Lee, interview with author, 15 Apr. 1989.

71. Ibid.

72. Ibid.

73. Gleason, interview with author, 29 Nov. 1989.

74. Rouse, interview with author, 4 Dec. 1988.

Chapter 5 — *Here Comes the Navy*

1. *The New York Times*, 21 July 1934, 14.

2. Gleason, interview with author, 29 Nov. 1989.

3. Rouse, interview with author, 4 Dec. 1988.

4. Lee, interview with author, 15 Apr. 1989.

5. "Arizona Goes Hollywood," *At 'Em Arizona*, 7 Apr. 1934, 1.

6. "Warner Brothers Stars Entertain Arizona," *At 'Em Arizona*, 14 Apr. 1934, 1, 3.

7. "The New Broadcast System," *At 'Em Arizona*, 4 Aug. 1934, 1.

8. Hughlett, interview with author, 16 Jan. 1989.

9. Byard, interview with author, 2 Dec. 1989.

10. Hubert, interview with author, 3 Dec. 1988.

11. Ibid.

12. Byard, interview with author, 2 Dec. 1989.

Chapter 6 — Man-of-War Life

1. Barker, interview with author, 1 Dec. 1988. *At 'Em Arizona*, 29 May 1937.

2. Bryan, interview with author, 3 Sept. 1990.

3. Vivirito, interview with author, 3 Dec. 1988.

4. Richardson, undated letter to Marks.

5. Bryan, interview with author, 3 Sept. 1990.

6. Huckenpoehler, interview with author, 31 Aug. 1990.

7. Amend, interview with author, 1 Dec. 1988.

8. Clunie, letter to author, 11 Mar. 1988. Barker, interview with author, 1 Dec. 1988.

9. McCafferty, interview with author, 2 Dec. 1988.

10. Pfeifer, interview with author, 3 Dec. 1989.

11. Clunie, letter to author, 11 Mar. 1988. Barker, interview with author, 1 Dec. 1988.

12. Clunie, letter to author, 11 Mar. 1988. Barker, interview with author, 1 Dec. 1988.

13. Amend, interview with author, 1 Dec. 1988.

14. Cole, interview with author, 1 Dec. 1988.

15. Byard, interview with author, 2 Dec. 1989.

16. Larson, interview with author, 4 Dec. 1989.

17. Lee, interview with author, 15 Apr. 1989.

18. Dodds, interview with author, 8 Apr. 1990.

19. Arnold, interview with author, 11 Apr. 1989.

20. Dodds, interview with author, 8 Apr. 1990.

21. McClintock, interview with author, 4 Oct. 1990.

22. Ibid.

23. Ibid.

24. Ibid.

25. Badger, interview with author, 1 Aug. 1989.

26. Amend, interview with author, 1 Dec. 1988.

27. Byard, interview with author, 2 Dec. 1989.

28. Zobel, interview with author, 30 Nov. 1988.

29. Lieutenant Commander H. Wesley Cole, letter of 19 Nov. 1984 to Hart, ed., *Arizona's Heart Beats*, volume 1, 23.

30. Gleason, interview with author, 29 Nov. 1989.

31. Clunie, interview with author, 1 Dec. 1988.

32. Ibid.

33. Gleason, interview with Marks, Nov. 1989.

34. Rourk, interview with author, 3 Dec. 1988.

35. Ibid.

36. Vlach, interview with author, 2 Dec. 1988.

37. Hubert, interview with author, 3 Dec. 1988.

38. Rouse, interview with author, 4 Dec. 1988.

39. Gleason, interview with author, 29 Nov. 1989.

40. Rourk, interview with author, 3 Dec. 1988.

41. Ibid.

42. Ibid.

43. Cutter, letter to author, 12 Feb. 1990.

44. Givens (formerly Giovenazzo), interview with author, 28 Nov. 1989.

45. Speedie, interview with author, 18 Mar. 1990.

46. Rouse, interview with author, 4 Dec. 1988. Hone, letter to author, 18 Jan. 1991.

47. Strauss, interview with author, 30 Oct. 1986.

48. Huckenpoehler, interview with author, 31 Aug. 1990.

49. Rouse, interview with author, 4 Dec. 1988.

50. Lager, interview with author, 1 Dec. 1988.

51. Rourk, interview with author, 3 Dec. 1988.

52. Fordyce, interview with author, 17 July 1989.

53. Schroeder, interview with author, 2 Dec. 1989.

54. Richardson, undated letter to Marks.

55. McCarron, interview with author, 2 Dec. 1989. Rhodes, interview with author, 3 Dec. 1989.

56. Rhodes, interview with author, 3 Dec. 1989.

57. Amend, interview with author, 1 Dec. 1988.

58. Barker, interview with author, 1 Dec. 1988.

59. Ibid.

60. Clunie, letter to author, 11 Mar. 1988.

61. McCarron, interview with author, 2 Dec. 1989.

62. Vivirito, interview with author, 3 Dec. 1988.

63. Barker, interview with author, 1 Dec. 1988.

64. Ibid.

65. Ibid.

66. Ibid. Cole, interview with author, 1 Dec. 1988.

67. Givens (formerly Giovenazzo), interview with author, 28 Nov. 1989.

68. Ibid.

69. Arnold, interview with author, 11 Apr. 1989.

70. Badger, interview with author, 1 Aug. 1989.

71. Campbell, interview with author, 1 Dec. 1989.

72. Rourk, interview with author, 3 Dec. 1988.

73. Arnold, interview with author, 11 Apr. 1989.

74. Cole, interview with author, 1 Dec. 1988.

75. Ibid.

76. Karb, interview with author, 5 Dec. 1988.

77. Huckenpoehler, interview with author, 31 Aug. 1990.

78. Lee, interview with author, 15 Apr. 1989.

79. Wylie Smith, interview with author, 3 Dec. 1988.

80. McCain, letters to Marks, 12 Sept. 1989 and 8 Oct. 1989; letter to author, 8 Jan. 1991.

81. McCain, letter to Marks, 8 Oct. 1989.

82. *Naval Ordnance*, 250. Captain C. S. Freeman, letter to the President of the Board of Inspection and Survey, 11 Mar. 1931, folder BB39/S8, Box 753, Record Group 19, National Archives.

83. Huckenpoehler, interview with author, 31 Aug. 1990.

84. Larson, interview with author, 4 Dec. 1989.

85. Hone, letter to author, 18 Jan. 1991.

86. O'Donnell, interview with author, 4 Dec. 1988.

87. Ibid.

88. Hone, letter to author, 30 Sept. 1990.

89. Krulak, interview with author, 11 Apr. 1989.

90. Huckenpoehler, interview with author, 31 Aug. 1990. Lee, interview with author, 15 Apr. 1989.

91. Clunie, interview with author, 1 Dec. 1988.

92. Arthur Williams, interview with author, 30 Nov. 1990.

93. Bryan, interview with author, 3 Sept. 1990.

94. Lager, interview with author, 1 Dec. 1988.

95. Ibid.

96. Lee, interview with author, 15 Apr. 1989.

97. Dybdal, interview with author, 2 May 1989.

98. Amend, interview with author, 1 Dec. 1988.

99. Huckenpoehler, interview with author, 31 Aug. 1990.

100. Amend, interview with author, 1 Dec. 1988.

101. Huckenpoehler, interview with author, 31 Aug. 1990.

102. Cole, interview with author, 1 Dec. 1988.

103. Ibid.

104. McCafferty, interview with author, 2 Dec. 1988.

105. Barker, interview with author, 1 Dec. 1988.

106. Campbell, interview with author, 1 Dec. 1989.

107. Huckenpoehler, interview with author, 31 Aug. 1990. Badger, interview with author, 1 Aug. 1989.

108. Rear Admiral William R. Cox, letter of 10 Apr. 1986 to Hart, ed., *Arizona's Heart Beats*, volume 2, 14–15.

109. Amend, interview with author, 1 Dec. 1988.

110. Vlach, interview with author, 2 Dec. 1988.

111. McCafferty, interview with author, 2 Dec. 1988.

112. Ibid.

113. McCarty, interview with author, 2 Dec. 1989.

114. McCafferty, interview with author, 2 Dec. 1988.

115. Ibid.

116. Ibid.

117. Burcham, interview with Marks, 6 Dec. 1990.

118. Ibid.

119. Ibid.

120. Traylor, interview with Marks, Dec. 1989.

121. Ibid.

122. McCarron, interview with author, 2 Dec. 1989.

123. Ibid.

124. Campbell, interview with author, 1 Dec. 1989.

Chapter 7 — Last Years of Peace

1. "A Welcome Installation," *At 'Em Arizona*, 21 July 1934.

2. "Overhaul Period Begins Monday," *At 'Em Arizona*, 21 Apr. 1934.

3. USS *Arizona*, 1934 deck log.

4. McKinney, interview with Marks, Nov. 1989.

5. Lee, interview with author, 15 Apr. 1989.

6. Arnold, interview with author, 11 Apr. 1989.

7. USS *Arizona*, 1934 deck log. Rouse, interview with author, 4 Dec. 1988.

8. Clunie, interview with author, 1 Dec. 1988.

9. USS *Arizona*, 1934 deck log.

10. Clunie, interview with author, 1 Dec. 1988.

11. Arnold, interview with author, 11 Apr. 1989.

12. Krulak, interview with author, 11 Apr. 1989.

13. Rear Admiral William R. Cox, letter of 10 Apr. 1986 to Hart, ed., *Arizona's Heart Beats*, volume 2, 17–18.

14. Ibid.

15. Arnold, interview with author, 11 Apr. 1989.

16. Badger, interview with author, 1 Aug. 1989.

17. Gleason, interview with author, 29 Nov. 1989.

18. Krulak, interview with author, 11 Apr. 1989

19. Ibid.

20. Baccala, 1936 diary.

21. Hughlett, interview with author, 16 Jan. 1989.

22. Baccala, 1936 diary.

23. Pfeifer, interview with author, 3 Dec. 1989.

24. The incident is covered in some detail in a series of documents, including Captain George Alexander's report and subsequent endorsements from Admirals Bloch, Stark, and Leahy. Folder BB39/L11-1, Box 752, Record Group 19, National Archives.

25. Larson, interview with author, 4 Dec. 1989.

26. McClintock, interview with author, 4 Oct. 1990.

27. "Navy Plane Dives in Sound; One Killed," *Seattle Post-Intelligencer*, 10 July 1937.

28. Amend, interview with author, 1 Dec. 1988.

29. Ibid.

30. McCarty, interview with author, 2 Dec. 1989.

31. Gasmann, interview with author, 3 Dec. 1989.

32. Schroeder, interview with author, 1 Dec. 1989.

33. Letter of 18 July 1938 to Captain Allan J. Chantry, Courtesy Naval Sea Systems Command. See also U.S. Naval Institute *Proceedings*, Jan. 1976, 79.

34. Board of Inspection and Survey report, 27 June 1938, folder BB39/S3-(5), Box 753, Record Group 19, National Archives.

35. Dodds, interview with author, 8 Apr. 1990.

36. Byard, interview with author, 2 Dec. 1989.

37. Kidd, interview with author, 29 Mar. 1990.

38. Ibid.

39. Dybdal, interview with author, 2 May 1989.

40. Holland, interview with author, 1 Dec. 1989.

41. Wylie Smith, interview with author, 3 Dec. 1988.

42. Rourk, interview with author, 3 Dec. 1988.

43. Holland, interview with author, 1 Dec. 1989.

44. Ibid.

45. Potter, *Nimitz*, 168. Holland, interview with author, 1 Dec. 1989. Vivirito, interview with author, 3 Dec. 1988.

46. Captain Jim Dick Miller, letter of 28 Mar. 1985 to Hart, ed., *Arizona's Heart Beats*, volume 1, 51.

47. Ibid.

48. Ibid.

49. Ibid, 52.

50. Dodds, interview with author, 8 Apr. 1990.

51. Fordyce, interview with author, 17 July 1989.

52. Ibid.

53. Richardson, undated letter to Marks.

54. Captain Jim Dick Miller, letter of 28 Mar. 1985 to Hart, ed., *Arizona's Heart Beats*, volume 1, 54.

55. McCafferty, interview with author, 2 Dec. 1988.

56. McCarron, interview with author, 2 Dec. 1989.

57. Barbara Reid, letter of 18 Oct. 1985 to Hart, ed., *Arizona's Heart Beats*, volume 1, 96–97. Reid, interview with author, 3 Dec. 1988.

58. Arthur Williams, interview with author, 30 Nov. 1989.

59. McCarty, interview with author, 2 Dec. 1989.

60. Wylie Smith, interview with author, 3 Dec. 1988.

61. USS *Arizona*, 1939 deck log.

62. Cole, interview with author, 1 Dec. 1988.

63. Captain Jim Dick Miller, letter of 28 Mar. 1985 to Hart, ed., *Arizona's Heart Beats*, volume 1, 53–54.

64. Federal Bureau of Investigation, Los Angeles office, report of 3 May 1941. Copy of summary supplied by FBI headquarters, Washington, D.C., in response to a freedom-of-information request.

65. Givens (formerly Giovenazzo), interview with author, 28 Nov. 1989.

66. McCarty, interview with author, 2 Dec. 1989.

67. Kidd, interview with author, 29 Mar. 1990.

68. Amend, interview with author, 1 Dec. 1988.

69. Ramsey, interview with author, 1 Dec. 1988.

70. Duerfeldt, interview with author, 5 July 1990.

71. Ibid.

72. Ibid.

73. Huckenpoehler, interview with author, 31 Aug. 1990

74. Hurst, interview with author, 2 Dec. 1989.

75. Cole, interview with author, 1 Dec. 1988.

76. O'Donnell, interview with author, 4 Dec. 1988.

77. Huckenpoehler, interview with author, 31 Aug. 1990.

78. Arthur Williams, interview with author, 30 Nov. 1989.

79. Cole, interview with author, 1 Dec. 1988.

80. Karb, interview with author, 5 Dec. 1988.

81. Burk, interview with author, 2 Dec. 1988.

82. Byard, interview with author, 2 Dec. 1989.

83. Hurst, interview with author, 2 Dec. 1989.

84. Captain Jim Dick Miller, letter of 28 Mar. 1985 to Hart, ed., *Arizona's Heart Beats*, volume 1, 53–54.

85. Langdell, interview with Marks, 26 Mar. 1990.

86. Ibid.

87. Langdell, interview with author, 4 Dec. 1988.

88. Flanagan, interview with author, 2 Dec. 1988.

89. Ibid.

90. Ibid.

91. Ibid.

92. Ibid.

93. Langdell, interview with Marks, 26 Mar. 1990.

94. Hurst, interview with author, 2 Dec. 1989.

95. Ibid.

96. McCurdy, interview with author, 18 Jan. 1989.

97. Ibid.

98. Ibid.

99. Vlach, interview with author, 2 Dec. 1988.

100. Ibid.

101. Burk, interview with author, 2 Dec. 1988.

102. Commander Paul H. Backus, "Why Them and Not Me?" in Stillwell, *Air Raid: Pearl Harbor!*, 160.

103. USS *Arizona*, 1941 deck log.

104. Flanagan, interview with author, 2 Dec. 1988.

105. Hurst, interview with author, 2 Dec. 1989.

106. Ibid.

107. Cole, interview with author, 1 Dec. 1988.

108. Karb, interview with author, 5 Dec. 1988.

109. Fuqua, undated speech to the New York Athletic Club.

110. Ibid.

111. Weller, unpublished manuscript titled "Pearl Harbor—1941."

112. Givens (formerly Giovenazzo), interview with author, 28 Nov. 1989.

113. Ibid.

114. Fuqua, undated speech to the New York Athletic Club.

115. Reid, interview with author, 3 Dec. 1988.

116. Ibid.

117. Byard, interview with author, 2 Dec. 1989. *Life*, December 1981, 46–48.

Chapter 8 — Day of Infamy

1. Fuqua, undated speech to New York Athletic Club.

2. Ibid.

3. Ibid.

4. Fuqua, action-report statement, 13 Dec. 1941.

5. Miller, action-report statement, 13 Dec. 1941.

6. Pecotte, action-report statement of 5 Jan. 1942; included in USS *Arizona* action report of 13 Feb. 1942.

7. Davison, action-report statement, 13 Dec. 1941.

8. Shapley, interview with Donnelly, 19 and 21 Jan. 1971.

9. Ibid.

10. McCurdy, interview with author, 18 Jan. 1989.

11. Ibid.

12. Ibid.

13. Ibid.

14. Ibid.

15. Ibid.

16. Ibid.

17. Ibid.

18. Ibid.

19. Nightingale, action-report statement, 15 Dec. 1941.

20. Fuqua, action-report statement, 13 Dec. 1941.

21. Nightingale, action-report statement, 15 Dec. 1941.

22. Ibid.

23. White, action-report statement, 13 Feb. 1942.

24. Ibid.

25. Ibid.

26. Ibid.

27. McCarron, interview with author, 2 Dec. 1989.

28. Ibid.

29. Ibid.

30. Ibid.

31. Weller, "Pearl Harbor—1941."

32. Ibid. Weller, letter to Vlach, 11 Sept. 1989.

33. Weller, "Pearl Harbor—1941."

34. Osborne, untitled recollections of 7 Dec. 1941.

35. Hurst, interview with author, 2 Dec. 1989.

36. Ibid.

37. Ibid.

38. Christiansen, interview with author, 2 Dec. 1988.

39. Edmondson, interview with author, 1 Dec. 1988.

40. Christiansen, interview with author, 2 Dec. 1988.

41. Ibid.

42. Ibid. Flanagan, action-report statement, 13 Dec. 1941.

43. Christiansen, interview with author, 2 Dec. 1988.

44. Flanagan, interview with author, 2 Dec. 1988.

45. Ibid. Flanagan, action-report statement, 13 Dec. 1941. Flanagan, interview with Marks, 6 Dec. 1990.

46. Flanagan, interview with author, 2 Dec. 1988.

47. Burcham, interview with Marks, 6 Dec. 1990.

48. Ibid.

49. Edmondson, interview with author, 1 Dec. 1988.

50. Ibid.

51. Ibid.

52. Ibid.

53. Stratton, interview with author, 1 Dec. 1988.

54. Ibid.

55. Friedman and others, *USS Arizona (BB 39)*, 41.

56. Graham and Lukasavitz, action-report statements, 13 Feb. 1942.

57. Burk, interview with author, 2 Dec. 1988.

58. Ibid.

59. Ibid.

60. Ibid.

61. Captain Jim Dick Miller, letter of 28 Mar. 1985 to Hart, ed., *Arizona's Heart Beats*, volume 1, 56–57.

62. Hein, action-report statement, 13 Dec. 1941.

63. Vlach, interview with author, 2 Dec. 1988.

64. Ibid.

65. Karb, interview with author, 5 Dec. 1988.

66. Ibid.

67. Ibid.

68. Ibid.

69. Vice Admiral Kleber S. Masterson, "*Arizona* Survivor," in Stillwell, *Air Raid: Pearl Harbor!*, 173.

70. Ibid, 173–74.

71. Ibid, 174.

72. McCurdy, interview with author, 18 Jan. 1989.

73. Ibid.

74. Henry Williams, interview with author, 17 May 1989.

75. Ibid.

76. Ibid.

Chapter 9 — Aftermath

1. Langdell, interview with Marks, 26 Mar. 1990; Langdell, interview with author, 4 Dec. 1988.

2. Ibid.

3. Burk, interview with author, 2 Dec. 1988.

4. Karb, interview with author, 5 Dec. 1988.

5. Fuqua, undated speech to New York Athletic Club.

6. Vlach, interview with author, 2 Dec. 1988.

7. McCarron, interview with author, 2 Dec. 1989.

8. Ibid.

9. Stratton, interview with author, 1 Dec. 1988.

10. Christiansen, interview with author, 2 Dec. 1988.

11. Ibid.

12. Ibid.

13. Flanagan, interview with author, 2 Dec. 1988.

14. Ibid.

15. Marcicano, interview with Langdell, date unknown.

16. Vlach, letter to author, 28 Dec. 1990.

17. Edmondson, interview with author, 1 Dec. 1988.

18. Ibid.

19. Reid, interview with author, 3 Dec. 1988.

20. Ibid.

21. Vlach, interview with author, 2 Dec. 1988. Miller, letter to author, 26 Nov. 1990.

22. Vlach, interview with author, 2 Dec. 1988.

23. Byard, interview with author, 2 Dec. 1989.

24. Vlach, interview with author, 2 Dec. 1988.

25. Vlach, telephone interview with author, 21 Feb. 1991.

26. Byard, interview with author, 2 Dec. 1989.

27. Baker, action-report statement, 13 Feb. 1942.

28. Byard, interview with author, 2 Dec. 1989.

29. Ross and Ross, *0755*, 18, 25.

30. Ibid, 45, 97–98, 117, 119–20, 143.

31. Burk, interview with author, 2 Dec. 1988.

32. Captain Jim Dick Miller, letter of 24 Feb. 1986 to Hart, ed., *Arizona's Heart Beats*, volume 2, 59–60.

33. Kidd, interview with author, 29 Mar. 1990.

34. Ibid; by telephone, 14 Feb. 1991.

35. Geiselman, action-report statement, 17 Dec. 1941.

36. Hone, "The Destruction of the Battle Line at Pearl Harbor." U.S.N.I. *Proceedings*, Dec. 1977, 49–59.

37. Ibid.

38. De Virgilio, interview with author, 16 Dec. 1990.

39. Ibid.

40. Ibid.

41. Ibid.

42. Ibid.

43. Hone, "The Destruction of the Battle Line at Pearl Harbor," 56–57. The Holtzworth report is reprinted in Friedman and others, *USS Arizona (BB39)*, 35–40.

44. De Virgilio, interview with author, 16 Dec. 1990.

45. Commandant Pearl Harbor Navy Yard, USS *Arizona* "War Damage Report," 7 Oct. 1943.

46. Ibid.

47. Lenihan, ed., *Submerged Cultural Resources Study*, 35.

48. Commandant Pearl Harbor Navy Yard, USS *Arizona* "War Damage Report," 7 Oct. 1943.

49. Lenihan, ed., *Submerged Cultural Resources Study*, 35.

50. Kirchner and Lewis, "The Oahu Turrets," 431.

51. Ibid.

52. Ibid, 431–32.

53. Ibid, 433.

54. Slackman, *Remembering Pearl Harbor*, 44.

55. Delgado, interview with author, 26 Feb. 1991.

56. Slackman, *Remembering Pearl Harbor*, 44.

57. Ibid, 57–60.

58. Ibid, 62–69.

59. Ibid, 72–74.

60. Ibid, 77–91.

61. Lenihan, ed., *Submerged Cultural Resources Study*.

62. Delgado, interview with author, 5 Mar. 1990.

SOURCES

Interviews with Author

Amend, John. Tucson, Arizona, 1 December 1988.

Arnett, Russell. By telephone, 15 November 1990.

Arnold, Admiral Jackson D., USN (Ret.). Rancho Santa Fe, California, 11 April 1989.

Baccala, Michael N. Pasadena, Maryland, May 18, 1988.

Badger, Captain Rodney J., USN (Ret.). Falls Church, Virginia, 1 August 1989.

Barker, Chief Boilerman Stacy, USN (Ret.). Tucson, Arizona, 1 December 1988.

Bryan, Captain William C., USN (Ret.). By telephone, 3 September 1990.

Burk, L. Howard. Tucson, Arizona, 2 December 1988.

Burke, Admiral Arleigh, USN (Ret.). Fairfax, Virginia, 17 February 1991.

Burke, Mrs. Roberta. Fairfax, Virginia, 17 February 1991.

Byard, Commander Ralph D., SC, USN (Ret.). Tucson, Arizona, 2 December 1989.

Campbell, Lieutenant Commander Hugh L., USN (Ret.). Tucson, Arizona, 1 December 1989.

Christiansen, H. Carl. Tucson, Arizona, 2 December 1988.

Clunie, Lieutenant Commander John, USN (Ret.). Tucson, Arizona, 1 December 1988.

Coffin, Rear Admiral Clarence, USN (Ret.). Tucson, Arizona, 3 December 1989.

Cohen, Chief Machinist's Mate Abraham, USN (Ret.). Tucson, Arizona, 2 December 1988.

Cole, Lieutenant Commander H. Wesley. Tucson, Arizona, 1 December 1988.

Cray, Harry B. Benson, Arizona, 30 November 1989.

Daniel, Vice Admiral John C., USN (Ret.). By telephone, 17 November 1990.

Davidson, Rear Admiral John F., USN (Ret.). Annapolis, Maryland, 23 August 1985 and 29 February 1988.

Delgado, Dr. James P. Annapolis, Maryland, 5 March 1990 and 26 February 1991.

De Virgilio, John. By telephone, 16 December 1990.

Dodds, Captain Charles R., USN (Ret.). Annapolis, Maryland, 8 April 1990.

Driscoll, Joseph C. Hartford, Connecticut, 17 July 1988.

Duerfeldt, Rear Admiral Clifford H., USN (Ret.). By telephone, 5 July 1990.

Dybdal, Rear Admiral Victor A., USN (Ret.). Honolulu, Hawaii, 2 May 1989.

Edmondson, Kenneth E. Tucson, Arizona, 1 December 1988.

Femia, Chief Boatswain's Mate Samuel, USN (Ret.). Tucson, Arizona, 2 December 1989.

Flanagan, Guy S. Tucson, Arizona, 2 December 1988.

Fordyce, Garland. Enfield, Connecticut, 17 July 1989.

Frisbie, Glenn H. Shell Knob, Missouri, 25 July 1988.

Gasmann, Lieutenant Howard P., USN (Ret.). Tucson, Arizona, 3 December 1989.

Givens, Chief Boilerman Joseph, USN (Ret.). Tucson, Arizona, 28 November 1989.

Gleason, Commander Carll, USN (Ret.). Phoenix, Arizona, 29 November 1989.

Grabowsky, Captain Leon, USN (Ret.). By telephone, 21 January 1991.

Henderson, Ralph. Tucson, Arizona, 1 December 1988.

Holland, Bernard. Tucson, Arizona, 1 December 1989.

Hubert, Chief Aviation Machinist's Mate Roy, USN (Ret.). Tucson, Arizona, 3 December 1988.

Huckenpoehler, Commander William B., USN (Ret.). Annapolis, Maryland, 31 August 1990.

Hughlett, Chief Electrician's Mate Charles, USN (Ret.). Easton, Maryland, 16 January 1989.

Hurst, Lieutenant Commander Milton T., USN (Ret.). Tucson, Arizona, 2 December 1989.

Karb, Chief Watertender Joseph F., USN (Ret.). Tucson, Arizona, 5 December 1988.

Kidd, Admiral Isaac C., Jr., USN (Ret.). Alexandria, Virginia, 29 March 1990. By telephone, 14 February 1991.

Krulak, Lieutenant General Victor, USMC (Ret.). San Diego, California, 11 April 1989.

Lager, Fred J. Tucson, Arizona, 1 December 1988.

Langdell, Joseph K. Tucson, Arizona, 4 December 1988.

Larson, Melvin S. Tucson, Arizona, 4 December 1989.

Lee, Edward P. Sunnyvale, California, 15 April 1989.

McCafferty, Chief Boatswain David, USN (Ret.). Tucson, Arizona, 2 December 1988.

McCarron, Chief Gunner John, USN (Ret.). Tucson, Arizona, 2 December 1989.

McCarty, Harold E. Tucson, Arizona, 2 December 1989.

McClintock, Captain David, USN (Ret.). By telephone, 4 October 1990.

McCurdy, Lieutenant Colonel Russell J., USMC (Ret.). By telephone, 18 January 1989.

O'Donnell, James. Tucson, Arizona, 4 December 1988.

Ogden, Ellsworth B. By telephone, 28 September 1990.

Pfeifer, John W. Tucson, Arizona, 3 December 1989.

Pride, Admiral Alfred M., USN (Ret.). Arlington, Virginia, 23 December 1988.

Ramsey, Winford R. Tucson, Arizona, 1 December 1988.

Ratcliffe, Ralph. By telephone, 24 October 1990.

Reid, Chief Machinist's Mate Everett O., USN (Ret.). Tucson, Arizona, 3 December 1988.

Reilly, John C. By telephone, 28 November 1990.

Rhodes, Chief Gunner Derward B., USN (Ret.). Tucson, Arizona, 3 December 1989.

Rourk, Lieutenant Charles, USN (Ret.). Tucson, Arizona, 3 December 1988.

Rouse, Jack. Tucson, Arizona, 4 December 1988.

Schroeder, Cletus. Tucson, Arizona, 1 December 1989.

Simpson, Claude. Tucson, Arizona, 30 November 1988.

Smith, Admiral Harold Page, USN (Ret.). Virginia Beach, Virginia, 26 October 1990.

Smith, Major Wylie A., USAF (Ret.). Tucson, Arizona, 3 December 1988.

Speedie, William. By telephone, 18 March 1990.

Stratton, Donald G. Tucson, Arizona, 1 December 1988.

Strauss, Rear Admiral Elliott B., USN (Ret.). 30 October 1986.

Vivirito, Chief Boatswain Joseph, USN (Ret.). Tucson, Arizona, 3 December 1988.

Vlach, Lieutenant Commander Vincent James, USN (Ret.). Tucson, Arizona, 2 December 1988. By telephone, 21 February 1991.

Warren, Commander H. Nelson, USNR (Ret.). By telephone, 15 November 1990.

Williams, Arthur S. Tucson, Arizona, 30 November 1989.

Williams, Captain Henry, Jr., USN (Ret.). By telephone, 17 May 1989.

Zobel, Chief Pay Clerk Herbert F., USN (Ret.). Tucson, Arizona, 30 November 1988.

Other Interviews

Ballentine, Admiral John J., USN (Ret.). With John T. Mason. Columbia University Oral History Collection, 11 April 1961.

Bennett, Lester. With Lorraine Marks. *Arizona* Reunion Association, 18 July 1990.

Boyle, Michael. With Joseph K. Langdell. *Arizona* Reunion Association, 4 December 1982.

Burcham, Chief Gunner's Mate Jimmie Lee, USN (Ret.). With Lorraine Marks. *Arizona* Reunion Association, 6 December 1990.

Flanagan, Guy S. With Lorraine Marks. *Arizona* Reunion Association, 6 December 1990.

Fore, Everett. With Bobby H. Johnson. Stephen F. Austin University Oral History Collection, 31 May 1983.

Foulds, Melvin R. With Joseph K. Langdell. *Arizona* Reunion Association, 3 December 1982.

Kinkaid, Admiral Thomas C., USN (Ret.). With John T. Mason. Columbia University Oral History Collection, 6 March 1961.

Kos, Martin. With Ellen Lomonaco. Special Collections, University of Arizona Library, 19 December 1984.

Langdell, Joseph K. With Lorraine Marks. *Arizona* Reunion Association, 26 March 1990.

Love, Ted. With Joseph K. Langdell. *Arizona* Reunion Association, 4 December 1983.

Marcicano, Jack R. With Joseph K. Langdell. *Arizona* Reunion Association, date unknown.

McKinney, Claude. With Lorraine Marks. *Arizona* Reunion Association, November 1989.

Shapley, Lieutenant General Alan, USMC (Ret.). With Major Thomas E. Donnelly, USMC. Headquarters Marine Corps, Oral History Collection, 19 and 21 January 1971.

Traylor, Thomas. With Lorraine Marks. *Arizona* Reunion Association, December 1989.

Books

Beigel, Harvey M. *Battleship Country: The Battle Fleet at San Pedro–Long Beach, California—1919–1940.* Missoula, Montana: Pictorial Histories Publishing Company, 1983.

Bowen, Vice Admiral Harold G., USN (Ret.). *Ships Machinery and Mossbacks.* Princeton: Princeton University Press, 1954.

Coletta, Paolo, editor. *American Secretaries of the Navy,* Volume II. Annapolis: Naval Institute Press, 1980.

Daniels, Josephus. *The Wilson Era: Years of Peace—1910–1917.* Chapel Hill: University of North Carolina Press, 1944.

Dyer, Vice Admiral George C., USN (Ret.), coauthor. *On The Treadmill to Pearl Harbor: The Memoirs of Admiral James O. Richardson, USN (Retired)*. Washington, D.C.: Naval History Division, Department of the Navy, 1973.

Friedman, Norman. *U.S. Battleships: An Illustrated Design History*. Annapolis: Naval Institute Press, 1985.

Friedman, Norman, Arthur D. Baker III, Arnold S. Lott, and Robert F. Sumrall. *USS Arizona (BB-39)*. Annapolis: Leeward Publications, 1978.

Hart, Nina, editor. *Arizona's Heart Beats*, two volumes. Lake Helen, Florida: privately published, 1986 and 1987.

Hough, Richard. *Dreadnought: A History of the Modern Battleship*. New York: Macmillan Publishing Company, Inc., 1964.

Jennings, Gary. *The Treasure of the Superstition Mountains*. New York: W. W. Norton & Company, 1973.

Jones, Ken, and Hubert Kelley, Jr. *Admiral Arleigh (31-Knot) Burke: The Story of a Fighting Sailor*. Philadelphia and New York: Chilton Books, 1962.

Keith, Francis Lovell, *United States Navy Task Force Evolution: An Analysis of United States Fleet Problems, 1931–1934*. College Park: University of Maryland master of arts thesis, 1974.

Lenihan, Daniel J., editor. *Submerged Cultural Resources Study: USS Arizona Memorial and Pearl Harbor National Historic Landmark*. Washington, D.C.: U.S. Government Printing Office, 1989.

Naval Ordnance: A Textbook. Annapolis: U.S. Naval Institute, 1939.

Potter, E. B. *Admiral Arleigh Burke: A Biography*. New York: Random House, 1990.

———. *Nimitz*. Annapolis: Naval Institute Press, 1976.

Ross, Captain Donald K., USN (Ret.), and Helen L. Ross. *0755: The Heroes of Pearl Harbor*. Port Orchard, Washington: Rokalu Press, 1988.

Slackman, Michael. *Remembering Pearl Harbor: The Story of the USS Arizona Memorial*, second edition. Honolulu, Hawaii: *Arizona* Memorial Museum Association, 1986.

Stillwell, Paul. *Air Raid: Pearl Harbor! Recollections of a Day of Infamy*. Annapolis: Naval Institute Press, 1981.

Wheeler, Gerald E. *Prelude to Pearl Harbor: The United States Navy and the Far East, 1921–1931*. Columbia: University of Missouri Press, 1963.

Magazine Articles

Corey, Herbert. "Across the Equator with the American Navy." *National Geographic* (June 1921).

Delgado, James P. "Surveying the Wreckage of the U.S.S. Arizona." *Sea Classics* (May 1989).

Hone, Thomas C. "The Destruction of the Battle Line at Pearl Harbor." *U.S. Naval Institute Proceedings* (December 1977).

Jensen, Ann. "USS Arizona: The Memories Do Not Die." *American History Illustrated* (December 1988).

Kirchner, Commander D. P., USN, and E. R. Lewis. "The Oahu Turrets." *The Military Engineer* (November–December 1967).

Murphy, Larry. "Diving on the Arizona." *Sea Classics* (May 1989).

"Our Latest Dreadnought, the 'Arizona'." *Scientific American* (25 November 1916).

Sims, Philip. "Freeboard Problems—1938." *U.S. Naval Institute Proceedings* (January 1976).

Snook, David. "British Naval Operations in the Black Sea, 1918–1920." Part I, *Warship International*, Number 1 (1989).

"They Do Remember." *Life* (December 1981).

Young, J. Russell. "When the President Takes a Vacation." *The Sunday Star Magazine* (19 April 1931).

Newspaper Articles

Army and Navy Journal, 13 July 1918 and 18 October 1919.

Army and Navy Register, 19 July 1919.

At 'Em Arizona, various dates, Manuscripts Division, Library of Congress; Special Collections, University of Arizona Library.

Courtland Arizonan, 26 June 1915.

Los Angeles Times, 28 August 1979.

Milwaukee Journal, 6 December 1977.

New York Evening Post, 26 March 1931.

New York Evening Sun, 17 March 1914.

New York Herald, 17 March 1914.

New York Herald Tribune, 22 March 1931.

New York Press, 17 March 1914.

New York Times, 20 June 1915, 18 October 1916, 25 March 1931, 28 March 1931, 29 March 1931, and 21 July 1934.

New York Tribune, 17 March 1914.

Norfolk Virginian-Pilot, 18 March 1931.

Seattle Post-Intelligencer, 10 July 1937.

Washington Herald, 23 March 1931.

Washington Post, 15 March 1931.

Washington Sunday Star, 19 April 1931.

Yavapai (Arizona) Associated, no date.

Youngstown (Ohio) Vindicator, December 1941.

Official Records

Arizona, USS (BB-39). Deck Logs, Record Group 24, National Archives.

Arizona, USS (BB-39). Ship's General Information Books, Record Group 19, National Archives.

Baker, Sergeant John MacR., USMC. Action-report statement, 13 February 1942. Operational Archives Branch, Naval Historical Center.

Board of Inspection and Survey, Folders BB39/S3-(5) and BB39/S8, Box 753, Record Group 19, National Archives.

Bureau of Construction and Repair records. Record Group 19. National Archives.

Bureau of Medicine and Surgery records. Record Group 52. National Archives.

Commandant, Pearl Harbor Navy Yard. USS *Arizona* "War Damage Report" to Chief of the Bureau of Ships, 7 October 1943. Record Group 19, National Archives.

Daniels, Josephus. Papers. Library of Congress.

Davison, Ensign Henry D., USN. Action-report statement, 13 December 1941. Operational Archives Branch, Naval Historical Center.

Flanagan, Ensign Guy S., USNR. Action-report statement, 13 December 1941. Operational Archives Branch, Naval Historical Center.

Fuqua, Lieutenant Commander Samuel G., USN. Action-report statement, 13 December 1941. Operational Archives Branch, Naval Historical Center.

Geiselman, Commander E. H., USN. Action-report statement, 17 December 1941. Operational Archives Branch, Naval Historical Center.

Graham, Aviation Machinist's Mate First Class Donald, USN. Action-report statement, 13 February 1942. Operational Archives Branch, Naval Historical Center.

Hein, Ensign Douglas, USN. Action-report statement, 13 December 1941. Operational Archives Branch, Naval Historical Center.

Lukasavitz, Seaman First Class Steven J., USN. Action-report statement, 13 February 1942. Operational Archives Branch, Naval Historical Center.

Miller, Ensign Jim Dick, USN. Action-report statement, 13 December 1941. Operational Archives Branch, Naval Historical Center.

Nightingale, Corporal Earl C., USMC. Action-report statement, 15 December 1941. Operational Archives Branch, Naval Historical Center.

Pecotte, Gunner's Mate Second Class Earl, USN. Action-report statement, 5 January 1942. Operational Archives Branch, Naval Historical Center.

White, Boatswain's Mate Second Class Thomas A., USN. Action-report statement, 13 December 1942. Operational Archives Branch, Naval Historical Center.

Letters

Arizona, USS (BB-39). Postcards, Special Collections, University of Arizona Library.

Clunie, Lieutenant Commander John, USN (Ret.). To author, 11 March 1988.

Cutter, Captain Slade D., USN (Ret.). To author, 12 February 1990.

Donovan, Edythe T. To author, 22 March 1988.

Driscoll, Bernard J. To author, 3 March 1990 and 30 May 1990.

Gesen, Margaret J. To author, 5 April 1990.

Hone, Thomas C. To author, 30 September 1990 and 18 January 1991.

McCain, James A. To Lorraine Marks, 12 September 1989 and 8 October 1989. To author, 8 January 1991.

Miller, Captain Jim Dick, USN (Ret.). To author, 26 November 1990.

Richardson, Nicholas W. To Lorraine Marks, undated.

Still, William. To author, 8 January 1991.

Vlach, Lieutenant Commander Vincent J., USN (Ret.). To author, 28 December 1990.

Weller, Lieutenant Commander Oree C., USN (Ret.). To Vincent J. Vlach, 11 September 1989.

Unpublished Manuscripts

Baccala, Michael N. 1936 diary. Courtesy Michael Baccala.

DeCelles, J. Howard. Undated questionnaire for U.S. Army Military History Research Collection. Carlisle Barracks, Pennsylvania.

Driscoll, Joseph C. 1917–21 journal. Courtesy Bernard Driscoll.

Frisbie, Glenn H. 1918 diary. Courtesy Glenn Frisbie.

Fuqua, Rear Admiral Samuel G., USN (Ret.). Undated speech delivered to New York Athletic Club. Special Collections, Naval Academy Library.

Greer, Chief Watertender Horace, USN (Ret.). "Fifteen Minute Talk." Courtesy of *Arizona* Reunion Association. Copy in Operational Archives Branch, Naval Historical Center.

Ingersoll, Commander Royal E., USN. 1920–21 diary. Courtesy Alice I. Nagle.

Johnson, Lawrence. 1917 diary. Courtesy Hans Henke.

Laning, Admiral Harris, USN (Ret.). Book-length memoir, circa 1940. Naval War College Library.

Leymé, George I. R. 1918–19 diary. Courtesy Mrs. Janet Joseph.

Marks, Lorraine, editor. *Memories* (a book-length compilation of individual recollections by former crew members).

Osborne, William T., Jr. Untitled recollections of 7 December 1941. Special Collections, University of Arizona Library.

Weller, Lieutenant Commander Oree C., USN (Ret.). "Pearl Harbor—1941." Courtesy Lorraine Marks.

INDEX

Note: Numbers that are italicized indicate the pages on which photos appear. Numbers in roman type apply to references in the text.

ABOUT THE AUTHOR

Paul Stillwell joined the staff of the U.S. Naval Institute in 1974 and is now director of oral history and editor-in-chief of *Naval History* magazine. He has a bachelor's degree in history from Drury College, Springfield, Missouri, and a master's degree in journalism from the University of Missouri-Columbia. From 1962 to 1988 he was in the Naval Reserve, including active duty from 1966 to 1969; he served in the tank-landing ship *Washoe County* (LST-1165) and the battleship *New Jersey* (BB-62).

Among his other publications are *USS South Dakota: The Story of Battleship X* (1972), *Air Raid: Pearl Harbor!* (1981), *Battleship New Jersey: An Illustrated History* (1986), and the Naval Institute's 1991 engagement calendar *A Century of U.S. Battleships*.

THE NAVAL INSTITUTE PRESS

BATTLESHIP ARIZONA
An Illustrated History

Designed by Karen L. White

Set in Galliard and
Printed on 60-lb. Glatco Matte
by Science Press, Inc.
Ephrata, Pennsylvania

Bound in Holliston Roxite B
by CHM Edition Bookbindery
Andalusia, Pennsylvania